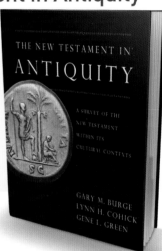

THE NEW TESTAMENT IN
ANTIQUITY

GARY M. BURGE
LYNN H. COHICK
and
GENE L. GREEN

ZONDERVAN

The New Testament in Antiquity
Copyright © 2009 by Gary M. Burge, Lynn H. Cohick, and Gene L. Green

This title is also available as a Zondervan ebook.
Visit www.zondervan.com/ebooks.

Requests for information should be addressed to:

Zondervan, 3900 *Sparks Dr. SE, Grand Rapids, Michigan 49546*

Library of Congress Cataloging-in-Publication Data

Burge, Gary M., 1952-
     The New Testament in antiquity / Gary M. Burge, Lynn H. Cohick, and Gene L.
Green.
          p. cm.
     Includes bibliographical references and index.
     ISBN 978-0-310-24495-0
     1. Bible. N.T.—Textbooks. 2. Bible. N.T.—Antiquities. I. Green, Gene L. II. Cohick,
Lynn H. III. Title.
     BS2535.3.B87 2007
     225.6'1—dc22   2006026524

Cover design: Chris Tobias—Tobias' Outerwear for Books
Cover photography: Harlan J. Berk Ltd. (www.harlanjberk.com)
Interior design: Sherri Hoffman

Printed in China

19 20 21 22 /ASC/ 30 29 28 27 26 25 24 23 22 21 20 19 18 17 16 15 14 13

To our many students
who continue to inspire us

CONTENTS

PREFACE

Today a variety of textbooks promise to survey the New Testament for the beginning student. Each volume comes with its own pedagogical, historical, even theological priorities. This volume is no different. We sought to write a textbook that is firmly rooted in our tradition, yet is conversant with the academic field we represent.

Four goals focused our efforts. First, we wanted to offer a volume that was academically rigorous. Too often evangelical introductions sacrifice academic thoroughness in order to make the text practical for the average reader. Each chapter provides an up-to-date examination of the subject informed by the best in current scholarship.

Second, we sought a volume that was accessible to the student. Technical jargon is kept to a minimum and explanations are generous for the reader with minimal background. Photographs, charts, and maps each illustrate the argument of the text to enhance understanding.

Third, the text of this book underscores the ancient context of the New Testament (hence the book's title). We believe that interpreting the New Testament requires an intimate understanding of its background, culture, and history. Numerous sidebars point the student to contextual insights and extrabiblical primary sources.

Fourth, we wanted a volume that is responsive to the confessional commitments of the evangelical tradition. Too often academic treatments of the New Testament view faith commitments as passé. We wanted a scholarly text that treated the pages of the New Testament *as Scripture*, which has spoken to the church through the centuries.

These, then, were our goals: academic, accessible, contextual, and confessional.

We represent over fifty years of experience teaching at the undergraduate level. We have devoted our careers to understanding and communicating to the alert undergraduate student. And we have taken those instincts for the classroom and applied them to a text that will serve that audience well. Nevertheless, beginning seminary students will discover this book to be ideal for those just starting their graduate work in theology.

For five years we worked collaboratively to build the present volume. Each of us brought to the text his/her own expertise in Pauline studies, Jewish backgrounds, Hellenism, or the Gospels. But in addition, we wanted to take advantage of the best in graphic design and illustration so necessary for the modern reader. Therefore, an ever larger team of artists, editors, photographers, and consultants grew to build *The New Testament in Antiquity*.

HOW THIS BOOK IS BUILT

While the book may be used profitably for personal study, it is ideally suited for classroom instruction. A quick look at the table of contents provides a good outline of its thematic approach. An introductory chapter explains to students why contextual work must be done in order to understand the New Testament effectively. It provides our methodological presuppositions and explains how each chapter is built. We then set out to reconstruct the historical and cultural setting of the New Testament period as concisely as possible. The major eras of intertestamental history run from Alexander to the second Jewish revolt against Rome. This is followed by chapters devoted to the cultural and religious setting of Jesus in Roman Judea and Galilee as well as the setting of Paul in the wider Mediterranean world.

We felt compelled to include a careful study of the sources for reconstructing the life of Jesus and the character of the Gospels. So much technical criticism is now in public debate that students must be abreast of current developments. We then provide a synthesis of Jesus' life and teachings from these gospels — which is followed by individual analyses of each of the Gospels.

A study of Acts (Ch. 12) opens our lengthy treatment of Paul and the early church. A summary of Act's historical and theological method is followed by a synthesis of Paul's life and work. This is then accompanied by a series of chapters on Paul's letters (Chs. 14 – 21), in roughly chronological order. The general epistles follow as well as a closing chapter on the Greek text of the New Testament, the development of the canon, and the work of translation. This final chapter is certainly technical, but it is designed for the nonspecialist and answers many of the residual questions about the New Testament we have heard time and again in class.

A note about sidebars and illustrations. One hallmark of this text is its numerous sidebars. In these we attempt to provide illuminating examples of what contextual study might yield. In many cases we cite primary sources; in other cases we use archaeology or cultural anthropology. Above all, we offer insights that will further advance the argument of the chapter.

The same is true of illustrations. Too often textbooks use pictures that are gratuitous and one wonders why they are there. Or the illustrations are of such poor quality that their impact is severely limited. Our photo researchers worked hard to provide the best illustrations available. The same is true of maps. We sought to build maps that were not only clear but that illustrate for the student how *location* can be critical for understanding most stories.

While an excellent textbook is vital for study of the New Testament, we cannot emphasize strongly enough the need to read the New Testament itself. We have observed a consistent temptation for students: the more thorough the textbook, the less inclined they are to read the original. Our hope is that this book will not replace the New Testament but rather will inspire a passionate and lifelong love for it.

Throughout *The New Testament in Antiquity* when citing the New Testament we have used Today's New International Version. We recognized the great legacy of the NIV (published in 1973 and 1978) and wanted to take advantage of the 2002 revision that has increased its clarity and power. Where other translations are used, they are noted.

We selected the *Judea capta* coin (see the cover) as a unifying thematic image. Not only is it perhaps one of the most arresting Roman coins from the first century showing Rome's conquest of Judea in AD 70, but it illustrates richly the difficult and often tragic interplay of Jewish life with Roman imperial power — a story evidenced throughout the New Testament.

ACKNOWLEDGMENTS

A significant number of people contributed to the writing, development, and design of this book. A number of our students provided research and editorial work. Among them: John Bonnell, Elizabeth Dias, Esther Giezendanner, Matt Harmon, Christopher Hays, Travis McMaken, and Mary Veeneman. Ben Gladd expertly indexed the volume.

Colleagues and researchers helped us locate impossible photo targets. Our many ancient coin images have come from the expertise and generosity of Shanna Berk Schmidt of Harlan Berk, Ltd., of Chicago. This is one of the premier sources for numismatics in the world, and we are deeply in their debt. Many of our photos come from the expert work of Zev Radovan (Israel) and Todd Bolen (USA). Graphics were helped by Hugh Claycombe and by Leen Ritmeyer in Jerusalem. In many cases their creative suggestions produced images we did not know existed. And in some cases, they tipped us off about new, interesting discoveries, such as a Roman soldier's sandal print found in a wall at the Greek city of Hippos, Galilee, in August 2007. Few would catch such little details.

At Zondervan the original encouragement for the book came from Jack Kuhatschek. A team of skilled editors worked with text, photos, layout, and design. Special thanks go to Katya Covrett (acquisitions), Verlyn Verbrugge (copyediting), David Frees and Kim Zeilstra (photos), Sarah Baar, Mark Sheeres, and Rob Monacelli (creative design and layout).

Our work on the book's chapters follows areas where each of us had pursued research or interests personally. Dr. Lynn Cohick brought her expertise in Jewish background and culture. Dr. Gene Green contributed on Paul and Hellenism. Dr. Gary Burge followed his interest in the Gospels and the history of the intertestamental era; he also served as the book's general editor.[1]

Our earnest hope is that this book becomes a beginning for further personal study for the New Testament, its background, and its message. We hope that it will become a tool for many classroom explorations of the meaning of our Christian faith and its New Testament legacy.

Gary M. Burge
Lynn H. Cohick
Gene L. Green

NOTES

1. Dr. Cohick wrote Chapters 8, 14, 17, 19, 21, 22, 23, and 26. Dr. Green wrote Chapters 4, 10, 12, 13, 15, 16, 20, and 24. Dr. Burge wrote Chapters 1, 2, 3, 5, 6, 7, 9, 11, 18, and 25. The final chapter on canon and hermeneutics (Ch. 27) was a collaborative effort.

ABBREVIATIONS

AB	Anchor Bible
ABRL	Anchor Bible Reference Library
ANTC	Abington New Testament Commentary
BECNT	Baker Exegetical Commentary on the New Testament
BNTC	Black's New Testament Commentary
BST	The Bible Speaks Today
CBC	Cornerstone Biblical Commentary
EBC	Expositor's Bible Commentary
ESV	English Standard Version
ICC	International Critical Commentary
IVPNTC	InterVarsity Press New Testament Commentary
JETS	*Journal of the Evangelical Theological Society*
KJV	King James Version
LCL	Loeb Classical Library
LEC	Library of Early Christianity
NAC	New American Commentary
NASB	New American Standard Bible
NCB	New Century Bible Commentary
NEB	New English Bible
NICNT	New International Commentary on the New Testament
NIGTC	New International Greek Testament Commentary
NIV	New International Version
NIVAC	NIV Application Commentary
NLT	New Living Translation
NovT	*Novum Testamentum*
NRSV	New Revised Standard Version
NTL	New Testament Library
NTS	New Testament Studies
PNTC	Pillar New Testament Commentary
RSV	Revised Standard Version
RTR	*Reformed Theological Review*
SBLDS	Society of Biblical Literature Dissertation Series
TNIV	Today's New International Version
TNTC	Tyndale New Testament Commentary
WBC	Word Biblical Commentary
ZNW	*Zeitschrift für die neutestamentliche Wissenschaft*

CHAPTER 1

STUDYING THE
NEW TESTAMENT

A rolling stone tomb complex from the first century, Nazareth.

PERSPECTIVE

The New Testament consists of twenty-seven individual "books" written in Greek almost two thousand years ago, and some or all of the New Testament has been translated into 1168 languages, something characteristic of no other book. Today about 2000 new translations are underway or completed.[1] But it is not mere curiosity that inspires this study. It is the story contained in these books, a story about a Jewish messiah and his followers that has led millions in every era to join the ranks of his disciples.

The New Testament is first and foremost about Jesus of Nazareth, a man called "Messiah" by his followers, who was killed in Jerusalem and who rose from the grave. His followers were transformed by what they saw and experienced, and they carried faith in Jesus to the entire Mediterranean world. The New Testament contains four Gospels outlining Jesus' life, a brief history of the early church, and a collection of letters from many of early Christianity's most prominent leaders. They were penned during the fifty years or so following Jesus' death and resurrection.

Today many Christians know the basic elements of this story and enjoy an intimate, deeply personal love for many passages of the New Testament. However, few understand the breadth of this story, much less how to interpret each book. Many of us gravitate to familiar texts but feel unconfident interpreting more difficult chapters. Some know the major characters such as Jesus, Peter, and Paul, but we are vague about the details of their lives or the more complex elements in their teachings.

P52 is the earliest papyrus NT text known (AD 100- 150). On one side (the recto) it shows John 18:31-33; on the reverse (the verso) it has John 18:37-38.

The aims of the book are simple: to assist students to become alert, capable readers of the New Testament — to guide them through its many books, giving not only essential background information, but also a digest of the New Testament's most important teachings.

METHODOLOGICAL PRESUPPOSITIONS

All authors come to the task of writing with presuppositions. For instance, historical optimism — or skepticism — will unwittingly surface in every study of the New Testament. The same is true of this book. Its goals are the same as many other surveys of the New Testament, but some crucial differences will stand out in our approach to reading the New Testament.

Scripture and Study

As Christians we are eager to affirm our commitment that the New Testament is *Scripture*. These words are not like other words; God has employed them — indeed, he still employs them — through the work of his Spirit in his church to reveal himself to the world. Therefore, we do not hold merely a historical or theological interest in the New Testament. Rather, God is at work in and through these chapters to bring life and transformation to all who seek him there. Thus, it is appropriate for us to refer to the New Testament (as well as the entire Bible) as *Scripture*, or the divinely inspired Word of God.

However, this high affirmation of the Bible does not mean that readers in the twenty-first century are capable of understanding the New Testament as if by magic. The message of the Bible may be timeless, but the form of that message is not. In order to accomplish his self-revelation in history, God necessarily had to embed that revelation in the historical and cultural context of its original readers. When Jesus told a parable, he framed it in ways that made sense to first-century farmers and fishermen. When Paul wrote a letter, he used not only his own personal cultural preferences, but he wrote to be understood, using words and ideas meaningful to a first-century audience. Today we may understand a great deal of that message, but probing its depths requires effort.

A Reader's Bias

Meaning can be missed not only by our ignorance of things presupposed by the New Testament's original audience, but also by the cultural framework we ourselves bring to the task of study. Without realizing it, we bring the cultural values and the historical framework of our own world to the text of the New Testament. This is understandable. We only make sense of something we read when the concepts we encounter register with something in our own experience. When we read about the "church" of Corinth, our own images of "church" leap quickly to mind. When Jesus refers to a "sower," our Western notions of farming and seed distribution fill in the picture. Readers bring their own understanding—sometimes called preunderstanding—to any text they encounter.

How do we cope with this? First, we work hard to understand *our own context*. That is, as interpreters of the New Testament we must become increasingly suspicious of our own preferences. For example, if we come from a highly individualistic culture (so common in the West) in which the church emphasizes private salvation, we may have difficulty understanding the biblical notion of corporate sin. Or we may be unprepared to see how Jesus' proclamation of "the kingdom of God" had social and economic implications. If we come from a society where religion and government are strictly separated, it may be impossible to see how Jesus' kingdom was bearing down on the political structures of his day.

Second, we must embrace the cultural context of the biblical world. If we do not share some of the reflexes of Paul's first readers, if we cannot appreciate the difficulties of Gentiles and Jews living side by side in first-century churches, it will be impossible to understand much of the New Testament.

Context, Context, Context

Words have a certain indeterminacy of meaning. That is, they gain meaning only when they are set firmly in a context. If a modern politician is referred to as "green," it could mean a variety of things: she could be "new" to the field; she could be deeply jealous; she could be an environmentalist; or she could belong to a party that wears green uniforms. Perhaps she is Irish. We have no idea. In other words, "green" has little meaning unless it is tied to a context. The meaning of the word itself is not "determined" without a context. It must fit its range of meanings, its *semantic range*.

In order for us to understand the New Testament effectively, therefore, we must rebuild the context of its words as carefully as possible. When John the Baptist introduces Jesus as the "Lamb of God" (John 1:36), does he mean that Jesus is meek? Or helpless? Or does it refer to lambs that are sacrificed at Jerusalem's temple? If this refers to sacrifice, what sacrificial ceremony does John have in mind? The daily sacrifices of temple worship? Or the great annual Passover sacrifices each spring? Knowing the context is the key. But without the context, the phrase "Lamb of God" has little usefulness or meaning. The job of interpretation thus requires humility of the first order because we are admitting that we are reading this story as foreigners and outsiders, not as readers who share its original context.

Our earliest picture of Jewish dress comes from the 3rd century synagogue of Dura-Europas on the Euphrates River, Syria. This fresco shows Samuel anointing David. However, note how the dress is strictly Hellenistic and no fringes are evident on the garments.

The title of this book is deliberate: *The New Testament in Antiquity*. Our primary responsibility is to gain the meaning of our Scriptures by understanding not only our own interpretative contexts, but also the original context of the New Testament. The *context of antiquity* should control how we understand the New Testament today.

RECREATING THE CONTEXT

What basic elements are necessary if we are going to be diligent in building this "context of antiquity?" Three important elements contribute to rebuilding the New Testament context. Every interpreter of the New Testament must have some mastery of each.

Knowing the Land

When Jesus moved through Galilee or traveled to Judea, he knew where he was. He knew the landscape, the roads, Hellenistic cities such as Scythopolis, and Jewish fishing villages like Capernaum. When Paul organized his missionary journeys, he had a good sense which cities would be strategic for the growth of the church. Such knowledge of geography — landscape, geology, climate, water resources, roads, settlement patterns, and political boundaries — is common among all societies. Most literature simply presupposes that its audience will know these things naturally. The Gospels refer to the Sea of Galilee without telling us its location. They also mention places such as Bethsaida and Cana as if they are familiar to us.

Our acquaintance with the specifics of biblical geography will play an important role in how we understand the story. When Jesus moves from Judea to Samaria, we must not only know where Samaria is but understand the ethnic differences between Jews and Samaritans. The far north was called "Galilee of the Gentiles" because of the rapid Hellenization going on. When Jesus moves around the landscape, sometimes he is in Greek regions; in other cases, in Jewish regions. His teaching and his activity are shaped by this setting. Therefore, if we cannot locate the city of Tyre or identify the Decapolis (a region known to every Galilean), we will be at a loss.

Geographical questions also follow any reconstruction of Paul's life and work. Famous cities such as Antioch on the Orontes, Ephesus, Troas, and Philippi were known intimately by Paul. The settlement pattern of Asia Minor played significantly in his plans and likely kept him from traveling north along the rim of the Black Sea. He spent eighteen months in Corinth founding a strategic church, yet it was this city's location as a maritime trading center and transit point that gave the city such value.

Knowing the History

Every culture likewise knows its history, so that allusions to people and events can happen in the most subtle manner. When a student announces he is from Richmond, Virginia, and he is a Southerner, he is saying more than providing geographical information. He is making a comment about history, the Civil War, and cultural orientation.

The New Testament period also had a history that everyone knew. The coming of Hellenistic culture behind the armies of Alexander the Great impacted Jewish life far more than we could imagine. This was followed by a series of regional Greek kings who sometimes encouraged assimilation but at other times brutally oppressed the Jews. Judaism's successful revolt against the Greeks and the subsequent Jewish nation formed in the second century BC inspired stories and writings current in Jesus' day.

No doubt the most important event for the average Jew was the conquest of Israel by Rome in 63 BC. The massive armies of Pompey quickly placed it under a Roman administration. The reality of this occupation—its tax burden, its Jewish collaborators, its Jewish resistors—shaped the world of Jesus and Paul. Of course participation in the empire had its benefits. Pompey had also cleansed the Mediterranean of pirates (Plutarch, *Life of Pompey*, 28:2). Suddenly trade, travel, and communication facilitated and protected by Rome was possible. The early church took advantage of these benefits as it moved its missionaries around the empire.

Therefore the parameters of our historical enquiry should begin in about 333 BC (Alexander's major defeat of a Persian army at Issus) and end with the second Jewish war with Rome in AD 132–135. Hellenism was changing the cultural landscape while the Roman occupation inspired collaborators like the Herodians as well as fighters like the Zealots. Jewish self-identity was in crisis, and many were asking if the successful revolts of the second century BC should serve as a model for how to treat the Romans.

Knowing history thus builds the context in which present events can be understood. In John

This coin, minted during the Bar Kokhba revolt of AD 132-135, shows symbolism that was recognized by every Jew: the four column entrance to the temple on one side, and on the other side, a *lulav*—a bundle of four branches used at the Feast of Tabernacles ceremonies.

10, for example, Jesus attends the Festival of Hanukkah. This celebration was popular since it retold the story of Judaism's guerrilla war against the Greeks and the rededication of the temple. When Paul writes a letter to Philippi, it helps to know something of the history of Macedonia and how Roman soldiers retired in the region. When Mary, Joseph, and the young Jesus return to Judea from Egypt, they bypass Bethlehem and slip into Galilee because a vicious son of Herod the Great is ruling the south (see Matt. 2:19–23). Without a strong grasp of the historical context, we may misunderstand or even misrepresent what is happening in a New Testament passage.

Knowing the Culture

Every society orchestrates its life with predictable reflexes and rituals. Social habits, religious traditions, political interests, even music and art contribute to values shared by generations. Rarely do they need to be defined overtly since we inherit them. One of the biggest hurdles for foreigners visiting another country is to understand what is going on. They may think they know, but they gradually sense they are missing a great deal. Humor, irony, and sarcasm presuppose much that is unsaid; what may be funny to one person may mean nothing to another. Try watching a film in a foreign theater. Americans will tell you that the British laugh at all the "wrong" places. (The British will say the same about Americans.)

One key to understanding Luke 11 is seeing that ovens were often shared in a community. This oven is still used today in rural Palestinian villages and is similar to those built 2,000 years ago.

Of course, the New Testament world shared many values that were understood but unspoken. Today these values are being studied. The advent of modern anthropology gave birth to an interdisciplinary effort to bring these academic skills to the study of the New Testament. Scholars look at the literature of the period, the archaeological remains, and even the evidence of village cultures for clues to how to understand the social reflexes presupposed in the Bible. For example, women were responsible for the transport and management of well or cistern water. Both the Old and New Testaments attest to this, but so does the culture of Middle East village life where it has been least disturbed by Western influences.

When we look at particular New Testament passages, asking questions about culture may lead us to entirely new levels of understanding. When a young son comes to his father and asks for his inheritance (Luke 15:11–12), what is the expected response? What will his older brother think? What happens when a neighbor awakens a man in the middle of the night asking for bread (Luke 11:5–6)? What leads the sleeping man to arise and share? Or what cultural assumptions drive a shepherd to leave ninety-nine sheep alone in search of one that is lost (Luke 15:4)? We dare not complete the picture with our own cultural assumptions since our culture is foreign to the story.

One key cultural value in the New Testament is the place given to shame and honor. Life was organized around the accumulation of honor and the avoidance of shame. For example, Jesus was once sitting in the home of Simon the Pharisee (Luke 7:36–50), having dinner with the village's religious and intellectual elite. When a woman interrupted the party by clutching Jesus' feet, wetting them with tears, kissing them, and drying them with her loosed hair, Simon discredited Jesus because he had violated principles of male/female contact by defending rather than rejecting the woman. *Simon concluded that Jesus was a man who had no honor.* But in addition, cultural values cascade over each other in dizzying swiftness: How did the woman get in? What did she intend? How was Jesus sitting so that his feet were accessible to her? Who was there at the meal? Why did Simon see the woman's deeds as sexually inappropriate? Why did Simon not wash Jesus' feet when he greeted him or anoint his head? What did Simon mean by his treatment of Jesus?

The interpreter will always bring cultural values to a story such as this. But the key is to limit the intrusion of our own cultural preconceptions and rebuild the context of the story using first-century values. For example, every culture has "greeting rituals." In the Luke 7 story, Simon has omitted these before other guests, shaming Jesus publicly. Without a clear understanding of "public shaming" and "greeting rituals," we are at a loss to understand what energizes this story.

The New Testament, however, represents more than one culture, and we must reconstruct each context accurately. Rural village life in Judea was different from urban life in Ephesus. Hellenistic Jews living throughout the Mediterranean often experienced clashes of culture that made them uncomfortable. Greeks and Romans had different assumptions about culture. We will discuss many of these in the pages that follow.

FEATURES

Sidebars. Throughout this book, sidebars provide illustrations for how the first-century context can be understood. These notes form illustrations of some of the ideas inherent in the New Testament passages under discussion. Other sidebars explain how to interpret troublesome passages and apply them responsibly to our own setting.

Notes from Antiquity. These notes provide background data such as archaeological research, anthropological insights, historical notes, or even citations of ancient texts to help us gain greater understanding of the New Testament.

Illustrations. Each chapter also uses a wide array of graphics and photographs, carefully chosen to aid us in reconstructing the world of the New Testament. Museum pieces, landscapes, maps, aerial photos, archaeological sites, and artist reconstructions each contribute to contextual material that will help our interpretation. Note especially the study of coins (numismatics). Coins served a much different purpose in the ancient world. Its value was directly related to its weight (a shekel, for instance, is a measurement of weight).

The image on the coin was "struck" by a government mint that authorized the coin's value. Thus, ancient coins served political purposes. They also distributed propaganda for the emperor — or they became an opportunity for dissenting peoples to resist any apparent participation with an occupier. The question given to Jesus in Matthew 22:15 – 17 about taxes is hardly innocent. It is about politics.

A Roman silver denarius showing the tools of minting: tongs, dyes, and hammer.

1. Are we giving deeper respect to the Bible when we say that it requires earnest study to unlock its deeper meaning? Why?

2. If the Bible is inspired by God, why should it take so much effort to understand it? Did God intend to make it so difficult?

3. If access to the deeper meaning of the New Testament can come only through thoughtful study, doesn't this exclude those who are unable to study? Are we making a "priesthood" of scholars who alone know the secrets of the New Testament?

4. If each of us brings some bias to our reading of the Scriptures, how can I know if any interpretation of a New Testament passage is correct?

5. What tools do scholars use to reconstruct the original context of the New Testament? Which do you think are most important?

BIBLIOGRAPHY
Introductory
Marshall, I. H., ed. *New Testament Interpretation: Essays on Principles and Methods*. Grand Rapids: Eerdmans, 1977.

Stambaugh, J. E., and D. L. Balch. *The New Testament in Its Social Environment*. LEC. Philadelphia: Westminster, 1986.

Tate, W. R. *Biblical Interpretation: An Integrated Approach*. Peabody, MA: Hendrickson, 1991.

Advanced
Klein, W., C. Blomberg, and H. Hubbard. *Introduction to Biblical Interpretation*. Second edition. Nashville: Nelson, 2003.

Osborne, G. *The Hermeneutical Spiral: A Comprehensive Introduction to Biblical Interpretation*. Revised and expanded. Downers Grove, IL: InterVarsity Press, 2006.

NOTES
1. See *www.wycliffe.org/about/statistics.aspx*.

CHAPTER 2

THE HISTORICAL SETTING
OF THE NEW TESTAMENT

Ancient ruins of the Hellenistic city Hippos, on the eastern shore of the Sea of Galilee.

The triumphal arch of Titus was built by the Roman Senate in AD 81 to commemorate Titus's conquest of Judea ten years earlier.

Produced following Rome's defeat of Judea, the coin depicts images of Vespasian (left) and Judea as a defeated woman (right).

PERSPECTIVE

Every culture is influenced by the historical forces that shape it. Events in history change who we are. Thus, it is impossible to understand the world of the New Testament without some grasp of the major political events that shaped its world and culture. Jerusalem's recovery from the Babylonian exile shaped the nature of Israel's priesthood. The cultural conquest of Hellenism changed the way people spoke and thought. Even the Roman Empire affected Judaism by bringing new possibilities of commerce and cultural exchange from the western reaches of the Mediterranean.

THE POST-EXILIC PERIOD, 539 – 332 BC

The turmoil described at the close of the Old Testament period set the stage for the Jewish faith we meet in the New Testament. Babylonian armies had sacked the walled city of Jerusalem and especially destroyed its temple in 586 BC. The sacred vessels of the temple and numerous exiles were carried off to Babylon, where the conquering king Nebuchadnezzar presented them as a part of his spoils of war. For a generation Judaism lived in despair, wondering if they could believe in a God who could be defeated like this. Lamentations reflects this numbing reality for Israel, and Psalm 137 echoes profound despair.

The defeat of Babylon by Persia in 539 BC changed Israel's fortunes immediately. While Babylon's policy for conquest had included the resettlement of defeated national groups (to disrupt their national identities), the Persians used these frustrated exiles as allies, promising to send them back to their homelands. Cyrus, the Persian monarch, permitted the Jews to begin this emigration soon after Babylon's fall. While many no doubt returned at once, the migration was likely gradual, taking decades to complete. But many other Jews chose to remain in Babylon, and by the first century, they enjoyed self-rule. Their community grew large, though little evidence remains that helps us reconstruct its size or welfare.

CYRUS THE GREAT

Xenophon was a prolific writer who served in the Greek cavalry in the late fifth century BC. Among his many works, the *Cyropaedia* ("Education of Cyrus") survives as a pseudo-historical account of Cyrus the Great's life. In 1.1.5 he describes the character of the Persian king:

> He ruled over these nations, even though they did not speak the same language as he, nor one nation the same as another; for all that, he was able to cover so vast a region with the fear which he inspired, that he struck all men with terror and no one tried to withstand him; and he was able to awaken in all so lively a desire to please him, that they always wished to be guided by his will. Moreover, the tribes that he brought into subjection to himself were so many that it is a difficult matter even to travel to them all, in whatever direction one begin one's journey from the palace, whether toward the east or the west, toward the north or the south.

Built by Nebuchadnezzar (605 - 562 BC), the Ishtar Gate was one of eight fortified inner gates of Babylon. Made of glazed brick it depicted ornate dragons and young bulls and opened the entrance to Babylon's "processional avenue" now traced to over one half mile.

The story of Israel's return can be traced in Ezra and Nehemiah and in the prophets Ezekiel, Haggai, Zechariah, and Malachi. Some scholars add Daniel and Esther to this list. Since the Exile was explained as divine judgment for Israel's covenant failings (Mal. 2:11), the Jewish leadership returned to Jerusalem with a profound desire to keep the law. Religious rigor characterized the call of Ezra, who not only demanded that the law be kept with care but called on Jews to separate themselves from those people living in the surrounding hills. The prophet Malachi reinforced this, prohibiting "mixed marriages" that would compromise faith (2:10–12) and calling for righteousness in everything from temple sacrifices (1:6–8) to wages given to the poor (3:5).

Haggai reminded Israel that faithfulness to God would return prosperity to the land (Hag. 2:19). And he pronounced a test on the nation's faith by calling for God's house (the temple) to be built before any of the city's neighborhoods (1:4–6). Many of the minor implements for the temple returned with the Jews, but most major items (such as the ark of the covenant) were lost. Work on a new temple began promptly and took about five years to complete (515 BC).

The full restoration of Jerusalem, however, was incomplete until Nehemiah began reconstructing the city's wall system (about thirteen years after Ezra's arrival). He had been a high official of the Persian king, but when he learned about the devastated condition of Jerusalem's infrastructure, he returned to Judea with the king's blessing. However, this development, combined with the rebuilding of the temple, signaled something ominous to those non-Jews living in the area. Ezra carried an authorization from the Persian king to resettle the

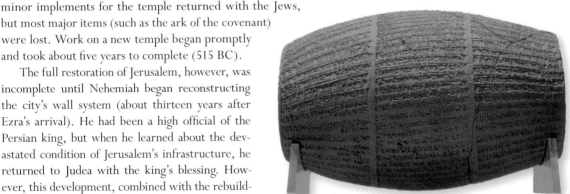

Dating from 536 BC, a cylinder seal such as this authorized the decree of Cyrus that permitted the Jews to be transferred from Babylon to Judah and rebuild their temple.

land (Ezra 1:2–4, 6:3–5), Nehemiah had an approval to reconstruct the walls (Neh 2:1–8), and now these returning refugees were acting on these pledges. At this time, political leadership in Jerusalem fell to the priesthood.

Judaism had changed during the exile. It adopted the popular use of Aramaic, a cognate Semitic language with Hebrew. This language had long been the *lingua franca* of the east and using it linked the Jews to the commercial and political channels of the emerging world. By the first century this was the common language of life in Israel and was likely Jesus' native tongue.

Judaism also had to come to terms with the meaning of faith *without* the temple and sacrifice. Piety was expressed through study, obedience, and prayer. This was possibly the origin of the synagogue, which began as a gathering of Jews who debated the Scriptures, prayed, and formed community centers. When the Jews rebuilt the temple, these village-based gathering places continued to flourish.

THE HELLENISTIC PERIOD (332 – 63 BC)

While the conquering empires of the east permitted the Jews to retain their cultural and religious identity, the coming of Greek culture — or Hellenism — in the fourth century made an indelible mark on Jewish life. Greek culture was missionary by nature, sweeping up new peoples and converting them to a new, "modern" way of life. Judaism soon found itself enticed to join the wider Mediterranean world.

Persian guards oversaw Jewish independence in Judah. This relief comes from the fifth century BC and was found at Persepolis.

TIMELINE OF POLITICAL EVENTS, 350 BC TO AD 135

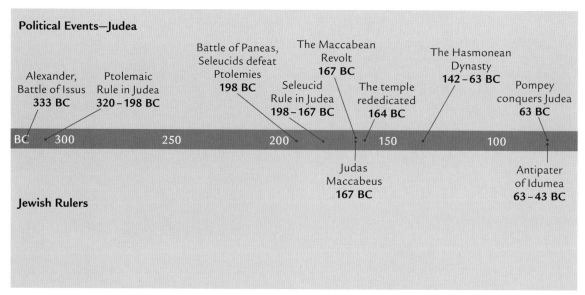

Political Events—Judea

Alexander, Battle of Issus **333 BC**

Ptolemaic Rule in Judea **320 – 198 BC**

Battle of Paneas, Seleucids defeat Ptolemies **198 BC**

Seleucid Rule in Judea **198 – 167 BC**

The Maccabean Revolt **167 BC**

The temple rededicated **164 BC**

The Hasmonean Dynasty **142 – 63 BC**

Pompey conquers Judea **63 BC**

BC 300   250   200   150   100

Judas Maccabeus **167 BC**

Antipater of Idumea **63 – 43 BC**

Jewish Rulers

Alexander the Great of Macedon

Few figures in the ancient world were as romanticized as Alexander the Great (356–323 BC). Images on coins and sculpture lived alongside biographies and legends, recalling his life for centuries. Rumors reported that he had descended from Zeus, that he read Homer on his campaigns, that he and his officers enjoyed lavish lives filled with finery, expensive food, and wine, and that his military instincts were as brilliant as they were severe.

As a Macedonian, Alexander's political goal was the defeat of the Persians who had controlled the eastern Aegean since about 513 BC. Alexander's father, Philip, was a charismatic leader who asserted Macedonian hegemony by defeating southern Greece—a region that viewed the Macedonians as hardly more than barbarians.

Throughout the Hellenistic era, Alexander's life had become legend. His image, like this one at Pompeii, decorated buildings throughout the Mediterranean.

Philip persuaded Aristotle to tutor his young son, which prepared Alexander for early leadership when his father was assassinated in 336 BC.

Alexander was only twenty at the time. But he picked up his father's mantle, won the allegiance of Philip's leading generals, and reasserted Macedonian nationalism. Alexander's first aim was to defeat the Persians who held Anatolia (Asia Minor). In 334 he visited Troy—the symbolic site of the Greek defeat of Asia—and then engaged the Persian satrap (governor) in his first battle at the Granicus River. This important victory led to the collapse of Asia. He moved south, freeing Greek cities (such as Ephesus, Sardis, and Miletus) along the Aegean and was cautiously hailed as a liberator.

As the agile Macedonians (30,000 strong) moved east, the Persian king, Darius III, knew he had to confront Alexander immediately. He raised an army of 100,000 and met his foe in

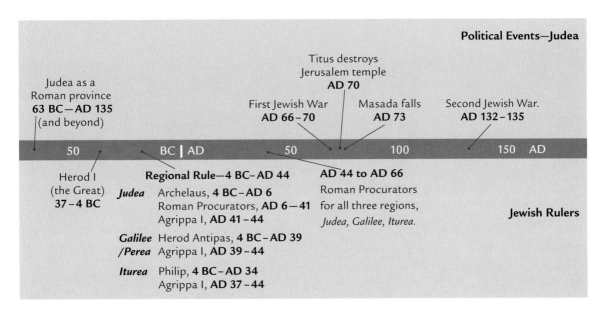

a narrow plain of Issus in 333 BC. The Persian army's superior size was constricted by the battlefield and his line was quickly breached by Alexander's swift, armored cavalry. Darius fled and the field belonged to the Macedonians.

Alexander continued his victory march south, stopping first to subdue the minor region of Judea. His main goal there was Egypt, which he occupied in 332 BC. Then he led his troops to the Euphrates and followed its course until he entered Mesopotamia. North of Babylon, Darius held a massive army of 200,000 at an open plain (Gaugamela) and assumed that his ability to outflank the smaller Macedonians would win the day. But he was wrong. Again Alexander drove his armored cavalry through the center of the Persian line and placed his opponent in disarray. Darius' conscripts collapsed; again, Darius fled and sought refuge this time in Bactria (modern Afghanistan), but there he was slain. Alexander (who was pursuing him) found his body on a roadside in 330 BC.

Alexander's military successes came from three strategic changes in field warfare. First, ancient war had generally consisted of wide lines of troops, many men deep, rushing at each other in a desperate melee. Philip and Alexander developed the Macedonian phalanx—a highly disciplined square of 256 men (sixteen per side) armed with a long eighteen-foot spear, the *sarissa*, that could outreach the enemy. The phalanx was heavily armed and disciplined, and could move independently with local commanders. Second, Alexander developed the heavy cavalry. These were horses well-protected with armor and men. Their charge could burst through most enemy lines. Finally, Alexander developed the siege train. These were wagons bearing supplies, catapults, ladders, and siege engines. Alexander (and every general) knew that an army's resupply was as important as its war-fighting ability. The Macedonians made such preparation a science.

This coin, the Judean *prutah*, was one of the most popular coins minted in Judea. Worth about one loaf of bread, it shows the influence of Alexander in its display of the Macedonian rosette.

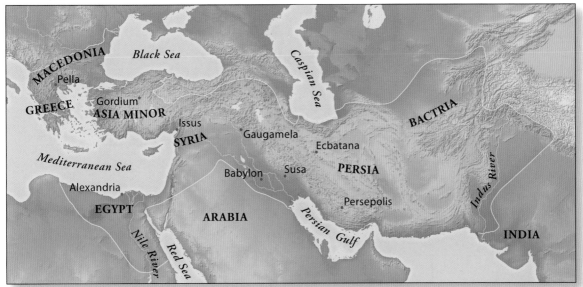

The Empire of Alexander

The swift collapse of the Persian military was unexpected. Suddenly Alexander viewed the prospect of unraveling the balance of Persia's great empire. He plundered the Persian treasuries, freeing its cities (such as Babylon), and later conquered the great Persian capital of Persepolis, which he burned. He continued to move east, hoping to build the greatest empire in history and see the "great ocean" of the east, which would mark the end of the world. He announced that he would cross the Hindu Kush Mountains and next take India. He defeated the Indian king Porus but had no idea how many kingdoms still lay ahead. His trusted veterans had crossed over 11,000

When Alexander defeated the Indian King Porus in 326, the Macedonians struck a silver coin showing Alexander, Porus, and his war elephants from the Punjab.

miles in eight years of constant campaign, and in western India they compelled Alexander to turn the army around. After two years, they made their way back to Babylon, where Alexander worked hard to build an administrative system for the empire. However in 323 BC at age thirty-three, he died.

THE ALEXANDRIAN BASE IN SAMARIA

NOTES FROM ANTIQUITY

When the Persians controlled the province of Judea, they chose Samaria as their base. Here were potential allies who hated Jewish rule yet understood local politics. When Samaria fell to Alexander in 332 BC he made this his base of regional control and stationed some of his Macedonian troops there.

Roman conquest in 63 BC again had a role for Samaria. It was one more vital Roman military outpost keeping an eye on Judea. During the Roman period, Herod the Great rebuilt Samaria splendidly, renaming it Sebaste (the Greek name of Emperor Augustus).

Samaria's use as a staging area for foreign rulers reinforced Judaism's antagonism toward the region and its people. Today remnants of Alexander's fortress along with numerous Roman remains can still be seen there.

When Alexander the Great conquered Judea, he fortified towers such as this in Samaria to control his rule of the region.

Alexander's death left his empire in the hands of his generals, who struggled for supremacy. Soon the empire was divided into political regions with each defended by powerful officers. Two dynasties affected Judaism's fortunes. In Egypt the Ptolemaic dynasty was founded in 323 with its capital in Alexandria. Ten years later the Seleucid dynasty was formed in Syria with its capital at Antioch. Judea was ruled from Egypt until 198 BC, when war changed the landscape dramatically.

While Alexander was committed to conquest, his legacy was more. The lands he conquered were quickly Hellenized. Cities were founded with features that reflected the values of his homeland: theaters, gymnasiums, schools, and municipal government. A universal monetary currency was established. Above all, Greek became the new language of a new world that united the cultures of Mesopotamia, Egypt, and the Mediterranean. Literature, commerce, medicine, religion, philosophy, and mathematics (to name a few) all used Greek. Greek culture dominated the eastern Mediterranean for almost nine hundred years and ended only with the coming of Islam in the seventh century. Greek became the language of the early Christian communities and of the New Testament.

Ptolemaic Rule (320–198 BC)

This coin depicts Zeus seated facing left and the name of Alexander on the right.

Ptolemy I Soter (*savior*) had been one of Alexander's most trusted generals, accompanying him throughout Asia. At Alexander's death, Ptolemy became governor of Egypt and with time was designated as king. Despite the turmoil of these years, Ptolemy successfully defended his hold on Egypt, based his capital at Alexandria, and Hellenized the northern cities of the country.

During this era, Judea enjoyed remarkable freedom as the Ptolemies considered it pacified. It was a small kingdom encircling Jerusalem and was viewed as a temple-state ruled by priests who merely had to pay taxes to the local Ptolemaic governor. Many Jews lived elsewhere outside Judea (called the Diaspora or Dispersion), and migration to cities like Alexandria was common, building permanent Jewish communities there.

The greatest threat to Jewish identity was the gradual assimilation of Hellenistic culture. Intertestamental literature records how Jerusalem's priests warned about the encroachment of these values. Theaters offered dramatic arts that were foreign to Jewish life. Gymnasium guilds enlisted young men at eighteen to join their social and athletic centers where sporting events were practiced nude. (Some young men even sought to reverse the signs of circumcision to avoid shame when they entered the games.) Clothing styles—always a potent symbol for the young—now made outlandish cultural statements. Jewish beards and flowing robes were being replaced with broad rimmed hats, short togas, and high laced sandals (2 Macc. 4:10–17). Hellenistic life was eroding traditional Jewish culture.

Jews began to use common Greek (or Koine Greek) as their common language. Thus, the Hebrew Scriptures were no longer understandable in the synagogues. According to the ancient *Letter of Aristeas*, the librarian of Alexandria called for the first-ever translation of the Hebrew Scriptures into Greek.

Josephus tells us the legend that followed this effort (*Ant.* 12.2.1–16 [17–23]). Jerusalem's high priest chose seventy-two men (six from each tribe) who were fluent in both Hebrew and Greek. They traveled to and worked in Alexandria for a mere seventy-two days translating the Hebrew Bible. They presented their efforts to the Egyptian king and placed a curse on any who might change anything. This translation was completed in about 250 BC and was sponsored by Ptolemy Philadelphus (285–246 BC). Among Greek-speaking Jews (such as Paul) this Bible became a standard text, serving both Judaism and the early church for centuries. Today scholars refer to it as the Septuagint (recalling its seventy-two translators).

While Alexander's tomb has never been found, the Istanbul Archaeological Museum has an ornate marble sarcophagus attributed to Alexander that was discovered in 1887 in Sidon, Lebanon.

ALEXANDER THE GREAT'S TOMB

On his deathbed, Alexander appointed his general, Perdikkas, as regent of the kingdom until his son (Alexander IV) was born. Perdikkas laid Alexander in an anthropoid sarcophagus, which in turn was encased in a gold casket and covered with a purple robe. A gold carriage carried this and all of Alexander's armor (Diodorus of Sicily, *The Library of History* 18.26.3). Perdikkas was intent on taking the king to Aegae in Macedonia, the traditional resting place of the Macedonian kings.

With Alexander's body in transit, Ptolemy I decided to travel to Syria to meet the assembly and (presumably) to pay his respects. But Ptolemy attacked the caravan, seized the mummy, and spirited it away to Egypt, where he buried it in his own kingdom. Alexander had once visited the famous Oracle of Ammon in the Egyptian desert in 331 BC, where he was declared "son of god." Soon stories serving Ptolemy's propaganda spread widely that this was Alexander's deathbed wish to return to the Oracle. Alexander's' tomb was finally located in Alexandria, the city named after him. The Ptolemaic kings used his burial to legitimize their rule and even claimed at one point to descend from him personally.

Seleucid Rule (198 – 167 BC)

Seleucus I Nicator (*conqueror*) was also one of Alexander's generals who vied for control of the fragmented empire. Along with Ptolemy I he became a powerful leader and eventually ruled Babylon, the upper Euphrates valleys, Syria, and Anatolia (or Asia Minor). In order to build a second capital for his western interests, he founded the city of Antioch on the Orontes, with its own Mediterranean seaport named Seleucia.

A silver *tetradrachma* minted during the reign of Seleucus I (305-281 B.C.) in Susa, Persia. Here Seleucus places Alexander's image on the coin as a unifying icon for his empire. On the obverse (front) of this coin appears a portrait of Alexander the Great wearing a leopard-skin helmet and the horns of a bull. The reverse shows a figure of Nike crowning a trophy.

The successors of Seleucus fought to hold this largest region of the empire and found enemies everywhere. New kings such as Antiochus III looked south as the only avenue to expand. A successful war with the Ptolemies in 198 (at Caesarea Philippi) led to Judea falling into Syrian hands. But the expanding power of Rome could be felt in western Asian Minor. At the Battle of Magnesia in 189 BC, the Seleucid Antiochus III lost 53,000 men (Rome lost 400) and fled for his life. He sued for peace but had to relinquish his fleet and his war elephants. By 190 BC all Asia Minor was paying tribute to Rome.

In 175 BC, following the murder of Antiochus III's successor (his son, Seleucus IV), his second son Antiochus IV gained the Seleucid throne and worked to consolidate his rule. In Jerusalem he joined the tradition of his predecessors and accepted the bribes of men who desired to be high priest. Soon Hellenizers like Jason and Menelaus were running the temple to the despair of the priestly families. Antiochus's presumption reached new heights when he assumed the title Epiphanes (*manifestation*, i.e., the revealing of God on earth) and sought to be worshiped.

Antiochus Epiphanes worked to increase his hold on Egypt as well, but there he encountered the Romans in 168 BC Antiochus returned north shaken and humiliated, and turned against perceived ethnic minorities that might weaken his slipping position. Jewish leaders witnessed his defeat in Egypt and attempted a rebellion. Antiochus viewed Jerusalem as rebellious and on his return from Egypt sacked the city, tore down its walls, and looted the temple treasury. He made decrees prohibiting temple festivals and circumcision, and it became illegal to possess the Scriptures. The worship of Greek gods became mandatory and soon festivals for the god Dionysius could be seen in Jerusalem's streets. In the winter of 167 BC the temple was turned over to the worship of Zeus and for three years pigs were sacrificed by Greeks on Israel's holy altar. In Jewish eyes, the temple had been desecrated (1 Macc. 1:41 – 61).

Maccabean War (167 – 141 BC)

Antiochus IV used repressive measures to Hellenize Judaism not long after he came to the throne in 175 BC. This gold coin issued in his kingdom during this period shows Zeus enthroned.

Resistance to Hellenism had been expressed for decades before this famous "abomination of desolation" at the temple. A group of Jews calling themselves the Hasidim (*pious ones*) saw the long-term implications of Hellenistic advances and openly criticized Jews who flirted with Hellenistic ways. Using Greek speech might lead to youth visiting Greek theaters — and then Greek racetracks and temples. But if some Jewish leaders were ever complacent about the assimilation of Hellenistic culture, much of it stopped in 167 BC. This tragedy brought an opportunity that the Hasidim now exploited. Antiochus had gone too far, and his offense to the temple proved to be the catalyst Judaism needed.

The story of Jews' resistance to their Seleucid oppressors became something legendary since it was retold every year at the feast of Hanukkah. The apocryphal book 1 Maccabees outlines its history and 2 Maccabees records heroic episodes of suffering and martyrdom. For example, we read about the faithful priest Eleazar, who refused pressure to sacrifice to Zeus and instead chose death (2 Macc. 6:18–31). These stories were well known in Jesus' day and inspired resistance to cultural compromise.

The passive resistance of the Hasidim quickly shifted to open warfare. Typical was the priest Mattathias, who refused to compromise under pressure and traveled to the village of Modein, a village west of Jerusalem. There ambitious young Greek soldiers demanded that he sacrifice to Zeus. Mattathias refused, drew a sword, killed the men, and destroyed their pagan altar. With his sons Judas, Simon, and Jonathan, Mattathias inspired a widespread revolt that stirred the villages of Judea and launched a guerrilla campaign to expel the Greeks from the land. Mattathias was killed and his son Judas led the war, gaining the nickname "Maccabeus" (*hammer*). Soon the revolt was called the Maccabean Revolt.

The Jewish fighters often won battles since they knew the terrain well and fought against an empire being challenged on every border. In 164 BC Judas gained the temple precincts and cleansed the sanctuary, inaugurating the feast we know as Hanukkah (*dedication*, 1 Macc. 4:36–51; Josephus refers to it as "the festival of lights," *Ant.* 12.7.7 [325]). The balance of the walled city had been planned as a Greek city and renamed Antiochia. Judas built a siege wall around it, defeated it, and razed it; then he built a Jewish palace on its grounds. His brother Jonathan gained a treaty with Rome, thus giving more threatening support to the war. Soon the Seleucids were in full retreat as they pulled back to Antioch and there awaited the coming Roman armies, who would conquer that capital seventy-five years later.

> ### JUDAS MACCABAEUS CLEANSES THE TEMPLE
> The most profound moment in the Maccabean war came in 164 BC when Judas and his brothers fought their way to Jerusalem and arrived at the temple. "They saw the sanctuary desolate, the altar profaned, and the gates burned. In the courts they saw bushes sprung up as in a thicket ... [and] they saw the chambers of the priests in ruins" (1 Macc. 4:38).
>
> Judas wept and cried out to heaven. Then he appointed priests to rededicate the temple and restore its offerings and sacrifices.

The Hasmonean Dynasty (141–63 BC)

The spoils of war now fell into the hands of the leaders of those campaigns. The family of Mattathias and its heirs formed the first Jewish dynasty in centuries, naming it the Hasmonean Dynasty. Since Judas and Jonathan had both died in battle, a popular assembly in Jerusalem proclaimed Simon a "high priest forever until a trustworthy prophet should arise"

THE HASMONEAN RULERS

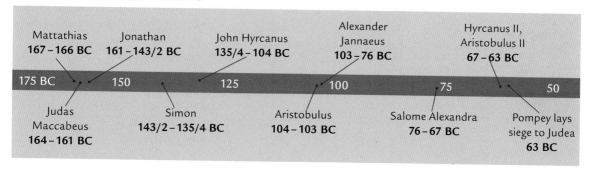

Mattathias 167–166 BC
Jonathan 161–143/2 BC
John Hyrcanus 135/4–104 BC
Alexander Jannaeus 103–76 BC
Hyrcanus II, Aristobulus II 67–63 BC

175 BC | 150 | 125 | 100 | 75 | 50

Judas Maccabeus 164–161 BC
Simon 143/2–135/4 BC
Aristobulus 104–103 BC
Salome Alexandra 76–67 BC
Pompey lays siege to Judea 63 BC

(1 Macc. 14:41). A Jewish calendar began with this *theocracy* as year 1. Note in 1 Maccabees 13:42 how documents and contracts were marked: "in the first year of Simon the great high priest and commander and leader of the Jews." For the first time since 586 BC Jewish coins were minted and the Jews enjoyed genuine autonomy.

The Hasmoneans consolidated their power and wealth and soon became a small aristocracy ruling Jerusalem. However, these efforts alienated many who had fought in the war but who now felt marginalized. Those with roots going back to the original Hasidim, for whom the war was inspired by a zeal for the law and the purity of the land, now recognized that they had little stake in the new government in Jerusalem. In a generation Judaism found itself torn three ways: Hellenized Jews, who still embraced Greek culture and life; Hasmoneans, who brokered power in Jerusalem; and Hasidim, who called for religious purity and warned of the corrupting dangers of power. Some went so far as to condemn the hereditary priesthood that began with Simon.

These tensions only increased as the Hasmonean princes expanded their borders and prosperity increased. Resistance to their rule focused on the Hasidim (known later as the Pharisees), whose power was localized in the numerous synagogues around the country. The Hasmoneans became an urban autocracy invested in the temple and the religious success of the Jewish nation. Struggle between these two groups intensified throughout the years 100–65 BC. Fearing a civil war, many Hasmonean kings tried to preempt rebellions. Alexander Jannaeus, for instance, ruled from 103–76 BC and in one year crucified 800 Pharisees in order to protect the status quo.

THE ROMAN PERIOD (BEGINS 63 BC)

Throughout the Seleucid period, the fledgling Roman Empire was expanding east. Two prizes were in its sights: Egypt (famous for its wealth, its academies, and its agricultural produce) and Syria (gateway to the Euphrates valleys). From the Taurus Mountains to Lebanon, the fertility of the land was unmatched. Moreover, control of the Upper Euphrates meant that Rome could halt any threat from its rival Parthia (or Persia). The empire therefore devised a plan. A swift march of legionnaires through Anatolia could capture Antioch, then move down the coast, controlling the corridor that would take them to Egypt.

Pompey's Conquest (63 BC)

Pompey the Great (106–48 BC), one of Rome's most celebrated commanders in the first century BC, had established his reputation through successful wars in Sicily, Africa, and Spain. In 67 BC he was assigned to bring Roman force to the boundary of the Seleucid domain. In 64 BC Syrian Antioch fell to Pompey. Immediately he began his march south, where Judea was his next strategic goal.

Pompey's march into Judea has been recorded in some detail by Josephus (*Ant.* 14.4.1–4 [57–71]; *War* 1.7.1–5 [141–151]). Conditions could not have been better for a siege. A civil war had erupted in Jerusalem between factions supporting rival brothers for the Jewish throne. Pompey followed the Orontes River south from Antioch. He liberated Damascus and the many Greek settlements

Pompey enjoyed a reputation as one of the leading military officers in first century BC Rome. When civil war broke out in Judea between the brothers Hyrcanus and Aristobulus, he exploited it masterfully, turning Judea into a Roman province.

Gerasa was a major Decapolis city located in the mountains of Gilead. Today the site is called Jerash (Jordan) and offers spectacular monumental remains from the Roman period. This is the main street (or cardo) that was once lined with public buildings.

and cities that had lived under merciless Hasmonean rule for a hundred years. Here he found auxiliary troops as well as abundant provisions. He promised that under Roman administration, this region — called *The Decapolis* (or League of *Ten Cities*) — would never again live under Jewish rule. The Greeks of Syria celebrated and eagerly joined Pompey's legions.

In 63 BC Pompey moved to Jericho and there began receiving peace overtures from a Jerusalem in disarray. He promptly marched west but when he arrived at Jerusalem's walls, some factions wanted to welcome him while others threatened hostilities. Pledges of peace from the city were evaporating, so Pompey prepared for war. He built a siege wall around the city, broke through the city's western defenses, and finally entered the temple where the priests were slain as they served. According to Josephus (*Ant.* 14.4.4 [69–72]), Pompey entered the temple sanctuaries and demanded to enter the Most Holy Place, something the high priest did only once each year (on the Day of Atonement). For Israel, it was a high sacrilege. He entered and looked around, but he did not touch the temple furniture or its treasures. In this one-day siege, 12,000 Jewish citizens of Jerusalem died.

THE DECAPOLIS CITIES

Following his successful conquest of the region, Pompey freed numerous cities from Jewish rule that the Roman governor of Syria administered. The Roman historian Pliny was the first to list them (*Natural History*, 5.16 [74]): Scythopolis, Gadara, Hippos, Dion, Pella, Raphana, Canatha, Damascus, Philadelphia, and Galasa (Gerasa). These cities formed a "league" and controlled important trade routes from Syria. Pompey also created a number of other autonomous Greek cities, setting them free from Jewish jurisdiction.

Jesus visited the Decapolis during his ministry (Mark 5:20; 7:31). For instance, the Gadarene demoniac was from Gadara (Mark 5:1–20). When Jesus visited here he was entering a strictly Greek world — hence the presence of swine in Mark 5:11–12.

Pompey freed many Hellenistic cities from Jewish rule and in turn enjoyed their military support. Among these cities was Gerasa located east of Galilee.

Pompey laid a heavy tribute on the city and appointed a high priest of his choosing (Hyrcanus II). He beheaded many of Jerusalem's leaders who resisted him and distributed rewards to those who had rendered support. After his departure, Roman rulers set about administering the new province, rebuilding the freed Decapolis cities and organizing two legions (9,600 troops) to quell any resistance.

Jewish Rulers under Rome

For the next two decades, Jewish leaders engaged a delicate game of political cooperation and passive resistance. Antipater (63–43 BC) was a wealthy Idumean (from the southern deserts) whose political help Pompey had valued immediately after the conquest. Antipater had supported the new high priest Hyrcanus and seemed cooperative. Rome needed him because he understood the local politics of Judea well—but as an Idumean he might not succumb to nationalistic urges. Antipater soon became the power behind Hyrcanus and because he won Rome's favor, Caesar made him a tax-free Roman citizen and governor of Judea. Permission to rebuild Jerusalem's walls came next, but in 43 BC he was poisoned by a rival. His two sons, however, had already become regional rulers:

The Roman Empire

Among Herod's greatest engineering achievements, the new port city of Caesarea stands out. Here an artificial harbor welcomed Roman ships from the west. The project began in about 22 BC and took Herod's engineers 12 years to complete. Recently scholars have located a hippodrome and a palace complex at the south perimeter of the city.

Phasael led Judea and Herod was running Galilee. Herod had aspirations to lead the entire country. With their father's death, both men were appointed joint rulers of the province.

In 40 BC the Parthian threat that Rome predicted now broke over Syria. Jerusalem was captured, Hyrcanus exiled, and Phasael killed. Herod fled for his life, running to Bethlehem, to the Dead Sea, then south to Egypt, where he was received in Alexandria by Cleopatra and took passage to Rome, vowing to return. The Roman Senate declared him "King of the Jews." Fortified with Roman troops, he returned to Jerusalem in 37 BC and attacked the city's defenders. The conflict was short-lived and established Herod on the throne.

Herod the Great (37–4 BC)

Herod ruled for thirty-three years and became expert at placating Roman interests in the region while keeping his Jewish province intact and prosperous. He built a series of fortresses around Judea, which accurately show his political concerns and vulnerabilities. All risks were to the east and south. The Parthians might return through Syria; the independent Arab Nabatean kingdom was just across the Dead Sea; and Cleopatra in Egypt had already gained ownership of Jericho (as well as Phoenicia and parts of Arabia).

Herod felt additional vulnerabilities as an "outsider" with the Hasmonean families of Jerusalem. Most viewed him as "half Jewish" since his mother was Arab (*Ant.* 14.7.3 [121–122]). He married one of the Hasmonean daughters, Mariamne, hoping to shore up his connections, but throughout his life he was always viewed as an interloper, well-connected to Rome but tenuously supported by leading Jewish families. He felt so

The theater at Caesarea has been completely excavated. It was rebuilt after Herod but still conveys something of the city's might. It seated about 4,000.

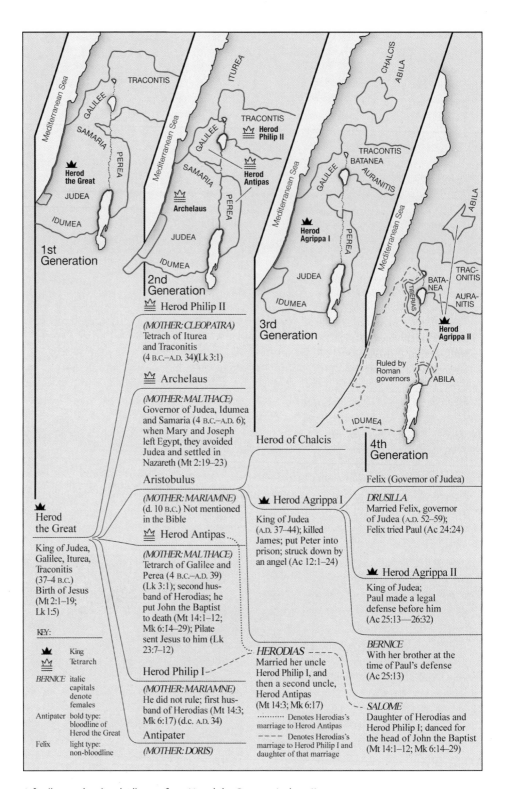

1st Generation

2nd Generation

3rd Generation

4th Generation

Herod the Great

King of Judea, Galilee, Iturea, Traconitis (37–4 B.C.) Birth of Jesus (Mt 2:1–19; Lk 1:5)

KEY:

♛ King

♛ Tetrarch

BERNICE italic capitals denote females

Antipater bold type: bloodline of Herod the Great

Felix light type: non-bloodline

Herod Philip II

(MOTHER: CLEOPATRA) Tetrarch of Iturea and Traconitis (4 B.C.–A.D. 34)(Lk 3:1)

Archelaus

(MOTHER: MALTHACE) Governor of Judea, Idumea and Samaria (4 B.C.–A.D. 6); when Mary and Joseph left Egypt, they avoided Judea and settled in Nazareth (Mt 2:19–23)

Aristobulus

(MOTHER: MARIAMNE) (d. 10 B.C.) Not mentioned in the Bible

Herod Antipas

(MOTHER: MALTHACE) Tetrarch of Galilee and Perea (4 B.C.–A.D. 39) (Lk 3:1); second husband of Herodias; he put John the Baptist to death (Mt 14:1–12; Mk 6:14–29); Pilate sent Jesus to him (Lk 23:7–12)

Herod Philip I

(MOTHER: MARIAMNE) He did not rule; first husband of Herodias (Mt 14:3; Mk 6:17) (d.c. A.D. 34)

Antipater

(MOTHER: DORIS)

Herod of Chalcis

Herod Agrippa I

King of Judea (A.D. 37–44); killed James; put Peter into prison; struck down by an angel (Ac 12:1–24)

HERODIAS

Married her uncle Herod Philip I, and then a second uncle, Herod Antipas (Mt 14:3; Mk 6:17)

·········· Denotes Herodias's marriage to Herod Antipas

– – – – Denotes Herodias's marriage to Herod Philip I and daughter of that marriage

Felix (Governor of Judea)

DRUSILLA

Married Felix, governor of Judea (A.D. 52–59); Felix tried Paul (Ac 24:24)

Herod Agrippa II

King of Judea; Paul made a legal defense before him (Ac 25:13—26:32)

BERNICE

With her brother at the time of Paul's defense (Ac 25:13)

SALOME

Daughter of Herodias and Herod Philip I; danced for the head of John the Baptist (Mt 14:1–12; Mk 6:14–29)

A family tree showing the lineage from Herod the Great to Agrippa II.

suspicious about these families that he arranged to have two of his sons by Mariamne killed "by accident." Altogether he executed forty-five Hasmoneans, fearing conspiracies.

In order to make Judea into one of Rome's finest provinces Herod embarked on an ambitious building program. A new fabulous harbor, one of the largest in the Mediterranean, Caesarea Maritima, gave access to ships from the west (*Ant.* 15.9.6 [331–341]). It was dominated by a temple to Augustus. In time it became the center for the Roman provincial

HEROD'S NEW HARBOR

Herod built Caesarea to impress its visitors. When his twelve-year project was done, it rivaled Piraeus, the port of Athens. Along a desolate forty-mile stretch of beach he constructed his port on the ruins of an abandoned village (Strato's Tower). Its breakwater used new hydraulic cement and formed a three and a half acre bay. The city of Caesarea (164 acres) was equally impressive: civic buildings with white marble façades, a theater, a hippodrome, and warehouses. The tides flushed its sewers each day making the city unprecedented in antiquity. Fresh water came to the city from an aqueduct that carried water from springs in the north.

Above all, Herod wanted the city to signal his allegiance to Rome. A temple dedicated to Caesar Augustus dominated the hill overlooking the harbor. Josephus describes it expansively: "And near to the mouth of the haven, upon an elevation, there was a temple for Caesar, which was excellent both in beauty and size; and therein was a Colossus of Caesar, not less than that of Jupiter Olympius, which it was made to resemble" (*War* 1.21.7 [414]).

Today excavations of Caesarea—both on land and in the harbor—have been continuing since 1972. Remarkable discoveries have shown the magnificence of the city. For example, blocks weighing 50 tons have been found in the breakwater. 100 huge vaults stretched along the coast to store the huge tonnage of goods moving through the port.

Left: The Herodium was a fortress built by Herod just east of Bethlehem. Today Roman baths, a synagogue, defensive walls, and massive sling stones (*ballista*) are among the material remains still in the fort. Pools and palaces graced the foot of the mountain. *Right:* The temple platform built by Herod I is enclosed behind Herod's retaining wall. The nearest corner of the platform is Jerusalem's southeast corner.

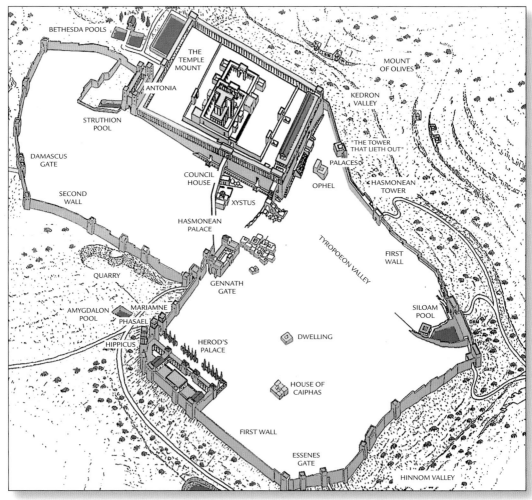

Herodian Jerusalem.

administration, where many Roman soldiers were billeted. Cornelius was a typical officer; in Acts 10 he became the first Gentile convert to the church.

In addition, Herod began construction projects elsewhere. His most important contribution was in Jerusalem, where he not only refurbished the walls and added theaters, a water system, a racetrack, and an opulent palace, but he reconstructed the temple—a project that began in 20 BC and was not completed until AD 63. The inner sanctuaries alone took eighteen months to decorate and required the training of priests, who alone could labor in the holy places. He added a "Women's Court" east of the place of sacrifice. The temple proper was surrounded by the "Court of the Gentiles." At its northwest corner Herod rebuilt an old Maccabean fortress to keep an eye on all temple activities—Fortress of Antonia (named after Mark Antony, the Roman who appointed Herod king).

Herod's paranoia was well placed. His successes only embittered the royal families, and such construction projects were financed by taxing the people to their maximum capacity. He was admired by Rome and despised by his own country. He was always watching for conspirators. Jesus was born during his reign and it comes as no surprise that a report of a "messianic child" in Bethlehem—a child whose story evoked expectations of messiah and promises of fulfillment—inspired him to send troops to the village on a horrific mission (Matt. 2:16–18).

Herod's temple looms large in the New Testament. When the disciples arrived once at Jerusalem, they were amazed at Herod's efforts: "Look, Teacher! What massive stones!" (Mark 13:1). The so-called "highest point of the temple" where Jesus was tested (Matt. 4:5) likely was the retaining

As ruler of Galilee, Herod Antipas struck his own coins. No bust appears on the coin out of deference for the Jewish avoidance of images.

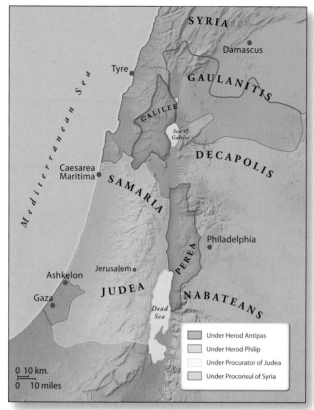

Divisions of Herod's Kingdom

wall's southeast corner. When Jesus cleansed the temple of moneychangers (21:12–17), this took place in the Court of the Gentiles. When he debated the temple leadership (ch. 23), he did so in the expansive porches surrounding its façade. Finally, when Jesus was arrested, he was taken to the "praetorium," which housed the Roman governor (27:27). Many scholars believe his interrogation with Pilate took place in the Antonia Fortress.

When Herod died in 4 BC of incurable diseases, few mourned his death. A funeral train carried him to one of his favorite fortresses, the Herodium, near Bethlehem, where he was buried.

The Division of Herod's Kingdom

After Herod's death, three of his sons divided the kingdom. **Archelaus's** rule of Judea (4 BC–AD 6) was vicious and feared. He was titled an "ethnarch" (ruler of a nation) because of the size of his rule (Judea, Samaria, and Idumea, Matt. 2:22). But the country was ready to explode in rebellion. Numerous guerrilla groups revolted but were defeated when the Syrian governor Varus sent as many as three legions into Judea (15,000 men) as well as numerous auxiliary troops. Over 2,000 Jewish captives were crucified. When Mary and Joseph were returning from Egypt with Jesus, they avoided Judea and returned to Galilee because "Archelaus was reigning in Judea in place of his father" (Matt. 2:22). Archelaus's brutality inspired delegations of both Samaritans and Jews to appeal to Augustus for his removal. In AD 6 Augustus agreed and banished him to Gaul. Archelaus's territory was then placed under the jurisdiction of Roman governors.

SEPPHORIS: A WINDOW INTO HELLENIZED GALILEE

The traditional capital of Galilee had always been Sepphoris, a town that sat on a hill as "the ornament of all Galilee" (*Ant.* 18.2.1 [27]). Today the excavations of the Joint Sepphoris Project have uncovered a huge and remarkable Hellenistic city nearby Nazareth.

The theater and mosaics there have offered up evidence of how Hellenized the first-century city had become. In one villa archaeologists uncovered panels that framed a dining room depicting a drinking rivalry between Bacchus and Hercules. Bacchus, the Greek god of wine, wins.

In 1987 archaeologists uncovered a significant villa in Sepphoris with a mosaic panel depicting woman now called "the Mona Lisa of Galilee."

Philip ruled regions northeast of Galilee and north of the Decapolis. His primary capital was Caesarea Philippi at the base of Mt. Hermon where numerous public buildings are now being uncovered. These are the ruins of the palace of Agrippa II.

Antipas retained his rule over Galilee and also controlled Perea, the region east of the Jordan River (4 BC – AD 39). Because he ruled a "part" of the kingdom, he was officially called a *tetrarch*, but he was allowed to use his family name of Herod, which enhanced his authority (Luke 3:19). Jesus' ministry began under Antipas's rule. Antipas rebuilt Galilee's ancient capital, Sepphoris, and made it his base. Since it was just north of Nazareth, Jesus and Joseph (who were tradesmen) may have worked there. Later Antipas built a new capital for himself on the western shore of the Sea of Galilee, calling it Tiberius (named after the emperor). The New Testament sometimes refers to the sea as "the Sea of Tiberias" (John 6:1).

Philip ruled as tetrarch over the northern regions of the kingdom (4 BC – AD 34): Gaulanitis, Auranitis, Batanea, Trachonitis, Paneas, and Iturea. These areas were chiefly Hellenistic, and he found little difficulty leading them. He built Caesarea *Philippi* (to distinguish it from Caesarea on the coast) as his capital near the ancient shrine to Pan on the Jordan

HOW PILATE OFFENDED THE JEWS

The attitude of the Roman governors toward Judea is illustrated by an incident recorded by Josephus (*War* 2.9.2 – 3 [169 – 174]). The temple leaders prohibited any images in Jerusalem because it violated the second commandment. All previous governors had respected this. But Pilate brought military standards bearing Tiberius's image directly to Jerusalem by stealth at night.

A Jewish delegation went to Caesarea and demanded their removal. For five days they knelt before his residence. Pilate's soldiers then surrounded them with weapons threatening to kill them if they would not relent. The Jews offered their necks, saying they would rather die than see the God's holy law profaned in the Holy City.

Pilate was stunned and removed the standards immediately.

Because of this incident (and many others) Philo found little to like in Pilate. He refers to him as by nature rigid and stubbornly harsh — merciless as well as obstinate (*The Embassy to Gaius* 38 [301]). Rome also disliked Pilate's efforts. He was recalled in AD 36 and one of his lieutenants, Marcellus, took his place as overseer until he was replaced by Marullus, the new prefect..

Excavators in Caesarea located a four-line dedicatory inscription with these words:

TIBERIEUM
[PO]NTIUS PILATUS
[PRAEF]ECT US IUDA [EA]
[FECIT D] E [DICAVIT]][1]

This is likely a building dedication honoring the emperor Tiberius. Translation: *Tiberium. Pontius Pilate, Prefect of Judea, has dedicated.*

The excavation of ancient Jerusalem since 1967 has uncovered much of the city's material culture from the first century. This collection of fine decorated pottery typifies the life of the upper classes in the first century.

River's headwaters. Here Jesus was identified as Son of God and Messiah for the first time (Matt. 16:13–16). Philip also built a southern royal city at the site of Bethsaida and renamed it Bethsaida Julias (honoring Augustus's daughter). Bethsaida was the original home of the disciples Peter, his brother Andrew, and Philip (John 1:44).

When Philip the tetrarch died in AD 34, the region was temporarily given to Syria. But the new emperor Caligula gave these areas along with Galilee to Agrippa I in AD 39.

Roman Prefects

Rome administered two types of provinces. Senatorial provinces were compliant with Roman rule, paid tribute, were ruled by a proconsul, and did not host a military legion. Gallio of Achaia was one such governor (Acts 18:12). Imperial provinces lived on the frontiers of the empire and were under the direct command of the emperor. If they held a Roman legion, they were governed by a *legate*. If the province was granted significant autonomy — as was the case with Judea — it was governed by *prefects* (after AD 44, called *procurators*). When Archelaus was exiled from Judea in AD 6, the emperor decided to place this important region under the direct control of Rome and thus give birth to the imperial province of Judea. We can reconstruct the names of these Roman governors (see chart on page 45), but only three are mentioned in the New Testament (Pilate, Felix, Festus). For three years (AD 41–44) Judea returned to the status of client kingdom but then in 44 returned to an imperial province.

In AD 26 Tiberius appointed *Pontius Pilatus* or **Pontius Pilate** as the fifth governor of Judea. At the excavation of Caesarea in 1961, an inscription bearing his name was uncovered. As governor, he had full control of the territory of Archelaus. He based himself in Caesarea with a large contingent of Roman soldiers and came to Jerusalem only when necessary, staying no doubt at the well-armed Antonia Fortress or Herod the Great's palace. The New Testament and Roman historians mention him as the governor who oversaw the trial of Jesus and called for his crucifixion (Tacitus, *Annals* 15:44; Luke 23:1).

Form	Title	Ruler	Dates	New Testament
Client Kingdom	King	**Herod the Great**	37–4 BC	Matthew 2:1
	Ethnarch	**Archelaus**	4 BC–AD 6	Matthew 2:22
Roman Province	Prefect	Coponius	6–9	
	Prefect	Marcus Ambivius	9–12	
	Prefect	Annius Rufus	12–15	
	Prefect	Valerius Gratus	15–26	
	Prefect	**Pontius Pilate**	26–36	Luke 3:1; 23:1
	Prefect	Marullus	37–41	
Client Kingdom	King	**Herod Agrippa I**	41–44	Acts 12
Roman Province	Procurator	Cuspius Fadus	44–46	
	Procurator	**M. Antonius Felix**	52–59	Acts 23:26–24:27
	Procurator	**Porcius Festus**	59–62	Acts 25
	Procurator	Albinus	62–64	
	Procurator	Gessius Florus	64–66[2]	

Later Jewish Rulers

Following Pilate a series of governors ruled the province of Judea without event. However, there were occasions when Jewish rule returned to Jerusalem, generally as a result of some palace intrigue in Rome. Two Jewish rulers are noted in the New Testament.

Many of the children of the Herodian dynasty — such as all the sons of Herod the Great — were educated in Rome and became friends with the imperial families. Herod's grandson **Herod Agrippa I** was given rule of Philip's tetrarchy by Emperor Caligula in AD 37. But when Caligula died, Agrippa's boyhood friend in Rome, Claudius, ascended to the throne (AD 41). Claudius immediately made Agrippa king over all Judea, thus retiring the system of governors. He even inherited the lands and wealth of Antipas, his uncle, who had ruled Galilee.

Agrippa is mentioned in the New Testament in Acts 12:1–2 as the ruler who executed James, the son of Zebedee, in Jerusalem. He also imprisoned Peter one Passover. When an angel miraculously released Peter, Agrippa ordered Peter's guards killed (12:19). Of all the Herods Agrippa was the most admired. Josephus records how he honored the temple upon his attainment to kingship. He offered the gift of a golden chain, a replica of one that had once imprisoned him. One of his first deeds was to enter the temple, stand on a platform, and with the high priest read the law. When he came to Deuteronomy's "law of kingship" (17:14–20), he wept. Jewish sources from the Mishnah to the Talmud record his piety.

But kingship also brought liabilities. Both Josephus (*Ant.* 19.8.2 [343–52]) and Acts 12:20–23 record similar accounts of his death in AD 44. He was in Caesarea wearing royal robes made of silver thread enjoying the flattery of the crowds, some of whom called him divine. A messenger from God then struck him dead.

When Agrippa died, his son, **Agrippa II**, was only seventeen and according to some, too young to rule. Thus, Roman governors returned to Caesarea (now called *procurators*). In AD 50 Agrippa II was given Chalcis (today central Lebanon) and in AD 53 obtained the old northeast tetrarchy of Philip. In AD 54 Emperor Nero gave him much of Galilee and in gratitude, he rebuilt Caesarea Philippi, renaming it Neronius (*Ant.* 20.9.4 [211]).

Roman governors commonly called on local rulers for counsel when they prosecuted provincial difficulties. In Acts 25 the governor Festus called on Agrippa II and his sister Bernice to adjudicate the case of Paul (25:13). Paul met with Agrippa and made his defense (26:1–29), whereupon the king advised Festus to free him.

Agrippa's rule (until AD 93) was without event until the outbreak of war in AD 66. He tried to stop the revolt but failed and throughout the conflict sided openly with Rome.

Titus' siege of Jerusalem took several months. The temple was entered by razing the Antonia fortress on the NW corner.

Evidence of Rome's violent destruction of Jerusalem has been recovered along the south wall of the temple where columns were hurled from the top of the temple and crashed onto the first-century street below.

TWO WARS WITH ROME

Judaism's history of revolt against foreign empires such as the Seleucids was retold every winter at Hanukkah. The Maccabees had proven that revolt could be successful, and aspirations for freedom lay hidden for decades. It only took a catalyst to make it explode.

The First Revolt (AD 66–70)

The burden of rule under the Roman governors shifted with each regime. Gessius Florus (AD 65–70) was unmatched for his personal corruption and contempt for the Jews. Appeals to the legate in Syria fell on deaf ears and soon Jewish plans to revolt erupted. A riot in Caesarea was followed by conflict in Jerusalem, where Florus crucified 3,600 people. He plundered the temple treasury, which inspired further outrage. Rome worried about a collapse of

---

THE FORTRESS OF MASADA

Masada rests on the top of a dramatic mountain outcropping 1,400 ft. above the west shore of the Dead Sea. Herod built a palace and fortress here guarding an escape route across the sea—one he used in 40 BC when he fled the Parthians.

Defenders saw Masada as impenetrable. Herod surrounded the mountain cliffs with a double wall and 110 defensive towers. Water was brought onto the mountain with an ingenious system that exploited a winter-flooding river nearby and aqueducts to run water into twelve cisterns that could hold 1.4 million cubic feet.

The Zealots captured the fortress and used it as their "last stand" against the Romans. Evidence of their occupation—such as a first-century synagogue and ritual baths—still remain. Titus assigned an officer, Flavius Silva, to lay siege to the mountain. Silva built a massive siege ramp over one of the aqueducts and, using Jewish slaves, built his way to the rim. According to Josephus, he found the grain stores burned and the defenders dead by suicide.

The final holdout for the Jewish resistance was on Herod's mountain fortress of Masada. According to Josephus the defenders committed suicide rather than surrender.

the eastern frontier, and Emperor Nero ordered Florus to increase severity lest the Parthians exploit an opportunity of Roman weakness.

The Jewish fighters (many of them Zealots) attacked Jerusalem's Antonia Fortress, burned Herod's Palace, and killed the Roman soldiers stationed in Jerusalem (after promising them safe passage from the city). They then occupied three of Judea's desert forts (*Herodium* near Bethlehem, *Masada* adjacent to the Dead Sea, and *Machaerus* on the Nabatean border). Remembering the successes of the Maccabees, they also attacked Greek cities like Sebaste (or Samaria) and Scythopolis. In August, AD 66, the temple stopped sacrificing to God on behalf of the emperor, which was, in effect, a declaration of war.

The Syrian legate, Cestius Gallus, decided to march south from Antioch with the Twelfth Roman Legion Fulminata (*thundering one*) and numerous auxiliaries. Even King Agrippa sent troops. Gallus arrived in Caesarea and obtained direction for his march east into Judea. Minor attacks were quickly repulsed. But when he saw Jerusalem's fortifications, he decided to retreat for unknown reasons. Gallus turned around and descended the mountain, using a shortcut to Caesarea along the narrow Beth Horon ridge. His men were relaxed and the legion was out of formation.

Many remains of Masada's defenders have been discovered. A rare sample of clothing provides a glimpse of Jewish life there.

Suddenly Zealot fighters ambushed them, showering the legion with arrows. No Roman defense could be formed and soon it was a rout. Rome lost 5,300 infantry and 380 cavalry (*War* 2.19.9 [555]) as well as the legionary eagle. The Zealots gained all of their equipment. On the ridge of

Beth Horon where Judas Maccabeus had won so many campaigns, the Roman Twelfth Legion was lost—something unprecedented in Roman history. Gallus fled with his officers back to Caesarea, and immediately a messenger was dispatched to the emperor.

The well-known general Vespasian and his son Titus formed a battle plan while the Jews of Galilee and Judea began to fortify the country. Vespasian organized an army with two complete legions (the Tenth and Fifteenth, each of which brought 6,000 troops), 23 cohorts (each bringing 600 men), six detachments of cavalry, and numerous auxiliary troops sent by regional kings. As he moved south, he devastated Galilee in AD 68. However, that same year Emperor Nero committed suicide following defeats in Gaul and Spain, and Vespasian returned to Rome eventually to assume the throne. Titus had sailed to Alexandria and formed an army centered on the Fifth Legion and now received orders to complete the war.

Titus Flavius Vespasianus, the oldest son of Vespasian, led the conquest of Jerusalem and later ruled as emperor from AD 79-81.

When Titus arrived in Caesarea, he now had four legions: the Fifth, Tenth, and Fifteenth, which were joined by the defeated and rebuilt Twelfth from Syria. He had at his disposal 60,000 experienced soldiers and numerous war engines. Titus quickly massed forces at every access road into Judea from Jericho to Emmaus. The Fifth Legion camped at Emmaus, the western gateway to Judea. The Tenth defeated Jericho and camped on the Mount of Olives, the eastern gateway. Troops controlled all roads north and south. No escape was possible for Jerusalem. Only its siege remained.

Titus marched into the mountains following a route not dissimilar from that used earlier by Gallus. Following a five-month siege, Jerusalem was sacked, its population killed or enslaved, and the temple—which Titus tried to save—burned to the ground. Titus's subordinates were then assigned to attack the remaining Zealot forts. Herodium and Machaerus fell in AD 71, and in 74 legend had it that 960 defenders of Masada chose to commit suicide rather than surrender to the Romans who surrounded them (*War* 7.8–9 [252–406]). Titus, meanwhile, began a meandering return to Rome through Antioch and Alexandria, where he celebrated his triumph with spectacular gladiatorial games and feasts. In AD 71 he joined his father Vespasian in Rome for a joint celebration of their defeat of the Jews.

The fall of Jerusalem and the destruction of the temple devastated Judaism. Before the city's siege, Zealot rebels had taken the city and killed any Jews who whispered suggestions of surrender. Of greatest consequence were the end of temple sacrifice and the disruption of the legal system and its schools. The Sanhedrin and many leading families fled, first to the western hills (Jamnia), then to Galilee, which became their home for centuries. The early Christian church in Jerusalem likewise fled. They hid in the Decapolis city of Pella (south of the Sea of Galilee) until the war was finished (Eusebius, *Eccl. Hist.*, 3.5.3). Many of them returned to Judea and formed the nucleus of the ancient church that still survives in the region to this day.

This bronze statue of Hadrian was found at the Decapolis city of Scythopolis.

Coins made a political statement. Kokhba's followers struck their own coins with a characteristic Judean palm indicating their autonomy from Rome. This coin likely dates from AD 132.

The Second Revolt (AD 132–135)

Titus left the Tenth Legion behind in Jerusalem to maintain order, and its general became the *de facto* governor of the city. His headquarters remained at Caesarea. Jerusalem had been so completely destroyed, Josephus notes that "there was left nothing to make those that came there believe it had ever been inhabited" (*War* 7.1.1 [3]).

Under Emperor Hadrian (AD 117–138) Rome decided to found a Roman colony in Jerusalem and rebuild the city, complete with pagan temples. Hadrian likewise forbade the practice of some Jewish customs, possibly circumcision. This provided the catalyst for another revolt. Its religious leader, the influential Rabbi Akiba, generated support from Jewish communities throughout the Diaspora. He recognized the military genius Simon bar Kokhba as the messiah-deliverer who would drive Rome out of Judea. Akiba called him "the son of the star" (bar Kokhba), taken from Numbers 24:17 ("a star will come out of Jacob"), which was generally understood as messianic.

Following the rebels' successful occupation of Jerusalem and the retreat of the Tenth Legion, a four-year war brought Roman control back to Judea with a vengeance. Bar Kokhba and Akiba were killed in AD 135 and their followers fled to caves above En-Gedi (near the Dead Sea), where they perished, leaving behind letters and remains recently discovered by archaeologists.

Hadrian now completed his plan for Jerusalem. The city was renamed *Aelia Capitolina*, and Jews were forbidden to step inside its walls. A temple dedicated to Jupiter was erected on the site of the Jewish temple and even a temple to Aphrodite (Venus) was built on what is now the traditional site of Jesus' tomb. Hadrian laid out the city plan for Jerusalem, which is still in use today within Jerusalem's present Old Walled City.

QUESTIONS FOR DISCUSSION ⦿⦿⦿⦿⦿⦿⦿⦿⦿⦿⦿⦿⦿⦿⦿⦿⦿⦿⦿⦿⦿⦿⦿⦿⦿

1. When did Hellenism first enter Judea and how did Jewish leaders react?
2. Why would some Jews welcome the occupation under Rome following the defeat of the Seleucids?
3. How deeply politicized was the environment in the New Testament period?
4. What features of Jesus' message about the kingdom of God would have resonated with the Jewish rebels fighting Rome?
5. How was Judaism permanently affected following the war of AD 70?

BIBLIOGRAPHY

Introductory

Bruce, F. F. *New Testament History*. New York: Doubleday, 1969.

Jeffers, J. S. *The Greco-Roman World of the New Testament Era*. Downers Grove, IL: Inter-Varsity Press, 1999.

Schürer, E. *The History of the Jewish People in the Age of Jesus Christ*. 4 vols., rev. and ed. G. Vermes, F. Millar, and M. Black. Edinburgh: T. & T. Clark, 1973–1987.

VanderKam, J. C. *An Introduction to Early Judaism*. Grand Rapids: Eerdmans, 2001.

Advanced

Reicke, B. *The New Testament Era: The World of the Bible from 500 BC to AD 100*. Philadelphia: Fortress, 1968.

Rhoads, D. M. *Israel in Revolution, 6–74 C.E.: A Political History Based on the Writings of Josephus*. Philadelphia: Fortress, 1976.

Schiffman, L. *From Text to Tradition: A History of Second Temple and Rabbinic Judaism*. Jersey City: Ktav, 1991.

NOTES

1. This reconstruction is from K. C. Hanson and D. E. Oakman, *Palestine in the Time of Jesus: Social Structures and Social Conflicts* (Minneapolis: Fortress, 1998), 78.

2. Source is J. S. Jeffers, *The Greco-Roman World of the New Testament Era* (Downers Grove, IL: InterVaristy Press, 1999), 122.

Chapter 3

THE WORLD OF JESUS IN HIS JEWISH HOMELAND

The Jordan River, less than a half mile south of the Sea of Galilee

PERSPECTIVE

Every person understands life though the set of cultural conventions shared from generation to generation. This was equally true for Jesus' earliest followers, who lived in a world vastly different from our own. Factors such as religious traditions, social habits, economic and agricultural customs, architecture, historical events, and even geographical features of the landscape each contributed to the "framework" or "lens" through which they saw life.

The penetration of Hellenistic culture into later Jewish life is seen here in the remains of the 4th century synagogue column from Chorazin decorated with a Medusa, a female monster in Greek mythology.

Today scholars are keenly aware of the need to reconstruct the social world of first-century Mediterranean society. A number of New Testament researchers have applied the tools of cultural anthropology to the New Testament and offered remarkable insights into first-century Palestine and the events in the Gospels.[1] The same is true for the life of Paul. Everything from the cultural forces of Hellenism to the shaping influences of trade routes influence how we view the apostle and his journeys.[2]

The challenge for the modern interpreter of the New Testament is that we read our Scriptures with entirely different cultural assumptions. Humility forces us to recognize that we are *foreigners to the biblical stories*, that they represent a different time and place from our own. When we try to understand them, we miss many cultural cues and may even misrepresent some of their stories.

Thus, in order for us to understand Jesus, Paul, and the world of the earliest Christians, we need to become cultural anthropologists. What did it mean for a Greek-speaking Jew like Paul to address an audience of philosophers in Athens? How did people travel and why does the New Testament emphasize hospitality? What is the difference between Galilee and Judea? This chapter will help us probe the world of Jesus centered on Galilee, Samaria, and Judea. Chapter 4 will concentrate on the wider Mediterranean world. In each case, we will try to reconstruct what the earliest Christians knew so that we can read the New Testament in its setting in antiquity.

THE LAND OF ISRAEL

It is difficult to overestimate the importance of the land of Israel to Jesus' contemporaries. Rabbis wrote with longing about life there. They called it a "goodly land" and a "land which is the most precious of all lands." It was viewed as "extensive and beautiful," "pleasant and glorious," and "promised to all those who remained faithful to God."[3] During festivals Jews traveled from great distances to come to Jerusalem (note Acts 2:9–11). Jews argued with each other about the obligation to live there—and many Jews sought at least to be buried there.

Fully 35 percent of the Mishnah was devoted to issues related to life in the land—and this only reflected the emphasis of the Old Testament, where residence in Israel was presupposed. Agricultural tithes, cities of refuge, and sacrifice assume one is living in Israel. However, it was temple worship and sacrifices that (according to the Mishnah) gave the land its high degree of holiness. The sacrificial altar would only accept animals and produce that had come from Israel itself. One rabbi, writing on Numbers 23:7, insisted that in every prayer after eating, the people should pray: "The Holy One, blessed be He, said, 'The Land of Israel is more precious to me than everything.'"

Geographical Setting of Israel

Israel is located at the eastern end of the Mediterranean Sea and forms a land bridge that connected great empires in antiquity. Because of the massive deserts of Arabia and Syria, trade and communication between Mesopotamia and Egypt passed along the upper Euphrates River and then south through Israel, continuing to Egypt (an area known as the Fertile Crescent). In time of peace, this brought prosperity; but in time of war, devastation. With the coming of the Greeks and Romans, for the first time control over Israel was oriented toward western Mediterranean cultures.

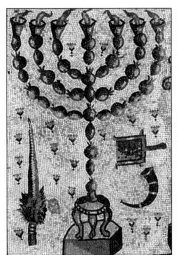

Left: This 4th century mosaic from the synagogue at Hammat Tiberius shows four images sacred to early Jewish use: the lulav bundle, the temple candelabra, an incense shovel, and the shofar (ram's horn). The lulav was used in antiquity at every Tabernacles feast. *Right:* The lulav, here with citrus, is used today in the Jewish holiday of Tabernacles.

The classic boundaries of biblical Israel generally began with the coastline along the Mediterranean. The natural eastern boundary was the Jordan River (Num. 34:12). The north/south limits were often described as "from Dan to Beersheba" (Judg. 20:1), which simply marked settlements in the rugged north Galilee mountains and the south central deserts (though Israel's rule often went further south).

Zone One: The Coastal Plain

Look carefully at the map on page 56. It is easiest to divide the country into a series of five longitudinal zones. Note how a major backbone of mountains runs north-south and then in northern Samaria it turns northwest and continues to the sea. This creates the first major zone — the coastal plain — which runs from Mount Carmel in the north to regions south of Gaza.

BURY ME IN THE HOLY LAND

Throughout the New Testament era Jews desired to be buried on the Mount of Olives east of Jerusalem where the Messiah might appear. Ancient tombs still abound on this hill — and today modern Jewish cemeteries cover the western face of the hill.

Following the second Jewish war of AD 135, burial around Jerusalem became impossible since Hadrian had prohibited it to Jews. The Sanhedrin moved to Galilee, and eventually the village of Beit She'arim became the first choice for burial. The great organizer of the Mishnah, Rabbi Judah ha-Nasi, lived and was buried there.

Evidence of the popular desire of Jews to be buried in the Holy Land from throughout the Mediterranean can be seen in the magnificent catacombs and architectural remains at Beit She'arim. Rock-cut tombs and sarcophagi abound in tunnel after tunnel. One vast catacomb (number 20) contains 200 single-grave wall niches and 125 standing stone sarcophagi.

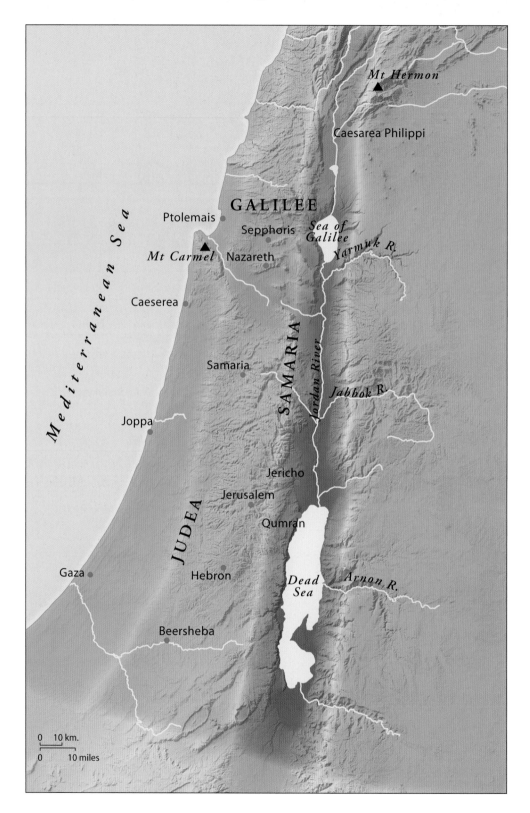

Mt Hermon

Caesarea Philippi

GALILEE

Ptolemais

Sepphoris

Sea of Galilee

Mt Carmel

Nazareth

Yarmuk R.

M e d i t e r r a n e a n   S e a

Caeserea

S
A
M
A
R
I
A

Jordan River

Samaria

Jabbok R.

Joppa

Jericho

Jerusalem

J
U
D
E
A

Qumran

Gaza

Hebron

Dead Sea

Arnon R.

Beersheba

0   10 km.

0   10 miles

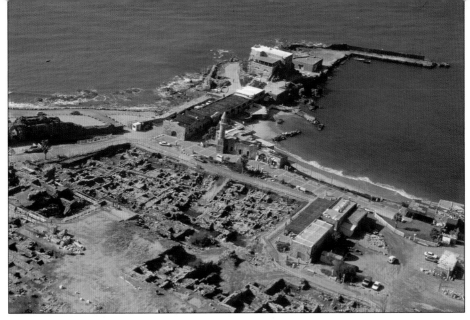

Caesarea Maritima was built by Herod the Great as the chief gateway into the country from the west. Today the ancient city and its port are being excavated.

In the New Testament era, this coast had a number of fishing villages, such as Joppa (see Acts 10). It also had coastal cities such as Azotus, Ascalon, and Caesarea, home to Cornelius (Acts 10:1) and site of Paul's two-year imprisonment (Acts 23–26). Caesarea became a critical harbor for Israel linking it with the rest of the Roman empire. The Roman political administration for the province was located here, and thanks to Herod the Great's architectural plans, it became one of the greatest ports in the entire empire. In the northern regions Ptolemais was built in the natural harbor that today shelters modern Haifa. From here a traveler could easily make his or her way east through valleys to Galilee's splendid capital, Sepphoris.

Zone Two: The Coastal Hills

Traveling east from the coast, we see low coastal hills that begin from near Beersheba in the south and continue north just east of Caesarea. Mount Carmel abruptly interrupts these hills and replaces them with dramatic vertical cliffs. The area is remarkably fertile and enjoys the rainfall of the coast without the problems of low-lying sand and swamp.

Various smaller villages have been discovered in these hills from the New Testament era. Perhaps the most famous is Emmaus. Luke 24:13–32 tells us about disciples who made the seven-mile journey from Jerusalem to Emmaus when the resurrected Jesus joined them. They continued to the village, where Jesus ate with them and explained the events of his death.

Zone Three: The Central Mountains

After the foothills is the central mountain range that begins south of Hebron and continues north to Samaria (where the mountains turn northwest toward the sea). These mountains rise as high as three thousand feet

From the coast, the hills of Judea begin to rise immediately. Here the Sorek River runs from the hills near Jerusalem to the Mediterranean Sea.

The coastal hills crest at the top of the Judean hills. This is near the headwaters of the Sorek River.

and are made of a hard limestone that is excellent for building. Because limestone is porous, it serves like a sponge, soaking up rainwater and holding it all year. Further down the mountain or in valleys the water escapes in a spring or can be tapped by a well. The mountains form deep valleys, and the limestone erodes into a rich soil that is excellent for agriculture (called "Mediterranean Brown" or *terra rosa*). Villages thus hugged the hillsides and farming was done either in the valley or along ancient terraces. In Matthew 5:14 Jesus referred to a "city on a hill"; he likely had such villages in mind.

In these mountains three great cities were like landmarks along the ridge: Hebron, Jerusalem, and Shechem. Hebron is the site where Abraham, Sarah, Isaac, Rebekah, Jacob, and Leah were buried (in the cave of Machpelah, Gen. 23:19; 49:29–31). In fact, in Jesus' day Herod the Great built a major shrine over the site commemorating the burial ground. Jerusalem, of course, lay at the heart of Judaism's religious life, and its temple was the site of regular pilgrimage for pious Jews.

To Jews in Jesus' day, these central mountains with Jerusalem at its center were called Judea and served as the heartland of Jewish life and thought. Even Galilee lived in its shadow.

HOUSES BUILT ON A ROCK

Jesus once compared obedient disciples to wise persons who built their houses on rock, and disobedient disciples to foolish persons who build houses on topsoil (see Matt. 7:24–27). Jesus likely is referring not to sandy beaches but has in mind the person who builds his home by carving its foundation out of mountain bedrock (a practice found everywhere among Palestinian villages). Cut limestone stacked on bedrock cannot be moved. The other category of people build on the topsoil of the valley, which often floods and is subject to instability.

However, an ethnic divide almost eight hundred years old still existed north of Judea. Just north of Jerusalem lived the Samaritans, who claimed a separate heritage, denied their Jewish identity, and located their own temple on a mountain above ancient Shechem. Hostilities between the two communities flared regularly, which made it all the more surprising that both Jesus (Luke 9:52; John 4:9) and the early Christians (Acts 8:25) reached out to them.

In addition to these main cities, numerous minor poor villages flourished in the hills. Bethlehem is perhaps the most famous of these, located about five miles south of Jerusalem.

The central mountains form the backbone of the country, and a short walk east

Jerusalem viewed from the Mt. of Olives in the east. The limestone wall in the foreground was built during Herod's refurbishing of the city in the first century BC.

of their main ridge delivers the traveler into an unexpected wilderness. Small villages hug the upper reaches of this eastern ridge (Bethphage, Bethany), but life here is difficult since the mountains have formed a rain shadow, converting Jerusalem's generous twenty-four inches of rainfall to just over eight.

East of Jerusalem, the landscape becomes a wilderness. This Judean Wilderness was the area where Jesus was tempted for 40 days.

Zone Four: The Jordan Valley

From the mountains, the wilderness landscape descends dramatically for almost ten miles, dropping almost 3,500 feet. The chief geographical marker in this desert is the Jordan River, which lies at the base of this deep depression. It is part of a far larger geological fissure that runs from Turkey to Africa for 3,700 miles, making the Dead Sea the lowest point on earth. The Jordan River begins in the far north in mountains above Galilee (near Mount Hermon) and feeds the Galilee Sea basin, which is already about 700 feet below sea level. It then continues its descent ending in the Dead Sea (about 1,200 feet below sea level). From the Jordan River, the valley climbs back up steep eastern cliffs that ascend as high as 3,600 feet.

The Jordan River decends into the desolate wilderness here near the Jabbok River. Viewed from the west facing modern Jordan.

Occasional oases such as Jericho permitted villages to grow, but without a natural spring or a clever water retention system (such as Qumran), life here was impossible. The wilderness was well known as a place of refuge and testing for everyone from King David to Jesus (1 Sam. 19–24; Matt. 4:1–11). John the Baptist used this region, and Jesus told stories about travel through this region. Jews coming to Jerusalem from Galilee often used this valley route, stopping at oases along the way. They arrived at Jericho and climbed west, ascending the Judean mountains, passing through Bethany and Bethphage, and arriving at Jerusalem. This desolate road was the setting for Jesus' famous parable of the Good Samaritan (Luke 10:29–37).

The wilderness ends at the Dead Sea. Nearby were located oases such as Jericho and nearby communities such as Qumran.

Zone Five: The Eastern Plateau

On the east side of the Jordan, a plateau rises precipitously, and its elevation is able to reclaim the rainfall that had been prohibited to the deep Jordan Valley. Here were cities that could grow cereal crops (thanks to fifteen inches of rainfall) and benefit from desert trading routes. Here were the cities of the Decapolis (see Ch. 2). The northern region just east of the Jordan River was known as Perea and was under the authority of Herod Antipas (along with Galilee itself). This explains why John the Baptist, who lived in this desert, could be pursued by Antipas. South of that was Nabatea, which had its capital at the famous canyon of Petra. Antipas feared the Nabateans and constructed a fortress on the border called Machaerus. Paul lived here for a while after his conversion (Gal. 1:17, called Arabia) and was threatened by the governor of Damascus, who served Aretas IV, king of Nabatea (2 Cor. 11:32).

Galilee

The geographical features that defined Judea and Samaria are absent in the northern region of Galilee. The north/south mountains disappear and a wide valley—the Jezreel Valley—separates Galilee from the central mountains. The chief feature of the region is a large (13 by 8 miles) freshwater lake, the Sea of Galilee, which is fed by the descending Jordan River. This sea was a chief source of fishing. To date, we have discovered the remnants of almost twenty ancient harbors surrounding the lake. Upper Galilee (the northern part) has mountains that are nearly four thousand feet in elevation. This region is desolate. In the Gospels when Jesus departs into the mountains to be alone, this was his destination.

Lower Galilee is much more dense in population. Villages like Nazareth (Matt. 2:23) and Cana (John 2:1; 4:46) were typical of conservative Jewish communities frequented by Jesus. Jesus eventually moved from Nazareth to Capernaum (Matt. 4:13) and began to call it his "home" (Mark 2:1). From here he called his disciples and began his ministry traveling to villages throughout Galilee. Most of his ministry was in a triangle formed by Capernaum, Bethsaida, and Chorazin.

The Gentile presence in Galilee was growing rapidly, however, and strict Jews referred to it derisively as "Galilee of the Gentiles" (Matt. 4:15). The ancient capital of Galilee, Sepphoris, lay in a valley just north of Nazareth, so that Hellenistic culture thrived not far from Jesus' childhood home. Jewish communities linked to Herodian ruling authority were likewise expanding: Bethsaida-Julias, Caesarea Philippi, and Tiberias.

Galilee's villages prospered for many centuries. A decorated column from Chorazim's Fourth Century synagogue.

Summary

Recent archaeological work in Galilee has changed how we think about Jesus' background and ministry. Trade was moving efficiently between village and city; political consciousness was well developed, making resistance to Roman rule common; and Hellenistic cultural values

Jewish fishing villages and Hellenistic cities surrounded Galilee's shores. Pictured the ancient (and) modern harbor of En Gev. The cone-shaped hill is ancient Hippos.

were spreading quickly. Jesus was exposed to all of this. He likely chose Capernaum as his teaching and healing base because the town was on a major trading route that moved north/south from the Mediterranean coastal plain to Damascus. It was no accident that the Romans built a tax station in Capernaum and fortified it with troops (Mark 2:14). Therefore, Jesus was known as a "Galilean"—he had an accent and wore regional clothing styles—and he was labeled critically by those living in Judea who heard him when he traveled south in order to celebrate the festivals at the Jerusalem temple (John 1:46; 7:52).

JEWISH VOICES IN THE FIRST CENTURY

Judaism in the first century proved to be a dynamic and vibrant religious experience for many. Prayer, Scripture readings, festival worship, the practice of the law, and temple sacrifice were values abundantly promoted by Jewish teachers. Like any religious faith, Judaism had a diversity of currents, each competing for the mainstream—and it is impossible to talk about the Jewish faith as if it had one voice.

Judaism was well known throughout the Roman Empire. Its native province (Judea to the Romans, Israel to the Jews) was populated by as many as 1.5 million. The Diaspora may have had as many as four million (or 7 percent of the Roman Empire), making Judaism a significant minority. Around the Mediterranean there were close to a thousand synagogues by AD 70.

These massive columns lay where they fell in the Decapolis city of Scythopolis. Such public architecture in one of Rome's largest cities in Judea projected the true power of the empire in Galilee.

Within Israel itself the majority of the people had been reduced to near-subsistence living (agriculture, trades, or fishing) because of the financial burden of the Roman occupation. Debt fueled resentment and rebellion—which may explain the power of Jesus' prayer, "forgive us our debts, *as we also have forgiven our debtors*" (Matt. 6:12). This widespread poverty made observance of Jewish law a luxury. In fact, most Jews likely spent the majority of their lives living in a state of "ritual uncleanness." They were often labeled derisively as the ᶜ*am ha-aretz* ("people of the land"). They were also the ᶜ*anawim* ("the poor"), for whom the burden of life seemed unbearable. Again, Jesus spoke to their condition, "Come to me, all you who are weary and burdened, and I will give you rest" (11:28). These people were Jesus' primary audience.

Left: The village of Gamla was located northeast of the Sea of Galilee (in today's Golan Heights). Destroyed in the first Jewish war, its remains reflect life in the first century. *Right:* The excavated synagogue at Gamla gives a rare glimpse at first century Jewish religious life. If Jesus visited most of the villages of Galilee (Matt 4:23), he likely came to Gamla.

Josephus outlines three sects among the Jews in the first century: the Pharisees, the Sadducees, and the Essenes (*Ant.* 13.5.9 [171]); there was also a "fourth philosophy," a generic grouping of those who resisted Rome violently (*Ant.* 18.1.6 [23]). But these do not reflect the mainstream of Jewish faith, for they represent barely 5 percent of the Jewish population. Yet we must understand who they are.

The Pharisees

Once the Maccabean revolt had succeeded in overturning Greek rule in the second century BC, the new Jewish dynasty—the powerbrokers of the war—no longer needed the religiously motivated sects that had given ideological support for the revolt. These deeply pious fighters (called "Hasidim") were soon marginalized from the politics of the country and focused instead on creating a world of religious rigor and separation from the corruption that followed the Jewish victory. The name "Pharisee" first surfaces when the Hasmonean ruler John Hyrcanus I (135/4–104 BC) persecuted the Pharisees for resisting the Hasmonean rule. They are often considered the descendents of the Hasidim (but this is uncertain).[4]

But a hundred years later, the Pharisees (*separated ones*) were widely known. They chastised those who flirted with Hellenism, promoted a vigorous adherence to the law, and anticipated a coming messiah who would bring a thoroughgoing righteousness to the land.

THE JEWS BURN JERUSALEM'S TAX ARCHIVE

The tax burden on the Jews was so severe that in AD 66 (during the war with Rome), once the Jewish rebels gained control of Jerusalem, they burned the tax record office:

> The king's soldiers were overpowered by the multitude.... The others then set fire to the house of Ananias the high priest, and to the palaces of Agrippa and Bernice; after which they carried the fire to the place where the archives were deposited and hurried to burn the contracts belonging to their creditors and thereby to dissolve their obligations for paying their debts.... This was done to persuade the poorer sort to join in their insurrection with safety against the more wealthy. (Josephus, *War*, 2.17.6 [426–427])

Josephus, himself a Pharisee, described them as "a certain sect of the Jews that appear more religious than others, and seem to interpret the laws more accurately" (*War* 1.5.2 [110]).

What distinguished the Pharisees from the other groups in Judaism was their emphasis on religious practice as an *individual, personal decision*. Ironically, this shift likely came from the individualism of the Hellenistic world (which the Pharisees resisted). Individual adherence to the law was one firm way to express Jewish cultural and religious identity. This helps explain the Pharisees' focus on tithing, Sabbath observance, and food purity laws.

Jesus referred to Pharisees who "sit in Moses' seat" (Matt 23:2). This was a seated position of authority, often in a synagogue. A 4th century stone "seat" was excavated in the Galilee synagogue of Chorazin.

The Pharisees appear with surprising frequency in the Gospels as primary opponents of Jesus. He took the Scriptures seriously and was skilled at their use — which gave him and the Pharisees much common ground. No doubt Jesus' tendency to interpret the law in his own way, his habit of breaking religious traditions to make a point (such as Sabbath rules), his claims of authority, and his popularity made him a lightning rod for the Pharisees' criticisms. While the Pharisees had central theological commitments — such as a strict theological determinism, the resurrection of the dead, and a messianic hope — it was their focus on external formalities that set them apart. But where this emphasis became rigid, they found a debating opponent in Jesus.

It would be wrong to think that all Pharisees succumbed to this tendency toward rigidity or that all Pharisees were "legalistic." Many Jews rejoiced in the law and in its adherence found life (see Ps. 119). Paul was a Pharisee, and he did not find his Jewish faith burdensome (see Phil. 3:3–8). In Acts 5:34 the Pharisee Gamaliel spoke up in defense of the apostles before the Sanhedrin (cf. also Acts 21:20).

The Sadducees

As a result of the Maccabean revolt, the Hasmoneans inherited the wealthy estates left by the Greeks and consolidated their power through their control of Jerusalem and the temple. By Jesus' day, they were called the Sadducees — the educated elites, landowners, and members of a Jerusalem urban class who had learned how to profit from the Roman occupation. For this reason, they were suspicious of any religious fanaticism that might upset the status quo; thus, they rejected the messianism common to the Pharisees.

While the Pharisees and the Sadducees are often studied, their differences are not easily compared. The Pharisees were committed to purity laws and the religious restoration of the country. The Sadducees were invested in *social position* and the benefits of the political architecture of the country under Rome. Many priests were likely Sadducees, and it is plausible that the Hasmonean rulers shared Saducean sympathies (some perhaps were Sadducees).

Josephus notes distinguishing marks of their belief. They disputed the notion of the resurrection and argued that "souls die with the bodies" (*Ant.* 18.1.4 [16]). They also debated the Pharisees' commitment to determinism, especially as it referred to an apocalyptic end to time. In the New Testament they only occasionally debated with Jesus. But since their influence was significant in Jerusalem, when they questioned him publicly, they were testing the threat his movement might bring to the city (Matt. 22:23).

The Essenes

A third Jewish sect discussed by Josephus was that of the Essenes, a small ascetic group (about four thousand total) who likely had communities throughout the country. Josephus, intrigued with this group, wrote about them more than any other (*Ant.* 13.5.9 [171–72]; 18.1.4–5 [18–22]; *War* 2.8.2–13 [119–61]). He gives remarkable detail about their lives: their vows of obedience to leaders, their initiation practices, their denial of luxuries and private property, even their dress (white garments), anointing practices, and communal meals. The seriousness of their lives inspired admiration even from Roman writers like Pliny who made the Essene "way" something known in the empire.

The origin of the movement probably began after the fragmentation of the Maccabean wars. Seeing the political corruption that quickly consumed Jerusalem, these Jews chose to live isolated, separated lives that avoided engagement with the growing Gentile population and most Jewish groups. Some members may have been married, others were strictly celibate. As one matured in the sect, personal discipline and purity were measured as tokens of devotion and dedication.

Most scholars think that the community at Qumran that produced the Dead Sea Scrolls was likely a branch of the Essenes. It was a rigorously pious monastic commune using Old Testament texts such as Isaiah 40:3 as their vision for life: "In the wilderness prepare the way for the LORD; make straight in the desert a highway for our God." This was an all-male monastic community living in isolation, critical of the temple, promoting regular water baptism, and awaiting God's intervention in history. Since this text was important to John the Baptist, some scholars argue he may have been influenced by this group.

> **NOTES FROM ANTIQUITY**
>
> **JERUSALEM'S ESSENE GATE**
> Josephus refers to an "Essene Gate" in the southwest region of the city (*War* 5.4.2 [145]). Today archaeologists are confident that they have found it, located in the Protestant Cemetery behind today's Jerusalem University College. This gate likely gave access to the "Essene Quarter" of the city, populated either by members of the movement or refugees from Qumran.

Many scholars believe that the Jewish settlement at Qumran at the northwest corner of the Dead Sea (shown here) was Essene.

The "Fourth Philosophy"

As we have seen, resistance to the Roman occupation or to Hellenistic cultural assimilation took many forms. Some decided to fight back with the sword. Some, such as the *Sicarii* (see sidebar), used psychological terror tactics, while others organized armed campaigns.

Judaism's commitment to military resistance, forged during the Maccabean campaigns, taught the Jews that guerrilla campaigns could work and that foreigners who occupied them would eventually find control of the country too costly. By the first century, the "politics of violence" was familiar to everyone. Various scriptural models of this type of resistance were celebrated, such as the zeal of Phineas (see Num. 25:1–13). The Jewish warriors who finally occupied and defended Jerusalem in AD 66–70 took up the name "Zealots" and made their last stand in the famous siege at the mountain fortress of Masada.

The excavation at Masada yielded numerous Jewish weapons from the first century. The Romans used this type of sword to quell Jewish rebellions.

We should expect that Jesus' ministry would be tested by movements such as these. The question about taxes given in Mark 12:14 is likely a probe about zealotry, which made sense since one of Jesus' followers was known as a (former) Zealot (Mark 3:18).

The Scribes

In addition to the four sects listed by Josephus, there are a number of other groups listed in the New Testament. Some represent professions, others are regional ethnic groups, others reflect political alliances.

In antiquity professionals who could read and write—and interpret the law—were in high demand. They served as secretaries and chroniclers, taught the law in synagogues, or adjudicated legal disagreements in court. Because of their strict devotion to the Scriptures and their role as custodians of Jewish tradition, many of the scribes were Pharisees (though not all Pharisees were scribes). Among the titles used for them, "teacher" and its Hebrew form "rabbi" were common (Matt 23:7–8). Much of their activity was concentrated in Jerusalem since it was the seat of Jewish learning and home of the judicial council (the Sanhedrin). Only the scribes who belonged to the Pharisees could enter the Sanhedrin and participate in judicial decisions.

The Samaritans

After the destruction of the northern kingdom of Israel, a remnant population survived around the city of Shechem. When the Jews returned from Babylon to rebuild their temple, these Samaritan people were viewed as deeply compromised. In addition, the Assyrians had moved many Persians into Samaria, who assimilated with the Israelites, and the Jewish leaders with Ezra and Nehemiah wanted nothing to do with them.

These Samaritans "revised" the Hebrew Scriptures (to promote their own place in history) and built a rival temple on Mount Gerizim that towered over Shechem. Hostilities between Samaritans and Jews ran high. In the Maccabean era, Jewish armies razed Samaria in war (*Ant.* 13.10.2 [275–279]). On another occasion, Samaritans tried to sabotage the Jerusalem temple at Passover by entering in disguise and spreading exhumed human bones throughout its chambers (*Ant.* 18.2.2 [29–30]).

Mt. Gerizim viewed from Shechem. The Samaritans viewed this mountain as sacred (John 4:20) and built a temple here in the 4th century BC.

This background makes the presence of Samaritans in the Gospels much more surprising. Jesus told a parable in which he made a Samaritan one of his heroes (Luke 10:25–37); even today, being a good "Samaritan" is a compliment. Jesus healed a Samaritan on one occasion and praised him for his gratefulness (17:15–19). At the well of Jacob in Shechem Jesus held his famous conversation with "the Samaritan woman" (John 4:1–38), whose testimony about Jesus led to the conversion of her village. Early Christian mission likewise came early to Samaria (Acts 8:5).

"I AM NOT JEWISH"

NOTES FROM ANTIQUITY

According to Josephus, the Samaritans refused any participation in the Maccabean wars by denying their Jewish heritage (*Ant.* 12:5.5 [257]. "When the Samaritans saw the Jews under these sufferings, they no longer confessed that they were of their family, nor that the temple on Mount Gerizim belonged to Almighty God. This was according to their nature. . . . And they now said that they were a colony of Medes and Persians—and indeed they were."

To save their temple, the Samaritans sent a letter to the Greek king Antiochus, honoring him with the title of "god" and offering to dedicate their temple on Mount Gerizim to Jupiter Hellenius (12:5.5 [261].

The Herodians

Mark and Matthew refer to opponents of Jesus called "Herodians" (Matt 22:16; Mark 3:6). Little is known about them, but they were probably political patrons living in the major cities of Galilee and Judea. They were the ones who questioned Jesus about paying taxes (Mark 12:13–14) in order to assess the threat he might bring to the status quo of Jewish political life. The Herodians had compromised with Rome and only saw the benefits of Jewish life in a Roman province.

Any from these circles who followed Jesus likely kept it secret since the social costs would be high. Nevertheless Luke tells us that the financial officer of Herod Antipas was named Chuza and that his wife helped finance Jesus' ministry (Luke 8:1–3).

THE JERUSALEM TEMPLE

It is difficult to overestimate the importance of the Jewish temple in first-century Judaism. It was a building of national as well as religious pride. Solomon's temple had been destroyed by the Babylonians (586 BC) but rebuilt by Ezra following the Exile. However, about 20 BC Herod the Great launched a monumental rebuilding program that promised to make this temple one of the greatest in the ancient world.

The project was in full construction during Jesus' life. Herod not only refurbished the inner courts, but he expanded the building's size so that it measured 360,000 square feet (equivalent to nine football fields). Fifty-ton stones were lifted into place—a process that still today defies explanation. When Titus's armies entered the temple courts in the Jewish war, they were stunned at its beauty and desired to preserve it (*War*, 5.9.2; [360–361]; 7:5:2 [112–113].

Not only was the size of the temple astounding, but much of the city's economic energies were invested in its functions. Twenty-four priestly families—numbering over 7,000 priests—worked alongside 9,600 Levites in the day-to-day tasks of maintenance, sacrifice, and worship schedules. Tithe money came in regularly and sacrifice became a major industry, making the temple remarkably wealthy.

Herod knew that the temple would likely be the site of any revolt against him. Thus, in the northwest corner he built a fortress, named it after Mark Antony, and staffed it with Roman auxiliary troops. This Antonia Fortress loomed over the temple courts below and sent a clear message to zealous pilgrim traffic. The temple was also the only location where the Romans permitted Jewish troops to be armed. They appeared at Jesus' arrest (Luke 22:52) and frequently did the bidding of the leading priests (Acts 5:26).

THE GREAT ROYAL PORCH

Herod had his engineers build a major covered porch at the south end of the temple that formed one perimeter to the Court of the Gentiles. Here four rows of forty columns (160 total) supported a massive wooden roof. Each column weighed five tons, was twenty-seven feet high, and, according to Josephus, was so wide that "three men might, with their arms extended, reach around it." Each was completed with a Corinthian capital. The Sanhedrin often met here, and teachers such as Jesus commonly conversed their students in its corridors (John 10:23).

When Titus destroyed Jerusalem in AD 70, this porch collapsed and most of its columns fell over the south retaining wall. Many were carried away for centuries-later building projects. But others remained buried, unearthed since 1968 in the excavation of the temple's southern wall.

The law stipulated that Jewish men were to travel to the temple to attend three pilgrimage festivals each year (Deut. 16:16). *Passover* began the Jewish festival cycle and celebrated new growth in field and flock in spring while telling the story of Israel's departure from Egypt. *Pentecost*, fifty days later, concluded the cereal harvest and called on Israel to study Israel's two years at Mount Horeb with Moses and the covenant written there. Finally, the

Left: Jerusalem was a temple with a city wrapped around it. Its walls protected a population of about 30,000 to 50,000 but its economy served the temple and its work.

Left: Capernaum was first identified in 1838 by the American scholar E. Robinson. It was rubble with the exception of a ruined building he correctly identified as a synagogue. This picture from 1898 shows how little was there. *Right:* Since 1968 the excavation of the village of Capernaum's entire 4th century synagogue has been completed. A first century village was located around its perimeter and the foundation of a first century synagogue was identified beneath the floor of the 4th century building.

autumn festival of *Tabernacles* or *Booths* marked the harvest of tree and vine and drew lessons from Israel's thirty-eight years of wandering in the desert.

It is impossible to know how many complied with the pilgrimage rule, and but perhaps the men only came at best to one festival per year. Diaspora Jews may have come only once in a lifetime. Jesus undoubtedly visited the city and its temple many times throughout his life. He was there during a Tabernacles feast (John 7:2), and he was arrested and crucified during a Passover feast.

THE SANHEDRIN

In antiquity every community gathered together its leading members to bring leadership and order to civic life. Jerusalem had its own lay nobility — men who were keenly invested in the success of Jerusalem and who worked closely with the temple priests to bring order. One example is Joseph of Arimathea, who supplied Jesus' tomb (Mark 15:43; John 19:38 – 42).

These elders joined together with select members of the priesthood (who were generally Sadducees) and leading Pharisees to form a "high council" called the Sanhedrin. Its tripartite structure gave wide representation to diverse interests and worked hard to give a fair and judicious hearing to legal complaints. It took its structure from the seventy elders appointed by Moses (Num 11:16; Mishnah, *Sanh.* 1:6). Seventy was considered the appropriate number needed to form a council in Judaism. Note how Jesus sent out seventy disciples as his delegates to Galilee (Luke 10:1 NASB).

The Jewish high priest (e.g., Caiaphas during Jesus' trial, Matt. 26:3) led the Jerusalem council. But this did not mean that this council convened for every decision. The Mishnah outlines how smaller groups of elders could decide cases (e.g., theft and personal injury took three judges). A "lower court" made up of twenty elders and the high priest heard intermediate cases (Mishnah, *Sanh.* 1:2 – 5). The stipulations for the prosecution and defense in trial are clearly laid out and impress even the most casual reader.

VILLAGES AND SYNAGOGUES

During the Babylonian exile Israel had to rethink its worship in the absence of a temple. Without sacrifice, worship centered on personal study, corporate prayer, and worship. When the Jews

WOMEN SYNAGOGUE LEADERS?

Synagogue meetings were convened when ten Jewish men gathered. However, newly found inscriptions suggest that some women were leaders in their communities. For example, in a second-century inscription from ancient Smyrna, a woman named Rufina was called the head or leader of her synagogue. The text reads:

> Rufina, a Jewess, head of the synagogue (*archisynagōgos*), built this tomb for her freed slaves and the slaves raised in her house. No one else has the right to bury anyone (here). Anyone who dares to do (so), will pay 1500 denaria to the sacred treasury and 1000 denaria to the Jewish people. A copy of this inscription has been placed in the (public) archives.

Rufina, and other women like her, were leaders in their communities, working for the good of others. Paul would have met such women as he traveled throughout the Roman world. Some, such as Phoebe (Rom. 16:1–2) and Lydia (Acts 16:14), became followers of Jesus and joined in Paul's ministry to spread the gospel message.

returned to Jerusalem, they brought these "assemblies" (Gk. *synagōgē*) with them, and despite the rebuilding of the temple, public meetings with study, discussion, and prayer continued.

By the first century, synagogues were commonplace in the villages of Israel. These may have been public gatherings to discuss civic issues or they may have been gatherings for religious debate and prayer. A quorum of ten Jewish men could convene a synagogue meeting at any time, and it brought a revolution to Jewish life. The synagogue was accessible to the average person compared with the temple's distance and formidable rituals. In this sense, the synagogue *decentralized* Jewish identity by bringing opportunities for religious expression to the village.

Moreover the synagogue became a network for expressing conservative Judaism. The Gospels depict Jesus as performing miracles in synagogues and teaching in many of them

Archaeologists have found few first century synagogues in Israel that were not rebuilt or destroyed over time. This small synagogue was built by the Zealot defenders of Masada during the first Jewish war.

(Mark 6:2; Luke 4:15), and it was here that he witnessed his fiercest debates with Pharisees. Through them, the influence of rabbis (or scribes) grew and the priesthood in Jerusalem came to be viewed with increased suspicion and cynicism.

The everyday life of a family in a Galilee village, however, did not revolve around temple sacrifice or synagogue attendance. These were vital, but Judaism also underscored the importance of personal purity, study, and observance, expressed in a living community and shaped by a family who would sustain faith for life. This helps explain why Jesus had his most effective results outside the formal religious structures of the temple and the synagogue. On hillside or grassy plains, crowds gathered and understood the personal care and grace of God, the importance of the Scriptures, and the pursuit of righteousness.

JEWISH LITERATURE

Another window into Jewish thought and life can be found through the literature read during the first century. Jesus (and his followers) would have known a number of these sources in the same way that we can make casual reference to well-known literature today. Of course, some of these sources were limited to scholars and others were the exclusive domain of isolated communities (e.g., the Dead Sea Scrolls).

The Scriptures

The Bible of the synagogues consisted of our Old Testament. It was called the *Tanak* (from the Heb. consonants T-N-K) as a shorthand expression for its three chief categories: the law (*Torah*), the prophets (*Nebiim*), and the writings (*Kithubim*). But it was also common to simply refer to any writings from this collection as "the law."

These Scriptures were generally read in Hebrew, but in the second century BC a Greek translation called the Septuagint (abbreviated LXX) became increasingly popular among Jews for whom Hebrew had become a dead language. Among Diaspora Jews, the LXX was the only "Bible" they knew.

The LXX also collected a series of writings from the intertestamental period commonly called the "Apocrypha." They contained historical works (such as 1 and 2 Maccabees), works of fiction (Tobit, Judith), and wisdom writing (Ben Sirach, the Wisdom of Solomon). While their inclusion in the LXX gave them an air of authority, still, they were not embraced by Hebrew scholars eager to create an authoritative canon of Scripture in the first century. Nevertheless these books are an important source when we reconstruct the intellectual life of Judaism in the century immediately preceding the New Testament.

Extracanonical Books

The search for Jewish writings that shed light on the first century world has netted surprising results. The Old Testament refers to books now lost to us (e.g., *The Book of the Wars of Yahweh*, see Num. 21:14), and we can imagine that Judaism had many others in the Herodian era that we are only now uncovering. Some were deemed inspired by religious communities; others were rejected. Modern collections of these works often refer to them as "Pseudepigrapha," which actually means "false signature"—referring to their spurious origins and frequent claim to have been authored by some biblical figure such as Baruch or Enoch.

The current collection, edited by James Charlesworth, includes fifty-two books that stem from 200 BC to AD 200.[6] These writings include apocalyptic books that give a vision of the end of history (*Enoch*), historical interpretations (*Jubilees*, *Assumption of Moses*), exhortations staged as blessings of Jacob to his twelve sons (*The Testaments of the Twelve Patriarchs*), and hymnic expressions of frustration and despair as Jews lived under Greek—then Roman—occupation (*Psalms of Solomon*). These writings teach us a great deal about the theological diversity in postexilic Judaism and how completely Hellenistic thought had penetrated Jewish thinking. Reading their pages sets the intellectual stage for interpreting a variety of New Testament passages.

Another collection, hailed as the most important archaeological find in the twentieth century, is the Dead Sea Scrolls (see on the Essenes, above). Here we have Jewish writings that precede the Jewish war (the settlement was destroyed about AD 68). Eight hundred manuscripts were located in eleven caves and represent everything from manuals of discipline to liturgies and commentaries. The three most cited Old Testament books are Psalms (36x), Deuteronomy (29x). and Isaiah (21x)—significantly the same books used most frequently in the New Testament.

The Qumran community produced extensive scrolls. This scroll, written in Hebrew, is from the "Community Rule" and outlines how community members should live.

Rabbinic Literature

A flourishing intellectual world came from the synagogues and schools of Israel, where Jewish scholars sought to interpret and apply specific scriptural texts. These writing often help us understand debates that Jesus engaged in with his opponents, such as the debate about the Sabbath in John 5:1 – 17.

Jewish scholars wrote commentaries on their Hebrew Scriptures. In some cases this could happen by an expansive rewriting of the story (*Jubilees*) or by supplying comments. Collections of these comments are called *midrash* (plur. *midrashim*; Heb., to "inquire"). Catalogues of legal collections exist (*Sipra* on Leviticus, *Mekilta* on Exodus) as well as narrative commentary (*Genesis Rabbah*).

Because many Palestinian Jews lived and worked in Aramaic, popular Aramaic paraphrases translated the Bible for them. These were called *Targums* (Aram. "translation"), and because they were considerably free with their rendering of the Old Testament, they give astounding insight into how Jewish teachers viewed the Bible in their day.

The disruption of the great rabbinic schools in AD 70 and 135 compelled leading scholars to formalize the teachings of their time. By the mid-second century, these schools saw a need

The Judean desert still holds many caves in which further ancient writings may be found. *Left:* The interior of Qumran cave 1, where seven scrolls were discovered. *Right:* This is the entrance of Qumran Cave 1.

to catalogue their primary laws that until then had been recited from memory. This "oral tradition" became a collection of sixty-three tractates (in six divisions) called *The Mishnah.* Here were rules governing everyday life from agriculture to legal damages. Since the Mishnah was formally compiled in the late second century, we cannot be sure how many of its provisions reflect the Jewish world during the time of Jesus.

Subsequent rabbis continued to provide guidance to the people, and they began to comment on the Mishnah itself. These commentaries were called the *Tosefta* ("supplements"). The final compilation used by New Testament scholars is *The Talmud* (from Heb. *lamad,* "to learn"). These volumes gather up scholarly rabbinic work from AD 200 to about AD 500 and helped later generations apply Mishnah in yet a new context. Two editions of Talmud exist. The oldest (and less complete) is the *Jerusalem Talmud,* which came from Israel and was organized around AD 400. The more famous is the thirty-six volume *Babylonian Talmud,* coming from the huge Jewish community living in Mesopotamia about AD 600.

Josephus

During the first Jewish war with Rome, a man named Josephus rose to leadership and became the defending general of Galilee. The north quickly fell to the Roman legions, and Josephus recognized that the Jewish revolt could not win and would likely lead to the utter destruction of Jerusalem. He accompanied the Roman general (and next emperor) Vespasian to Judea and then followed Vespasian's son Titus to Jerusalem, trying to persuade his former allies to surrender. After the war, Josephus retired to Rome, where he wrote his famous *Antiquities of the Jews* and an account of the war (*The Jewish War*).

Josephus is of crucial importance because he provides a firsthand account of the war, an early Jewish interpretation of Jewish history, and the earliest non-Christian references to Jesus. But we must keep in mind that Josephus is often idiosyncratic and deeply polemical. He writes to bolster his own role in Roman eyes and to demonstrate that the rebels who fought the Roman legions never represented the mainstream of Jewish leadership.

Philo of Alexandria

Among the few Jewish works that have survived from the first-century Jewish Diaspora, the writings of Philo of Alexandria (called Philo Judaeus) are among the most important. Philo lived in Alexandria, Egypt, during the lifetime of Jesus and Paul. His birth is often dated at about 20 BC and his death at about AD 50.

Philo's works give us insight into the mind of a Diaspora Jew precisely where the tensions between Hellenism and Judaism were evident. In this sense, Philo helps us understand some New Testament books that may reflect this same milieu. John's Gospel (cf. John 1:1), Paul's letters (e.g., Colossians), and particularly Hebrews may share this setting. Hebrews shares many patterns of thought with Philo and has led some to recommend Apollos, a native of Alexandria, as its author.

However, there is the danger of reading Philo (or Josephus) and concluding that his words are typical of the Jewish communities of the Mediterranean. His is only one voice, though an important one. Philo has been deeply influenced by the dualism of later Platonic thought, but this was not necessarily the case with Jews in synagogues throughout the Mediterranean.

PHILO'S SYNAGOGUE IN ALEXANDRIA

Diaspora Jews such as Philo met regularly in buildings they referred to as "places of prayer" (Greek, *proseuchai*). Prayer and the teaching of the law were central. Philo explains his own experience in Alexandria:

> Each seventh day there stand wide open in every city thousands of schools of good sense, temperance, courage, justice and the other virtues in which the scholars sit in order quietly with ears alert and with full attention, so much do they thirst for the draught which the teacher's words supply. (*On the Special Laws* 2:62)

The Alexandrian Jewish community (home of Apollos, Acts 18:24) was huge. This mosaic, found at Scythopolis in Israel, shows a voyage down the Nile and names "Alexandria."

1. Name the villages in Galilee that were most important in Jesus' public ministry. Why did he choose to anchor his efforts in Capernaum?

2. Why did John the Baptist become an opponent of Herod Antipas? What geographical insights are essential in this answer?

3. What did Jesus have in common with the Pharisees and why did they become his foremost opponents?

4. What would be the most faith-shaping experiences of a Jewish child as they grew up in a village like Capernaum?

5. Select some cultural elements from Jesus' ministry that cannot be understood without a background knowledge of the first-century world.

BIBLIOGRAPHY
Introductory

Malina, B. *Windows on the World of Jesus: Time Travel to Ancient Judea.* Louisville: Westminster John Knox, 1993.

Murphy, F. J. *The Religious World of Jesus: An Introduction to Second Temple Judaism.* Nashville: Abingdon, 1991. Revised as: *Early Judaism: The Exile to the Time of Jesus.* Peabody, MA: Hendrickson, 2002.

Stambaugh, J. E., and D. L. Balch. *The New Testament in Its Social Environment.* LEC. Philadelphia: Westminster, 1986.

Vanderkam, J. C. *An Introduction to Early Judaism.* Grand Rapids: Eerdmans, 2001.

Advanced

Hanson, K. C., and D. E. Oakman. *Palestine in the Time of Jesus: Social Structures and Social Conflicts.* Minneapolis: Fortress, 1998.

Safrai, S., and M. Stern. *The Jewish People in the First Century.* 2 vols. Assen/Minneapolis: Van Gorcum/Fortress, 1974, 1976.

Sanders, E. P. *Judaism: Practice and Belief, 63 BCE — 66 CE.* Philadelphia: Trinity Press International, 1992.

NOTES

1. W. Stegemann, B. Malina, and G. Theissen, eds., *The Social Setting of Jesus and the Gospels* (Minneapolis: Fortress, 2002); B. Malina, *Windows on the World of Jesus* (Louisville: Westminster John Knox, 1993); idem, *The New Testament World: Insights from Cultural Anthropology* (Louisville: Westminster John Knox, 2001³); K. C. Hanson and D. Oakman, *Palestine in the Time of Jesus: Social Structures and Social Conflicts* (Minneapolis: Fortress, 1998); J. Stambaugh and D. Balch, *The New Testament in Its Social Environment* (LEC; Louisville: Westminster John Knox, 1986).

2. J. Murphy-O'Connor, *Paul the Letter Writer: His World, His Options, His Skills* (Collegeville, MN: Glazier, 1995); J. Neyrey and B. Malina, *Paul, in Other Words: A Cultural Reading of His Letters* (Louisville: Westminster John Knox, 1990).

3. W. D. Davies, *The Territorial Dimension of Judaism* (Minneapolis: Fortress, 1991), 19.

4. E. Schürer, *The History of the Jewish People in the Age of Jesus Christ*, rev. and ed. by G. Vermes, F. Milar, and M. Black, 4 vols. (Edinburgh: T. & T. Clark, 1973–1987), 1:212; E. P. Sanders, *Judaism: Practice and Belief, 63 BCE to 66 CE* (Philadelphia: Trinity Press International, 1992), 380–412.

5. H.C. Kee and L. H. Cohick, ed., *The Evolution of the Synagogue* (Harrisburg, Pa.: Trinity Press International, 1999), 10; cf. 9–26

6. J. Charlesworth, ed., *The Old Testament Pseudepigrapha*, 2 vols. (New York: Doubleday, 1983, 1985).

CHAPTER 4

THE MEDITERRANEAN WORLD OF THE APOSTLE PAUL

The City of Corinth and the Gulf of Corinth

PERSPECTIVE

Paul arrived in the city of Corinth around the middle of the first century AD, having traversed the Roman road system from Antioch in Syria all the way to Troas on the western coast of Asia Minor. He and his companions crossed the Aegean Sea to Neapolis, the port of Philippi, and then walked through the eastern cities of Macedonia. After preaching in Berea, they again paid passage on a ship to Athens. From there it was a short overland trip to Corinth. The roads they walked were paved and filled with pedestrians, horses, mules, and carts.

Throughout the journey Paul spoke Greek and, as a Roman citizen, could converse in Latin as well. He also encountered peoples whose language he did not know. While the vast region he and his associates traveled was under Roman rule, the Macedonians of Berea had a distinct cultural heritage from the Greeks in Athens, and the Galatians' history was markedly different than that of the inhabitants of the Antioch in Syria. Romans from Italy could be found in many cities, and Corinth itself was a Roman colony on Greek soil. Paul undoubtedly heard the sounds of the flute during worship in the temples, smelled the meat in the market next to the temple of Apollo, saw orators in the central forum making a good show before the crowds who praised them, and witnessed the dozens of clients who followed a rich man as he strode toward the public basilica. This was the Gentile world where Paul, the Jew from Tarsus, proclaimed the gospel.

Paul took up the issues and debates of his day and constantly pointed men and women to the new thing that God was doing through a crucified and resurrected Jew called Jesus. He engaged the current thinking on the nature of the gods, the world, and the values by which

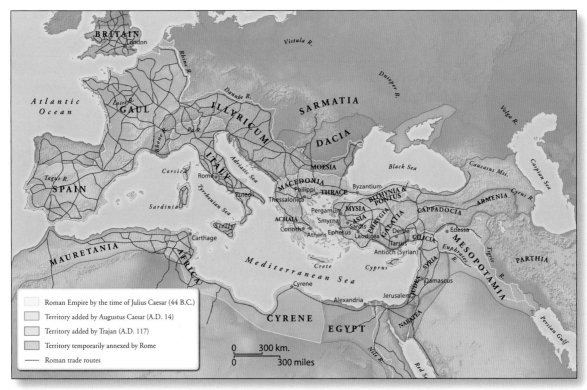

The Roman Empire

Some cities, such as Thessalonica, had both Latin and Greek speaking inhabitants as this two language inscription reveals. *Left:* Monument with Greek at top, Latin at bottom. *Above:* Enlarged Greek inscription.

people should live. As an orator in the forum, he proclaimed publicly that only Jesus, not the emperor or any of the gods, was Savior and Lord. The apostle heralded the message of salvation, which offered hope in the midst of the anxious insecurities of life. His words spoke powerfully and pointedly to the peoples of the Mediterranean.

THE GEOGRAPHY, THE JOURNEY, AND THE PEOPLES

During the days of the apostles, the Roman Empire extended from southern Britain and Spain in the west to Syria and Judea in the east. North Africa, including Egypt and the Nile River valley, was under Rome's dominion, while the northern boundary followed the Danube basin. The Roman world surrounded the whole Mediterranean Sea, which came to be known simply as "Our Sea." Beyond the borders lived many peoples who were often hostile to Roman interests, such as the Parthians to the east and Germanic tribes in the north.

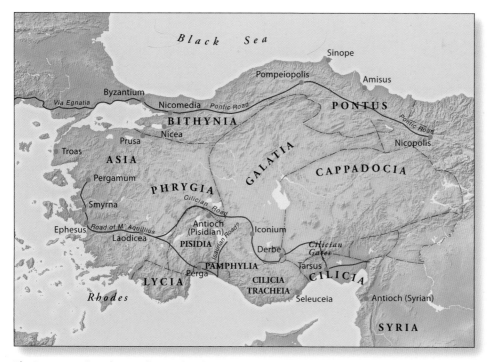

The Roman provinces in Anatolia or Asia Minor.

Cenchreae was the port city of Corinth on the Aegean.

The provinces of Macedonia and Achaia

The New Testament story plays out over a large portion of this vast empire. The center of the early Christian mission quickly moved from Jerusalem in Judea north to Antioch, the third largest city in the empire (called "The Pearl of the East") and the city Pompey made in 67 BC as the capital of the eastern part of the empire. By Paul's time, the Romans had organized Asia Minor (modern-day Turkey) into provinces. In the three southern provinces—Cilicia, Galatia, and Asia—Paul established churches.

Cilicia was Paul's home province, from the city of Tarsus. The Galatian churches, located in the southern section of Galatia, received one of Paul's earliest letters while Asia, located in the southwest corner of Asia Minor, had the great city of Ephesus as its capital. The book of Revelation was written to seven churches scattered throughout this Roman province as well (Rev. 1:4; 2:1–3:22).

But the gospel also extended to the northern provinces of Asia Minor (a region sometimes known as Anatolia) early in the church's history. First Peter circulated among the believers in the provinces of "Pontus, Galatia, Cappadocia, Asia

The Appian Way is a typical Roman road linking Rome to the eastern port of Brundisium.

and Bithynia" (1 Peter 1:1). By this time the Romans had united Pontus and Bithynia into a single province bordering the Black Sea, which was bisected by the Pontus Road. Cappadocia was located south of Pontus and north of Cilicia. The ancient region of Galatia was also in the north, but when this former kingdom was reorganized as a Roman province it was joined with lands to the south.

On the other side of the Aegean Sea were the provinces of Macedonia and Achaia. Macedonia spread across present-day northern Greece as well as portions of Macedonia and Albania. The Roman road that cut across the province was known as the Via Egnatia. Paul founded churches in Philippi and Thessalonica, principal metropolitan centers situated along this road. He wrote the Roman believers that "from Jerusalem all the way around to Illyricum [located northwest of Macedonia], I have fully proclaimed the gospel of Christ" (Rom. 15:19). At some point he must have traveled the length of the Via Egnatia, which reached Illyricum on the coast of the Adriatic.

The province of Achaia was the land of southern Greece, including the great peninsula known as Peloponnesus. Corinth was situated on the strategic narrow isthmus between the mainland of Greece and the Peloponnesus. The only other Achaean city mentioned in the New Testament, apart from the port city of Corinth called Cenchreae, is the famed Athens (Acts 17:15–34).

Midway through the first century AD we have evidence of Christians in Italy and Rome (Acts 18:2). Neither Paul nor Peter was the first to proclaim the gospel there although both were martyred there

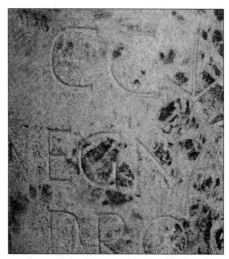

A "millarium" or mile marker from outside Thessalonica which identifies the Roman proconsul Gnaeus Egnatius as the person responsible for the construction of this highway through Macedonia.

The Roman Empire extended also to North Africa

during Emperor Nero's reign. Paul's vision even extended further to Spain (Rom. 15:24, 28), also a Roman province, and he may have traveled there after his release from imprisonment after Acts 28. Spain stood at the western mouth of the Mediterranean, and the ancient city of Gades (modern day Cádiz) was sometimes called "the ends of the earth."

Travel throughout the empire was facilitated by a network of all-weather roads that the Romans constructed. The Via Appia was the "queen of roads," extending from Rome to Brundisium, a city on Italy's southeastern coast. The Via Egnatia traversed the province of Macedonia between Apollonia on the Adriatic Sea and Byzantium (modern Istanbul). The Cilician Road crossed the southern portion of Asia Minor, connecting Ephesus in the province of Asia with the cities of Syria. The roads were signposted with *milaria* (mile markers) at strategic

ANTIPATER OF THESSALONICA ON THE DANGERS OF SEA TRAVEL

During the early part of the first century AD, Antipater wrote many epigrams about the dangers of travel by sea. In one he said, "Ill-starred Nicanor, wasted by the grey sea, naked you lie on a foreign shore or by the rocks.... Ah pitiable, your life is over, and your labours served only fishes and the sea." Another warned, "Trust not the fatal sea, mariner, not even when at anchor, not even if the beach holds your stern-cables. Ion fell into the harbour, and the sailor's hands, so swift to dive, were fettered by wine. Avoid dances on deck; the sea is the wine-god's enemy."[1]

points and *itineraria* were available, which informed travelers about distances between cities and places to stop. A network of other roads radiated from the main, paved highways. Through these great arteries of the empire flowed the message of salvation.

Travel along these roads was arduous and could be dangerous, especially in isolated places (see 2 Cor. 11:26). Paul traveled in the company of others both for protection and to help carry provisions (Acts 13:5). Inns for travelers were known for their poor food, bad wine, and worse company, so travelers preferred to stay in private homes of friends and patrons (Acts 16:15; 17:5–7). The virtue of hospitality was highly prized across the Mediterranean world (1 Peter 4:9).

Travel by sea on cargo vessels (no ships carried only passengers) was much quicker than by road, although more precarious. On foot, a band of travelers could cover fifteen to twenty miles a day and in a carriage twenty-five to thirty miles. But with favorable winds a ship could cover a hundred miles. Contrary winds would slow this pace considerably (cf. the two-day journey from Troas to Neapolis in Acts 16:11 and the five-day return journey in 20:6). Sea travel could be treacherous because of storms and shipwreck (Acts 27; 2 Cor. 11:25–26) and because of pirates, even though Augustus had cleared the sea of many of these brigands. Between October and May the sea lanes were virtually shut down (cf. 2 Tim. 4:21). Seamen were particularly superstitious and would not sail on ill-omened days, such as Friday the thirteenth.

What motivated early Christians to subject themselves to such adversity? The apostles were responding to Jesus' commission to his disciples to "be my witnesses in Jerusalem, and in all Judea and Samaria, and to the ends of the earth" (Acts 1:8; cf. Matt. 28:18–20; Luke 24:46–49). In the midst of a pluralistic world, they were also driven by the conviction that there was only one God who created the first human from whom all people are descended and therefore all peoples were responsible to him (Acts 17:24–31; 1 Cor. 8:4–6). Only through Jesus Christ can humanity approach him (1 Tim. 2:5) since his death was a sacrifice for everyone's sins (1 John 2:2).

Since the time of Alexander the Great, Greek was the universal tongue that facilitated trade and politics. The Greek spoken during the New Testament era is commonly called *koinē* ("common") Greek. When the Romans conquered, they did not attempt to Latinize their conquered peoples, although the affairs of government were carried out in Latin.

During this era, an educated person would speak both Latin and Greek (Suetonius, the Roman historian, called these "our two languages," *Claudius* 42.1). Greek became so entrenched that Horace could say, "Captured Greece took captive her savage conqueror and brought civilization to rustic Latium" (*Epistles* 2.1.156). Those both within and outside the empire who did not speak Greek were simply known as "barbarians" (Rom. 1:14). For example, Acts relates Paul's encounter with those who spoke the Lycaonian language in Lystra (Acts 14:6), and he testified of his sojourn among the Nabateans in Arabia, people whom he likely evangelized (Gal. 1:15–17). Paul hints at the evangelization of the uncivilized Scythians who lived around the Black Sea (Col. 3:11). Since there is one God and Christ's death was for all, the gospel opens the door to all peoples and breaks down the ethnic boundaries between them.

> **REGULATION OF THE SLAVE TRADE**
> Slave markets were regulated to protect the buyers. One ancient regulation stated, "Let care be taken that the bill of sale for each slave be written in such a way that it can be known exactly what disease or defect each one had, and which one is a runaway or a wanderer, or not innocent of any offence" (Aulus Gellius, *Attic Nights* 4.2.1).

NOTES FROM ANTIQUITY

ἐπρίατο ὁ Ἀπόλλων ὁ Πύθιος
παρὰ Σωσιβίου Ἀμφισσέος ἐπ᾽
ἐλευθερίαι σῶμ[α] γυναικεῖον,
ἁι ὄνομα Νίκαια, τὸ γένος
Ῥωμαίαν, τιμᾶς ἀργυρίου
μνᾶν τριῶν καὶ ἡμιμναίου.
προαποδότας κατὰ τὸν νόμον
Εὔμναστος Ἀμφισσεύς. τὰν
τιμὰν ἀπέχει.τὰν δὲ ὠνὰν
ἐπίστευσε Νίκαια τῶι Ἀπόλλωνι
ἐπ᾽ ἐλευθερίαι.

Apollo the Pythian *bought* from Sosibius of Amphissa, *for freedom*, a female slave, whose name is Nicaea, by race a Roman, *with a price* of three minae of silver and a half-mina. Former seller according to the law: Eumnastus of Amphissa. The *price* he hath received. The purchase, however, Nicaea hath committed unto Apollo, *for freedom*.

Manumission inscription from Delphi which recorded the freedom granted a slave. The usual formula is: "Date. N.N. sold to the Pythian Apollo a male slave named X.Y. at the price of – minae, for freedom, (or on condition that he shall be free, etc," followed by conditions and the names of witnesses.[2]

THE ORDER OF SOCIETY

Roman society was highly stratified and the Romans recognized that every person had his or her place within the established order (Latin *ordo*). One's position was determined by a number of factors, including whether they were free or slave, had wealth or not, and were a citizen or foreigner. Greater honor was ascribed to those who enjoyed higher status. The world where the gospel was first proclaimed was hierarchical and far from egalitarian.

Slaves, Libertini, and Free

The lowest status people in society were slaves. Above them were freedmen and women who had formerly been slaves, while the highest status was reserved for those born free. Even if a former slave attained great wealth, the stigma of once having been a slave could not be erased.

Slavery was widely practiced throughout the Roman world, and the institution itself was unquestioned. Within Italy there was approximately one slave for every three free persons, though in other parts of the empire the ratio was not as high. Wealthy people sometimes owned slaves numbering into the hundreds, and this became an indicator of a person's status. But even those of the lower artisan classes who made their living in local trades could own a few slaves.

Free people became slaves when they were captured as prisoners of war or were kidnapped and sold into slavery (1 Tim. 1:10). Some were slaves because they had been born to slave parents, while others sold themselves or even their children into slavery because they could not repay debts. Unwanted children, especially females, were left out exposed either to die or to be found by strangers who, in turn, could raise them and then sell them as slaves. Slaves were human property (called "a living tool") and were bought and sold as any other commodity. They could be rented to others, a convenient way to recoup the cost of purchasing a slave. The master had complete *dominium* over the slaves.

SLAVES ON THE FARMS

In *On Agriculture* 1.17.1 – 2, Varro makes the following classification: "Now I turn to the means by which land is tilled. Some divide these into ... three parts: the class of instruments which is articulate, the inarticulate, and the mute; the articulate comprising the slaves, the inarticulate comprising all cattle, and the mute comprising the vehicles."

Slaves constructed, cleaned, served as cooks, nurses, beauticians, barbers, midwives, doctors, cleaners, prostitutes, painters, and even pedagogues who looked after children and, when the children were old enough, conducted them to school (Gal. 3:24 – 25). Some slaves held responsible positions as managers while others ended up as gladiators. Those severely ill-treated believed running away was their only recourse. Slaves could be given ID collars, one of which read, "I have run away. Capture me. When you have returned me to my master, Zoninus, you will receive a reward" (*CIL* 15.7194).

Slaves could obtain their freedom (a process called "manumission") and join the ranks of the *libertini* or freedmen. Sometimes the slaves could purchase their freedom by saving up gifts and the small allowance they received, or if their family or friends could supply the funds. Some masters manumitted slaves to impress others with their wealth while others freed slaves in their wills. At times, a slave master would free a female slave in order to marry her. Freed slaves were commonly granted citizenship. Paul encourages slaves to avail themselves of manumission if such an option became available (1 Cor. 7:21). The *libertini* were recognized by the freedman's beanie, a cap made out of felt.

Those born free within Roman society all shared the common advantage of enjoying higher social status than slaves or even freedmen and women. However, not all free people were of the same social class. Some would be loosely classified as the *humiliores*, those of low birth and status, while people of the higher orders of society were the *honestiores* or those who were given honor is society.

Honestiores

The highest class of aristocrats in the empire were the *senators*. They owned property that was valued at least one million sesterces, a sum equivalent to 250,000 denarii (each denarius was equivalent to a day's wage). The wealth of some senators greatly exceeded this amount. The New Testament names some who were senators, such as Sergius Paulus, the proconsul of Cyprus (Acts 13:7), and Gallio, the proconsul of Achaia (Acts 18:12).

SENECA'S ADVICE ON HOW TO DEAL WITH CAPTIVES NEWLY ENSLAVED

Seneca writes in his *Essay about Anger* 3.29.1 – 2:

If a captive who has suddenly been reduced to slavery hangs on to remnants of his former freedom and does not run quickly to perform degrading and laborious services, if he does not keep up with the pace of his master's horse or carriage because he is out of shape from previous inactivity, if sleep overwhelms him because he is exhausted by his demanding daily duties, if he refuses to do farm work or does not do it vigorously when he has been transferred to this hard labor from service in the city with its holidays — let us carefully distinguish whether he *cannot* do the work or *will not*.

THE VALUE OF A GOOD MIND

"Lucius Voltacilius Pilutus is said to have been a slave and even to have been chained to the doorpost as a doorman until he was manumitted because of his intelligence and interest in education.... Then he became a teacher of rhetoric" (Suetonius, *On Rhetoricians* 27).

OBLIGATIONS OF THE *LIBERTINI* AND THEIR PATRONS

Roman law as well as social custom underscored a freedman's or woman's obligation to their former master and the duty of the patron to the client. One Roman law stated: "A freedman must provide services and supply his own food and clothing. But if he cannot support himself, food must be provided to him by his patron" (*Digest of Laws* 38.1.18).

Below the senatorial order were the *equestrians*, those born Roman citizens who had accumulated wealth totaling at least 400,000 sesterces (100,000 denarii). Some of the governors of Judea, such as Pontius Pilate, Marcus Antonius Felix, and Porcius Festus, were from the equestrian order (Luke 3:1; Acts 24:1–3, 27). Below the equestrian order were the *decurions*, who were freeborn aristocrats whose wealth needed to total at least 100,000 sesterces. Erastus, the city treasurer of Corinth (Rom. 16:23), was a decurion as was Dionysius of Athens, a man who served in the Areopagus (Acts 17:34).

Humiliores

The enormous wealth of the empire was in the hands of the *honestiores* and not the vast majority of the population known as *humiliores*. A middle class did not exist, and the economic gap between the *honestiores* and the people of low birth and status was huge. The *humiliores* were free people (either born free or *libertini*) who owned small farms or businesses or worked as barbers, moneylenders, potters, shippers, tanners, butchers, weavers, wine and oil makers, soldiers, or other kinds of artisans. Because of their low status in society, they were not considered virtuous. Most people in the early church were *humiliores* and slaves, the very people society considered less virtuous.

Honestiores had the most honored seats at public events, such as in the stadium in Delphi.

Patrons and Clients

Patronage was a central feature of the Roman world. A person would come under the protection and care of a patron, and clients, in turn, would render services for the patron. Clients followed their patrons as they went about their business and supported their cause in public. The patrons' public honor was greatly enhanced by their number of clients as well as by the social status of the clients. The higher the class of clients, the higher the status of the patron. Patrons offered legal protection to their clients, rewarded them with food and presents, and sometimes invited them to banquets.

A patron could, in turn, be a client of a person of higher social status. Higher

JUVENAL AND PERSIUS ON PATRONS

Juvenal, the Roman satirist, describes the less-than-refined dinner experience of a client invited to his patron's banquet:

> When bidden to dinner, you receive payment in full for all your past services.... See with what a grumble another [slave] has handed you a bit of hard bread that you can scarce break in two, or bits of solid dough that have turned mouldy.... See now that large lobster being served to my lord, all garnished with asparagus.... Before you is placed on a tiny plate a shrimp hemmed in by half an egg — a fit banquet for the dead. (*Satire* 5.12 – 90)

Another Latin author, Persius, satirizes a patron: "You know how to present a shivering client with a threadbare cloak, and then you say, 'I love the Truth; tell me the truth about myself!'" (1.54 – 55).

Inscription which honors a benefactor, "one who does good."

status clients were sometimes euphemistically called "friends," a sense that is behind Jesus' statement, "I no longer call you servants . . . I have called you friends" (John 15:15). The greatest patrons were the emperors themselves, who, among their many honorific titles, were called "benefactor" (*euergetēs*). In the New Testament, Jesus is sometimes viewed as the one who is the greatest benefactor of all (see Acts 10:38).

Citizens and Aliens

Paul was a Roman citizen (Acts 22:25 – 29), but not because he was born and lived in the Roman Empire. Many within the provinces of the empire, although free persons, did not enjoy the rights of citizenship, which included exemption from humiliating forms of punishment (such as crucifixion) and punishment without trial (Acts 16:37 – 39). While Paul was beheaded when finally condemned in Rome, Peter was crucified since his legal status was that of an alien. Roman citizens in the provinces could appeal to Caesar if they believed their

CICERO AND SENECA ON CLIENTS

The senator Cicero commented on the services a client would render to a patron:

> Men of the lower class have only one way of either earning or repaying favors from our class, and that is by working on our political campaigns and following us around.... This constant attendance, which we have come to expect for men who are honorable and generous, is an appropriate activity for friends [a euphemism for 'client'] who are of a lower class and not busy.... As they themselves often say, they cannot plead cases for us, or pledge security, or invite us to their homes. Yet they ask all these things from us, and they think that the favors which they receive from us can be repaid by their service. (*Speech in Defense of Murena* 70 – 71)

Seneca is a bit more cynical: "Clients, you say? Not one of them waits upon you, but rather what he can get out of you. Once upon a time, clients sought a politically powerful friend; now they seek loot. If a lonely old man changes his will, his morning visitor goes to someone else's door" (*Letters* 19.4).

case was not considered fairly by provincial authorities (Acts 25:10–12). Moreover, Roman citizens could vote.

Some were born citizens of Rome because their parents were citizens, as was the case with Paul, or one could purchase citizenship (Acts 22:28). Those who were freed from slavery were often granted citizenship and those who served in the auxiliary military forces became citizens upon discharge. Citizenship helped ensure their loyalty to the imperial power (Acts 21:39). The New Testament reflects on the theological meaning of citizenship (Phil. 3:20) and alien status (1 Peter 2:11).

The Family

The hierarchical social structure within Roman society was also present in the family. The father of the family, known as the *paterfamilias*, had absolute authority (*patria potestas*) over the entire household—spouse, children, extended family, and slaves. He held rights over all the property and financial affairs of the family and also could determine whom his children married. If a child was born to his wife, he had authority to "expose" the child (thus killing it) if it was unwanted. Children continued to be obligated to their father even after they moved out of the family home. The father also directed the religious life of the family.

Marriages were arranged, although there could be genuine affection between husbands and wives. Women were commonly married early in their teens while men entered marriage much later. Marriages were governed by contracts, which had to do primarily with economics and inheritance.

Women were under contract to remain faithful to their husbands while husbands

Juno was the goddess of marriage, here depicted standing behind the couple. The marriage contract is in the form of a scroll.

were given wide latitude to satisfy their sexual desires outside the family home. Plutarch even wrote, "If therefore a man in private life, who is incontinent and dissolute … commit some peccadillo with a paramour or a maidservant, his wedded wife ought not to be indignant or angry, but she should reason that it is respect for her which leads him to share his debauchery, licentiousness, and wantonness with another woman" (*Advice to Bride and Groom* 140B). Above all, a woman was expected to obey her husband, be faithful, worship only his gods, and manage the household well.

Women were expected to pass from being subject to their fathers to being subordinate to their husband. Livy once said, "Never, while their men survive, is feminine subjection shaken off; and they themselves abhor the freedom which the loss of husbands and fathers produces" (*History of Rome* 34.1.12). However, during the Roman period, the model of the "new woman" was emerging as many women found themselves with great wealth and less supervision by men who were absent during war and on administrative duty. These women were more socially self-determined in many matters, including financial affairs, political participation, and even sexuality.

The New Testament discussion about the role of women is carried out between the poles of the traditional roles of women and the new emerging definitions. While the Gospels and letters are sometimes viewed as advocates for traditional roles, the presence of women in the church who provided significant leadership shows that the church was advocating models that diverged from the extremes of the surrounding culture (Acts 18:24 – 26; Rom. 16:1 – 7; Phil. 4:2 – 3; Col. 4:15).

Children were expected to obey their parents, especially their fathers, and to honor them in a way similar to how a person would honor the gods. Fathers were expected to discipline and be strict with their children as an expression of love, while mothers were considered to be more tender.

Fathers taught their sons a trade. Mothers likewise disciplined their children and were afforded respect from their children. They were the sole persons responsible for the education of their daughters in the skills of domestic life and moral development.

A child's toy from the Roman empire

LESBIA

Valerius Catullus wrote about Lesbia, who embodied the image of the new woman:

Lesbia hurls abuse at me in front of her husband,
That fatuous person finds it highly amusing!
Nothing gets through to you, jackass, for silence would signal
That she'd been cured of me, but her barking and bitching
show that not only haven't I been forgotten,
But that this burns her, and so she rants and rages. (Poem 83)

THE GOVERNMENT OF THE EMPIRE

The Emperors

Augustus.

"Caesar" was the family name of Julius Caesar, which Augustus, his adopted son, took and was subsequently used by the succeeding emperors. The title "emperor" comes from the Latin *imperator*, which was originally granted to generals after victory in battle. Julius Caesar adopted it as a permanent title to designate himself as the supreme military authority in Rome. Tiberius, for example, said, "I am *dominus* [lord] of my slaves, *imperator* of my troops, and *princeps* [first citizen] of everyone else" (Dio Cassio, *Historia* 57.8.2).

Augustus wanted to restore the religious traditions of Rome and thus adopted the title *pontifex maximus* as well. He was also called *pater patriae*, "the father of the fatherland," a title that suggested not only his protective care but his unrivaled authority (similar to *paterfamilias*). These titles highlight how exalted the emperor became in the first century. The culmination of this process was the emperor cult, which flourished especially in the East.

When Augustus became emperor, he added to his title *divi filius* ("son of god", i.e., son of the deified Julius Caesar). Augustus became known as "the god and savior, emperor" and Nero was hailed as of "the lord of the entire world." The Christian proclamation that Christ was the true Lord and only Savior was a direct challenge to the exalted status of the emperor (Phil. 2:11; Titus 2:13). Only Jesus could be rightly called the "Son of God" (John 3:16; 1 John 5:5).

The tradition of worshiping a ruler as divine was common in the East, as Nebuchadnezzar demanded (Dan. 3) or as the adoration that the pharaoh received in Egypt. This notion was given wider circulation through the conquests of Alexander the Great and the cult that flourished in the wake of his own divinization. The ruler cult only slowly spread to Rome itself. These men were considered to have done great deeds that were those one would expect of the gods.

Augustus had established peace in the empire (*pax Romana*) and was acclaimed as the universal benefactor. His name Augustus (Gk. *Sebastos*) means something like "his reverence" or "his worship" and has divine overtones. Despite such high honors, we should not assume that the imperial cult was simply a religious affair. The emperors were the greatest patrons in the empire, controlling vast wealth to promote their interests. Cities that were recipients

THE EMPERORS

Augustus (Octavian)
Augustus
31 BC – AD 14
Luke 2:1

Tiberius
AD 14 – 37
Luke 3:1

Caligula (Gaius)
Caligula
AD 37 – 41

Claudius
AD 41 – 54
Acts 11:28; 18:2

Nero
AD 54 – 68
Acts 25:10; 28:19

Galba
AD 68

Otho
AD 69

Vitellius
AD 69

Vespasian
AD 69 – 79

Titus
AD 79 – 81

Domitian
AD 81 – 96

Nerva
AD 96 – 98

Trajan
AD 98 – 117

Hadrian
AD 117 – 138

A model of the imperial temple of Augustus in Ankara, Turkey.

Augustus was considered to be the "son of god" (*divi filius*) that is, the son of the deified Julius Caesar.

of imperial patronage returned the favor by honoring such an exalted patron with a temple erected for his veneration, complete with sacrifices and priesthood. This overwhelming act of thanksgiving to the patron was calculated to ensure future benefits.

The Senate

During the Roman republic, which lasted until the time of Augustus, the Senate ruled supreme over all affairs, domestic and foreign. This body of approximately three hundred was composed of men of the highest social class. Only those with the greatest wealth could be members of the Roman Senate, and they held their position for life. But after the assassination of Julius Caesar in 44 BC, the senate lost its prestige and power as the emperor, beginning with Augustus, gained supremacy. The Senate was allowed to govern certain of the less problematic provinces of the empire, but in many ways it became more of a club of the Roman aristocracy.

THE IMPERIAL CULT IN THE EAST

One of the ways which citizens of cities in the eastern part of the empire honored the emperor for his generous patronage was to establish a temple and priesthood as part of the imperial cult. A fragmentary inscription from Thessalonica records the construction of such a temple in that Macedonian city:

> ...proconsul...of Latomia buil[t the] tem[ple] of Caesar. In the time of priest and agon[othete of Im] perator Caesar Augustus son [of god]...-ōs son of Neikopol[eōs, priest] of the gods, Dō [... son of...] -pos, and (priest) of Roma a[nd Roman] benefactors, Neik[... son of] Paramonos. In the term of the Politarchs Diogenēs son [of...] Kleōn son of P..., Zōpas son of Kal..., Eulandros son of..., Prōtogenēs son of..., and the superin[tendent] of the work, trea[surer of the city] Sōsōnos s[on of...] [In the term of the] architec[t] Dionysiu[s son of...].[4]

Corinth was a Roman colony on Greek soil. Viewed from the nearby mountain, Acrocorinth.

The Cities and the Provinces

We are accustomed to governments that have well-defined structure and boundaries and little variation from region to region. The Roman Empire, however, was characterized by diversity in its governmental institutions. While much of the empire was organized into provinces, there were also vassal states. Governors were prefects, legates, or proconsuls, depending on the type of administrative district they governed and their own status within the empire. Cities were classified in various ways, with some enjoying free city status while others were Roman colonies. Vassal states could become provinces and provinces could move from being imperial to senatorial, and then back again. During the New Testament era, Judea was sometimes a vassal kingdom and at other times governed directly by the Romans as a province (see Ch. 3).

The cities. The Roman Empire was basically a commonwealth of autonomous cities that were the political and economic backbone of the Roman Empire. A city was a social and economic unit that exercised control over a large geographical area—its hinterland or *territorium*. Produce from the country was brought into the city markets. These products were also the source of much of the riches of the aristocracy, who owned most of the arable land. The seat of government over the surrounding area was in the city, similar to our county governments.

Though the Jesus movement began in the rural regions of Galilee, it soon became an urban phenomenon. In fact, when Paul spread the gospel throughout the Roman world, his center of operations were the cities and via these the surrounding countryside was influenced (see Acts 19:10; 1 Thess. 1:8). He proclaimed he had filled the whole region from Jerusalem to Illyricum with the gospel (Rom. 15:19) even though he limited his ministry to significant urban centers.

> COLONIAE I
> IVLIAE ·
> CORINTHIENSI ·
> Q · GRANIVS · Q · F ·
> BASSVS · S · P · D · D
> PROC · AVG ·

Colonies were governed by Roman law. This inscription identifies Corinth as a Roman Colony.

Thessalonica was a "free city" and not a colony. The grant of freedom is commemorated in this coin.

Two types of cities are relevant for our study of the New Testament. (1) The first is the *colony* of Roman citizens (*coloniae civium romanorum*). The program of colonization began with Julius Caesar and continued under succeeding emperors. Colonies were often populated with veterans of the Roman legions, as Philippi (Acts 16:12), or with members of the proletariat who had no land and lived from the sale of their labor, as Corinth (which was populated largely with *libertini* from Italy).

The colonies mirrored life in the imperial city of Rome. Except for the excluded classes, such as slaves and foreigners, their populations enjoyed Roman citizenship. They were exempt from taxes paid to Rome and Roman law was their law. The gospel spread through various Roman colonies during the early Christian mission, such as Pisidian Antioch, Lystra, Iconium, Troas, Philippi, Corinth, Ptolemais (Acts 21:7), and Syracuse (28:12).

(2) The empire also had numerous *free cities*, such as Ephesus, Smyrna, Tarsus, Antioch in Syria, and Thessalonica. These cities could govern themselves according to local tradition, could mint their own coins, and were exempt from many of the taxes normally paid to Rome. Here the democratic Greek system of government prevailed with the highest ruling authority being the *ekklēsia* ("assembly," a word commonly used to describe the "church" in the New Testament) of the *dēmos*, the people or the free citizens of the city (Acts 19:30, 33). This assembly had final say in political/legislative as well as judicial matters. Meetings of the *ekklēsia* included prayers and sacrifices to the local deity. Free cities also had a *boulē* or senate, and frequently we find inscriptions speaking of *hē boulē kai ho dēmos* ("the council and the people"). The Areopagus of Athens was one such body (Acts 17:19, 34); the Sanhedrin in Jerusalem functioned in a similar way. The leading magistrates in some

Tarsus, the home of the Apostle Paul, was one of the many free cities in the empire.

Macedonian cities were called "politarchs" (Acts 17:6, 8) while in other cities they are simply "rulers" (Matt. 20:25; Rom. 13:3; Titus 3:1).

The provinces. The Roman Empire was divided into administrative districts called "provinces" (see Acts 23:34; 25:1), which were classified as either imperial or senatorial. (1) Imperial provinces (e.g., Cilicia, Syria, Egypt, Galatia, Cappadocia, and Pamphylia), were the more problematic and came under the direct control of the emperor. Judea was especially problematic for Rome because of the number of its violent uprisings. One or more Roman legions were garrisoned inside an imperial province to maintain order (legions were about 6,000 soldiers strong). For Judea, a legion was located both in Egypt and in Syria. These provinces were governed by legates of senatorial rank (*legatus*), although the minor imperial provinces could be administered by a prefect (*praefectus*), who could be an equestrian. Jesus was crucified by Pontius Pilate, the *prefect* of Judea.

Pontius Pilate was a Roman prefect, as noted in this inscription.

(2) Senatorial provinces were those that posed no threat to the empire. These had only a small garrison of troops. Senatorial provinces mentioned in the New Testament are Macedonia, Achaia, Asia, Crete (united with Cyrene in Africa), Bithynia (united with Pontus in 74 BC), and Cyprus. The governor of these provinces was called a proconsul (see "Honestiores," above).

Vassal Kingdoms

The Roman Empire also had vassal kingdoms. Although governed by kings or royalty of lower status, these enjoyed a modicum of freedom under the authority of the emperor and had the liberty to govern their internal affairs as long as they remained loyal to Rome. They could collect taxes and even maintain an army. They could not develop their own foreign relations and their power to mint their own money was limited. They paid tribute to Rome and had to assure that the frontiers were secure. Galatia was a vassal kingdom until 25 BC; Judea under Herod the Great and his descendants was another.

RELIGION IN THE MEDITERRANEAN WORLD

When the early Christian messengers spread the gospel across the Mediterranean world, every city they entered contained numerous temples, altars, and shrines dedicated to local deities as well as gods worshiped throughout the empire. When Paul wrote 1 Corinthians, he

---

NOTES FROM ANTIQUITY

PAUSANIUS ON THE GODS IN ATHENS

Writing in the second century AD, Pausanius describes in great detail the religious environment in Athens, making note of the multiple temples and images along with the myths that stand behind them. He writes, "Near the statue of Demosthenes [the orator] is a sanctuary of Ares, where are placed two images of Aphrodite, one of Ares made by Alcamenes, and one of Athena made by a Parian of the name of Locrus. There is also an image of Enyo, made by the sons of Praxiteles. About the temple stand images of Heracles, Theseus, Apollo binding his hair with a fillet" (*Description of Greece* 1.8.4). Pausanius even mentions the "altars of the gods named Unknown" (1.1.4), a description strikingly similar to Paul's discovery of the Athenian altar dedicated "To an Unknown God" (Acts 17:23).

The temple of Hephaestus was one of the many temples and altars which filled the agora in Athens.

discussed what he called the "so-called gods, whether in heaven or on earth" (1 Cor. 8:5); in Athens he became distressed because "the city was full of idols" (Acts 17:16).

Atheists were not common, and almost everyone believed that that there were multiple gods who governed the affairs of humanity and the world. Jews and Christians, by contrast, acknowledged only one God and considered that the fundamental movement of salvation was to forsake the worship of those gods and turn to the one true and living God (1 Thess. 1:9). Ancient pagans correctly perceived Christianity as an attack on the worship of idols (Acts 14:11–18; 17:22–31; 19:23–41) since the heralds of the gospel condemned such worship and called people to serve the true and living God (e.g., Rom. 1:22–25; 1 Cor. 5:11; 6:9; 10:14–22; Gal. 5:20–21; 1 John 5:21; Rev 21:8; 22:15). During that era, society was critical of those who abandoned the gods of their community and family, for rejecting the family deities or the gods of the city was seen as an antisocial act, for the gods were regarded as patrons of the community.

Paganism, Judaism and Christianity

Christians were not alone in their rejection of pagan notions about the divine. Judaism too differentiated itself from pagan beliefs and practices. In the first place, pagans had various temples in different places to worship their deities and could sacrifice to their gods even if there were no temple. The Jews, however, only sacrificed in the temple in Jerusalem. For their part, the Christians gathered in any convenient location, although most often in private houses. Worship was not tied to any particular locality and, in some respects, Christian practices mirrored those of the synagogue.

The temple housed the image of the deity, as in the temple of Artemis in Ephesus.

Temples of the same god could be found in various cities, such as these temples of Jupiter in Pompeii and Athens.

Second, the function of a temple in the Roman world was to house the image of the deity. The temple was the dwelling of the deity, not a religious meeting place for worshipers. But in the temple of God in Jerusalem there was no image (Ex. 20:4–6). The temple was holy since it was dedicated to the worship of the God who lived there (Matt. 23:21; 27:51; Heb. 6:19). Yet early Christian apologetic was critical of the notion that God could be confined to the temple in Jerusalem (Acts 7:48–50), and Paul declared that the gathering of God's people was his temple and his presence dwelt in their midst (1 Cor. 3:16; 2 Cor. 6:16).

Third, the worship of Yahweh was expensive. The priesthood in the Greek and Roman temples was an honorary position, underwritten by those who served as priests. The priests were from the aristocracy, and those that wanted to advance in society sought out a priesthood. But in Judaism the priesthood was hereditary, and Jewish society maintained the priests. While the gods of the Greeks and Romans ended up with little of the sacrifice (normally only the bones since the meat of public sacrifices was sold in the market, cf. 1 Cor. 10:23–30), the sacrifices in Jerusalem consumed most of the animal (although priests and worshipers received a considerable portion of certain sacrifices). Early Christians looked to Christ as their great high priest (Heb. 3:1; 4:14–15) and did not acknowledge any other person as priest who mediated between humanity and God. Those who did serve as ministers of the gospel could expect to be supported by the churches they served (Luke 10:7; 1 Cor. 9:7–12; 1 Tim. 5:17–18).

Fourth, a feature that distinguished Judaism from pagan religion was the subjection of the whole life of the worshiper to Yahweh. Among the Gentiles, ethics was a subject of philosophy, alongside metaphysics, and was not connected to one's religious allegiances. But within Judaism, religion and ethics were intimately intertwined.

The "pious" pagan was not necessarily a moral person but rather one who faithfully performed the necessary obligations before the gods, as well as family and country. Religion had nothing to do with the morality of the worshipers. In fact, a number of cults promoted lifestyles that were viewed immoral by Christians. Dionysus was the god of wine and drunkenness; Aphrodite was the patroness

Votive offerings from the Serapeum, the temple of Serapis, in Thessalonica.

of prostitutes. Christianity shared with Judaism the conviction that faith in God results in an ethical life subject to God's will. Conversion to the living God includes serving him (1 Thess. 1:9) as obedient children who hear God's call, "Be holy, because I am holy" (1 Peter 1:13–16).

Pagans and Christians on the Relationship with the Divine

In the Greco-Roman world, the relationship with the gods was viewed as a transaction: "Do this for me and I'll do that for you." Votive offerings were given to the gods in anticipation of receiving some benefit, such as an answer to prayer. When the ancients dedicated sacrifices and prayers to the gods, they expected some return on their investment. Thanksgivings for benefits received were not mere expressions of gratefulness but carried with them the expectation that future benefits would be granted. In offering to the gods, the worshiper had to follow the established formulas. If one made a mistake, the ritual had to begin over again. Christians, however, embraced a different approach to God, whom they viewed as their Father (Matt, 6:7–13).

The gods were often viewed as capricious. The very same god could bring a person tragedy or blessing. Antipater shows how perplexed people could be as they tried to understand the gods' behavior: "Easy-going is Hermes, shepherds, pleased at libations of milk and honey from the oak. Not so Heracles; he demands a whole ram or a fat sheep, or anyway exacts a whole victim. But he keeps the wolves away. But what good is that if what is protected is killed, whether by wolves or by the protector?"[5] Much Roman cult activity was devoted to keeping the gods on your side in the hope of maintaining the *pax deorum* ("peace with the gods"). Keeping the proper relationship with the gods was the essence of *pietas* ("piety"). The unwavering and self-sacrificial love of God, as understood by the Christians, stood in bold relief to these popular notions about the gods (John 3:16; Rom. 8:31–39).

Other Religious Trends in the Mediterranean World

Although the established cults of the cities and the empire were the dominant religious force in the Roman world, from the time of the Roman republic new religions from the East began to establish their roots. These so-called "mystery religions" promised the worshiper a more personal communion with the divine. Initiation into the cult and its secrets was often a dramatic and emotional event, through which the initiate came into union with the deity, obtained salvation, and was promised bliss in the afterlife. These religions, such as the worship of Mithra,

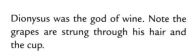
Dionysus was the god of wine. Note the grapes are strung through his hair and the cup.

JOSEPHUS ON RELIGION AND ETHICS
Josephus comments on how religion and ethics go hand in hand in Judaism:

> The reason why the constitution of this legislation was even better directed to the utility of all than other legislations were, is this, that Moses did not make religion a part of virtue, but he saw and he ordained other virtues to be parts of religion; I mean, justice, and fortitude, and temperance, and a universal agreement of the members of the community with one another; for all our actions and studies, and all our words [in Moses' settlement], have a reference to piety towards God. (*Against Apion* 2.17 [170–171])

Isis, Cybele, Demeter, and Dionysus, resonated with the themes of death and rebirth, which were tied with the agricultural cycle of sowing and reaping.

Although some scholars have attempted to understand the rise of Christianity as part of this movement, significant differences exist between the Christian story and that of the mysteries. The death and resurrection of Christ, for example, is not an annual cyclical event but a once-for-all occurrence. And, although the Christian faith offers personal communion with God, it does not promise that the initiate will become absorbed by the deity.

Religion in the Mediterranean world was not limited to the temples and public altars. Private religion included such practices as divination, magic, and astrology. In the first century, Antipater of Thessalonica notes the prevalence of astrology in one of his many epigrams: "The experts in astrology tell of an early death for me; though it be so, I care nothing for that, Seleucus. All men have the same way down to Hades; if mine is quicker than others', I shall be face to face with Minos the sooner."[6] People understood the gods to speak through dreams, visions, and oracles.

By using curses, often inscribed on lead tablets and thrown into wells or buried, a person could attempt to banish their enemies to the underworld. One such tablet read: "Spirits of the netherworld, I consecrate and hand over to you, if you have any power, Ticene of Carisius. Whatever she does, may it all turn out wrong. Spirits of the netherworld, I consecrate to you her limbs, her complexion, her figure, her head . . . [and] if I see her wasting away, I swear that I will be delighted to offer a sacrifice to you every year" (*Corpus Inscriptionum Latinarum* 10.8249; cf. Luke 6:28; Rom. 12:14!). "Demons" (*daimōn*) filled the gap between the gods and humans, and exorcism for those possessed by spirits was widely known and practiced.

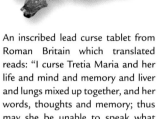

An inscribed lead curse tablet from Roman Britain which translated reads: "I curse Tretia Maria and her life and mind and memory and liver and lungs mixed up together, and her words, thoughts and memory; thus may she be unable to speak what things are concealed, nor be able..."

PHILOSOPHY IN THE MEDITERRANEAN WORLD

Philosophy played a central role in ancient Greco-Roman society. Philosophers wrote and gave public lectures throughout the cities of the Empire; we meet many of them face to face, with characteristic garb and beard, in statues that survive from the period. The Roman philosopher Gellius once quipped, "*Video barbum et pallium, philosophum nondum video,*" which translates, "I see the beard and the mantle, but I do not yet see the philosopher."

Athens retained something of its classical flavor as philosophers could be found declaiming in the central agora (Acts 17:17–18). Cicero (first century BC) was largely responsible for

---

IT'S MAGIC!

While the purpose of religion was to placate the gods, the goal of magic was to control the powers by using prescribed formulas and incantations. Ephesus was known as a center of magic (Acts 19:18–20). If the ritual is performed in the proper way, one could expect the desired results. Cato the Elder described a chant by which one could cure a dislocated limb:

> A dislocation can be remedied with this chant. Take a green reed, about four or five feet long, split it down the middle, and have two men hold it against their hips. Begin to chant: *motas vaeta daries dardares astataries dissunapiter.* Continue until the two halves of the reed come together. Wave an iron knife over the reed. When the halves have joined and are touching one another, take the reed in your hand and cut it on the right and on the left. Fasten it to the dislocation or fracture, which will then heal. Continue to chant every day: *huat hauat huat ista pista sista dannabo dannaustra.* Or: *huat haut haut istasis tarsis ardannabou dannaustra.* (*On Agriculture* 160).

NOTES FROM ANTIQUITY

Reconstructed stoa in Athens. The Stoics took their name from this place.

mediating Greek philosophical trends to the Roman people, though they were much more reluctant to engage in philosophical speculation, considering it something of a waste of time.

Philosophy was principally concerned with reason (or how to know the world), metaphysical issues (or how to understand the world), and moral questions (or how one is to live to assure happiness). The nature of the gods was commonly discussed, as were practical aspects of daily life. For example, Plutarch's *Moralia* includes essays on "The Delays of the Divine Vengeance" and "Fate" as well as tracts on "The Love of Wealth," "Compliancy," "Envy and Hate," and "Praising Oneself Inoffensively." He also wrote "Advice to Bride and Groom."

In the encounter with the philosophical trends of the era, we find Christianity co-opting the place of philosophy as it had the place of religion within society. Paul, like the philosophers, makes his case in the marketplace (Acts 17:16–31), and the themes he addressed were part of the current debates. New Testament moral teaching addresses the common topics of philosophical discussion, such as the proper conduct expected of each one according to his or her station (the household codes in Eph. 5:21–6.9; Col. 3:18–4:1). Christians also discussed moral issues, such as the vice and virtue lists in Galatians 5:19–23 (see also Rom. 1:28–32). Yet while the *form* of the teaching is strikingly similar, the understanding of the *sources* of vice and virtue are distinct. Christian ethics find their foundation and motivation in the character of God and his redemptive work (1 Peter 1:13–16).

Two of the most prominent philosophical schools during the first century were the Epicureans and the Stoics. Paul encountered adherents to

Epicurus

both these philosophies in the city of Athens (Acts 17:18). The Epicureans, founded by Epicurus around 300 BC, did not believe in the existence of the gods, or, if they did truly exist, they were far distant from the world and did not exert any influence over it. Hence, they denied the notion of divine providence and affirmed that everything happens by chance. They therefore rejected all forms of divination and prophecy. They also rejected the notion of a future divine judgment. In the field of ethics they emphasized the importance of pleasure—not simply the sensual kind but the pleasures of the mind, and tranquility or the state of being free from passions and fears.

The small theater (or "odeon") in Ephesus used for musical performances or speeches.

The Stoics, founded by Zeno also around 300 BC, received their name from the Stoa, a building in Athens where they taught. These placed emphasis on "reason," which governed the universe. Theologically they were pantheists so the relationship between God and the world is like that between the soul and the body. Against the Epicureans, they affirmed divine providence and immanence. They argued that one should live in harmony with nature. In ethics they emphasized the need for acting according to the reason, which indwells all things, self-sufficiency, and obedience to one's obligations. Contrary to Epicurean belief, they expected a final destruction of the world by fire, after which a new world is born (regeneration).

RHETORIC IN THE MEDITERRANEAN WORLD

Among the educated, rhetoric was an essential topic of study. It was taught in the schools of the rhetoricians, and experts in rhetorical technique sought to promote their ideas and acquire students. Rhetoricians followed the principles and techniques laid out by writers

TACITUS ON RHETORICAL TRAINING

Among our ancestors, a young man was trained for public speaking in the following manner. Once he had been prepared by instruction at home and had been crammed full of worthwhile learning, he was taken by his father or a close relative to an orator who held a prominent position in the state. The young man would then accompany him and follow him about and be present during all his speeches whether in the law courts or the assembly meetings, so that he listened to debates and heard legal disputes and learned to fight battles by being, I think I may say, right in the battle. Under this system, young men acquired, right from the start, a great deal of experience, self-possession, and good judgment because they were studying in broad daylight and in the very middle of the battle.... Therefore young men were immediately imbued with true and perfect eloquence. (*A Dialogue on Orators* 34.1–4)

like Aristotle, who composed the famous *Ars Rhetorica*. He defined rhetoric as "the faculty of discovering the possible means of persuading in reference to any subject whatever" (1.2.1).

Rhetoricians gave public lectures in various locations in the cities. Those who sought their instruction wanted to enter public office or to become professionals in rhetorical technique. Such people were also equipped to serve as ambassadors or legal counsel.

Aristotle classified public discourse into three categories: deliberative, judicial, and epideictic rhetoric. Deliberative rhetoric was used in discourses that had to do with the future, and its purpose was to exhort or dissuade. Judicial rhetoric was oriented to the past, and its purpose was to accuse or defend. Epideictic rhetoric concerned the present, and its purpose was to praise or blame. Aristotle taught that the epideictic style was especially suited for written compositions, and it should come as no surprise that the majority of the letters in the New Testament are filled with praise for good behavior and blame for bad conduct (see, e.g., Rev. 2–3). On occasion, Paul had to defend himself because of his lack of refined rhetorical skill (1 Cor. 2:4; 2 Cor. 10:10) and felt compelled to distance himself from those who used their rhetorical finesse for their own self-interest (1 Thess. 2:1–12). Paul did not come as a rhetor to the city but as a herald who proclaimed the message of Christ crucified in the power of God (1 Cor. 2:1–5).

QUESTIONS FOR DISCUSSION ◎◎◎◎◎◎◎◎◎◎◎◎◎◎◎◎◎◎◎◎◎◎◎◎◎◎◎◎◎◎

1. Why is it important for the student of the New Testament to understand the history and culture of the Greco-Roman world, especially considering that Christianity finds its roots within Judaism?

2. How did the Christian proclamation of the "kingdom of God" impact the existing political structures of the day?

3. How do the early Christian authors interact with their surrounding culture? Do they adopt, challenge, or "Christianize" existing values?

4. How did Christianity respond to the challenges presented to it by religious pluralism? What guidance can contemporary Christians find in the New Testament as they seek to understand their faith in midst of a pluralistic world?

5. How does Paul "contextualize" the gospel as he takes the faith that was born in Palestine and spreads it throughout the Greco-Roman world?

BIBLIOGRAPHY

The Loeb Classical Library. Cambridge, Mass.: Harvard University Press. (This collection contains original texts and translation of Latin and Greek authors.)

Introductory

Bell, A. A., Jr. *Exploring the New Testament World*. Nashville: Nelson, 1998.

Jeffers, J. S. *The Greco-Roman World of the New Testament*. Downers Grove, IL: InterVaristy Press, 1999.

Stambaugh, J. E., and D. L. Balch. *The New Testament in Its Social Environment*. LEC. Philadelphia: Westminster, 1986.

Advanced

Evans, C. A., and S. E. Porter, eds. *Dictionary of New Testament Backgrounds*. Downers Grove, IL: InterVarsity Press, 2000.

Ferguson, E. *Backgrounds of Early Christianity*. Grand Rapids: Eerdmans, 2003.

Hornblower, S., and A. Spawforth, eds. *The Oxford Classical Dictionary*. Oxford and New York: Oxford Univ. Press, 1996.

NOTES

1. A. S. F. Gow and D. L. Page, *The Greek Anthology* (Cambridge: Cambridge Univ. Press, 1965), 2:21–23.

2. Adolph Deissmann, *Light from the Ancient East*, trans. L. Strachan (New York: Kessinger, 2003), 322.

3. Robert K. Sherk, ed. and trans., *The Roman Empire* (Cambridge: Cambridge Univ. Press, 1988), 41–50.

4. H. Hendrix, "Thessalonicans Honor Romans" (Th.D. diss.; Harvard Univ, 1984), 107–8.

5. Gow and Page, *Greek Anthology*, 1:73.

6. Ibid., 1:35.

CHAPTER 5

SOURCES FOR
THE STORY OF JESUS

The Sea of Galilee looking west toward Tiberius and Magdala.

The central interest of the New Testament is the person of Jesus Christ. His life, death, and resurrection are the focal point of every New Testament sermon. While Paul and the other letter writers of the New Testament concentrate on Jesus' death and resurrection, it is the four Gospels (Matthew, Mark, Luke and John) that invite us to study the events of Jesus' earthly life.

For the last two centuries the critical study of the Gospels has preoccupied many New Testament scholars. They want to reconstruct the "historical Jesus," and yet they also want to weigh the value of our sources about him. This debate increased sharply toward the end of the twentieth century as book after book sifted the evidence once more. The so-called "Jesus Seminar" (see below) is just one example of scholars trying to reframe the portrait of Jesus. Such research has raised questions. Should Mark be preferred as a source over Matthew and Luke? Did Matthew and Luke use an ancient lost source code named "Q?" Do extrabiblical books supply credible historical evidence about Jesus? Today some scholars answer "yes" to each of these questions.

As these scholars work in this area, their results are an abstraction of modern scholarship, a reconstruction dependent on historical research whose methodologies were born during the last two hundred years. In every instance such reconstructions must be seen as tentative; in some cases, they are simply hypotheses.

Excavators at Magdala discovered a mosaic depicting a first century fishing boat, the only image of such a vessel we possess. It is now located on the grounds of Capernaum.

It is of utmost importance that what we possess about Jesus in our canonical sources is trustworthy and reliable; did the things we read about him actually happen? We must use restraint when we "fill in" his portrait using political, cultural, or religious assumptions that may come from our own world. African, Asian, Arab, and Hispanic Christians may have entirely different lenses through which they read this story, and these may challenge, correct, or reinforce our portraits of Jesus.

SOURCES OUTSIDE THE GOSPELS
Pagan Sources

Among the thousands of pages that have survived from the first-century Roman Empire, nothing mentions Jesus. The first reference comes in the early second century, from a Roman governor named Pliny living somewhere in the Roman province of Bithynia. Pliny wrote to Emperor Trajan about a religious cult called "Christians" that was growing in his province and wondered if he should prosecute them. Pliny mentions that the group worshiped Jesus, but we find no information about Jesus himself.

About the same time, the Roman historian Suetonius wrote about riots that took place during the reign of the Emperor Claudius (AD 41 – 54) that centered on a man named "Chrestus." This too is an authentic reference to Jesus (misspelling "Christ"), but all it can do is fix the Christian community in Rome at this time. Perhaps fighting had erupted when followers of Jesus proclaiming his lordship confronted either Jewish or Roman opponents.

A few years later (AD 120), we hear from Tacitus whose ambition was to record the history of the Roman Empire from roughly AD 14 (the coming to power of Tiberius) to AD

68 (the end of Nero's rule). Our set of his "annals" is incomplete, and while the period that describes Jesus has not survived, Tacitus does refer to Jesus in his description of a fire in Rome in AD 64. Tacitus describes this cult as a superstitious religion, meaning that it was dangerously antisocial and decidedly irrational. Nevertheless, he does say that Jesus was executed at the hands of Pontius Pilate during the reign of Tiberius (*Annals* 15:44).

These references are helpful in reconstructing second-century Christianity, but they do not contribute to our portrait of Jesus in the first century.

Jewish Sources

Early Judaism likewise left behind a rich trove of written documents, and some scholars are convinced that we can find references to Jesus in them. But most of these are controversial. Note that we are seeking *independent* information about Jesus that supplements what we have in the Gospels.

The emperor Trajan (*Marcus Ulpius Traianus*) ruled from 98-117 and was contacted by Pliny the Governor of Bithynia about what to do with Christians in his province. This silver denarius shows his profile on one side, a camel on the reverse.

There is a huge body of other Jewish writings that may be of use to us. However in virtually every case, these documents were penned well into the Christian era and if they refer to Christ, they may be responding to Christian writings already in circulation. Examples of this include the Mishnah (Judaism's oral traditions written down in about AD 200), the Tosefta (later rabbinic commentary), the Targums (Aramaic translations and expansions of the Bible), and the Talmuds (commentary on the Mishnah stemming from about six hundred years after Jesus). No helpful references to Jesus are among these.

For instance, the Babylonian Talmud (*Sanh.* 43a) offers an example of someone killed on the eve of the Passover and tells us his name is "Yeshu." He was a criminal, we learn, because he practiced magic, beguiled people, and led them astray.

Far more important is the Jewish historian Josephus, who wrote a history of the Jewish people sometime after AD 100. Josephus was a Galilee commander in the Jewish war against Rome (AD 66–70), was captured by the Romans, and accompanied the commander Vespasian and later his son Titus in their siege of Judea and Jerusalem. Thanks to his helpful counsel to the Romans, Josephus was rewarded and retired comfortably in Rome, where he wrote both *The Jewish War* (telling the story of the Roman conquest of Judea) as well as the much longer *The Jewish Antiquities* (which begins with Adam and Eve). Both survive in excellent texts to this day (having been preserved by Christian scribes).

TACITUS

As Tacitus describes the great fire that swept through Rome in AD 64, he indicates how Nero blamed it on Christians (even though Nero himself was suspected as the culprit).

> To dispel the rumor, Nero substituted as culprits and treated with the most extreme punishments, some people popularly known as Christians whose disgraceful lives (he claimed) were notorious. The source of their name, Christus, had been executed when Tiberius was emperor by order of the procurator Pontius Pilatus. But the deadly cult though checked for a time, was now breaking out again not only in Judea, the birthplace of this evil, but even throughout Rome—where all the nasty and disgusting ideas from all over the world pour in and find a ready following. (*Annals* 15:44)

Since Jesus was crucified forty years before the fall of Jerusalem, it is perhaps not surprising that Josephus does not refer to Jesus in the *War*. However in his *Antiquities*, we find two intriguing passages. Josephus describes the transition between two governors of Judea (Festus and Albinus). While Albinus was enroute to Judea, the high priest Annas decided to kill criminals in his prisons. Josephus writes:

When, therefore, Annas was of this disposition, he thought he had now a proper opportunity [to exercise his authority]. Festus was now dead, and Albinus was but upon the road; so he assembled the Sanhedrin of judges, and brought before them the brother of Jesus, who was called Christ, whose name was James, and some others [or, some of his companions]; and when had formed an accusation against them as breakers of the law, he delivered them to be stoned. (*Ant.* 20.9.1 [197–203])

This passage corroborates the New Testament view that Jesus had a brother named James (Mark 6:3; Gal. 1:19), and it points to the priest Annas (John 18:13). But note that Josephus cannot identify James by referring to his family lineage ("James, father of x"). Rather, he notes James's brother Jesus, whom Josephus must believe is easily recognizable to his reader. Of course, the passage offers a cynical view of Jesus (called "the Christ"), but this is what we'd expect since Josephus never became a Christian.

A more perplexing text in Josephus appears in *Ant.* 18.3.3 [63–64]. Since Josephus evidently did not believe that Jesus was the Messiah, it is surprising to find the following:

Now there was about this time Jesus, a wise man, if it be lawful to call him a man; for he was doer of wonderful works, a teacher of such men as receive the truth with pleasure. He drew over many of the Jews and many of the Gentiles. He was [the] Christ. And when Pilate, at the suggestion of the principal men among us, had condemned him to the cross, those that loved him at the first did not forsake him; for he appeared to them alive again the third day, as the divine prophets had foretold these and ten thousand other wonderful things concerning him. And the tribe of Christians, so named from him, are not extinct at this day.

This passage is no doubt an insertion into the text of Josephus penned by a Christian scribe. Not only does Josephus seem to embrace Jesus as the Messiah but he announces the resurrection! Some scholars believe we should edit the paragraph, removing all of the explicitly confessional elements to find a core that may have been written by Josephus himself. If this reconstruction is correct, we may have an important second reference to Jesus:

At this time there appeared Jesus, a wise man. For he was a doer of startling deeds, a teacher of people who receive the truth with pleasure. And he gained a following both among many Jews and among many of Greek origin. And when Pilate, because of an accusation made by the leading men among us, condemned him to the cross, those who had loved him previously did not cease to do so. And up till this very day, the tribe of Christians (named after him) has not died out.[1]

Even with these passages from Josephus, we have limited new information about Jesus coming from Jewish sources. They refer to Jesus and a group of followers, but that is about all.

Second- and Third-Century Christian Sources

In recent years, scholars have revisited a collection of Christian writings produced in the two or three centuries following the writing of the New Testament. An important category of sources is the so-called "apocryphal gospels." These are Christian writings stemming from the centuries following the New Testament, which in some cases record fantastic legends (such as in the *Infancy Gospel of Thomas*) or may simply rebuild and embellish the New Testament Gospels themselves (such as the *Gospel of the Nazarenes*).[2] For the most part, this material offers no help with our questions.

But two ancient gospels deserve special mention. In about 1886 French archaeologists in Egypt uncovered a gospel manuscript that would stir controversy a hundred years after its discovery. The second-century apocryphal *Gospel of Peter* is sometimes promoted as the oldest form of the passion story (called "the Cross Gospel"), and this story was supposedly used by Mark when he wrote his gospel.[3] The weight of scholarly opinion has been severely critical of any suggestion that the *Gospel of Peter* precedes the canonical Gospels or provides material.[4] But such an example is fair warning to beginning students of the New Testament. Suggestions such as this abound, and in each case, the theories must be examined with judicious scholarship before they are accepted. Sensational discoveries will always be exploited, and the student must be careful to follow the lead of specialists who will weigh them in time.[5]

A few years before the discovery of the Dead Sea Scrolls, archaeologists found a library of Christian documents in the ruins of an ancient monastery in the village of Nag Hammadi in southern Egypt, mostly copied in the 300s by Gnostic Christians. While much of the library is of dubious value to research the historical Jesus, some scholars now argue that one book, *The Gospel of Thomas*, provides sayings of Jesus that are authentic and historically reliable. *Thomas* consists of 114 sayings of Jesus (with no narration) that are strung together thematically. Some scholars immediately related this to the sayings source "Q" (see below). The trouble with this work, however, is that it is suffused with a Gnostic theological outlook that supplies the framework for understanding any of the sayings. While recent studies have argued that *The Gospel of Thomas* depends on the canonical Gospels, some scholars (such as Helmut Koester) still insist that "nearly all biblical scholars in the United States" agree that Thomas gives authentic sayings of Jesus. Many New Testament scholars would dispute this.

Summary of Sources

It may be surprising to see how little information we have about Jesus outside the New Testament Gospels. For the most part, the canonical gospels provided the substance of what the church knew about Jesus, and later writings generally embellished that story in order to make it more compelling to new audiences around the Mediterranean. But in the main,

Christian communities (no doubt mentored by their Jewish counterparts) conserved their traditions about Jesus. Communication among the earliest Christians was excellent. Roads and sea lanes were good and couriers moved regularly among churches carrying all variety of Christian writings. In other words, *the early Christians were talking to each other*. They could discuss what gospels were important and reliable and they could weigh the merits of new offerings to their archives of Christian writings.

THE GOSPELS AS SOURCES FOR JESUS' LIFE

When we turn to a gospel as a source of Jesus' life, a long list of questions immediately confronts us. What sort of literature is this? How would the ancient world classify it? What were the aims of its authors? Why do we have four gospels? Is there a literary relationship among them — and if so, which gospel is oldest? Above all, do these gospels represent the historical Jesus accurately or are they embellishments based on the Jesus worshiped in the early church? New Testament scholarship has wrestled with each of these questions for two centuries, and it is important for us to understand briefly the contours of this contemporary conversation.

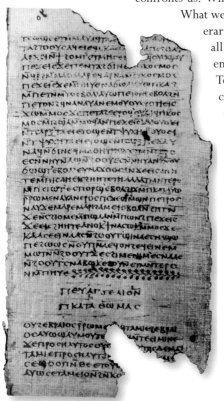

A page from the Gospel of Thomas. Fragments of the gospel were discovered at the Egyptian village of Oxyrhynchus in 1897, 1903, and 1905. A Coptic manuscript was found in a nag Hammadi in 1945.

The Genre "Gospel"

Every literature fits into its surrounding culture by using recognizable forms of style and composition. It would be interesting to ask how an ancient librarian from the great library of Alexandria might have classified the gospel of Mark. He would notice that Mark opens his text by saying that this "is the beginning of the gospel of Jesus Christ." But there a problem emerges. In antiquity "gospel" (Gk. *euangelion*) was not used for a written document. It was a "great announcement" or a proclamation. In non-Christian circles, it might refer to the emperor's birth or a victory in battle, but never a book. Perhaps this hint betrays something about Mark's theological purposes: His writing is indeed a "great announcement" and is penned to announce something unparalleled that God has done in history.

But our librarian has not solved the problem. In the past, scholars tried comparing the gospels with a variety of ancient literature types (from "memoirs" to "miracle working" stories). Many even viewed the gospels as a unique genre, unparalleled in ancient writing. This last option seems unlikely. Writers try to communicate by using forms that readers/hearers will easily understand. Today scholars are inclined to view the gospels as "biographies" (Greek, *bioi*). In antiquity Roman biographies existed in abundance (e.g., Plutarch's *Lives*; Suetonius's *Lives of the Caesars*). These sophisticated writings both chronicled the fascinating events in their subjects' lives and built a profile of them. Plutarch, for example, provides an outline of the work of the biographer in his introduction to his biography of Alexander the Great:

> It is not Histories that I am writing, but Lives; and in the most illustrious deeds there is not always a manifestation of virtue or vice, nay, a slight thing like a phrase or a jest often makes a greater revelation of character than battles where thousands fall, or the greatest armaments, or siege of cities. Accordingly, just as painters get the

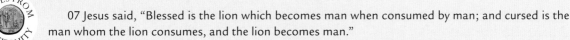

THE GOSPEL OF THOMAS

The *Gospel of Thomas* found in 1945 in Southern Egypt contains 114 sayings of Jesus without any narrative. Some parts echo what we find in the canonical Gospels. Others are a complete Gnostic reworking of Jesus' original sayings. Today scholars debate whether any of these sayings are authentically from Jesus and thus can be used to build his historical portrait.

Here are some sample sayings of *The Gospel of Thomas*:

05 Jesus said, "Recognize what is in your sight, and that which is hidden from you will become plain to you."

07 Jesus said, "Blessed is the lion which becomes man when consumed by man; and cursed is the man whom the lion consumes, and the lion becomes man."

82 Jesus said, "He who is near me is near the fire, and he who is far from me is far from the kingdom."

92 Jesus said, "Seek and you will find. Yet, what you asked me about in former times and which I did not tell you then, now I do desire to tell, but you do not inquire after it."

114 Simon Peter said to them, "Let Mary leave us, for women are not worthy of life." Jesus said, "I myself shall lead her in order to make her male, so that she too may become a living spirit resembling you males. For every woman who will make herself male will enter the kingdom of heaven."

likenesses in their portraits from the face and the expression of the eyes, wherein the character shows itself, but make very little account of the other parts of the body, so I must be permitted to devote myself rather to the signs of the soul in men, and by means of these to portray the life of each, leaving to others the description of their great contests. (Plutarch, *Alexander* 1)

Ancient *bioi* were unlike modern biographies in at least one respect. Rarely did they probe beneath the surface looking for signs of development. This was long before the advent of psychology. Instead, the biographer worked to unveil the true identity of a man or woman and thereby explain his or her great deeds.

The Literary Criticism of the Gospels

The more pressing question is the quality of history we can find the gospels. Can we rely on them as a source to reconstruct the life of Jesus? From the beginning of the nineteenth century, New Testament scholarship recognized that three of four gospels (Matthew, Mark, and Luke) have a great deal in common. They have been termed the "synoptic" gospels. About 93 percent of Mark can be found in Matthew or Luke; 58 percent of Matthew can be found in Mark and Luke; and 41 percent of Luke can be found in Matthew and Mark.[6] Let's put this another way: Of Mark's 661 verses, Matthew holds 606 of them and Luke holds 308; only 31 verses in Mark are not found in either Matthew or Luke. How do we explain this? The parallels among the synoptic gospels are so precise (seen particularly in Greek) that most scholars think that there must have been some literary dependency.

One option would be to say that each gospel was dependent on some earlier "pre-gospel." Some point to the remark of the bishop Papias (who lived in Hierapolis in Asia Minor, c. AD 60–130), who said that Matthew composed the "oracles" (Gk. *logia*) of Jesus in Hebrew and everyone translated them as best they could. Today a number of scholars are intrigued with this view and while they might not argue that Matthew, Mark, and Luke are independent

Matthew 8:16-17	Mark 1:32-34	Luke 4:40-41
16 When evening came,	32 That evening after sunset	10 At sunset
many who were demon-possessed were brought to him,	the people brought to Jesus all the sick and demon-possessed.	the people brought to Jesus all who had various kinds of sickness,
and he drove out the spirits with a word and healed the sick.	33 The whole town gathered at the door, 34 and Jesus healed many who had various diseases. He also drove out many demons,	and laying his hands on each one, he healed them.
		41 Moreover, demons came out of many people, shouting, "You are the Son of God!"
	but he would not let the demons speak because they knew who he was.	But he rebuked them and would not allow them to speak, because they knew he was the Messiah.
17 This was to fulfill what was spoken through the prophet Isaiah: "He took up our infirmities and bore our diseases,"		

A synopsis is a book that prints each gospel in columns so that parallel passages may be compared. Note here the parallels among Matthew 8:16–17; Mark 1:32–34; Luke 4:40–41.[7] Note how Mark contains elements of Matthew and Luke.

of each other, they wonder if a primitive gospel existed that preceded the others. We might diagram this arrangement thus:

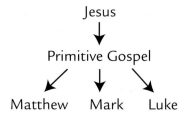

The church fathers recognized this literary puzzle and attempted to find solutions that pointed to one gospel using the other as a literary source. One of the earliest theories (first attributed to Augustine) understood Matthew as the first gospel, Mark abbreviated Matthew, and Luke used both of them in his third gospel. This solution, generally illustrated thus:

Matthew

↓ ↘

Mark → Luke

Later scholars argued that Mark abbreviated both Matthew and Luke. Note, for example, Matthew 8:16/Mark 1:32/Luke 4:40. Matthew describes Jesus as healing people "in the evening"; Luke says it was "sundown." But Mark conflates the two, saying that it was "in the evening, at sundown." This solution (generally attributed to J. J. Griesbach) can be illustrated thus:

Matthew

↓ ↘

Luke → Mark

No portraits of St. Augustine of Hippo (354–430) exist. This picture, sketched in the nineteenth century, was taken from an eleventh-century fresco at the Church of St. Ambrose, Milan, Italy [8]

Other passages, however, point in another direction. For instance, in the story of the paralytic (Matt 9:1–8/Mark 2:1–12/Luke 5:17–26) Jesus is impressed with the faith of the paralytic's friends because they break open the roof of the house and lower the man to Jesus through the crowd. Matthew tells us that Jesus is "amazed at their faith," but he does not convey the story of the removal of the roof! Matthew assumes you know that detail. This seems to follow a pattern. While Mark's gospel is shorter, each of Mark's narratives is longer, and often details are removed in Matthew (but still assumed). Thus, many scholars today assume that in some manner, Mark must be the earliest gospel written.

On close examination, Mark seems to be the oldest (see sidebar on "Aramaic Words in Mark"). In addition, Matthew seems to make adjustments to Mark. For instance, in Mark 6:14 we are told that Herod Antipas was a "king." Matthew 14:1 amends this to say that Antipas was a "tetrarch." In Mark 6:5 we learn that Jesus "could not do any miracles [in Nazareth]." Matthew appears to supplement this potentially embarrassing admission by saying Jesus did no mighty work there "because of their lack of faith" (Matt. 13:58). As New Testament scholar G. M. Styler once put it, "Given Mark, it is easy to see why Matthew was written. Given Matthew, it is hard to see why Mark was needed."[9]

Mark

↓ ↘

Matthew → Luke

J.J. Griesbach (1745-1812) was a New Testament scholar most famous for his work in textual criticism. His Greek New Testament (1775) became the tool of scholars for generations. That same year he was appointed professor at the Univ. of Jenna, Germany.

The cumulative evidence has made the majority of scholars affirm what we call "Markan Priority" in the formation of the gospel tradition. But if it is so, the next question is whether Matthew used Luke or Luke used Matthew. Note, for example, that when Matthew and Luke make editorial changes to Mark, none of Matthew's changes show up in Luke and vice versa. If Matthew had known Luke — or if Luke had known Matthew — then surely some of the changes would be apparent. This has led scholars to suggest that Matthew and Luke are each dependent on Mark, but they are not using each other.

But note too that there is a body of verses commonly shared between Matthew and Luke, but is not in Mark (about 250 verses). This material is code-named "Q" (from the German *Quelle*, "source"), and scholars suggest that perhaps this is an early "pre-gospel" collection of Jesus' sayings that stood alongside Mark (but was unknown to Mark). This new diagram of synoptic relationships can be illustrated thus:

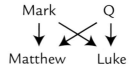

Moreover, both Matthew and Luke each made original contributions in the production of their gospels (Matthew has 300 unique verses; Luke, 520 verses). Matthew, for example, has a Christmas story with elements unknown elsewhere (such as the story of Herod and the wise men); Luke has the story of the shepherds of Bethlehem visited by an angel.

The solution (often credited to B. H. Streeter) that is most popular today is the "four source" hypothesis to the synoptic problem; it suggests that each gospel saying and story can be attributed to one of four sources. Note in this illustration how Matthew and Luke each used three sources for his gospel:

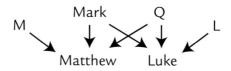

This view has been so well received that some scholars refer to this result as an "assured finding."[10] Yet today this popular hypothesis is weathering criticism. Just when we thought that at least one historical question could be put to rest, another generation of scholars has argued that it is completely wrong. W. R. Farmer wrote in the 1960s that Mark was the last of the three synoptics to be written and that Matthew was first—and Farmer has a growing following.

Many other scholars see the process of gospel writing as more organic and deny the clean lines of literary dependence shown by these illustrations (above). For them, the "Jesus traditions" were held by those in Jerusalem who served as the custodians of this archive. This was a fixed pool of sayings and stories whose linguistic forms were memorized and preserved. Matthew may have written an early Aramaic gospel (recall the words of Papias above) and drawn on these traditions. Peter may have been one of these custodians and drawn on this pool as well—finally contributing to the writing-up of Mark. Luke 1:1–4 tells us that he did genuine research on what was being held by eyewitnesses—and reading what others had penned. No doubt these earliest Christian leaders were talking with each other, sharing notations, comparing memorized bodies of material.

B. H. Streeter (1874-1937) was a pioneer in gospel studies and spent most of his life at Oxford University. He is well-known for *The Four Gospels, A Study of Origins* (1924)

When all is said, we must sound a note of caution. We are dealing here with hypotheses. Q particularly is hypothetical, for no such document has ever been found. And many who work in this area are trying to find "the original gospel," with the assumption that such a gospel is more historically reliable to build a portrait of Jesus; they thus ascribe levels of credibility to the existing gospels, which is a dangerous thing to do.

In our discussion we have barely touched on John's Gospel as a source for Jesus' life. For most of the twentieth century, John's gospel was viewed by critical scholars as secondary to the synoptics—late, and not reliable historically. But in the last twenty years we have seen a shift in emphasis. John is increasingly viewed as an independent (and trustworthy) recorder of events from Jesus' life. Scholars who once viewed John as a Hellenistic rewriting of the gospel now recognize that John relies heavily on rabbinic thinking, is accurate when using geography, and is faithful to the tradition. The best reconstructions of Jesus' life today take seriously John's claim as an eyewitness of that life.

The Historical Criticism of the Gospels

In addition to the issue of sources, scholars have also asked what happened during that mysterious period between Jesus' death and the writing up of the gospels. If Q and Mark are the earliest documents, what sources contributed to them? Were Aramaic stories of Jesus circulating among Jesus' followers and if so, could these be discovered within the texts of the canonical Greek gospels?

In 1919 a young German scholar named Karl Ludwig Schmidt turned the key that opened this door. He noted that the gospels consisted of a series of episodes set in a framework with connecting narrative material that served as "bridges" between episodes. Mark 1:16–45 provides a good example, which is a series of stories with a limited chronological sequence: Jesus calls his disciples, he exorcizes a man in Capernaum, he heals Simon's mother-in-law, and he heals a leper. Each of these episodes is "linked" by narrative that gives the story coherence, but in the end, the stories themselves appeared to Schmidt to be independent.

William R. Farmer challenged the assumption of Markan priority in 1964 with his famous book, *The Synoptic Problem*. It was reprinted in 1976.

Schmidt argued that these brief episodes circulated orally in the earliest Christian communities and that Mark and the other writers picked these up and "threaded" them together by narrative. This means we can locate the "pre-gospel" stratum of the gospels as well as the "bridge" material inserted by the gospel writers. In subsequent study, these units of tradition were called "forms" and classified (miracles, parables, legends, etc.), and their study was soon called "form criticism."

Jesus

↓

Oral Tradition

↓

Gospel

But the aim of form criticism was not merely to classify these events but to make some historical judgment about their value. The passion for gospel research grew rapidly as scholars anticipated that now we were looking under the surface, finding out how the stories of Jesus were formed and preserved. Many viewed this pre-gospel era skeptically, believing that the early Christians not only shaped the words of Jesus to fit their own circumstances, but also created new words of Jesus, generally in the context of worship.

Form critics claimed that the gospel materials were preserved not necessarily because they came from Jesus, but because they met some need in the Christian community. Each had a setting in the early church that explained to some degree what was happening at that time. For instance, the early Christians had numerous conflicts with the leadership of Judaism (see 1 Thess. 2:13–16). Thus, stories from Jesus' life that illustrated this persecution were preserved because of their usefulness in preaching. For example, Mark 2:23–28 shows Jesus criticized for harvesting grain on the Sabbath. The episode does not explore what happened but moves quickly to Jesus' summary comment: "The Sabbath was made for people, not people for the Sabbath" (2:27). These words are an incisive critique for all those

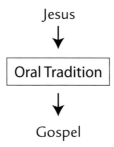

THE JESUS SEMINAR

In 1985 Robert Funk founded the Jesus Seminar along with thirty other scholars. The goal of the seminar—and its many "fellows" (now claiming two hundred)—was to sift the gospels and locate the true historical Jesus, employing the best higher critical methods.

The committee quickly became a lightning rod of criticism not only because it included sayings of Jesus in the apocryphal gospels (such as the *Gospel of Thomas*), but it urged that most of the materials we have in the gospels are inauthentic. Its first major publication assessing the "sayings" of Jesus appeared in 1993: *The Five Gospels: The Search for the Authentic Words of Jesus*. Of Jesus' sayings only 18 percent were deemed authentic. In 1998 a second publication weighed the 176 events in Jesus' life and was published as *The Acts of Jesus: The Search for the Authentic Deeds of Jesus*. In this study, only 16 percent were deemed authentic.

who would criticize Jesus' Jewish followers who did not strictly observe Jewish Sabbath regulations. In fact, some felt the early church may have even doctored these stories to fit their situation.

The Authenticity of the Gospels

The most important question for Christians today is to gain confidence that indeed the words of Jesus uttered in first-century Palestine are accurately represented in our gospels. When I read the gospel of Matthew, am I reading what Jesus himself said, or am I reading the musings of Christian prophets and leaders—inspired as they might be—who wrote about Jesus decades after his death? Of course, these questions center directly on our understanding of the authority of our Scriptures.

The best way to approach this subject is to be sure we understand the nature of the problem. Historical criticism posits that following the death of Jesus, the "Jesus tradition" was preserved for approximately thirty or forty years before it was finally written down in the gospels we possess today. The heart of the question is this: *Was the church in this earliest era successful in preserving Jesus' sayings and deeds so that the gospel record is accurate?*

Our confidence in the success of this process can be helped by keeping various things in mind. **(1) The stylistic forms of Jesus' sayings.** Many of the sayings of Jesus in the gospels reflect forms that could easily have been retained through these decades. Parables, proverbs, riddles, poignant phrases ("the first will be last—and the last first!"), catch-phrases ("the kingdom of God") each would aid historical preservation. In addition we have Aramaic—both transliterated words and grammatical phrases—that hint at the earlier, Aramaic world of Jesus. In other words, the era of the historical Jesus is indeed reflected in the gospels even though the gospels are written later for Greek-speaking audiences.

(2) The terminology of tradition. Paul was a rabbi, trained in the skills of handling religious materials passed down orally (see, e.g., 1 Cor. 11:2, 23; 1 Thess. 2:13; 2 Thess. 2:15; 3:6). This reflects the well-honed Jewish ability to retain vast amounts of material and transmit them to a new generation. The Mishnah (the oral law of Judaism) was preserved in just this way for generations. Thus, it comes as no surprise that the apostles, living in this Jewish context, knew how to handle sacred stories coming from Jesus. They treated Jesus' words as carefully as any rabbi treated sacred traditions brought to him.

NOTES FROM ANTIQUITY

THE IPSISSIMA VOX JESU

When scholars defend "authentic" words of Jesus in the gospels, they allow for the possibility that the gospel writers may have paraphrased Jesus' words, particularly since he commonly spoke in Aramaic. Hence they distinguish the *ipsissima verba Jesu* ("the very words of Jesus") from the *ipsissima vox Jesu* ("the very voice of Jesus"). An authentic "word" of Jesus may well represent his "voice," though not his exact words.

Paul Feinberg, a conservative evangelical, writes, "Inerrancy does not demand that the sayings of Jesus must contain the *ipsissima verba*, only the *ipsissima vox*. When a New Testament writer cites the sayings of Jesus, it need not be the case that Jesus said those exact words."[11] This careful definition permits variations in parallel gospel accounts of Jesus' sayings. Thus in Matthew 27:54 and Mark 15:39 the centurion's cry at the cross records, "Surely he was the Son of God." In Luke 23:47 he says, "Surely this was a righteous man." For a Roman—Luke's audience–"righteous person" was the meaning of "Son of God."[12]

(3) The function of apostles. In the first half of the first century, the apostles were regarded as the guardians and the transmitters of the authoritative traditions about Jesus. This was a stable community, anchored in Jerusalem, to which even leaders like Paul came to confirm the essence of their teaching (Gal. 1:18; 2:2–10). In one important respect, they behave like the scribes of Judaism, whose teaching was devoted to the recitation of Judaism's great traditions.

(4) The cultural role of memory. Contemporary Westerners depend on the written word and often assume that memorizing large bodies of material is impossible or at least unreliable. But this is a cultural prejudice that has no place in discussions of ancient societies, where the majority of people could not read. First-century Judaism taught through memorization and expected young people to hold secure large portions of Scripture. "Good students are like good cisterns," one saying went, "They never lose a single drop." Leading Jewish teachers spoke orally and were measured by their students and followers who sat at their feet and repeated verbatim what they heard. For some scholars, this explains why we have a limited number of sayings from Jesus. He moved from village to village repeating his parables and sayings with great frequency.

(5) Eyewitnesses and the lapse of time. It is helpful to remember that the same generation who heard Jesus speak in Galilee was also alive during the writing of the gospels. These were eyewitnesses, who could now read the Gospel of Mark and make a judgment about its truth. If the gospels had departed significantly from the historical memory of Jesus, objections would have been lodged and quickly corrected.

(6) Written records? We know that following the war of AD 70, rabbinic students frequently took written notes of their teacher's sayings. Today scholars dispute whether this practice occurred during the era before the war. If it did, this opens up the possibility that written records existed during the earliest years of the church—and perhaps even during the ministry of Jesus. And so, it adds to our confidence that these sayings of Jesus were preserved.

(7) Christian prophecy and caution. It is not true that during the earliest era of the church, Christian prophets had free reign to speak whatever they wanted in the name of the Lord and so produce sayings of Jesus. New Testament communities were cautious with regard to prophets. In 1 Corinthians 14, for example, Paul warns the Corinthians about giving too much power to prophets and expects that the prophets in their community will check each other before speaking. Further, the heresy addressed in 1 John 4:1–6 stemmed from prophets who believed they were anointed with the Spirit and could dismantle orthodox teaching about Jesus. John warns about them and tells the community to be wary of such teachers and prophets (2:18–27).

(8) Respect for the sayings of Jesus. The early church carefully distinguished the sayings of Jesus from its own teachings and did not pretend to invent sayings. Paul, for example, explains when he has a word from the Lord and when he doesn't (1 Cor. 7:8, 10, 12, 25, 40). Also, since Paul wrote before the gospels were penned, we might expect to find some of Paul's sayings in the gospels. There is not one example of this.

(9) Dissimilarity of interests. If the formative era of the church could create sayings of Jesus, we should expect some correlation between what we know to be the concerns of the early church and the primary themes of the gospels. But we do not. For example, important issues in the life of the early church centered on the Gentile mission, circumcision, food laws, the Holy Spirit, and even the notion of the church itself. Jesus says little about any of these. The early church did not try to settle a dispute by putting words in his mouth.

Moreover, the gospels talk a great deal about the kingdom of God and refer to Jesus repeatedly as the Son of Man. Oddly, perhaps, no other literature from this era shows an interest in either of these. What does this mean? Simply that the gospels reflect a context that is *dissimilar* from the context of the early church—and the burning issues that troubled earliest Christianity do not show up in the gospels.

Summary

Each of these points is important because their cumulative effect shifts the burden of proof. It is fully defensible to argue that the works and words of Jesus as recorded in the gospels reliably reflect the Jesus of history, that the gospels are "innocent until proven guilty." Students of the gospels can confidently sustain a reasonable argument that the gospels' portrait of Jesus is accurate and reliable.

Jesus' teaching ministry included the mentoring of a circle of close followers (the apostles), whose task in part was to learn what he taught and to carry that teaching to new places (Mark 6:7). When Jesus died, this community of Galileans took up residence in Jerusalem and from there served as custodians of the traditions that stemmed from Jesus. They preserved these as carefully as anyone would in the Jewish ethos—and more so. They believed that Jesus was not merely an itinerant preacher from Galilee, he was the Messiah, a messenger from God whose words rivaled those of Moses. Their archive of sayings and stories became a wellspring of materials that quickly took shape and within years provided the gospel writers with their raw materials.

1. Why do scholars not believe that each gospel writer worked independently and that their parallel accounts buttress the authority of the gospel record?

2. Why do scholars work so hard to discern which of the gospels is earliest? What inspires their labor? What do they hope to achieve?

3. How does "Q" disappear if we posit that Matthew and Luke used each other?

4. What safeguarded the "Jesus tradition" from alteration during those formative years between Jesus' death and the writing of the gospels?

5. What are the theological implications for us if we decided that some of the sayings of Jesus in *The Gospel of Thomas* were authentically from Jesus?

BIBLIOGRAPHY
Introductory

Blomberg, C. *Jesus and the Gospels*. Nashville: Broadman & Homan, 1997.

_____. *The Historical Reliability of the Gospels*. Downers Grove, IL: InterVarsity Press, 1987.

Wilkins, M. J., and J. P. Moreland. *Jesus under Fire: Modern Scholarship Reinvents the Historical Jesus*. Grand Rapids: Zondervan, 1995.

Wright, N. T. *The Contemporary Quest for Jesus*. Minneapolis: Fortress, 2002.

Advanced

Bauckham, R., ed. *The Gospels for All Christians: Rethinking the Gospel Audiences*. Grand Rapids: Eerdmans, 1998.

Borg, M., and N. T. Wright. *The Meaning of Jesus: Two Visions*. San Francisco: HarperSanFrancisco, 1999.

Gerhardsson, B. *The Reliability of the Gospel Tradition*. Peabody, MA: Hendrickson, 2001.

NOTES

1. J. P. Meier, *A Marginal Jew: Rethinking the Historical Jesus* (New York: Doubleday, 1991), 61.

2. For an exhaustive catalogue of these, see E. Hennecke and W. Schneemelcher's two-volume study, *The New Testament Apocrypha*, trans. R. M. Wilson (Philadelphia: John Knox, 1991).

3. J. D. Crossan, *The Cross That Spoke: The Origin of the Passion Narrative* (San Francisco: Harper, 1988); H. Koester, *Ancient Christian Gospels* (Valley Forge, PA: Trinity International, 1992), 216–40. For the text of the Gospel of Peter, see www.earlychristianwritings.com or R. E. Brown's translation in *The Death of the Messiah*, 2 vols. (ABRL; New York: Doubleday: 1994), 1317–49. See also idem, "The Gospel of Peter and Canonical Gospel Priority," *NTS* 33 (1987): 321–43.

4. J. W. McCant, "The Gospel of Peter: Docetism Reconsidered," *NTS* 30 (1984): 258–73; J. Green, "The Gospel of Peter: Source for a Pre-Canonical Passion Narrative?" *ZNW* 78 (1987): 293–301.

5. Students may one day read about the so-called *Secret Gospel of Mark* discovered in 1958 — which supplements Mark with about twenty previously unknown sentences. But today these verses have stirred a whirlwind of controversy. One scholar remarked, "To use such a

small fragment of dubious origins to rewrite the history of Jesus and the Gospel tradition is to lean on a reed" (J. P. Meier, *A Marginal Jew* [ABRL; New York: Doubleday, 1991], 121).

6. John, by comparison is utterly different; only 8 percent of John is shared by the other three.

7. K. Aland, *Synopsis of the Four Gospels* (Stuttgart: United Bible Society, 1976), 36.

8. W. Wood, *The Hundred Greatest Men* (New York: Appleton, 1885), 159

9. G. M. Styler, "The Priority of Mark," in C. F. D. Moule, *The Birth of the New Testament* (London: A. & C. Black, 1962), 223–32.

10. W. Marxsen, *Introduction to the New Testament* (Philadelphia: Fortress, 1968), 118.

11. Paul Feinberg, "The Meaning of Inerrancy," in *Inerrancy*, ed. N. L. Geisler (Grand Rapids: Zondervan, 1979), 270, cited in G. Osborne, "Historical Criticism and the Evangelical" *JETS* 42 (March 1999): 193–210.

12. Osborne, "Historical Criticism and the Evangelical," 193–210.

° °

CHAPTER 6

THE STORY OF JESUS

The northern coast of the sea of Galilee was dotted with numerous fishing villages. Fishing was abundant thanks to fresh water springs in the area. The site of Heptapegan (*seven springs*) is located in the trees along the shoreline.

Recovering the story of Jesus' life has today become one of the great pursuits of our time. Not only have literary and historical analyses of the Gospels advanced (see Ch. 5), but today our understanding of the cultural environment that shaped Jesus' world has also matured. The disciplines of comparative anthropology and archaeology (to name only two) have given us access to the world of Jesus in ways unimaginable only fifty years ago.

The first surface survey of Sepphoris began in 1930 but work started in earnest in 1985. Its huge archaeological park (Heb., Zippori) was opened in 1992.

Yet we must be clear about the limitations of our pursuit. Jesus was an itinerant preacher in one of the remote provinces of the Roman Empire. He had no "international" prestige and hence limited public recognition from the great record-keepers of society. Thus, a full-orbed portrait of his life and work may not be possible. But what we do have in our Gospels squares nicely with what we are learning about the first century. These discoveries supplement the gospel story, giving us a more accurate view of Jesus' world.

For example, the excavation of Sepphoris (the capital of Galilee, close to Jesus' hometown of Nazareth) informs us about the Hellenization of Galilee. It is also disclosing its secrets about the economic relationships between the rural villages and the urban centers of the region. This city of

The theater of Sepphoris was in use during Jesus day and sat 4500 in its audience. This may explain Jesus' knowledge of Greek stage names such as "hypocrite," Matt 6:2, which was a Greek actor.

thirty thousand was in full reconstruction during Jesus' adolescence, and Jesus and his father Joseph may have worked there.

CHRONOLOGY

Building a chronology for Jesus' life has always been difficult. In the first century, calendars began with the founding of the city of Rome (754 BC or year 1 for Rome). However in the sixth century AD, a Christian monk (Dionysius Exiguus of Scythia) proposed instead a "Christian calendar," which started with the birth of Jesus. Unfortunately, he failed to take into account the death of Herod the Great, who was certainly alive during Jesus' infancy (Matt. 2:1). Herod died in 4 BC, which means that Jesus was likely born sometime between 5 and 7 BC.

The crucifixion, of course, is tied to the duration of Jesus' ministry (determined by counting the number of annual Passover Festivals in his ministry). If he had a three-year ministry that began in AD 26 or 27, his crucifixion likely occurred in the spring of AD 30 (or later). Even though the precise year is unclear, every gospel writer agrees that Jesus was crucified on a Friday afternoon, in spring, during Passover.

> **JESUS AND THE MANGER**
> We often use European/American conceptions of the setting of Jesus' birth. Public inns were rare, especially in small villages like Bethlehem. Peasants lived in small one-room houses or caves divided in two parts, one for animals and an elevated area for the family. Mary and Joseph tried to find space in the guest room of a family home (Gk., the *katalyma*, Luke 2:7). Instead they were offered a small section inside a peasant's home where animals were kept. The manger was likely a feeding trough carved out of stone in the wall or the floor.

BIRTH AND EARLIEST YEARS

Matthew and Luke tell the story of Jesus' birth (during the reign of the Emperor Augustus, 43 BC – AD 14). An angel (Gabriel) appeared to the priest Zechariah in Jerusalem and to a young, unmarried woman named Mary in Nazareth. Zechariah's wife, Elizabeth, will give birth to John, who will become a prophet, and Mary will give birth to Jesus, who will be known as "the Son of the Most High God" (Luke 1:32). Since Mary and her fiancé, Joseph, are not married, Mary's pregnancy will be a miracle (Matt. 1:20).

Following their marriage, Mary and Joseph were forced to travel south to Bethlehem, where a Roman census required each family return to its ancestral homeland for registration. The Roman census was an instrument of occupation designed to control and tax (see sidebar); it brought extreme hardship to all. Mary and Joseph's entrance into this scene evokes images of terror and displacement: They are a young, poor couple, pushed into a distant village by the military and forced into a peasant's hovel to give birth to Mary's first son.

Matthew and Luke develop different aspects of the story while agreeing on its essential elements. Matthew records details about Joseph, the star, the visit of the Magi, the attack of

This form of the silver denarius was struck during the last three years of Augustus' reign and was copied as the principal form by his son Tiberius. The reverse shows Augustus' wife Livia holding a scepter and sheaf—posed intentionally like the god Pax (or Peace, e.g Pax Augusta). Such coins were used commonly by Mary and Joseph.

LACTANTIUS ON THE ROMAN CENSUS

Lactantius was a Roman scholar who converted to Christianity in about AD 300 and soon became the tutor of the Emperor Constantine's son Crispus. As a devout Christian, he was critical of the brutality of Roman public policy. Here he writes about a typical Roman census:

The census-takers appeared everywhere, and produced a tumult wherever they went. The fields were measured clod by clod; every grapevine and fruit tree counted, every head of livestock of every kind was listed, the exact number of people noted, and in the autonomous cities the urban and rural population were herded together until the market places were filled with the collected families. All came with their whole band of children and slaves. Everywhere was heard the screaming of those who were being interrogated with torture and beatings. Sons were forced to testify against their fathers, the trustiest slaves driven to bear witness against their masters, and wives against their husbands. When all other means had been exhausted, the victims were tortured until they gave evidence against themselves, and when pain had at last conquered, taxable property that did not exist was registered. Neither age nor illness won exemption. The ill and the infirm were dragged before the examiners; age was set down by estimate and the age of [tax-free] minors was raised while that of the old [who were likewise exempt] was lowered. The market places rang with lamentations. (*De mortibus persecutorum* 23.1ff.; cf. 26.2ff.)

Herod's soldiers, and the family's flight into Egypt. For him an important theme is the parallel between the birth of Moses and of Jesus. Luke includes the story of John the Baptist's family and birth, the visit of the shepherds, the purification of Mary, the naming of Jesus, and hymns from Mary (Luke 1:46–55), Zechariah (1:68–79), and Simeon (2:29–32). Luke is interested in God's unexpected visitation to the "poor" and lowly, who, like models of salvation in the Old Testament, become agents of salvation.

It is difficult to know how long Mary and Joseph remained in Egypt following Jesus' birth. Certainly they waited until Herod's death (4 BC) since when they return, Herod's son Archelaus is ruling Judea (Matt. 2:22). Archelaus was notorious for his ineptitude and arrogance and the Romans deposed him in AD 6. So Joseph's family bypassed Judea and settled in Galilee (2:22–23).

Jesus grew up in the Galilee village of Nazareth, secluded in the mountains of "lower" Galilee but nevertheless near to the expanding city of Sepphoris and the busy trade routes moving through the valleys. Jesus was probably educated in the local synagogue each morning from age five or six and each afternoon worked at his father's trade. Joseph was a *tektōn* ("carpenter"; Mark 6:3), which refers to someone who works in wood, metal, or stone. Woodworkers were needed for construction. Hence Jesus knew hard labor and probably followed his father to nearby Sepphoris, working there to rebuild the new Greek city.

Like other boys in his village, from the age of six to ten Jesus became literate in Hebrew through study of the Torah in the Nazareth synagogue, and he memorized vast quantities

The "shepherd's" fields outside Bethlehem in the 19th century. Today they are in the village of Beit Sahour and still host scenes such as this.

of Scripture. From ages ten to twelve he became acquainted with the oral laws under the direction of the synagogue teacher and custodian, the *hazzan*. At this point, he ended his schooling and began working full-time with his father. The only event from this time recorded in the Gospels is Jesus' visit to a Passover in Jerusalem at age twelve.

From the age of thirteen until the beginning of his public ministry (about thirty), Jesus worked in Nazareth and joined the village men at the synagogue for discussion and debate. These exclusively male gatherings sharpened understanding of the law and were as raucous as they were inspiring. Thus, Jesus had almost twenty years experience debating in his local synagogue before he began teaching in the synagogues of Galilee. By the time he was an adult, he was a skilled craftsman, literate, knowledgeable in the traditions and history of his people, and adept at public discourse.

JESUS AND THE GALILEE CARAVAN

How did Mary and Joseph lose track of Jesus at age twelve (see Luke 2:41–51)? Jewish boys were under the care of their mothers until puberty. At age thirteen they associated with village men, formally became "sons of the law," and were permitted to be a legal witness, lead in prayer, and enjoy a legal independent status.

Cultural anthropologists offer insights into what may have happened. When Mary and Joseph traveled to Jerusalem they probably did so with a large caravan, and the men and women traveled separately. Since Jesus was at a transitional age, Mary likely thought Jesus was with Joseph and Joseph thought he was with the women. At night they discovered their error.

Records found in rabbinic Judaism in the century after Jesus give us some idea what life was probably like in the first century. As a faithful Jew, Jesus likely traveled to Jerusalem yearly to celebrate Passover, Pentecost, and Tabernacles. He was surrounded by the "markers" of his Jewish faith. The front door of his home had Scriptures (likely Deut. 6:4–9; 11:12–21) nailed to the right upper post (the *mezuzah*). He also dressed in a long cloak with double tassels on each of the four corners of its hem—but unlike the Greeks, he made one thread at each corner blue, signaling his identity as a Jew. Twice each day he recited the

Today modern Nazareth, with its large Arab Christian population, remains on the same site as ancient Nazareth, in the mountains of S. (or lower) Galilee seated in a deep valley (beyond the tree line).

Shema (Deut. 6:4–9), which explains how he can readily refer to it when asked in Matthew 22:34–40. He kept a kosher diet, wore his hair and beard long, and observed the many rules regulating the Sabbath.

BAPTISM AND TEMPTATION

The public ministry of Jesus opens with a preliminary scene describing John the Baptist. As an adult, John took on the role of a prophet, traveled into the eastern deserts and along the Jordan River, and called the residents of Judea to repentance (Matt. 3:5–10; Luke 3:7–9). Many of the leaders of Jerusalem came to him and pressed him to explain himself (John 1:19–28).

Jesus made his first public appearance at the Jordan River with John. When he entered the water, the Spirit descended on him and God's voice confirmed, "You are my Son, whom I love" (Mark 1:11). John told the crowds that Jesus was "the Lamb of God, who takes away the sin of the world" (John 1:29) and that he would "baptize with the Holy Spirit" (1:33).

Jesus then entered the wilderness alone and was tested for forty days by Satan (Matt. 4:1–11). His triple test evoked memories of Israel in the wilderness—perhaps also the testing of Adam—but Jesus prevailed, citing passages from Deuteronomy 6–8 in response to each provocative offer. Satan weighed in on Jesus' understanding of sonship and the empowering that came at his baptism. Would Jesus exploit his power for self-interest? Would he exchange his divine calling for a secular understanding of power? In each case, Jesus refused.

Jesus was baptized in the Jordan River which near Mt. Hermon in the far north, flows into the Sea of Galilee near Bethsaida, and flows out south to the Dead Sea.

The Judean wilderness lies between Jerusalem and the River Jordan. This is the region of Jesus' forty-day testing.

THE BEGINNING OF THE GALILEE MINISTRY

Jesus and John worked side by side in the Jordan Valley; gradually some of John's followers changed their allegiance to follow Jesus (John 1:35–42). Jesus moved quietly between the Jordan Valley and Galilee, gaining disciples and establishing his reputation. His first miracle was at Cana in Galilee (John 2).

Jesus' world changed abruptly with the arrest and imprisonment of John the Baptist. The prophet's moral exhortations condemned the illicit marriage of Herod Antipas (the political ruler of that area) to Herodias (his brother's wife, Mark 6:17–18). Josephus tells us the full story (*Ant.* 18.5.1–2 [109–119]). When Antipas decided to marry Herodias, he also shamed his first wife, the daughter of King Aretas of Nabatea (an Arab kingdom just south of Perea). When this princess fled home, her father was enraged, and John's preaching contributed to his fury. Antipas killed John at his fortress of Machaerus on the Nabatean border to silence his critic and avoid a possible border war. King Aretas did attack Antipas in AD 36 and destroyed his

These first century stone jars were discovered in Jerusalem and illustrate the water jars used by Jesus in John 2:6. Unlike pottery jars, these jars could not become "unclean" through common use (Lev 11:33) and thus could hold purification water.

army. Many Jews saw this defeat as God's judgment on Antipas for killing John (*Ant.* 18.5.2 [116 – 119]).

With the arrest of John, Jesus moved north, no doubt to escape these political dangers (Mark 1:14). His destination was the familiar hills of Galilee, and soon he became a public figure, moving from village to village, gathering disciples, and establishing his reputation as a healer, an exorcist, and as a teacher of unusual talent. Nevertheless Herod Antipas was not amused, and superstitious rumors gathered momentum in Galilee that in fact, Jesus was actually John the Baptist, now returned to life (Mark 6:16).

Despite his reputation as a "Nazarene," Jesus never returned to Nazareth permanently and instead moved to the fishing villages on the north end of the Sea of Galilee. Capernaum became his new home (Mark 2:1), a fishing village that lay on the main highway connecting central Galilee with the mountain villages of the Golan Heights — as well as in far-off Damascus. It was also on the border with Philip's territory and thus a tax station for commerce moving down the highway. If Jesus was ever pursued by Antipas, he could just slip across the border by boat (6:45). Capernaum even had its own Roman garrison. A centurion from its barracks helped build Capernaum's synagogue (Luke 7:4 – 6).

One of Herod's Fortresses, Marchaerus, occupied a defensive position against the desert Nabatean kingdom but also, according to Josephus, was the location of John the Baptist's death.

A Jewish ritual bath yet to be excavated at Herod's Machaerus.

GAMLA: A FIRST CENTURY COMMUNITY UNCOVERED

In the Golan Heights northeast of the Sea of Galilee archaeologists in 1967 discovered a village well-known among Jewish historians. Gamla was destroyed at the beginning of the great war with Rome (AD 66–70) and was never rebuilt.

Excavations continue today. Over six hundred sickle blades have been found, showing that Gamla was an agricultural center. Likewise loads of military gear testify to the last fight at the town. Above all, a first-century synagogue has been completely excavated.

If Jesus visited the many villages of Galilee, he certainly came to Gamla. At this remote site we can revisit the world of the first century and an actual synagogue where Jesus preached.

GROWING POPULARITY

As Jesus' popularity grew, he was followed by groups of people who hung on his every word. "A large crowd" from both Galilee and Judea followed him (Mark 3:7). He spoke from the coves on Galilee's shores and on some occasions used moored boats as his platform. On one occasion he gathered them on the side of a mountain and delivered his famous "Sermon on the Mount" (Matt. 5–7), after which the audience was stunned at his authority, contrasting it with the efforts of Jewish teachers of the law.

The term "disciple" (Gk. *mathētēs*, "learner") referred to the wider public that followed Jesus. In order to further advance his work and to develop a circle of uniquely trained disciples, Jesus chose twelve men (called "apostles" or "the Twelve"; see Mark 3:13–19). The Twelve played a role well known in Judaism. They were authorized representatives or agents who carried their patron's authority. They could speak for him and act in his name. These men were entrusted to go into the villages of Galilee, preaching what Jesus taught them and casting out demons, all under the authority of Jesus.

Their efforts moving in twos throughout Galilee (Luke 9:1–6) no doubt spread word about Jesus rapidly. Many people traveled to find him, so that when Jesus arrived in their towns, he found audiences who were expectant and receptive. This strategy was so effective that at one point Jesus appointed seventy-two people to accomplish the same purpose (Luke 10:1–20).

Gamla was one of Galilee's many villages. It occupied a precipitous ridge, here seen with the excavated village's walls and buildings. (See chap. 3 for a photo of Gamla's synagogue.)

A further index of Jesus' growing fame is the great feeding miracles. Once in western Galilee about five thousand men (and additional women and children) listened to his teaching for so long that they needed to be fed. Jesus repeated this feeding miracle on the east side of the sea, perhaps near Bethsaida (Mark 8:1–10). Here four thousand were fed with seven loaves and a few fish.

One characteristic of Jesus' following was its unexpected mix of people. Jesus eagerly crossed social boundaries that we might miss when we read the Gospels today. For instance, when he visited Tyre and Sidon (Mark 7:24) or moved through the Decapolis (the Greek cities in northeastern Galilee), he was with Gentiles (7:31). These were unexpected contacts

Matthew opens the public ministry of Jesus with the Sermon on the Mount which took place on the hills near Capernaum.

for a Jewish teacher. He likewise responded to a request for healing from a Roman centurion in Capernaum (Matt. 8:5). Similarly, he had a ministry among the "outcast" Samaritans (John 4) and sent his followers into their villages to preach (Luke 9:52).

Moreover, Jesus associated with women as well as men (Luke 8:43; 10:38; John 4:7). Some women were deeply troubled, such as Mary of Magdala (Mark 16:9) and the woman caught in adultery (John 8:3), while others were established leaders in the community who helped pay Jesus' expenses (such as Susannah and the wife of Herod's financial minister, likely from Sepphoris, Luke 8:3).

Jesus also ministered to those who lived on society's margin: tax collectors, lepers, adulterers, and "sinners." Even one of his apostles was a political revolutionary (Matt. 10:4). In this sense Jesus failed to maintain "social boundaries" that promoted the Pharisees' notion of separation and purity, and he incurred criticism for making misguided social choices (Mark 2:16).

Cultural anthropologists wonder if Jesus was labeled a "bad son" by some of his contemporaries. He rejected conventions held deeply in his society (such as diet, Sabbath-keeping, and social boundaries). He did not marry, devote himself to Joseph's trade, or become an established member of Nazareth. In a poignant text in Mark 3:31–35, the crowd directed him to his immediate family who was calling to him — and he publicly separated himself, redefining what it means to be "family." It is little wonder that his brothers did not follow him (John 7:5). The story is also silent regarding his father, Joseph, whose expectations for his "firstborn" son would have been significant.

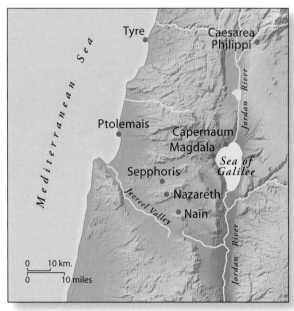

Galilee during Jesus' ministry.

GROWING OPPOSITION

The source of opposition to Jesus is a critical question among modern researchers. Discovering its source to a large degree discloses what is at the heart of Jesus' self-consciousness and mission. Was he a religious reformer within Judaism who threatened its leadership? Was he challenging the social and political injustices of his day and so jeopardized Israel's uneasy equilibrium with Rome?

Jesus' critics felt they had good grounds to object to him. One of the major components of the Gospels is the sheer number of stories of conflict wherein different groups—Sadducees, Pharisees, and scribes—expressed resistance to his teaching and behavior. Two areas provoked conflict. First, Jesus was known as someone who "broke the Sabbath." Multiple stories show him openly violating Sabbath law and not refraining from work (Matt. 12:1–14; Mark 2:23–28; 3:1–6; Luke 13:10–17; 14:1–5; John 5:1–18). In each of these stories, Jesus' offensive "work" could have waited until the next day. But he saw this activity as prophetic, acting out a message that expressed criticism of intricate Sabbath legislation. His explanation is remembered in the succinct maxim, "The Sabbath was made for people, not people for the Sabbath" (Mark 2:27).

Second, Jesus seemed too relaxed about purity laws. Mark 7:1–4 outlines the Pharisees' concern about washing and utensils and notes their criticism of Jesus: "Why don't your disciples live according to the tradition of the elders instead of eating their food with defiled hands?" On another occasion, Jesus expressed apparent disregard for food laws (kosher) and declared all foods "clean" (Mark 7:15, 19). Dietary rules and Sabbath observance were principal markers in Judaism that set Jews apart from Gentiles. Jesus failed to hold to these boundaries.

Other controversies followed Jesus (such as his treatment of divorce law, Mark 10:1–12), but in each of them Jesus expressed himself as having an authority not subject to human tradition or rule. He

Magdala was one of many fishing ports bordering the Sea of Galilee. However today little remains of the ancient village. Magdala took its name from Hebrew "migdal," meaning "tower" which probably referred to small towers used in the first century to stack fish in salt for commercial markets.

Jesus' teachings could provoke. It would be better to have one of these heavy basalt millstones tied around your neck and be cast into the sea than to lead a little one to sin (Luke 17:2).

might quote from the Torah, but then follow it with an authoritative "I" statement: "You have heard that it was said . . . but I tell you. . . ." He reinforced this with the odd prelude to many of his sayings, "Truly I tell you . . ." (Matt 5:18; cf. John 3:3). He defended his commitment to the law (Matt. 5:17) but delivered a severe prophetic critique to its practitioners: They practiced outward forms of religion for public viewing, but failed to pursue the inner values the law promoted. He claimed that such people were "hypocrites" (6:5). The implication of this language seemed clear: Jesus spoke with a voice authorized by God.

Moreover, Jesus deemed that obedience to his personal words affected a person's relationship with God (Matt. 7:21-27; John 5:23). In fact, Jesus could explain that his own efforts and words actually represented the work of God in the world. These concerns coalesced one Sabbath in Jerusalem. Jesus "worked" on Sabbath by healing a lame man but defended himself with an argument based on the rabbinic opinion that God *alone* could work on Sabbath (John 5:16 – 18). As Jesus' ministry matured, his audiences increasingly perceived that he bore a presence and power that were unique. He performed healings, raised the dead, exorcized demons, forgave sins, and silenced storms. It is no wonder that occasionally they looked at him in amazement and were filled with fear (Mark 6:50).

At the base of Mt. Hermon near Caesarea Philippi springs feed river systems that give birth to the Jordan River.

Today visitors can visit Caesarea Philippi where Peter identified Jesus as the Messiah. The ruins of its impressive temple complex are still visible.

JESUS "SETS HIS FACE" TOWARD JERUSALEM

A turning point came at the apex of Jesus' ministry in Galilee. At Caesarea Philippi, Jesus turned toward his followers and asked them to identify him. They explained the public's many incorrect views of him, but then Peter gave the correct answer: "You are the Messiah" (Mark 8:29). Matthew 16:16 gives a fuller wording, "You are the Messiah, the Son of the living God." This judgment was confirmed the next week when Jesus took Peter, James, and John with him to a high mountain (likely Mount Hermon) and there was "transfigured," showing his radiant glory alongside Elijah and Moses (Mark 9:2–13).

Following these remarkable events, Jesus (lit.) "set his face" to go to Jerusalem for the last time (Luke 9:51). The gospel writers note that during the trip, Jesus made three explicit predictions of his coming betrayal and death: at Caesarea Philippi (Mark 8:31–33), in central Galilee near Capernaum (9:30–32), and near Jericho (10:32–34). Each time he became increasingly specific about what would happen in Jerusalem. As they heard these predictions, the disciples' responses changed: Initially they rebuked him and were confused (8:32), later they were afraid to ask him what he meant (9:32), and finally they were filled with fear (10:32). As he moved south, even sympathetic Pharisees warned him about what lay ahead (Luke 13:31).

WHY CAESAREA PHILIPPI?

Caesarea Philippi began its Roman life when the Emperor Augustus gave it to Herod the Great to rule in 20 BC. As a tribute of thanks, Herod built a pure white marble temple in honor of Augustus. After Herod's death, the city passed on to his son Philip, who rebuilt it and made it the capital of northeast Galilee.

Philip also chose this site because of its sacred traditions. One of the sources of the Jordan River flowed from a cave here, and shrines and temples to the Roman nature god Pan were built (its most ancient name is Paneas). Soon the city was called "Caesarea of Philip" (Caesarea Philippi) to distinguish it from Caesarea "on the sea." But for most ancient historians, the traditional link to Pan remained. Pliny referred to the city as Caesarea Panias (*Natural History*, 5.71, 74)

NOTES FROM ANTIQUITY

THE FINAL WEEK

Jesus' arrival in Jerusalem begins the story of his last week. It was springtime, the season of Passover, and pilgrims from everywhere were pouring into the city. Jerusalem had become for Jesus a "theological symbol" representing the city that resisted God's messengers (Luke 13:34–35).

Jesus' journey took him to Jericho and from this oasis he climbed the Roman road west into the desert. Here in the Judean mountains, a short walk from Jerusalem, he stayed with friends in the village of Bethany (Mary and Martha); when he first arrived, he electrified the village by raising Lazarus from death (John 11:1–45). Upon entering Jerusalem, he was greeted by crowds of residents and Passover pilgrims as a great messianic figure. Most wanted to see him—others wanted to see Lazarus and confirm the story of his resurrection (John 12:9–11). Some were deeply devoted to Jesus' teaching, while others were caught up in

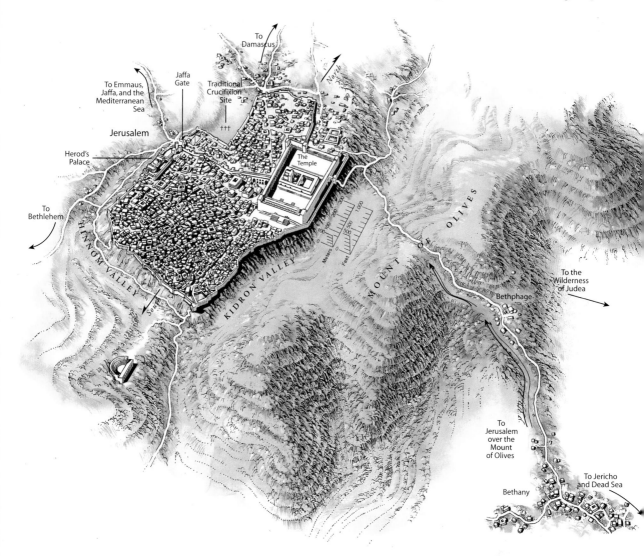

This artist's reconstruction depicts Herod's refurbished and expanded city of Jerusalem during Jesus' lifetime.

Left: This scale model of first century Jerusalem shows the details of Herod's magnificent city. The full model is on the grounds of the Holy Land Hotel, W. Jerusalem. *Right:* The fig was a symbol of Israel and its destruction by Jesus symbolic of the judgment that would come on Jerusalem (Mark 11:12-14).

political dreams of Jesus' talk about "the kingdom of God" (Luke 19:11). Soon palms were waving and shouts of Jewish nationalism could be heard: "Blessed is he who comes in the name of the Lord!" "Blessed is the coming kingdom of our father David" (Mark 11:9–10)! Jesus rode a donkey, evoking memories of Zechariah's prophecies (Matt. 21:5; cf. Zech. 9:9).

A common Old Testament theme is that God's prophets will bring judgment first to God's house, the temple (Jer. 7:1–15; 26:1–15; Mal. 3:1–5). When Jesus entered Jerusalem, he astonished even his disciples. Crossing the Kidron Valley he cursed a fig tree because it had no edible fruit (Mark 11:12–14). In the Old Testament the fig was a common symbol of Israel itself (Jer. 8:13; 29:17; Hos. 9:10; Joel 1:7), and its destruction symbolized the judgment on the nation (Isa. 34:4; Hos. 2:12; Luke 13:6–9).

Jesus then entered the temple courts, expressed outrage at its commercial activities, disrupted the moneychangers, and interrupted the sacrifices — an act of civil disobedience that confirmed the authorities' commitment to have him arrested. For the remainder of the week, Jesus entered into a sustained critique of Jerusalem's leadership and daily debated them inside the spacious courtyards of the temple (Matt. 23; Mark 12). He even climbed

NARD

Nard was extremely precious and imported from northern India. Nard is a shrub whose leaves and shoots were harvested and taken by caravan to the west. Sometimes it was mixed with its own root to increase its weight. Note that Mary's gift is called "pure," meaning that it had no additives. Nard smelled like *gladiolus* perfume and had a red color. It was used as medicine, as an aromatic wine, as a breath scent, and as perfume (see Pliny, *Natural History* 12:24–26 [41–46]).

A pound was huge and lavish. Its value of three hundred denarii represents a year's wages for a day laborer. Cheaper nard from Gaul, Crete, or Syria cost a hundred denarii per pound, but Mary owned the very best.

In antiquity, the blossoming almond tree was the welcomed harbinger of spring and Passover. Its flowers precede its leaves and it can bloom in pink or white. Its symbolism was found in the temple where the golden lampstand was fashioned to represent a blossoming almond (Exod 25:31-40). Jesus pointed to such trees (in this case a fig tree) as signals of his second coming (Luke 21:29-31).

Today's Jerusalem not only has a thriving modern population of Arabs and Israelis, but has been the site of intensive archaeological work. This view is from the south showing the excavation of the southern entrances to the temple.

Jesus was arrested in the Kidron Valley east of Jerusalem. There he found an olive orchard where he prayed and was later betrayed. The name Gethsemane comes from the Aramaic *gat semen*, or olive press.

the Mount of Olives just east of the city and prophesied not only the demise of Jerusalem and its temple but the judgment of the world (Matt. 24; Mark 13; Luke 21).

The Jerusalem leadership started talking about stopping Jesus; some underscored the threat he was posing to the security of the nation, in that a popular uprising could lead to a Roman military response (John 11:48). The high priest Caiaphas drew this conclusion easily: It was expedient that Jesus should die since it would be a sacrifice for the whole nation's well-being (11:50). In this context, one night in Bethany Jesus' good friend Mary (the sister of Lazarus and Martha) took an alabaster jar of pure nard and anointed him generously. It was as much a disturbing symbol as a luxurious gift. Mary was saying goodbye and readying his body with burial spices (Matt. 26:6–13; Mark 14:3–9; John 12:1–8).

Each Passover season anticipated the ritual slaughter of lambs, which was followed after sundown by a Passover meal. This year, the Passover meal began on a Thursday evening. Following Jewish tradition, Jesus secured a room within the walled city, sent two disciples to prepare the tables and the food (Luke 22:8), and hosted his final meal with the Twelve. This ritual meal recalled the exodus from Egypt, God's redemption of his people, and the sacrificed lambs whose blood covered their homes (see Ex. 12–13).

But during the middle of the meal, Jesus interrupted the festivities, broke a loaf of bread, poured a cup of wine, and announced that these would now represent his broken body and shed blood (Matt. 26:26–28). In the Old Testament each covenant was sealed with sacrifice (Gen. 15:9–18; Ex. 24:3–8). Jesus is doing the same here: "This is my blood of the [new] covenant, which is poured out for many for the forgiveness of sins" (Matt. 26:28).

THE ROMAN *TRICLINIUM* AND THE PASSOVER

Every culture has rules for festival meals. At Judaism's Passover festival, participants dined reclining on cushions at low tables, reaching for common bowls. First-century Jews had adopted the Roman *triclinium* table, a low three-sided table shaped like a "U." Guests reclined on cushions while the interior of "U" provided access for servers. The body was supported with the left arm (or elbow), the right hand was used for eating, and the feet were extended away from the table.

This explains why "the beloved disciple" (John) can lean his head back, rest it on Jesus' chest, and ask him a question (John 13:23–25). They were reclining side by side, John to the right, Jesus to the left.

In antiquity all Jews celebrated the Passover with the ritual slaughter of a lamb. Today this practice continues only among the Samaritans north of Jerusalem.

ARREST, TRIAL, AND CRUCIFIXION

Jesus then walked outside of the city and entered an olive orchard not far from the road that would take him back to Bethany. Here he prayed fervently and was burdened by the dread of his coming suffering (Mark 14:32–42). The evening was interrupted when Judas, who had received thirty silver pieces (Matt. 26:14–16), led a determined band of men to arrest Jesus. Priests, temple police (Luke 22:52), and even a detachment of Roman soldiers (John 18:3, 12) arrived with weapons and torches. With the signal of a kiss Judas identified Jesus, and he was arrested.

Jesus' trial was quickly carried out since the authorities feared a furious reaction from the masses, many of whom came from Galilee (Luke 22:2). The high priest Caiaphas gathered a cadre of leaders at his residence, and his father-in-law, the now-retired high priest Annas, began the interrogation (John 18:13). This was followed by witnesses who made unsuccessful charges against Jesus (Matt. 26:60).

Left: A scale model of first century Jerusalem here reconstructs the four-tower Antonia Fortress, likely site of Jesus' interrogation before Pilate. *Right:* The Antonia Fortress was destroyed when Titus sacked Jerusalem in AD 70. Today its courtyard paving stones can be found in the lower levels of the Sisters of Zion convent.

Because the witnesses contradicted themselves about details (Mark 14:56), Caiaphas himself entered the fray. He first prodded Jesus to speak in his own self-defense, hoping to find some incriminating evidence on his own lips. Finally, he asked him forthrightly: "Tell us if you are the Messiah, the Son of God?" (Matt. 26:63). It was considered blasphemy to claim divine honors for oneself. Jesus answered by describing himself as an apocalyptic judge who would possess a heavenly role with God (Mark 14:62). This was enough. After calling for a test vote, he handed Jesus over to the temple police to be guarded.

For each gospel writer, the scene is tragic. Jesus was alone, and even his leading disciple, Peter, who followed and stood outside the priest's house and was known for his bravado, denied knowing Jesus three times. Early on Friday morning Caiaphas called for a plenary meeting of the Sanhedrin in order to formalize the decision (Mark 15:1). Because the Jews had lost the privilege to execute a criminal (John 18:31), Caiaphas had to defer to the Roman governor (Pontius Pilate), who was in Jerusalem because of the Passover festival. Pilate's interrogation of Jesus likely took place at the Antonia Fortress.

The Sanhedrin's charges of blasphemy would make little impact on Pilate. Thus Caiaphas reframed the charges against Jesus, implying that he was guilty of political sedition: "We have found this man subverting our nation. He opposes payment of taxes to Caesar and claims to be Messiah, a king" (Luke 23:2). Thereupon Pilate probed Jesus' understanding of politics. "Are you the king of the Jews?" Jesus agreed but was wary of Pilate's meaning

Left: Jesus walked to Golgotha on the «way of suffering» (Via Dolorosa) in Jerusalem (pictured). This roman arch betrays the Roman history of the city embedded in its modern walls. *Right:* The crataegis thorn which grows in Israel and is commonly viewed as the source of Jesus' "crown of thorns."

and reinterpreted the title: "My kingdom is not of this world" (John 18:36). But the Sanhedrin voices returned, claiming Jesus had disturbed the peace, made trouble in Galilee, and now was bringing unrest to Jerusalem.

When Pilate heard that Jesus was from Galilee, he decided to send him to the Jewish ruler of Galilee, Herod Antipas, who was in Jerusalem. This was a stroke of genius. Pilate could still get Jesus condemned, but shift the blame to a Jewish ruler. But Jesus refused to talk to Herod. Because Antipas had killed John the Baptist, Jesus had little respect for him (Luke 23:6–16).

Jesus' case returned to Pilate, and the governor appealed to a Passover amnesty tradition to release a prisoner (John 18:38–40). But the crowd outside his fortress called instead for the release of Barabbas, a man described in Greek as a *lēstēs*. This term should be translated as "bandit patriot" (today, we would call him a "terrorist"), describing someone who fought against the Roman occupation. Pilate was troubled by this turn of events. He handed Jesus to some of his troops, had him thoroughly whipped, and presented him to the crowd, hoping to evoke pity (John 19:1–11). But this was only met with a cry for Jesus' death.

Following considerable pressure from the Sanhedrin leaders (John 19:12–15) and concerned about his own fate, Pilate handed Jesus over to his troops to commence the crucifixion. Jewish executions generally practiced stoning. However in the ancient world, various rulers began to use public crucifixion as a deterrence (cf. Josh. 10:26). Antiochus Epiphanes used crucifixion against his enemies in 167–166 BC (*Ant.* 12.5.4 [255–256]). The Maccabean ruler Alexander Jannaeus crucified eight hundred Pharisees who opposed him (*Ant.* 13.14.2 [379–380]). In 4 BC the Roman general Varus crucified two thousand Jewish rebels in Judea (*Ant.* 17.10.10 [295]). Jews detested the practice and, in Jesus' day, viewed it as a sign of the Roman occupation.

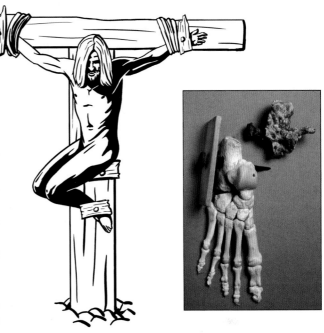

Left: This artist's model gives a credible option for understanding how Jesus was crucified. Note the seat for the victim to rest called the sedile. Josephus called this "the most wretched of deaths" (*The Jewish War* 7.6.4 [203]). *Right:* The ankle bone of the crucified man still shows the nail used in his death. A model foot is next to it showing how the original nailing would have looked.

A victim was thoroughly beaten with a special bone or metal-tipped whip, cutting the back to promote copious bleeding. He was then forced to carry the horizontal cross-beam to the site. After Jesus was beaten (Mark 15:15), he was also mocked with a crown of thorns and robe, poking fun at his claim to be the Jewish king. As he walked to his crucifixion outside the city walls (called Golgotha, "the place of the skull"), he became so weak that he could not carry the beam. A visitor to Jerusalem, Simon from Cyrene, was forced to carry it for him (Mark 15:21). Women wailed as they watched Jesus walking through Jerusalem's streets, leaving a heavy trail of blood.

Soldiers oversaw the final execution. Crosses were not tall and victims were roped or nailed to them with their feet not far from the ground. Victims were also crucified naked,

A CRUCIFIED MAN FOUND IN 1968

In 1968 at Giv'at ha-Mivtar in Jerusalem, a first-century bone box (or ossuary) was discovered containing the skeleton of a man who had been crucified. His heel bones were still fastened together by a single iron nail 5.5 inches long. The man's ankles had been placed sideways and on top of each other, and the nail was driven through a piece of acacia wood (that functioned like a washer) and the ankles into the olivewood cross. When he was taken down, the nail could not be removed and he was buried with the nail, the acacia wood, and a fragment of olivewood.

increasing the shame and dread of the method. (This is why the soldiers gamble for Jesus' garments, John 19:23–24). From their crosses men might dictate their will or hold conversations with their families. Jesus thus speaks from the cross since he is surrounded by his closest friends, his mother, and a circle of Jewish women.

BURIAL AND RESURRECTION

As a crucified criminal, Jesus should have been buried in a field adjacent to Jerusalem (*Ant.* 5.1.14 [43–44]). This is what happened to Judas Iscariot when he regretted his deed, committed suicide, and was buried in a field purchased by the priests with his bribe money (Matt. 27:3–10).

In Jesus' case, a wealthy member of the Sanhedrin named Joseph from the village of Arimathea came forward. Joseph believed in Christ secretly and did not agree with the Sanhedrin's decision (Matt. 27:57; John 19:38). Together with Nicodemus (see John 3:1ff; 7:50), they asked for Jesus' body. It was a custom of respect in Judaism to bury bodies before sundown (John 19:31). Joseph possessed a new tomb that was unused and offered it immediately. Certainly the authorities had to assess if Jesus were dead. Using a mallet, they crushed the legs of the two men crucified with Jesus (John 19:32) but they did not hit him. Instead, one soldier took his lance and stabbed him in the side. But Jesus' life had already expired.

Joseph and Nicodemus—no doubt aided by the women at the cross—removed Jesus' body and carried it to Joseph's tomb not far away. Archaeologists have found about nine

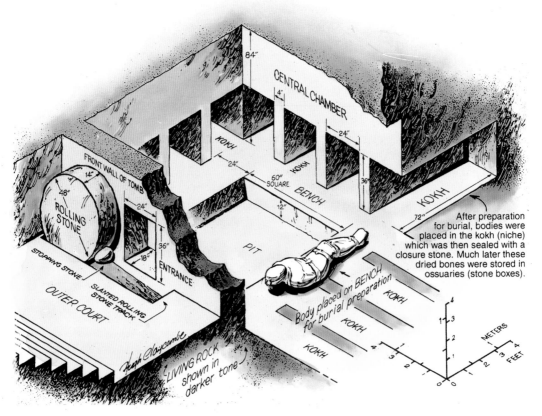

Some first century tombs had characteristic designs. This tomb (based on a variety that have been found) shows a rolling stone, an interior reception area, a burial bench, and burial niches called "kokhim."

Rolling Stone tombs such as this one at Khirbet Midras were well-known in the hills of Judea.

hundred tombs from this period and so we have a good idea how this one was built. In one type, Jews carved cave tombs into the limestone hills outside Jerusalem's walls. A low door led to a square burial chamber (or receiving room) inside, which was encircled by a stone bench running along the room's perimeter. Six foot shafts (or niches, Heb. *kokhim*) could be seen above the bench for final placement of the body. Many of these tombs were sealed with a movable "rolling" stone door.

Jesus was laid on the stone bench and wrapped loosely in linens dusted with spices; his head was given a burial napkin, and he was surrounded by seventy-five pounds of myrrh and aloe—an expensive gift from Nicodemus (John 19:39). Because Sabbath was beginning, no doubt they thought they would return to place Jesus in a wall niche and complete the burial later. Therefore, the rolling stone was closed. Fearing that his body might be stolen, the priests requested a guard at the tomb, sealing it for the duration of the Sabbath.

Early on Sunday morning, well before sunrise, a group of women arrived at the tomb prepared to complete Jesus' burial (Mark 16:1–2). They worried about moving the heavy locking stone at the cave's entrance. But when they arrived, what looked at first like a disaster—the tomb was open, the body was gone—turned their sorrow into joy. Angels appeared telling them that Jesus was alive and that they should tell the others. Then Jesus surprised them by appearing himself in the garden, telling them how his promises had been fulfilled. Soon the disciples were rushing to see for themselves.

Jesus met with his disciples that evening, showing them his wounds and fulfilling his promise that he would never abandon them (John 14:18). He also surprised some disciples on the road to Emmaus west of Jerusalem (Luke 24:13–27). He continued to appear to them in Jerusalem (Luke 24:36–49) and in Galilee (Matt. 28:16–20) for forty days (Acts 1:3). On one occasion he appeared to five hundred people (1 Cor. 15:6).

The gospel writers are remarkably modest in their presentation of "proofs'" for the resurrection. On occasion, the details of their stories collide as if written by independent and excited witnesses. But they stand in firm agreement that this event, this divine vindication of the truth of Jesus' life and message, lies at the very center of Christian faith and experience.

QUESTIONS FOR DISCUSSION ⊙⊙⊙⊙⊙⊙⊙⊙⊙⊙⊙⊙⊙⊙⊙⊙⊙⊙⊙⊙⊙⊙⊙⊙⊙⊙

1. Explain some of the chief reasons Jesus was successful in his public ministry.

2. In what ways was Jesus' behavior different from the scribes and Pharisees in his day?

3. Was Jesus affected by political issues during his life? How did he embrace them or avoid them?

4. What was the Sanhedrin's chief complaint against Jesus? Why were its members persuaded that he had to die?

5. What are the literary and theological connections between the Old Testament Passover traditions and Jesus' death in the Gospels?

BIBLIOGRAPHY

Introductory

Barnett, P. *Jesus and the Rise of Early Christianity*. Downers Grove, IL: InterVarsity Press, 1999.

France, R. T. *The Man They Crucified: A Portrait of Jesus*. Downers Grove, IL: InterVarsity Press, 1975.

Harrison, E. F. *A Short Life of Christ*. Grand Rapids: Eerdmans, 1968.

Advanced

Bock, D. L. *Jesus according to Scripture: Restoring the Portraits of the Gospels*. Grand Rapids: Baker, 2002.

Meier, J. P. *A Marginal Jew: Rethinking the Historical Jesus*. 3 vols. ABRL. New York: Doubleday, 1991, 1994, 2002.

Stanton, G. N. *The Gospels and Jesus*. Oxford: Oxford Univ. Press, 1999.

CHAPTER 7

THE TEACHINGS
OF JESUS

A first century Jewish ritual bath (*mikveh*) from the Galilean village of Gamla.

Jews practiced "secondary burial" in which the decomposed body's bones were placed in ornately carved limestone boxes. Jesus compared these with the Pharisees (Matt 23:27). This Jewish burial box (or "ossuary") is from the New Testament era.

Throughout the Gospels Jesus is recognized as a great teacher. The Greek term for "teacher" (*didaskalos*) translates the Hebrew word *rabbi* ("my great one," Matt. 23:8, John 1:38) and was used as an exalted title for teachers of the Jewish law. When Jesus moved from village to village, particularly in Galilee, the crowds immediately recognized a skill and an authority that surpassed what they met in the synagogues. Note Matthew 7:28–29: "When Jesus had finished saying these things, the crowds were amazed at his teaching, because he taught as one who had authority, and not as their teachers of the law."

When we imagine Jesus' teaching in his own time and place, we cannot use profiles of teachers from our own world to understand the nature of his work. Our culture is heir to the Greek tradition, where abstract reasoning and verbal prowess are the measure of the teacher. Jesus' world was different. He communicated through word pictures, dramatic actions, metaphors, and stories. Rather than lecture about religious corruption, Jesus refers to the Pharisees as "whitewashed tombs." Rather than outline the failings of the temple, he curses a fig tree. This means that we should think of Jesus as a "metaphorical theologian" for whom drama, humor, and storytelling were all a part of his method.[1]

But was Jesus a *sophisticated* teacher? Some scholars have a romantic view of him as a rural village carpenter who offered pithy and simple insights about God. Jesus was indeed a craftsman, but rabbis commonly held such practical jobs. Paul was a tentmaker, and the famous rabbi Shammai was a stonemason. The Mishnah described the law as a "crown" worn by the teacher, but it could not be used to glorify oneself or to gain profit. Instead, the rabbi was to have an occupation through which God granted the means to teach (Mishnah, *Aboth* 4:5).

Jesus' teaching ministry focused on the villages of Galilee, many of which could be found by the sea. This view looks east, over the shoulder of Mt. Arbel, a region known intimately by Jesus.

Jesus' most famous teachings, such as the Sermon on the Mount, took place in the hills on the Galilee's northwest shore. This region was known as the Plain of Gennesaret (Matt 14:34, Mark 6:53) with its chief city Magdala (or Tarichea) which had a fleet of 230 boats (Josephus, *War* 2.21.4,8 [608, 635]). This view looks west toward Mt. Arbel.

As noted in chapter 6, as a young man Jesus met regularly with men who studied and debated the Jewish law over late-night communal meals. Such men called themselves *haberim* ("friends") and took their mandate from Psalm 119:63, "I am a friend [*haber*] to all who fear you."[2] The Jews at Qumran did this regularly every night (*Damascus Document*, Geniza A, Col. 6:2–10). Jesus had honed debating skills for many years and was adept at theological discourse.

JESUS' AUTHORITY

Jesus' audiences frequently recognized he had "authority." For example, Mark writes after Jesus taught in the synagogue in Capernaum: "The people were amazed at his teaching, because he taught them as one who had authority, not as the teachers of the law"

WHY DIDN'T JESUS WRITE A GOSPEL?

We have no evidence that Jesus wrote down any of his own sayings—much less that he wrote a book. The great scholars of Jesus' day were recognized by the number of students (*talmid*) they could attract, not the books they wrote. Communication was verbal and memorization commonplace. Thus the rabbinic scholars Johannan ben Zakkai, Gamaliel, Hillel, and Shammai did not leave their own writings behind, but rather their teachings were collected and preserved by their followers (like Jesus).

This also explains the repeated mention of the great crowds that followed Jesus. He begins with twelve "disciples," and at one point five thousand flocked around him. By every first-century measure, Jesus was a respected teacher and speaker.

(Mark 1:22). "Authority" is one of the most frequent descriptors for Jesus. Sometimes it is linked to his power (Luke 4:36). At other times the Jewish religious leaders recognize it (Mark 11:27–33). Even a Roman centurion sees it (Matt. 8:5–13).

Among religious teachers, authority rarely referred to inherent authority or something tied to personality or formal study. Authority (Heb. *reshuth*) was *conveyed* by a rabbi through a solemn rite performed from Jesus' day up to the third century AD. A rabbi conveying authority "leaned" (*samakh*) on his disciple, placing his hands on the disciple's head. This ritual of ordination was called Semikah or "leaning," and through it a rabbi "communicated his personality [and] his status to the disciple."[3] Within Jewish tradition, Moses' commissioning of Joshua provided a model for subsequent leaders (Deut. 34:9; cf. Num. 11:25).

Judaism viewed itself as living within a "stream of tradition." The Scriptures as well as traditions were carried by that stream to each new generation. But the capacity to bear those traditions forward required that one be authorized to do so. This was one of the chief functions of "rabbinic authority." If this chain of *reshuth* is broken, Jewish survival might be at risk. In the war of AD 132–135 Hadrian hoped to defeat Judaism by forbidding this ordination, but Rabbi Judah ben Baba laid hands on numerous disciples of the deceased Rabbi Akiba and was killed for sabotaging Hadrian's plan.

How did *reshuth* begin? The headwaters of this stream of tradition began with Moses who was the only man ordained directly by God. Since rabbinic authority was secondary and indirect, the rabbi taught what lived inside the stream, what went before, what began with Moses. Thus, when a rabbi taught in a synagogue, he would sit in Moses' seat (see sidebar).

But if this was the nature of authority, how did Jesus gain his? This question recurs with surprising frequency in the Gospels (Matt. 21:23). Jesus not only behaves like a rabbi, but he has disciples and extends his own authority to them (Mark 6:7). He even interprets the traditions, contrasting his own views with Moses, and he breaks traditions (such as work rules for the Sabbath). Such behavior led to an inevitable deduction: Jesus was claiming an ordination not by human hands, but by God, *just like Moses*. Thus, he stood outside the stream of Jewish tradition and claimed an entirely new trajectory of tradition. His teaching was thus like new wine that broke old wineskins (Mark 2:22). Obeying him was equivalent to obeying God (Matt. 7:21–23).

DISCOVERING A "MOSES SEAT"

When Jesus criticized the Jewish leaders in the temple, he said, "The teachers of the law and the Pharisees sit *in Moses' seat*. So you must obey them and do everything they tell you. But do not do what they do, for they do not practice what they preach" (Matt. 23:2–3). In Jesus' culture, teachers sat when they taught, and because the rabbi represented the authority of Moses, that chair was called "the Moses Seat."

Such stone seats have been discovered in the excavations of fourth-century synagogues at Hammath Tiberias and at Chorazin. The most prominent elder sat on this stone seat, on a raised platform adjacent to the box (or ark) containing the Scripture scrolls; from here he interpreted the teachings of Moses.

NOTES FROM ANTIQUITY

The 4th century "Moses Seat" uncovered at the synagogue of Chorazin, just north of Capernaum.

Four languages were known in first-century Judea: Latin, Greek, Hebrew, and Aramaic. But since the New Testament was written in Greek for Greek readers, what we hear is a translation of Jesus' words. But the Gospels betray hints of another language; Jesus was speaking a different language—likely Aramaic.

Aramaic (a cognate language to Hebrew) was used in the villages of Jesus' day. That Jesus spoke Aramaic seems assured (see sidebar on "Aramaic Words in Mark" in Ch. 5). Some scholars also believe Jesus knew Hebrew, for he read from the Hebrew Scriptures. But this was probably not the language he used regularly in rural villages.

Jesus probably did not know Latin, the language of Rome. But some scholars argue that he knew Greek, thanks to its common use in the country. Yet Jews used it less than we think. Josephus admitted to his lack of ability in Greek and probably had translators render his Aramaic into Greek (*Against Apion* 1.9 [50]). When Titus laid siege to Jerusalem in AD 70, he was unable to talk to the defenders in Greek, but sent Josephus to speak to them "in their own language" (*War* 5.9.2 [361]).

Such suggestions of authority made conflict with the Jewish leaders inevitable. Among his followers, it led to reflection about Jesus' true identity. His authority implied something important about his identity in relation to God.

JESUS' TEACHING STYLE

According to the Gospels, Jesus was an outstanding teacher. Crowds were impressed not only by his authority, but by his teaching skill. Simplicity was one of his hallmarks. He rarely used technical theological speech. Jesus also liked to tell stories. But here we need a word of cultural warning: *Simplicity and story-telling do not betray a lack of profundity.*

The effectiveness of Jesus' work stemmed from *how* he said things. If we recognize these verbal strategies, we will not misinterpret his words. For example, Jesus (and his culture) enjoyed overstatement and gross exaggeration. In Mark 9:43–47 Jesus does not ask his disciples to mutilate themselves but wants to underscore *dramatically* the importance of sin. "If your hand causes you to stumble, cut it off...." The truest meaning of such verses is found in their figurative sense. Jesus talks about straining out gnats and swallowing

Jesus commonly used images drawn from his own culture such as these camels (Matt 23:24).

camels. He describes how we see specks in another's eye, but miss the log in our own. These are a few examples of humorous and dramatic exaggerations meant to rivet audiences.

Jesus also used puns where wordplay in the original language created intriguing and amusing meanings. Some of these are in Greek: In Matthew 16:18 Jesus says, "And I tell you that you are Peter [*petros*], and on this rock [*petra*] I will build my church, and the gates of death [*Hadēs*] will not overcome it." The Aramaic word was *kepha* (Cephas; cf. John 1:42; 1 Cor. 3:22). Other puns are in Aramaic: in Matthew 23:24 Jesus contrasts a gnat and a camel chiefly because in Aramaic they sound similar (gnat, *galma*; camel, *gamla*).

Similes and metaphors provided colorful illustrations of his message. Disciples should be wise as serpents and innocent as doves (Matt. 10:16). Faith should be like a grain of mustard seed (Luke 17:6). The Pharisees were like whitewashed tombs (Matt. 23:27). Disciples should both be the salt of the earth and the light of the world (5:13–16).

Other techniques included proverbs, which expressed wisdom in a memorable or pithy form. "Where your treasure is, there your heart will be also" (Matt. 6:21). Paradoxes created intriguing contradictions that needed unraveling to be understood. How can a widow who contributes to the treasury two tiny copper coins be credited with the largest gift (Mark 12:41–44)? How can the first be last and the last first (10:31)? And how can someone gain life only by losing it (Luke 17:33)?

Jesus stood in the tradition of the Old Testament prophets when he used parabolic acts in order to demonstrate the meaning of his message. Instead of merely lecturing about God's love for the outcast, he ate meals with tax collectors and sinners (Luke 19:1–6). He underscored his criticism of Judaism's many Sabbath rules by breaking them (Mark 2:23–27). Rather than lecturing about corruption in the Jerusalem temple, he caused a public disturbance by upending tables and scattering coins (Mark 11:15–19).

This activity helps explain Jesus' many miracles and exorcisms. These were not only acts of compassion, for they also signaled how God's power was at work in Jesus and how his messianic kingdom was entering the world. Curiously in Mark 1:27 after Jesus' first exorcism in Capernaum, the crowd shouts, "What is this? A new teaching—and with authority! He even gives orders to evil spirits and they obey him."

The mustard seed (*sinapis alba*) was used medicinally in antiquity and as a metaphor for faith in Jesus' teaching.

JESUS' PARABLES

Almost a third of Jesus' teaching comes in the form of parables. The background of Jesus' parables can be found in the old Hebrew custom of figurative speech, the *mashal*. A *mashal* could be any figurative saying—a proverb, a riddle, even an allegorical story. This explains why so many of Jesus' different teachings are figurative. Proverbs (Luke 4:23), similes (Matt. 10:16), brief stories (Luke 15:1–10), even longer narratives (Luke 15:11–32) are all called "parables."

The characteristic form of Jesus' parables was the brief, clever word picture, and little has been found among Jesus' contemporaries to parallel it (although almost two thousand parables have been discovered for rabbis in the period following Jesus). Jesus used commonplace themes from his world to catch the attention of his audience and help them understand his message. But while the parables strove to make things clearer, they also had an enigmatic quality that could make the hearer puzzled. Parables both exclude listeners as well as invite them in. Following some of Jesus' sayings, he must even take his disciples aside to explain them (Mark 4:33–34). In this sense, parables *provoke a response* and lead us to probe deeper, to react in frustration, to depart perplexed, or to step nearer seeking answers.

One most interesting discovery in recent years has been a literary analysis of the parables. Scholars have shown that the parables not only use images and metaphors unique to the biblical period, but they employ a *poetic form* that made them poignant to hear and easy to retain. Some refer to the symmetry of the parables and how they provide repetitive structures that enhance the parable's interest. In some cases it is a simple reversal, such as we find in Mark 2:27. Note how the terms "Sabbath" and "people" reverse order, forming an X like a Greek letter *chi* (giving this form the title, *chiasmus*).

The *Sabbath* was made for *people*,
not *people* for the *Sabbath*.

THE PARABOLIC SAYINGS OF JESUS

Jesus' ministry was characterized by his use of parables and imagery. The following list sets out the synoptic parables organized by the periods of Jesus' ministry. In John's gospel Jesus does employ imagery and metaphor (4:1–42; 10:1–42; 15:1–16) but nothing similar to the synoptic parables.[4] (Where available, parables in the *Gospel of Thomas* are listed for comparison.)

The Sermon on the Mount (Matthew)

The salt of the earth (Matt. 5:13; Mark 9:49–50; Luke 14:34–35)

The light of the world (Matt. 5:14–15; Mark 4:21; Luke 8:16; cf. 11:33; John 8:12)

On treasures (Matt. 6:19–21; Luke 12:33–34; cf. 16:9)

The sound eye (Matt. 6:22–23; Luke 11:34–36)

On serving two masters (Matt. 6:24; Luke 16:13)

The birds of the air and the lilies of the field (Matt. 6:26–30; Luke 12:24–28)

The speck in the eye (Matt. 7:3, 5; Luke 6:41–42; cf. *Thomas* 27)

On profaning the holy (Matt. 7:6)

The two ways (Matt. 7:13–14; Luke 13:23–24)

The wolves in sheep's clothing (Matt. 7:15–20; cf. 3:10; Luke 6:43–45; cf. 3:9)

The house built on the rock (Matt. 7:24–27; Luke 6:47–49)

Galilean Ministry

The harvest is great (Matt. 9:35–38; cf. 4:23; 14:14; Mark 6:6, 34; Luke 8:1; 10:2; John 4:35)

The two debtors (Luke 7:41–43)

He who has ears to hear, let him hear (Matt. 11:15; 13:9, 43; Mark 4:9, 23; Luke 8:8; 14:35)

The sign of Jonah (Matt. 12:38–42; 16:1–4; Mark 8:11–12; Luke 11:16, 19–32; John 6:30)

The parable of the sower (Matt. 13:1–9; Mark 4:1–9; Luke 8:4–8; cf. *Thomas* 8)

The reason for speaking in parables (Matt. 13:10–17; Mark 4:10ff., 25; Luke 8:9f., 18; John 9:39)

The interpretation of the parable of the sower (Matt. 13:18–23; Mark 4:13–20; Luke 8:11–15)

Jesus' true family (Matt. 12:46–50; cf. 7:21; Mark 3:20–21, 31–35; Luke 8:19–21; John 15:14)

The seed growing secretly (Mark 4:26–29)

The wheat and the weeds (Matt. 13:24–30)

The mustard seed (Matt. 13:31–32.; Mark 4:30–32; Luke 13:18–19; cf. *Thomas* 20)

The leaven (Matt. 13:33; Luke 13:20–21)

Jesus' use of parables (Matt. 13:34–35; Mark 4:33–34)

The interpretation of the parable of the weeds (Matt. 13:36–43)

The hidden treasure and the pearl of great price (Matt. 13:44ff.)

The fish net (Matt. 13:47–50)

Treasures old and new (Matt. 13:51f.)

The unforgiving servant (Matt. 18:23–35)

On the Way to Jerusalem (Luke)

The good Samaritan (Luke 10:29–37)

The friend at midnight (Luke 11:5–8)

Light (Luke 11:33; cf. 8:16; Matt. 5:15; Mark 4:21)

The sound eye (Luke 11:34–36; Matt. 6:22–23)

The rich fool (Luke 12:16–21; cf. *Thomas* 64)

On treasures (Luke 12:33f.)

The barren fig tree (Luke 13:1–9; cf. Matt. 21:18–19; Mark 11:12–14)

The mustard seed (Luke 13:18–19; Matt. 13:31–32; Mark 4:30–32)

The leaven (Luke 13:20–21; Matt. 13:33)

The great supper (Luke 14:15–24; cf. Matt. 22:1–14)

The cost of building a tower and going to war (Luke 14:28–33)

Salt (Luke 14:34–35; Matt. 5:13; Mark 9:49–50)

The lost sheep (Luke 15:1–7)

The lost coin (Luke 15:8–10)

The lost (prodigal) son (Luke 15:11–32)

The unjust steward (Luke 16:1–9)

On serving two masters (Luke 16:13; Matt. 6:24)

The rich man and Lazarus (Luke 16:19–31)

On being unprofitable servants (Luke 17:7–10)

The unjust judge (Luke 18:1–8)

The Pharisee and the tax collector (Luke 18:9–14)

Ministry in Judea

On riches (Matt. 19:23–30; Mark 10:23–31; Luke 18:24–30)

The laborers in the vineyard (Matt. 20:1–16)

The pounds (Luke 19:11–27; cf. Matt. 25:14–40; Mark 13:34)

Final Ministry in Jerusalem

The two sons (Matt. 21:28–32)

The vineyard and the laborers (Matt. 21:33–46; Mark 12:1–12; Luke 20:9–19; *Thomas* 66)

The great supper (Matt. 22:1–14)

The poor widow (Mark 12:41–44; Luke 21:1–4)

The fig tree (Matt. 24:32–36; Mark 13:28–32; Luke 21:29–33)

The exhortation to watch (Mark 13:33–37; cf. Matt. 25:13–15; Luke 19:19–19; 21:34–36)

The flood, watching, and the thief in the night (Matt. 24:37–44; Luke 17:26–36; 12:39–40; cf. Mark 13:35)

The good and wicked servants (Matt. 24:45–51; cf. 25:21; Luke 12:41–46; cf. 19:17)

The ten virgins (Matt. 25:1–13; cf. Mark 13:33–37; Luke 12:35–38; 13:25–28)

The talents (Matt. 25:14–30; cf. Mark 13:34; Luke 19:11–27)

The sheep and the goats (Matt. 25:31–46)

Another form can be found in Luke 11:9–10. In each paragraph, the words "ask," "seek," and "knock" provide an artful symmetry:

1 *Ask* and it will be given to you;

　2 *Seek* and you will find;

　　3 *Knock* and the door will be opened to you.

1' For everyone who *asks* receives;

　2' those who *seek* find;

　　3' and to those who *knock*, the door will be opened.

In the parable of the lost sheep (Luke 15:4–7) three lines frame a series that invert their themes. As generally happens, the central idea of the structure is found in the turning point: God's celebration of the one who is lost.[5]

A What one of you, having a hundred sheep

B and having lost one of them

C does not leave the ninety-nine in the wilderness

　1 and go after the *lost* on

　　2 until he *finds* it, and having *found* it

　　　3 he places it upon his shoulders *rejoicing*

　　　　4 And coming *to the home*

　　　　4' he calls *to the friends* and neighbors

　　　3' saying to them, *rejoice* with me

　　2' because I have *found* my sheep

　1' which was *lost*.

A' I say to you that thus there is more joy in heaven

B' over one sinner who repents

C' than over ninety-nine righteous persons who need no repentance.

There is considerable discussion among scholars on how to interpret the parables. Our instinct to allegorize each of them down to the smallest detail has now been rejected. Many recent scholars have emphasized that at the heart of each parable lies a crisis—a point or points of stark contrast that shock us, forcing us to make a value judgment on a theme or character. For instance, the foolish barn builder seems to be living with God's blessing evidenced by his material wealth, until suddenly he hears God's voice, "You fool! This very night your life will be demanded from you" (Luke 12:20). Suddenly we are surprised, forced to realign our thinking.

Some of the parables do have allegorical elements (e.g., the parable of the sower), but this is secondary to the crisis of decision. Moreover, the most important issue is to understand the cultural elements at work in each parable. These are stories told from another culture and time, and we read them as foreigners. What does it mean when a young son asks for his inheritance? Or when a coin is lost? The parables are like music being played out with rhythms from another world. If we cannot recognize this music—or worse yet, if we fail even to admit our own foreignness to its sounds—we will miss their deeper meanings and misrepresent what Jesus intended to teach.

THEMES IN JESUS' TEACHING
The Kingdom of God

The primary theme of Jesus' teaching was his announcement of the arrival of God's kingdom (Mark 1:15). This topic was at the center of his teaching (Matt. 4:17, 23; Mark 1:15; Luke 9:11; Acts 1:3). The phrase "kingdom of God" or "kingdom of heaven" (which are synonyms) occurs with marked frequency in each gospel (Matthew 55x, Mark 20x, Luke 46x, John 5x). If we account for parallel sayings, we have about eighty separate sayings where Jesus teaches about his kingdom.

But what was this kingdom? Was it a political entity that might compete with Roman rule? Did it imply a revolution? Roman bureaucrats were familiar with provincial kingdoms, and if Jesus' kingdom was tied to nationalism and political resistance, it would be immediately suppressed. Or was this kingdom a heavenly reality whose benefits were only spiritually available—either now or sometime after death?

The notion that God ruled and sustained the universe was commonplace in Jewish thinking (Ps. 22:28). Above all, he was deemed the only rightful king of his people (Ps. 47), whose throne was located in Jerusalem (Ps. 48). But the Old Testament prophets also looked forward to a future period when God's kingdom would be asserted with determination—when Israel's enemies would be vanquished (Isa. 34:12), exiles would come home (52:7–12), and an everlasting kingdom would be established in Jerusalem (Zech. 14:9–17).

In northern Israel (Qasrin), scholars have created models of residential life in 4th century Israel (a period similar culturally to the 1st century). Here an oven for baking bread stands inside a Jewish home.

Many of Jesus' most dramatic teachings took place when he arrived in Jerusalem and entered the temple. The excavation of Herodian Jerusalem uncovered these first-century stairs on the south side of the temple which were in heavy use during Jesus' lifetime.

This *eschatological* (or "climactic") coming was felt fervently in Jesus' era and gave birth to an entire literature devoted to explaining it. Such *apocalyptic* literature (e.g., *Jubilees, 1 Enoch, Psalms of Solomon*) announced the *imminent* conclusion to world history and a dramatic in-breaking of God's rule. The sectarian Jews in the deserts of Qumran, for example, anticipated that God would soon come in power to lead them in victory (see sidebar on "God's War Plans," p. 158).

Jesus' affirmation of God's sustaining care of the universe came as no surprise to his Jewish audiences (Matt. 6:25 – 34). Nor did it surprise them when he spoke about the kingdom as an experience in heaven, meant for those who would banquet after death with God's people of old (Matt. 8:11 – 12; Mark 10:17 – 30). Even Jesus looked forward to this time (Luke 22:16, 18). When he arrived in Jerusalem on his final visit, the crowds thought that his coming would be a catalyst for the birth of this kingdom (Mark 11:10; Luke 19:11). But they were wrong. Jesus believed that such a final judgment would only come with his own second coming in power (Mark 8:38; 13:26; 14:62; Luke 17:24 – 30).

What set Jesus apart from others in Judaism was his announcement that something dramatic and epochal was happening *in the present*, that in some way not foreseen the rule of God's kingdom was *now taking hold of the world*. He tells his followers that the kingdom is

JESUS' POLITICS ARE TESTED

Jesus' frequent discussion about a "kingdom" led some to worry about his political aspirations. After he fed five thousand people in Mark 6, even Herod Antipas began making worried inquiries about him.

On his last visit to Jerusalem, assistants to the temple leadership disguised themselves as disciples and approached Jesus in public, asking him: "What is your opinion? Is it right to pay taxes to Caesar or not" (Matt. 22:17)? This question was not simply about tax revenue. It was a veiled political probe. One of the earliest revolts against Roman rule used the refusal to pay taxes as a form of resistance. Thus we can reframe the question: "Teacher, do you support the Jewish resistance against Rome?" Read Matt. 22:18 – 22 to see how artfully Jesus disguises his answer.

MESSIANIC ZEAL

Some Jewish groups held a fervent expectation that God would send an anointed (Heb. "messiah") messenger who would be a catalyst for the arrival of God's rule on earth. He would end the Gentile occupation of Judea and bring about the resumption of the great kingdom of David (2 Sam. 7). The most explicit outline of this expectation can be found in the *Psalms of Solomon*, written within seventy-five years of Jesus' ministry:

See, Lord, and raise up for them their king, the son of David, to rule over your servant Israel.... Undergird him with the strength to destroy the unrighteous rulers, to purge Jerusalem from gentiles.... He will gather a holy people whom he will lead in righteousness.... He will distribute them upon the land according to their tribes; the alien and the foreigner will no longer live near them.... And he will have gentile nations serving him under his yoke, and he will glorify the Lord in (a place) prominent (above) the whole earth.... And he will be a righteous king over them, taught by God.... There will be no unrighteousness among them in his days, for all shall be holy, and their king shall be the Lord Messiah. (from *Psalms of Solomon* 17:21-32).[6]

something that can be entered (Matt. 5:20; 7:21), that people can now be "in" the kingdom (Matt. 13:41, 43), and that it is a gift to people (Luke 12:32). This kingdom was presently appearing (Luke 19:11).

Note, for example, in Matthew 12:28 (also Luke 11:20) how Jesus indicates that his defeat of a demon through an exorcism signals far more than a healing miracle; it unveils the power of his kingdom overturning Satan's power and breaking his grip on the world. An era had changed, and the relationship between God and the world would never be the same.

Jesus describes this kingdom as experiencing resistance and hostility (Matt. 11:12). When he sent his followers out to preach, the arrival of this new order was at the heart of their message (Matt. 10:5–7). In Luke 17:20–21, when Jesus fields a question about the coming kingdom and the end of the world, he gives an unexpected response: "The coming of the kingdom of God is not something that can be observed, nor will people say, 'Here it is,' or 'There it is,' because the kingdom of God is in your midst."

The advancement of this kingdom can best be seen in Jesus' so-called "parables of growth." Jesus compares kingdom growth to seed scattered on the ground that grows unexpectedly (Mark 4:26–29), to a mustard seed that begins small only to become a tremendous bush (4:30–32), or to yeast that spreads mysteriously through dough (Matt. 13:33). Since this kingdom has now made its arrival, judgment of the world has become inevitable. Weeds grow along with the wheat (Matt. 13:24–30), but at the climax of history, there will be a great "sorting out" when useless weeds are removed and judged.

Therefore, every person *must make a decision* whether or not to belong to this kingdom. Jesus is like a sower, and the only pertinent question is whether we permit this seed to germinate (Matt. 13:1–9). Have we discovered this kingdom as the

A woman in an Arab village near Hebron bakes traditional flatbread that likely reflects traditions that reach back to antiquity. "The kingdom of heaven is like yeast that a woman took and mixed into about sixty pounds of flour until it worked all through the dough" (Matt 13:33).

most precious thing we own, like a precious pearl sought for a lifetime or a treasure discovered by surprise (Matt. 13:44–46)?

In sum, Jesus altered the basic framework of Jewish eschatology. Rather than seeing the kingdom arrive in a climactic, definitive event, Jesus spoke of an interim state—the time of the church—when God's power would be active through the Spirit. The church still awaits its final redemption in Christ's second coming.

Discipleship in the Kingdom

In establishing his kingdom, Jesus formed around himself "disciples" whose main task was to obey him and his words. Jesus did not simply recall Jews to their traditions, admonishing them to greater faithfulness to Moses (though this was important, Matt. 5:17–18). Nor did he only promote a revival of wisdom or ethics (though this was important too, 5:19–20). He called men and women *to himself*. This is one of the distinct features that set Jesus apart from other rabbis of his day. People left their trades to become his followers (Mark 1:16–20) and were told that personal obedience to him and his words meant everything (Luke 6:46–49). Jesus was forming a self-conscious messianic community, where they would find qualities of forgiveness, generosity, love, and devotion absent in the rest of the world. They would transform the world.

Jesus formed this circle of followers from those who lived on the margins of society: tax collectors, sinners, prostitutes. He was willing to have direct contact with lepers and risk defilement (Mark 1:40–41), and with women, even if their illness would put his entire ministry in jeopardy (Luke 8:43–48). He sometimes answered his critics with parables reminding them that God was like a shepherd in search of a lost sheep or a woman in search of a lost coin (Luke 15:1–10)—or more powerfully, like a father scanning the horizon for his lost son (15:11–32). At other times he answered his critics with a proverb: "It is not the healthy who need a doctor, but the sick. I have not come to call the righteous, but sinners" (Mark 2:17).

Jesus' unique compassion for humanity was shaped by his unique vision of God as Father of everyone—sinner and pious, Jew, Samaritan, and Gentile. God is referred to as "Father" fifteen times in the Old Testament (e.g., Isa. 63:16), though these lacked a personal element. But this was Jesus' typical way of referring to God (in Mark 14:36 we even have the Aramaic term "*Abba*"). *Abba* was an informal word used generally by children for their fathers. Jesus' habit was so well known that even Greek-speaking Christians used *Abba* (Rom. 8:15–16; Gal 4:6).

Jewish disciples who had prayed their entire lives listened to Jesus and asked him to teach them to pray (Luke 11:1). His prayers were different. He did not pray in Hebrew or use the

Jesus used poignant images from local culture to depict his central teaching. God is like a shepherd, he taught, searching for and protecting his sheep (Luke 15:3-7; John 10:1-18).

stock liturgical phrases. His model prayer was an outline of intimate conversation with God (the Lord's Prayer; Matt. 6:7–15; Luke 11:2–4).

Similarly he told parables about prayer that emphasized God's eagerness to respond to our need (Luke 11:5–13); our only requirement is to come to him with humility (18:9–14). In a world where religious symbols were often on public display, Jesus called for profound authenticity in every spiritual endeavor. Public things like fasting and tithing should be hidden (Matt. 6:1–6, 16–18) while more difficult signs of faith, like reconciliation and love (5:23–24, 43–46), should hallmark his community.

The Ethics of the Kingdom

It would be a mistake to think that discipleship in this kingdom is only a matter of spiritual renewal and private devotion to Jesus. Jesus also sought a transformation in his followers' lives. Jesus taught that the reign of God, now empowered by the Spirit, would open new possibilities to human righteousness. Men and women are placed under the ethics of the kingdom and can live out those ethics through his Son. The seemingly impossible standards of the Sermon on the Mount can only portray "the ideal of the person in whose life the reign of God is absolutely realized."[7]

The starting point for these ethics is the righteousness of the inner life — a righteousness that ought to exceed that of the Pharisees (Matt. 5:20). Or more precisely, the starting point consists of a "renewed heart." Thus while adultery still remains a sin, Jesus calls us to curb lust (5:27–30). And while murder is condemned, anger must likewise be resolved (5:21–26). Love must be exhaustive, shown even to those who are enemies (see Luke 6:35). Jesus said, "But love your enemies, do good to them, and lend to them without expecting to get anything back. Then your reward will be great, and you will be children of the Most High, because he is kind to the ungrateful and wicked" (Luke 6:35). How else could such courageous decisions be lived except through a transforming encounter with God?

This is why at the heart of Jesus' teaching is a demand that his hearers make a critical decision, that they repent, turn, and become a disciple (Matt. 13:45–46). Any commitment that stands in the way must be jettisoned at once. The rich young ruler must give up his wealth (Mark 10:17–22). Suddenly Jesus' paradoxical statements come clear: Unless you lose your life, you really cannot find it (Matt. 10:39).

The first ethical demand of the kingdom is to love God wholly (Matt. 22:37–38). And the second follows it quickly: " 'Love your neighbor as yourself.' All the Law and the Prophets hang on these two commandments" (22:40). The ethics of Jesus thus spring from this encounter, and what one learns about God's affection, grace, and forgiveness must then be borne to others. To do otherwise will falsify one's claim to kingdom membership; it will fulfill the role of "hypocrite" (Luke 6:42).

When asked about the most important law, Jesus recited the great *Shema* recited twice each day and taken from Deut. 6 (see Matt 22:37-38). Shown here in Hebrew.

But to integrate religious experience into life means rethinking major questions of life: Who are my neighbors and what are my obligations to them (Luke 10:30–35)? How many times must I forgive (Matt. 18:21–22)? How much wealth may I collect (Luke 12:16–20)? These questions signal the dawning of the kingdom in the world. Lives lived under such discipleship will become "a light on a hill" that is visible for the entire world to see (cf. Matt. 5:14–16).

The Cross and the Kingdom

Once Jesus' public identity was confirmed among his disciples at Caesarea Philippi (Mark 8:27–30), the Gospels indicate that he chose to reframe his messiahship as a "way of the cross": "Whoever wants to be my disciple must deny themselves and take up their cross and follow me" (Matt. 16:24). Three times Jesus made predictions about dying, and each gained greater and greater detail. As he moved toward his final Jerusalem visit, his death became a prominent theme in his teaching, and the disciples became increasingly wary (Mark 10:32–33).

This expectation of death appeared early in Jesus' ministry. He once described himself as a bridegroom whose presence at his wedding banquet naturally led to feasting and celebration. But then, he added, "the time will come when the bridegroom will be *taken* from them, and on that day they will fast" (Mark 2:20). This verb "taken " (Gk. *apairō*) is a term for violent removal (such as kidnapping; cf. Isa. 53:8). Not long after saying this, Jesus found himself in conflict with some of the Pharisees who were dismayed at his violation of Sabbath law. In an exquisite example of foreshadowing, Mark tells us that immediately these men went out and plotted how they might kill him (Mark 3:6).

Once in Jerusalem during his final week, Jesus offered one of his most important parables to explain his approaching death (Matt. 21:33–46; Mark 12:1–12; Luke 20:9–19). This story describes a vineyard whose tenants refuse to give its owner the rightful portion of the vineyard's yield. The owner sends couriers to the tenants, but they are rejected. Then he sends his son. Thinking that if they kill the owner's heir they might gain the vineyard for themselves, the son is expelled from the vineyard and murdered. The imagery of a vineyard and frustrated expectation comes directly from Isaiah 5:1–7. God had sent his prophets repeatedly to call for "fruit" from his people and now judgment must result. Here Jesus poignantly shows that his own mission is that of the final Son, whose death brings tremendous offense to God himself.

But Jesus' death in the Gospels is not an accident. He knew he was accomplishing something purposeful for the kingdom he was establishing. We hear this first from John the Baptist, who introduces Jesus publicly with the words: "Look, the Lamb of God, who takes away the sin of the world" (John 1:29). Jesus' life will end with a voluntary death, a sacrificial death, no different than the lamb sacrificed each day at the temple.

Following his third and final prediction of the cross (Mark 10:33–34), a quarrel broke out about greatness in the kingdom. James and John wanted places of

Scholars at the Tantur Ecumenical Institute near Bethlehem here attempt to reconstruct the cross as it may have been seen in antiquity.

honor among the twelve apostles. Jesus corrected their presumptuous quest for prestige: "The Son of Man did not come to be served, but to serve, and to give his life *as a ransom* for many" (Mark 10:45; cf. John 6:51). Here Jesus is explaining the meaning of his death as a "ransom" (Gk. *lytron*). This was a payment that in some manner freed a captive. Jesus here suggests that his death will supply some substitution, some exchange for others in jeopardy. Jesus may well have had in mind the poignant image of the Suffering Servant of Isaiah 53:11.

Perhaps the most profound hours of teaching came when Jesus gathered with his apostles for a last Passover meal. Despite the distress of this crisis, he taught them carefully about his own return (John 16:16–24), the promise of the Holy Spirit who would comfort and equip them (14:16, 26; 15:26; 16:13), the impending persecution that would follow (15:18–27), and the quality of love that should characterize the community of believers (13:34–35; 15:12–17). During this meal, he picked up a loaf of bread, broke it, and ceremonially named it as representing his body: " 'This is my body given for you; do this in remembrance of me.' In the same way, after the supper he took the cup, saying, 'This cup is the new covenant in my blood' " (Luke 22:19–20).

Each of Israel's covenants had been established with the shedding of blood (Ex. 24:1–10). Even the Exodus required the sacrificial death of a lamb (12:22–23). Now Jesus intimated that his death was such a sacrifice and that it would establish a new covenant for this new kingdom. The earliest Christians saw profound symbolism in Jesus' crucifixion. *He was a Passover lamb slain for God's people.* John reports that when Jesus was on the cross, his legs were not broken, just like the Passover lamb (John 19:36; cf. Num. 9:12). When Jesus was cut with a spear (John 19:34), blood flowed freely from his side, fulfilling yet another requirement of slain lambs (that their blood flow freely, Mishnah, *Hullin* 2:6).

Grape production was common in the first century. Using the imagery from Isaiah 5, Jesus compared Israel with a tended vineyard (Mark 12:1-12).

Ancient Roman pottery such as this discovered in Jerusalem likely served the final Passover of Jesus. "After taking the cup he gave thanks and said, 'Take this...'" (Lk 22:17).

Christology

The accelerating revelation of who Jesus was in his earthly ministry climaxed with the resurrection. At once his followers needed new categories to understand him. In John's language, he had been "glorified" (John 12:23; 21:19), and the cross, rather than a place of abandonment and shame, could be seen as a "lifting up" as he began his movement back to the Father (John 8:28; 12:32, 34). This reflection no doubt prompted the earliest Christians to think about the events in Jesus' life from a new vantage. In this sense, the resurrection forced the question of Christology and made the church probe his earthly life (his miracles, his sayings, his deeds) as well as his birth, exploring them for signs of his true identity.

For example, Jesus once prayed the following:

> "I praise you, Father, Lord of heaven and earth, because you have hidden these things from the wise and learned, and revealed them to little children. Yes, Father, for this was your good pleasure.
>
> "All things have been committed to me by my Father. No one knows the Son except the Father, and no one knows the Father except the Son and those to whom the Son chooses to reveal him." (Matt. 11:25 – 27)

Jesus' own self-understanding thus included a keen awareness of his unique place with God, a place shared by no other human. Suddenly Jesus' uncanny authority began to move into focus, as did his uncompromising victory over Satan. The people then understood that in him was something far greater than they ever imagined possible.

How did Jesus exhibit this understanding of his role with God? For one, he often assumed divine prerogatives. For example, when he forgave the sins of a paralytic, the scribes immediately took offense: "Who can forgive sins but God alone" (Mark 2:7). He repeated this with a marginalized woman who tried to rescue him at a hostile banquet, and again the Jewish leaders became angry (Luke 7:49). Jesus also viewed himself fulfilling roles reserved for God. He saw himself as God seeking out lost sheep (Luke 15:3 – 7). He defended breaking the Sabbath to heal a man by arguing that such work God himself was doing through him (John 5:1 – 24).

Jesus even cited the Old Testament law and followed such citations with a predictable formula: "You have heard that it was said . . . but I tell you . . ." (Matt. 5:22, 28, 32, 34, 39, 44). When he taught, he reinforced his sayings with a finality that had no parallel in Judaism. He prefaced them with a phrase, "I tell you the truth" (NIV) or "truly" (TNIV, RSV, NRSV). This translates the word *amēn*, a Hebrew term that means "surely" or "firmly."

Was it not enough to follow and obey Jesus? Was it necessary to embrace some commitment to *who he was*? Matthew and Luke offer nativity stories that give us important hints that in the virgin birth we have evidence of a person who exceeds the role of the average child. God was at work in his birth in unprecedented ways. Mark begins his gospel with an affirmation that his record tells not simply the gospel, but the "good news about Jesus the Messiah" (Mark 1:1). Of course this is Mark's own confession of faith, but it signals to his readers that the story he is about to tell us is about a man whose identity rests with God.

What the Synoptic Gospels record with subtlety, John's gospel makes explicit. Not only does John's Jesus evoke all of the synoptic hints of unique identity, but Jesus himself explains how his person and work stem directly from God. Jesus once said, "The words I say to you I do not speak on my own authority. Rather, it is the Father, living in me, who is doing his work" (John 14:10).

The gospel writers give us clues to Jesus' identity through the list of titles that appear throughout their stories. For us to understand him we must understand these carefully in their own original context. (1) *Messiah* is a transliteration of the Hebrew *mashiach* and refers to "the anointed one," a title used in the Old Testament to describe kings and prophets — and in the intertestamental period, an "anointed king" who would usher in the eschatological kingdom of Israel. This term was translated into Greek as "Christ."

(2) *Son of God* (or Son) was another Old Testament title used for Israel's kings as well as heavenly beings such as angels. It was associated with the coming Messiah, and in the Gospels it lays claim to Jesus' intimate and unparalleled relationship with the Father.

(3) Jesus' favorite self-designation was *Son of Man* (found 69x in the Synoptic Gospels and 13x in John). In Hebrew the phrase simply meant "man," but in Daniel 7:13 and elsewhere in early Judaism it likely took on a specialized use for a celestial figure (e.g., *1 Enoch* 46:4; 48:2; 62:9, 11; 71:17).

Jesus' call to discipleship demanded a serious commitment. "No one who puts a hand to the plow and looks back is fit for service in the kingdom of God," Luke 9:62. This Palestinian farmer demonstrates the plowing technique of antiquity.

Each of these titles have been studied at length. They help clarify Jesus' identity. Each gospel writer sought to explain who Jesus was. And in some cases, Jesus' true self exceeded their ability to describe him.

1. What are the essential elements in Jesus' conflict with the Pharisees and the scribes? What fundamental theological ideas did they find in him that were unnerving?

2. What is the relationship between the "kingdom" announced by Jesus and the church that we experience from day to day?

3. What are some guidelines that will assure us that when we interpret a parable, we will not misrepresent Jesus' intention?

4. Why are Jesus' ethical teachings so popular—even among those who profess no faith in Christ?

5. Jesus' serious ethical demands are sometimes sharply contrasted with Paul's emphasis on grace. Is there a way to synthesize these emphases?

BIBLIOGRAPHY
Introductory

Bailey, K. E. *Poet and Peasant* and *Through Peasant Eyes: A Literary Cultural Approach to the Parables in Luke*. Combined ed. Grand Rapids: Eerdmans, 1983.

Blomberg, C. *Interpreting the Parables*. Downers Grove, IL: InterVarsity Press, 1990.

Green, J., S. McKnight, and I. H. Marshall. *Dictionary of Jesus and the Gospels*. Downers Grove, IL: InterVarsity Press, 1992.

Advanced

Dunn, J. D. G. *Jesus Remembered*. Grand Rapids: Eerdmans, 2003.

Ladd, G. E. *A Theology of the New Testament*. Grand Rapids: Eerdmans, 1974, 1993.

Wright, N. T. *Jesus and the Victory of God*. Minneapolis: Fortress, 1996.

NOTES

1. K. E. Bailey, "Jesus the Metaphorical Theologian and the Rabbinic World," in *Jacob and the Prodigal: How Jesus Retold Israel's Story* (Downers Grove, IL: InterVarsity Press, 2003), 21–22.

2. S. Safrai, "Religion in Everyday Life," in S. Safrai and M. Stern, eds., *The Jewish People in the First Century* (Philadelphia: Fortress, 1976), 2:803–4.

3. D. Daube, "Rabbinic Authority," in *The New Testament and Rabbinic Judaism* (London: Athone, 1956), 207.

4. C. Brown, ed., *The New International Dictionary of New Testament Theology* (Grand Rapids: Zondervan, 1976), 2:749–51.

5. K. E. Bailey, *Finding the Lost: Cultural Keys to Luke 15* (St. Louis: Concordia, 1989). Bailey also does this for the parable of the lost son. The translation here is formal.

6. J.H. Charlesworth, ed., *The Old Testament Pseudepigrapha*, (Garden City, NY: Doubleday, 1983), 2:667.

7. G. Ladd, *A Theology of the New Testament* (Grand Rapids: Eerdmans, 1993), 127; N. T. Wright, *Jesus and the Victory of God* (Minneapolis: Fortress, 1996), 282–87.

CHAPTER 8

THE GOSPEL ACCORDING TO MATTHEW

Jesus taught in coves such as this on Galilee's north shore. On occasion he taught from a boat using the cove as a natural theater (Matt 13:2).

As the opening book of the New Testament, the early church gave Matthew's gospel deep respect for centuries. It came from the pen of an apostle and reflected an intimate acquaintance with the Jewish customs of Jesus. In the early second century, Papias, the bishop of Hierapolis, said Matthew was the first to record Jesus' story (Eusebius, *Eccl. Hist.* 3.39.16). Augustine elevated Matthew above the other canonical Gospels and for a thousand years Matthew's priority was taken for granted (see Ch. 5).

Matthew offers stories that set his gospel apart, such as the familiar Christmas story of the Magi bringing gifts to Jesus and Herod the Great's plan to kill this new "king." The compelling ethics of the Sermon on the Mount — a compendium of Jesus' wise and parabolic sayings — has been studied as a gateway into Jesus' innermost thoughts about loving God and discipleship.

Matthew's audience was primarily Jewish, so he addressed issues close to the Jewish heart. Jesus respected the law and claimed to fulfill it. Matthew's cadence flows between teaching and action. Scripture continues to be fulfilled, and God's plan is not frustrated *despite Jesus' death on the cross.* Jesus rises from the tomb, thereby vindicating his messiahship through the resurrection.

ANCIENT ANTIOCH

Ancient Antioch (possibly where Matthew's readers lived) stood adjacent to the important Orontes River. With its port Seleucia, it stood at a strategic gateway: Commerce traveling from Italy or Greece could enter here and continue east, moving down the Euphrates River to Babylon, up the Orontes into central Lebanon, or overland to Damascus.

Antioch had been the capital of the Seleucid Empire. In New Testament times it was well networked to the entire Roman Empire. It is not surprising that an important church grew here. Following the destruction of Jerusalem in AD 70, Antioch became a leading city of Christianity for five hundred years.

Very little of ancient Antioch has been discovered, for the modern city of Antakya sits on the ancient site.

THE SETTING OF MATTHEW'S GOSPEL

Because Matthew exhibits a keen interest on matters of Jewish law and custom, many scholars believe this gospel originated either in Palestine or Syria. When Papias said Matthew wrote in the Hebrew "dialect" (Gk. *dialecto*), many suggest he was not referring to the Hebrew language but a Hebrew writing style. Matthew shows no clear signs of being translated from Hebrew to Greek, but indications of "Hebraic style" abound. This gospel, then, may have come from a Jewish Christian group anchored within a larger Jewish community, such as Syrian Antioch.

MATTHEW'S RELATIONSHIP TO JUDAISM

Matthew likely writes his gospel after the failed First Jewish Revolt; as such, it reflects the issues of devastation and renewal. Matthew selects stories about Jesus that speak powerfully to his context in history. For example, Matthew likely debated with other Jews about the validity of Jesus' interpretation of the law. He gathers up numerous stories about Jesus' interaction with Jewish leaders and through them explains Jesus' teachings and directives for his followers.

Note the watchtower in the olive grove and vineyard. The caretakers of the vineyard would stand guard over the property from the tower. In Jesus' parable, the tenants observe the son, perhaps from their watchtower, and plot the latter's destruction.

Some have suggested that Matthew's theology harshly rejects Judaism in favor of the church. But the focus of his criticism is on Jerusalem's leadership and their inadequate understanding of God's law. Matthew makes it clear that Jesus was Jewish, as was each of his apostles. Matthew is hardly rejecting Judaism.

In Matthew's gospel, Jesus redefines God's people to include both Jews and Gentiles who believe his message. But this does not mean Matthew is shy about recording Jesus' prophetic criticism of his own people. His parable of the tenants and the vineyard (21:33–46) retells Isaiah's famous song of the vineyard (Isa. 5), where Israel is described as a vineyard cultivated and protected by God. In Jesus' story, the tenants kill the vineyard owner's son in a futile attempt to inherit the property. The owner will return and give it to "others" who will yield good fruit. The Jewish leaders realize that Jesus is speaking about them (21:45). New leaders are necessary for Israel; Jesus and his disciples are that new leadership.

THE LITERARY FORM OF MATTHEW'S GOSPEL

Studies of Matthew have frequently noted its symmetry, for the gospel's story alternates between narrative and discourse. Matthew gathers Jesus' teachings into five sections: the Sermon on the Mount (chs. 5–7), the Missionary Discourse (ch. 10), the Parables of the Kingdom (ch. 13), the Church and the Kingdom (ch. 18), and the Judgment Discourse (chs. 24–25). Each segment concludes with the phrase, "when Jesus had finished saying these things." Some even suggest that in Matthew, Jesus is the new Moses for Judaism, who offers a new "Torah" (*Torah* is Genesis to Deuteronomy, written by Moses).

Yet to focus solely on the five discourses minimizes the importance of Matthew's record of Jesus' birth and death. Clearly Matthew wants to emphasize how Jesus fulfills Old Testament prophecies in his birth and death. In chapters 1–2 alone, Jesus is described as fulfilling five prophecies. Matthew's Passion narrative is indispensable to understanding Jesus as Messiah, his authority, and even his intentions in building his church. Matthew's portrait of Jesus is driven by a theological conviction that in Jesus Christ, God has revealed his plan of salvation for all peoples.

OUTLINE OF MATTHEW'S GOSPEL

I. Prologue (1:1–2:23)

A. Genealogy (1:1–17)
B. Birth Narrative (1:18–2:23)

II. Introduction to Jesus' Ministry (3:1–4:11)

A. Jesus' Baptism (3:1–16)
B. Jesus' Temptations (4:1–11)

III. Jesus' Galilean Ministry (4:12–18:35)

A. Narrative: Call of Repentance (4:12–44)
B. Discourse: Sermon on the Mount (5:1–7:29)
C. Narrative: Jesus' Ministry and Miracles (8:1–9:35)
D. Discourse: Missionary Discourse (9:36–11:1)
E. Narrative: Jesus' Ministry and Teachings (11:2–12:50)
F. Discourse: Parables of the Kingdom Discourse (13:1–53)
G. Narrative: Jesus withdraws from Galilee (14:1–17:20)
H. Discourse: Kingdom of Heaven Discourse (18:1–35)

IV. Jesus' Jerusalem Ministry (19:1–28:20)

A. Narrative: Jesus' Instructions for Christian Life (19:1–22:46)
B. Discourse: Judgment Discourse (23:1–25:46)
C. Narrative: Jesus' Passion and Resurrection (26:1–28:20)
   1. The Last Supper (26:1–35)
   2. Jesus' Arrest and Trial (26:36–27:26)
   3. Jesus' Crucifixion and Resurrection (27:27–28:20)

THE GENEALOGY OF JESUS IN MATTHEW AND LUKE

Matthew begins his gospel with the genealogy of Jesus (1:1–17). Luke also includes a genealogy (Luke 3:23–38). Judaism had a keen interest in genealogies because proof of priestly and royal lineage brought privilege and power (Ezra 2:62). Herod the Great once burned the archives of Jewish families in Jerusalem, fearing that some would claim his throne based on Davidic ancestry. Jews also speculated on the lineage of the Messiah. Some believed his heritage would be priestly and others that he would come from the line of David. Matthew's and Luke's selective genealogies send a spiritual message: Jesus bears the line of David (and thus qualifies to be the Messiah), Jesus is genuinely linked to the human race (and so can be called the Son of Adam), and Jesus likewise is the Son of God.

How do we account for the differences of names in Matthew's and Luke's genealogies? Some have argued that both lists belong to Joseph—one traces his biological ancestry, the other his legal ancestry. Others have argued that Luke gives the genealogy of Mary and

Matthew speaks of Jesus' birth and first months of life in Bethlehem.

Matthew that of Joseph (cf. Luke 3:23, Jesus "was the son *as was supposed* of Joseph," NRSV). A variation of this second view states that Mary had no brothers and her father Eli *adopted* Joseph to be his heir, but we have no evidence for this.

MATTHEW'S STORY OF JESUS
Prologue and Introduction (1:1 – 2:23)

The story of Jesus' birth in Bethlehem is filled with intrigue. An angel appears to Joseph and explains that the child Mary is carrying is "from the Holy Spirit" (1:20). This child is nothing less than the fulfillment of God's design, for a prophet had spoken generations ago that "a virgin will conceive and give birth to a son, and they will call him Immanuel" (1:23; see Isa. 7:14). Four more times in the birth stories, Matthew refers to prophecy being fulfilled: Jesus' birth in Bethlehem (2:6 – 7; cf. Mic. 5:2); King Herod's murdering infants in Bethlehem (2:17 – 18; cf. Jer. 31:15); Jesus' family's return from Egypt (2:15; cf. Hos. 11:1); and Jesus' childhood in Nazareth (2:23; cf. Judg. 13:5 or Isa. 11:1).

Above all, Matthew finds in Moses' young life the template for how Jesus' life begins. Moses and Jesus both narrowly escape an attempt on their lives not long after birth. Rulers who abused God's people pursued both children. Moses and Jesus are called from Egypt—and each of them possesses a saving mission for God's people. The comparison with Moses continues in Matthew's gospel.

FULFILLING THE SCRIPTURES

Matthew has been chided for finding fulfillment where there is none—for example, how could Hosea possibly have been referring to Jesus' life when he writes "out of Egypt I have called my son" (Matt 2:15)? Was Matthew grasping at straws to bolster his argument that Jesus fulfills God's promises?

Other scholars delve more deeply into Matthew's purpose. Because modern readers today tend to think that a prophecy can have only one historic fulfillment and must be tied closely to its original context, they miss what Matthew is doing. Matthew is not thinking merely of one sentence in Hosea 11:1, but is recalling the entire context, wherein Hosea speaks of God's compassion to the wayward Israel and God's promise to "settle them in their homes" (Hos. 11:11). The promise of a new exodus, which brings God's people into the kingdom of heaven, is the picture Matthew is creating for his readers by recounting Jesus' departure from Egypt.

JESUS AS GOD'S SPECIAL CLIENT

In the ancient world, the relationship of "patron" and "client" was critical (see discussion in Ch. 4). At Jesus' baptism, God reveals himself as Jesus' patron, for he announces that Jesus is due special honors as God's Son. The people's proper response is to acknowledge Jesus' high status by honoring him or risk the wrath of his Patron. In other words, to honor Jesus is to honor God. To reject Jesus is likewise to reject God.

In this relationship of patronage, Jesus is given special opportunities. He alone possesses unique knowledge (see 11:27) and is given unique powers (see 28:18). Because of the honor bestowed on Jesus by his Father-Patron, all should give Jesus praise and admiration.

At the end of his ministry, Jesus views his disciples as *his* special clients. If the public honors them, then also Jesus, their patron, will be honored. Note 25:40: "Whatever you did for one of the least of these brothers and sisters of mine, you did for me."

Jesus' Baptism in Matthew's Gospel (3:1–4:11)

John hesitates to baptize Jesus because he recognizes Jesus' superiority. But Jesus insists that John baptize him "to fulfill all righteousness" (3:15). What does Jesus mean? John himself recognized that Jesus does not need a baptism of repentance. But Jesus insists on being baptized because he is starting his public ministry. He knows that the Holy Spirit, which alights on him at baptism, will consecrate him as he begins to teach and to heal. Jesus hears God confirm that ministry: "This is my Son, whom I love; with him I am well pleased" (3:17). Jesus identifies himself with all people and their need for forgiveness.

GALILEE'S NATURAL AMPHITHEATERS

How did Jesus speak to such large audiences in Galilee? Scholars who have studied the region around Capernaum note that its coves form natural amphitheaters where crowds could sit and listen to Jesus standing near the shore. Evidence within Matthew for this may come from Jesus' occasional decision to teach from a boat anchored in the cove (13:2).

Jesus' Galilean Ministry in Matthew's Gospel (4:12–18:35)

After John is arrested (4:12), Jesus leaves the region of the Jordan. Probably the danger posed by Herod Antipas (who arrested John) threatens Jesus as well. When Jesus reaches Galilee, he leaves his home in Nazareth and settles in Capernaum, a fishing village on the Sea of Galilee's north shore. He then gathers disciples and quickly establishes a reputation as a healer of every disease. Soon his name was known throughout Galilee and southern Syria, where he travels and preaches in synagogues about "the good news of the kingdom" (4:23).

The opening event in Matthew is the "Sermon on the Mount" (chs. 5–7). Vast crowds follow Jesus, so he moves to a hillside to address them. The parallel with Moses is striking. Moses ascended a mountain, where God met him and revealed to him the Ten Commandments. Jesus does something similar, as he teaches his "beatitudes" (5:3–12). In this case, however, the people join him on the mountain rather than wait below as they did for Moses (Ex. 19). Matthew creates a picture of direct access to God's revelation.

Jesus' voice carried well to the large groups who followed him because he used Galilee's natural amphitheaters to present his message.

Matthew details Jesus' teachings that juxtapose his word with that of Moses. For example, Jesus says, "You have heard that it was said"—then he cites a law, "You shall not commit adultery." This is followed by a teaching formula, "But I tell you"—and an interpretation, "Anyone who looks at a woman lustfully has already committed adultery with her in his heart" (Matt. 5:27–28). Again and again Jesus reinterprets the law, not abrogating its place but driving to its very heart.

Among the Pharisees the pursuit of righteousness and purity was critical. The Mishnah (ca. 200) contains almost two hundred pages in a modern translation on provisions for purity. These debates cover issues such as the proper way to wash hands before meals and making kosher meals. In the Pharisees' intense emphasis on purity, Jesus claims that concern for the well-being of others took a backseat. Jesus teaches that righteousness includes mercy toward others and the pursuit of social justice (25:31–46).

Jesus practices what he teaches. After he descends the mountain and enters Capernaum, his call to generosity, even to one's enemies, is displayed in his healing of the Roman centurion's slave. The powerful words he preached on the mountain come to life in his calming the storm (8:23–27), his healing of the Gadarene demoniacs

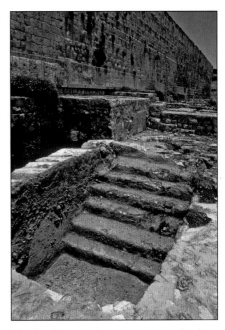

Ritual purity was an important concern for those Jews living in Jerusalem, in the vicinity of the temple of God. Today, many Jewish women use a purification bath or mikvah after their monthly period.

(8:28–43), and his bringing to life the daughter of the synagogue leader (9:18–26). Having demonstrated his power over forces of nature, illness, and even death, Jesus asks the disciples to do the same. Matthew 10 records Jesus' lengthy teaching to the disciples about what hardships they will face as his emissaries. He presents them with a daunting task of preaching the gospel at great personal cost. Yet he also promises: "Whoever publicly acknowledges me I will also acknowledge before my Father in heaven" (10:32).

After instructing the twelve disciples about their "mission," Jesus continues to preach and teach in Galilean cities. Jesus chastises the crowds for their fickleness in rejecting John as too ascetic and dismissing Jesus as a glutton and drunkard (11:19). The Pharisees' frustration over Jesus and his disciples eating from grain fields on the Sabbath reveals the same lack of perception. Jesus charges them with failing to understand God's true desire in the law: "mercy, not sacrifice" (12:7; cf. also 9:13).

A central theme in Jesus' teachings is the kingdom of heaven. In chapter 13 he speaks extensively in parables, often introducing them with the phrase, "the kingdom of heaven is like...." The kingdom Jesus announces is politically inauspicious, socially unimportant, and numerically insignificant, but it will grow to encompass far more than the first disciples can

Peter confesses Jesus as the Christ in the Gentile city of Caesarea Philippi (16:15-16). Pictured is Agrippa's palace.

envision. Imagine, he says, a mustard seed. It is small and barely visible. Yet when planted, it grows into a bush so large the birds build a nest in it (13:31–32).

Jesus does not promote a political kingdom, but a divine work proven by his power. Miracles are a demonstration of kingdom power. Exorcisms demonstrate that the world, once under Satan, is now visited by God's Son. This kingdom brings a crisis into the lives of those who encounter it. It is a discovery so precious—like a treasure in a field or a pearl of great value—that all is sold in order to attain it.

In the far north at the impressive Greek city of Caesarea Philippi, Jesus asks his disciples the central question of his ministry, "Who do you say that I am?" Peter responded, "You are the Messiah, the Son of the living God" (16:15–16). After praising Peter for his confession, Jesus describes to the disciples his own imminent sufferings and the hardships that await any who "take up their cross and follow him" (16:24, NRSV). This picture is not the final word, however, for six days later Jesus takes Peter, James, and John up a mountain and there reveals his dazzling glory. These three men hear God declare that Jesus is "my Son, whom I love; with him I am well pleased. Listen to him" (17:5). The words echo those spoken at Jesus' baptism: Jesus is God's Son. Note also the centurion who draws the same conclusion, "Surely he was the Son of God!" (27:54).

Matthew refers to the church (Gk. *ekklēsia*), a common Greek term that means "assembly" (16:18; 18:15–20). No other gospel uses this term. The sense of community is heightened further with Jesus' promise of his own presence in their midst: "For where two or three come together in my name, there am I with them" (18:20). Even though Jesus places a high priority on the church in Matthew, the gospel acknowledges the reality of sin and imperfection within this community (cf. Jesus' parable of the weeds in the field in 13:24–30, 36–43). Only at the harvest will the weeds and wheat be separated.

Jesus Moves toward Jerusalem (19:1 – 28:20)

Jesus moves south toward the destiny that awaits him in Jerusalem. As he travels, some Pharisees asked him about marriage and divorce. Among the Pharisees, opposing factions disagreed over the proper grounds for divorce. In effect, they were challenging Jesus to choose sides. Jesus declares that God established marriage to be a lifelong commitment between a man and a woman. Surprisingly, Jesus' own disciples are dumbfounded by Jesus' words: "If this is the situation between a husband and wife, it is better not to marry" (19:10). Their reaction highlights the common attitude among Jewish men that divorce is not something to be avoided at all costs. Jesus recognizes his teaching as revolutionary (19:11).

Jesus arrives at Jericho, where he dramatically heals two blind men (20:29–34). He then directs his disciples to go into the village of Bethphage, just east of Jerusalem, and secure a donkey for him to ride into the city. The prophet Zechariah wrote that Israel's king would come to the city riding on a donkey (Zech. 9:9). When Jesus approaches Jerusalem, the crowds recognize what he is doing. Soon cloaks and palms are spread before him and the crowd begins to shout, "Hosanna to the son of David," proclaiming Jesus as the heir to David's throne (Matt. 21:9; cf. 2 Sam. 7:16).

Matthew intensifies the scene by writing that all Jerusalem is shaken with the prospect of Jesus' arrival. Immediately he enters the temple and disrupts those selling animals and exchanging money. Jesus is here redefining the purpose of the temple as a place of healing and relief—a place known for prayer and worship, not for commercialism.

Response to Jesus' actions in the temple is swift and negative. The chief priests and the scribes challenge his authority to teach and heal as he does. Yet for the next few days, Jesus remains in the temple debating with its leadership. For instance, the Pharisees ques-

Jesus used everyday examples and images to explain how his church would grow, including the metaphor of a field ready to be harvested (13:24-30).

On his way to Jerusalem to face his death, Jesus stops at Jericho, and heals a blind man (20:29). Beyond the riverbed is Herod the Great's winter palace in Jericho.

tion him about paying taxes—a clear plan to trap Jesus as either a rebel against Rome or a Roman collaborator. Jesus offers the enigmatic line, "Give back to Caesar what is Caesar's, and to God what is God's" (22:21). He also challenges the Sadducees' view that there is no resurrection by pointing out that Israel's God is a living God.

Jesus then gives his final discourse, a strong warning of judgment to come. He attacks the basic assumptions of the pharisaic perspective. Repeatedly he charges, "Woe to you, teachers of the law and Pharisees, you hypocrites" (23:13; see also 23:15, 23, 25, 27, 29). He indicts them as being blind guides and neglecting "the more important matters of the law—justice, mercy and faithfulness" (23:23). He warns his disciples of persecutions they may face (24:9). He prophesizes the temple's destruction and foreshadows the impending last days of false prophets and terrible sufferings. To the disciples he preaches watchfulness, "because the Son of Man will come at an hour when you do not expect him" (24:44).

JUDAISM AND DIVORCE

Among Pharisees in Jesus' day, two main groups discussed the legal implications of God's law for marriage and divorce. "The House of Shammai say, 'A man should divorce his wife only because he has found grounds for it in unchastity, since it is said 'because he has found in her indecency in anything' (Deut 24:1). And the House of Hillel say, 'Because he has found in her indecency in anything.' R. Aqiba says, 'Even if he found someone else prettier than she, since it is said, 'And it shall be if she find no favor in his eyes' (Deut 24:1)" (Mishnah, *Gittin* 9:10).

Jesus' own teachings are similar to the House of Shammai since both reject divorce except for adultery. An underlying assumption shared by all three views is that the husband is the one able to initiate divorce. In John 4 we meet a woman who has had "five husbands." The grounds for her divorces may have been trivial, but Jesus does not judge her as to her sinfulness. In another story (John 7:53–8:11) where Jesus meets a woman caught in adultery—a different issue—he stops her accusers, shows her grace, and says, "Has no one condemned you? ... then neither do I."

The chief priests plot to capture Jesus. Judas, one of the Twelve, makes a pact with the chief priests to betray Jesus. But this does not happen until Jesus shares his final meal with his disciples. Then they depart to spend the night in prayer at the foot of the Mount of Olives. There Judas springs his plan and the temple leadership arrests Jesus.

Matthew follows Mark's gospel closely in his telling of the Passion. Yet Matthew adds details that highlight his own interests. For example, he stresses the fulfillment of prophecy at Jesus' betrayal (26:54). Judas's suicide too fulfills Jeremiah's prophecy concerning the thirty pieces of silver (27:3–10). Matthew also reminds us that Jesus could have called on thousands of angels to defend him. Pilate's wife's dream warns against having anything to do with Jesus' condemnation. The emphasis on dreams takes us back to Jesus' nativity, when God spoke to the Magi in a dream (2:12) and to Joseph in two dreams (2:13, 19).

Only Matthew tells us that the chief priests and Pharisees request Pilate to put guards at Jesus' tomb to prevent his disciples from "fraudulently" claiming Jesus rose from the dead (27:62–66). These same guards are soon frightened and become "like dead men" (28:4) when an earthquake shakes the ground and an angel opens the sealed tomb. This is Matthew's second reference to an earthquake heralding God's activity. The first one opened the tombs of the faithful when Jesus died on the cross (27:51–53).

AUTHORSHIP AND DATE

Throughout its history, this gospel has been credited to Matthew, one of Jesus' disciples (9:9), though the book itself mentions no author. That is why some scholars prefer to view this gospel as anonymous. A variety of arguments are generally put forward to refute Matthew's role as author: (1) Would an eyewitness such as an apostle have used Mark as a source? This question assumes the synoptic theory of Mark's priority (see chs. 5 and 9) and suggests that an eyewitness apostle would not reach for sources. (2) Some say that the Trinitarian formula in 28:19 represents a theological sophistication unexpected from a contemporary of Jesus. (3) Others believe Matthew's name was attached to the gospel in the second century in order to shore up the authority of this anonymous gospel.

But each of these claims is open to debate. (1) We have already seen that the priority of Mark in the synoptic problem is not certain, though it is the majority view. But this question of eyewitnesses betrays an assumption about the behavior and options available to an apostle. The apostles viewed themselves as custodians of the words of Jesus, and the synoptic evidence suggests a great deal of sharing went on in every direction. Therefore to say that

Matthew would not consult with Mark (who was likely Peter's assistant) is not reasonable. (2) The early church grew quickly in its theological sophistication. Paul's letters, penned before Matthew was written, use Trinitarian categories freely. We should not be surprised to find such language as commonplace within Matthew's era. (3) The church father Tertullian, writing at the end of the second century, explains that Christians did not hold as authoritative those works whose authorship could not be verified. Tertullian castigates the heretic Marcion for publishing a version of Luke without an author's name (*Against Marcion*, 4:2). Therefore, it is doubtful that Matthew would have had a wide, anonymous circulation.

Herod's engineers quarried enormous stones to rebuild the temple. The largest weighed 370 tons. These stones are some of the largest cut stones in the world.

Dating Matthew's gospel is closely tied to the question of authorship. If Matthew wrote it, then the gospel stems from the apostolic period. Further, if Matthew used Mark, we must allow time for Mark's gospel to be published and to circulate. Scholars also examine Matthew's references to Judaism and the church. If Matthew's followers have completely broken with Judaism, then the date of the gospel must be late first century. For example, note how the phrase "their synagogue" is used five times (4:23; 9:35; 10:17; 12:9; 13:54). Does this imply a distancing from Judaism? No simple answer will satisfactorily address these questions. Some date this gospel in the 60s, while others suggest the decade of the 80s.

THE SPLENDOR OF HEROD'S TEMPLE

Herod the Great followed in the pattern of great Hellenistic kings in his desire to build monumental architecture. One of his most ambitious projects was to expand the temple in Jerusalem. Josephus claims some of the stones were as big as 65 ½ feet long, 7 ½ feet high, and 9 feet wide. The outward face of the temple was covered with plates of gold and, at the rising of the sun, reflected back a fiery splendor that made people look away (*War* 5 [222]). What was not covered in gold was pure white limestone; from a distance it looked like a snow-covered mountain.

It is no wonder that such an edifice impressed Jesus' disciples. They cried out, "Look, Teacher! What massive stones! What magnificent buildings!" (Mark 13:1). But Jesus, suspicious of its place in this city, predicted its doom: "Do you see all these things? . . . Truly I tell you, not one stone here will be left on another; every one will be thrown down" (Matt. 24:2).

NOTES FROM ANTIQUITY

QUESTIONS FOR DISCUSSION ⊙⊙⊙⊙⊙⊙⊙⊙⊙⊙⊙⊙⊙⊙⊙⊙⊙⊙⊙⊙⊙⊙⊙⊙⊙⊙⊙⊙⊙

1. Did Matthew write this gospel? Did he write it in Hebrew? What is at stake in your answers?

2. Is Matthew's gospel anti-Jewish? Why or why not?

3. How does Matthew organize his gospel? How does this structure further Matthew's message?

4. Do you think that the Sermon on the Mount's ethics are applicable today? How should they be applied?

5. How does Matthew treat the law? Should Christians today follow the law?

BIBLIOGRAPHY

Introductory

Aune, D. E., ed. *The Gospel of Matthew in Current Study*. Grand Rapids: Eerdmans, 2001.

McKnight, S. "Gospel of Matthew." Pages 526–41 in *Dictionary of Jesus and the Gospels*. Ed. Joel B. Green, Scot McKnight, and I. Howard Marshall. Downers Grove, IL: InterVarsity Press, 1992.

Neyrey, J. H. *Honor and Shame in the Gospel of Matthew*. Louisville: Westminster John Knox, 1998.

Saldarini, A. J. *Matthew's Christian-Jewish Community*. Chicago: Univ. of Chicago Press, 1994.

Advanced

Carter, W. *Matthew and Empire*: *Initial Explorations*. Harrisburg, PA: Trinity Press International, 2001.

Davies, W. D., and D. C. Allison Jr. *A Critical and Exegetical Commentary on the Gospel according to Saint Matthew*. ICC. 3 vols. Edinburgh: T. & T. Clark, 1988–1991.

France, R. T. *Matthew, Evangelist and Teacher*. Downers Grove, IL: InterVarsity Press, 1989.

Nolland, J. *The Gospel of Matthew*. NIGTC. Grand Rapids: Eerdmans, 2005.

Keener, C. S. *A Commentary on the Gospel of Matthew*. Grand Rapids: Eerdmans, 1999.

CHAPTER 9

THE GOSPEL ACCORDING TO MARK

Mark's opening scene finds John the Baptist in the wilderness calling Israel to repentance. This is the wilderness of Judea looking east, over the Jordan Valley.

Mark's story of Jesus is known for being quick-paced and dramatic. In fact, its story is so compelling when read aloud (and reflects so many features of Hellenistic theater) that many scholars are convinced that this gospel was originally intended for oral presentation. Its unfolding drama compares favorably with Hellenistic dramas of antiquity. In Mark 1–3 exorcisms, miracles, and conflict stories appear in rapid succession as Jesus launches his ministry in Galilee. Immediately his authority is established as he demonstrates his power over disease, demons, and even nature. Jesus' authority even encompasses privileges normally reserved for God: the ability to forgive sin and work on the Sabbath—and this inspires harsh criticism from his opponents.

As we read Mark's drama we wonder: Who will understand that this is the Son of God (cf. 1:1)? If this is the Jewish Messiah, who will embrace and promote his emerging kingdom? In the first half, Mark shows Jesus' public successes in Galilee and in adjacent Hellenistic areas north and east of Galilee (both climaxed by a feeding miracle). Suddenly—at a critical turning point in the story—Jesus turns to his followers near a mountain in the far north and he asks them what they think about him (8:27). After two wrong answers, Peter says, "You are the Messiah" (8:29).

Mark then shifts the direction of his story sharply. Jesus begins to move south, toward Judea, toward his fate at the hands of the Jerusalem temple hierarchy. He predicts his own death three times, and each time Mark explains how Jesus is misunderstood. Finally, Jesus arrives at Jerusalem during Passover in the midst of crowds of cheering Galilean pilgrims, who have celebrated his message in the north. But as his popularity swells, so does his opposition. The religious leadership of Jerusalem moves quickly to check Jesus' growing celebrity status. He confronts them with courage, prophesies God's judgment on their world, and is promptly taken into custody. He is crucified, but not defeated. Mark ends his story with an empty tomb, dazed followers, and angels proclaiming his resurrection. In crisp dramatic form Mark closes the story telling us that Jesus' disciples are silenced in their astonishment and filled with fear (16:8).

Mark organizes Jesus' ministry into two simple locales: first Galilee and then Judea. The Sea of Galilee with its many villages saw the bulk of Jesus' ministry. Sunset looking west toward Tiberius.

During a renovation in the 1940s, the Syrian Orthodox Church found a 6th century Aramaic inscription here that referred to St. Mark. Today it is a chapel commemorating his residence in Jerusalem.

THE SETTING OF MARK

Some scholars see hidden in Mark's narrative hints of the gospel's intended audience. By the end of the second century, Clement of Alexandria said with confidence that Mark wrote his gospel from Rome. This is no doubt linked to the widely held tradition of Peter's martyrdom in Rome and Mark's connection with him as the recorder of his memoirs. At best we can reconstruct some features of Mark's audience by reading between the lines.

Most of Mark's readers/hearers spoke Greek and did not know Hebrew or Aramaic. Hebrew names and Aramaic words are translated (3:17; 7:34; 15:22, 34). In 7:1–4 Mark outlines Jewish purification rituals for those who do not understand Judaism. But this audience does know some of the rudiments of the Christian message. In 15:1 he does not have to explain who Pilate is, nor does he have to explain the Pharisees or the high priest. Words like "rabbi," "Gehenna," and "amen" are used without explanation. In 15:21 Mark refers to Simon of Cyrene as the father of "Alexander and Rufus." These two men are likely Christians known to Mark's audience; if we could place them, we could fix the locale of the gospel.

MARK'S LITERARY FORM

Most agree that a decisive turning point in this gospel occurs when Peter confesses the true identity of Jesus at Caesarea Philippi (8:29). But this confession is also mirrored by two other announcements that frame the ends of the gospel. In 1:1 the gospel begins with Mark's

On one occasion Jesus demonstrated his authority over the Sabbath by letting his followers "harvest" grain on the Sabbath (Mark 2:23). This led to an immediate controversy.

own personal testimony of faith: "The beginning of the good news about Jesus the Messiah, the Son of God" (cf. TNIV note]. At the close of the gospel we hear a Roman centurion at the cross proclaim, "Surely this man was the Son of God!" (15:39). Hence three confessions — by our author, by the leading Jewish apostle, and by a Gentile — frame the gospel, hinting at Mark's purposes. Mark wants to persuade us to see Jesus as the Messiah embraced by all the world.

In order to accomplish this evangelistic goal, Mark builds his case for Jesus by writing his story in two major divisions. Jesus is introduced *in public* to the communities of Galilee. Evidence for his messiahship mounts with each new miracle, exorcism, and parable. When Jesus is furthest from Jerusalem (Caesarea Philippi), he challenges his followers to identify him accurately. Peter does this, and immediately Jesus heads toward Jerusalem and teaches them *privately* how he must die when he arrives.

Jesus' successes in Galilee suddenly reverse themselves. Though crowds cheer Jesus' arrival, authorities plot his demise. Within three chapters, Jesus is dead. When Mark's audience is at its lowest ebb, a handful of women arrive at the tomb carrying burial spices. Suddenly, the story reverses again. The tomb is empty and angels proclaim that even death cannot defeat Jesus.

OUTLINE OF MARK'S GOSPEL

I. The Ministry of Jesus in Galilee (1:1 – 8:26)

    A. Prologue (1:1 – 13)
    B. The First Phase of the Galilean Ministry (1:14 – 3:6)
    C. The Second Phase of the Galilean Ministry (3:7 – 7:23)
    D. The Third Phase of the Galilean Ministry (7:24 – 8:26)

II. The Suffering of Jesus in Jerusalem (8:27 – 16:8)

    A. Jesus Travels to Jerusalem (8:27 – 10:52)
    B. Jesus Enters Jerusalem (11:1 – 13:37)
    C. Jesus Dies in Jerusalem (14:1 – 16:8)

THE MINISTRY OF JESUS IN GALILEE (1:1 – 8:26)

The first half of Mark's gospel demonstrates how Jesus' power and authority validate his claim to be Judaism's Messiah. Fifteen miracle stories reinforce how Jesus is uniquely equipped to bring the power of his kingdom to bear on the forces of this world. Nevertheless, no one understands him and recognizes his identity except demons, whom he defeats. In both divisions of the gospel we find a lengthy "anchor" parable that summarizes the purpose of the section. In the first half, Jesus is a sower casting seed among a variety of soils, watching for their growth or response.

Prologue (1:1 – 13)

Mark opens by introducing us to John the Baptist, a prophet who is fulfilling the call of Malachi 3:1 and Isaiah 40:3. His appearance evokes strong memories of Elijah, who likewise

WHY WAS JOHN THE BAPTIST ARRESTED?

The region of the Jordan where John worked was called "Perea," which shared a border with Nabatea. Mark explains that John was arrested because of his prophetic critique of the wrongful marriage of Herod Antipas to his brother's wife Herodias (6:14–29). Before Antipas married Herodias, he was married to the daughter of the Nabatean king in Petra. The princess returned to her father in shame.

John the Baptist condemned this well-known scandal, inflaming a possible war. Herod's arrest of John was thus a political move designed to silence this critic. Josephus tells us John was imprisoned in the fortress of Machaerus, which guarded the Nabatean border.

Today followers of John the Baptist still venerate him as the one true messenger of God. This community (called the Mandeans) lives along the Tigris River in Iraq, practices river baptisms, and follows a secret religion preserved by a handful of Mandean priests.

stood outside Israel calling the nation to repentance. But John is not merely calling Israel to repent; he is "on stage" to announce the messianic age soon to be inaugurated by the arrival of Jesus. This Messiah will usher in the messianic kingdom and baptize his followers with the Holy Spirit, empowering them in a manner reminiscent of his own anointing by the Spirit.

Jesus arrives at the Jordan River; when he is baptized, a heavenly voice confirms his identity and the Spirit descends on him. At once we know we have met the hero of Mark's drama. Endowed with the power of the Spirit, Jesus is "sent" deeper into the desert to see if his faithfulness to God is greater than the tests of Satan. This test recalls the testing of Israel in the desert (forty years, forty days), but we see the true valor and success of Israel's Messiah.

The First Phase of the Galilean Ministry (1:14–3:6)

The opening verses of Jesus' public ministry must be read with care. John has been arrested, yet Mark gives no hint at any opposition. Why? Who has been angered? This is a sign foreshadowing what will come.

Mark next distills the essence of Jesus' public announcement, "The time has come.... The kingdom of God has come near. Repent and believe the good news" (1:15). John was preparing Israel for the inbreaking of God's salvation in history; Jesus is the catalyst of this new kingdom. But its announcement must first take place in Galilee. Because of the violent removal and imprisonment of John from the Jordan, Jesus moves north. (In ch. 6, Mark relates the full story of John's arrest and the fears of Herod Antipas.)

The exciting opening Galilean stories of Mark serve to reinforce the importance of what is happening in Israel. This new kingdom is a realm of power, whose king bears unique authority to challenge the powers of the world. Jesus calls people from their

John the Baptist was likely killed at Herod's border fortress with the Nabateans called "Machaerus." This is located today in Jordan, near the Dead Sea.

careers—and they respond immediately. He teaches with authority, and the crowds give him undivided attention. With authority he casts out demons, heals Simon Peter's mother-in-law, cures a leper, and restores the legs of a paralytic. He even forgives the sins of a man. Each of these stories underscores that defeating human affliction, sin, suffering, and the demonic are the necessary work of the kingdom of God. But these do not stand alone. Jesus' teaching is intimately linked to these powerful works.

From these earliest days, Jesus' popularity grew swiftly. Crowds from everywhere press about him, whole cities gather in their synagogues, and even the religious leadership begin to question him. Mark builds a picture of Jesus' fame as he moves through the villages of the Galilee.

The Second Phase of the Galilean Ministry (3:7–7:23)

Jesus' popularity continues to grow, his authority and power are demonstrated in more dramatic scenes, and opposition continues to test him. Jesus' following takes a form that

Jesus returned frequently to Capernaum and used it as his ministry base in Galilee. This is an artist's reconstruction of the synagogue that stood in Capernaum in the 4th century. Evidence of a black basalt first century synagogue is beneath it (see photos, p. 185).

can be measured. Twelve leaders are appointed, who assist not only in representing the kingdom throughout Galilee's villages but in managing the crowds, who now number in the thousands.

Mark lists the twelve men (3:13–19)—a symbolic echo of the twelve tribes of Israel. Jesus is like a new Moses, tested in the desert, now leading twelve new tribes into a new kingdom. These twelve "apostles" (6:30) receive unique privileges. They leave their occupations and join Jesus in his itinerant ministry in Galilee. They not only learn by observing his life of faith, but they are given inside teaching unavailable to the masses (4:34). Jesus even invites three among them (Peter, James, John) to observe breathtaking scenes: the

Top: Some scholars believe that we may have found the residential area of Capernaum used by Peter and his family (Mk 1:30). Note the small size of the rooms and their black basalt construction. *Bottom Left:* Jesus first miracle in Mark was an exorcism that took place in Capernaum's synagogue. The white limestone structure seen today is from the 4th century. *Bottom Right:* The excavation of Capernaum's 4th century white limestone synagogue revealed that it rests on the foundation of a first century black basalt synagogue (seen here).

raising up of a little girl (5:37) and his transfiguration (9:2). These three will later ask him privately about his teachings (13:3) and accompany him in the night of prayer before his arrest (14:33).

But Jesus also has a mission for his disciples. He sends them out to preach and to have authority over demons. At one point, they strike out on their own in pairs, visiting villages and trusting God for provisions (6:7–13), where they discover they are agents of Jesus' kingdom, extending its reach in ways they never imagined. They *can* heal. They *can* defeat Satan. And they *can* explain in public venues what is happening in the land. In a word, they not only represent Jesus but they now bear his kingdom power.

Mark includes a representative selection of Jesus' parables, whose central aim is interpreting the meaning of this new kingdom. The kingdom reminds Jesus of "scattered seed" (4:26) or a grain of "mustard seed" (4:31). But the most significant parable is the parable of the sower (4:1–20), which represents everything happening in the public ministry: Jesus is a farmer casting seed onto a variety of soils. Most receive the seed and it takes root—but only a few seeds find "good soil" that permits the seed to produce a generous yield. Such parables are typical of Jesus' teaching style (4:2, 33–34), veiling to many the true secrets of the kingdom (4:11–12).

Along the Sea of Galilee, a man demonstrates the ancient art of throwing a "cast net."

FISHING ON THE SEA OF GALILEE

Net fishing was the typical method of fishing for who lived on the sea; the Gospels point to Jesus' knowledge of these.[1] Hook-and-line fishing was known but used far less since it yielded fewer fish. Three net systems were in use.

The *drag net* (cf. Matt. 13:47–48) was the most ancient form and is attested early in Egypt. A wall-like net with weights on the bottom and cork on the top is pulled along the coast. Then the lead rope is swept across the sea by boat and pulled back to shore, pulling in fish as it comes. The fish are then sorted and distributed to the workers.

The *cast net* (cf. Mark 1:16–17) is circular. It has lead sinkers attached to its edges and is tossed into the sea by a lone fisherman. It lands on the water like a parachute, sinking and catching unwary fish. The fisherman either dives into the water and pulls the fish out individually, or dives down, gathers the weights together, and lifts the net into his boat.

While net fishing was the most common practice, fish hooks were also in use. Jesus referred to them in Matt. 17:27.

The *trammel net* (cf. Mark 1:19–20) has three "layers" of net connected at the top by a head rope (with cork) and a foot rope (with lead weights). The outer nets have wide openings while the inner net is finely meshed and loose, flowing easily in and out of the outer nets. The net is spread in the water generally at night in a long line and held while other fishermen scare the fish toward it (with splashing). The fish enter the first net easily, push against the fine mesh net, and then carry the fine net into the third outer net, entangling themselves hopelessly. The fishermen haul the net ashore, disentangle the fish, and repair the many breaks. In the story of the miraculous catch of fish (Luke 5:1–7) the men have already fished all night and now are repairing their trammel nets. Jesus tells them to set sail again and drop the net once more. This was a genuine act of faith!

Since a number of Jesus' apostles are fishermen, we often find him using boats either to teach in (4:1) or to cross the Sea of Galilee. On two occasions storms arise, placing the crew in jeopardy (4:35–41; 6:45–52). On each occasion, Jesus rescues the boat by silencing the storm. Jesus can control the primeval forces of chaos that reside in the seas.

Jesus' more aggressive posture in Galilee is noticed. In chapter 6 Mark recounts what actually happened during John's arrest and death—not simply to complete the story, but to interpret the political atmosphere of the Herod's Galilean tetrarchy. Herod Antipas is now wondering about Jesus. But Herod knows Jesus had been with John and is haunted by the prospect that now John the Baptist has returned from the grave to haunt him. Mark's implications are clear. Jesus must be wary of the political forces in Galilee that will execute him on a whim. Thus, Jesus begins to move away to "a quiet place" (6:31), possibly beyond Herod's reach.

But word of Jesus' movement has also reached Jerusalem's leadership, and they send emissaries to interrogate him (7:1). Jesus uses their questions as an opportunity to unmask their true spiritual jeopardy. He cites harsh words from Isaiah 29 ("They worship me in vain."), then illustrates by citing two examples of the misuse of God's law. The razor edge of his prophetic rebuke comes in Mark 7:9, "You have a fine way of setting aside the commands of God in order to observe your own traditions!"

In 1986 two men from the Israeli kibbutz Nof Ginosar discovered a sunken fishing boat from the first century at the bottom of the Sea of Galilee. Today it has been restored and rests in the kibbutz museum.

Fishing was a major industry in Galilee. Fish were used for local consumption and exported throughout the province. These fish (talapia) are common in the Sea of Galilee.

The Third Phase of the Galilean Ministry (7:24–8:26)

The Jordan River inlet to the Sea of Galilee (on its north shore) served as a political and cultural boundary in Galilee. The Decapolis to the east was influenced by the Greek culture; the regions to the west were Jewish. Politically, this line also marked the boundary between Philip and Herod Antipas. Thus when Jesus moves into Bethsaida (6:45), he is moving into a different world, free of Herod's threats. When he exorcises demons from the man in Gerasa (5:1), he is in Gentile territory (cf. the pigs that become host to the demons, 5:11).

Jesus' transition into Gentile territory now takes on a more deliberate form. He travels to the far north, beyond Galilee, and enters the Gentile cities of Tyre and Sidon, where he meets a Greek woman who exhibits a devotion he had sought among the Jews. He moves

Jesus' decision to move to eastern Galilee brought him into contact with Gentiles from the Decapolis. This site named Kursi held a Greek fishing village and recalls the locating of Jesus driving demons into a herd of pigs.

Herod Antipas was building his own kingdom in Galilee. These rare coins stem from his rule (4 BC – AD 39). One side shows an upright palm with "Herod the Tetrarch." The reverse: a wreath with the name of Tiberius where it was minted.

directly into the Decapolis (7:31) and following a healing, the Greeks there compliment him. He feeds four thousand people, showing his growing popularity even in this region. Jesus' eating practices are criticized in 7:1–5, and in 7:14–23 Jesus argues against such rules, declaring "all foods clean." He is now signaling a key aspect of his new kingdom where division of "clean and unclean" no longer applies.

Jesus moves back and forth between the two political sections. Then he returns to Bethsaida, healing a blind man (8:22–26). This story is as much parable as it is miracle story. After his eyes are anointed the first time, the blind man can only see partially. Jesus must anoint him again, and this restores his sight perfectly. Partial sight is exactly the condition of the apostles (8:21), who now must be given clear vision.

THE SUFFERING OF JESUS IN JERUSALEM (8:27 – 16:8)

The second half of Mark follows Jesus' movement from Caesarea Philippi to Jerusalem during the season of Passover. Once Peter accurately identifies Jesus, Jesus begins the first of his three predictions of the cross (8:31; 9:31; 10:33). Each prediction increases in specificity and is surrounded by ironic responses among the apostles. When Jesus reaches Jerusalem, the confrontation hinted at throughout the gospel comes to a climax.

Jesus Travels to Jerusalem (8:27 – 10:52)

Caesarea Philippi, in the foothills of Mount Hermon, was the capital of this northeastern region ruled by Philip. Here Jesus probes his followers' understanding of his identity. They report the rumors that are swirling around them; then Peter offers what we have not heard yet in the gospel: "You are the Messiah." It is no accident that this confession occurs far from Jerusalem. In Mark's mind, faith has been discovered far from the epicenter of Jewish practice—among the Gentiles no less—and when Jesus moves toward Jerusalem, faith will seem faint and cynicism and hostility will grow.

Immediately following Peter's confession, Jesus must redefine what it means to be the Messiah as he heads south. In 8:32 Peter tries to correct Jesus' statement but is rebuked. When Jesus is transformed on the peak of a mountain (likely Mount Hermon), Peter offers the foolish suggestion to stay there and bask in the glory and power of the moment. But Jesus leads them down the mountain to a scene of chaos and service, where his truer mission is realized.

In chapter 9 Jesus again predicts his Passion, and this is followed by an argument concerning which of his disciples is greatest (9:33–37). If Jesus is going to die, they are already positioning themselves for his succession. As he nears Jerusalem, the dreaded reality of this mission hangs over them and they walk behind him, fearful and amazed (10:32).

Caesarea-Philippi was the northern capital of Galilee ruled by Philip. Today ancient ruins can still be found such as this Roman arch used as a bridge over a small river.

Following the third prediction (10:33) there is another ironic dispute. If Jesus dies, then James and John want to be sure they have privileges due their rank in heaven.

These teachings on the road to Jerusalem bridge the mission of Jesus with the call to discipleship. "Whoever want to be my disciple must deny themselves and take up their cross and follow me" (8:34). "Whoever wants to be first must be slave of all" (10:44). Sacrifice is the first hallmark of membership in this kingdom: "For even the Son of Man did not come to be served, but to serve, and to give his life as a ransom for many" (10:45). Models of true discipleship can be found in children (9:36; 10:14). They can also be found in the blind, such

THE MESSIANIC SECRET

One peculiar feature of Mark's presentation of Jesus is that Jesus frequently conceals his true identity. For instance, he tells demonic spirits to be silent as they are expelled (1:25, 34; 3:11–12), and he orders people who have been healed to keep their experience secret (1:44; 5:43; 7:36; 8:26). After Peter's confession at Caesarea Philippi, Jesus even tells him to be silent (8:30), and when Peter, James, and John return with him from Jesus' transfiguration, he charges them not to report what they have seen (9:9). Jesus clearly wants people to know who he is. So why does he refuse to let them speak openly about it?

The best explanation for Mark's "messianic secret" is found in the underlying political forces that shaped messianic expectation in Jesus' day. He does not want to become a pawn serving the agenda of militant Jewish groups, nor does he want to incite a violent revolt against Rome. Some of his actions (such as the cleansing of the temple, the feeding miracles) could lend themselves to this interpretation, and he needs to control the true nature of his mission. Power is not the gateway to understanding Jesus—it is the cross. Thus Mark presents a Roman centurion (a man of war) who recognizes Jesus only as he stands at the foot of the cross (15:39).

as the man in Jericho, whose request stands in contrast to that of James and John. He cries for mercy and a gift; they demand privilege and power.

Jesus Enters Jerusalem (11:1 – 13:37)

When Mark mentions Jericho, Jesus has almost reached his destination. The usual road followed by pilgrims and merchants from Galilee to Jerusalem went south down the Jordan Valley. At the oasis of Jericho it climbed the mountain heading west, following switchbacks for its 3,500 foot ascent. Jesus passes through two villages on the east side of the crest (Bethany and Bethphage) without stopping.

Evidence of the Roman occupation of Judea can be seen in the many artifacts of material culture that have been discovered from the New Testament era. This is a Roman medicine box with compartments for different medicines.

Here Mark's story accelerates. Jesus arrives in the city in triumph, cheered by pilgrims who also have come for Passover from Galilee and recognize him. His confrontation with the temple now is overt. He expresses outrage at the commercial industries of the temple's courts and with the fury of a prophet, judges what he sees. As he crosses back and forth between Bethany (where he stays, 11:11) and Jerusalem, he curses a fig tree — a symbol of Israel and its temple — because it provides no fruit, and the fig dies. This too is a prophetic gesture.

Jesus is now interrogated by the leading figures in Jerusalem society: Pharisees, Herodians, Sadducees, and scribes (12:13, 18, 28). In his debates Jesus offers his second major narrative parable that anchors the deeper meaning of the second half of this gospel. The parable of the vineyard and the tenants (12:1 – 11) echoes Isaiah's song of the vineyard (Isa. 5:1 – 7), expressing despair for Israel's failure to produce a nation pleasing to God. Then Jesus applies the story to himself: He is the son of the vineyard owner. But the hubris of the tenants prevails. They murder the son, cast him from the vineyard, and hope to claim the destiny of the vineyard for themselves. Instead, the vineyard will be judged. From the Mount of Olives Jesus scans the city of Jerusalem and announces its downfall.

Jesus Dies in Jerusalem (14:1 – 16:8)

The authorities now determine to kill Jesus (12:12), but are unable, thanks to his popularity among the pilgrims. But death looms over the story. Jesus is anointed for burial in Bethany, one of his disciples chooses to betray him, and Jesus reinterprets his final Passover as a meal recognizing his imminent death. As Jesus prays in an olive grove beneath the Mount of Olives, his captors come and spirit him away to the high priest, Caiaphas. Here Jesus openly acknowledges his identity and is condemned, sent to the Roman governor Pilate, and beaten as preparation for crucifixion.

Mark's crucifixion scene is deeply ironic inasmuch as six times Jesus is referred to as "king" (15:2, 9, 12, 18, 26, 32) and three times is mocked on the cross. But he is a king, bringing a kingdom to Israel that Caiaphas and Pilate cannot recognize. He is buried by a rich man and tended by women disciples. They represent polar opposites of Israel: the pious leadership of the nation, the poor from Galilee.

When the women arrive at the tomb on Sunday morning, they are greeted by a heavenly messenger announcing that Jesus is alive, fulfilling his threefold promise of resurrection (8:31; 9:31; 10:34). But instead of obeying the angel and reporting back to the others, they flee in fear, awestruck by what they have seen. Most scholars are convinced that Mark's gospel ends at 16:8, giving a poignant ending to the drama (see sidebar). The readers wonder: What happened? Where is Jesus? Where do the women go? The climax of Mark's gospel is taut with mystery and intrigue and it prods us to complete the drama with our own belief.

AUTHORSHIP AND DATE

Unlike most Hellenistic biographies, no gospel bears reference to its author. But such anonymous writing was not unusual for books not being written for the "book trade." The prolific writer Galen (AD 129–199), court physician to Marcus Aurelius, tells us in his essay "On My Own Books" that he gave his works "without a title to my friends or pupils," since he did not have publication in mind. When these things were published for public consumption, "everyone gave them a different title." It is clear that in the world of antiquity, publishing was conceptualized much differently than it is today.[2]

The Gospels were likely personal documents, written within the communities they served. Thanks to effective travel and trade routes, Christians began reading each other's texts regularly. Some time in second century, the phrase "According to Mark" was attached either to the end or the beginning of this gospel (or even in the margin). Can this later scribal identification be trusted? Who was this "Mark"?

The most important early church record of the tradition that associates Mark with our gospel comes from Papias, bishop of Hierapolis in Phrygia in the early second century (in words recorded by Eusebius):

> The elder used to say this, "Mark became the interpreter of Peter and wrote down accurately (though not in order) all that he remembered of what was said or done by the Lord. For he had neither heard nor followed the Lord; but later (as I said) he followed Peter, who used to give teaching as necessity demanded—but he [Peter] did not did not make an orderly account of the Lord's sayings. So Mark did no wrong in writing down some things as he recalled them. For he made it his aim to leave out nothing he had heard and to state nothing falsely. (*Eccl. Hist.*, 3.39.15)

Mark is clearly linked with Peter and his aim is to write an accurate (not necessarily chronological) account of Jesus' life. One argument in support of the accuracy of this tradition is how unlikely it would be for someone to choose the name "Mark" as pseudonym. "Mark" was one of the most popular names in the Roman world and would hardly distinguish the gospel. A better pseudonym would be the name of an apostle to give the gospel more credibility. We have an ample supply of these pseudonyms in the New Testament apocrypha (*The Gospel of Peter, Thomas*, etc.).

In the New Testament only one person named Mark is mentioned. Philemon 24 and 2 Timothy 4:11 refer to an associate of Paul's named Mark, and Colossians 4:10 adds that he was the cousin of Barnabas. Acts refers to someone named Mark once (Acts 15:39), but three times mentions "John whose surname is Mark" (12:12, 25; 15:37). First Peter may have originated from Rome and refers to Mark as Peter's spiritual son (1 Peter 5:13).

Many scholars see these references as the same person, whose composite profile may be simply reconstructed: Mark was a Greek-speaking convert, who knew some Aramaic, became a Christian, and worked closely with Peter. He joined Paul in his first journey and in later years served both Peter and Paul before their deaths in Rome.

But is this New Testament figure the same as the one Papias attaches to the second gospel? Nothing prohibits it. In the gospel itself, there is indirect evidence that indeed Peter is closely linked to the author. Peter is the most significant leader among the apostles but ironically, also the object of much criticism, leading out with bravado and failing miserably. When Papias says that Mark "interpreted" Peter, this probably means that Mark made a composite sketch of stories from the reservoir of Peter's preaching.

Jesus predicted the destruction of Jerusalem (Mark 13:2) and it was fulfilled in AD 66–70. The heat of fire was so intense that burning shops along the temple's south wall have left a scorched shadow.

Is it possible to indicate *when* Mark wrote? Early church traditions either tell us that Mark wrote just before (so Clement of Alexandria) or just after Peter's death (so Irenaeus). Peter likely lived in Rome during the 50s and 60s and was martyred sometime later in Nero's reign (54–68). This dates the writing of Mark to sometime in the 60s.

A watershed event for dating the Gospels is undoubtedly the catastrophic destruction of Jerusalem in AD 66–70. Mark writes as if the temple is still standing and says nothing about a revolt. His reference to the temple's future destruction (13:2) and to the "abomination that causes desolation" (13:14) make little sense if the temple was already in ruins.

If Mark served as a source for Matthew and Luke (see Ch. 5), there is wide consensus that these two Gospels stem from the 70s or 80s. If so, Mark had to circulate for some time to gain recognition, which again urges for a date before 70. But if Mark was penned *before* the great war, he may even have written earlier, perhaps in the 50s. Some scholars have even suggested a first draft in the late 40s.

QUESTIONS FOR DISCUSSION ⊙⊙⊙⊙⊙⊙⊙⊙⊙⊙⊙⊙⊙⊙⊙⊙⊙⊙⊙⊙⊙⊙⊙⊙⊙⊙⊙

1. What literary features of Mark's gospel make it a compelling dramatic presentation?

2. Why does Jesus choose Capernaum as an ideal base from which to work in Galilee?

3. Is Mark using a geographical motif in his gospel? Is Jesus treated differently in Judea, Galilee, and the Diaspora?

4. If people cannot comprehend Jesus when they encounter him (as in the first half of Mark), what are the practical implications of this for evangelism today?

5. The disciples frame Jesus' messiahship in their own terms, and Jesus has to correct them. Does this happen today? What political, social, or religious agendas from our culture have shaped how we understand Jesus' kingdom?

BIBLIOGRAPHY
Introductory
Bock, D. L. *Matthew, Mark*. CBC. Carol Stream, IL: Tyndale, 2006.
Garland, D. *Mark*. NIVAC. Grand Rapids: Zondervan, 1996.
Lane, William. *Mark*. NICNT. Grand Rapids: Eerdmans, 1974.

Advanced
Evans, Craig. *Mark 8:27 – 16:20*. WBC. Dallas: Word, 2001.
France, R. T. *The Gospel of Mark*. NIGTC. Grand Rapids: Eerdmans, 2002.
Guelich, Robert A. *Mark 1:1 – 8:26*. WBC. Dallas: Word, 1989.
Marcus, Joel. *Mark 1 – 8*. New York: Doubleday, 2000.

NOTES
1. See M. Nun, *The Sea of Galilee and Its Fishermen in the New Testament* (Ein Gev: Sea of Galilee Fishing Museum, 1989).

2. Galen, "On My Own Books," *Selected Works*, ed. and trans. by P.N. Singer (Oxford: Oxford Univ. Press, 1997), 3.

CHAPTER 10

THE GOSPEL ACCORDING TO LUKE

Hellenism assimilated into Judaism by the first century as seen here in the decorate façade to the Sanhedrin Tombs, Jerusalem.

Luke's gospel was originally the first scroll of a two-volume work (the second scroll being Acts). These volumes comprise approximately one quarter of the New Testament, making Luke-Acts together the largest New Testament book. Contemporary readers can easily miss that these books tell one continuous story since John's gospel now separates them. But when originally composed and sent to Theophilus (Luke 1:1–4; Acts 1:1–2), they were read as a single narrative about Jesus and his disciples.

Luke's account speaks eloquently of God's salvation sent first to the Jewish people and then to the Gentiles throughout the Mediterranean world. This story of the empire-wide spread of the gospel is told in a way that also emphasizes how this salvation is offered to all people, those "far off" (Acts 2:39), regardless of ethnicity or nationality, social class, gender, or age.

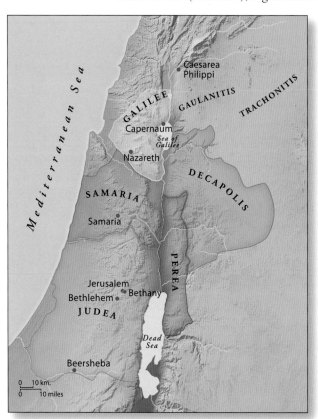

Luke called all the land where the Jews resided, including Galilee, "Judea."

Here we watch the church proclaim the message not only to Jews but also to Samaritans, an Ethiopian official, Romans, Macedonians, Greeks, and "barbarians" as the gospel spreads "to the ends of the earth" (Acts 1:8). In Luke's gospel the poor have the gospel preached to them, women become full participants in God's salvation, and even children are welcomed by Jesus. People who are social pariahs (e.g., tax collectors and those classified as "sinners") enter into God's kingdom. Luke's story is about the offer of salvation to those who are on the outside, to those marginalized by society.

THE SETTING OF LUKE'S GOSPEL

Luke is the only gospel that names its recipient—"most excellent Theophilus" (Luke 1:3; Acts 1:1). This name means "beloved by God," and some suggest he received this name after being baptized as a Christian. However, before the Christian era "Theophilus" appeared in inscriptions and ancient documents referring to both Jews and Gentiles. Theophilus is most likely the person's given name.

Theophilus enjoys high social status since Luke calls him *most excellent* Theophilus (cf. Acts 23:26; 24:3; 26:25 where procurators Felix and Festus are similarly addressed). This title identifies him as someone of higher social rank than Luke, possibly a member of the equestrian order. Theophilus possesses considerable economic means and is likely the literary patron who financed the copying of these scrolls, both for Theophilus and for others.

We do not know where Theophilus and the others are located, although Rome and Greece have been suggested. Perhaps these books are distributed to Paul's churches. The readers are likely Gentiles, for when Luke presents Jewish customs, he includes explanatory phrases that help his readers understand their meaning. For example, in 22:1 Luke says, "Now the Festival of Unleavened Bread, called the Passover, was approaching." A Jewish audience would hardly need this explanation about the Passover (cf. also 22:7). What Matthew calls a "scribe" (Matt. 23:13), Luke calls a "lawyer" (Luke 11:52 NASB), a term more understandable to Gentiles. The way Luke traces Jesus' genealogy back to Adam instead of Abraham (Luke 3:38; cf. Matt. 1:2) underscores that salvation is for the Gentiles (e.g., Luke 2:29 – 32).

Theophilus is likely a believer. The events surrounding the opening of the gospel "have been fulfilled *among us*," and Theophilus is someone who has already been "taught" the gospel (1:1, 4; this verb denotes instruction in Acts 18:25; Rom. 2:18; 1 Cor. 14:9; Gal. 6:6). As new believers living in a world that held hostile attitudes toward Christians (see Acts 17:6; 21:21, 24; 28:22), we can easily understand why Theophilus and the others need to "know the certainty of the things" they have been taught (1:4).

LUKE'S STORY ABOUT JESUS

The author's main interest lies in the presentation of God's salvation as revealed in Jesus Christ. I. Howard Marshall notes, "But whereas the stress in Mark is on the person of Jesus, in Matthew on the teaching of Jesus, and in John on the manifestation of eternal life in Him, Luke's stress is on the blessings of salvation which he brings."[1] This "salvation" has numerous nuances, such as healing from disease (17:19; 18:41 – 42), liberation from demonic control (8:36), restoration of life to the dead (8:50), and rescue from disaster (6:9). But salvation is also tied to the forgiveness of sins (7:49 – 50) and is a response to faith (7:50; 8:48). Yet the realities of forgiveness, liberation, and healing are not separate and distinct but are aspects of the total salvation that Jesus Christ brings.

The combined volumes of Luke-Acts emphasize the significance of this salvation on a broader scale. Stephen spoke of the deliverance of Israel from Egypt (Acts 7:25), an event that prefigured the salvation God offers to all humanity (13:47, quoting Isa. 49:6). Salvation for Luke is the deliverance God brings in the age to come, which has already dawned (Acts 2:16 – 17, 21). Jesus proclaims to Zacchaeus, "For the Son of Man came to seek and to save what was lost" (19:10). God is the ultimate source of salvation, which he accomplishes through his Son.

Various deities, such as Asclepius (the god of healing, here pictured), Isis and Sarapis, along with various deified rulers, such as emperors, were called "savior." Luke presents Jesus as the one who is the only true Savior.

The two volumes of Luke-Acts narrate a single continuous story. The books are structured in similar ways and common themes appear in both volumes, such as the role of the Holy Spirit (Luke 4; Acts 2) and the theme of salvation. The pattern in which the history of Jesus and the early church are presented is symmetrical (see chart of "Luke and Acts Compared").[2]

LUKE AND ACTS COMPARED

Luke	Acts	Theme
3:21 – 22	3:21 – 22	Prayer (1:14, 24) and reception of the Holy Spirit
4:14 – 21	2:14 – 39; 13:16 – 41	Proclamation which focuses on fulfillment and rejection
4:40	28:9	Healing
5:17 – 26	3:1 – 10; 14:8 – 11	Healing of paralytic
8:40 – 56	9:36 – 41; 20:9 – 10	Raising the dead
21:15	6:10	Wisdom
22:69	7:56	Jesus as the exalted Son of Man
23:34, 46	7:59 – 60	Prayer for forgiveness

Moreover, the unity of the two books is seen in the way that Acts presents the fulfillment of events predicted in Luke, such as the witness of the disciples (Luke 24:48; Acts 1:8) and the persecutions they will suffer (Luke 21:12 – 23; Acts 4:3; 5:18 – 25, etc.). The disciples proclaim the same message of the kingdom of God that Jesus announces.

We can understand Luke's literary structure by identifying its four principal sections.

1. After the introductory prologue (1:1 – 4), Luke describes Jesus' infancy (1:5 – 2:52) and John the Baptist's ministry (3:1 – 4:15).
2. Luke follows Mark closely as he tells of Jesus' ministry in Galilee (4:14 – 9:50). The response of the people is favorable.

JOSEPHUS ON WRITING HISTORY

Josephus makes a spirited defense of his method in writing history that is similar to Luke's opening prologue. He claims he did not make up the account of the things he recorded but thoroughly investigated what had actually occurred as he sought understanding:

There have been indeed some bad men, who have attempted to malign my history, and took it to be a kind of scholastic performance for the exercise of young men. A strange sort of accusation and false charge this, since everyone that undertakes to deliver the history of actions truly ought to know them accurately himself in the first place, as either having been concerned in them himself, or informed of them by such as knew them. Now both these methods of knowledge I may very properly pretend to in the composition in both my works. (*Against Apion* 1.10 [53 – 54]).

Josephus carefully lays out his qualifications as a historian and affirms, "How impudent then must those deserve to be esteemed that undertake to contradict me about the true state of those affairs!" (ibid., 1.10 [56]). Luke too is well aware of the challenges to the Christian story in his day and seeks to deflect the critics.

3. Then follows Luke's "travel narrative," where Jesus travels from Galilee to Jerusalem (9:51–19:27; note 9:51, 53; 13:22; 17:11; 18:31–34; 19:28). The central theme is the rejection of Jesus and the seeming failure of his ministry. It begins with the Samaritans' rejection of Jesus (9:51–56) and ends with Jesus' lament over unresponsive Jerusalem (19:41–44).

4. Luke returns to Mark's outline as he describes Jesus' work in and around Jerusalem (19:45–21:38), his passion (22:1–23:56), and finally his resurrection and ascension (24:1–53).

OUTLINE OF THE GOSPEL OF LUKE

I. Prologue (1:1–4)

II. The Infancy Narrative (1:5–2:52)

III. The Beginnings: John and Jesus (3:1–4:13)

    A. The Ministry of John the Baptist (3:1–20)
    B. Jesus' Baptism and Temptation (3:21–4:13)

IV. The Galilean Ministry (4:14–9:50)

    A. The Proclamation In and Around the Synagogues of Galilee (4:14–44)
    B. Calling and Teaching the Disciples (5:1–6:49)
    C. The Authority of Jesus (7:1–50)
    D. The Proclamation of the Kingdom (8:1–9:17)
    E. Jesus: The Messiah Who Will Die and Rise Again (9:18–50)

V. The Journey to Jerusalem (9:51–19:44)

    A. The First Announcement of the Journey to Jerusalem (9:51–13:21)
    B. The Second Announcement of the Journey to Jerusalem (13:22–17:10)
    C. The Third Announcement of the Journey to Jerusalem (17:11–19:27)
    D. Jesus' Arrival in Jerusalem (19:28–44)

VI. The Jerusalem Ministry (19:45–21:38)

VII. The Crucifixion of Jesus (22:1–23:56)

VIII. The Resurrection and Ascension (24:1–53)

THE PROLOGUE (1:1 – 4)

Luke's prologue outlines his methodology in composing Luke-Acts and reveals his purpose in writing. He is not the first to attempt to give an account of the life of Jesus. "Many" have written about "the things that have been fulfilled among us." "Fulfilled" reflects Luke's emphasis on the fulfillment of God's plan (1:20; 4:21; 9:31; 21:22, 24; 24:44–47). Luke's sources are the "eyewitnesses and servants of the word" (1:2), that is, persons committed to the realities they proclaimed and who handed down the story as a sacred tradition (cf. 1 Cor 11:23; 15:3–4).

In 1:3–4 Luke adds a comment about his own contribution, stating that he has "investigated" everything, which implies something more than "investigated." Josephus uses this word to suggest the idea of following "an account or events so as to understand them."[3] Luke has exercised great care in his quest for accuracy. Thus, he can offer Theophilus this "orderly account" in order to confirm his faith.

ELIJAH WILL COME

The expectation that Elijah would come to reform Israel before the day of the Lord is echoed in Jewish literature. Sirach 48:9–10 says of Elijah, "You were taken up by a whirlwind of fire, in a chariot with horses of fire. At the appointed time, it is written, you are destined to calm the wrath of God before it breaks out in fury, to turn the hearts of parents to their children, and to restore the tribes of Jacob." Later Jewish tradition ascribed other roles to him, such as settling disputes (Mishnah, *Baba Mesia* 3:3–4; *Eduyyot* 8:7) and even raising the dead (Mishnah *Sotah* 9:15). Apparently during Jesus' day it was common belief among the scribes (Matt. 17:10; Mark 9:11–13), the Jewish populace (Matt, 16:14), and Jesus himself that Elijah would appear to inaugurate the new age.

THE INFANCY NARRATIVE (1:5 – 2:52)

Before telling the story of Jesus' birth, Luke recounts the announcement of the birth of John the Baptist, the harbinger of the Messiah (1:5–25). The account begins with the tragic situation of Zechariah and Elizabeth, who are childless (1:5–7). Luke notes their lineage and character and, since childlessness was considered a reproach (Lev. 20:20–21; Jer. 22:30), he informs the reader that that their childlessness is not due to any moral fault.

The focus of the story is on John's special place in preparing Israel for the coming day of the Lord. According to 1:15–17, he will be filled with the Spirit of God, which means the prophetic voice will return to Israel after centuries of prophetic silence. But John is more than a prophet (see 7:26–27; Mal. 3:1) since he fulfills the prophetic hope of Malachi 4:5–6 that Elijah would return before the day of the Lord (see also Matt. 17:10–13).

The scene shifts to the private meeting of Gabriel with Mary in Nazareth (1:26), which begins Luke's account of Jesus' birth (1:26–2:21). Mary is betrothed to Joseph when the angel arrives. Jewish marriage was a two-staged event. The engagement (1:27) consisted of a formal witnessed agreement to marry and the payment of the bride price to the bride's father. The marriage ceremony and celebration took place about a year later. Gabriel's announcement includes the proclamation that Mary will have a son who should be named "Jesus" (1:31). He will be called the Son of God (1:32), which in Israel was a royal title (2 Sam. 7:14; Ps. 2:7) but in the Roman world was associated with the ruler cult. Jesus' birth is a direct challenge to the imperial claims of Augustus Caesar.

Zechariah, the father of John the Baptist, received a revelation from an angel while offering incense in the temple (Luke 1:8-20).

For Luke, the title "Son of God" is also linked with Adam (3:38). Jesus is the second Adam. Gabriel also announces that he will be an heir to the Davidic dynasty in fulfillment of the ancient promise made to David (1:32–33; 2 Sam. 7:12–17), held dear by the Jewish people.

The emperor Augustus was the adopted son of the deified Julius Caesar, and was therefore known as *divi filius* or "the son of god."

Nazareth was not a prominent village in Galilee, but it was located a mere five miles from the important town of Sepphoris (Zippori in Hebrew, a place which Josephus called "the ornament of Galilee") which lay on the intersection of the Via Maris and the Acre-Tiberias roads.

THE COMING KING OF THE LINE OF DAVID

The first century BC pseudepigraphical book known as the *Psalms of Solomon* (17:21–25) echoes the hope for a coming king who will be a descendant of David and who will liberate God's people from the Gentiles:

> See, Lord, and raise up for them their king, the son of David,
> to rule over your servant Israel in the time known to you, O God.
> Undergird him with the strength to destroy the unrighteous rulers,
>   to purge Jerusalem from Gentiles, who trample her to destruction;
>   in wisdom and in righteousness to drive out the sinners from the inheritance;
>   to smash the arrogance of sinners like a potter's jar;
>   to shatter all their substance with an iron rod;
>   to destroy the unlawful nations with the word of his mouth;
>   at his warning the nations will flee from his presence;
>   and he will condemn sinners by the thoughts of their hearts.[4]

The expectation of this psalm is that the coming King will liberate Israel from their Gentile oppressors (the Romans), gather the scattered Israelites (the Diaspora), and cleanse the nation of unrighteousness (17:26–32). The hope is that "their king shall be the Lord Messiah" (17:32).

Upper Left: As in ancient times, some houses in Bethlehem are attached to caves which served as shelter for livestock. The stable where Jesus was born was not like the wood structures depicted in contemporary Christmas nativity scenes *Upper Right:* Bethlehem lay under the shadow of the Herodium, one of the palace-fortresses of Herod the Great. *Left:* Bethlehem, the birthplace of Jesus, and the Herodium, where Herod the Great is most likely buried.

Instead of seeking some sign as Zechariah did (1:18), Mary asks a simple and practical question about how she can conceive without ever having had sexual relations (1:34). Gabriel answers (1:35) that his conception will be due to direct divine intervention.

Luke's juxtaposes the birth of Christ with political history (2:1–2). The Roman census, which compelled Joseph and Mary to travel to Bethlehem, was part of the administrative reform of Augustus as he attempted to establish more firmly the tax base in the empire. Augustus himself was considered to have inaugurated a new era of peace, but in Luke's view he is simply one whom God uses to accomplish his plan.

While in Bethlehem Mary's time comes to give birth (2:6–7). There was no guest room, so the child is laid in a manger. The houses there used many caves as part of the house, with stables usually attached to the dwelling.

THE CENSUS UNDER QUIRINIUS

According to ancient records, Quirinius was the governor of Syria from AD 6–7, sometime after the birth of Jesus Christ (see Luke 2:2; Josephus comments on a census under Quirinius when Archelaus was banished; *Ant.* 17.13.5 [355]; 18.1.1 [1–10]). Luke, however, places the birth of Jesus during his administration although Jesus was born before the death of Herod the Great in 4 BC. This tension between Luke's account and that of ancient records has generated a number of attempts to resolve the problem.

Sherwin-White[5] mentions a gap in the historical records with regard to the Syrian legates and suggests that Quirinius filled the gap between 4 BC and 1 BC. Another proposal is that "governor" means simply "administrator" here, allowing that Quirinius may have administered the census under the rule of the legate Saturnius (6–4 BC). Luke seems aware of a later census under Quirinius since he notes that this one was the "first." Despite these considerations, to date we do not have a fully satisfactory solution.[6]

An angel announces Jesus' birth to shepherds, who represent the lowly and the humble to whom God offers salvation through his Son (2:10–11). The announcement is replete with divine and royal titles as the infant Jesus is called Savior, Christ, and Lord. Angels break into a chorus of praise to God for his act and proclaim divine peace, which rests on those who receive his favor (2:14).

THE BEGINNINGS: JOHN AND JESUS (3:1 – 4:13)

As in 2:1, Luke locates the beginning of John and Jesus' ministry within the political and religious history of the era (3:1–2a). John's ministry fulfills the Old Testament expectation of a harbinger to precede the coming of the Lord (Isa. 40:3–5 in Luke 3:2b–6). The coming one is none other than the Lord himself, who will usher in God's salvation (3:6). John's message in 3:7–14 is that judgment is near (3:7–9) and therefore people are called to true repentance (3:8). Conversion results in treating others with compassion and justice (3:10–14). John baptizes in the Jordan River, a rite that is a sign of conversion.

John points to one mightier than him, who will bring both salvation and judgment (3:15–17). Luke's presentation of the baptism of Jesus (3:21–22) does not emphasize the theme of fulfillment (cf. Matt 3:13–17) but rather the divine testimony with regard to his person. The Spirit comes on Jesus, endowing him with power for ministry (4:18; Acts 10:36–38). A voice comes from heaven that includes an affirmation of Jesus' Sonship, echoing the Old Testament (Ps. 2:7; Isa. 41:8; 42:1) and revealing Jesus' kingly rule, his intimate relationship with the Father, and his identification with the Suffering Servant of Isaiah.

Like Matthew, Luke recounts both the genealogy and temptation of Jesus (3:23–4:13; see Ch. 8), after which Jesus begins his public

Tiberius Caesar was the Roman emperor during Jesus' ministry.

Galilee, ruled by Herod Antipas, included Gentile cities such as Sepphoris, where this mosaic was found.

ministry in Galilee in the power of the Spirit (4:14 – 15). In his genealogy, Luke, a Gentile, underscores the universality of Christ as Savior and Lord of all human beings.

THE GALILEAN MINISTRY (4:14 – 9:50)

Luke introduces Jesus' Galilean ministry with a summary statement (4:14 – 15), which highlights characteristic themes in Luke: Jesus carries out his ministry in the power of the Spirit (4:14), he engages in a vigorous teaching ministry (4:15a; cf. 6:17 – 49), and "everyone praised" his ministry (4:15b).

The first full picture of Jesus' teaching takes place in the synagogue in Jesus' hometown, Nazareth (4:16 – 29). The reading of Scripture and an exposition were common components of a synagogue service.

Jesus presents himself as the Spirit-anointed prophet who fulfills Isaiah 61:1 – 2 and 58:6. After the reading he proclaims that the time of fulfillment has come (4:21). The blessings described are the signs of the messianic age — the Spirit has returned and is upon him, the good news has come, and the liberation of Israel is breaking in. But the recipients of these blessings are society rejects: the poor, the prisoners, the blind, and the oppressed. In his exposition, Jesus stresses that that the gospel is also for those outside Israel, just as in the past (4:24 – 28). The hostile reaction to this declaration is the first sign of Jesus' rejection by his own people (4:23, 29). The cross is foreshadowed from the very inception.

As in Matthew, the opening phase of Jesus' ministry is marked by the call and teaching of the first disciples (5:1 – 6:49), the demonstration of his authority to heal and forgive (7:1 – 50), and his proclamation of the mes-

---

READING SCRIPTURE IN A SYNAGOGUE SERVICE

NOTES FROM ANTIQUITY

The tractate *Megilla* (3 – 6) of the Mishnah presents guidelines for a synagogue service for a period after the writing of the New Testament. But many of these aspects seem to have been practiced earlier. On reading Scripture, *Megilla* 4:4 instructs:

He that reads in the Torah should read no fewer than three verses. He may not read to the translator [who would translate from Hebrew to Aramaic] more than a single verse [at a time, so the translator will not err], and, in the case of the prophetic lection [a reading from the Prophets], three. If the three constitute three distinct pericopae, they read them one by one. They skip [from place to place] in the prophetic lections but not in the Torah lections.

Interpretation of the reading is also prescribed.

sage of the kingdom (8:1 – 9:17), a ministry that the apostles are commissioned to share (9:1 – 6). The lifestyle prescribed for these missioners is distinct from that of other traveling orators in the ancient world. They are not to have great entrances and seek fine receptions but to be content with basic provisions. The climax of the revelation of Jesus' teaching and power is Peter's confession, in which he recognizes Jesus as the promised Messiah (9:18 – 20).

"THE MESSIAH OF GOD"

When Jesus asks Peter who the disciples think Jesus is, Peter responds, "God's Messiah [*christos*]" (9:20). "Christ" or "Messiah" means "Anointed One," a title that marked the bearer as the king (Ps. 2:2, 6). The Jewish people expected God to raise up a ruler from the line of David (2 Sam. 7:4 - 17). His coming would be a day of mercy: "May God cleanse Israel for the day of mercy in blessing, for the appointed day when his Messiah will reign" (*Psalms of Solomon* 18:5). Peter and the disciples understand that the day has begun.

This revelation is quickly followed by the declaration that the Messiah will not come in power to triumph over the Roman oppressors but will suffer, be killed, and be raised on the third day (9:21 – 22). The sufferings are a necessary part of God's plan for the Messiah (9:22), a thought unheard of in Jewish theology. This is a new messianic vision — the apocalyptic and royal Son of Man (9:22a; cf. Dan. 7:13 – 14) who comes in power and glory is identified with the Servant of the Lord of Isaiah 53, who suffers for the sins of the people. His disciples likewise will suffer for the kingdom (Luke 9:23 – 27).

THE JOURNEY TO JERUSALEM (9:51 – 19:44)

The journey to Jerusalem dominates the middle section of the gospel and contains most of the information about Jesus' ministry that is unique in Luke. The fact that Jesus and his disciples are on their way to Jerusalem is noted at various points along the way (9:51; 13:22; 17:11; 18:31; see also 9:57; 10:38; 14:25; 18:35).

The design of the synagogue in Nazareth would have been similar to this synagogue in Gamla located in the Golan Heights, NE of the Sea of Galilee.

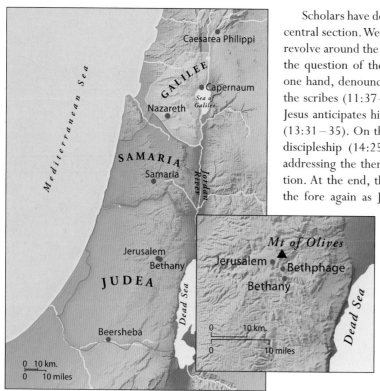

Left: Jesus' journey from Galilee to Jerusalem is a noted feature of Luke's gospel. *Right*: Jerusalem and the surrounding region

Scholars have debated about the overall purpose of this central section. We suggest it deals with the problems that revolve around the conflict with the Jewish leadership and the question of the nature of discipleship. Jesus, on the one hand, denounces the leadership of the Pharisees and the scribes (11:37–54). Conflict with them widens, and Jesus anticipates his rejection by the whole of the nation (13:31–35). On the other hand, Jesus also focuses in on discipleship (14:25–35), with chapters 15–18 largely addressing the theme of discipleship in the face of rejection. At the end, the Davidic kingship of Jesus comes to the fore again as Jesus comes near Jerusalem (Jericho) and is recognized as "Son of David" (18:38).

As the journey to Jerusalem comes to an end, Jesus heads into the city from the east, coming near through Bethphage and Bethany, over the Mount of Olives (19:28).

As Jesus begins his ministry in the holy city, Luke shows that Jesus is in control of the situation. In 19:28–44 he tells the disciples how to procure a colt for his entry. As he enters the city, he is hailed as the coming King with the people using Psalm 118:26. The disciples lead the cheers, and the atmosphere is charged as they praise God for the mighty deeds Jesus has done (19:37). At this very point the opposition to Jesus raises the first objection (19:39), but Jesus will not silence the praise (19:40). In 19:41–44 Jesus weeps over Jerusalem and announces her judgment.

A CHALLENGE TO HONOR

The type of public debate that Jesus and his opponents engage in was well known in the ancient world. This "challenge-riposte" was a kind of "social tug of war, a game of social push and shove." Such interchanges usually have three parts: "(a) *challenge* in terms of some action (word, deed, or both) on the part of the challenger; (b) *perception* of the message by both the individual to whom it is directed and the public at large; and (c) the *reaction* of the receiving individual and the evaluation of the reaction on the part of the public."[7]

Jesus makes the first claim by entering the social space of the leadership, the temple, and challenges their authority (19:45–46). He is then countered by the leaders (20:1–2) with regard to his authority. The question of honor is central in this social push and shove. Such honor challenges only took place among equals, and therefore the question of Jesus' status comes to the fore. Luke shows how Jesus is on equal footing with the religious leaders. He responds to each challenge and then goes on the offensive. In other words, Jesus is the one who has higher honor and status. He has a rightful claim to the authority demonstrated by cleansing the temple.

This coming cataclysmic event is predicted as judgment for not receiving the Lord, "because you did not recognize the time of your visitation from God" (19:44, NRSV). "Visitation" means that God comes to his people, either for blessing or judgment. He had come to bless them (Gen. 50:24–25; Job 10:12; Isa. 23:17), but they did not recognize his hand. What is left is severe destruction.

JERUSALEM MINISTRY (19:45–21:38)

Luke highlights the conflict between Jesus and the leaders of the nation. They try to trap him, especially in reaction to his dramatic move of cleansing the temple. When his authority is questioned, he responds with a series of rebuttals, including questions concerning the source of John's and his own authority (20:1–8), a parable that shows that the present Jewish leadership is on the way out (20:9–19), a teaching about paying taxes (20:20–26), and another about the resurrection (20:27–40). In these controversies Jesus responds with such wisdom that the opposition is silenced (20:7, 19, 26, 40, 44).

THE CRUCIFIXION, RESURRECTION, AND ASCENSION OF JESUS (22:1–24:53)

After Jesus' final Jerusalem ministry, Luke recounts the crucifixion and triumph of Christ. After the Last Supper (22:1–38), Jesus is arrested and tried. A central point is the absolute innocence of the Lord. Both Pilate (23:1–5) and Herod (23:6–12) examine him and find him innocent (23:4, 14–15; cf. 23:47). This message is important for Theophilus and other Christians who need to understand why the Savior was crucified. The only reason why Pilate yields is the pressure of the crowd. The crucifixion is viewed as the travesty of justice.

Jesus was led to the home of the high priest along a path like these first century steps in south Jerusalem

Cicero called crucifixion the *crudelissimum taeterrimique supplicii* ("that cruel and disgusting penalty"; *Against Verres* 2.5.165) and the *summo supplicio* ("the extreme penalty"; 2.5.168). It was considered the most wretched of deaths. Roman citizens and, in particular, members of the upper class were exempted from this form of execution. Death on a cross was limited to foreigners and people of the lower class, especially slaves.

CICERO ON ROMAN CITIZENS AND CRUCIFIXION

Cicero writes in *Pro Rabirio* 16:

How grievous a thing it is to be disgraced by a public court; how grievous to suffer a fine, how grievous to suffer banishment; and yet in the midst of any such disaster some trace of liberty is left to us. Even if we are threatened with death, we may die free men. But the executioner, the veiling of the head and the very word "cross" should be far removed not only from the person of a Roman citizen but from his thoughts, his eyes and his ears. For it is not only the actual occurrence of these things or the endurance of them, but liability to them, the expectation, nay, the mere mention of them, that is unworthy of a Roman citizen and a free man.

Top: The traditional site of Jesus' death and burial, The Church of the Holy Sepulchre, Jerusalem. *Middle:* Inside the church of the Holy Sepulchre, two first-century tombs. *Bottom:* Luke comments that the place of the ascension was in "the vicinity of Bethany" (24:50). The Church of the Ascension upon the Mount of Olives near Bethany marks the traditional location of the ascension. The church was constructed by Helena, the mother of Constantine, in AD 392.

The crucified Jesus, however, is raised from the dead. The first witnesses are women (24:1–12). They hear the witness of the two angels and remember Jesus' words (24:7–8). The implication is that they believe, a point evidenced by their witness (24:9–10). They keep repeating these things to the apostles (24:10), who consider their words to be only "so much nonsense."

Luke's gospel ends with the encounters of Jesus with the disciples on the road to Emmaus (24:13–35) and his appearance to the disciples in which he gives them tangible evidence that he is no mere phantasm (24:36–43). Luke's final account is the ascension of Jesus (24:50–53), which stitches this volume together with his second scroll, Acts (Acts 1:1–11).

AUTHOR AND DATE

While Luke-Acts supplies evidence about the identity of the first reader(s), the authorship of these two volumes is a more elusive question. The book does not name its author, but external evidence points to Luke, the travel companion of the apostle Paul, as the person who composed these volumes. If this identification is correct, then Luke-Acts is the only book in the New Testament written by a Gentile.

The person who wrote Luke and Acts was a well-educated person who could write fine literary Greek. He was also highly influenced by the Septuagint (LXX), especially in the speeches of Acts, yet he does not betray any direct knowledge of Hebrew Scripture. These evidences suggest the author is either a Greek or a Hellenistic Jew. He is not an eyewitness of the life of Jesus (Luke 1:2), though he identifies himself as a participant in the gospel (1:1).

In certain sections of Acts the narrative shifts from the third to the first person plural. These so-called "we" sections indicate that the author is an eyewitness of some of the events in early Christian history. For instance, this person is with Paul in Troas and Philippi during Paul's second missionary journey (Acts 16:8–10). He apparently remains behind in Philippi during that trip (16:17, 40). Later he rejoins Paul during the third tour when the apostle returns to Macedonia (20:3–5), and he even accompanies him to Jerusalem (21:17). He also travels with Paul on his imprisonment journey to Rome (27:1–28:16) and remains with him there.

Some scholars have suggested that these "we" sections are an artistic invention or that sources used by

The narrative in Acts occasionally shifts to the first person plural and from these "we" sections in Acts we can trace some of the movements of the author of Luke-Acts (indicated here by the use of dashed lines).

the author were written in the first person plural but were not changed to "they." But the simplest solution is probably the correct one. The author of Luke-Acts is someone who travels with Paul and ends up with him at Rome, but his name is not mentioned in Acts. Silas and Timothy are excluded as authors since they are mentioned in the third person (Acts 16:6–8; 15:40; 16:1–3), as are Mark, Barnabas, Apollos, and numerous others (20:4). Among the companions who appear with Paul in Rome, known through the letters he wrote from that city, we encounter Luke (Col. 4:14; Phlm. 24)—though Luke is not Paul's only unnamed companion. Based on this evidence, it is not implausible that Luke is the author, but we cannot prove it either.

The church was unanimous in crediting this book to Luke. Clement of Alexandria (AD 190–202) quoted the gospel frequently and attributed it to Luke, as did Tertullian (AD 190–220). The Muratorian Fragment (AD 170–200), an early canonical list, refers to the gospel and associates Luke the *medicus* ("physician") with it. Jerome (AD c. 345–c. 419) sums up ancient opinion: "Luke, a physician of Antioch as his writings indicate, was not unskilled in the Greek language. An adherent of the apostle Paul, and companion of all his journeying, he wrote a Gospel" (*De viris illustribus* 7).

LUKE AND SEUTONIUS

When the Roman historian Suetonius wrote about the life of Augustus, he explained how he handled his material: "Having given as it were a summary of his life, I shall now take up the various phases one by one, not in chronological order but by categories, to make the account clearer and more intelligible" (*Augustus* 9). Luke, as a historian of his time, selects and arranges the events of the life to Jesus in a way that underscored his portrait of the character and work of Jesus.

The earliest date for Luke-Acts is two years after Paul's arrival in Rome as a prisoner (Acts 28:30) or around AD 62. The fact that Acts ends so abruptly suggests this is the time of its composition. Since Luke is deeply concerned with central figures in the early church such as James (Jesus' brother), Peter, and Paul and the death of none of these is mentioned (James died in 62, Peter in 64/65 and Paul in the late 60s), an early date — in the early 60s, perhaps even AD 62 — appears a likely time of composition.

But some scholars have underplayed the importance of Luke's final statement, underscoring that the author's concern is to show how the gospel arrived at Rome and not to give a full account of Paul's life and ministry. Also, if Mark was the first canonical gospel written and if Luke used Mark, then the date of the book is likely later than the early 60s. Those who hold to a later date suggest a time after the fall of Jerusalem and the destruction of the temple (AD 70).

LUKE AS HISTORIAN

Luke writes as a participant in the early history of the church. His presence during Paul's journeys added credibility to his work in the eyes of ancient readers. But as a Gentile convert he relies on sources to garner information about the life of Christ and even admits this in his prologue (Luke 1:1–4). Luke is aware of the existence of other gospels, perhaps including Mark and a collection of Jesus' sayings such as "Q" (see Ch. 5). Some of the events he describes were handed down to him as sacred tradition (1:2) by those who observed Jesus' life, likely including Mary (1:5–2:52).

Luke has used great care in his research. In 1:3–4 he notes how he "followed" or "investigated" everything, suggesting that he not only knows his sources well but faithfully hands on what he has found. On the basis of this diligent research he can offer Theophilus this orderly account in order to confirm his faith. This book is not for those inside the church but for those who need to "know the certainty" of the teaching they have received, given the hostility leveled against the Christian faith during this era (Acts 17:6; 28:22). The word "certainty" was a favorite term in antiquity to denote a true philosophy as opposed to a superstition. Concern for certainty is also reflected in Acts 1:3, in which Luke tells Theophilus that, after his resurrection, Jesus gave the apostles "many convincing proofs that he was alive."

QUESTIONS FOR DISCUSSION ◎◎◎◎◎◎◎◎◎◎◎◎◎◎◎◎◎◎◎◎◎◎◎◎◎◎◎◎◎◎

1. How would you compare Luke's telling of the nativity story with that of Matthew? What are the prominent differences in their telling of the history and their theology?

2. Some scholars believe that Luke's "opening story" of Jesus in the Nazareth synagogue foretells the entire gospel (see Luke 4). Do you agree?

3. If we say that Luke presents theological themes in this gospel, does this present a difficulty for understanding the Gospels as historical records of Jesus' life?

4. If Luke underscores how Jesus includes those on society's margin and women as recipients of God's salvation, what should the church do today to make this a reality in its ministries?

5. Do you agree with those liberation theologians who contend that this gospel presents a "preferential option for the poor"? Why or why not? Frame your response in light of Luke's presentation of the gospel.

6. What does the message of "salvation" mean for contemporary people? How can we proclaim this message while being both faithful to the gospel and relevant to society?

BIBLIOGRAPHY
Introductory
Bock, D. L. *Luke*. IVPNTC. Downers Grove, IL: InterVarsity Press, 1994.

Ellis, E. E. *The Gospel of Luke*. NCB. Grand Rapids: Eerdmans, 1974.

Morris, L. *The Gospel According to St. Luke*. TNTC. Grand Rapids: Eerdmans, 1988.

Stein, R. H. *Luke*. NAC. Nashville: Broadmand & Holman, 1993.

Tannehill, R. C. *Luke*. ANTC. Nashville: Abingdon, 1996.

Advanced
Bock, D. L. *Luke*. BECNT. 2 vols. Grand Rapids: Baker, 1994, 1995.

Fitzmyer, J. A. *The Gospel According to Luke*. AB. 2 vols. Garden City, NY: Doubleday, 1981, 1985.

Green, J. B. *The Gospel of Luke*. NICNT. Grand Rapids: Eerdmans, 1997.

Marshall, I. H. *The Gospel of Luke*. NIGTC. Grand Rapids: Eerdmans, 1978.

Nolland, J. *Luke*. 3 vols. WBC. Dallas: Word, 1989, 1993.

NOTES

1. I. H. Marshall, *Luke: Historian and Theologian* (Exeter: Paternoster, 1970), 117.

2. Based on J. D. G. Dunn, *The Acts of the Apostles* (Harrisburg, PA: Trinity International, 1996), xiv.

3. D. L. Bock, *Luke*, 2 vols. (Grand Rapids: Baker, 1994–1995), 1:60. See Josephus, *Contra Apion* 1.53 [1.10]; 1.218 [1.23].

4. J. H. Charlesworth, *The Old Testament Pseudepigrapha*, 2:667.

5. A. N. Sherwin-White, *Roman Society and Roman Law in the New Testament* (Oxford: Clarendon, 1963), 162–71.

6. For a full discussion of the problem, see Bock, *Luke*, 1:903–9.

7. See B. J. Malina and J. H. Neyrey, "Honor and Shame in Luke-Acts: Pivotal Values of the Mediterranean World," in *The Social World of Luke-Acts*, ed. J. H. Neyrey, (Peabody, MA: Hendrikson, 1991), 29.

CHAPTER 11

THE GOSPEL ACCORDING TO JOHN

The great cardo or main street of Ephesus looking toward the Ephesian harbor. This is the traditional location of John's community.

The gospel of John is a careful retelling of Jesus' life that takes us deeper into the meaning of his life and work. John likely assumes we understand the basic outline of the Synoptic Gospels and therefore probes beneath the surface, supplying numerous stories untold elsewhere. Using irony, drama, and subtle theological nuance, John illustrates how Jesus' arrival fulfills and upends major Jewish festivals and institutions of worship.

Many unforgettable sayings of Jesus come from this gospel. Note, for example, the "I am" sayings (see sidebar, below). John also provides astounding affirmations of Jesus' divine nature and origin: "Before Abraham was born, I am" (8:58); "I and the Father are one" (10:30). It is John who takes the most creative step of describing Jesus as the Word of God through whom all creation came into being (1:3). His most dramatic turn comes in 1:14, when he tells us that this Word, which shares every feature with the Father, has become flesh, living among us.

In chapters 1–12, John describes Jesus' entry into the world and how Jesus offers "signs" as evidence of his identity. Jesus' "trial" begins the moment he is examined by the world, and throughout these chapters witnesses are brought forward demonstrating Jesus' truth and innocence. In chapters 13–21 John describes Jesus' movement toward his "glorification" on the cross: his arrest, trial, crucifixion, and burial. But this is no tragedy, but rather a further opportunity to unveil Jesus' true mission from God. With unexpected irony, John views the cross as Jesus' royal coronation, as a place of glory from which new life will flow to everyone who believes.

THE SETTING OF JOHN'S GOSPEL

A strong early church tradition places the location of John's ministry in Ephesus. According to fourth-century historian Eusebius and the theologian Irenaeus, John lived in Ephesus.

THE _I AM_ SAYINGS IN JOHN'S GOSPEL

_I am_ the bread of life. (6:35, 51)
_I am_ the light of the world. (8:12; 9:5)
_I am_ the gate for the sheep. (10:7, 9)
_I am_ the good shepherd. (10:11)
_I am_ the resurrection and the life. (11:25)
_I am_ the way and the truth and the life. (14:6)
_I am_ the true vine. (15:1, 5)

Jesus also uses the so-called "absolute" _I am_. Here the grammar defies logic. This _I am_ likely refers to the name of God given to Moses on Mount Sinai:

Unless you believe that _I am_, you will surely die in your sins. (8:24)
When you lift up the Son of Man, then you will realize that _I am_. (8:28)
Before Abraham was, _I am_. (8:58)
When it does happen, you may believe that _I am_. (13:19)

Sometimes the use is ambiguous. In some cases Jesus is simply identifying himself; in others, he is alluding to God:

_I am_ [or, it is I], don't be afraid. (6:20)
Jesus said to them, _I am_ [he]. (18:5)

Jesus visited numerous rural villages throughout Galilee. This rural village near Hebron (Der-Samet) reflects many of the architectural features of first century villages.

A generation after John, Ignatius of Antioch writes of the faithfulness and strength of the Ephesian church (*Ign. Eph.* 8–9).

If the traditions of early Christianity are correct, John became a leader in this region of Asia Minor. Ephesus may have been his base of ministry if he had jurisdiction over the seven leading churches of Asia (Rev. 1–3). John no doubt traveled to places such as Pergamum, Sardis, and Thyatria. He was the historian and theologian who brought to them the story of Jesus. He was a valued eyewitness to the life of Jesus (John 19:35).

In later years, John stood with the church in times of persecution and conflict. When it seemed that the fledgling community's struggle with the prestigious synagogue community would overwhelm them, John held to a courageous witness to Jesus Christ. When internal conflict later came to the church, John again was the community's strength, writing letters (1–3 John) to encourage them (see Chapter 25).

THE LITERARY FORM OF JOHN'S GOSPEL

This gospel betrays evidence of its literary history. If you read the entire gospel without regard for its chapter divisions, you will notice its natural literary divisions. In chapters 1–12 Jesus is at work in public, showing signs and teaching diverse public audiences. In chapters 13–17 he is in private speaking to his followers, almost saying "farewell" to them. The story ends with a detailed passion/resurrection account (chs. 18–21).

The setting of John's Gospel was likely in a Hellenistic city where Jewish and Hellenistic culture met. This Greek tomb from Ephesus depicts the female monster of Greek mythology, Medusa.

John alone tells us about the healing of a paraplegic man in Jerusalem at the five-porch pool of Bethesda (John 5:2). The pool is also mentioned at Qumran on the *Copper Scroll* (3Q15 11:12-13). This model reconstruction in Jerusalem shows its probable design.

Chapter 12 is therefore the climax to Jesus' public ministry. It ends with a "summing up" of Jesus' efforts, a cry of despair concerning disbelief, and a final reaffirmation of the divine origins of Jesus' words. John 13:1 moves to the Passover, remarks that Jesus is now departing from the world, and narrows the stage to those who have followed him. Chapter 17 ends a lengthy prayer. A shift to the Kidron Valley (ch. 18) moves us to Jesus' arrest, trial, and death.

These natural divisions are often labeled the "Book of Signs" (chs. 1–12), since they record Jesus' revelatory miracles, and the "Book of Glory" (chs. 13–21), since John interprets the cross as a place of Jesus' glorification (13:31).

The Book of Signs (John 1–12)

The Book of Signs begins with a prelude serving like an overture, a curtain-raiser to the drama that begins at verse 19. This is followed by a unit centered on John the Baptist and his disciples (and their earliest contacts with Jesus). Then the story moves quickly from scene to scene: a miracle at Cana, cleansing the temple, Nicodemus, and so on.

Clearly, these sections are *topically arranged*. From chapters 2–4 Jesus is working miracles on institutions in Judaism; from chapters 5–10 he is making appearances at a series of Jewish festivals (each festival is actually named). In other words, Jesus is replacing Jewish symbols with abundance, messianic abundance. For instance, at a Passover (ch. 6), which recalls the Exodus and God's provision of manna, Jesus feeds the crowd bread and then announces he is the true bread from heaven (6:41)!

John repeatedly refers to "hour" (Gk. *hōra*; e.g., 1:39; 2:4; 5:25; 7:30; 8:20; 12:23). Usually, *hora* refers to an hour of the day, but John frequently uses it to signal a specific period in Jesus' life. For example, at Cana when Mary tells Jesus that the wedding is out of wine, he responds, "My hour [*hora*] has not yet come" (2:4). He tells the Samaritan woman that "a time [*hora*] . . . has now come" for true worshipers to worship the Father in spirit and truth (4:23).

This phrase provides a rhythm for the entire gospel and indicates that Jesus' life was oriented toward one event: his glorification and return to the Father through the cross. Once Jesus returns to Jerusalem for the last time (ch. 12) and is betrayed and arrested (ch. 13), the "hour" of glory is underway, to be completed when he is raised from the dead. In this "hour" many great things happen. His sacrificial work on the cross is completed (19:30), he gives the Spirit (20:22), and he begins his return to glory (17:5, 24).

OUTLINE OF THE BOOK OF SIGNS (JOHN 1 – 12)

I. The Prologue (1:1 – 18)

II. Jesus and the Baptist (1:19 – 51)

III. Jesus and the Jewish Institutions (2:1 – 4:54)

    A. At Cana, Purification Vessels (2:1 – 12)
    B. In Jerusalem, the Temple (2:13 – 25)
    C. In Jerusalem, a Rabbi (3:1 – 21)
       {An additional excursus on the Baptist (3:22 – 36)}
    D. In Samaria, a Sacred Well (4:1 – 42)
    E. Return to Cana (4:43 – 54)

IV. Jesus and Jewish Festivals (5:1 – 10:42)

    A. Sabbath (5:1 – 47)
    B. Passover (6:1 – 71)
    C. Tabernacles (7:1 – 9:41)
    D. Rededication [Hanukkah] (10:1 – 39)
    E. Return to John the Baptist (10:40 – 42)

V. Foreshadowing Jesus' Death and Resurrection (11:1 – 12:50)

    A. Lazarus: A Paradigm of Death and Life (11:1 – 57)
    B. Jesus Anointed for Death Enters Jerusalem to Die (12:1 – 50)

A careful examination of the Book of Signs reveals *internal markers* that subdivide each section. For example, stories in Cana frame the section on Jewish institutions. The festival section clearly refers to each respective festival, exploits a major symbol in the festival (Sabbath/work, Passover/bread, Tabernacles/water and light, Rededication/Jesus' consecration), and generally offers a discourse expanding the meaning of the symbols (see 6:15 – 35 as a comment on Passover). The final reference to John the Baptist (10:40 – 42) refers back to the beginning of the entire sequence of signs (1:19ff.), making another closing frame and reiterating the value of Jesus' signs. The closing two chapters serve as a sobering warning of what is to come. In chapter 11, the death and raising of Lazarus foreshadows the death and raising of Jesus,

In John 9 Jesus directs the blind man to go wash in the "pool of Siloam." This pool, south of the temple, was used daily during the Festival of Tabernacles.

LIVING WATER IN FIRST CENTURY JUDAISM

In a land that frequently experienced drought, Israel was keenly aware of water sources and water quality. Springs and rivers that ran all year were few and so the land used systems to catch the winter rains and store them (cisterns) or dug wells. In Jewish culture, "dead water" was standing, stored water. "Living water" was moving water (e.g., rivers, springs, and rainfall); such water came directly from God and did not have to be transported by human hands (up a well or cistern). Only living water could serve as water for ritual washings.

This distinction explains why the woman of Samaria is so amused when Jesus claims to know where living water is. Samaria has no river. If Jacob had to cut a well here, how can Jesus be superior?

Jesus mentions living water again at Jerusalem's autumn Feast of Tabernacles (7:37–39). In this period of drought, everyone prayed for renewing rains to end the dry summer. At the festival Jesus makes an extravagant claim: Anyone looking for living water should come to him and drink, for he is the source of such renewing water directly from God.

NOTES FROM ANTIQUITY

In John 4 Jesus' offer of living water referred to ritual water used for purification. This Jewish ritual bath (*mikveh*) at Qumran was "purified" by running ("living") water brought down by channels from cliffs west of the site.

and in chapter 12, Jesus cries out about Jewish unbelief while Greeks come to the disciples eagerly seeking "to see" Jesus.

As we examine this structure, we see the topical arrangement (at least in chs. 1–12), even though the stories themselves have a clear historical character. Foremost on John's agenda is the theological meaning of Jesus Christ and his impact on Judaism. As readers who watch the drama unfold, we come away with a clear understanding of Jesus' identity; in light of his coming, every religious position has been called into question.

The Book of Glory (John 13–21)

The same theological agenda can be found in the Book of Glory. Jesus turns in private to his disciples during his final Passover. He teaches them about servanthood, washes their feet, explains the coming Holy Spirit in terms of personal revelation and persecution, and prays at length for his followers and their disciples.

Chapter 18 opens the story of the trial and death of Jesus. It reads much like the Synoptics, moving quickly from scene to scene. The cross is followed by a detailed resurrection account in which Jesus anoints his followers with the Spirit. Chapter 21 is likely an addition about resurrection stories in Galilee and Jesus' lengthy discussion with Peter.

It is important to see that the cross is carefully reinterpreted in John's gospel. The anguish described by the Synoptics in Gethsemane does not appear here. Jesus moves confidently toward "the hour." At his arrest, he steps forward and gives orders. At his trial, he asks the questions. He is robed like a king and "lifted up" on the cross under a sign announcing in the languages of the world that he is "the King of the Jews."

OUTLINE OF THE BOOK OF GLORY (JOHN 13 – 21)

I. The Passover Meal (13:1 – 30)

    A. The Foot Washing (13:1 – 20)
    B. The Betrayal of Judas (13:21 – 30)

II. The Farewell Discourse (13:31 – 17:26)

    A. Jesus' Departure and Provision (13:31 – 14:31)
    B. The True Vine (15:1 – 17)
    C. The Disciples and the World (15:18 – 16:33)
    D. The Priestly Prayer of Jesus (17:1 – 26)

III. The Suffering and Death of Jesus (18:1 – 19:42)

    A. Arrest and Interrogation (18:1 – 19:16)
    B. Crucifixion and Burial (19:17 – 42)

IV. The Resurrection (20:1 – 31)

V. Epilogue (21:1 – 25)

THEOLOGICAL THEMES IN JOHN'S GOSPEL

John's stories contribute to a theological portrait that has been deeply valued in the history of the church. They weave themselves throughout John's gospel.

John's Central Affirmation

The most important affirmation of this gospel is that God has appeared in human history in the man Jesus Christ. In him we see the glory of God (1:14). Despite the unrelenting darkness of this world, God has entered our world, which stands in enmity with him. But he does

---

THE CROSS AND PASSOVER

In 1:29, 36, John the Baptist introduces Jesus as the "lamb of God." This title may refer to the sacrificial lamb that was killed daily in the temple (Ex. 29:38 – 46) or the lamb of Isaiah 53:7. But more likely John sees Jesus as the Passover lamb, whose death marked the central event of the Passover—the blood of a lamb that covered the doors of the Israelites in Egypt and saved them (Ex. 12).

Jews coming to Jerusalem to celebrate the Passover had to supply (or purchase) a perfect young lamb for sacrifice. No bones could be broken. No disease could be present. The Levite watched for running blood when the lamb was sacrificed to verify the lamb was alive.

At his final Passover, Jesus uses the meal to show that his death is a sacrifice (Mark 14:17 – 31). In John, the cross becomes an altar where Christ, the Passover lamb, is slain. The hyssop used at the cross was also used at the Passover (cf. John 19:29; Ex. 12:22). Jesus' legs are not broken (19:33), which fulfills a Passover rule (John 19:36; Ex. 12:46). Blood runs freely from his wound (19:34), showing that his life is being exchanged for others.

John tells us that when Jesus was on the cross, hyssop was used to extend a drink of wine to him (19:29). Hyssop was also used by the Israelites in Egypt at Passover to cover their homes in lamb's blood (Exod 12:22)—a symbol John no doubt valued.

---

so through human flesh, embracing our own creatureliness. This revelation is so potent that darkness cannot defeat it. Even though Jesus is persecuted, tried, and crucified, John affirms that the light cannot be extinguished (see 1:5).

But Christ's gift is not simply his revelation of the Father (14:9). "In him was life and the life was the light of all people" (1:4 NRSV). There is hope for the world. John's message is also one of sacrifice and redemption. Those who embrace this revelation by identifying with the light will gain eternal life. The life of the Son is poured out in sacrifice, thereby creating the community of the redeemed (17:6–12, 20–26). They bear Christ's Spirit, which sustains them.

Thus, John writes to explain this revelation and redemption and all their possibilities. In 20:31 he makes clear this aim, "But these are written that you may believe that Jesus is the Messiah, the Son of God, and that by believing you may have life in his name." Here all of John's major themes converge: belief, acknowledgment of Jesus' sonship, and the promise of life.

Circumstances John Must Address

John is likely written for Christians who, already knowing the rudiments of Christ's life and Christian truth, now wish to go further. Not only is there an uncompromising maturity of thought in this gospel, but also its narratives imply it is written to address certain practical

ANTI-SEMITISM AND JOHN'S GOSPEL

For some scholars, the gospel of John has contributed directly to the anti-Judaism of the past two thousand years. Seventy-one times the phrase "the Jews" appears in this gospel. Matthew and Luke, by comparison, only use the term five times each.

Anti-Semitism has been the dark heritage of the church. But those who read John as endorsing anti-Semitism deeply misread it. Jesus and the apostles are Jewish. So are his opponents. Jesus does not wrestle with "the Jews" — he is a Jew! He is not condemned by "the Jews" — he is condemned by the brokers of religious power in first-century Jerusalem. In most cases "the Jews" refers either to the "Judeans" (7:1) or to Jewish leaders.

circumstances in the church. John asserts Christian truth amidst unsympathetic forces and clarifies Christian doctrines at an early stage of church development.

For instance, John gives attention to the relationship between Jesus' followers and Judaism. The Synoptic Gospels contain many conflict stories between Jesus and the Pharisees. John not only deepens the conflict but explains it (cf. 8:31–59; 10:19–39). The "Jews" virtually becomes a technical term in John for those who reject Jesus. His messiahship and his relationship to the festivals and institutions of Judaism are emphasized. Jesus has come to replace what is offered in the Jewish institutions. Such an emphasis likely springs from a Christian community that is experiencing marked conflict with the synagogue.

John's gospel also emphasizes themes important to the development of Christian life and thought throughout the first century. At the time the gospel was circulating publicly the early Christian church had grown and diversified considerably. Thus, John includes historic materials relevant to Christian needs in his generation. But we must not think these needs became the controlling force in John's literary design.

(1) John the Baptist. Did the Baptist have followers who refused to follow Jesus? Luke 3:15 and Acts 19:1–7 suggest this while later writings confirm it. This gospel affirms, however, that the Baptist was not the Messiah (John 1:20; 3:28) or the light (1:8–9), and that Jesus is superior (1:30; 3:29–30; 10:41). We even witness certain disciples of John becoming Jesus' first converts (1:35–42).

(2) The person of Christ. In a fashion unparalleled by the Synoptics, John affirms the oneness of Jesus and the Father (10:30; 14:9–10), their distinction from each other (14:28; 17:1–5), and their unity of purpose (5:17–18; 8:42). In the formation of later Trinitarian doctrine, John played a notable role. This was particularly true at the Council of Nicea (325), when Arius denied the eternal nature of the Son and Athanasius affirmed Jesus as the eternal Logos (1:1). Both

When Jesus visited Samaria (John 4), the region had developed its own distinct history, culture and religious traditions. Mt. Gerizim was the site of the Samaritan temple (4:20), which was destroyed in 128 BC. It is here depicted (with steps) on a fourth-century Samaritan oil lamp.

Greek and Jewish listeners would immediately recognize in this title a profound statement. Greeks would think of the seminal forces that sustain the universe; Jewish minds would think back to Genesis 1, where the word of God was the means of creation.

In Jesus' day, the word of God took on personal creative attributes (Ps. 33:6, 9) and was viewed as an apt description for divine Wisdom. In Proverbs 8, Wisdom coexisted with God from the beginning. Through Wisdom — the Logos — God extended himself into

John's gospel ends with Peter meeting Jesus on Galilee's north shore. This site, today called St. Peter's Primacy, has been venerated by Christian pilgrims at least since the 4th century.

the cosmos, creating the world. Jesus shares the very same essence as God: He existed before time and was the agent of all creation. In perhaps the most surprising verse penned by an apostle, John writes that this Logos, this Wisdom, became flesh and lived among us as a human being (1:14).

For Jews who might struggle with the divinity of Christ, this category of Wisdom gave a ready-made explanation. No rabbi would doubt that divine Wisdom came from God since the beginning of time. No rabbi doubted the personal coexistence of Wisdom with God. John echoes this conviction: What God is, so the Logos is. And the Logos is Christ (cf. 1:1–2).

Thus, John asserts the *divinity* of Christ in the strongest terms. If anyone were inclined toward *adoptionism* (that Jesus was merely a divinely inspired man), the gospel gives an unrelenting rebuttal. But the Greek world was comfortable with divinities and, if anything, hesitated to affirm Jesus "full humanity" (*docetism*). In John Jesus was eternally divine and fully incarnate—fully God and fully human.

(3) The Holy Spirit. John provides us with a wealth of information concerning the Spirit. His treatment moves in two directions. (a) John emphasizes how the Spirit is an integral feature of Jesus' experience of God. During Jesus' baptism, for instance, the Spirit *remains* on Jesus (1:32–33), underscoring the permanence of God's indwelling in him. God has given him the Spirit without measure (3:34). The Spirit is a source of living water (4:10), which later we learn flows from within Jesus himself (7:37–39). The release of the Spirit is dependent on Jesus' death (7:39): "Unless I go away, the Advocate/Paraclete will not come to you" (16:7). This imagery that joins Spirit and Christ may be at work in the cross when Jesus is wounded and water (along with blood) flows from him (19:34).

(b) John promises the Spirit to believers. He records Jesus' nighttime conversation with Nicodemus in which he challenges the rabbi to be born again (3:1–10). This is a work not of intellectual or moral conversion, but of spiritual activity. The same is true for the Samaritan woman, a character who stands theologically and socially opposite Nicodemus. The living water she seeks (4:15) is later defined as the Spirit (7:37–38), and Jesus takes advantage of Samaria's cultural rift with Judaism to talk about true worship that engages the Spirit (4:24). The work of the Spirit culminates in Jesus' lengthy farewell discourse (chs. 14–16), where the Spirit is described and promised for all believers. John even records Jesus' giving the Spirit to his disciples on Easter day as a final gift before his departure (20:22). To be united with Jesus is to experience his Spirit, which is set free for the world at the cross.

LAZARUS' BURIAL

The death, burial, and resurrection of Lazarus in John 11 are an ironic foreshadowing of Jesus' passion in the Fourth Gospel. In Jewish custom, a person was usually buried on the day he died. The body was washed, perfumed, and wrapped, and mourning continued for one week. Visitors visited the tomb to pray and recite Scripture. Emotion was public in this culture, so wailing was loud and raucous. Many believed that the spirit of the person left the body and they would be unrecognizable.

This explains Martha's grief in John 11:39. Four days have passed for Lazarus and all hope is lost. Jesus' power, however, can overcome even this obstacle. This also explains Jesus' burial for three days. The women are distraught because if Jesus' body cannot be found immediately, he may not be recognizable. Jesus' return before Monday puts their concerns to rest.

(4) The sacraments. John has a "sacramental" view of history inasmuch as the incarnation of Christ for him means the genuine appearance of God in history. Worship can affirm such genuine appearances when worship symbols (baptism, the Lord's Supper) take on the real properties of that which they depict. Hence they are called "sacraments." While scholars debate the role of the sacraments in this gospel, his main message about each (found in 3:1–21 and 6:52–65) is corrective: Without the Holy Spirit these expressions of worship become powerless rituals void of their original purpose.

(5) Our future hope: eschatology. Many early Christians longed for the second coming of Christ and anticipated an imminent end to history. This explains the cherished sayings of Jesus about his second coming in the Synoptics (see Matt. 24; Mark 13; Luke 21). How did they cope when this hope was frustrated (cf. 2 Peter 3:1–12)? John, while maintaining this hope (John 5:25–30; 1 John 2:28), introduces a fresh emphasis: The longed-for presence of Jesus is mediated to us *now* in the Spirit. Jesus has come back and is with us already in the Spirit. In technical terms, John emphasizes a *realized eschatology* in contrast to the apocalyptic hope of the Synoptics.

(6) Irony. John invites us to explore a theme that has troubled interpreters. Is it possible for us to comprehend Jesus' words and actions, or do we always filter them through our own experiences? If the original audience of Jesus had difficulty understanding him, will it be difficult for us who now read his words in English centuries later?

Jesus frequently came to Jerusalem by climbing the mountains of Judea. Here a Roman aqueduct remains from that road

John's gospel creates a drama on a stage. We sit in the audience watching characters move in and out, making contact with Jesus. Remarkably, many misunderstand what is happening and either race to the wrong conclusion (6:15), reject him outright (7:43–44), or debate among themselves (7:12–13).

In 11:2 and 12:3 John identifies Mary of Bethany as the one who anointed Jesus with perfume from bottles such as these the week prior to his burial.

Nicodemus, for instance, hears Jesus say that he must be born again, and he wonders if he must return to his mother's womb (3:4). The Samaritan woman hears Jesus offer her living water and promptly wonders how he can offer her water when he has no bucket and there are no streams nearby (4:11). Later, Jesus' disciples bring him food and encourage him to eat, but he says he has other food they don't know about. Immediately they wonder, "Could someone have brought him food?" (4:33). Jesus even tells the Pharisees that he is going someplace where they cannot follow (heaven), but they speculate that he must be making a trip to visit Greeks (7:35)! Sometimes a person makes an ironic, misunderstanding statement and does not even know its significance. In 11:50 Caiaphas is plotting politics when he says that it is good that one man should die for the sake of the nation; no truer words were ever uttered.

What is going on here? Following many of Jesus' speeches, the audience argues over the meaning of his identity. In some cases, when they perceive who he really is, some want to arrest him while others want to become his disciples (7:43–44). In 9:35–41, Jesus announces that a blind man now can see—and the sighted Pharisees have become blind!

The secret is found in 1:5 and 3:19–21. John understands that the world lives in darkness and so cannot understand the reality of things around it. *Divine revelation is inaccessible to the world.* In fact, when God's light penetrates that darkness, exposing the unreality of the world's life, many flee deeper into the darkness because they prefer it. The darkness hates the light. Only the transforming power of God's Spirit can reverse our incomprehension

When Jesus referred to the vine (John 15) he took advantage of one of Israel's most familiar images. Note how the lintel on this Jewish tomb near Jerusalem uses the same images.

and make us children of God able to see things clearly. Only later do the disciples really understand the meaning of Jesus (2:22). Only when they gain the Spirit do they understand (16:12–13).

(7) The world. One of the most frequently used words in John's gospel is "the world" (*kosmos*). The term appears seventy-eight times in his gospel (and twenty-four times in his letters). No other gospel has anything similar. In Greek-speaking Jewish thought, *kosmos* refers to the heavens and the earth created by God in Genesis 1. John shares this thought (1:3, 10; 17:5, 24) but takes the concept further. The "world" is more specifically the "universe" of humanity. For example, see John 1:10, "Though the world was made through him, the world did not recognize him" when he came. The second "world" refers to humanity.

John understands that this world—though good—is hostile to the things of God. It is controlled by a darkness that cannot comprehend the light and resists it (3:19). It is dead and needs life (6:33, 51), yet it hates the very One who can save it (7:7). The root problem is that the world is under the dominion of Satan (12:31), who will one day be judged. Nevertheless, God loves the world (3:16), that is, sinful humanity arrayed against him. Jesus thus dies to take away the sin of the world (1:29) and bring it the only prospect for life.

Christ wants his disciples to have an honest assessment about the world. They too will be despised (15:18; 17:14), and the Spirit within them will engage the world in its errors (16:7–11). Above all, Jesus' gives his followers a word of assurance: "In this world you will have trouble. But take heart! I have overcome the world" (16:33).

AUTHORSHIP AND DATE

John's gospel, like the others, provides no explicit internal evidence concerning its author. It may, however, provide us with clues concealed in the enigmatic figure of the "disciple whom Jesus loved" (the "beloved disciple"). This title occurs in six passages in John (13:23; 19:26–27; 20:2–10; 21:7, 23, 24). This last passage describes him as the one "who testifies to these things and who wrote them down." Therefore the origin of the gospel must in some way be connected to this person.

But who is he? Some have suggested he is an idealized literary figure. To a degree this is true (he is faithful and intimate in his knowledge of Jesus). But this hardly excludes the possibility of a genuine historical person. Lazarus is sometimes nominated. He is the only figure of whom it is said that Jesus loved him (11:3, 11, 36). Furthermore, these texts occur only after Lazarus is introduced in chapter 11. But this solution is unlikely. Why would Lazarus's name be mentioned in chapters 11–12 but then left shrouded in subsequent accounts?

Some have suggested *John* Mark as the author. We do know that a man named John Mark was a part of the early church (Acts 12:12) and that he was associated with Peter. This may explain the mild rivalry between Peter and the beloved disciple in this gospel (cf. 20:2–8; 21:7–14); further, if Mark was related to the Levite Barnabas (Col 4:10), this would also explain how the beloved disciple knows the high priest in 18:15. But there is a strong patristic tradition that Mark authored the second gospel, not this one; besides, the beloved disciple is certainly one of the Twelve (13:23), which Mark was not.

The most recent suggestion points to Thomas as the beloved disciple. Throughout the gospel Thomas is presented as a person of leadership (11:16). His story with Jesus even concludes the gospel (assuming that ch. 20 originally ended the book). Above all, Thomas asks to see the wound in Jesus' side, and the beloved disciple was the only one who saw the piercing of Jesus (19:35).

Stone jars such as these were used in Jewish homes in the first century. They were made of stone (not pottery) because stone did not take on the properties of ritual impurity.

But the best solution is the traditional one: John son of Zebedee (Mark 3:17; Acts 1:13). This man was one of the Twelve, and along with James and Peter formed an inner circle around Jesus. This is the origin of his eyewitness testimony and penetrating insight. In the Synoptics John appears with Peter more than with any other, and in Acts they are companions in Jerusalem (Acts 3–4) as well as in Samaria (8:14). In fact, John and Jesus may have been cousins. (A careful comparison of the names of the women at the cross suggests that Jesus' and John's mothers may have been sisters.) This explains two things. In John 19:25–27 Jesus entrusts Mary to John because of a natural family relation, and in 18:15–16 John is known by the high priest through Mary's priestly relatives (Luke 1:5, 36).

Later patristic evidence also points to the apostle John. Irenaeus (AD 200) says that the beloved disciple was John and that John wrote the gospel at Ephesus. Irenaeus also writes that he knew Polycarp, bishop of Smyrna (c. AD 69–155), who claimed to have been tutored by John himself. Eusebius (c. AD 300) records this John/Polycarp/Irenaeus connection in the same way. John's association with this gospel is also confirmed by Clement of Alexandria (c. AD 200) and the Muratorian Canon (AD 180–200).

If John son of Zebedee wrote this gospel, we can make some conclusion about its date. The sources of John must be early and have their roots in first-generation Christianity. But fixing a certain date for the publication of the gospel is difficult because objective data are slim. The latest possible date is AD 125. Recently in Egypt two papyrus fragments of John (Rylands Papyrus 457 [P52, see p. 442] and Egerton Papyrus 2) have been dated to the first half of the second century. Allowing time for John to circulate, we can say that John could not have been completed after 110.

The earliest possible date for the gospel is more difficult. If John knows and uses the Synoptics (and this is disputed), then AD 70 or 80 is appropriate. In John 9:22; 12:42; and

A medieval basilica dedicated to John commemorates his death in Ephesus. However excavations beneath it show a 3rd century mausoleum that may point to the authenticity of the tradition about John's death in this city.

16:2 we read about Jewish believers being excommunicated from the synagogues. In AD 85 the rabbis of Palestine instituted such expulsions for Christians. Therefore we find a remarkable consensus of scholarly opinion that John was published somewhere between AD 80 and 100.

Nevertheless, an earlier date may be possible. Current research has challenged John's literary dependence on the Synoptics (esp. Mark and Luke). If anything, John may know pre-Synoptic traditions. Above all, the way in which John describes Jerusalem, his knowledge of the geographical and political divisions in Judaism, and his use of metaphors all point to a date approximating that of the Synoptic writers. The great watershed date of AD 70 is critical: John presupposes a Judaism before this war. With his critical disposition toward the temple (John 2:13–25; 4:21–25) and severe conflicts with Jewish leadership (cf. chs. 5, 8, 10), we are surprised to find no hint of this catastrophic event.

If Jesus and Nicodemus met in the temple courts (John 3), Jesus may have entered the temple via these southern steps. This area from the first century has now been excavated.

QUESTIONS FOR DISCUSSION ⊚⊚⊚⊚⊚⊚⊚⊚⊚⊚⊚⊚⊚⊚⊚⊚⊚⊚⊚⊚⊚⊚⊚⊚⊚⊚⊚

1. What are the chief differences between John's Gospel and the Synoptics?

2. Why does John describe each of Jesus' miracles as a "sign"?

3. How many times in this gospel does Jesus' audience "divide" — some people believe, others become antagonistic? What does this say about the "world"?

4. In some stories in John (e.g., chs. 1, 4, 9) the narrative itself parades before us a catalogue of theological names for Jesus. What does John want us to understanding about the chief character in the story?

5. What is the relationship between signs and faith in John's gospel? Does John view miraculous signs as genuine avenues to a strong faith?

BIBLIOGRAPHY
Introductory
Blomberg, C. *The Historical Reliability of John's Gospel*. Downers Grove, IL: InterVarsity Press, 2002.

Burge, G. M. *John*. NIVAC. Grand Rapids: Zondervan, 2000.

Morris, L. *The Gospel according to St. John*. Revised edition. NICNT. Grand Rapids: Eerdmans, 1995.

Advanced
Ashton, J. *Understanding the Fourth Gospel*. Rev. ed. Oxford: Oxford Univ. Press, 2007.

Brown, R. E. *The Gospel according to John*. AB. 2 vols. New York: Doubleday, 1966, 1970.

Keener, C. *The Gospel of John: A Commentary*. 2 vols. Peabody, MA: Hendrickson, 2003.

Köstenberger, A. *John*. BECNT. Grand Rapids: Baker, 2003.

CHAPTER 12

THE ACTS OF
THE APOSTLES

Paul was accused before Gallio, the Roman proconsul of Achaia, at the *bema* (latin: *rostrum*) in Corinth (Acts 18:12-17).

Acts serves as a "bridge document" that links the Gospels to the New Testament letters. Here we learn about the fate of Christ's earliest followers—how they consolidate the early church in Jerusalem and envision a mission that will send missionaries as far as Rome.

Luke recounts the compelling story of the establishment of the first churches throughout the empire, although his history does not comprehensively describe all the activities of all the apostles. He traces the spread of Christianity to Jews and Gentiles from every social stratum throughout the empire. His subject is God's salvation in Jesus Christ, intended for all people, regardless of class or ethnicity (cf. Rom 1:16). While Luke writes this history for Theophilus and others (1:1), we discover ourselves in this narrative since, in Peter's words, God's promise is "for all who are far off—for all whom the Lord our God will call" (2:39).

THE SETTING OF ACTS IN THE NEW TESTAMENT

The placement of Acts after John is somewhat confusing since Luke composed this story as the second volume of a book written to Theophilus (cf. 1:1–2 and Luke 1:1–4). These two scrolls should be read and understood together as one continuous narrative (see Ch. 10 for a comparison of Luke and Acts).

Luke-Acts traces the geographic progress of the gospel. His life of Jesus begins in Jerusalem when John the Baptist's father, Zechariah, goes to fulfill his priestly duty in the temple (Luke 1:9). Jesus is circumcised and presented in the temple as an infant (2:22) and, at the age of twelve, goes with Mary and Joseph to Jerusalem (2:41–51). While his public ministry centers in Galilee (4:14–15), Jerusalem is the place of his crucifixion, resurrection, and ascension.

Just before his ascension, Jesus commands his disciples to spread the gospel from Jerusalem out to the wider world (Luke 24:44–47). Acts begins with this command and expands on it: "You will be my witnesses in Jerusalem, and in all Judea and Samaria, and to the ends of the earth" (Acts 1:8). Acts tells how this command is fulfilled in Jerusalem (2:14–36), around Judea and Samaria (8:1), then all the way to Rome (23:11; 28:11–16).

Luke also wants to demonstrate the place of the gospel within Roman history. Jesus was born during the reign of Caesar Augustus and the rule of Quirinius, governor of Syria (Luke 2:1–2). Jesus' public ministry and crucifixion occurred when Pontius Pilate was procurator

---

"THE ENDS OF THE EARTH"

Ancient authors identified "ends of the earth" with various distant points. First-century geographer Strabo, for example, links the phrase to Gades in Spain (near modern Cadiz; see *Geography* 3.1.8). This may be why Paul is so concerned to bring the gospel to Spain (Rom. 15:24, 28).

But Strabo also views the world as an island, so any distant place that borders the sea can be identified this way. He notes how Homer viewed Ethiopia as the "ends of the earth" (*Geography* 1.1.6). The unknown author of the *Psalms of Solomon* speaks of the Roman general Pompey (who conquered Jerusalem in 63 BC) as having come "from the end of the earth" (*Pss. Sol.* 8:15). Thus, Acts 1:8 may refer to extending the gospel to the imperial city.

But this phrase also has ethnic associations. In Isaiah 49:6, God commissions the Servant of the Lord: "I will also make you a light for the Gentiles, that my salvation may reach to the ends of the earth" (cf. Acts 13:47). Acts 1:8 may therefore refer not only to the geographic but also the ethnic expansion of the Christian faith.

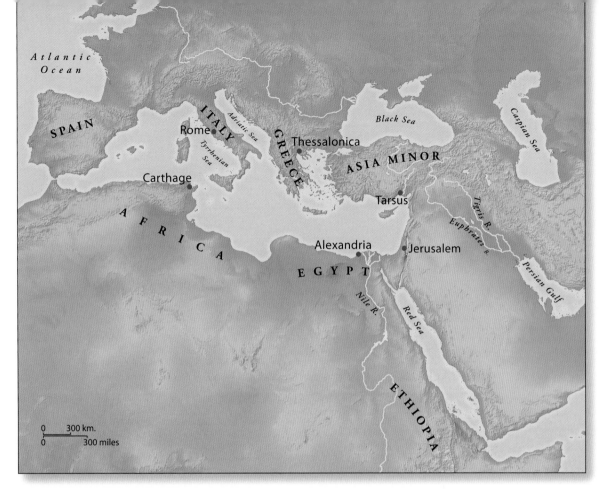

Both Spain and Ethiopia, as well as Rome, were sometimes called "the ends of the earth."

of Judea (Luke 3:1). Luke mentions a famine in Jerusalem (Acts 11:28) and expulsion of Jews from Rome (18:1–2) during the reign of Claudius. Paul was tried before two governors of Judea, Felix (24:1–2) and Porcius Festus (25:1–7).

Luke is also interested in theology, seen especially in the speeches in Acts. As Hengel observes, "We only do justice to the significance of Luke as the first theological 'historian' of Christianity if we take his work seriously as a source, i.e., if we attempt to examine it critically, reconstructing the story he tells by adding and comparing other sources. . . . He does not set out primarily to present his own 'theology.'"[1]

LUKE'S HISTORY OF THE EARLY CHURCH

Many commentators understand Jesus' commission in 1:8 as a synopsis of the book: "You will be my witnesses in Jerusalem, and in all Judea and Samaria, and to the ends of the earth." Acts is about the spread of the gospel in Jerusalem and Judea (chs. 1–7), then to Samaria and to Antioch (chs. 8–12), culminating with Paul's three missionary journeys throughout the empire (chs. 13–28).

But the story in Acts also revolves around people. Peter is the main protagonist in the first part of the book (chs. 1–12) while Paul becomes the central figure in the second part (chs. 13–28). The lives of these two apostles are paralleled repeatedly.

Luke shows the spread of the gospel throughout the northern Mediterranean, reaching as far west as Rome, where the temple of Divus Romulus, the founder of Rome, is located.

PARALLELS OF PETER AND PAUL IN ACTS

Peter	Paul
Sermon in Jerusalem (2:22–36)	Sermon in Pisidian Antioch (13:26–41)
Lame man healed (3:1–10)	Lame man healed (14:8–11)
Filled with Spirit (4:8)	Filled with Spirit (13:9)
Extraordinary healings (5:15)	Extraordinary healings (19:12)
Laying on hands to receive Spirit (8:17)	Laying on hands to receive Spirit (19:6)
Conflict with magician (8:18–24)	Conflict with magician (13:6–11)
Tabitha raised from the dead (9:36–41)	Eutychus raised from the dead (20:9–12)
Miraculously released from jail (12:6–11)	Miraculously released from jail (16:25–41)

THE HISTORIAN'S TASK

Commenting on the historian's task, Lucian writes in *How to Write History* 55:

> After the preface ... let the transition to the narrative be gentle and easy. For all the body of the history is simply a long narrative.... [The historian] will make everything distinct and complete, and when he has finished the first topic he will introduce the second, fastened to it and linked with it like a chain, to avoid breaks and a multiplicity of disjointed narratives; no, always the first and the second topics must not merely be neighbors but have common matter and overlap.

Another prominent structural element in the book is Luke's summary statements, which stitch his narrative together around the growth of the church and the expansion of the gospel (6:7; 9:31; 12:24; 16:5; 19:20), with a final summary statement at the end (28:30–31). These summaries divide the text up into six sections or panels.

These various structural elements make deciding how best to outline the story of Acts difficult. But ancient ideals about writing history apparently move Luke to bind the various incidents together into a cohesive unit. The "common matter and overlap" in Acts (see sidebar on "The Historian's Task") helps the reader understand the story as a cohesive unit and not as a simple collection of historical vignettes, but it does make outlining the book problematic. But Acts 1:8 is still the best way to give the overall framework of Acts (see outline).

OUTLINE OF ACTS

I. Beginnings in Jerusalem (1:1–26)

II. Mission in Jerusalem (2:1–8:3)

  A. Early Witness to the Jewish Populace in Jerusalem (2:1–3:26)
  B. Early Persecution and Life of the Church (4:1–8:3)

III. Mission in Judea, Samaria, and the Surrounding Regions (8:4–12:25)

  A. Peter's Testimony to the Samaritans (8:4–40)
  B. Call of Saul (9:1–31)
  C. Peter's Miracles and Mission to Gentiles in Caesarea (9:32–11:18)
  D. Spread of the Gospel to Gentiles to Antioch (11:19–30)
  E. Death of Herod Agrippa I (12:1–25)

IV. Mission to the Ends of the Earth (13:1–28:31)

  A. Paul's First Missionary Journey and the Jerusalem Council (13:1–15:35)
    1. Mission to Cyprus and Southern Galatia (13:1–14:28)
    2. Jerusalem Council (15:1–35)
  B. Paul's Second Missionary Journey (15:36–18:22)
    1. Return to the Galatian Churches (15:36–16:5)
    2. Mission to Macedonia and Achaia (16:6–18:22)
  C. Paul's Third Missionary Journey (18:23–20:38)
    1. The Mission to Ephesus (18:23–19:41)
    2. The Return to Macedonia, Achaia, and Troas (20:1–12)
    3. Address to the Ephesian Elders (20:13–38)
  D. Paul's Return to Jerusalem (21:1–22:21)
  E. Paul's Imprisonment in Jerusalem, Caesarea, and Rome (22:22–28:31)
    1. Imprisonment and Witness in Jerusalem (22:22–23:22)
    2. Imprisonment and Witness in Caesarea (23:23–26:32)
    3. Journey to Rome and Witness (27:1–28:31)

THE BEGINNINGS IN JERUSALEM (1:1–26)

Before his ascension (1:9–11), Jesus commissions the apostles in response to their question, "Lord, are you at this time going to restore the kingdom to Israel?" (1:6). During the first century, most Jews longed for liberation from Rome and the reestablishment of the Davidic monarchy. Some even attempted to bring about this liberation through armed conflict (5:36–37; 21:38).

The burning hope was for reestablishment of the twelve tribes, the conquest or conversion of the Gentiles, a purified and glorious temple, and purity and justice in the worship and moral life of Israel. This was the disciples' hope as well, but their hopes were dashed with Jesus' crucifixion (Luke 24:21). Now that Jesus is raised from the dead, their hope is revived. In Acts 1:7, the apostles are thinking of the kingdom in terms of the promises made to Israel and the restoration of national sovereignty, but Jesus has in mind a larger vision of the kingdom. Before it comes, the church must proclaim the gospel of Jesus Christ to all people everywhere in the power of the Spirit (1:8). Then the ascended Jesus will return and fully establish his kingdom (1:9–11).

Before embarking on this mission, however, the church must select a replacement for Judas to be the twelfth apostle (1:15–26). He is chosen by casting lots, a well-known form of discovering the divine will in the ancient world. Appointment to positions by casting lots was a well-known practice. Philo calls casting lots "that uncertain and fortuitous divider, the lot" (*Quis Rerum Divinarum Heres* 179), whereas the Roman Quintus states that discerning the divine will by lot "is not in itself to be despised" (*De Divinatione* 1.18.34).

THE MISSION IN JERUSALEM (2:1 – 8:3)

The coming of the Spirit occurs on Pentecost (2:1–4), a feast that, during the first century, celebrated the renovation of the old covenant (see *Jubilees* 6:17, "The feast of weeks [Pentecost] ... [is] to renew the covenant in all (respects), year by year." On this feast day God's people receive his Spirit as the blessing of the new covenant according to his promise (Jer. 31:33; Ezek. 11:19; 36:26–27). In his sermon (Acts 2:14–36), Peter understands the event as fulfilling Joel 2:28–32 and as a sign of the advent of the "last days" (Acts 2:14). But the central focus of his message is Christ and proclamation. Peter includes four basic points (2:22–39): the fulfillment of prophecy; a summary of Jesus' ministry, death, and triumph (resurrection and ascension); quotations of the Old Testament that testify about the Messiah; and a call to repentance. In response to Peter's preaching, approximately three thousand express their faith and repentance through baptism (2:37–41).

Luke also presents a number of cameos on communal life in the early church (2:42–47; 4:32–5:16; 6:1–6). "All the believers were one in heart and mind" (4:32), and private property was used to benefit those in need. They gave to the neediest among them (2:45b) and "no one claimed that any of their possessions was their own, but they shared everything they had" (4:32). In so doing, the church embodies the classical ideal of friendship.

As a result of this *koinōnia* ("sharing"), there are no needy members of the congregation (4:34). Barnabas is a prime example of the ideal of true friendship (4:36–37) while Ananias and Sapphira violate it by embezzling what they previously dedicated to the Lord for those in need (5:1–11). Their act echoes the sin of Achan (Josh. 7). At one point, longstanding prejudices between Aramaic-speaking and Greek-speaking Jewish Christians from the Diaspora hinder the church from responding in true friendship to widows (6:1–6).

As the church vigorously carries out the commission to preach the gospel, opposition to the community arises. The Jewish leadership is "greatly disturbed" because of how the apostles are "teaching the people [and] proclaiming in Jesus the resurrection of the dead" (4:2).

Although Peter and John are arrested and warned not to preach or teach in Jesus' name (4:18), they declare their obligation to God (4:19) and continue to give bold witness to the gospel (4:23–31), empowered by the Spirit

Multiple *mikvehot*, baths for ritual washing, could be found south of the temple mount in Jerusalem. This was one place in Jerusalem where 3,000 people could easily be baptized in a day.

(4:31; 5:12–16). They proclaim Jesus as the Messiah (5:17–42) with significant results (6:7). The persecution reaches a peak after Stephen's martyrdom (6:8–8:3).

Stephen's account of Israel's history highlights two fundamental points. First, the Israelites have a history of rejecting God's servants sent to them, such as Joseph (7:9), Moses (7:23–29, 39–40), and the prophets (7:52a); even now they reject Jesus, "the Righteous One" (7:52b). But God was with those whom his people rejected (7:9, 30–35, 38). Second, God's presence with his people does not depend on any sacred site. God appeared to Abraham in Mesopotamia (7:2), was with Joseph in Egypt (7:9), and revealed himself to Moses at Mount Sinai (7:30–34, 38). Their ancestors had the tabernacle, which went everywhere with them (7:44–46). God does not dwell in houses made by human hands (7:48–50; cf. 1 Kings 8:27; Isa. 66:1–2).

Stephen's sermon, therefore, is pivotal in Luke's narrative. Jesus is presented again to the Jewish nation, and once again, they reject the call to repent and believe that Jesus is the promised Messiah. The door is now open to take the gospel out to the wider world, and worship of God is not linked to the temple in Jerusalem. The next step is the mission to the Gentiles.

KOINONIA AND FRIENDSHIP

The statement "friends are one soul" (cf. Acts 4:32) was proverbial in antiquity. When Aristotle was asked, "What is a friend?" he replied, "A single soul dwelling in two bodies" (Diogenes Laertes, *Lives of Eminent Philosophers* 5.20). Aristotle quotes a proverb of his day, "Friends' goods are common property," and then affirms, "This is correct, since community [*koinōnia*, 'sharing'] is the essence of friendship" (*Nichomachean Ethics* 8.9.1 [1159B]).

In the church, the ideal community of friends, no rule demands each to hand over his resources for distribution to all (see 5:4). Rather, the early Christians respond to the necessity of others (4:35). This perspective accords with Aristotle's comment on sharing property: "For individuals while owning their property privately put their own possession at the service of their friends and make use of their friends' possessions as common property" (*Politics* 2.2.5 [1263A]).

THE MISSION IN JUDEA, SAMARIA, AND THE SURROUNDING REGIONS (8:4 – 12:25)

The persecution that now breaks out is severe (8:1–3). Many leave Jerusalem and are scattered throughout the surrounding regions, preaching the gospel as they go (8:4). But the expansion of Christianity is ethnic as well. Philip goes to Samaria (8:5–25). The Samaritans were descendants of the non-Jewish settlers in the northern kingdom after the Assyrian conquest (2 Kings 17:24–41), though the Samaritan considered themselves true descendants of Israel.

Luke emphasizes that the inclusion of the Gentiles in the church is fully legitimate in two ways. First, their inclusion comes through divine intervention. Both Peter and Cornelius have similar visions (10:1–23), and these visions are retold in the following narratives (10:30–32; 11:5–10). Moreover, through the Holy Spirit the Lord tells Peter what to do (10:19–20; 11:11–12). Divine confirmation comes while Peter is speaking — the Lord pours out his Spirit on the Gentiles gathered at the house of Cornelius (10:44–47; 11:15–17). The conclusion is inevitable. Peter says, "Surely no one can stand in the way of their being baptized with water. They have received the Holy Spirit just as we have" (10:47). The church in Jerusalem agrees: "So then, even to Gentiles God has granted repentance that leads to life" (11:18).

Second, this admission of the Gentiles to the church is led by none other than Peter himself, the principal leader of the church, and is subsequently confirmed by the church in Jerusalem.

The mission of the church continues with the spread of the gospel north to Antioch and west to the island of Cyprus (11:19–30). Antioch, the third largest urban center in the empire known as the "Pearl of the East," became the hub of the church's mission out to the wider world (see Ch. 13 and beyond). This comes as no surprise since the city was a political and military center.

Nothing appears able to detain the spread of the gospel, including rulers such as Herod Agrippa I, grandson of Herod the Great (Acts 12). Luke records his opposition to the gospel and his untimely end, an account paralleled in Josephus.

The apostles and the rest of the disciples met and preached in Solomon's Portico in the temple (Acts 3:11; 5:12). In this model, Solomon's porch is on the upper left.

THE MISSION TO THE ENDS OF THE EARTH (13:1 – 28:31)
Paul's First Missionary Journey and the Jerusalem Council (13:1 – 15:35)

With Paul's first missionary journey, the church adopts a new policy with regard to evangelism. The church begins a direct mission to the Gentiles instead of simply evangelizing them as a result of the dispersion generated by the persecution in Jerusalem (11:19 – 20).

The church launches this mission from Antioch, not Jerusalem, under divine direction and with the affirmation of the whole church in that city (13:1 – 3). Paul and Barnabas set sail for Cyprus, Barnabas's home (4:36; 15:39). The gospel reaches the highest corridors of power in the evangelization of the proconsul Sergius Paulus, a name known also from ancient inscriptions (13:4 – 12). But the Jewish false prophet Elymas, a court magician (13:6 – 7), opposes the gospel and is struck blind by God. In this way, Luke demonstrates the superiority of the gospel over ancient magic (see also 8:9 – 24; 19:18 – 20).

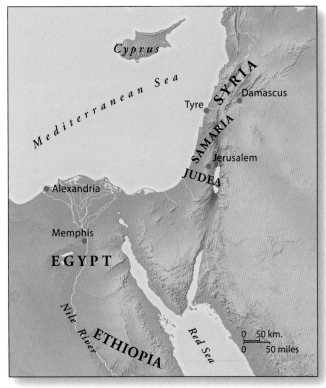

The gospel spreads beyond Judea to Samaria, Ethiopia and Syria

Paul and Barnabas make their way into Galatia, where Paul preaches in the synagogue in Pisidian Antioch (13:13 – 52), a sermon that parallels Peter's Pentecost address in Acts 2. For the first time we hear Paul's declaration of justification by faith (13:38 – 39), a theology he discusses at length in Romans and Galatians (see, e.g., Rom. 1:16 – 17; 3:21 – 24). After Jewish rejection of the gospel in the city, Paul announces his mission to the Gentiles, citing Isaiah 49:6 (Acts 13:47 – 48; see 1:8).

GOD-FEARERS

Cornelius, the Roman centurion, was a "God-fearer" — a person who "feared God" (10:2). God-fearers (cf. also 13:16, 26, 43; 16:14; 17:4, 17; 18:6 – 7) were Gentiles who sympathized with Judaism and adopted some, but not all, of Jewish theology and practice. They did not become full proselytes, which required circumcision for men and baptism for men and women. Epictetus, a Stoic philosopher, notes the difference between a God-fearer and a proselyte:

> Why do you act the part of a Jew, when you are a Greek? Do you not see in what sense men are severally called Jew, Syrian, or Egyptian? For example, whenever we see a man halting between two faiths, we are in the habit of saying, "He is not a Jew, he is only acting the part." But when he adopts the attitude of mind of the man who has been baptized and has made his choice, then he both is a Jew in fact and also is called one. (Cited in Arrianus, *Dissertationes* 2.9.19 – 20)

Left: Herod completely rebuilt Samaria, naming it after Augustus, whose Greek name was Sebaste. Temples, a basilica, even a stadium have all been excavated. *Right:* The city of Caesarea, where the Roman soldier and God-fearer Cornelius was converted, was a Gentile city.

After Paul and Barnabas evangelize Iconium, Lystra, and Derbe, they return through the cities to strengthen the churches and establish leadership. Then they return to Antioch in Syria (Acts 14). The evangelization of the Gentiles, though ordained by God, generates a dispute as some Jewish believers insist that the male Gentile converts be circumcised like male proselytes to Judaism (Acts 15:1). Since Jesus was the Jewish Messiah, this insistence on circumcision is understandable (see Gen. 17:10 – 14, 23 – 27; Ex. 12:44, 48).

From the Gentile perspective, this "salvation without circumcision" was welcomed since the thought of such surgery was abhorrent for the Greek. This seeming mutilation of the body was a barrier to Gentile conversion to Judaism — but now this bar-

JOSEPHUS ON THE DEATH OF HEROD AGRIPPA I

Luke's account of the death of Herod Agrippa I (12:20–23) is strikingly similar that of Josephus (*Ant.* 19.8.2 [344–350]):

> On the second day of these shows, [Herod] put on a garment made wholly of silver, and of a contexture truly wonderful, and came into the theatre early in the morning; at which time the silver of his garment being illuminated by the fresh reflection of the sun's rays upon it, shone out after a surprising manner, and was so resplendent as to spread amazement over those that looked intently upon him; and presently his flatterers cried out, one from one place, and another from another ... that he was a god.

Josephus then recounts his dreadful death.

rier is abolished. This is the first issue dealt with in the Jerusalem council, although the larger question is whether discipleship of Christ first entails conversion to Judaism and the relationship of Christianity to Judaism. The second issue taken up in the council is how those Jewish Christians who remain faithful to the Jewish law can sit at table and have fellowship with Gentiles who are ritually unclean and whose food is ceremonially unclean because they have not adhered to the ceremonial laws. Fellowship around the Lord's table would be difficult in such situations, but this is addressed in the council's discussion (15:20; cf. Gal. 2:11–14).

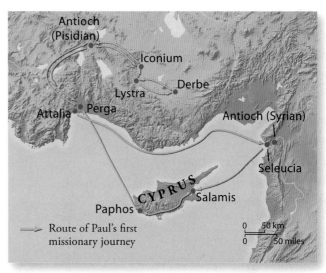

Paul's first missionary journey

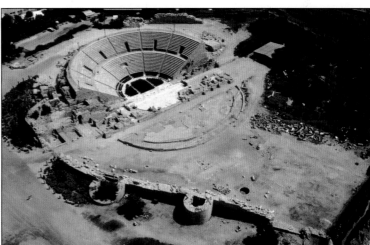

Left: The city of Antioch in Syria was the third largest urban center in the Roman empire. Although located 24 miles inland, the city enjoyed access to the Mediterranean via the Orontes River. A 19th century view of the river. *Right:* The theater at Caesarea where Herod Agrippa I received divine accolades has been reconstructed and is in use today.

Paul's Second Missionary Journey (15:36–18:22)

Paul's second missionary journey (15:36–18:22) brings him back through the churches founded on the first missionary journey and on to the Aegean port city of Troas, where he receives the well-known "Macedonian call" (15:36–16:10). In a vision Paul sees a Macedonian man who implores him, "Come over to Macedonia and help us" (16:9).

Because of a conflict with Barnabas over taking John Mark along, Paul takes Silas (15:36–40) and adds Timothy to his company (16:1–4). The author of Acts, Luke, joins them at Troas since the narrative in Acts is told in the first person plural (16:10–13). Luke apparently remains in Philippi since the narrative continues in the third person (see the other "we" sections in 20:5–15; 21:1–18; 27:1–28:16). Paul and his companions evangelize the Roman province of Macedonia, preaching in the Roman colony of Philippi (16:11–40), the free city of Thessalonica (17:1–9). and Berea, the seat of the confederation of Macedonian cities, called the *koinon* (17:10–13).

Paul and his companions must flee Berea; they sail by ship (likely embarking from Dion) and travel the costal waters down to nearby Roman colony of Corinth, which stands on the isthmus between mainland Greece and the Peloponnese (18:1–17).

An inscription from Pisidian Antioch bears the name of Sergius Paulus who had been the proconsul of Cyprus (Acts 13:4-12). Paul and his associates may have gone to Pisidian Antioch at the suggestion of Sergius Paulus whose family owned an estate in the area.

Through his account of these journeys, Luke emphasizes the mounting and severe hostility that Paul and the early Christians endure. But the important story for the first readers of Acts is that Paul and his companions are innocent of all charges; those who profess faith in Christ pose no threat to the empire. Any opposition is due to financial loss (16:19), jealousy (17:5), false charges and social prejudice (16:20–21), incitement (17:13), philosophical arrogance (17:18, 21), and hostility from the unbelieving Jewish community (17:5, 13; 18:6, 12). Luke shows Theophilus how Paul is vindicated before the authorities in Philippi, Athens, and Corinth (16:35–40; 17:19–20, 32–33; 18:12–17). Moreover, though severe opposition arises, God is with Paul and his companions (16:25–34; 18:9–10).

Luke repeatedly emphasizes that the gospel is sent "to the Jew first," as Paul himself notes (Rom. 1:16). Paul first preaches the gospel to the Jewish community in a city; if they reject Jesus as the Messiah, Paul turns to the Gentiles (16:13–15; 17:1–4, 10–12, 17; 18:5–6). The early church faced a dilemma: Why were so many Gentiles becoming followers of Jesus the Messiah while God's own people were not? Had God forsaken his people (see Rom. 9–11)? Luke records the repeated offer of the gospel to the Jews and, in his final summary, observes, "Some were convinced by what [Paul] had said, but others would not believe" (28:24). So Paul states, "Therefore I want you to know that God's salvation has been sent to the Gentiles, and they will listen!" (28:28).

A third emphasis in this section is the relationship between faith in Christ and other systems of belief. The gospel is the fulfillment of Jewish hopes contained in Scripture, and Luke repeatedly highlights how Paul returns to the sacred text to expound the message of

Paul's second missionary journey

Left: The forum in Philippi where Paul was accused and flogged before the authorities of this Roman colony (Acts 16:19-24). *Right*: Paul was accused before Gallio, the Roman proconsul of Achaia, at the *bēma* (Latin: *rostrum*) in Corinth (Acts 18:12-17).

Christ in the synagogue. In Thessalonica, for example, Paul goes to the synagogue "and on three Sabbath days he reasoned with them from the Scriptures, explaining and proving that the Messiah had to suffer and to rise from the dead. 'This Jesus I am proclaiming to you is the Messiah,' he said" (17:2–3). Likewise in Berea, he goes to the synagogue and lays out the message; the Jews of that city receive the message and eagerly examine the Scriptures to see whether Paul is right (17:11). In Athens and Corinth he proclaims Jesus as the Messiah in the synagogues (17:17; 18:5).

But Luke also shows how the gospel is superior to popular religion (16:16–18) and the philosophical constructs popular during the era (17:16–34). In Athens, Paul confronts Epicurean and Stoic philosophers (17:18). His address to the council of the city, the Areopagus, is an artful refutation of the tenets of these philosophies.

While Paul does not specifically quote Scripture in his message in Athens, he repeatedly refers to biblical truth: God is the creator of all (17:24; cf. Ps. 146:6), all humans have been formed from one ancestor (17:26; cf. Gen. 1:27–28; 2:7), and God has determined the boundaries for people (17:26b; cf. Deut. 32:8). Luke's presentation of the gospel repeatedly demonstrates that, although the church is persecuted and embroiled in legal disputes, the gospel is the true way of salvation.

Paul's Third Missionary Journey (18:23–20:38)

Paul's third missionary journey begins after he returns to Jerusalem and then travels to Antioch in Syria (18:22–23). After visiting the churches founded on his previous travels, Paul arrives in Ephesus (18:24–19:21), the "mother city" of the province of Asia located at the terminus of the Cilician Road.

THE "MACEDONIAN MAN"

In his vision (16:9), Paul sees a Macedonian man who is likely dressed in traditional Macedonian garb. Antipater of Thessalonica refers to L. Calpurnius Piso, the Roman proconsul in Macedonia, who himself took up the region's traditional costume (note how the hat does the talking): "A broad-brimmed hat, from olden times the Macedonian's comfortable gear, shelter in snowstorm and helmet in war, thirsting to drink your sweat, valiant Piso, I come, an Emathian [an ancient name for Macedonia] to Italian brows."[4]

ON ADMITTING FOREIGN DEITIES IN ATHENS

The charge against Paul in Athens that he was "advocating foreign gods" (17:18–20) echoed the charge leveled against Socrates centuries before: "Socrates is guilty of rejecting the gods acknowledged by the state and of bringing in strange deities: his is also guilty of corrupting the youth" (Xenophon, *Memorabilia* 1.1.1). Paul's presentation before the Areopagus may have been an initial hearing of the type needed before new and foreign deities could be added to the Athenian pantheon.

NOTES FROM ANTIQUITY

Most of Luke's account of this journey records the gospel's penetration into Ephesus (19:1–41) and his address to the Ephesian elders (20:17–38). Between these events, Paul travels back through Macedonia and Achaia (20:1–6; see his plans in 19:21), spends a brief time in Troas (20:7–12), then bypasses Ephesus and stops at Miletus (20:13–16). Paul's ministry in Ephesus lasts for three years (20:31). Ephesus was a "free" city, not a Roman colony (like Philippi and Corinth). It was the capital of Asia Minor and its most populous city (between 200,000 and 250,000).

Luke's account of the Ephesian ministry highlights the evangelism of those who had only heard the message of John the Baptist (19:1–7), evangelism in the synagogue and rejection of the gospel by the Jewish community (19:8–10), and the extraordinary miracles God works through Paul (19:11–20). The superiority of Christ over Jewish exorcists and the compelling claims of Christ over against magic make for a powerful story for those facing the frightful power of demons and seeking protection from magic spells.

The Thessalonians had constructed an imperial temple in the city to honor Julius Caesar and his adopted son, Augustus (here pictured).

The Roman Agora in Athens was filled with altars, images of the gods and temples

A reconstruction of the Stoa in Athens where Paul likely stood before the city council, the Areopagus, whose duties included the admission of new deities to the Athenian pantheon.

Ephesus was also the center of the Artemis cult; the temple dedicated to her was one of the wonders of the ancient world. Pilgrims from everywhere visited this religious center as Artemis was becoming a universal deity. So effective is the evangelization of Ephesus through the powerful proclamation of the gospel, however, that the trade in silver shrines commemorating Artemis is severely diminished, and a near riot ensues because of the way the goddess appears to be brought into dishonor (19:23–41). Paul's proclamation of the gospel does include a direct attack against idolatry (19:26; cf. 14:8–18; 17:16–31).

Paul's final address to the Ephesian elders given in Miletus upon return from Macedonia and Achaia (20:17–38) summarizes the apostle's ministry and serves as his last testament. With this sermon Paul's Aegean ministry comes to a close.

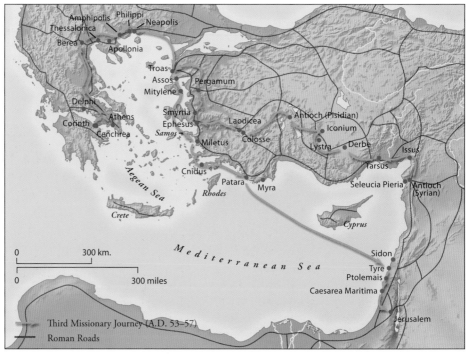

Paul's third missionary journey

The theater in Ephesus (Acts 19:23-41, see v. 38).

Paul's Return to Jerusalem and Subsequent Imprisonments (21:1 – 28:31)

As chapter 20 ends, an even more dangerous chapter opens as predicted by the prophecies given to Paul (21:4, 10 – 14). The last part of Acts is taken up with Paul's return to Jerusalem (21:1 – 22:21) and his imprisonment in Jerusalem, Caesarea, and Rome (22:22 – 28:31). Familiar themes resurface: the persecution of the apostle and his innocence before all charges (26:30 – 32), the presentation of the gospel to Jews in Jerusalem and Rome and their rejection of it (21:37 – 22:29; 28:17 – 27), and the offer of the gospel to the Gentiles (21:17 – 19; 22:21; 28:28). Paul goes to the imperial city as an "ambassador in chains" (23:11; 26:32 – 27:1; 28:16; see Eph. 6:20).

In 9:15, God told Ananias that the apostle Paul was God's "chosen instrument to proclaim my name to the Gentiles and their kings and to the people of Israel." In chapters 24 – 26 Paul testifies before King Agrippa II and the Roman governors of Judea, Felix, and then Festus. In the end, he travels to Rome, where he will present his gospel before Emperor Nero. Luke ends the story only telling of Paul's two-year imprisonment in Rome, where he continues to preach the gospel (28:30 – 31). Nothing can quench his burning passion to proclaim Christ.

JEWISH EXORCISTS AND "EPHESIAN LETTERS"

Magic was such a dominant feature of life in Ephesus that many magical incantations were known as "Ephesian Letters" (Plutarch, *Table Talk* 7.5). The potency of magic spells was bound up with their secrecy. To reveal the secret was to render the spell powerless. The scene in Acts 19:18 – 19 is not only one of repentance but of destroying the power of magic. The book burning is a clear sign that these believers have renounced their former life. Burning books to control ideas was known in antiquity (1 Macc. 1:56), but this action in Acts is voluntary.

THE TEMPLE OF ARTEMIS IN EPHESUS

In his second century AD travelogue, Pausanius comments on the glory of the temple of Artemis: "The land of the Ionians has the finest possible climate, and sanctuaries such as are to be found nowhere else. First because of its size and wealth is that of the Ephesian goddess" (*Description of Greece* 7.5.4). Antipater of Thessalonica found it to be one of the grandest sights in the ancient world: "I have set eyes on the wall of lofty Babylon . . . and the statue of Zeus by Alpheus, and the hanging gardens, and the colossus of the sun, and the huge labor of the high pyramids, and the vast tomb of Mausolus; but when I saw the house of Artemis that mounted to the clouds, those other marvels lost their brilliancy."[5]

The Artemis temple in Ephesus. Note the image of the deity in the coin.

Column base from the Artemis temple in Ephesus. Note that the relief images also appear in miniature around the column bases on the coin depicting the temple.

COMPOSING THE STORY

Luke uses various sources in writing this two-volume work, including eyewitness accounts and written documents (Luke 1:1–2). The sources for this second volume include testimony that came from the early Palestinian church as well as the apostle Paul. Luke's "we" sections (16:10–13; 20:5–15; 21:1–18; 27:1–28:16) suggest that the author himself was Paul's traveling companion and an eyewitness to part of the history described in the scroll. Ancient historiography considered that the presence of an historian at some of the events described added credibility to the account.

There has been considerable debate about the literary genre of Luke and Acts (see Ch. 10). Is it a novel, a scientific treatise, a biography, or a history? The question of genre is important because genre raises certain expectations and suggests a particular strategy for reading the document. Luke-Acts presents itself as both a biography and a history (see sidebar).

Ancient historians remark on their concern for faithfulness in their writing. The father of ancient historiography, Thucydides, noted that while he found it difficult to record the exact words spoken by some figure, he attempted to remain faithful to the actual sense of what was said:

> With reference to the speeches in this history, some were delivered before the war began, others while it was going on; it was hard to record the exact words spoken, both in cases where I was myself present, and where I used the reports of others. But I have used language in accordance with what I thought the speakers in each case would have used, adhering as closely as possible to the general sense of what was *actually spoken*. (*History of the Peloponnesian War* 1.22)

Insofar as we can verify his history, Luke's presentation is strikingly accurate. Colin Hemer noted in his comparative study of Acts and ancient historical sources:

> Here we discovered a wealth of material suggesting an author or sources familiar with the particular locations and at the times in question. Many of these connections have only recently come to light with the publication of new collections of papyri and inscriptions. . . . By and large, these perspectives all converged to support the general

reliability of the narrative, through the details so intricately yet often unintentionally woven into the narrative.[6]

The prevailing skepticism regarding Luke's faithfulness to the events recorded in Acts is not warranted.

AUTHOR AND DATE

The assessment about the authorship and date of Luke (see Ch. 10) holds true for Acts since this two-volume work was composed by the same person for the same recipient. As noted in the discussion on Luke, the testimony of the early church is unanimous that Luke was truly the author of these books.

Our assessment of the date of composition will depend, in part, on our understanding of the purposes of the book in light of the statement in 28:30: "For two whole years Paul stayed there in his own rented house." Was Luke-Acts composed at the end of that two-year period, giving us a date of composition of about AD 62, well before the martyrdom of Peter and Paul under Nero? Or, since Luke's concern is to tell the story of the movement of Christianity from the Jewish confines to the "ends of the earth," could the volumes have been written even after Paul's death (which is hinted at in 20:25, 38; 21:13; 25:11). In other words, would the first reader have come to these verses and said, "Paul's death happened as predicted"?

HISTORY OR BIOGRAPHY?

The debate about whether Luke-Acts should be regarded as a history or a biography is based on ancient discussion on these two genres. Plutarch, for example, said, "For it is not Histories that I am writing, but Lives" (*Alexander* 1.2). For him, writing history meant chronicling the flow of events while in biography the concern was with character portraits (see sidebar on "Luke and Plutarch" in Ch. 10 for quote).

The first-century BC Latin biographer Cornelius Nepos similarly distinguished these genres in *Pelopidas* 1.1 "I am in doubt how to give an account of his merits; for I fear that if I undertake to tell his deeds, I shall seem to be writing a history rather than a biography."

ANCIENT HISTORIANS ON WRITING HISTORY

Polybius (*Histories* 2.56.10–12) distinguishes historical writing from poetry saying:

> A historical author should not try to thrill his readers by such exaggerated pictures, nor should he, like a tragic poet, try to imagine the probable utterances of his characters or reckon up all the consequences probably incidental to the occurrences with which he deals, but simply record what really happened and what really was said, however commonplace. For the object of tragedy is not the same as that of history but quite the opposite. The tragic poet should thrill and charm his audience for the moment by the truth of the words he puts into his characters' mouths, but it is the task of the historian to instruct and convince for all time serious students by the truth of the facts and the speeches he narrates.

History was concerned with "a faithful narration of facts" (Tacitus, *Agricola* 10). Lucian in his essay *How to Write History* repeatedly advocates for such faithfulness. Luke presents his two-volume work as an historical narrative (Luke 1:1) based on the best historical testimony available to him, including that of eyewitnesses (1:2). He is diligent in his investigation and makes significant attempts to arrange his narrative in an orderly way (1:3).

QUESTIONS FOR DISCUSSION ⊙⊙⊙⊙⊙⊙⊙⊙⊙⊙⊙⊙⊙⊙⊙⊙⊙⊙⊙⊙⊙⊙⊙⊙⊙⊙⊙⊙

1. Compare the message of the apostles in the sermons in Acts 2, 13, and 17 with our contemporary telling of the gospel. How is our message the same as theirs? How is it different?

2. Miracles, including speaking in tongues and prophecy, were a common element of the apostolic proclamation and the life of the early church. Are such phenomena for the church today? Frame your response with reference to Luke's presentation of the Spirit's coming and theology of the Spirit in Acts.

3. Discuss the key elements of Christian mission according to Acts, including the message, the method, and the recipients of the gospel.

4. How can we proclaim the gospel in a world of religious pluralism? What lessons can we learn from Acts as we reflect on this present-day issue?

5. Who are the excluded people in our society? Does the church reach them with the gospel of Christ? Do our current practices reflect Luke's emphasis on the gospel to the excluded?

BIBLIOGRAPHY
Introductory
Bruce, F. F. *The Book of Acts*. NICNT. Rev. ed. Grand Rapids: Eerdmans, 1988.

Larkin, W. J. *Acts*. IVPNTC. Downers Grove, IL: InterVarsity Press, 1995.

Marshall, I. H. *The Acts of the Apostles*. TNTC. Grand Rapids: Eerdmans, 1980.

Stott, J. R. W. *The Message of Acts*. BST. Downers Grove, IL: InterVarsity Press, 1990.

Advanced
Barrett, C. K. *The Acts of the Apostles*. ICC. 2 vols. Edinburgh: T. & T. Clark, 1994, 1998.

Fitzmyer, J. A. *The Acts of the Apostles*. AB. New York: Doubleday, 1998.

Witherington, B. *The Acts of the Apostles: A Socio-Rhetorical Commentary*. Grand Rapids: Eerdmans, 1998.

NOTES
1. Martin Hengel, *Acts and the History of Early Christianity* (Philadelphia: Fortress, 1980), 67.

2. G. H. R. Horsley, *New Documents Illustrating Early Christianity* (North Ryde, N.S.W.: Macquarie Univ. Press, 1986), 6:192–93.

3. W. D. Davies, *Paul and Rabbinic Judaism* (Philadelphia: Fortress, 1980), 121.

4. Gow and Page, *Greek Anthology*, 1:37.

5. Ibid., 1:69.

6. C. J. Hemer, *The Book of Acts in the Setting of Hellenistic History* (Tübingen: Mohr, 1989), 412.

CHAPTER 13

PAUL OF TARSUS:
LIFE AND TEACHINGS

The Cilician road passed through Tarsus, Paul's home.

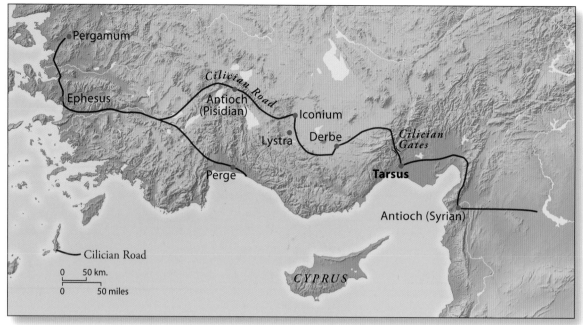

The city of Tarsus was located on the Cilician Road, the major east-west road in southern Asia Minor.

Besides Peter, the most prominent leader in the early church was Paul, a man from the Greek city of Tarsus. His conversion is a cornerstone in Acts, where Luke describes the event three times (Acts 9:1–9; 22:3–21; 26:1–23). Through his vision on the Damascus road, Paul becomes a witness of Christ's resurrection (1 Cor. 15:3–11) and an apostle with a special commission to proclaim the gospel among the Gentiles (Gal. 2:7–8). From both Acts and Paul's letters, we can develop his life and teachings.

Peter describes Paul as a "dear brother" who wrote many letters but whose message was distorted by some within the churches (2 Peter 3:15–16). Echoes of his teaching can be heard in other New Testament letters, such as 1 Peter and Hebrews, and the leaders of the postapostolic church recount many of the traditions surrounding his life, including his martyrdom in Rome under Nero. Paul's influence on theology has been enormous. He offers

THE ZEAL FOR GOD

The zeal Paul demonstrated in persecuting the church is not simply religious fanaticism. Paul saw his devotion for God and his law as part of a noble history in Israel, which lauded those who showed outstanding courage to defend and avenge what was holy.

For example, Scripture remembered Phinehas's zeal, which led him to violence against an Israelite man and a Midianite woman indulging in sexual sin and the worship of Baal (Num. 25:1–15). Later, 1 Maccabees 2:54 recalls the event, "Phinehas our ancestor, because he was deeply zealous, received the covenant of everlasting priesthood" (see also 2:58). According to Sirach 45:23, "Phinehas son of Eleazar ranks third in glory for being zealous in the fear of the Lord."

Paul understood his persecution of the church as part of this tradition. His righteous zeal was the source of his greatest sin (1 Tim. 1:12–14). Yet precisely at this point Paul realizes he became the recipient of God's gift of grace: "I was shown mercy because I acted in ignorance and unbelief. The grace of our Lord was poured out on me abundantly, along with the faith and love that are in Christ Jesus."

The principal route which connected the eastern section of the empire with Rome passed through the narrow pass through the Taurus mountain range known as the Cilician Gates, located about 30 miles from Tarsus.

the clearest and most detailed exposition of the Christian faith. Although he worked hard and suffered severely for the gospel, he refused to seek honor for himself since he knew that his efforts were divinely empowered: "To this end I strenuously contend with all the energy Christ so powerfully works in me" (Col. 1:29). To understand the shape and history of early Christianity, we must explore the life and teachings of Paul.

SAUL OF TARSUS

Paul was a Jew and also a Roman citizen (Acts 16:37–38; 22:25–29; 23:27), born in the free city of Tarsus, the capital of the province of Cilicia. As a Roman Paul would have had three names: *praenomen, nomen,* and *cognomen.* A Roman's *cognomen* acted as a surname and, in the apostle's case, this was the Latin *Paullus* (Gk. *Paulos*), which identified him as a member of the *Paulli* family. He was known also as Saul (Gk. *Saulos,* a transliteration of the Semitic *Shaul* (Acts 7:58; 8:1; 13:9). The name was likely his *supernomen,* a kind of nickname used chiefly with Jews.

Tarsus was "no ordinary city" (Acts 21:39), lying thirty miles south of the pass through the Taurus Mountains called the Cilician Gates along the great Cilician Road, which crossed the southern section of Asia Minor.

The inhabitants of Tarsus were so well known for learning that Strabo, the Roman geographer, remarked, "The people at Tarsus have devoted themselves so eagerly, not only to philosophy, but also to the whole round of education in general, that they have surpassed Athens, Alexandria, or any other place" (*Geography* 14.5.13). However, Strabo continues that the inhabitants who study there "complete their education abroad"; Saul followed this pattern by studying in Jerusalem under the rabbi Gamaliel, grandson of the famous rabbi Hillel (Acts 22:3; cf. 5:34). Strabo makes special note of the schools of rhetoric in Tarsus, and Paul's letters evidence his familiarity with ancient rhetorical discourse. Although he received rigorous training in Torah, Saul could also

This Roman road which runs to Syria from Petra is similar to the road to Damascus on which Paul encountered the risen Christ. "Damascus Road" has become a metaphor for conversion because of the story of Paul's vision along this highway.

have read Homer, Euripides, and other Greek literature without the fear of incurring "uncleanness" or ritual defilement (Mishnah *Yadayim* 4:6).

Paul presents a detailed summary of his Jewish heritage in Philippians 3:5: "circumcised on the eighth day, of the people of Israel, of the tribe of Benjamin, a Hebrew of Hebrews; in regard to the law, a Pharisee." That he was an Israelite by birth is clear from his reference to circumcision according to Jewish law. Since Saul was zealous for the traditions of his people (Gal. 1:14), he likely married as most Jewish men did their early twenties. However, in Acts Paul is a single man (1 Cor. 7:8), and we can only speculate what may have happened to his spouse.

PERSECUTOR AND CONVERT

We first meet Saul at Stephen's martyrdom (Acts 7:54–58; 8:1; 22:20), after which he launched an aggressive wave of persecuting any Jews who acknowledged Jesus as the promised Messiah (Acts 8:3). Paul was enraged by this new sect and set out to destroy it (Gal. 1:13, 23; 1 Cor. 15:9; Phil. 3:6). He deemed belief in Jesus as Messiah blasphemy, and in his zeal (Gal. 1:13–14) he set out to persecute Jesus' disciples, sowing terror and deep fear (Acts 9:26).

But God had other plans for Saul. We cannot understand Paul's theology apart from his encounter with the risen Christ on the road to Damascus where, by his own account, he was "taken hold" by Jesus Christ (Phil. 3:12).

At his conversion Paul saw a light and heard Christ's voice, but he also saw the Lord (Acts 9:17; 22:14). Paul recalls this event in his letters: "Have I not seen Jesus our Lord?" (1 Cor. 9:1); "and last of all he appeared to me also" (1 Cor. 15:8; cf. Gal. 1:15–16). Paul was struck blind and led by the hand into Damascus (Acts 22:11). The powerful Saul was now helpless. His whole life had become radically reoriented.

In a world that held faithfulness to tradition as a high value, Saul's conversion must have appeared confusing. In fact, that type of change was hardly commendable according to the ancient worldview. Cicero, for example, quotes the Stoic opinion that "the wise man never 'supposes' anything, never regrets anything, is never wrong, never changes his mind" (*Pro Murena* 61). Paul explains his unusual change by appealing to divine intervention, which he viewed as the outworking of God's plan for him before he was born (Gal. 1:15–16). He became convinced that the crucified Jesus of Nazareth was indeed alive. In fact, contrary to all Jewish teaching, Paul came to understand that it was necessary for the Messiah to suffer death and rise from the dead and that this Jesus was the Messiah (Acts 17:3). In reality, his conversion was not an abandonment of his ancestral heritage but the fulfillment of it.

Petra was the capital of the Arabian kingdom of the Nabateans.

HERALD OF THE GOSPEL

Paul's conversion included Jesus' instruction that he would be a witness to what he had seen and heard. Soon he felt compelled to proclaim this experience both to his own people and to Gentiles (Acts 9:15; 22:14–15; 26:15–18). In fact, Paul began immediately to proclaim in Damascus that Jesus indeed was the long-anticipated Messiah, the promised King (9:19b–22). Sometime during this period, Paul went away to "Arabia" (see sidebar) and then returned to Damascus, where he stayed for three years (Gal. 1:15–18a). Reaction to his preaching became so severe that he had to escape the city by night (Acts 9:23–25; 2 Cor. 11:33). From Damascus, he went away back to Jerusalem (Gal. 1:18b).

During Paul's brief visit to Jerusalem with Peter he also met with James (Gal. 1:18–19) and was presented to the church in the city by Barnabas (Acts 9:26–29). The accounts in Galatians and Acts are difficult to reconcile here since in Galatians he notes that he saw no apostle save Peter and then James, the Lord's brother. In Acts, however, Barnabas presents him to the apostles. Most likely the apostles whom Luke mentions in Acts are only Peter and James (who was considered an apostle). While Paul seeks to demonstrate to the Galatians his independence of Jerusalem, Luke emphasizes Paul's acceptance by the Jerusalem church.

Paul spoke openly in Jerusalem about Jesus as the Messiah and became a lightning rod for conflict (Acts 9:29). Therefore he quickly left and traveled to northern Syria (Antioch?) and finally arrived in Cilicia, where his home of Tarsus was located (Gal. 1:21). Following his departure from Judea, Luke says with a touch of irony, "Then the church . . . enjoyed a time of peace" (Acts 9:31).

The following years in Paul's ministry were taken up with his mission to the Gentiles (Gal. 2:6–9). We are acquainted with his journeys through his letters addressed to his churches, but much of our knowledge about this missionary enterprise comes from Acts, which recounts three missionary journeys (see Ch. 12), with Paul traveling extensively on the roads and sea lanes of the empire.

After his third missionary journey Paul was arrested in Jerusalem and sent to Caesarea, where he was imprisoned until his journey to Rome as a captive (Acts 21:27–28:31). Acts ends rather abruptly without saying what became of Paul there. We know Paul wrote a number of letters during his imprisonment (his so-called "Prison Epistles":

Romans could obtain passage to the ports of the Mediterranean on cargo vessels (Acts 28:11). Safe sea lanes and the roads gave Romans a high degree of mobility.

Paul's journey to Rome, recorded in Acts 27–28

Ephesians, Philippians, Colossians and Philemon). Despite his captivity, Paul continued to proclaim the gospel of Jesus Christ to all who came into contact with him. In fact, he describes himself as an "ambassador in chains" (Eph. 6:20; see Phil. 1:7, 13). He considered himself a "prisoner of Christ Jesus" (Eph. 3:1; 4:1; Phlm. 1, 9, 23). He even proclaimed the gospel to Caesar's elite Praetorian Guard (Phil. 1:13). Although Nero provoked a wholesale persecution against the Christians, accusing them of setting the city of Rome on fire (which he himself is rumored to have set), Paul does not appear to have been martyred as was Peter during this assault. Shortly before the great fire, he had been released from imprisonment and presumably set out to visit his churches (Eusebius, *Eccl. Hist.* 2.22.2): "Tradition has it that after defending himself the Apostle was again sent on the ministry of preaching, and coming a second time to the same city suffered martyrdom under Nero."

CHRISTIANS

The New Testament uses various terms to describe the followers of Jesus: "believers" (1 Thess. 1:7), "saints" or "holy people" (Phil. 1:1), "Nazarene sect" (Acts 24:5), "disciples" (Acts 11:26), and followers of "the Way" (Acts 9:2; 19:9, 23; 22:4, 14, 22). "Christian," however, was not a self-designation of the believers. The name identified them as partisans of Christ, similar to the "Herodians" (Mark 3:6; 12:13), and early on the name took on a pejorative sense.

The Roman historian Tacitus, commenting on the persecution under Nero's reign, derided the believers as people "whom the crowd styled Christians" (*Annals* 15.44). We are not surprised, therefore, that Peter urges the believers, "However, if you suffer as a Christian, do not be ashamed, but praise God that you bear that name" (1 Pet. 4:16). From earliest times, that term for believers was not honored; instead, it was a source of shame. At times Roman authors misconstrued the name, calling the believers "Chrestianoi," as if the founder of the group were named "Chrestus." Suetonius appears to commit such a gaff when he comments that Claudius expelled the Jews from Rome "on account of disturbances at the instigation of Chrestus" (*Life of Claudius* 25; cf. Acts 18:5).

Paul sailed from the ancient harbor in Caesarea, bound as a prisoner on his way to Rome. Pictured: the remains to the Caesarea hippodrome for horse races.

ON THE ROAD AND ON THE SEA

Roman dominance over the landscape is illustrated by the system of roads that stretched throughout the empire and linked Italy and the provinces with Rome. Along these all-weather highways traveled Roman officials and soldiers, colonists, those engaged in trade (both men and women), heralds of various religions, philosophers, and pilgrims. Roman mile markers dotted the highways and itineraries offered travelers information about where towns were located and the distances between them. Both Pompey and Augustus pacified the Mediterranean, clearing out most of the pirates. Thus, travel became relatively quick and easy.

While exiled in Thessalonica, Cicero once complained about how crowded the Via Egnatia and other roads had become. Yet there were dangers. Robbers could fall on an ill-armed company, and the sea was known for its treachery (see Acts 27). Antipater of Thessalonica once said, "Approve not the grievous labor of the treacherous ocean or the heavy toil of perilous seafaring. As a mother is more delightful than a step-mother, by so much is the earth more desirable than the gray sea."[1]

Paul agreed: "Three times I was shipwrecked, I spent a night and a day in the open sea, I have been constantly on the move. I have been in danger from rivers, in danger from bandits, in danger from my own people, in danger from Gentiles; in danger in the city, in danger in the country, in danger at sea" (2 Cor. 11:25–26). Yet he kept on the move, bringing the gospel to city after city.

But the apostolic calling to proclaim the gospel to the Gentiles always lies in tension with Paul's concern for the newly founded congregations: "Besides everything else, I face daily the pressure of my concern for all the churches" (2 Cor. 11:28). It is out of this tension that he wrote his letters to his previously established churches.

As Christ's *authoritative messenger*, therefore, Paul spoke with Christ's authority (2 Cor, 13:3), and to set aside the message he proclaimed meant to reject Jesus Christ who sent him (1 Thess. 4:2, 8). The apostles were invested with authority and power of Christ (Matt. 10:1–2; 2 Cor. 12:12), though no apostle was greater than the One who sent him (John 13:16).

NERO'S PERSECUTION OF THE CHRISTIANS

Tactius recounts the terror of the blaze that consumed ten of Rome's fourteen districts. "Nero was seeking the glory of founding a new capital and endowing it with his own name" (*Annals* 15.40). But Nero needed a scapegoat to blame in order to deflect the suspicion that the blaze was set by imperial order: Therefore, "Nero substituted as culprits, and punished with the utmost refinements of cruelty, a class of men, loathed for their vices, whom the crowd styled Christians" (15.44). Tacitus describes Nero's cruelty:

First, then, the confessed members of the sect were arrested; next, on their disclosures, vast numbers were convicted, not so much on the count of arson as for hatred of the human race.... They were covered with wild beasts' skins and torn to death by dogs; or they were fastened on crosses, and, when daylight failed were burned to serve as lamps by night.... Hence there arose a sentiment of pity, due to the impression that they were being sacrificed not for the welfare of the state but to the ferocity of a single man (15.44).

From his last letters and the testimony of the early church, we can reconstruct some of Paul's activities between his two Roman imprisonments. The Pastoral Epistles (1–2 Timothy, Titus) contain a number of casual references to places Paul visited, journeys not recorded in Acts. Apparently he evangelized Crete (Titus 1:5) and traveled to Nicopolis, Troas, and Miletus (Titus 3:12; 2 Tim. 4:13, 20).

Some question remains whether Paul ever reached Spain (the Roman province *Hispania*) during this period (cf. Rom. 15:24, 28). Corduba (the modern Córdoba) was the home of the philosopher Seneca and his brother Gallio, who became the proconsul of Achaia (Acts 18:12), while the orator Quintilian and later three emperors came from the province. The New Testament is silent on whether Paul was able to reach this goal. Gades in Spain (modern Cadiz) was identified in ancient literature as "the ends of the earth," and Paul may have been driven to evangelize it because of the Lord's commission in Acts 1:8 (see sidebar on "The Ends of the Earth" in Ch. 12).

After Paul's first imprisonment in Rome, he traveled to various places such as Crete, Nicopolis, Troas, Miletus and possibly Spain.

The forum in ancient Rome. Paul had planned to pass through Rome on his way to Spain.

Clement of Rome, who wrote at the end of the first century, comments that Paul did reach "the limits of the West" (*1 Clement* 5:7 — perhaps meaning Spain). The Muratorian fragment, a list of books considered canonical by the Roman church written near the close of the second century, comments that Acts does not include "Paul's journey when he set out from Rome for Spain."

Paul later returned to Rome. He may have been at Corinth when the persecution in Rome broke out (2 Tim. 4:20), and news of the violence likely spread to the church in that Roman colony. Did Paul return to aid the suffering believers in the imperial city? We can only speculate, but we know that he was captured again. During this second Roman imprisonment Paul wrote 2 Timothy, where he clearly anticipates his imminent demise (2 Tim. 4:6). This second Roman imprisonment ended in martyrdom according to Eusebius: "It is related that in his [Nero's] time Paul was beheaded in Rome itself and that Peter likewise was crucified" (*Eccl. Hist.* 2.25.5). Paul's last recorded words demonstrate the confidence in his work and the level of his hope even in that dark hour:

> For I am already being poured out like a drink offering, and the time for my departure is near. I have fought the good fight, I have finished the race, I have kept the faith. Now there is in store for me the crown of righteousness, which the Lord, the righteous Judge, will award to me on that day — and not only to me, but also to all who have longed for his appearing. (2 Tim. 4:6–8)

Paul's apostolic legacy survived his death, and he still speaks to the church today through his letters.

A BRIEF CHRONOLOGY OF PAUL'S LIFE

Assembling a chronology of Paul's life is no easy task since we do not have a full account of his early years nor do the New Testament documents include much information about his travels between the first and second imprisonment in Rome. Moreover, events mentioned in his letters are sometimes not recounted in the Acts (e.g., see his list of sufferings in 2 Cor. 11:23–27). Nevertheless, we can reconstruct many of the details of his life.

A CHRONOLOGY OF PAUL'S LIFE
(Note that all dates are AD and approximate)

Paul's Life		Paul's Letters	
5–10	Paul's Birth		
[30 (or 33)	Crucifixion of Jesus]		
32/33 (or 34)	Paul's Conversion		
35 (or 36)	First Visit to Jerusalem		
46 (or 47)	Second Visit to Jerusalem		
47–48	First Missionary Journey	48	Galatians (South Galatia theory date)
49	Jerusalem Council		
49–52	Second Missionary Journey	50–51	1 and 2 Thessalonians
		51	Galatians (North Galatia theory date)
52–57	Third Missionary Journey	54	1 Corinthians
		56	2 Corinthians and Romans
57–59	Caesarean Imprisonment		
59	Trial before Festus and Agrippa II		
59–60	Voyage to Rome		
60–62	First Roman Imprisonment		
		60–62	Ephesians, Philippians, Colossians, Philemon
62–64	Release and Travels		
		65–66	1 Timothy and Titus
67–68	Reimprisonment	67–68	2 Timothy
68	Martyrdom in Rome		

PAUL'S TEACHINGS
Some Critical Issues

We know the contours of Paul's teaching through his many surviving letters, though not all of Paul's writings survived. We do not have a letter sent to the Laodicean church (Col. 4:16) or the first letter he wrote to the Corinthians, penned before our 1 Corinthians (1 Cor. 5:9). Some scholars have questioned whether all of the Pauline letters in the New Testament were truly written by him. While no one doubts the authenticity of Romans or 1 Corinthians, books such as the Pastoral Epistles have come under severe attack (see Ch. 21). In outlining Paul's theology, should we include the letters whose authenticity is questioned? Nevertheless, scholars of all persuasions have summarized Paul's theology and confidently attested to his accessibility to us. No other New Testament author, apart from Luke, gives us so much material to work with.

Yet even with his rich collection of writings, questions remain regarding whether Paul's theology is entirely consistent. Since he wrote in response to situations as they arose, some insist we should not expect any internal coherence in his teaching. Others argue that Paul's theology should be divided into stages, since there is development in his thought. Among those who search for some center of Paul's theology, there is no consensus on which doctrine should be viewed as the focal point. Instead of a "center," should we describe his thought in a manner that is less static and more dynamic? Does the very notion of a "center" minimize important aspects of his thought?

Moreover, discussion of Paul's theology has taken a dramatic turn in recent years as the traditional reading of Paul, inherited from the Reformers, has come under attack by the so-called "new perspective" on Paul. The serious student of Paul's thought is faced with a dizzying array of questions as she or he seeks to tease out the fundamental structures of the apostle's teaching.

But although Paul's letters take up a broad spectrum of problems, he addresses these issues within a coherent theological framework that recalls God's act of creation, his salvation through the cross and resurrection of Christ, and the final consummation when Christ returns. Thus, when dealing with the error of idolatry or the issue of asceticism, Paul orients his response around God's creative act (Rom. 1:22–25; 1 Tim. 4:3–4). When facing human sin, the agony of death, or the division between Jews and Gentiles, he responds with reference to the cross and resurrection of Christ (1 Cor. 15:3–4; Eph 2:11–16; 1 Thess. 4:13–16). When commenting on the rejection of Christ in his day or the disorder in the universe, his gaze is on Christ's return (Eph. 1:9–10; Phil. 2:9–11).

Foundational Ideas for Paul

Paul, who spoke publicly as this Greek orator, denounced polytheism and idolatry as he proclaimed the one true God (1 Thess. 1:9).

Paul's starting point is a belief in the unity of God. The *Shema*, the Jewish confession Israelites repeated every morning and evening, is Paul's foundation: "Hear [Heb. *Shema*], O Israel: The LORD our God, the LORD is one" (Deut 6:4–9). Paul echoes the *Shema* in his letters, such as in his statement that God wants all people to be saved and to come to know the truth, "for there is one God" (1 Tim. 2:5). The claim that God is one means for Paul that there is one Savior for all humanity (2:6). In a world awash in religious pluralism, Paul boldly declares, "For even if there are so-called gods, whether in heaven or on earth (as indeed there are many 'gods' and many 'lords'), yet for us there is but one God, the Father, from whom all things came and for whom we live" (1 Cor. 8:5–6).

Paul understands the worship of idols, the creation of human hands, as the central source of sin since humans reject the revelation of the one God and worship and serve that which is created rather than the Creator (Rom. 1:18–25). His proclamation of the gospel among the Gentiles, therefore, begins with a call to abandon idols in favor of the one God of all (Acts 14:11–18; 17:22–31; see 1 Thess. 1:9). Paul refuses to give traditional religions place alongside the gospel. While respectful and no blasphemer of other religions (Acts 19:37), he does not recognize them as a source of salvation (Rom. 1:24–25).

Through the Damascus road event God showed Paul that there is also only "one mediator between God and human beings, Christ Jesus, himself human" (1 Tim 2:5). Paul undoubtedly knew the stories about Jesus even before his encounter with the risen Christ. When speaking to Agrippa II, he declared, "The king is familiar with these things, and I can speak freely to him. I am convinced that none of this has escaped his notice" (Acts 26:26). None of this escaped Paul's notice either. But when Paul encountered the risen Jesus and heard his voice (Acts 9:17; 22:14–15; 1 Cor. 15:8), he understood Jesus to be the royal "Son of God." He was descended from David, according to the promise of 2 Samuel 7:11–16, but he was also the one "who through the Spirit of holiness was appointed the Son of God in power by his resurrection from the dead: Jesus Christ our Lord" (Rom. 1:4).

Jesus as Lord and Savior

Among the Gentiles Paul's announcement that Jesus is the Christ (or Messiah) would not have been readily understood. Paul's central proclamation among them was that "Jesus Christ is Lord" (Phil. 2:11). "Lord" was commonly recognized as a title of both deities and rulers as part of the imperial cult. This Christian proclamation directly challenged these other claims to lordship. Paul writes to the Corinthians that while there were many called "lords," in fact "there is but one Lord, Jesus Christ, through whom all things came and through whom we live" (1 Cor. 8:6).

In a similar way, Paul proclaimed that Jesus is the "Savior" (Phil. 3:20; 2 Tim. 1:10; Titus 1:4), and this title likewise linked Jesus with God (Isa. 43:11). This title was also ascribed to a variety of deities and appears in the imperial cult. Augustus was styled as "the god and savior, emperor" and various deities, such as the god of healing Asclepius, were called "savior."

People longed for salvation from disaster, disease, and death. Temples dedicated to "Zeus the savior" could be found at harbors (Strabo, *Geography* 9.1.15). The Egyptian goddess Isis was thought to offer healing and immortality. The common concern for salvation found its hope and fulfillment in Jesus Christ (Acts 16:29–32). Through Jesus Christ, those who believe are saved (1 Cor. 1:21; 15:2; Eph. 2:8). While salvation is a process that begins in the present (1 Cor. 1:18) and includes the Spirit's work of washing and renewing a person (Titus 3:5), Paul frequently speaks of Christ's salvation as a future event—we will be saved from God's wrath through him (Rom. 5:9).

Given Paul's liberal use of the titles "Lord" and "Savior" for Jesus Christ, we are not surprised to hear him call Jesus "God." In Titus 2:13 Paul speaks of the "blessed hope" that is "the appearing of the glory of our great God and Savior, Jesus Christ." Similarly, Romans 9:5 speaks of "the Messiah, who is God over all, forever praised! Amen." The exalted status of Christ is so high that Paul describes him as the one who brought the world into existence and the one for whom creation exists (Col. 1:15–16; "firstborn" implies his preeminence as in

---

MANY "LORDS"

The title *kyrios* ("lord") was a mark of respect (similar to "sir") or a term meaning slave master (Eph. 6:9; Col. 4:1). For the Greek-speaking Jews, *kyrios* was also the divine title for YHWH used in the Greek Old Testament (the Septuagint).

But Gentiles also used *kyrios* to refer to deities. For example, if you were inviting someone to dine with you at the temple of the Egyptian deity Serapis, you might write, "Nikephoros asks you to dine at a banquet of the Lord [*kyrios*] Serapis in the Birth-House on the 23rd, from the 9th hour."[2] The gods Isis, Apollo, Artemis, Athena, Hermes, Asclepius, and Dionysus were all called *kyrios*. Moreover, in the imperial cult that honored the emperor as a deity, *kyrios* is often found. Even Nero is called "the lord of all the world."

Left: Asclepius, the god of healing, was one of the many deities called "savior." *Right*: The temple of Epidaurus in Greece was the center of the healing cult of Asclepius, although temples to the god were erected in other cities as well, including Corinth

Ps. 89:27). He exercises authority over all as Lord (1 Cor. 15:25 – 26; cf. Ps. 110:1). Paul's high Christology contrasts sharply with modern attempts to reduce Jesus to nothing more than a moral teacher, a traveling sage, or a cultural ideal.

But Paul also rigorously affirms the humanity of Christ. He "made himself nothing by taking the very nature of a servant, being made in human likeness. And being found in appearance as a human being, he humbled himself by becoming obedient to death" (Phil. 2:7 – 8). God's saving purposes are accomplished through him since God, "sending his own Son in the likeness of sinful flesh and for sin . . . condemned sin in the flesh" (Rom. 8:3 NRSV).

The Death and Resurrection of Christ

For Paul, the crucifixion of Jesus was a sacrifice for the sins of humanity (Rom. 4:25; 1 Cor. 15:3; Gal. 1:4). This death for sin fulfilled the promise of the ancient Scriptures: "Christ died for our sins according to the Scriptures" (1 Cor. 15:3; see Isa. 53:12). During Paul's time, Jewish theology did not understand Isaiah 53 as a messianic prophecy; to preach "Christ crucified" (1 Cor. 1:23) was a patent contradiction. How could the promised Messiah be subject to such shameful treatment? Paul's challenge in the synagogue, therefore, was to show from Scripture that "the Messiah had to suffer" (Acts 17:3).

The message of the cross was likewise difficult for the Gentiles to accept, as Paul acknowledges: "We preach Christ crucified: a stumbling block to Jews and foolishness to Gentiles" (1 Cor. 1:23). To preach that a crucified Jew was Savior and Lord would have been hard to accept. Moreover, crucifixion was the ultimate torture (see sidebar on "A View of the Cross"). But Paul states: "To those whom God has called, both Jews and Greeks, Christ [is] the power of God and the wisdom of God" (1 Cor. 1:24).

Paul saw Christ's death through the sacrificial system of the temple in Jerusalem. He declares to the Corinthians that "Christ, our Passover lamb, has been sacrificed" (1 Cor. 5:7); his death is "a sacrifice of atonement" that turned away God's wrath (Rom. 3:25). The repeated references to Christ's blood return us to the sacrificial nature of Christ's death since that blood was poured out in death for sin (1 Cor. 11:25; Eph. 1:7; Col. 1:20). The significance of Christ's death does not end, however, at the cross; its twin theme is the resurrection, when Jesus' life is vindicated by God. On his journey to Damascus, Paul saw the risen Christ and proclaimed that Jesus was truly alive (Acts 25:19). His understanding of the resurrection was also rooted in the prophetic testimony that Christ would be raised, as he says: "He was raised on the third day according to the Scriptures" (1 Cor. 15:4; cf. Acts 2:24–32).

Paul elaborates on the resurrection in 1 Corinthians 15 in response to some within the church who denied that deceased believers would be raised (15:12). While Paul affirms an intermediate conscious state between the death and resurrection of the believer (2 Cor. 5:6–8; Phil. 1:20–23), his hope is fixed on the resurrection of the dead since, indeed, Christ was raised from the dead (1 Thess. 4:13–18). So united is the resurrection of the believers with the resurrection of Christ that Paul viewed the Corinthian denial of the believers' resurrection as entailing the denial of Christ's resurrection (1 Cor. 15:12–19).

As a result of Christ's work on the cross and his resurrection, God has inaugurated the *new covenant*, as represented in the Lord's Supper (1 Cor. 11:23–26). The blessings of the new covenant were that God would write his law on his people's heart, they would all have the knowledge of God, and God would forgive their sins (Jer. 31:31–34). Paul emphasizes these benefits of forgiveness (Eph. 1:7; Col. 1:14), knowing God through Christ (Gal. 4:8–9; Eph. 1:17; Phil. 3:8, 10), and fulfilling the law by the power of the Spirit (Rom. 8:4; cf. 2:15). The death and resurrection of Christ have also *justified* believers (4:25; 5:1, 9), meaning they are "declared righteous" in Christ through faith (3:21–26). Through Christ's death God is both the righteous Judge who deals with sin and the One who acquits those who have faith in Christ. Furthermore, those who were enemies of God because of their sin are now *reconciled* to him and are at peace with him (5:1, 10–11; Eph. 2:13). Through Christ's redemptive act we are saved from the wrath of God (Rom. 5:9–10).

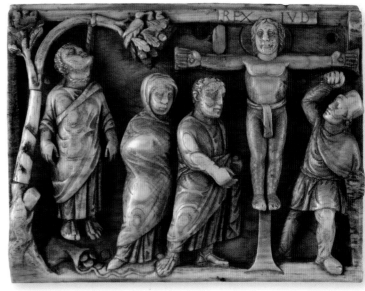

Paul boldly proclaimed the message of "Christ crucified" (1 Cor 1:23). This fourth century A.D. depiction from a small casket is our earliest portrayal of his crucifixion

THE NEW PERSPECTIVE ON PAUL

In the 1970s a debate erupted among New Testament scholars trying to understand Paul's theology in light of his Jewish context.[3] This debate has resulted in a "new perspective" on Paul that today challenges many conventional interpretations of the apostle.

Traditionally, many have thought that Paul saw Judaism as a religion that required a person to earn their salvation through meritorious works of religious law. Because of our inability to obey God's law, our relationship with him is broken—and only Christ's work on the cross has solved our need for righteousness. Our justification, then, is a gift that compensates for our sin—that offers us grace. In this view, Paul inherited a severe legalism from Judaism that taught that by obeying the law, God's wrath could be appeased. God's grace in Christ is truly good news because it offers us a way of escape. Paul, therefore, was converted *to Christ*, but more importantly, converted *from Jewish legalism*.

Slaves were common in Rome and Christians eagerly included them. Here two women slaves fight as gladiators in the arena. This plaque recognizes their release from slavery and gives their names, Amazon and Achillia.

But today many question whether Judaism embraced such a view of the law. In this new view, the legalism Christians have projected onto first-century Judaism originated with Luther's struggle with the legalism of medieval Catholicism. Keeping the Jewish law, according to the new perspective, was a response to God's grace and commitment, not a means of achieving it. A Jew does not obey the law in order to earn salvation; Jews obey the law because of their status as members of God's covenant community. But then why did Paul emphasize grace as if it were contrasted to the law? The answer: the Gentile mission of the church. Gentiles who did not have the Jewish law would view it as an obstacle to conversion. Thus, Paul underscored the power of grace without law among non-Jews.

If then Paul had no complaint with his Jewish heritage (cf. Phil. 3:4–6), in what sense can we say he was "converted?" According to the new perspective, Paul's conversion began in the discovery of Jesus of Nazareth, the resurrected Messiah. He was critical of things such as circumcision and dietary rules because they impeded the Gentile mission and kept Jewish Christians and Gentile Christians apart. But does this mean that in Paul's mind Judaism outside of Christ is a sufficient and saving faith? Scholars are divided. Some believe that to find some inadequacy in Judaism anchors an anti-Jewish attitude in the heart of Paul's theology. These scholars develop a "two covenant" theology for Paul. But a majority believes that Paul presented Christ as a necessary continuation of God's saving work in history, which Jews also must join. There is one covenant, one means of salvation in Christ.

While this debate about first-century Judaism and the law will continue, it has offered an important corrective to our understanding of the New Testament and its world. The characterization of the Jewish faith as nothing more than legalism ignores not only the rich teaching of the Old Testament about the grace and mercy of God but also the many writings of Jews in antiquity who knew that obedience to God could only spring from experiencing his grace.

Paul argues in Romans that both Gentile and Jew are under sin and subject to God's wrath and that Christ's justification is effective for both peoples (Rom. 3:21–31). While Paul's conversion was truly not in the same category as that of the Gentiles who turned to God from idols, he did undergo a radical transformation in his perspective regarding God's Messiah. In this conversion he affirmed the promises made to his ancestors that are now fulfilled in Christ. Paul also found that the righteousness by which he stood before God was the righteousness of God through Christ (2 Cor. 5:21; Phil. 3:8–9).

THE IMPLICATIONS OF THE GOSPEL

For Paul, justification has social dimensions regarding Jewish and Gentile fellowship (Gal. 2:11–21), and this reconciliation extends to the whole cosmos (Eph. 2:16; Col. 1:20). The salvation of Christ also has dramatic effects in the life of the believers. They are formed together into a new community, the church, which has both local manifestations (1 Cor. 1:2; 1 Thess. 1:1) and a universal dimension (Eph. 1:22–23). God has taken both Jew and Gentile and made them into one new humanity (2:14–15) and, together, they are reconciled to God (2:16–17).

The social distinctions that separated humanity — gender, ethnicity, socioeconomic status — are of no importance as this new and diverse community comes together as one (Gal. 3:28; Col. 3:11). The Roman Empire was hardly egalitarian in its perspective on social class. A person was expected to stay within their order, though some social mobility was possible (e.g., a slave becoming a freedman). People were classified as either slave or free, citizens or noncitizens, patricians or plebs, Romans, Greeks, Macedonians, Jews, or "barbarians."

Gender distinctions were also important. The amazing social mix within Christianity, however, caught the attention of Pliny the Younger, governor of the Roman province of Bithynia around AD 112. In writing to Emperor Trajan about the "Christian problem" he stated:

> This made me decide it was all the more necessary to extract the truth by torture from two slave-women, whom they call deaconesses. . . . I have postponed any further examination and hastened to consult you. The question seems to me to be worthy of your consideration, especially in view of the number of persons endangered; for a great many individuals of *every age and class*, *both men and women*, are being brought to trial, and this is likely to continue. It is not only the towns, but villages and rural districts too which are infected through contact with this wretched cult. (*Epistles* 10.96)

Paul's view of Christ's cross embraces his understanding of the Christians' participation in the victory over sin. Since the blessing of the new covenant included the writing of God's law on the heart as well as forgiveness, Paul regarded union with Christ in his death as a death to sin. This is symbolized in baptism and framed as a liberation from the slavery to sin (Rom. 6:1–23). Paul knows full well that humanity is incapable of doing what God requires because of our fallen human nature, the "flesh" (*sarx*, 7:13–25). Yet Christ has not only justified believers (8:1) but also empowered his people with the Spirit so that they can do what pleases God (8:1–13). The high moral standards he describes in his letters (see, e.g., Rom. 12–15; Eph. 4–6; Col. 3–4) form a roadmap for those liberated by Christ from sin's slavery and enabled by God's Spirit.

Paul's theology is also oriented to the future. In a world marked by violence, disease, death, and despair, Paul was filled with hope. When he faced his darkest moment during his second Roman imprisonment, he knew that a crown of righteousness awaited him (2 Tim. 4:6–8). Because of Christ's resurrection those who died in Christ would be raised at his return (1 Thess. 4:13–18), an event he calls the *parousia* (1 Cor. 15:23; 1 Thess. 2:19; 4:15; 5:23; 2 Thess. 2:1).

This return of Christ is the consummation of human history, a time when all will confess that Jesus is Lord (Phil. 2:9–11). He will have then "destroyed all dominion, authority and power" — all forces natural and supernatural that are against God. He reigns now and will continue to do so "until he as put all his enemies under his feet," including death itself (1 Cor. 15:24–26). Then God will be all in all.

QUESTIONS FOR DISCUSSION ⊚⊚⊚⊚⊚⊚⊚⊚⊚⊚⊚⊚⊚⊚⊚⊚⊚⊚⊚⊚⊚⊚⊚⊚⊚⊚

1. In what ways does Paul's theology help us understand the place of Christianity in the midst of a society marked by religious pluralism?

2. Compare Paul's proclamation about Christ with the understanding of salvation preached in the contemporary church. How is the contemporary message similar and how does it differ from what Paul proclaimed?

3. What are the implications of the "new perspective" on Paul? Compare the fundamental observations of this perspective with the preaching you have heard.

4. What are the social effects of salvation? Does Paul reflect on the role of Christians in the wider society?

5. What place does eschatology (the teaching about the "last things") have in the theology of the church today? What place does eschatology have in your understanding of the Christian faith and your present life? Compare Paul's emphasis, including the link between eschatology and ethics.

BIBLIOGRAPHY
Introductory
Bruce, F. F. *Paul: Apostle of the Heart Set Free*. Grand Rapids: Eerdmans, 1977.

Marshall, I. H. *New Testament Theology*. Downers Grove, IL: InterVarsity Press, 2004.

Polhill, J. *Paul and His Letters*. Nashville: Broadman & Holman, 1999.

Schreiner, T. R. *Paul: Apostle of God's Glory in Christ*. Downers Grove, IL: InterVarsity Press, 2001.

Advanced
Dunn, J. D. G. *The Theology of the Apostle Paul*. Grand Rapids: Eerdmans, 1998.

Murphy-O'Connor, J. *Paul: A Critical Life*. Oxford: Clarendon, 1996.

Neyrey, J. H. *Paul: In Other Words*. Louisville: Westminster John Knox, 1990.

Ridderbos, H. *Paul: An Outline of His Theology*. Grand Rapids: Eerdmans, 1975.

Schnabel, E. J. *Early Christian Mission*. Vol. 2. *Paul and the Early Church*. Downers Grove, IL: InterVarsity Press, 2004.

NOTES
1. Gow and Page, *Greek Anthology*, 2:57.
2. Horsley, *New Documents Illustrating Early Christianity*, 1:5.
3. See E. P. Sanders, *Paul and Palestinian Judaism* (Philadelphia: Fortress, 1977).

CHAPTER 14

THE LETTER TO
THE GALATIANS

The ancient theater of Psidian Antioch, a major city in the Roman province of Galatia.

Pisidian Antioch

Galatians has always captivated those eager to understand the essence of the gospel message. Martin Luther called it "my own epistle, to which I have plighted my troth, my Katie von Bora [his wife's name]" (*Works* 26). Paul the apostle here contrasts his theology to his opponents' "gospel" (1:6). He explains his past "in Judaism" (1:13) and his new life "in Christ" (2:17–21) to persuade the Galatians against the intruders. He clarifies God's redemptive plan in Christ as fulfilling earlier promises made to Abraham. He expounds on life in this new age as empowered by the Spirit.

WHERE WAS GALATIA?

"Galatia" could refer to the region where ethnic Gauls lived. In the third century BC, migrating Celts moved into northern Asia Minor (Strabo, *Geography* 12.5.1, 567). Pompey established a client kingdom under Galatian leadership there. But by 25 BC, Rome reorganized Asia Minor and created a province of Galatia that reached from the northern region almost

RAMSAY TRAVELS TO ASIA MINOR

William Ramsay traveled to Asia Minor regularly to pursue his passion for the regions of New Testament history. Another well-traveled Victorian, Gertrude Bell, shared many of these trips with Ramsay and his wife. Notes from Bell's journals give insight into their adventures:

Madan Shehar

Saturday, May 25, 1907

The Ramsays arrived yesterday. I was in the middle of digging up a church when suddenly two carts hove into sight and there they were. It was about 3 in the afternoon. They instantly got out, refused to think of going to the tents, Lady Ramsay made tea (for they were starving) in the open and Ramsay oblivious of all other considerations was at once lost in the problems the church presented. It was too delightful to have someone as much excited about it as I was.

to the Mediterranean Sea. It included cities such as Pisidian Antioch, Lystra, Derbe, and Iconium, which Paul visited on his first missionary tour.

Two hypotheses discuss the location of the Galatian churches. The North Galatian theory identifies Galatia as the area of ethnic Gauls in the northern Asia Minor. This theory connects Paul's meeting with Peter, James, and John in 2:1–10 with the Jerusalem Council of Acts 15. Paul's visit to Galatia occurs *after* this conference, on his second missionary journey, and Galatians was written on his third journey. This view was held by most patristic, medieval, and Reformation commentators and is popular today.

The North Galatian theory has its weaknesses. If the Jerusalem Council determined that circumcision was not necessary for Gentile Christians, why are some teaching the Galatians that they must be circumcised? This theory also fails to explain why Paul does not refute his opponents by referring to the council's decision. And why does Peter withdraw from fellowship with Gentiles in Antioch (2:11–14) if he and the council agreed on a policy?

The South Galatian theory (proposed in the nineteenth-century by Sir William Ramsay) begins by demonstrating that the imperial province of Galatia extended to the south. Thus when Paul visited Pisidian Antioch on his first missionary journey, he was in Galatia. The South Galatian theory concludes Paul used the Roman provincial name for his churches, while Luke used the ethnic designation for the region Paul visited on his second journey (Act 16:6).

This view usually connects Paul's visit to Jerusalem in 2:1–10 with his "famine visit" recorded in Acts 11:27–30. However, James Dunn's modified South Galatian theory argues that Galatians 2:1–10 fits with Acts 15.[2] Paul refers to Barnabas frequently (2:1, 9, 13) as if the Galatians know him, but Barnabas was with Paul *only* on his first tour. This suggests that Paul founded the Galatian churches on his initial journey. Additionally, Paul's encounter with Sergius Paulus, the proconsul of Cyprus (see Acts 13:7–12), whose family was from Pisidian Antioch, may have led Paul to preach in that city.

Moreover, a southern locale for Galatia puts it within the perceived jurisdiction of the Jerusalem church (Antioch was a "daughter" church of Jerusalem). Thus, Paul's opponents from Jerusalem would feel justified in "checking up" on Paul's new churches. We will follow a South Galatian theory.

JERUSALEM COUNCIL: JEW AND GENTILE CHRISTIANS

James declared at the Jerusalem council: "It is my judgment, therefore, that we should not make it difficult for the Gentiles who are turning to God" (Acts 15:19–21). He then asks that Gentiles abstain from sexual immorality and meat polluted by idols. Paul felt the council secured his own position that Gentiles should be welcomed as full members of the family of God. Yet other Jews were convinced that the Messiah did not dismantle circumcision. Gentiles who were not circumcised could still adhere to Judaism (they were known as "God-fearers"; see the sidebar on "God-Fearers" in Ch. 12). The "people from James" who convinced Peter to withdraw from eating with Gentile Christians likely held this position (Gal. 2:12).

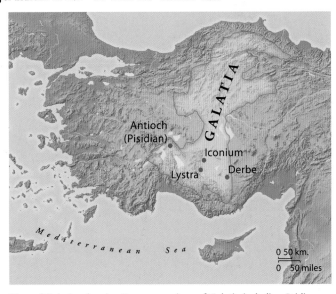

Map of Galatia, showing Roman province of Galatia including Psidian Antioch, Lystra, Derbe, and Iconium

SETTING IN GALATIA

In his letter, Paul is explicit that the Galatians are Gentiles (4:8–9). Living in the Roman province of Galatia, their society had an indigenous layer, a Greek layer, and a Roman layer. Common to all three tiers was paganism. People in that area worshiped the local goddess Agdistis (Gk. Cybele), as well as Greek gods. Paul and Barnabas were identified as Hermes and Zeus by those in Lystra (Acts 14:11–12). The Galatians also believed in "elemental spirits" (4:8–9 NRSV)—forces that shaped daily life and ruled capriciously over humans, holding them in slavery (4:9).

Curiously, the Galatian Christians seem to struggle more with questions concerning Judaism and less with their pagan environment than other churches started by Paul. Both archaeological remains and textual references demonstrate that Jews prospered in cities such as Thessalonica and Corinth. Yet issues of circumcision and the Sabbath play almost no role in those churches' debates. Why are the Galatians churches different? To answer this, we must look at Paul's opponents and at Paul's sending church, Antioch.

Paul calls the intruders troublemakers and agitators, perverting the gospel of Christ (1:6–7, 5:10, 12). He charges them with proclaiming a gospel of Christ *plus* circumcision (6:12–13). Scholars have labeled this movement "Judaizing."

In adding circumcision to faith in Christ, the opponents established a gospel with the social boundaries of Judaism. To Paul's great dismay, they even influenced Peter in Antioch. Paul levels this charge against him: "You are a Jew, yet you live like a Gentile and not like a Jew. How is it, then, that you force Gentiles to follow Jewish customs?" (2:14). These Jewish Christian missionaries saw the law as sufficient, while Paul saw the law as fulfilled in Christ and his Spirit (3:17, 25).

Cybele was worshiped throughout the Roman Empire, especially in Asia Minor where she was often known as Agdistis.

Why were these Jewish Christian missionaries so effective in the Galatian churches? Those churches probably felt a connection to Jerusalem. "People from James" came to Antioch in Syria and apparently confronted Peter (2:12). Perhaps a similar group also traveled to the Galatian churches. Paul challenged his opponents' motives by declaring that these interlopers just "want to impress others by means of the flesh . . . to avoid being persecuted for the cross of Christ" (6:12). In Paul's time, Jewish followers of Jesus could still be part of their local synagogue. But if a Jew accepted Gentiles as equal members of God's family, he could be charged with polluting the congregation and expelled.

Paul also equated his opponents' message with the slavery experienced under paganism (4:9–10), insisting that their position of Christ *plus* circumcision contradicted the gospel message. It entrapped the gospel within the old age, but Christ brought in a new era. The Christian has died with Christ, and now lives in a new reality (2:19–21).

JUVENAL AND GENTILE JUDAIZING

Juvenal accuses Gentiles of Judaizing: "Some who have had a father who reveres the Sabbath adore nothing but the clouds . . . and see no difference between eating swine's flesh, from which their father abstained, and that of man. In time they take to circumcision. Having been wont to flout the laws of Rome, they learn and practice and revere the Jewish law, and all that Moses handed down in his secret tome. . . . For all of this the father was to blame" (*Satire* 14.96–106).

THE MESSAGE OF GALATIANS

The structure of Paul's letter is a matter of debate among scholars. Some point to ancient letter-writing handbooks as the best parallel for understanding Galatians. Hellenistic letters generally consisted of an opening, a thanksgiving, a body, an ethical section, and a closing. Within this model, letters took various shapes according to their purpose.

The "rebuke letter" type is similar to Galatians. Such a letter was sent to someone who failed to follow instructions or foolishly changed his mind. There is generally a close relationship between the sender of the letter and its recipient. A rebuke letter has no opening thanksgiving; note, for example, P.Oxy. I 123.5 – 9: "I am very much surprised [*thaumazō*], my son, that till today I have not received any letter from you, telling me about your welfare."[3] In many "rebuke letters" the sender simply asks the addressee to write, though it may also include instructions for business or personal conduct. A unique aspect of Galatians is that it similarly has no thanksgiving. Rather,

The philosopher on this ancient sarcophagus is shown with his scrolls.

Paul begins, "I am astonished [*thaumazō*] . . ." (1:6). Paul wants the Galatians to change their minds and behaviors, returning to the true gospel he preached to them.

Others point to oral rhetorical forms to interpret Galatians. Rhetoric was commonly used in antiquity to persuade. Aristotle describes three forms of persuasion: *ethos*, *pathos*, and *logos*. "The first kind depends on the personal character of the speaker [*ethos*]; the second on putting the audience into a certain frame of mind [*pathos*]; the third on the proof, or apparent proof, provided by the words of the speech itself [*logos*]" (*Rhetoric* 1:2).

Paul draws from these three forms to persuade the Galatians to return to his gospel. For example, he presents himself as a model of behavior (*ethos*) in describing his new life in Christ (2:19–20). His character as an apostle (1:1) called by God to go to the Gentiles (1:15–17) buttresses his argument. Paul uses proof derived from *pathos* as well, speaking to their hearts with his cajoling reminder of their love for him (4:14) and his sarcastic denunciation of his opponents (5:12; 6:12). Paul also used *logos* in employing proof by example (e.g., Abraham).

OUTLINE OF GALATIANS

I. Greetings (1:1–5)

II. Rebuke (1:6–4:11)

- A. Paul's Rebuke to the Galatians (1:6–9)
- B. Paul's Autobiographical Narrative (1:10–2:21)
  1. Paul's Call (1:10–17)
  2. Paul Meets Apostles in Jerusalem (1:18–2:10)
  3. Paul Confronts Peter in Antioch (2:11–21)
- C. Theological Argument on Law and Promise (3:1–4:11)
  1. Abraham's Example (3:1–14)
  2. The Law and the Promise (3:15–29)
  3. Heirs of God (4:1–11)

III. Request (4:12–6:10)

- A. Paul's Personal Appeal (4:12–20)
- B. Theological Argument Using Sarah and Hagar (4:21–5:1)
- C. Ethical Appeals (5:2–6:10)
  1. Circumcision Is of No Value (5:2–15)
  2. Live in the Spirit (5:16–6:10)

IV. Closing Summary and Greetings (6:11–18)

Paul's Greeting (1:1–5)

Paul's greeting contains key ideas he will develop throughout his letter. He insists he is a divinely appointed apostle (1:1). Paul foreshadows the letter's argument in his description of Jesus, who "gave himself for our sins to rescue us from the present evil age" (1:4). The power of Christ's death reinforces both Paul's dispute with Peter (2:15) and his theological argument about the law and the promise (3:21–24).

Paul's Rebuke (1:6–4:11)

Paul immediately launches his rebuke: "I am astonished that you are so quickly deserting the one who called you by the grace of Christ and are turning to a different gospel" (1:6). He holds the Galatians responsible to reject the intruders' new message. He lays down a curse on anyone who would alter his gospel.

Next Paul reminds the Galatians of his own behavior in Christ. His life as a Pharisee was filled with zeal and passion for the law (1:13–14). Then he encountered the risen Christ and life in the Spirit, which sets the stage for his request that they too walk in the Spirit (5:16). He offers himself as a suitable model to follow. These biographical details help establish his argument that the law no longer plays a key role in God's salvation plan.

God gave Paul an assignment—to preach to Gentiles about God's Son, Jesus (1:15–16). His language mimics Amos, Isaiah, and Jeremiah—prophets called by God to perform a particular task (Isa. 49:1–6; Jer. 1:4–5; Amos 7:14–15). Paul implies his independence from the Jerusalem church in showing his actions between his conversion and his first trip to Jerusalem.

Paul makes a second trip to Jerusalem, probably eleven years later—likely the Jerusalem Council of Acts 15. During this visit, the apostles in Jerusalem (James, Peter, and John) accepted Paul's commission. But they did not spell out exactly how Jews and Gentiles should relate to each other in individual congregations. This sets up the disagreement with Peter in Antioch (2:11–14).

To better appreciate the conundrum, we must understand something about Gentile "God-fearers" who became part of the synagogue. Many were recognized as "righteous" because they forsook idols and acknowledged the one true God. But they did not become full Jews unless they underwent circumcision. Unlike the temple where priests demanded that "unclean" Gentiles remain outside, the synagogue was not a "sacred" space. Gentiles could listen to the reading of the law and participate in festivals.

A third-century AD inscription from Aphrodisias, southern Asia Minor, records over fifty God-fearers who enjoyed the company of the synagogue.[5] Nine were leaders of the city council, a job that required them to be present at pagan sacrifices. The Jews did not demand circumcision unless a Gentile wanted to be part of Israel. Many Jews reasoned that eventually, God would include God-fearers among those saved, but they remained Gentiles.

Paul shares the belief that in the end times, Gentiles will follow God (3:14). He sees this fulfilled in the church: Gentiles are equal members with Jews in Christ. Both are part of the "Israel of God" (6:16). Thus, observance of the law (circumcision) rebuilds a barrier that Christ's death tore down (2:18). The Galatians fail to see the ramifications of Christ's death and resurrection in their own lives (3:1).

This early third century AD inscription from Aphrodisias, Asia Minor, provides clear evidence that Gentile god-fearers were part of Diaspora synagogues.

ABRAHAM IN JEWISH THOUGHT

Paul highlights Abraham's response of faith. God blessed Abraham with the promise, "Look up at the heavens and count the stars—if indeed you can count them.... So shall your offspring be" (Gen. 15:5). But most Jews in Paul's day focused on Genesis 17:10 with its command of circumcision. Note Sirach 44:19–21, which reads in part: "Abraham ... certified the covenant in his flesh [circumcision], and when he was tested he proved faithful [sacrifice of Isaac, Gen. 22]. Therefore the Lord assured him ... that he would make him as numerous as the dust of the earth."

Paul therefore asks, "You foolish Galatians! Who has bewitched you?" (3:1). He develops three crucial contrasts: the law and the Spirit, the law and the promise, and the law and faith. In each case, Paul understands the law to have served its purpose and to be eclipsed by Christ's work. Here is Paul's understanding of the gospel message. It goes back to the garden of Eden, when sin entered the world (1:4). It traces God's work in Israel, including his dealings with Abraham and the giving of the law (3:6–18). It assumes Christ's incarnation (4:4) and focuses on the crucifixion (2:20–21) and resurrection (5:5). Its culmination is yet to come, but until Christ's return, believers are to live in the Spirit (5:16).

Paul anticipates the readers' next question, "What, then, was the purpose of the law?" (3:19). He explains that sin had infiltrated the world. God provided an interim remedy through the law's sacrificial system and its injunctions to remain separate from idolatry. But the law was like a *paidagōgos*, the family slave in charge of delivering a son safely to school. Once the child grows up, the slave is no longer needed. Thus, the law is no longer required now that Christ has come.

Paul declares: "So the law was put in charge of us until Christ came that we might be justified by faith. Now that this faith has come, we are no longer under the supervision of the law" (3:24–25). What does Paul mean "justified by faith"? The word family for "to justify" and "just" or "righteous" has been understood in two basic ways. To some this family carries a forensic meaning, a transfer of status implying a "right relationship" with God; others stress the sense of ethical renewal or uprightness. In general, Protestants have emphasized a forensic meaning, while Catholics have pointed to the ethical emphasis.

Today the debate continues. While most Protestants hold that a believer's sins are *imputed* or charged to Christ (see 2 Cor. 5:19–21), *how* Christians are credited with Christ's righteousness is debated. Recently, some scholars recommend that Paul's understanding of justification has three aspects to it: (1) a past element, the death and resurrection of Christ, (2) a present component, where each believer by faith is made righteous and (3) a future aspect, wherein "we eagerly await through the Spirit the righteousness for which we hope" (Gal. 5:5).

Debates rage as well over how to translate the phrase "faith in/of Jesus Christ" in 2:16. Some write "faith *in* Jesus Christ," with Christ as the recipient of our trust. Others suggest "faith/faithfulness *of* Jesus Christ," emphasizing his obedience unto death for our salvation. Paul uses this expression seven times in his letters: twice in 2:16 and in 3:22 (see also Rom. 3:22, 26; Eph. 3:12; Phil. 3:9). In Paul's time, faith also describes the patron-client relationship. In this case, faith refers to the patron's dependability to make good on promises for assistance. The clients' faith in the patron means they *trust* his goodwill. Likewise, the patron must *trust* that the clients will be grateful for their aid.

Looking at 3:22 may offer a way forward, "so that what was promised, being given through faith in Jesus Christ, might be given to those who believe [have faith]." Paul appears to use both emphases here—the objective work of Jesus Christ for humanity's salvation, and the subjective response of belief incumbent on his followers.

Paul's Request (4:12–6:10)

Paul has described his own character and Abraham's faith as exemplary. He has pointed to the gospel's superiority over against the law. He has leveled charges against the Galatians' disbelief and change of heart. Now he makes his request: "I plead with you, brothers and sisters, become like me, for I became like you" (4:12). He "became like them"—*outside* the law. But he asks them to become as he is—one who is *in* Christ. If they are in Christ, they are not outsiders; they are God's children and heirs of the promise (4:7).

To fulfill his injunction to "become as I am," the Galatians must resist those who promote "slavery" (circumcision). For Paul, it is a matter of life and death—if they succumb to circumcision, they have cut themselves off from Christ. But he saves his hottest anger for his opponents: "I wish they would go the whole way and emasculate themselves!" (5:12).

After so much talk about slavery, Paul introduces a term that sums up his letter's central idea, freedom: "It is for freedom that Christ has set us free" (5:1). Using a common farming image of yoked oxen, Paul illustrates the unyielding bondage of false teachings (5:2). Those promoting circumcision and other Jewish rites like Sabbath and food laws are in effect enslaving Gentiles to the Jewish way of life.

Paul declares that freedom leads to a choice: Christians can follow the "flesh" or the Spirit. Those who live after the flesh reveal it by their actions: idolatry, fornication, envy, drunkenness, and jealousy (5:20–21). Paul asks the Galatians to live by the Spirit (5:16) and walk in the Spirit (5:25; cf. Deut. 13:4–5; Isa. 33:15; Jer. 44:23). Having crucified the flesh, they can help each other avoid sin (Gal. 6:1) and support each other in tough times (6:2). When they do this, they "fulfill the law of Christ" (6:2).

Paul's Spirit-based ethics is not antithetical to the law. Many Jews in Paul's day understood that the law must be done from the heart. Deuteronomy insists that simply going through the motions of fulfilling the requirements of the law does not satisfy God (Deut. 30:6). Philo, the first-century Jew from Alexandria, criticizes those who "are uncircumcised in their hearts, as the law expresses it, and by reason of the hardness of their hearts they are stubborn" (Philo, *Special Laws* 1.305). Paul picks up the promise given in Jeremiah that a new covenant will be written on the heart (Jer. 31:31–34). He promotes a circumcision of the heart through the Spirit, who frees believers to walk in righteousness and faith (Gal. 5:6; cf. Rom. 2:28–29; 2 Cor. 3:3, 6).

Paul's Closing (6:11–18)

Paul's final section summarizes his message. He repeats his challenge to those who threaten to derail the Galatians' faith (6:12–13). He reiterates the importance of the cross: As Christ

> **"BECOME AS I AM"**
>
> Paul points to himself as a model for the Galatians to follow. His request matches those made by philosophers to their students. Seneca advocates this in his letter to his friend Lucilius. "We can get rid of most sins, if we have a witness who stands near us when we are likely to go wrong.... Happy is the man who can make others better.... Choose a master whose life, conversation, and soul-expressing face have satisfied you; picture him always to yourself as your protector and your pattern" (*Epistles* 11:8–10).

was crucified, so too Paul was crucified to the world and his flesh (6:14). The Galatians also can live as new creations (6:15), dead to the old order that stresses the physical. Instead, Paul declares that the mark of a Christian reflects the marks of Jesus. Those who are a new creation are the true "Israel of God" (6:16).

AUTHOR AND DATE

Scholars are virtually unanimous that the apostle Paul wrote this letter to churches in Galatia. When? The answer depends on which region in Asia Minor the letter was sent to. Those holding a North Galatian theory date the letter to Paul's third missionary journey, suggesting AD 53. The South Galatian theory holds that Paul wrote Galatians after his first missionary journey, before the Jerusalem council and before writing 1 – 2 Thessalonians (winter of 47 – 48). Dunn's modified South Galatian theory argues that Galatians was written from Corinth about the same time Paul wrote 1 – 2 Thessalonians (AD 51). No theological doctrine hinges on the date of this letter, though the date does have ramifications for establishing the chronological ordering of Paul's letters.

QUESTIONS FOR DISCUSSION ⊚

1. Explain the differences between the North and South Galatian theories.

2. What was the central issue dealt with at Paul's meeting with James, Peter, and John in Jerusalem? With Peter in Antioch?

3. What are the chief concerns of those who opposed Paul in Galatia?

4. When Paul refers to "works of the law," what does he mean? Who is promoting "works of the law," and why?

5. Explain how the Spirit is integral to Paul's understanding of the Christian life.

BIBLIOGRAPHY
Introductory

Aune, D. E. *The New Testament in Its Literary Environment*. LEC. Ed. Wayne A. Meeks. Philadelphia: Westminster, 1987.

Esler, P. F. *Galatians*. New Testament Readings Series. New York: Routledge, 1998.

Longenecker, R. N. *Galatians*. WBC. Dallas: Word, 1990.

Stowers, S. K. *Letter Writing in Greco-Roman Antiquity*. LEC. Ed. Wayne A. Meeks. Philadelphia: Westminster, 1986.

Advanced

Betz, H. D. *Galatians: A Commentary on Paul's Letter to the Churches in Galatia*. Hermeneia. Philadelphia: Fortress, 1979.

Bruce, F. F. *Commentary on Galatians*. NIGTC. Grand Rapids: Eerdmans, 1982.

Martyn, J. L. *Galatians*. AB. New York: Doubleday, 1997.

Nanos, M. D., ed. *The Galatians Debate: Contemporary Issues in Rhetorical and Historical Interpretation*. Peabody, MA: Hendrickson, 2002.

NOTES

1. From *The Letters of Gertrude Bell* (1927), 1:239, cited in S. Neill, *The Interpretation of the New Testament, 1861–1961* (Oxford: Oxford Univ. Press, 1964), 141.

2. J. D. G. Dunn, *The Epistle to the Galatians* (BNTC; Peabody, MA: Hendrickson, 1993), 12–20.

3. See N. A. Dahl, "Paul's Letter to the Galatians: Epistolary Genre, Content, and Structure" 117–142, in *The Galatians Debate*, ed. M. D. Nanos (Peabody, MA: Hendrickson, 2002), 119. P.Oxy. I 123.5–9 is dated to the third or fourth century AD.

4. For an English translation of the inscription, see B. Brooten, *Women Leaders in the Ancient Synagogue* (Brown Judaic Studies 36; Chico: Scholars Press, 1982): 158, no. 6. For a discussion of implications for patron/client relationships, see L. M. White, *The Social Origins of Christian Architecture* (Valley Forge, PA: Trinity International, 1990), 1:77–78.

5. J. Reynolds and R. Tannenbaum, *Jews and Godfearers at Aphrodisias* (Cambridge: Cambridge Univ. Press, 1987).

CHAPTER 15

1 AND 2 THESSALONIANS

A decorative grave stele depicting two Roman residents from the Macedonian city of Thessalonica.

The two letters to the Thessalonians are among Paul's earliest letters. Soon after establishing this church during his second missionary journey (AD 50), Paul, Silas, and Timothy were forced to leave town because civil disturbances broke out in the wake of their proclamation of the gospel. Despite repeated attempts, Paul was blocked from returning to this fledgling church. The persecution that resulted spilled over to these new believers. Would the Thessalonians stand firm in the faith?

Cassander founded the city of Thessalonica in 316 BC. The city would become the principal port of the Macedonian kingdom.

Paul traveled on to Berea and then south by sea to Athens, where he decided it was better to be left alone and to send Timothy back to Thessalonica. While anxiously awaiting a report about the church, Paul traveled to Corinth. Timothy finally arrived with news—and it was good. Despite severe opposition, the Thessalonians continued in their new faith. First Thessalonians was written right after Timothy's report. The letter is, above all, a thanksgiving to God for the faith, love, and enduring hope that marked this church.

We do not know how much time elapsed between 1 and 2 Thessalonians, though it was not long. Paul was probably still in Corinth when further news about the Thessalonians arrived. Persecution intensified, and in response Paul assured the Thessalonians of God's intervention to both punish their persecutors and to give believers relief from suffering. Moreover, some in the church were proclaiming that the day of the Lord had already come. Finally, some believers were not working, contrary to Paul's teaching and example.

THE SETTING OF 1 AND 2 THESSALONIANS
The City of Thessalonica

Antipater of Thessalonica (first century AD) wrote an epigram in which he referred to his hometown as "the mother of Macedonia." The city was a mixture of native Macedonians and Roman immigrants. It exhibited great loyalty to the emperor and the Roman people and enjoyed the benefits of that relationship.

Coin of Andriscus who claimed to be the son of the last Macedonian king Perseus.

Cassander, king of Macedonia, founded the city in 316 BC and named it after his wife Thessaloniki, half-sister of Alexander the Great. When the Romans attempted to rule the Mediterranean world, the Macedonians fought three wars against them. In 168 BC, Rome gained the final victory and dismantled the Macedonian monarchy, dividing the former kingdom into four districts and making Thessalonica the capital of the second administrative area.

In 149 BC Andriscus, a man who claimed to be the son of the former king Perseus, organized a revolt against Roman domination. Thessalonica sided with the Romans and hailed Metellus, the Roman commander, as their "savior and benefactor." Rome remembered the loyalty of the city and named Thessalonica as the capital of the reorganized province of Macedonia.

A century later, after the assassination of Julius Caesar, assassins Brutus and Cassius fought a decisive battle against Octavian (Augustus) and Mark Antony for control of the empire just outside the Macedonian city of Philippi. Thessalonica sided with Octavian and Mark Antony, who won. As a reward for her loyalty, Antony granted Thessalonica the high honor of becoming a "free city." As such, Roman troops were not garrisoned there, and the citizens of Thessalonica were allowed to govern themselves according to their traditional laws and customs.

When Octavian and Mark Antony later fought against each other, Thessalonica sided with Octavian, a wise and strategic move since Octavian defeated Antony at the Battle of Actium in 31 BC. As in the past, Thessalonica was favored by Rome, who remembered her loyalty.

Thessalonica prospered under Roman rule. Many Romans immigrated to the city, bringing their wealth with them. These Romans were honored with public inscriptions that praised them for their benefactions. The city established a cult to honor the "goddess Rome and the Roman benefactors" and also built a "temple of Caesar" to honor Julius Caesar and his adopted son, Augustus. Thessalonica enjoyed great privileges and benefited immensely from the Roman presence and rule.

Tetradrachm of Alexander, minted by Lysimachus, and gold stater minted by Brutus. Note the similarities, including the Horn of Ammon.

THE GOSPEL COMES TO THESSALONICA

During Paul's second missionary journey, he, Silas (Acts 17:4), and Timothy (see 16:1–3; 17:14–15; 1 Thess. 1:1; 2:7, 13) arrived in Thessalonica to preach the gospel. They had traveled down the Via Egnatia from Philippi, where Paul and Silas had been beaten and jailed without trial (Acts 16:16–40; 1 Thess. 2:2). Despite this suffering, these Christian messengers gathered courage to proclaim the gospel in Thessalonica, even in the face of great opposition.

Thessalonica was granted free city status due to its loyalty to Mark Antony and Octavian as commemorated in this coin.

Acts 17:1–9 records Paul's ministry in Thessalonica. He went into the Jewish synagogue where, during three Sabbath days, he used the Scriptures to persuade those gathered that the anticipated King of Israel, the Messiah, had to suffer and that Jesus was this Messiah (Acts 17:3; cf. 9:22; 18:5, 28). While some Jews believed, the larger response came from the "God-fearing Greeks (17:4; see sidebar on "God-Fearers" in Ch. 12). The apostles apparently undertook a wider evangelistic effort among the Gentiles since most in the church had "turned to God from idols to serve the living and true God" (1 Thess. 1:8–9)

RELIGION IN THESSALONICA

Thessalonica, as other cities of the empire, was full of idols. The epigramist Philip of Thessalonica records the names of twenty deities. He preserves for us a prayer to Artemis for the emperor ("Artemis ... dispatch this very day that hateful sickness away from the best of Emperors.... For Philip will offer the smoke of frankincense above your altars, and will make splendid sacrifice of a mountain-roaming boar"), and to Apollo from a sailor ("Be gracious in return, and send upon the sails a favorable breeze running with us to the harbors of Actium").[1]

Antipater, another epigramist, preserves the prayer of a woman to Aphrodite: "Bithynian Cythera dedicated me, the marble image of your form, Cyprian goddess [Aphrodite], according to her vow. Do you make a large gift in return for a small one, as your custom is; a husband's loving heart is all she asks."[2] Another woman, blind and childless, offers hers to Artemis ("Both prayers were heard by Artemis, midwife in child-bearing and light-bringer of white-gleaming rays").[3]

Poseidon, Aphrodite, Sarapis, Isis—Thessalonica, as most ancient cities, was marked by religious pluralism.

Since so many God-fearers were persuaded by Paul's explanations and proofs, including many prominent women (Acts 17:4), those of the synagogue who were not persuaded became jealous and managed to stir up a mob against Paul and Silas. The riot that ensued soon inflamed the whole populace.

The charges leveled against Paul and his companions before the city officials (Gk. *politarchas*; see Acts 17:6, 8) were well calculated: "These men who have caused trouble all over the world have now come here" (Acts 17:6). News about how the gospel had caused civic unrest in places like Philippi had reached Thessalonica (cf. 16:19–24). Rome did not tolerate civil disturbances, and even a free city like Thessalonica would be expected to deal severely and quickly with anyone accused of inciting them.

The second part of the accusation was that Paul and Silas, along with those like Jason (their patron) were "defying Caesar's decrees, saying that there is another king, one called Jesus" (Acts 17:7). These imperial decrees, which had been emitted under the reigns of Augustus and Tiberius, made it illegal to predict the death of any person, especially the emperor. The apostolic prediction of a coming king implied the passing of the current ruler.

Paul's proclamation of "another [coming] king" (see 1 Thess. 1:10; 4:16; 5:2–3; 2 Thess. 2:3–8) may have sounded like the promise of a renewed monarchy for the Macedonians. Upon hearing such accusations, the city officials knew they had to act

The central agora is currently under excavation. Although most of the remains in this photo are from the second century AD and later, archaeologists have recently uncovered first century structures.

because the city's privileged status with the Romans was at stake. Consequently, Paul and his companions fled the town under the cover of night (Acts 17:10).

Paul, Silas, and Timothy traveled to Berea, where they proclaimed the gospel. But after disturbances broke out there, the Berean believers sent Paul to the coast, and he sailed to Athens (Acts 17:10–15). Soon afterward Silas and Timothy joined Paul in Athens (cf. Acts 17:15; 1 Thess. 3:1), but then returned to Macedonia, leaving Paul on his own.

Paul repeatedly tried to return to Thessalonica but was hindered by circumstances, which he attributes to satanic opposition (1 Thess. 2:17–18). He was deeply concerned about this church since they were recent converts, now on their own, who were suffering persecution because of their faith (1:6; 2:14; 3:3–4). They were also experiencing moral problems (4:1–8) and theological confusion (4:13–5:11). Paul's anxiety moved him to send Timothy back to Thessalonica to encourage the believers and to find out whether "in some way the tempter might have tempted you and that our efforts might have been in vain" (3:5).

From Athens Paul traveled to Corinth (Acts 18:1). The wait for Timothy's return from Thessalonica must have been agonizing. Paul saw himself as the Thessalonians' father in the faith (1 Thess. 2:11), and his care for them was as tender as a nursing mother's (2:7). Would they stand firm in the faith despite the suffering they were facing?

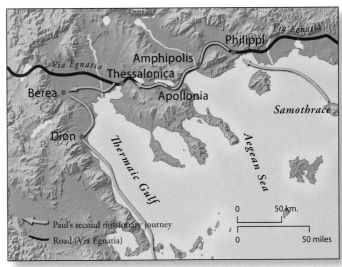

Note how Paul traveled off the Via Egnatia to arrive at Berea. He perhaps sailed for Athens from Dion.

The names of the politarchs are both Macedonian and Latin. The politarchs are mentioned in Acts 17:6 and 8.

OUTLINE OF 1 THESSALONIANS

THE MESSAGE OF 1 THESSALONIANS

Paul wrote 1 Thessalonians promptly after Timothy's arrival in Corinth (1 Thess. 3:6; cf. Acts 18:5). Timothy brought "good news" of the church's faith, love, and steadfastness in hope, even amidst their persecutions (1 Thess. 1:3; 3:6, 8). These believers had continued steadfast in faith despite the overwhelming conflict they endured. Hearing Timothy's report, Paul overflowed with thanks to God and joy over the Thessalonians (3:9; see also 1:3; 2:13) and offered earnest and constant prayers to God that he and his companions might return to the church supply "what is lacking in your faith" (3:10 – 11).

Following ancient convention, Paul begins the letter with the names of the authors, followed by that of the recipients and then a salutation (1:1 – 2). He goes on to offer an extended thanksgiving for the Thessalonian believers (1:3 – 10). Paul commonly uses these thanksgivings to introduce the main topics of the correspondence, and 1 Thessalonians is no exception. He reminds the readers of how the gospel came to them (vv. 3 – 5) and of their reception (vv. 6 – 10; topics repeated in 2:1 – 2 and 2:13 – 16, respectively). Woven in here are notes about the character of the gospel messengers (1:5b), the sufferings endured (1:6), the mission of the church (1:8), and their eschatological hope (1:10).

Although Timothy delivered a good report about the steadfastness and Christian character of the Thessalonian believers, the news was not altogether good. Paul and his companions felt compelled to defend their personal character (2:1 – 12), most likely because of some accusation concerning why Paul had not returned. Paul responds that they were genuinely concerned for the well-being of the Thessalonians and did not preach with questionable motives. He reminds the church that he and his companions had entered the city to preach in spite of great opposition (vv. 1–2) and that their message, methods, and motives were pure (vv. 3–5). They did not come looking for honor or financial gain but genuinely cared for them as a nursing mother (vv. 6–9). Their character was blameless and, like a father, they encouraged the moral progress of the church (vv. 10–12).

Other scholars, however, contend that Paul's purposes in chapter 2 are didactic, not apologetic. Paul forwards himself and his companions as moral examples for this congregation to follow. But 2:1–12 is attached to a large section (2:13–3:13) that records Paul's attempts to provide continuing pastoral care for this fledgling congregation. He was not neglecting them or failing to show interest in them, for he made every effort to return and, when he was hindered from accomplishing this, sent Timothy in his stead (2:17–3:5). When Timothy finally returned from Thessalonica, Paul rejoiced over the Thessalonians' faith, love, and steadfastness and declared his longing and prayers to see the church again (3:6–13). While 2:1–12 appeals to what they know about the sincere motives of Paul and his companions, 2:13–3:13 tells the story of their continued care for the well-being of the church.

But there were other problems in the church. Paul delivers a stern warning to those Thessalonians who dismissed his commands about sexual morality (4:1–8). He advises them that he "who rejects this instruction does not reject a human being but God, the very God who gives you his Holy Spirit" (4:8).

The Thessalonian congregation also apparently has some questions for Paul, which they conveyed via Timothy (cf. 4:9). Their first concern was about *philadelphia* ("love among the members of this

In the very heart of the city at the agora (market) archaeologists have found the remains of a first century circular bath next door to a brothel.

THE *PAROUSIA* OF CHRIST

Paul's description of Christ's *parousia* ("coming," 4:15) echoes contemporary accounts of the *parousia* of an emperor to a city, an occurrence that marked the beginning of new eras and was celebrated by the minting of coins and the erection of ceremonial structures. Usually a delegation of officials out of the city went out to meet the coming dignitary. Josephus records the coming of Vespasian to Rome:

> And as this goodwill to Vespasian was universal, those that enjoyed any remarkable dignities could not have patience enough to stay in Rome, but hurried to meet him at a very great distance from it; nay, indeed, none of the rest could endure the delay of seeing him, but did all pour out of the city in such crowds, and were so universally possessed with the opinion that it was easier and better for them to go out than to stay there, that this was the very first time that the city joyfully perceived itself almost empty of its citizens; for those that stayed within were fewer than those that went out. But as soon as the news was come that he was close by, and those that had met him at first related with what good humor he received everyone that came to him, then it was that the whole multitude that had remained in the city, with their wives and children, came into the road, and waited for him there; and for those whom he passed by, they made all sorts of acclamations, on account of the joy they had to see him, and the pleasantness of his countenance, and styled him their benefactor and savior, and the only person who was worthy to be ruler of the city of Rome. And now the city was like a temple, full of garlands and sweet odors. (Josephus, *War* 7.4.1 [68 – 72])

Paul writes that both the resurrected and living believers will file out to meet the coming Ruler (1 Thess. 4:16 – 17), implying that they will return with him.

family" of believers, see 4:9 – 10). Perhaps the striking mix of people from different ethnic groups, social strata, and gender gave rise to strains in the social fabric of this new community. The second question concerned the destiny of the dead in Christ (4:13 – 18). Some in the church had died since Paul's departure, and the Thessalonians were grief-stricken since they did not fully understand the doctrine of the resurrection of believers. Paul responded that as Christ died and rose again, so the believers who died would be raised (4:13 – 16). This resurrection would occur at Christ's advent or *parousia* (4:15).

The church also asked Paul when the day of the Lord would arrive (5:1 – 11). While Paul does not speculate about the time, saying that the day will come unexpectedly, like a thief in the night (5:2), he does tell them that one can be prepared by living a moral life and wearing the armor of God: faith, love, and hope (5:8).

Timothy also informed Paul that the new leaders were not being recognized as they should have been (5:12 – 13). Moreover, some members of the church were not working (5:14; cf. 4:11 – 12). Paul classifies them as the "disruptive" since they refused to live by the community rule on this matter (see also 2 Thess. 3:6 – 15). After teaching the Thessalonians about good relationships with others, both inside and outside the church (5:14 – 15), and with God himself (5:16 – 18), Paul instructs them about receiving and evaluating prophetic messages (5:19 – 22). The letter closes with a final prayer for their sanctification (5:23 – 24), greetings, and a blessing (5:25 – 28).

OUTLINE OF 2 THESSALONIANS

THE MESSAGE OF 2 THESSALONIANS

Three topics taken up in 1 Thessalonians return in this letter: persecution, the day of the Lord, and work. Probably the messenger who carried 1 Thessalonians to the church returned to Paul in Corinth with further news about the believers and their situation. After the epistolary greeting (2 Thess. 1:1 – 2), Paul offers his thanks to God for the church, as he did in the first letter (1:3 – 4). He underscores the Thessalonians' faith, love, and perseverance through persecution, which is the fruit of hope (cf. 1 Thess. 1:3; 3:6 – 8; 5:8). These characteristics mark the Thessalonians to such a degree that Paul can lift them up as an example to other churches.

Then Paul discusses the topic of persecution (2 Thess. 1:5 – 9). The Thessalonians' persecution (cf. 1 Thess. 1:6; 2:14; 3:2 – 4) has continued and intensified. Paul reminds them that they are suffering for the kingdom and that their persecutors will be judged by God (2 Thess. 1:5 – 10). These verses graphically describe the cataclysmic nature of this divine retribution: The Lord Jesus will be "revealed from heaven in blazing fire with his powerful angels," and the Thessalonians' persecutors "will be punished with everlasting destruction." By contrast, relief is promised to these believers (1:7), and Paul reminds them that they will glorify the Lord at his return (1:10). Chapter 1 ends with a reminder of Paul's constant prayers that the name of the Lord be glorified among them and that they be glorified "in him" (1:11 – 12).

Second Thessalonians 2:1 – 12 is an interpretive jungle. The Thessalonians not only faced external persecution but also internal doctrinal confusion that threatened to destabilize them. A teaching was circulating among the believers that the final consummation, which included the return of Christ and the resurrection/rapture of the church (2:1), had "already come" (or, possibly, was "right at hand"). Paul does not know the source of this unsettling perspective—perhaps a "prophecy" (lit., "spirit"; cf. 1 John 4:1 – 3), a message, or a letter with Paul's name falsely inscribed on it.

In response, Paul assures the Thessalonians that two events will precede the day of the Lord (2:3). (1) "Rebellion" (*apostasia*) is commonly used to speak of apostasy from the faith.

A "rebellion" could be any movement against an established authority, either religious or political, but the word is commonly used to speak of an apostasy from the faith. Such an event is characteristic of the last times (1 Tim. 4:1)—a perspective also found in Jewish apocalyptic writings. (2) The "man of lawlessness" will be revealed. Paul no sooner mentions this figure than he highlights his final doom (2:3). This figure, who demands worship as a god, would be readily recognized in the ancient world where rulers were often given divine status and honored with both temple and cult. Even Thessalonica had a temple that honored the emperor as divine.[9]

Paul does not identify this "man of lawlessness" with any current or past emperor, but he does note that some (unidentified) power is "holding him back" (2:6–7). Is it the empire, the emperor, government, the law, the preaching of the gospel, Paul himself, God the Father, or the Holy Spirit (all of these have been suggested)? We simply do not know, though Paul assumes the Thessalonians do know because of his initial instruction (2:5). In any case, 2:7 does not imply that the Holy Spirit will be taken out of the world, and with him the church, as some who propose a "pre-tribulation" rapture of the church argue. Some authors suggest that this power who "holds it back" should be understood as an agent who prefigures and anticipates the coming of the "man of lawlessness." Paul's main aim is to remind the church of these events and to assure them of Christ's final victory over all hostile powers (2:8–12), including this "man of lawlessness" and those who are deceived by him.

After thanking God for the church (2:13–14), calling the Thessalonians to adhere to the teaching they have already received (2:15), and pronouncing a blessing on them (2:16–17), the apostle asks for prayers for his mission (3:1–2). He then underscores his settled assurance in the Lord's ability to take care of his own (3:3–5; cf. 1 Thess. 5:23).

The third major issue Paul addresses has to do with work (3:6–15), another matter he has previously instructed them about (3:10; cf. 1 Thess. 4:11–12) and offers himself as an example (2 Thess. 3:7–9). Despite his teachings and warnings, some have remained "disruptive," not heeding the apostolic instruction and refusing to work (3:11). Many argue that the reason why some Thessalonians are not working is because of their expectations concerning the day of the Lord. If that day has come or is soon to come (2:2), why continue to work? However, though Paul must correct the Thessalonians' understanding about eschatology, he does not make any connection between that issue and the problem of work.

Another reading of the situation is that some Thessalonians continue to act as dependent clients, relying on rich patrons in the city or the church for benefits such as money, food, and even public representation. Such personal patronage was a significant feature of economic life in the Roman Empire. Clients often arose early to appear at the house of their patron to give him or her a morning greeting. While Paul encourages benefaction toward those with genuine need (1 Thess. 4:9–10; 2 Thess. 3:13), he calls the believers to abandon their status as dependent clients and work for their living. In 3:6–15, he calls the church to undertake disciplinary action toward those who are disorderly. These who refuse to work should be noted, admonished, and shunned, though they are not to be viewed with hostility as enemies. Note too that no patron in the church has any obligation to support them (3:11–15).

AUTHORSHIP AND DATE

Paul wrote 1 Thessalonians from Corinth on his second missionary journey. The book opens with the names of Silas and Timothy, the cofounders of the church along with Paul (1 Thess. 1:1). The letter has many verbs in the first person plural ("we"), which may indicate that Silas and Timothy had a significant role in the letter's composition. Paul only occasionally steps out of the group to express his particular concerns (2:18: 3:5; 5:27). Joint composition of letters was known in the ancient world. For example, in Cicero's letter *Ad Atticum* he says, "For my part I have gathered from your letters—both that which you wrote in conjunction with others and the one you wrote in your own name . . ." (11.5.1). Paul, however, had the major hand in writing (cf. 5:27).

Early external evidence that supports the authenticity of 1 Thessalonians is firm though not extensive. Eusebius regarded 1 Thessalonians as a genuine Pauline letter. References to the book appear early in such writings as the second-century *Didache*, the *Letters of Ignatius* (d. 135), and the *Shepherd of Hermas*. Tertullian comments that even the heretic Marcion considered the book to be genuine (AD 207/208), and Tertullian concurs. In the second half of the second century, the Muratorian Canon and Irenaeus regarded it as an authentic work by Paul. Currently scholars universally regard this epistle as authentic.

Second Thessalonians is another matter. This letter enjoyed the same solid support in the early church. In the second century, Ignatius and Justin Martyr make use of it, while Polycarp and Irenaeus attribute it to Paul, as do Clement of Alexandria and Tertullian in the third century. The Muratorian Canon also classifies this letter as authentic.

But in the nineteenth century, some scholars raised questions. One argument was that the style is so strikingly similar to that of 1 Thessalonians (though this phenomenon can also be used to argue in favor of Pauline authorship). A second argument against Paul's authorship is that 2 Thessalonians addresses a more general situation. But the specific situation of the church is clearly defined in all three chapters (the persecutions, the questions about day of the Lord, and the problem of work).

Finally, some say this letter reflects "post-Pauline" theology. For example, the eschatology of the letter is not linked with joy. Also, there appears to be a tension between 1 Thessalonians 5:1–11, which speaks of an unexpected end, and 2 Thessalonians 2:1–12, which outlines the events that will precede the day of the Lord. Moreover, the author speaks about the "tradition" handed down to the Thessalonians (2:15), a marker that appears to class this

JUVENAL ON HOW CLIENTS ARE ENTERTAINED

NOTES FROM ANTIQUITY

The Thessalonian believers who are not working are acting like any client of a socially superior patron. Juvenal, the Latin satirist who wrote near the end of the first century AD, penned his fifth satire about the meager rations and dishonorable treatment that clients sometimes received when invited to a banquet by their patron. See sidebar on "Juvenal and Persius on Patrons" in chapter 4 for a quote.

book with the post-Paulines. But the serious tone of the eschatological teaching in chapter 1 is generated by the severity of the suffering the church is facing. The tensions between an imminent end and signs that precede the end are found in Jewish eschatology and even in Jesus' teachings (Mark 13). The mention of the "tradition" is common piece in Paul's teaching (e.g., 1 Thess. 2:13; 4:1–2; cf. 1 Cor. 15:1–8). Most scholars today affirm its Pauline authorship.

The recipients of the book are believers in Thessalonica, organized into an "assembly" (*ekklēsia*; 1 Thess. 1:1). The majority are Gentiles who have "turned . . . from idols" (1:9), with some Jewish believers (Acts 17:4). Most are of the artisan class, who worked with their hands to make a living (1 Thess. 4:11).

The Gallio inscription from Delphi dates the term when L. Iunius Gallio served as proconsul of the province of Achaia: "Tiberius Claudius Caesar Augustus Germanicus, 12th year of tribunician power, acclaimed emperor for the 26th time, father of the country, sends greetings to [_____]. For long I have been well-disposed to the city of Delphi and solicitous for its prosperity, and I have always observed the cult of the Pythian Apollo. Now since it is said to be destitute of citizens, as my friend and proconsul L. Iunius Gallio recently reported to me..."[11]

Since the occasion of the letter is Timothy's return from the Thessalonian church (1 Thess. 3:6), the date of composition can be set during Paul's visit to Corinth when Timothy, along with Silas, arrived from Macedonia (Acts 18:5). Paul spent a year and half in that city, during which time Gallio was named as the proconsul of the Roman province of Achaia (Acts 18:11–12). An inscription from Delphi indicates that Gallio was named to this post in AD 51, which gives us the approximate date for 1 Thessalonians.

First Thessalonians is one of the earliest epistles of the apostle Paul, second only perhaps to Galatians, which was written at the end of the first missionary journey (see Ch. 14). Second Thessalonians appears to have been written not long after the first letter during Paul's same eighteen-month stay in Corinth. Some of the same themes appear in both letters, such the persecutions, questions about the end, and the problem of the "disruptive" who refused to work.

Some scholars, however, argue that the canonical order of the books is based on the fact that 1 Thessalonians is longer and has nothing to do with which one was written first. A few modern authors have argued that some evidence points to 2 Thessalonians as being first. However, note how 2 Thessalonians 2:15 looks back to a previous letter written to the church: "Stand firm and hold to the teachings *we passed on to you*, whether by word of mouth or *by letter*"—most likely 1 Thessalonians.

QUESTIONS FOR DISCUSSION ◉◉◉◉◉◉◉◉◉◉◉◉◉◉◉◉◉◉◉◉◉◉◉◉◉◉

1. Isolate Paul's teaching on suffering in 1 and 2 Thessalonians. How does the apostle construct a "theology of suffering" for these persecuted believers? Why are these believers able to stand firm in their faith in the face of severe opposition?

2. How does Paul use the teaching about the last things to help the Thessalonian believers? Are his concerns speculative or pastoral and moral?

3. Describe the character of good Christian leadership according to these letters. How does Paul's leadership ethic compare to that of contemporary Christian leaders?

4. What importance does Paul place on sexual ethics? How does he underscore the importance of sexual purity?

BIBLIOGRAPHY
Introductory

Green, G. L. *1 and 2 Thessalonians*. PNTC. Grand Rapids: Eerdmans, 2002.

Holmes, M. W. *1 and 2 Thessalonians*. NIVAC. Grand Rapids: Zondervan, 1998.

Marshall, I. H. *1 and 2 Thessalonians*. NCB. Grand Rapids: Eerdmans, 1983.

Morris, L. *The First and Second Epistles to the Thessalonians*. NICNT. Grand Rapids: Eerdmans, 1991.

Advanced

Bruce, F. F. *1 and 2 Thessalonians*. WBC. Waco, TX: Word, 1982.

Malherbe, A. *1 Thessalonians*. AB. Garden City, NY: Doubleday, 2001.

Wanamaker, C. *The Epistles to the Thessalonians*. NIGTC. Grand Rapids: Eerdmans, 1990.

NOTES

1. Gow and Page, *Greek Anthology*, 1:303.

2. Ibid., 1:19.

3. Ibid., 1:79.

4. Cassius Dio, *Hist.* 56.25.5–6, as quoted in E. A. Judge, "The Decrees of Caesar at Thessalonica," *RTR* 30 (1971): 3. See also a similar decree from Tiberius, p. 4.

5. Cassius Dio, *Hist.* 57.15.8, as quoted in ibid., 4.

6. Dio Chrysostom 12.5; 8.33; cf. 12.5; 32.11; 77/78.27; Plutarch, *Moralia* 78A; 131A.

7. Epictetus 3.23.32.

8. Epictetus 3.23.23–24. On this theme, see especially B. W. Winter, "Entries and Ethics of the Orators and Paul (1 Thessalonians 2:11–12)," *TynBul* 44 (1993): 61–63; A. J. Malherbe, "'Gentle as a Nurse': The Cynic Background to 1 Thess ii," *NovT* 12 (1970): 214.

9. See H. L. Hendrix, "Thessalonicans Honor Romans" (Th.D. diss., Harvard University, 1984), 107–8.

10. Cited in ibid., 107–8.

11. J. Murphy-O'Connor, *St. Paul's Corinth* (Collegeville, MN: Liturgical, 1990), 161.

CHAPTER 16

1 CORINTHIANS

The *diolkos* served as a dry canal between the Saronic Gulf and the Gulf of Corinth to pull ships overland.

The Corinthian congregation was embroiled in a variety of problems as its members were pulled between the demands of their newly acquired faith and the cultural values surrounding them. Divisions were a hallmark of this church. It was broken into disputing factions that hailed one minister of the gospel over another as if each preacher were nothing more than a leader of a philosophical school. Members took each other to court, and some used their Christian liberty in ways harmful to others in the congregation. Socioeconomic differences separated members at the Lord's table. The church was polarized over the gifts of the Spirit, with some members acting as if they were superior. Furthermore, many in the church engaged in immoral sexual practices, including visiting prostitutes. The Corinthian church also had doctrinal issues. Certain believers denied a future resurrection of the dead, a perspective Paul viewed as a tacit denial of the resurrection of Christ.

This letter is an impassioned attempt to correct these problems as well as to respond to inquiries about aspects of Christian faith and practice. Although written to a group of Christians whose social world was distinctly different from ours, its message is a powerful one for the church today; our problems are, in many ways, not so distant from theirs. We too must find our way between apostolic teaching and contemporary culture, and we sometimes confuse the two.

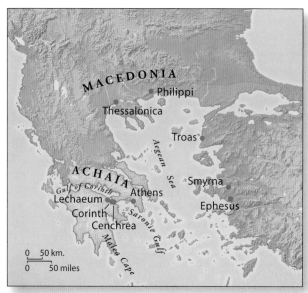

The Roman provinces of Macedonia and Achaia

Corinth and the surrounding *territorium*

THE SETTING OF 1 CORINTHIANS
The City of Corinth

Paul arrived in Corinth midway through his second missionary journey (Acts 18:1–18), after having been in Macedonia and Athens (see Ch. 15). In that great city, the capital of Achaia, he evangelized and taught the new believers for eighteen months (Acts 18:1, 11).

Corinth's location greatly enhanced its importance. It stood on an isthmus between mainland Greece and the Peloponnesus; thus, it controlled all north-south travel and trade. But more important, Corinth was a strategic hub for one of the east-west routes in the empire. Ships sailing from Italy docked at Lechaeum, Corinth's port on the Gulf of Corinth. Those sailing from Asia arrived at Cenchrea, on the Saronic Gulf (see Acts 18:18–19; Rom. 16:1). Seafarers preferred to avoid sailing around the Peloponnese on these east-west journeys because this route added six days to the trip and the waters around Maleae on the southern part

The temple of Apollo in Corinth is one of the structures from classical Corinth that survived until Roman times.

of the Peloponnese were treacherous. Strabo recalls the ancient dictum, "But when you double Maleae forget your home" (*Geography* 8.6.20–23).

In order to facilitate east-west trade, a dry canal, called the *diolkos*, was constructed in the sixth century BC and continued in use up through the ninth century AD Sometimes goods were carried across the isthmus on a stone track; at other times ships were hoisted on wheeled wagons and rolled to the other side. Corinth controlled all this trade and grew rich as a result. The city played host to travelers from across the Mediterranean world. This rich cosmopolitan center built its economy on the many people who came through her gates. Into this bustling city, Paul came to preach the gospel.

The Coming of the Romans

During the third century BC Corinth was a Greek city-state in alliance with other cities of Achaia to form the Achaean League. Rome's eastward expansion ended in a military showdown with Corinth in 146 BC. Mummius descended on Corinth with 32,000 Roman infantry and 3,500 cavalry. He captured the city, ordered the men to be killed, and handed the women and children over to slavery. He sent Corinth's wealth to Rome and destroyed its walls and buildings. Corinth was left practically deserted for a hundred years.

The Babbius monument reads, "Gnaeus Babbius Philinus, aedile and pontifex, had this monument erected at his own expense, and he approved it in his official capacity as duovir."[2] This former slave not only served as city manager (*aedile*) and priest (*pontifex*), but became one of the two principal governing officials of Corinth (*duovir*).

THE ROMAN DESTRUCTION OF CORINTH (146 BC)

Ancient authors who describe the defeat of Corinth tell a tale of brutality and pain. Pausanius graphically paints this picture:

> As soon as night fell, the Acheans who had escaped to Corinth after the battle fled from the city, and there fled with them most of the Corinthians themselves. At first Mummius hesitated to enter Corinth, although the gates were open, as he suspected that an ambush had been laid within the walls. But on the third day after the battle he proceeded to storm Corinth and set it on fire. The majority of those found in it were put to the sword by the Romans, but the women and children Mummius sold into slavery. (*Description of Greece* 7.16.7 – 8)

Antipater of Thessalonica composed an epigram which pulses with the pathos of that moment:

> I, Rhodope, and my mother Boisca, neither died of sickness,
> nor fell by the enemy's sword.
> But we ourselves, when fierce Ares burnt the city of Corinth,
> our fatherland, chose a brave death.
> My mother slew me with the slaughtering knife,
> nor did she, sorrowful woman, spare her own life,
> But tied the noose around her own neck, for to die in
> freedom was better than slavery.[1]

Roman Corinth

Shortly before his assassination in 44 BC, Julius Caesar ordered the recolonization of Corinth, naming it *Colonia Laus Julia Corinthiensis*. The colonists were mostly freedmen, plebeians (common Roman citizens), and Roman legionary veterans. Rome secured the deep loyalty of these colonists by granting them land allotments (six to seven acres per colonist) and placing them in an environment that had lost none of its strategic advantage, which meant prosperity for many of them. But such success was the exception rather than the rule.

Left: Although Corinth was located on Greek soil, first century Corinth was a Roman colony, as evidenced by the predominance of Latin inscriptions in the city *Right*: The Isthmian Games were supervised by Corinth. Shown in the picture are the remains of an ancient starting line used in the Isthmian Stadium. Paul makes reference to them in 1 Corinthians 9:24-27.

Paul appeared before the proconsul Gallio at the *bēma* located in the Corinthian *agora*.

Rebuilt Corinth was a strategic boon for Rome since it gave her a point from which to expand her influence east and to facilitate trade. It became the largest city of Roman Greece, with a population at around 80,000 in the city and another 20,000 in the surrounding countryside. Although located on Greek soil, the new colony was a thoroughly Latin city, with mostly Latin inscriptions. The main exceptions were those related to the Isthmian games, since those who participated in this biannual event came from the Greek-speaking world. The city's architecture was Italian and the images of the emperor were portrayed with Roman dress.

But why were Paul's Corinthian letters (and Romans, for that matter) written in Greek and not Latin? Corinth began to experience a gradual increase in the presence of Greeks in the city. These were not citizens but *incolae* (foreign residents without full civic rights) and not therefore part of the social elite. By the second century Favorinus wrote that Corinth, "though Roman, has become thoroughly Hellenized." The fact that the letter was written in Greek may reflect the Christian reality—the gospel made the greatest inroads among those of the lower classes who spoke Greek (see 1 Cor 1:26).

Corinth was the capital of Achaia and the seat of the Roman proconsul. L. Iunius Gallio, brother of the great philosopher Seneca, was the proconsul during part of Paul's eighteen-month stay in the city (Acts 18:12). Gallio assumed the post on July 1, AD 51, but left early. Seneca commented on his untimely departure: "When, in Achaia, he began to feel feverish, he immediately took ship, claiming that it was a malady of the place" (*Letters* 104.2). Acts 18:12–17 underscores Gallio's judicial power as Paul stood before him at the *bēma* (Gk.) or *rostrum* (Latin), a speaker's platform erected during the Augustan period.

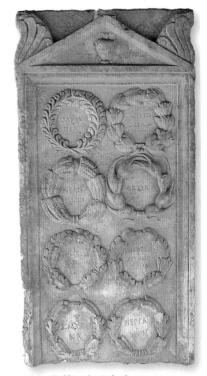

This relief found at Isthmia commemorates the prizes won by an athlete at various games, including the Isthmian games

Erastus was the *aedile* of Corinth. The person honored in the inscription may be the same Erastus named in Romans 16:23

The city itself had two chief magistrates (*duovirs*) elected each year by the assembly of citizens. It also had a senate. The business managers of the city (*aediles*) were also elected annually. They took care of public works (buildings, streets, market supervision) and managed the city's income. An inscription found near the theater names one of these officials: "Erastus in return for his aedileship laid (the pavement) at his own expense" (in Latin: *ERASTVS PRO AEDILIT[at]E S(ua) P(ecunia) STRAVIT*). Since the inscription dates from around AD 50, Erastus may be the "city treasurer" (*oikonomos*) mentioned in Romans 16:23 (Romans was written from Corinth).

Strabo once noted that "Corinth is called 'wealthy' because of its commerce, since it is situated on the Isthmus and is master of two harbors, of which the one leads straight to Asia, and the other to Italy" (*Geography* 8.6.20a). A number of the rich in this city opened their arms to the gospel, such as Erastus (Rom. 16:23; 2 Tim. 4:20) and those with households large enough to accommodate the believers for a common meal (1 Cor. 11:17–18). A significant group of believers in the church enjoyed a high socioeconomic status.[3]

But not everyone had access to such wealth. Paul comments that this church was filled with those who had neither economic power nor social status (1 Cor. 1:26). When the whole church gathered to eat the Lord's Supper, some went hungry (11:21). The weak and the strong believers' different responses to eating of idol meat may be due to the economic disparity between the rich, accustomed to meat regularly, and the poor, who consumed meat only on special occasions. The second century AD orator Alcifrón commented on the stark economic disparity he witnessed in the city: "No more did I enter Corinth than I realized that shamelessness of the rich there and the disgrace of its poor" (*Letters of Parasites* 24 [3.60]).

THE GOSPEL COMES TO CORINTH

Paul evangelized Corinth during his second missionary journey (Acts 18:1–18). He arrived there distressed (18:9–10; 1 Cor. 2:3), especially after the ill-treatment he suffered in

Macedonia and the dishonoring ridicule he endured in Athens. Silas and Timothy joined him after their return from Macedonia, arriving with an offering from the Macedonian churches for his support (Acts 18:5; 2 Cor. 11:7–9). Aquila and Priscilla also joined him (Acts 18:2–3; see 1 Cor. 16:19). Paul spent eighteen months in Corinth (Acts 18:11) and wrote the Thessalonian letters during this period.

After Paul left Corinth, Apollos came to the city and the Corinthian church received him warmly (Acts 18:27–19:1). Apollos was an eloquent Alexandrian Jew trained in rhetoric (18:24–25), whose oratorical skills were notably stronger than Paul's (1 Cor. 2:4; 2 Cor. 10:10). His presence in Corinth accounts for his prominence in the minds of some Corinthians (1 Cor. 3:4–6).

After leaving the city, Paul wrote his first letter to the Corinthian church, a document that has not been preserved but is referred to in 5:9–11. Around AD 55, while Paul was in Ephesus on his third missionary journey (Acts 19; 1 Cor. 16:8, 19), "some from Chloe's household" in Corinth arrived with news about the congregation (1 Cor. 1:11–12). These were likely Chloe's slaves or business associates who had become believers. A more official delegation visited Paul (16:15–18), who presumably brought a letter to Paul from the church asking him various questions (7:1; cf. 7:25; 8:1; 12:1; 16:1, 12). Paul wrote what we now call 1 Corinthians in response to the report from Chloe's people and to answer these questions.

Around the same time Paul sent Timothy to Corinth (4:17; 16:10–11). Paul had previously dispatched Timothy to Thessalonica to aid the church there (1 Thess. 3:1–5; Timothy's later missions are noted in Phil. 2:19–22; 1 Tim 1:3). Paul seems to expect that his letter will arrive before Timothy.

THE MESSAGE OF 1 CORINTHIANS

The problems in Corinth have been evaluated in various ways. Some scholars have attempted to find "a common source"[5] to all the issues, variously identified as Gnosticism, Hellenistic-Jewish wisdom speculation, factionalism, a conflict with Paul, or dualistic thought coupled with an over-realized eschatology. Others adopt a more eclectic reading of the evidence, looking at the Corinthian situation as a patchwork of issues. Witherington, for example, identifies five basic problems in this church: partisan attachments to Christian leaders, continued adherence to cultural values, pride and insult in using spiritual gifts, sexual issues, and disagreement over eschatology, including the resurrection and the believer's present reign.[6] He and others argue that we should identify the variety of cultural, philosophical, and religious influences that impinged on this church located at one of the major crossroads of the Roman empire.

CRINAGORAS ON CORINTH

Not long after the city was refounded in 44 BC, the poet Crinagoras lamented the low level of society that characterized the city from the start: "What inhabitants, O luckless city, have you received, and in place of whom? Alas for the great calamity to Greece! Would, Corinth, that you be lower than the ground and more desert than the Libyan sands, rather than wholly abandoned to such a crowd of scoundrelly slaves, you should vex the bones of the ancient Bacchiadae."[4] The Bacchiadae were the ancient aristocratic rulers of classical Corinth. The social composition of the Roman city was quite different from its glorious past.

OUTLINE OF 1 CORINTHIANS

Division in the Church

After opening greetings (1:1–3) and thanksgiving (1:4–9), Paul addresses the problem of divisions in the church (1:10–4:21). Paul has been informed of factionalism that has arisen among the members of the church as they align themselves behind various Christian leaders: "One of you says, 'I follow Paul'; another, 'I follow Apollos', another, 'I follow Cephas'; still another, 'I follow Christ'" (1:12; see 3:4). Paul was the founder, Apollos was an eloquent Alexandrian Jew who ministered there (Acts 18:24–28), and Cephas is the Aramaic name of Peter (John 1:42), who apparently traveled through Corinth (1 Cor. 9:5). There was either a final "Christ group" or Paul himself interjects his correction to their factionalism—he simply belongs to Christ.

Paul is not quoting the Corinthians' exact words, as though they are making such childish claims, but rather employs the rhetorical technique called "impersonation," displaying an adversary's thoughts as if they were expressing them themselves. Borrowing language that was often employed to encourage political concord and peace, Paul exhorts the Corinthians authoritatively in the name of the Lord Jesus Christ "that all of you agree with one another in what you say and that there be no divisions among you, but that you be perfectly united in mind and thought" (1:10).

From there he launches a discussion about wisdom and the message of the cross (1:18ff.). Traveling experts in rhetoric, known as sophists, were well known in Corinth. Orators drew crowds and attracted students by their rhetorical expertise. Philo of Alexandria notes that sophists were "winning the admiration of city after city, and ... drawing well-nigh the whole world to honor them" (*On Agriculture* 143). Some Corinthian believers are viewing the Christian messengers as nothing more than sophists who came to town and, accordingly, divided into rival schools around each one. Paul, for his part, distances himself from the rhetorical finery of the sophists (2:1–5). The Corinthians, however, are concerned about form over content.

Paul knows that the heart of the problem is a fundamental misunderstanding of the gospel. The message of the cross is not just another brand of philosophical "wisdom" (1:18–25; 2:4–5), but a demonstration of God's power and wisdom (1:22–25). Moreover, to emphasize rhetorical form and eloquence empties the cross of its power (1:17). In Paul's view, the power to persuade rests in God (2:4–12). So while the world views God's means of salvation, the cross, as foolishness and weakness (1:18, 23), those who believe this "foolishness" of the cross are saved (1:21). This "foolishness" of God is wiser than human wisdom, and his supposed "weakness" is stronger than any human accomplishments (1:25). By contrast, human wisdom cannot lead a person to know God (1:21).

Paul also counters the Corinthians' factionalism by underscoring the true position of Christian ministers. They are not sophists to be praised and defended, but rather "servants" (3:5) and "co-workers" under God (3:9). One plants, another waters, but God causes the growth (3:6–7). Thus, the church does not belong to any minister but to God (3:9). For this reason, the Corinthians should not exalt one minister over another (3:5; 4:6).

Immorality in the Community

Chapter 5 deals with incest in the church. A man has entered an illicit sexual relationship with his stepmother, possibly marrying her after his father died (5:1). Perhaps this is a wealthy family who could lose the inheritance of the deceased husband were she to marry into another family. This kind of relationship was prohibited by both the Old Testament (Lev. 18:7–8; 20:11; Deut. 22:30; 27:20; Ezek. 22:10–11) and Roman custom. *The Institutes of Gaius* 1.63 said, "Neither can I marry her who has aforetime been my mother-in-law or step-mother." Cicero commented: "The mother-in-law marries the son-in-law, no one looking favorably on the deed, no one approving it, all foreboding a dismal end to it. Oh, the incredible wickedness of the woman . . . unheard of since the world began! Oh, the unbridled and unrestrained lust! Oh, the extraordinary audacity of her conduct!" (*Pro Cluentio* 5.14–6.15). Yet the Corinthians are boasting about this union and take no disciplinary action (5:2), perhaps since this individual is a member of the elite.

Paul addresses the man's sin (his step-mother does not appear to be a church member) and exhorts the church to excommunicate him (5:3–4), although he holds out the hope for the person's redemption. While the Corinthians tolerate such sin in their midst, they paradoxically disassociate themselves from unbelievers, having misinterpreted Paul's earlier teaching about church discipline (5:9–13). The church must be pure and should take action to maintain its purity, but this does not mean they should distance themselves from people in the surrounding culture.

Moreover, some Corinthian believers are taking each other to court (6:1–11). Paul discourages believers from trying their legal cases before "the unrighteous" (6:1 NRSV). Roman courts were known for corruption, and the way legal proceedings were conducted would hardly promote *concordia* ("harmonious agreement") among the Corinthians. Paul encourages arbitration in the church to settle disputes (6:5) and, in the end, states that suffering wrong is better than doing wrong (6:7–8; cf. Matt. 5:38–42; Rom. 12:17, 19; 1 Peter 2:23; 3:9).

In 6:12–20 he returns to the problem of sexual immorality, addressing the practice of consorting with prostitutes. Jews normally did not visit prostitutes, but for the Greeks and Romans, prostitution was considered acceptable and became a "Main Street" affair. Prostitutes registered with a city magistrate (the *aedile*), and moralists like Cicero and Cato condoned it as a safeguard against adultery (see sidebar).

The Corinthians argued that sex was a natural function of the body. As the body needed food, so the body needed sex (6:13). But Paul insists that such behavior cannot be allowed in the church. How can someone take the members of Christ and join them to a prostitute? As in 1 Thessalonians 4:3–8, he calls believers to a life of sexual purity. Their bodies are not their own but have been redeemed at the price of Christ's death and become the temple of God's Spirit. The body has a role in God's plan since it will be raised up. So our bodies are for the Lord, and we must honor God with them (1 Cor. 6:13–20).

Corinthian Questions — On Marriage

In chapter 7 Paul begins to answer the questions the Corinthians have written to him (7:1). He begins with sexuality, marriage, divorce, the single life, widows, and "virgins." In light of Paul's Jewish heritage, the fact that he prescribes the single life is shocking (7:7); Jews viewed marriage positively (cf. Gen. 2:18–25). Sometime after Paul, the Talmud records the words of Rabbi Johanan: "He who is twenty years old and not married spends all of his days in sin" (*b. Kidd.* 29b).

Paul's concerns are not simply about marriage but on sexual relationships within marriage (7:1–7). Some of the Corinthians were arguing for celibacy although married. Paul states that while there may be cause for abstention, this should be by mutual consent, only for a season, and for only one reason: prayer. Marital relationships should resume so that Satan does not take advantage of lack of self control.

Paul echoes Jesus' teaching about divorce in 7:10–16 (see Matt. 5:31–32; 19:3–12), but adds that a believer should not separate from an unbelieving spouse simply because they do not share the faith (cf. 1 Peter 3:1–6). Nor should a believer's new existence be used as an excuse to change one's social status (7:17–24). Paul concludes his teaching on marriage with a curious section on the "virgins" — likely women betrothed but not yet married (7:25–40).

THE STOICS AND CYNICS ON MARRIAGE

During the first century, a debate raged between the philosophical schools of the Stoics and the Cynics about marriage. Marriage brings great responsibilities, so should one enter into such a union? Stoics stated that the universe is governed by divine principle and one must live in harmony with it; this includes marriage. Cynics understood marriage simply as a social convention. They longed for freedom to pursue philosophy, unencumbered by the concerns of this life, including marriage.

The macellum or meat market (today often called "The North Market") was located next to the temple of Apollo. An inscription found at Corinth notes that Quintus Cornelius Secundus, along with his wife, sons and daughter built "the meatmarket [...] along with [...] and the fishmarket."

Paul in no way prohibits marriage, but he does offer the advantages of unmarried life (7:32–35).

Corinthian Questions—On Meats Offered to Idols

Next Paul discusses the pressing question of whether Christians may eat food offered to idols (1 Cor. 8–10). The first issue is whether a Christian may eat meat sacrificed in pagan temples and subsequently sold in the marketplace.

Next is whether one may eat at the tables located in the idol temples. While Paul allows Christians to eat idol meat, he does insist that if such actions provoke a weak brother or sister to eat in violation of their conscience, the strong believer should not eat such meat (8:7–13). But the Christian's freedom does not extend to eating meat in the idol temple since such action necessarily involves one in the idol cult (10:14–22).

A third question concerns an invitation to eat at an unbeliever's house. Should a Christian do so, especially if the meat served has been sacrificed to idols (10:27–30)? While Paul deals specifically with eating idol meat and the question of community, the issue of how to act toward one's patron runs through this section. Should believers risk dishonoring patrons by refusing? This presented a dilemma to some.

How does chapter 9 fit into Paul's discussion? Here Paul addresses the topic of Christian freedom (9:1) but also the attendant social responsibility placed on Christians (9:19). Certain social circumstances should limit the believer's use of Christian freedom, and Paul places himself as an example of such limitation (9:3–7, 12b, 15, 19). Not using freedom for the sake of another in the community does not mean a person has lost freedom.

JEWISH REFLECTIONS ON MARITAL RELATIONS

Paul is not the only Jewish author to comment on the frequency of sexual relations in marriage and reasons for abstention (1 Cor. 7:5). The Mishnah reflects early debates on this issue:

He who takes a vow not to have sexual relations with his wife—the House of Shammai say: [He may allow this situation to continue] two weeks. And the House of Hillel say: For one week. Disciples go forth for Torah study without [the wife's] consent for thirty days. Workers go out for one week. The sexual duty of which the Torah speaks [Exod 21:10]: (1) those without work [of independent means]—every day; (2) workers—twice a week; (3) ass-drivers—once a week; (4) camel drivers—once in thirty days; (5) sailors—once in six months. The words of R. Eliezer. (m. Ketub. 5:6)

The *Testament of Naphtali* 8.8 likewise affirmed, "There is a time for having intercourse with one's wife, and a time to abstain for the purpose of prayer." Paul's advice in 1 Corinthians 7:5 seems to have been something of a commonplace.

Corinthian Questions — On Worship

In chapters 11 – 14, Paul discusses worship issues. He begins with an often-discussed section on head coverings for men and women (11:2 – 16). Some Corinthian men appear to have participated in the Corinthian worship services with their heads covered (11:4) while some women were praying and prophesying with their heads unveiled (11:5). In this context Paul discusses gender roles, which, from his cultural perspective, were expressed through head coverings (11:3, 7 – 12).

Why would some Corinthian men in the church cover their heads in worship? The Jewish custom of head-covering in prayer postdates the New Testament and so does not help us understand the problem. But Roman men and women who officiated in pagan cults covered their heads with part of their flowing Toga as they offered sacrifices. Those who participated as priests were of the social elite, and the Corinthian men Paul refers to were likely of this class. In *Roman Questions*, Plutarch asks, "Why is it that when they worship the gods, they cover their heads, but when they meet any of their fellow-men worthy of honor, if they happen to have the toga over the head, they uncover?" (*Moralia* 266C).

The temple of Asclepius in Corinth housed dining rooms with couches like this where the worshipers could dine.

The deceased is reclining at this funerary banquet.

Second, Paul insists that the women should be veiled in worship and not leave their heads uncovered (11:5–6). Women, at least those of the upper class, are most frequently depicted with their head uncovered in Roman portraits. But the evidence is not unanimous. Veiling seems to have something to do with a woman's relationship to her husband; according to Plutarch, this was the common practice of Roman women. So why are some Corinthian women throwing off the veil? The Villa of the Mysteries in Pompeii depicts women devotees of the Dionysus cult with their heads (and more) uncovered and hair down. In such cults, women could take part in ways normally inaccessible to them in their male-dominated societies. Perhaps, therefore, women in the Corinthian church, as in the Dionysus cult, are throwing off their head-covering (which would have indicated their proper relationship to their spouse) and using the Christian cult as a form of "social liberation."

Paul discusses gender roles and the Christian church in a way that emphasizes both men and women's dependency on each other (11:11–12) and "headship" (11:3). Being the "head" has been understood as either "source" or "authority," but not "superiority of nature." The authors of this book understand that Paul's emphasis is on the mutual dependence of men and women and do not interpret "headship" as granting authority to the man. However, Christians will probably continue to debate this issue (hopefully, charitably) for years to come.

Next Paul discusses the Lord's Supper, the symbolic sharing of the bread and wine that Jesus instituted among the disciples. In the early church, it was celebrated in the midst of a common banquet (11:17–34; cf. Matt. 26:26–29; Mark 14:22–25; Luke 22:14–20). Banqueting as a religious ceremony was common in the ancient world, often done to remember the dead.

Food and wine were served at these annual events to commemorate the life of the deceased or of some hero. These were private feasts and only a select group participated. The Corinthian believers are following contemporary custom by celebrating a Christian banquet in honor of Christ's death, but at these events, some are excluded and go hungry (11:20–21). Others get drunk (even though the wine commonly served was a mixture of wine and water). These groups have their "own private suppers" (11:21); from Paul's perspective, this is not the Lord's Supper, which symbolizes the common life of the church (10:16–17).

Paul returns the Corinthians to the fundamentals of the Lord's Supper, which recalls and proclaims the sacrificial death of Christ, the new covenant, and the promise of Christ's coming kingdom (11:23–26). He warns the Corinthians against partaking in this meal "in an unworthy manner" (11:27)—referring to the manner in which the supper was taken, which was divisive and exclusive. Taking the Lord's Supper together as a celebration of our common salvation implies that believers act and live together as Christ's body.

Paul's next worship issue is his discussion of the gifts of the Spirit (chs. 12–14). While he pays particular attention to tongues and prophecy in chapter 14, he mentions many other gifts in the Corinthian church (12:7–11, 28–30; cf. 1:7; Rom. 12:6–8; 1 Thess. 5:19–22). From Paul's perspective, the gifts of the Spirit are not given to a special elite group but to believers for the benefit of other believers (1 Cor. 12:7). In chapter 14 he repeatedly reminds the Corinthians that the gifts must be used for building up other members of the community (14:3–5, 12, 26; cf. 1 Peter 4:10–11).

The development of Paul's argument emphasizes this very point. He first presents the gifts (12:1–11), then discusses the body of Christ (12:12–27), and then returns to the issue of the gifts (12:28–31). Next is a lengthy discourse on love (13:1–13). Each member must use his or her gifts for the benefit of others, in love, and for the church's upbuilding (see Rom. 12:4–10, where Paul runs the same argument). This is Paul's antidote to the factionalism of this church.

On the Resurrection

In the last major section, we learn that some Corinthians deny the (future) resurrection of believers (15:12), perhaps because of the Greek notion that "when you're dead, you're dead." Aeschylus said, "When the earth has drunk up a man's blood, once he is dead, there is no resurrection" (*Eumenides* 647–648). But since the resurrection of the believers is linked inextricably with Christ's resurrection, Paul argues that to deny the believer's resurrection is, in fact, to deny Christ's (15:13, 16; cf. Phil. 3:21). For Paul, the Christian hope is not life eternal in heaven (though cf. 2 Cor. 5:6–10; Phil. 1:20–24), but the resurrection of the dead. If Christ has not been raised, our faith is in vain and we have no salvation (15:14–19). Christianity is more than ethics but the promise of immortality and the triumph over death and hell (15:54–57).

Paul ends his letter with an exhortation about the collection for the poor believers in Jerusalem (16:1–4; cf. 2 Cor. 8–9), his forthcoming visit (16:5–9), and the visit of Apollos (16:12). He closes with the final greetings (16:13–24), which includes the Aramaic prayer "Maranatha!" ("Come, Lord!").

COMPOSING 1 CORINTHIANS

The array of issues the apostle takes up in 1 Corinthians is almost dizzying. Divisions, questions about marriage and sexuality, litigation and idol meats, head coverings, banqueting and the Lord's Supper, spiritual gifts, and the resurrection give the letter an eclectic feel. Some students of the letter have concluded that its fragmented nature demonstrates that the letter is a compilation of various letters Paul wrote to the Corinthian church. But this eclectic nature stems rather from the multifaceted nature of the Corinthians' problems as they worked out the meaning of their new faith in Christ. We should also remember that

THE AMANUENSIS

Ancient authors often used a secretary or "amanuensis" when composing documents. These people took dictation, sometimes using a form of shorthand, but they could edit what they were given to write or could even be instructed to compose a letter around certain themes. Nevertheless, the author assumed full responsibility for what was written. The presence of a scribe is sometimes indicated in the letter itself (see Rom. 16:22; Gal. 6:11; 1 Peter 5:12), but often we become aware of a secretary's presence because of a change in handwriting at the end, where the author adds the final greeting.

Paul "wrote" his letters using an amanuensis, who would have taken dictation on wax tablets before transcribing the work onto papyrus (see 16:21, where Paul adds his final greeting). Thus, we are more surprised by the document's cohesion than its multicolored contents.

AUTHOR AND DATE

Contemporary scholars have not seriously questioned the authenticity of 1 Corinthians. Paul wrote it in Ephesus on his third missionary journey (1 Cor. 16:8, 19; cf. Acts 19:1–41). He was closely associated with Aquila and Priscilla and their house church in Ephesus, who, along with others, conveyed greetings to the Corinthians (16:19–20). Paul's Ephesian ministry lasted around three years (see 20:31), although the exact duration of his stay appears to have been closer to twenty-seven months (19:8, 10). This period has been variously dated, with late AD 52 until early AD 55 being the most likely dates. Most scholars believe that 1 Corinthians was written partway through Paul's Ephesian ministry, sometime around the spring of AD 54 (1 Cor. 16:8).

QUESTIONS FOR DISCUSSION ⊙⊙⊙⊙⊙⊙⊙⊙⊙⊙⊙⊙⊙⊙⊙⊙⊙⊙⊙⊙⊙⊙⊙⊙⊙⊙⊙⊙⊙

1. The misuse of the gifts of the Spirit (chs. 12 – 14) is one factor that contributed to the divisions in the church. Identify the problems and note how Paul corrects them. Does he restrict or prohibit the use of the gifts in the church?

2. Is Paul's teaching on eating meat offered to idols (chs. 8 – 10) relevant for us who live in societies where such practices are nonexistent? What principles have significance for us?

3. Discuss Paul's teaching on sexuality in contrast with contemporary sexual norms.

4. Should Christians ever go to court against each other? Compare the Corinthians' situation and context with modern litigation. How does Paul's teaching apply today?

5. How do members of your church understand the Christian hope in the face of death? Compare and contrast 1 Corinthians 15 with our current views about the fate of the deceased.

BIBLIOGRAPHY

Introductory

Blomberg, C. *1 Corinthians*. NIVAC. Grand Rapids: Zondervan, 1995.

Bruce, F. F. *1 and 2 Corinthians*. NCB. Grand Rapids: Eerdmans, 1980.

Hays, R. B. *First Corinthians*. Interpretation. Louisville: John Knox, 1997.

Advanced

Fee, G. D. *The First Epistle to the Corinthians*. NICNT. Grand Rapids: Eerdmans, 1987.

Garland, D. *1 Corinthians*. BECNT. Grand Rapids: Baker, 2004.

Thiselton, A. C. *The First Epistle to the Corinthians*. NIGTC. Grand Rapids: Eerdmans, 2000.

Witherington, B., *Conflict and Community in Corinth: A Socio-Rhetorical Commentary on 1 and 2 Corinthians*. Grand Rapids: Eerdmans, 1995.

NOTES

1. Gow and Page, *The Greek Anthology*, 7:493.

2. J. Murphy-O'Connor, *St. Paul's Corinth* (Wilmington, DE: Glazier, 1983), 27.

3. B.Witherington, *Conflict and Community in Corinth* (Grand Rapids: Eerdmans, 1995), 22 – 23.

4. Gow and Page, *Greek Anthology*, 9.284.

5. This phrase comes from C. Blomberg, *1 Corinthians* (NIVAC; Grand Rapids: Zondervan, 1995), 23.

6. Witherington, *Conflict and Community in Corinth*, 74.

7. Murphy-O'Connor, *St. Paul's Corinth*, 30.

8. Horsley, *New Documents Illustrating Early Christianity*, 1:5.

CHAPTER 17

2 CORINTHIANS

Acrocorinth was a monolithic rock mountain standing over the Hellenistic city of Corinth. In the classical period before Paul the famed temple of Aphrodite stood here.

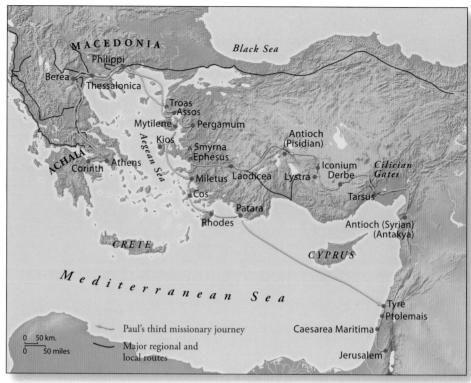

Paul's third missionary journey

PERSPECTIVE

In 1 Corinthians, Paul answered questions posed to him and tried to restore the unity of the church. But that letter did not remedy the situation. He soon learned about outsiders gaining influence within the congregation. These "super-apostles" (11:5) contradicted Paul's teachings, discredited his stature as an apostle, and promoted themselves as the sole interpreters of the faith. They argued that Paul lacked spiritual prowess, eloquence, and rhetorical skill, and they attacked Paul's gospel message. He had to confront these false teachers directly but not imitate their tactics. Paul here offers a poignant definition of ministry and suggests that weakness is the measure of godly leadership.

PAUL'S THORN IN THE FLESH (12:7)

Paul tells the Corinthians that a "thorn" was given to him to keep him from being too elated. What was this "thorn"? Interpreters offer three solutions: (1) Some believe Paul suffered from personal anxiety or spiritual torment. (2) Others hold that Paul had a physical illness, such as headaches, malaria, epilepsy, an eye ailment, or a speech impediment. (3) Still others suggest that Paul uses "thorn" as a figure of speech implying persecution.

Paul explains he was given this thorn in order not to be overly exalted by visions. He contrasts his own experience with the boastful "super-apostles." He recognizes it is all too easy for a human to become "puffed up" over such revelations.

PAUL'S VISITS AND LETTERS TO THE CORINTHIANS

Over seven years, Paul visited the Corinthians three times and wrote four letters.

First visit (Fall 50 – Spring 52): on Paul's second missionary journey (Acts 18:18)

First letter (ca. 52): now lost (1 Cor. 5:9)

Corinthians write Paul (1 Cor. 7:1)

Second letter (Spring 54): 1 Corinthians, written from Ephesus (1 Cor. 16:8)

Second visit (Summer or Fall 54): a painful one (2 Cor. 2:1)

Third letter (Spring 55): a letter of tears (2 Cor. 2:3 – 4; possibly 2 Cor. 10 – 13?)

Fourth letter (Fall 56): 2 Corinthians, written from Macedonia (2 Cor. 7:5 – 7)

Third visit (Winter, 56 – 57): three-month stay

HISTORICAL CONTEXT

To understand 2 Corinthians we must identify the outsiders opposed to Paul. Their recent presence within the church surprised and worried him. During his third missionary tour Paul remained in Ephesus over two years but also maintained contact with the Corinthians. If the wind was blowing favorably Corinth was merely five to six hours across the Aegean by ship. He had visitors from Corinth (1 Cor. 1:11) as well as couriers who brought him a letter (7:1) — likely Stephanas, Fortunatus, and Achaicus (16:17). Paul replied with 1 Corinthians, which the three men took back to Corinth. But soon Timothy arrives with news that Paul's authority has been seriously challenged (16:10 – 11).

At this point scholars are unclear what happens. Most believe that Paul made a quick trip to Corinth (unrecorded in Acts) to confront the Corinthians directly. But he was rejected by the church and calls this a "painful" visit (2 Cor. 2:1; 12:14, 21; 13:1 – 2). After returning to Ephesus, he writes a "tearful letter" of rebuke (2:4) and sends it with Titus, a deeply trusted colleague. Paul not only admonishes the Corinthians for failing to defend him, but also tests their loyalty by asking them to punish those who insulted him (2:1 – 11; 7:8 – 13). He wants Titus to gauge the church's reaction to his exhortation and then meet him in Macedonia.

Paul leaves Ephesus and travels north to Troas and then on to Macedonia to meet Titus (2:12 – 13) to find out the condition of the church *before* he arrives in Corinth. Titus brings good news that the church is filled with shame over their treatment of Paul (7:5 – 7). But Titus also has some bad news. People with letters of recommendation (3:1) have infiltrated the church, attacking Paul's ministry and authority.

Filled with relief and dread, Paul writes 2 Corinthians in the fall of AD 56. He then travels from Macedonia to Corinth for a third visit and stays three months, leading many scholars to surmise Paul's relationship with the Corinthians has improved. From Corinth, Paul writes Romans.

THE UNITY OF 2 CORINTHIANS

Scholars wonder whether 2 Corinthians is a composite of several of Paul's Corinthian letters pieced together. Note how Paul changes from a conciliatory tone in chapters 1 – 9 to more combative remarks in chapters 10 – 13. He seems to equivocate in his attitude toward the Corinthians, for in 7:4, 16, he expresses confidence in them, while in 11:2 – 4, he fears they will be led astray.

Many scholars believe chapters 1 – 9 form a literary unit and chapters 10 – 13 are a separate letter later appended. Some view chapters 10 – 13 a part of Paul's earlier

This first century bronze statue of Mercury has the god dressed in typical traveler garb with hat and cloak

"tearful letter," in which he is confronting those who rejected him during his "painful visit." Others think these four chapters originate from a setting *following* Paul's reunion with Titus when new conditions arose at Corinth.

Such fragmentary theories fail to explain how or why an ancient editor joined two separate letters. Did someone remove the greetings from chapter 10 and the closing from chapter 9, and then join the two together? The evidence from Greco-Roman letters is inconclusive. While preserved letters of Plato and Demosthenes have both greetings and closings, letters by Plato's contemporary Isocrates are often missing both (Isocrates, *To Nicocles* 2.1).

Not a few scholars argue for the unity of the entire letter. No Greek manuscript evidence supports a division of the book, and there is only one opening formula (1:1–2) and one concluding formula (13:11–13). They also argue the letter shows an internal coherence.

In our view the "tearful letter" is lost. The change of tone between chapters 9 and 10 reflects Paul's shift of focus as he turns from the Corinthians' response to his "tearful letter" to address the threat of the "super-apostles." To win their trust, Paul first establishes a rapport with the Corinthians (chs. 1–9) and then tackles the difficult topic of the "super-apostles" (chs. 10–13). This type of rhetoric is called *epideictic*, where the author focuses on both praise and blame to persuade his readers.[1]

Note also that in letter-writing conventions in Paul's day, some authors attached a post-script, indicating their own personal hand. Cicero attached postscripts even longer than chapters 10–13 (see *Letters to Friends* 12.12.5 [387]). Paul may have added a lengthy argument to his "finished" letter because new information has reached him or because he wants to convey sensitive information.

PAUL'S EXHORTATION FOR CORINTH

Second Corinthians follows the general letter pattern of the day: greetings, thanksgiving, body opening, body middle, body closing, and letter closing. It holds together with two supporting themes: Paul's authority and Paul's visits. In the opening chapters, Paul declares that despite grave dangers inherent in traveling (1:8–11), he yearns to see them (1:17–19). Chapter 6 lists the trials he faces in his travels (6:3–10). Titus's previous trip (see 7:13) introduces Paul's upcoming visit to take up the famine collection (8:1–9:15). In chapters 10–13, Paul warns that in his impending visit, he will not be lenient (13:2). Paul's relationship with the Corinthians is indeed fragile.

OUTLINE OF 2 CORINTHIANS

I. Greetings (1:1–2)

II. Thanksgiving (1:3–7)

III. Paul's Reason for Not Visiting (1:8–2:13)

    A. Death Sentence (1:8–11)
    B. Failure to Visit (1:12–2:2)
    C. "Tearful Letter" (2:3–13)

IV. Paul's Defense of His Ministry (2:14–6:13)

    A. Ministry of the New Covenant (2:14–4:18)
    B. Gospel Brings Reconciliation (5:1–6:13)

V. Personal Appeal to the Corinthians (6:14–7:16)

VI. Appeal for Contribution to Judea (8:1–9:15)

VII. Defense of His Ministry (10:1–11:21)

    A. Paul's Boasting within Limits (10:1–18)
    B. The Super-Apostles (11:1–21)

VIII. Paul's Boasts as a "Fool" (11:22–12:13)

IX. Paul's Plan for a Visit (12:14–13:10)

X. Closing (13:11–13)

THE RECONCILIATION OF PAUL AND THE CORINTHIANS (1:1–9:15)

These chapters are Paul's most personal and autobiographical section, revealing relief, anxiety, grief, indignation, and delight. He recalls his long history with the church (1:1–2:17) in order to underscore his extensive investment in their lives. He then moves to the theological core of the letter (3:1–7:16), where he outlines the essence of Christian leadership and the paradox of Christian weakness. One important test of the Corinthians' repentance and living by faith is whether they will follow through in the famine offering Paul is collecting (8:1–9:15).

Paul and His Travel Plans to Corinth (1:1–2:13)

As the Corinthians vacillate over their allegiance to Paul and his gospel, he explains why his travel plans changed, and he introduces two key themes: suffering and consolation. Paul did not visit them as initially planned because of unexpected suffering—a life-threatening menace faced in Asia (1:8–11). Most scholars think Paul was imprisoned and believed he might be executed. Moreover, he wants to spare them pain (2:1–2), concerned he may have to rebuke them again, and wants to avoid such a confrontation.

Paul and Christian Leadership (2:14–7:16)

Paul is fearful that the Corinthians still may not understand the dangers of those who have infiltrated their church. He deprecates the outsiders' efforts with statements such as "unlike so many, we do not peddle the word of God for profit" (2:17). Paul compares his opponents to hucksters who preyed on people during festivals or the Isthmian games.

On this coin, a Roman soldier stands over a Jewish female slave representing Judea captured during the First Revolt (66–70 AD). Paul experienced the might of Rome in his imprisonments under Roman guard.

Paul asks, "Do we need, like some people, letters of recommendation to you or from you?" (3:1). His opponents claim a religious authority that rivals Paul, comparing their own experience with that of Moses. Paul challenges such a model by announcing that his ministry of the Spirit has far more glory than Moses' message and fulfills the prophet Jeremiah's promise (Jer. 31:31–34) of a "new covenant." Israel has failed to recognize the temporary nature of the old covenant and disregarded God's new work in Christ (2 Cor. 3:10–11). Thus, Israel still has the veil over its heart, but it is removed in Christ (3:13–14). In a brilliant show of rhetorical skill, Paul claims that the Corinthians, not the "recommended" opponents, show the glory of the new covenant (3:18).

Paul then reframes the Corinthians' perception of authority and leadership by contrasting the indescribable glory of Christ with the utter weakness of humanity. The might of the Holy Spirit, which empowers Paul's ministry, is held in "jars of clay," a euphemism for the body (4:7). This highlights the surpassing greatness of Christ's glory, which is revealed not in pomp and ceremony, but in persecution and death. He reveals his eschatological perspective: "We fix our eyes not on what is seen, but on what is unseen, since what is seen is temporary, but what is unseen is eternal" (4:18).

Clay jars were widely used in the Greco-Roman world. Paul speaks of our body (jar) as containing a heavenly treasure.

The mature Christian church should cultivate the discernment required to view people with different eyes, to look for transformed men and women in whom the Spirit is at work (5:17). Paul describes his role in helping the Corinthians understand this as his "ministry of reconciliation" (5:18), with himself as "Christ's ambassador" (5:20).

Paul's Collection for Judea (8:1–9:15)

At the end of chapter 7, Paul declares "complete confidence" in the Corinthians (7:16). With his accolades ringing in their ears, Paul now challenges the Corinthians to preserve his confidence in them by following through with their contribution to the Judean famine relief fund. He promotes material self-emptying—generosity—as an indication that the Corinthians are genuine in their love (8:8). He raises this issue because his opponents have provoked questions in the Corinthians' minds as to the legitimacy of this collection (8:20–21).

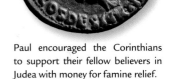
Paul encouraged the Corinthians to support their fellow believers in Judea with money for famine relief.

Paul also capitalizes on Corinth's relationship with its neighbors. Corinth's historic rival was Macedonia, and he excites the Corinthians' competitive nature by noting that the Macedonians have already been generous (8:1–2). The famine relief collection is Paul's special project, and he writes about it extensively with his churches in Galatia (Gal. 2:9–10), Macedonia (2 Cor. 8:1–2), and Corinth (1 Cor. 16:1); he also refers to it in Romans 15:25–32. Paul is concerned about the plight of his fellow Jews in Judea. But the famine gift also represents key theological concerns. Paul describes it with words like *eulogia* ("blessing," 2 Cor. 9:5; Gal. 3:14), *charis* ("grace," 1 Cor. 16:3; 2 Cor. 8:6), and *koinō-nia* ("sharing," Rom. 15:26; 2 Cor. 8:4). For Paul, Gentiles' giving to Jews concretely demonstrates unity between the two segments within the church.

LEADERSHIP AND HARDSHIP

Paul's confessions of weakness must have sounded odd to people used to the Stoic celebration of stability. Seneca, Paul's contemporary, praised the Stoic's goal of inner calm against the external hardships and struggles of the world. Human reason "makes us joyful in the very sight of death, strong and brave no matter in what state the body may be, cheerful and never failing though the body fail us" (*Moral Epistles* 30.3). Adversity is inconsequential and insignificant.

Paul's goal, however, is not happiness in the midst of struggles, but comfort from the Lord (1:4–7; 7:6–13). He distrusts human wisdom and courage, relying instead on God's power, made all the more evident in his weakness (11:30; 12:9). This is a true leader's strength (4:7–11).

PAUL'S CONFRONTATION (10:1 – 13:13)

Aristotle spoke of the importance of rhetoric and oratory skill. Paul declares that his own power comes from God, not human speech.

Paul reserves his harshest language for the "super-apostles" (11:5; 12:11), who presented letters of recommendation (3:1) and turned the Corinthians away from Paul and his gospel. His anger is evident: "Such persons are false apostles, deceitful workers, masquerading as apostles of Christ. And no wonder, for Satan himself masquerades as an angel of light" (11:13–14). Paul is planning another visit (12:14), where he will face his accusers and not spare them (13:2–3).

How did these "super-apostles" gain a foothold in the Corinthian church? They initially accepted money as payment for ministry, which impressed the church. But the church was also awed by their eloquence and rhetorical skills. They bore letters of recommendation (3:1) and claimed superior spiritual experiences (cf. 1 Cor. 12–14 for the church's interest in spiritual gifts).

The super-apostles taunt Paul about his weak presence, his failure to accept financial support, and his lack of special powers (visions, signs, and miracles). Their first criticism reflects a common view that public speakers should look healthy. One's message suffers if he looks "thin and pale" (Epictetus, *Discourses* 3.22.86–87). Paul objects to being judged by human standards of oratory skill. He insists that he "take[s] captive every thought to make it obedient to Christ" (10:5). On his supposed lack of special powers, Paul asserts that he demonstrated "among you the marks of a true apostle, including signs, wonders and miracles" (12:12).

Paul follows this claim with a sarcastic comment that he did all this free of charge, but the Corinthians seem offended (12:13). The issue of financial support was an important one to the Corinthians and tied closely to accusations of weakness. To fully appreciate the situation, we must understand the Roman social system of patron/client relationship (*clientela*). When a benefactor gave a gift, the recipient (client) was obliged to offer thanks. With due praise given, the benefactor bestowed more gifts to the client, and so the cycle continued. If Paul refused a gift, it was a serious social error, and the church might feel slighted. Yet if Paul accepted a gift, he would give the impression that he was a client of the church or indebted to it. Thus, Paul insisted on working manually as a tentmaker, which was socially demeaning.

The relief fund for Jerusalem presents another problem. Will Paul use the collection to get their money indirectly without taking on the social obligations inherent in the patron/client system? Paul vigorously defends himself against such slander and promises he will have nothing to do with the collection or its delivery to Jerusalem (8:17–23).

AUTHOR AND DATE

Few scholars have argued against Pauline authorship for 2 Corinthians. The critical debate concerns the unity of the letter (see above). The date of writing is generally placed in fall of AD 56 (see the timeline of Paul's relationship with the Corinthians, above). After Paul traveled to Macedonia from Ephesus (Acts 20:1), he wrote 2 Corinthians.

1. The Corinthian church had evidently been taken over by "false teachers." What were they teaching?

2. Examine Paul's approach to the so-called "super-apostles" in chapters 10–13. How does he contrast his own tactics with their ministry?

3. Can Paul's message of Christian suffering work in today's society of instant gratification and individualism?

4. Explain why scholars have frequently suggested that 2 Corinthians 10–13 is a separate letter. What benefits/drawbacks are there in this view?

5. What is the profile of Christian leadership that Paul promotes in this letter? What would that look like in a real-world setting today?

BIBLIOGRAPHY

Introductory

Belleville, L. L. *2 Corinthians*. IVPNTC. Downers Grove, IL: InterVarsity Press, 1996.

Garland, D. E. *2 Corinthians*. NAC. Nashville: Broadman & Holman, 1999.

Hafemann, S. *Second Corinthians*. NIVAC. Grand Rapids: Zondervan, 2000.

Murphy-O'Connor, J. *St. Paul's Corinth: Texts and Archaeology*. 3rd ed. Collegeville, MN: Liturgical, 2002.

Advanced

Barnett, P. *The Second Epistle to the Corinthians*. NICNT. Grand Rapids: Eerdmans, 1997.

Furnish, V. P. *II Corinthians*. AB. New York: Doubleday, 1984.

Harris, M. J. *The Second Epistle to the Corinthians*. NIGTC. Grand Rapids: Eerdmans, 2005.

Martin, R. P. *2 Corinthians*. WBC. Waco, TX: Word, 1986.

Peterson, B. K. *Eloquence and the Proclamation of the Gospel in Corinth*. SBLDS 163. Atlanta: Scholars, 1998.

NOTES

1. See S. Stowers, *Letter Writing in Greco-Roman Antiquity* (LEC; Philadelphia: Westminster, 1986).

2. See G. Bowersock, *Greek Sophists of the Roman Empire* (Oxford: Oxford Univ. Press, 1969), 61–62.

3. See J. L. White, *Light from Ancient Letters* (Philadelphia: Fortress, 1986), 118.

4. R. Hock argues that Paul's labor in a shop would not have hindered his message (*The Social Context of Paul's Ministry: Tentmaking and Apostleship* [Philadelphia: Fortress, 1980).

CHAPTER 18

THE LETTER TO
THE ROMANS

Evidence of a Jewish community near Rome was found in Ostia in the Tiber River. These ruins may well stem from a synag

At the end of his third missionary tour, Paul remained in Corinth for three months and reflected on his future ministry. Once again, he looked west, wanting to go as far as Spain. But first he hoped to go to the imperial capital of Rome, where a Christian community was already growing.

Paul's letter to the Romans is his longest (which explains why it is first in the New Testament canon of Paul's letters). While some view it as his best systematic treatment of the Christian faith, Paul nevertheless writes with an awareness of critical issues that need to be addressed. Although he has never visited this church, Christian couriers commonly brought news of developments throughout the Mediterranean. The Roman Christians were thus well known in Greece (Rom. 1:8; 16:3ff.), so Paul can write to them addressing specific issues.

THE CITY OF ROME

Rome was an astonishing city. By the first century an extensive system of aqueducts provided most of the city with clean water. Sewer systems, public latrines, and public baths increased levels of sanitation. Multistoried buildings with internal plumbing were common. Augustus (27 BC–AD 14) installed a police force and fire prevention units. Monuments, government buildings, libraries, racecourses, and theaters displayed impressive feats of engineering and architecture.

Rome had served as the capital of the entire Mediterranean world for nearly two centuries and was a famous cultural and intellectual center. The lure of this city with its thousands of miles of paved roads brought scores of people from all corners of the empire—civilized and uncivilized (cf. 1:14). Medical colleges and gladiator spectacles were equally popular. By the end of the second century AD Rome reached the pinnacle of its power, prosperity, and population—estimated at nearly one million.

Religion was central to Roman political and social life. Priests frequently counseled the senate on issues like making war and interpreting the law. Religious oracles were consulted

Left: A temple dedicated to all Rome's gods, the Pantheon was built in open fields outside the ancient city (the *Campus Martius*). It stood prominently in Paul's day. *Right:* Access to Rome was via the Tiber River which flowed into the Adriatic Sea at the city of Ostia. A great maritime city since the 4th century BC, Christians in Rome would know the port well. This coin from Nero (AD 54-68) shows the Ostia harbor lighthouse (with statue), Neptune reclining below and four successive uses of the harbor: two ships entering at full sail, two being rowed out, a large ship at anchor (whose sails are being gathered in), and a ship alongside a quay being unloaded.

to predict the future. Extravagant religious festivals were part of the fabric of everyday life. It was not, however, one religion, but a blend of many. The Romans usually assimilated the gods of conquered people, merging them with the Roman pantheon, and required those conquered to adopt Roman divinities. To desecrate any temple in the empire was a capital crime. This is why the Romans struggled with Jewish (and later, Christian) claims to theological exclusivity. Refusal to embrace the imperial religious spirit deemed Jews and Christians haughty, exclusive, and intolerant. Eventually this led to persecution.

Paul is fully aware of the religious and social climate of this city. He knows that the Roman church is Gentile, but is also anchored in a Jewish community. This multicultural environment brings its own challenges. Jews might seek privileges in their ethnic heritage; Gentiles might discriminate against Jewish fellow believers.

THE SETTING OF ROMANS

Paul is facing a major transition in his ministry (15:19–23). Having preached the gospel "from Jerusalem all the way around to Illyricum" (present-day Bosnia and Serbia), he concludes, "There is no more place for me to work in these regions." Thus, Paul hopes to visit Rome on his way to Spain.

Paul mentions two people whose names help us locate this writing in the city of Corinth: Gaius, Paul's host while visiting the church in Corinth (cf. Rom. 16:23; 1 Cor. 1:14) and Phoebe (Rom. 16:1), a deacon in the church in Cenchrea (a port six miles east of Corinth). Paul's commendation of Phoebe (16:1–2) indicates that she will be delivering this letter. Most scholars agree that Paul writes this letter at the end of his third missionary journey (cf. Acts 20:2–3). Therefore we must think of him as a veteran of many years, experienced in theological debate and having well-formed ideas about the church and its beliefs.

Paul has just completed a collection of money from his Gentile churches and is planning to give it to the poorer churches

One of the most famous Roman gladiators was Spartacus, who escaped from gladiator school in 73 BC and organized such a volatile slave revolt that it threatened the Roman republic. His throng of runaway slaves and rebel gladiators defeated three Roman armies on the slopes of Mt. Vesuvius.

GLADIATORS

Gladiators (from *gladius*, "sword") were fighters who dueled to death for the public in Rome. In AD 107 Emperor Trajan sent ten thousand gladiators into the arena over a period of four months.

Gladiators fought with a variety of weapons. The *Samnites* entered hand-to-hand battle with a large shield, a visor, a helmet, and a short sword; the *retiarius* ("net man") attempted to entangle his fully armed opponent and finish him off with a trident; the *essedarii* ("chariot men") fought from chariots; the *lauearii* ("lasso men") aimed to lasso their opponent; the *andabatae* fought on horseback with closed visors (i.e., blindfolded!).

Exhibitions usually began with sham fights with wooden swords and javelins. During the real fighting, a losing gladiator could appeal for mercy to the crowds, who signaled either to spare his life (thumbs up) or to continue with his death (thumbs down).

NOTES FROM ANTIQUITY

The Romans occupied southern Spain (or Iberia) from the 2nd century BC but Augustus completed its conquest from 26-19 BC. This Roman bridge is found in Salamanca, Spain.

in Judea (Rom. 15:25–27; cf. 1 Cor. 16:1–4; 2 Cor. 8–9). As he writes Romans, the delicacy of this gesture is on his mind. Will the ethnic tensions, racial pride, and theological differences between Gentile and Jewish Christians surface again? Will Jewish believers in Jerusalem reject this gift and jeopardize the fragile unity of the church?

Then there are his opponents in Judea whom he has known since he was a young Pharisee. Will they continue to pursue him (15:31)? Paul thus asks that the Christians in Rome pray for his protection and that the contribution he takes to Jerusalem "may be favorably received by the Lord's people" (15:31).

One plausible view is that Paul writes this extensive letter because he has ominous feelings about what will happen in Judea (15:30–33). If he is arrested or even killed, this letter

THE EDICT OF CLAUDIUS

The Roman historian Suetonius writes that Claudius "expelled the Jews from Rome because they were constantly rioting at the instigation of Chrestus" (*Life of Claudius* 25.4). Who is Chrestus, and why would Claudius banish the entire Jewish population and not just this "troublemaker"?

The spelling and pronunciation of this common Greek name is close to the Greek word *Christos*, meaning "Messiah." Suetonius has most likely confused the two words. Tensions probably flared up when Jews returning from Jerusalem claimed that Jesus of Nazareth was indeed the long-awaited *Christos*. Claudius's edict likely affected both Jews and Jewish Christians, since the Romans considered both part of the same group.

will be a theology legacy, guiding the Roman church (and perhaps others) in his absence. But Paul is also looking to the Roman Christians for practical financial support. His journey to Spain will be expensive, and so the Roman church can offer him help (15:26–29).

THE CHURCH IN ROME

The origins of Christianity in Rome are uncertain. By the first century BC Rome possessed a large Jewish population, perhaps as many as fifty thousand. Many Jews arrived as slaves after 63 BC when Pompey conquered Jerusalem. The strong commercial ties between Rome and Judea attracted even more Jews. Archaeologists know of nearly a dozen synagogues in Rome. It is plausible to assume that the Roman congregation began in these synagogues the early decades of the first century (cf. Acts 2:10).

But Gentiles likely joined as well, raising a variety of disputes well known to Paul. Evidence of widening tensions *within* the Jewish community comes in the late 40s when the Emperor Claudius expelled Jews and Jewish-Christians from the city (AD 49; cf. Acts 18:1–2). As a result, the leadership of Roman Christianity rapidly became Gentile.

Claudius's expulsion affected the Christian couple Aquila and Priscilla, who fled to Corinth and hosted Paul there (Acts 18:1–3). But they returned to Rome, and Paul anticipates seeing them again (Rom. 16:3). The motif "first to the Jew, then to the Gentile" (1:16), which runs throughout Paul's letter, evidences the ethnic diversity of the Roman congregation. But little more can be known.

Paul is aware, of course, that he is addressing Christians with Jewish heritage. He speaks of circumcision, the law of Moses, Abraham's significance, and the fate of unbelieving Israel as if his readers enjoy a deep Jewish heritage. He even identifies with them by referring to Abraham as "the forefather of us Jews" (4:1) and greets his fellow Jews in chapter 16 (Priscilla, Aquilla, and others, vv. 3–4, 7, 11).

At the same time, Paul clearly has Gentile Christians in mind in this letter. The sins of idolatry catalogued in chapter 2 are characteristic of the pagan world. Paul assures these Gentiles that they are among those called to "belong to Jesus Christ" (1:5–6) and are central to God's plan of salvation (11:13–25). Moreover, they are the focus of Paul's commission (see 15:15–17, cf. 1:13).

THE PURPOSE OF ROMANS

We have already summarized a few of the reasons Paul may have written Romans, particularly as he moves further west to expand his mission into new frontiers. He is in Corinth and wants to work in the far west; Rome and Spain are now his new destinations. His journeys in the eastern half of the Mediterranean were supported by the church of Syrian Antioch (Acts 13:1–4). Now as he moves further west, he wants to locate a different "anchor church," one with the vision and resources to assist him expand his mission into new frontiers.

Paul knows that the Christians there understand the gospel, but perhaps there are errors in their belief or teachers have criticized Paul's teachings. Romans 1:16; 3:8; and 9:1–2 imply that Paul feels under attack and needs to defend himself and his understanding of the faith. This explains his frequent use of rhetorical questions (apparently) raised by his opponents, whether real or hypothetical (i.e., 2:17–24; 3:1, 5–8). If Paul is

Claudius ruled from AD 41-54 and was famous for his decree to expel Jews from Rome who were caught up in a debate about "Chrestus" (a misspelling of the Latin *Christus*), referring to Christ.

The temple of Romulus in Rome. According to a legend known since the 3rd century BC, Rome was founded by the twins Romulus (Lat. The Roman) and Remus who were rescued from the Tiber River and raised by a wolf.

going to rely on this church as a strategic ally in his mission, he must establish himself as a decisive teacher, dispel any doubts about his positions, and lay out "my gospel" (2:16).

However Paul's interest in the Roman church is not simply pragmatic. He also cares for their pastoral needs and no doubt has a good idea of what they are. The diversity of this community leads naturally to the subject of conflict. Thus, his argument in 9:1–11:36 shows how Gentiles and Jews have both participated—and will participate—in the program of God's salvation. He wants them to experience a genuine unity as "one body . . . liv[ing] in harmony with one another" (12:5, 16) and to pursue a life of righteousness (12:1–15:13) with no discrimination between the "weak" and the "strong" regarding the law (14:1; 15:1, 7).

TERTIUS WROTE ROMANS?

In Romans 16:22 Paul's scribe identifies himself: "I, Tertius, who wrote down this letter, greet you in the Lord" (16:22). This raises an interesting question: How much editorial influence did Tertius exercise on the content of this letter?

Writers in antiquity usually enlisted an amanuensis, or scribe, to help compose letters. Authors gave scribes varying degrees of freedom in the actual wording of the text, ranging from much freedom in composition to dictation word for word. Most likely Paul dictated Romans to Tertius. The study of letter writing in antiquity shows that the repetition of the word "for" (*gar* in Greek) signals a process of dictation—and it occurs 144 times in Romans. Furthermore, Romans closely resembles some of Paul's other letters, which probably had different scribes.

AUTHORSHIP AND LITERARY UNITY

Paul's authorship of Romans is rarely disputed. It claims to be from Paul (1:1) and was upheld through the earliest centuries. Its language echoes that of other so-called undisputed letters (Galatians, 1–2 Corinthians, and Philippians).

A more complex question is the literary unity of the letter. Some scholars doubt that chapter 16 was a part of Paul's original letter. Some early manuscripts end the letter at 16:24. The final "benediction" (16:25–27) even appears elsewhere (e.g., after 14:23 or 15:33). Some speculate that Paul originally wrote chapters 1–14 (or 1–15) with the doxology as his original ending. Some argue that the list of greetings in 16:1–24 stems from another copy of the letter sent to Ephesus, which would explain how Paul knows so many people.

However, no Greek manuscript omits chapter 16, and its extensive list of names may be explained by Paul's extensive travels and contacts throughout the Mediterranean. Priscilla and Aquila (16:3) are a good example. Paul met them in Corinth, yet they were originally from Rome.

THE LITERARY FORM OF ROMANS

Many interpreters agree on the major divisions of the letter. This is because Paul incorporates several literary devices and grammatical features that signal the beginning and end of sections. Paul opens and closes his letter in typical ancient fashion: greeting, thanksgiving, reason for writing, and his theme. His conclusion includes upcoming plans, commendations, and a doxology.

The first century witnessed an explosion of literary production. Books circulated on papyrus scrolls, and letters were sent on smaller sheets of papyrus (seen here from Pompeii). In the late 1st century or the early 2nd century, Christians began using the sewn papyrus codex or book.

Within this framework, Paul develops two main sections: doctrinal instruction and ethical exhortation. In the first section he uses a number of questions and answers with the internal logic of the gospel. In the second section he describes first its impact on the life of the church and then on the community at large.

OUTLINE OF ROMANS

I. Salutation and Introduction (1:1–17)

II. Theological Explanation of the Gospel (1:18–11:36)

A. The Human Dilemma: Universal Sin and Guilt (1:18–3:20)

B. The Divine Solution: Justification (3:21–5:21)

C. The Christian Prospect: Sanctification (6:1–8:39)

D. God's Plan for Israel: Rejection and Restoration (9:1–11:36)

III. Ethical Exhortation: Practical Implications of the Gospel (12:1–15:13)

A. Practicing Righteousness in the Body (12:1–21)

B. Practicing Righteousness in the World (13:1–14)

C. Christian Liberty and Christian Charity (14:1–15:13)

IV. Conclusion (15:14–16:27)

A. Paul's Upcoming Ministry, Travel Plans, and Prayer Requests (15:14–33)

B. Recommendation of Phoebe and Greetings (16:1–16)

C. Final Remarks and Doxology (16:17–27)

THE THEOLOGICAL ARGUMENT OF ROMANS
Salutation and Introduction (1:1–17)

The introduction immediately sets the tone and direction and echoes many other letter openings of Paul. For instance, he identifies himself as an apostle (1:1), greets the saints with "grace and peace" (1:7), and gives thanks for their faith (1:8). Aware of his need to build rapport with a church he has never visited, Paul expands his greeting (1:1–7) to reveal the credibility of his apostolic calling and Gentile ministry. He explicitly mentions his frustrated attempts to visit despite his longing to see them (1:8–15).

Above all, Paul's introductory paragraphs offer the thesis that will be defended throughout the letter (1:16–17): The gospel offers the power of God for salvation to everyone who believes, both Jews and Greeks. In it the righteousness of God has been revealed — in a manner that fully conforms with Old Testament principles of righteousness (1:17; Hab. 2:4). Paul is now ready to discuss the theological and ethical implications of this thesis.

A Theological Explanation of the Gospel (1:18–11:36)

The human dilemma: universal sin and guilt (1:18–3:20). In 1:18 Paul launches his first doctrinal section on the nature of the human condition. He describes the sinfulness and guilt of Gentiles (1:18–32), Jews (2:1–3:8), and all humanity (3:9–20). God's wrath is revealed against sinful humanity for repudiating his truth (1:18). Paul reaches back to the beginning to highlight the universality of sin (1:19–23): Human rebellion is a willful attempt to reject God and usurp his role as Creator. This results in inappropriate sexual relations (1:24), misdirected worship (1:25), and corrupted ethics (1:26–32) that destroy the very fabric of human society.

The Roman Christians were ordinary citizens of the empire such as this Roman couple whose sculpture was completed during the late Republican period (1st century BC).

Even the Jews, God's people privileged with the custodianship of his Word (3:2), have rejected his truth. They too will be judged, for "God does not show favoritism" (2:11). Jews should not place confidence merely in having the law, for breaking it puts them in a worse position than Gentiles (2:17–27). True Jewishness, Paul clarifies, focuses on the importance of the inward work of the Spirit over against ethnic identity markers, like circumcision (2:28–29).

Paul concludes this section with numerous quotes from the Psalms: "Jews and Gentiles alike are all under the power of sin . . . there is no one righteous, not even one" (3:9–10; cf. Ps. 14:1–3). Indeed, all human beings are sinful and without excuse, rightfully condemned for not living according to conscience (Gentiles) or the law (Jews).

The divine solution: justification (3:21–5:21). Paul then develops his solution. The sacrificial death of Christ is the basis for justification, and we appropriate the benefits of his death by faith (3:21–26). Since Jew and Gentile alike are justified by faith alone, there is no room for personal boasting (3:27–31). To illustrate the principle of righteousness by faith Paul highlights the story of Abraham (4:1–25), using as his key text Genesis 15:6: "Abraham believed God, and it was credited to him as righteousness" (Rom. 4:3ff.). Abraham's righteous status was declared *before* his circumcision (Gen. 17:10–14), which set in place an important pattern. Works of the law cannot be a precondition for salvation. Therefore, righteousness by faith is freely available to Jews and Gentiles alike — thus making Abraham the spiritual father of all believers.

Acquiring a new position with God brings remarkable results: peace with God, grace that transforms character, and hope in the midst of suffering (5:1–11). This new status of righteousness is given to us by Christ, the new head of a new humanity (5:12–21). As Adam imputed to humanity a propensity to sin from which there is no escape, Christ as head can now do the same in reverse, repairing what was broken in Eden.

PAGAN TEMPLES IN ROME

Religion thrived in Roman culture. The Romans developed complex mythologies. Jupiter (god of lightning, thunder, and rain; Greek Zeus) headed the Roman pantheon. Devotion to these gods took concrete form in impressive structures of worship, like the temple of Jupiter.

Likely Paul has this background in mind when he writes: "Although they claimed to be wise, they became fools and exchanged the glory of the immortal God for images made to look like mortal man and birds and animals and reptiles" (1:22–23).

The Christian prospect: sanctification (6:1–8:39). The gospel not only offers freedom from condemnation, but also a way of escape from the dilemma of our moral paralysis. It offers *restoration*, a return to human goodness and holiness that can only be regained by a renewed relationship with God. Therefore Paul discusses the tyranny of sin (Rom. 6), the condemnation brought about through the law (ch. 7), and the hopeful restoration given through the work of the Spirit (ch. 8).

Some might exploit God's offer of free grace saying that Paul's teaching inspires *antinomianism*—sinning so that God's grace may forgive that much more. This view betrays a misunderstanding of baptism (6:1–14) and conversion (6:15–23). Union with Christ in baptism frees us from the *compulsion* to sin: "Sin shall no longer be your master" (6:14). Thus, we can yield our lives to God rather than to sin. The benefits are remarkable: freedom (not to do anything we want, but to live as we were designed), holiness (to be like God), and eternal life (6:23).

Paul sustains this discussion by moving through a variety of metaphors. Slavery (6:20–23) and marriage (7:1–3) model how a new relationship with the law has come about. Through redemption we have acquired a new Master in God, who now owns us (6:22). Likewise, the death of a spouse changes the binding obligations of a marriage, and so our death to the law (our former spouse) enables us to conduct our lives for God. The struggle to fulfill the law (7:14–20) is the hallmark of a life lived in the flesh, a life in bondage to sin. God's work in the gospel offers a new prospect: that sin no longer reigns (6:12; 8:2), that our captivity is over (7:23), and that we now live safe from condemnation (8:1).

The hopeful prospect of the gospel is not only found in the work of Christ. Paul now turns to the transforming work of the Holy Spirit (8:1–30). He sees two opposite choices before us: the flesh (or "sinful nature") and the Spirit (8:5). The former refers to a life lived in captivity to sin that results in death; this life cannot obey the law or please God (8:5, 7). The alternative is the Spirit of God (mentioned nineteen times in Rom. 8). Just as justification is a gift of God's goodness, so sanctification is another expression of his grace. The Spirit indwells and transforms (8:9), implants holy desires (8:5), controls the mind (8:6), gives life (8:11), puts to death evil deeds (8:13), leads to self-control (8:14), confirms our spiritual adoption (8:15), and intercedes on our behalf with the Father (8:26).

Above all, the Spirit confirms within us that God continues to be on our side, giving us a new status as his adopted sons and daughters (8:14–17). Despite our suffering and feelings of futility, God remains on our side, promising a future that holds a glorious promise of both our own redemption and that of the entire earth (8:18–25). *This is the fundamental source of our peace (5:1).* God is in control, and for those who love him every good plan is in place (8:28–30). No object—celestial or creational—can separate us from God's love (8:37–39).

God's plan for Israel: rejection and restoration (9:1–11:36). At the center of Paul's consciousness is a deep and troubling anguish about the Jewish people (9:2). He believes that Jesus is the Messiah, that his resurrection vindicates every claim about him, and that his own conversion is personal proof that God is at work in Christ. But Judaism has not completely embraced its Messiah. Everywhere he goes, Paul finds strong resistance to his preaching. His discussion in this section no doubt represents countless hours of argument in synagogues during his three missionary tours.

One debater's voice looms large: If Jesus Christ is central to God's program for righteousness—and since his Jewish people have not universally acclaimed this program—has God's effort failed (9:6)? Paul feels so deeply here that he would sacrifice himself for his own people if it were possible (9:3–4).

Paul sees the problem as organized around multiple foci. First, there is the obvious problem of Israel's unbelief. Here Paul argues that God's so-called "failure" is only apparent; all through history some Israelites believed and others did not. It is possible to descend from "Israel" but not belong to "Israel" (9:7; cf. 2:28). God has kept in history those who are faithful—a remnant (9:27; 11:5). This preservation of the faithful is God's own doing (9:11–12).

But if God is responsible for this believing remnant, then is his mercy capricious? How can he still find fault (9:19)? Paul says that this divine freedom is the freedom a potter has over clay. The clay only becomes what it is, thanks to the potter's hand. Every gesture is an act of mercy since the clay is useless in its natural state. God acts to save, and he has saved many Jews who now proclaim Jesus' messiahship.

If ethnicity is no guarantee to becoming "God's people" (9:25–26), the way is then open for Gentiles to become God's children. Moreover, this means that Israel's zeal for religion based on works is misdirected (9:32). Their effort promoted a righteousness born not from God but from within Judaism.

In every case, it is not the person's pedigree that matters but his or her faith. It is one's desire to yield to God's purposes in history that matters. Paul demonstrates this principle by citing Jeremiah, Isaiah, Leviticus, Deuteronomy, Joel, and the Psalms to show this as an old theme. Paul also notes that Isaiah and Moses ushered a warning for those who continue in their disobedience (10:21).

WHO IS THE "I" IN ROMANS 7?

Is Christian perfection possible? Proponents who say either yes or no must come to terms with Romans 7:14–25. In this text the person speaking is obviously struggling with sin. But who is this "wretched man" who cries out for deliverance (7:24)? Does this "I" refer to Paul before or after his conversion, or perhaps to something else?

Three interpretations are common: (1) Paul describes his struggle before conversion, as a Jew representing Israel's experience with the law ("I" = unregenerate Paul/Israel). (2) Paul describes his own experience after conversion ("I" = regenerate Paul). (3) Paul is not writing autobiographically but rather symbolically for all humanity ("I" = Adam/humanity).

Therefore, God has not failed or rejected his people because Paul himself and the many whom God has preserved now represent the true faith of his people. But a remnant implies another larger body that has failed to attain the goal. What of them? Paul sees this as another opportunity for grace since as a result of Israel's unbelief, the Gentiles have now entered God's family or been grafted into God's olive tree (11:17–24). This unexpected development will provoke Jewish envy (11:11–12), so that they may eventually be grafted back into the tree.

Paul's heartfelt desire is for the salvation of *all fellow Jews* (11:28–36). He acknowledges that even though unbelieving Jews are "enemies" of the gospel, God loves them for the sake of their ancestry because God does not revoke his covenant love on a whim. God loves Israel — which reminds Gentiles that any anti-Jewish sentiments are sin. And yet by refusing Christ, these Jews have entered the deepest tragedy yet: separation from the very ancestral olive tree that has sustained them.

Paul needs to remind the Gentile Christians of their heritage as well as the tragedy of Israel's loss (Rom. 11:17-24). Christian Gentiles are like branches grafted into the trunk of an olive tree — God's historic people, the Jews. Unbelieving Jews, however, are like branches broken off who may be grafted in when they embrace Christ.

Ethical Exhortation: The Practical Implications of the Gospel (12:1–15:13)

In Paul's mind, right thinking and believing produce right living. Paul now outlines four areas that require sincere Christian reflection: community ethics (12:1–21), political ethics (13:1–7), personal ethics (13:8–14), and the relationship of the "strong and the weak" (14:1–15:13). This final section is so long it suggests that Paul may be addressing a common problem either troubling the Roman church or his churches in general.

No system of ethics is successful without the moral and spiritual transformation of the practitioner (12:1–2). When this happens, genuine, reasoned worship takes place. Yet the opposite is often the case. Christians become proud of their status and damage the community in which they live. Paul reminds the Romans that all gifts are tokens of God's mercy and are given in order to strengthen and serve others. The community of faith thus becomes a place where service trumps competition and humility outweighs pride. Generosity, love, liberality, and patience are hallmarks of a redeemed life.

But no Christian community can live in isolation from the social and political realities of the world. The church must live within the empire. So Paul charges the church to submit to the authorities and live as good citizens (13:1–7). However, what sets apart the church is not its good citizenship but its belief that the state is not the final authority in matters of truth. The state must answer to God. Hence Christians are not called to blind political obedience but to be subject when the state conforms to its calling under God.

Life in the empire is also life in the marketplace, with legal transactions, property rights, and friendships. Here too Paul calls on Christians to be exemplary in their conduct (13:8–14). The church should be the one place where people act differently toward one another, where Christians do not simply look after one another but where goodness is extended to others regardless of their faith. This is what it means to be a light to the world.

THE VOICE OF JESUS IN ROMANS

In chapters 12–16 Paul unveils the ethical implications of the gospel. These commands often parallel the teachings of Jesus. As a result, scholars suggest that Paul has access to some of the same sources used by gospel writers.[1] Compare, for example, the following texts:

Romans	Gospel Parallel	Paul's Instruction
12:14	Luke 6:27–28	Bless those who persecute you; bless and do not curse.
12:17	Matt. 5:39	Do not repay anyone evil for evil.
13:7	Mark 12:17	If you owe taxes, pay taxes; if revenue, then revenue.
13:8–9	Mark 12:31	Love your neighbor as yourself [sum of commandments].
14:10	Matt. 7:1–2	You, then, why do you judge your brother or sister?
14:14	Luke 11:41; Mark 7:19	I am convinced … that nothing is unclean in itself.
16:19	Matt. 10:16	Be wise about what is good, and innocent about what is evil.

Finally, Paul reflects on the problem of religious and ethnic diversity that was characteristic of the first-century church (14:1–15:13). What happens when someone with strict and conservative scruples (like the Jew) decides to live in a community that celebrates its freedom in Christ? Tensions develop. The unity of the church and the preservation of the weaker believer should rank higher than our own freedom. Paul knows that food laws have disappeared in Christ (14:14), yet he refuses to injure a brother or sister for the sake of his own freedom.

When Paul tells the Roman Christians to support those in public authority (13:1-7), he is walking a delicate line between politics and pagan religion since religious structures were a part of Roman society. In Pompeii, the public forum housed public courts (basilica), the market (macellum), as well as temples such as the great Capitolium (or the temple of Jupiter), dedicated to the gods Jupiter, Juno, and Minerva. Mt. Vesuvius is in the background.

Conclusion (15:14 – 16:27)

Paul closes his letter by returning to several themes of the introduction (cf. 1:8 – 15). He describes more fully his ministry to the Gentiles, his reasons for writing, and his future travel plans (15:14 – 33). A recommendation of Phoebe (16:1 – 2) and numerous greetings to believers (16:3 – 16) give a warm relational tone. Paul concludes with a warning about false teachers (16:17 – 20), final greetings from his coworkers (16:21 – 24), and a doxology (16:25 – 27).

THE CENTRAL THEME OF ROMANS

From the time of the Reformation most Protestants studying Romans have emphasized the personal justification of the believer before God. Individual salvation, justification by faith, and freedom from God's wrath were located at the center of Paul's letter. This debate turned a sharp corner in 1963 when Krister Stendahl wrote an article in the *Harvard Theological Review* entitled "The Apostle Paul and the Introspective Conscience of the West."[2] Stendahl argued that Paul is not preoccupied with matters of personal salvation and that we can find this emphasis only if we read Romans through the lens of Augustine's or Luther's anxieties about sin and justification.

For Stendahl and many subsequent interpreters of Paul, Paul's interests lie in a deeper question of how Gentiles who do not possess the law gain full access to God's promises for salvation. In this view, the climax of Paul's thought is found in Romans 9 – 11, where Paul redefines the meaning of "Israel" theologically as God's people within which both Jews and Gentiles can cohere in one people in Christ. This "new perspective" on Romans thus sees Jew-Gentile relations as the epicenter of Romans. Both Jews and Gentiles share equal jeopardy before God's wrath — and both share equally in his grace.

This view does acknowledge numerous secondary themes in Romans. Individual salvation is one of them, but it is subsidiary to a wider concern about the law, Gentile hope, and Jewish advantages. As some scholars today prefer, Romans should be viewed as a "dialogue with Judaism."[3] Or, as James Dunn puts it, Paul is dialoguing with himself — Paul the Jewish rabbi talking with Paul the Christian apostle.[4] For instance, when Paul argues against "works of the law," is he arguing against religious efforts by Jews trying to secure their place with God, or is he thinking about Jewish "identity markers" such as circumcision and food laws that isolated Israel from other nations? If the latter, then Paul is arguing against an assumed sense of privilege that hinders the gospel among Gentiles. This shift from a "vertical" to a "horizontal" understanding of Romans determines how interpreters organize and interpret the letter.

In response, it seems difficult to doubt that Paul is addressing an individual crisis in Romans. He writes not simply about a Jewish and Gentile problem but about a human problem. The individualism of Romans can certainly be defended, though it cannot be brought into the center of the apostle's thought. For Paul it is the *individual* Jew or Gentile who is fallen, who benefits from Christ's work on the cross, who exhibits faith, and who then is rescued from Adam's curse. But this individual never lives a privatized spiritual life outside of a redeemed community. The redeemed community has moved from a status "in Adam" to a place "in Christ" and now must seek its relation to the historic people of God known as "Israel."

Keeping this debate in mind, interpreters have often seen Paul's interest as centered on the law (mentioned seventy-two times in Romans)[5] or on the righteousness of God attained through faith (1:17). Others see this complex of ideas as one idea subsumed in "the gospel," which Paul mentions at the beginning (1:1, 2, 9, 15) and end of his letter (15:16, 19). The gospel is even the main theme of Paul's thesis statement in 1:16, "I am not ashamed of the gospel. . . ."[6]

But what is the content of this gospel? Here key themes merge: Paul is making clear that both Jews and Gentiles live under a parallel jeopardy — the threat of the law, which discloses our failure to satisfy God's righteousness. But that righteousness has now been met by God himself. In Christ, God satisfied the law and made his righteousness alive within the community of faith. *This is the good news of the gospel.* Since it is appropriated by faith and not the law, it is accessible to both Jews and Gentiles. Through grace, God offers genuine human renewal. And if we do not recognize this new work of God in Christ, if we continue to pursue the law (9:30–31), a renewed community made up of Jews and Gentiles — a new Israel — is impossible.

QUESTIONS FOR DISCUSSION ⊙⊙⊙⊙⊙⊙⊙⊙⊙⊙⊙⊙⊙⊙⊙⊙⊙⊙⊙⊙⊙⊙⊙⊙⊙⊙⊙⊙⊙⊙

1. How do the details from Paul's situation (i.e., his missionary context) and the Roman church (i.e., Jewish and Gentile diversity) help us understand Romans?

2. Why does Paul send a letter of such theological complexity to a congregation he has neither established nor visited?

3. How does Paul explain the despair of human sinfulness, yet maintain the dignity of the human race?

4. What distinctive themes does "the new perspective on Paul" sound in the interpretation of Romans?

5. In Romans 11 Paul recognizes the special status of Jews in God's plan of salvation. How, if at all, should this theological understanding affect international politics with modern-day Israel?

BIBLIOGRAPHY

Introductory

Bruce, F. F. *Romans*. TNTC. Grand Rapids: Eerdmans, 1985.

Moo, D. J. *Romans*. NIVAC. Grand Rapids: Zondervan, 2000.

Osborne, G. R. *Romans*. IVPNTC. Downers Grove, IL: InterVarsity Press, 2004.

Stott, J. *Romans*: *God's Good News for the World*. Downers Grove, IL: InterVarsity Press, 1994.

Advanced

Dunn, J. D. G. *Romans*. 2 vols. WBC. Waco, TX: Word, 1988.

Fitzmyer, J. *Romans*. AB. New York: Doubleday, 1993.

Moo, D. J. *The Epistle to the Romans*. NICNT. Grand Rapids: Eerdmans, 1996.

Schreiner, T. R. *Romans*. BECNT. Grand Rapids: Baker, 1998.

NOTES

1. C. Blomberg, *The Historical Reliability of the Gospels*, (Leicester, England: Inter-Varsity Press, 1987), p. 223.

2. The original article can be found in *HTR* 56 (1963): 199–215 and later was reprinted in K. Stendahl, *Paul among Jews and Gentiles* (Philadelphia: Fortress, 1976). See also Sanders, *Paul and Palestinian Judaism*.

3. D. Moo, *The Epistle to the Romans* (NICNT; Grand Rapids: Eerdmans, 1996), 28.

4. J. D. G. Dunn, *Romans* (WBC; Waco, TX: Word, 1988), 1:lxiii.

5. See F. Thielman, *Paul and the Law*: *A Contextual Approach* (Downer's Grove, IL: Inter-Varsity Press, 1994).

6. D. Moo, *Romans* (NIVAC; Grand Rapids: Zondervan, 2000), 26.

CHAPTER 19

EPHESIANS AND COLOSSIANS

The theater of Ephesus and the Arcadian way, which led to the port of Ephesus

Map of Asia Minor

In Jerusalem after his third missionary journey, Paul was greeted with hostility by the temple leadership and arrested. Following two years imprisonment in Caesarea (Acts 23–26), Paul was transferred to Rome, awaiting trial (Acts 27–28). Most scholars think he wrote four so-called "prison epistles" while at Rome: Ephesians, Colossians, Philippians, and Philemon.

Ephesians and Colossians reveal how deeply these churches were rooted in Hellenistic thought. Paul does not debate Jewish law with these churches as he did in Romans and Galatians. Instead, he strengthens the church against the influences of Jewish and pagan religious and philosophical systems. He emphasizes that faith in Christ requires no supplemental religious experience drawn from the local temple rituals. In Ephesians, Paul offers perhaps his most eloquent profile for the life and mission of a unified Christian church. In Colossians, he

PAUL'S IMPRISONMENT IN ROME

In antiquity prisons held people accused of crimes until their sentencing. Then they were freed, executed, or exiled. A judge might coerce obedience by jailing an offender, but imprisonment was rarely a form of punishment.

Prisons were oppressive, dark, holding cells, but Paul's circumstances in Rome were significantly different; he seems to have been allowed to rent an apartment (Acts 28:16), though such rooms were expensive and often dangerous because of their construction. Seneca decries "tenement walls crumbled and cracked and out of line" (*De Beneficiis* 6.15.7). Strabo reminds us how many fires the city witnessed (*Geography* 5.3.7).

Paul was probably chained to a soldier, but he could receive visitors and speak freely. He also likely took advantage of the public food rations provided for all Roman citizens over age fourteen residing in the city.[1]

paints an awe-inspiring picture of the cosmic Christ, who stands above all creation. In both letters, Paul outlines how to be a Christian within the Greco-Roman milieu and how the Christian faith shapes social categories such as marriage, family, slavery, and politics.

THE CONTEXT OF COLOSSIANS

Colossae was a small town in the Roman province of Asia, located about a hundred miles east of Ephesus and close to two more prominent neighbors, Laodicea and Hierapolis. Because of its fertile soil, Colossae produced figs and olives, as well as "Colossian" wool, known for its distinctive black color (see Strabo, *Geography* 12.8.16).

Phrygian Worship of Cybele

Rome's conquest of Colossae introduced Roman religious deities and practices, but these had not percolated down into the local population. Generally, people followed traditional Phrygian gods and goddesses. Agdistis (Gk. Cybele) was the most popular goddess in Anatolia and was worshiped in numerous cultic festivals along with her consort, Attis. Cybele had compelled Attis to castrate himself so that he would not be drawn to another lover.

Cybele was a defender of mountains and fortresses. She is often pictured with a crown, which resembles the walls of the city.

Worshipers of Cybele sang loudly, played flutes, drums, and cymbals, and danced wildly. Her more devoted male worshipers might castrate themselves in their frenzied adulation, mimicking Attis (Ovid, *Fasti* 4.181). Paul may be referencing such practices in his comments about "their self-imposed worship . . . and their harsh treatment of the body" (2:23).

Jewish Worship in Asia Minor

Cities like Colossae also hosted large Jewish populations. Estimates suggest as many as 11,000 Jews, who practiced Jewish piety, such as reverence for the temple and observance of Sabbath, festivals, circumcision, and food laws. "Jews from . . . Asia" stirred up the crowd against Paul in Jerusalem, claiming "this is the man who teaches everyone everywhere against our people and our law and this place [temple]" (Acts 21:28).

Stoicheia and Astrology

In antiquity, most people lived in great fear of angelic or spiritual forces. They were terrified of powers emanating from astral bodies, from the underworld, even from ancestors. Unpredictable gods and goddesses and inscrutable Fate made daily life unpredictable.

The Greco-Roman world believed that their daily lives were tightly controlled by the sun, moon, planets, and stars, which explain their deep involvement with astrology and the zodiac. A second-century AD papyrus collection of magical spells includes this advice to an initiate:

> Now when the god comes in, do not stare at his face, but look at his feet ... then ask, "Master, what is fated for me?" And he will tell you even about your star, and what kind of daimon [spirit] you have and your horoscope and where you may live and where you will die. And if you hear something bad, do not cry out or weep, but ask that he may wash it off or circumvent it, for this god can do everything. (*Papyri Graecae Magicae* 13.708–14)

At the beginning of the Empire period, Roman rulers were favorably disposed to astrologers and often relied on their predictions of the future. This coin shows Augustus with his zodiac sign, Capricorn.

Paul's warning in 2:8 about the "elemental spirits [*stoicheia*] of the universe" (NRSV) fits this context.

Jewish communities were not exempt from such speculation. The *Testament of Solomon* 18:1 – 5 (first century BC) reports "Solomon's" experience:

> Then I commanded another demon to appear before me. There came to me thirty-six heavenly bodies, their heads like formless dogs.... I asked them, saying, "Well, who are you?" With one voice, they said, "We are thirty-six heavenly bodies [*stoicheia*], the world rulers of the darkness of this age."... Then I, Solomon, summoned the first spirit and said to him, "Who are you?" He replied, "I am the first decan of the zodiac (and) I am called Ruax. I cause heads of men to suffer pain and I cause their temples to throb."

Efforts to control these powers involved magic, which attempts to manipulate supernatural forces. Pagans and some Jews used magic to win another's love, to beat their competitor at the games, or to prosper in business. Some Jews incorporated magic with esteemed Jewish figures such as Moses and Solomon. These Jews were eclectic: God was entreated to handle some concerns, while magic was chosen to fix other problems. It is precisely this false dichotomy that Paul addresses in Colossians.

Often magic was enhanced by ascetic practices. For example, fasting supposedly enhanced magic's potency. Asceticism was also advocated by the mystery cults. A devotee of Isis wishing to join her cult was required to undergo ten days of purification, which included fasting.[2] The Colossian "philosophy's" admonition, "Do not handle! Do not taste! Do not touch!" (2:21), is similar to the taboos listed in the magical incantations and initiation rites. The Colossians heard claims from numerous sources that a god/goddess could be persuaded or a magical spell enhanced by ascetic practices.

THE MESSAGE OF COLOSSIANS

The Colossian believers are being attacked on two fronts, one ideological (who controlled the universe?) and one sociological (should the Colossians separate from larger society through asceticism?). These two tensions threatened to

Attis, Cybele's consort, is identified by his signature Phrygian headdress.

pull apart the church, because they worked against each other. Asceticism tends to draw tight boundaries around its group, but the borders of the Colossian beliefs were eclectic and porous. Their "philosophy" promoted that Christians could believe in many different powers in the world, but they could only manipulate that spiritual world through narrow ascetic practices.

Paul speaks to the ideological issues by proclaiming Christ as the all-powerful deity, in control of all things (1:15 – 19). He attacks the problem of asceticism by declaring that in baptism, a believer has put off the old self (2:12). All efforts to control the body with self-abasing practices are misguided and futile.

The Colossians saw around them frenzied and violent religious celebrations. But it was not their previous worship of a pagan deity that troubled Paul. Rather, the insidious quality of eclecticism within paganism threatened to undermine the exclusivity of Christ. Their mindset undermined the singular claims of Christ's sovereignty over *all* spiritual forces. Paul had to teach them that Christ could not be manipulated by external acts of ritual piety (2:20 – 23).

OUTLINE OF COLOSSIANS

I. Greetings (1:1 – 2)

II. Thanksgiving (1:3 – 14)

III. Majesty of Christ (1:15 – 23)

IV. Mystery of Christ (1:24 – 29)

V. Call to Steadfastness (2:1 – 7)

VI. Warnings against the "Philosophy" (2:8 – 23)

VII. Practical Exhortations (3:1 – 4:6)

    A. The Basis of Christian Living (3:1 – 4)
    B. The Christian's New Life (3:5 – 17)
    C. The Christian Household (3:18 – 4:1)
    D. Prayer for Paul in Prison (4:2 – 6)

VIII. Personal Notes and Closing (4:7 – 18)

Paul focuses on four tasks in Colossians. After his introduction and thanksgiving, he describes the divine glory and majesty of Christ (1:15 – 2:7) and contrasts this exalted vision with the debased viewpoint of the "philosophy" (2:8 – 23). He then turns to the behaviors characteristic of a believer convinced of the power and authority of Jesus Christ (3:1 – 4:6). He ends with a list of greetings (4:7 – 18).

ELCHASAI, AN EXAMPLE OF CHRISTIAN SYNCRETISM

During the reign of Trajan (AD 98 – 117), a teacher named Elchasai mixed ideas from Judaism, astrology, and magic together with Christian teachings. The resulting syncretistic philosophy encouraged its followers to plan their lives around a calendar focused on Sabbath and cycles of the moon. The group cautioned against the powerful and evil stars (angels) that threatened humans. They promoted a syncretistic Christianity that blended Jewish rites with astrological speculations. Hippolytus declared Elchasai's teachings as heresy.[3]

Paul seems to have a chiastic structure here. "Chiasmus" is rooted in the Greek letter X (chi) and refers to an argument whose central point is in its middle, with parallel points made on each side. This was common in the Old Testament and in first-century rhetoric, and some scholars today argue for extensive use of chiasmus by Paul.[4] The body of the Colossians letter fits this pattern well. It contains the teachings about the exalted Christ and the resulting behaviors and attitudes of his faithful followers (1:15 – 2:7 and 3:1 – 4:6). The center holds Paul's denunciation of the aberrant philosophy (2:8 – 23). In this structure, Paul's argument with his adversaries is central, and we can understand why he writes the letter.

Emperors promoted their power through inscriptions on coins. Julius Caesar stressed his own divinity by associating himself with Aeneas, the mythical founder of the Roman race and Venus, Aeneas' mother.

Paul writes with Timothy, his solid supporter and young pastor (1:1). The Colossian church is made up largely of Gentiles, who have turned from paganism to follow Jesus (3:7). Paul does not know the Colossians personally (2:1), for his coworker Epaphras founded the church (1:7, 4:12).

In his thanksgiving, Paul mentions several important ideas that play a key role in his subsequent argument: faith, love, hope, wisdom, darkness, and kingdom. The first three are well known to readers of Paul, for these are used extensively elsewhere (e.g., 1 Cor. 13; 1 Thess. 1:3). His specific battle with the "philosophy" at Colossae centers on the definition of wisdom, which Paul understands as God's discrete acts of history, especially through Israel and Jesus, the Messiah. The "philosophy" has defined wisdom as esoteric and hidden knowledge of heavenly spirits, planets and stars, and powers such as Fate. None of these has any connection to actual history.

Paul repudiates the "philosophy's" teachings about the nature of the world and contends that they leave the person in darkness. God's kingdom has brought in a new age with Christ's death and resurrection. The old things — the elemental spirits and unseen powers — fade before the surpassing power of God in Christ. In 1:15 – 20, he provides a breathtaking description of the divine Christ, in which each characteristic counters the "philosophy's" view of Christ and the world.

Christ is the image of God (1:15); he carries all the power and authority of the Most High God. Through him creation came into being (1:16), including the unseen world of spirits, demonic forces, planetary powers, and Fate. All things are also ruled by Christ. He represents ultimate power, the power of God. Paul describes Christ three times as the "head" (1:18, 2:10, 19) of the body, the church; that is, he is the source of life for the church (2:19). Christ has been raised, and Paul describes him as "the firstborn from among the dead" (1:18). Both these descriptions intimately connect Christ to the church and its hope of resurrection.

Because God's fullness resides in Christ (1:19), Christ can reconcile humans to himself. This incredible power breaks any holds that capricious gods/goddesses or planetary powers might have on humans. Christ reveals the mystery of God, which is the reconciliation of people to God through him (1:27). This mystery is firmly rooted in the story of Jesus' life in Palestine, not in esoteric musings about mythic cycles of dead and rising gods/goddesses.

If all this is true, the Colossian believers must live in line with this reality. Their behavior will change based on three truths: their position in Christ, their new life in Christ, and their new nature. (1) They have been raised with Christ (3:1), so they can now seek heavenly things. If the Colossians want to know about heaven, they must do so through Christ, not the elemental spirits. In addition, believers can live in hope of the new age, for although Christ inaugurated the new age with his resurrection, more is still to come. Some day Christ will appear in glory (3:4).

(2) New life in Christ is possible only through death (cf. this same theme in Rom. 6:4; Gal 2:20). Through our union with Christ's death, all evil behaviors, including idolatry, are also put to death (3:5).

(3) A new life results in a new nature (3:10), which reflects the image of Christ (3:10). All ethnic and social boundaries are broken down (3:11), and social relationships within the church are built up (3:12–4:1).

The center of the letter is Paul's attack against the "philosophy." Yet as serious as this disease is, scholars have struggled to understand its nature in the Colossian context. Some have labeled it a Jewish heresy; others see a pagan cult, while still others fall back on general "syncretism." While each of these is true, what provides the central key is the vast influence of magic and folk religion throughout Asia Minor.

The "philosophy" is best understood as an amalgam of Jewish, pagan, and folk religious ideas blended by arrogant teachers within the Colossian church who mocked believers who did not accept their ways (2:16, 18). Paul sees it as linked to human thinking and earthly perspectives. It is part of the present evil age, is founded on human traditions, and leads to a glorification of the flesh. It devalues Christ's unique work of redemption and instead promotes magic to heal illness and control evil forces.

THE CONTEXT OF EPHESIANS

For some scholars, Ephesians is the greatest of all Paul's writings. His eloquence is surpassed only by the depth of his reflection on the nature and mission of Christ's church. Unlike Galatians or Colossians, Paul does not refer to local crises or controversies. Instead, he develops themes that have broad appeal in the churches. Many suggest that Ephesians is a general letter sent to various churches in Asia.

The style of Ephesians is unique. Paul's language is almost liturgical. For example, in the first chapter alone, he writes a single sentence that stretches across twelve verses (1:3–14).

Ephesus was a vital port city along the Aegean Sea, which served Asia Minor by carrying tons of goods to and from Greece. The temple of Artemis was one of the wonders of the ancient world, and people traveled from great distances to see it. Paul spent over two years in Ephesus on his third missionary tour, and this is probably the origin of the church.

THE DIVIDING WALL OF HOSTILITY

Ephesians 2:14 refers to "the dividing wall of hostility" that has been broken down in Christ. When Jews entered the temple precincts, they walked across a public court and then came to fourteen steps on top of which stood a five-foot wall. This wall surrounded the inner sanctuaries (*Ant.* 15.11.5 [417]; *War* 5.5.2 [193]). Gentiles could enter the "outer court," but signs posted on this perimeter wall warned that no uncircumcised male could go beyond it without risking death.

Paul's announcement is dramatic: Christ has torn down this dividing wall through his death. Jews and Gentiles now stand as one as they approach God.

OUTLINE OF EPHESIANS

I. Greeting and Prayer (1:1–23)

    A. Greetings (1:1–2)
    B. Prayer of Praise (1:3–14)
    C. Prayer of Blessing (1:15–23)

II. The Church and the Work of Christ (2:1–3:21)

    A. The Mystery of Our Salvation (2:1–10)
    B. The Mystery of the Church (2:11–22)
    C. The Ministry of the Church (3:1–21)

III. The Obligations of the Church (4:1–6:16)

    A. Unity (4:1–16)
    B. Righteousness (4:17–5:20)
    C. Authority and Order (5:21–6:9)
    D. Spiritual Warfare (6:10–17)

IV. Closing Exhortation (6:18–24)

THE MESSAGE OF EPHESIANS

Two clues in the letter point to Paul's purpose: He is writing to Gentiles, and he is concerned about cosmic spiritual powers. Paul identifies his readers as Gentiles (2:11; 3:1) and cautions them not to return to their former ways (4:17). Rather, he turns their attention to the majesty and power of Christ, who unites Jew and Gentile in his church.

Paul uses various terms translated as "powers" more frequently in Ephesians than in any other letter (1:19, 21; 2:2; 3:10, 15; 4:27; 6:11, 12, 16). He does not want Gentiles to fall

Against the backdrop of Ephesus' marketplace Paul proclaimed the gospel of Jesus.

back into their old habits, relying on spiritual forces, astrology, and magic instead of the superior power of Christ. He writes to shape and reinforce their identity as united followers of the all-powerful, cosmic Christ.

If Colossians centers its message on Christology (and how Christ defeats the cosmic powers), Ephesians concentrates on ecclesiology (or the doctrine of the church). The first half (1:3–3:21) is a lengthy and eloquent prayer for the life of the church and includes the benefits enjoyed by those who have embraced faith in Christ. This prayer is like an overture in which Paul describes not only the quality of the personal life of the Christian—a theme that will find attention in later chapters—but the miracle of the church's corporate life: Jews and Gentiles are now becoming one in Christ.

In the second half, Paul offers specific pictures of what such oneness looks like. Paul contends for one body, one baptism, one faith, and one God and Father of all (4:4–6). He concludes that the gifts extended by God—apostles, prophets, evangelists, pastors, and teachers (4:11)—enable believers to build the church. He calls the Ephesians to reject a lifestyle filled with greed, anger, and impurity (5:3–5).

Along with general indictments against shameful behavior, Paul offers positive exhortation for the family (see also Col. 3:18–4:1). In Greco-Roman society, the family was a microcosm of the state, and even of the universe. Each element knew its proper relation to the others. A hierarchy existed for the good of all. In society, the wealthy few must not lord it over the poor masses, and the poor must not greedily desire the position of the wealthy.

Against this backdrop, Paul explains how Christ's work on the cross redeems even ordinary relationships. He begins this section with an overall principle, that within the church, the believers should "submit to one another out of reverence for Christ" (Eph. 5:21). Paul then details how such behavior should look between husband and wife, parents and children, and slaves and masters. People likely filled several roles, so that a wife might also be a slave owner, and a child might be either a slave or an owner's son or daughter. Slaves could not be legally married, but they might have informal unions. Paul is concerned that in all these relationships, humility and service to each other out of love for Christ must be foremost. Thus a master cannot be harsh with a slave, even if such treatment was legal, because that behavior dishonors their Master, Jesus. Again, a husband cannot be harsh with his wife, even if such behavior was legal, because that contradicts Christ's own love for his bride, the church.

Paul's description of husbands and wives begins at 5:21, not 5:22. In verse 21 he calls for all believers to "submit to one another out of reverence for Christ." Verse 22 depends on the grammar of verse 21, for it has no verb (literally it translates: "wives to your husbands as to the Lord"). Paul asks wives to be subject to their husbands in the same way as all members of the church submit to each other.

In antiquity women were viewed as incomplete men. According to Aristotle (*Generation of Animals* 729b, 737–38), if a fetus comes to full term, it will be a male; if something interferes with its proper development, it will be female. Thus, females are substandard humans, physically and intellectually inferior. This view was widespread and influenced the thinking of the church for a millennium.

Greco-Roman families ordered themselves with this fundamental assumption. Daughters were under the legal control of their fathers. At marriage, many young brides remained under their father's control even while moving to their husband's house. This was a new development in Roman history, for in the early Republic, most fathers transferred brides to their husband's control. Paul, by contrast, sees deference as a universal calling—not only one held by women. When he reaches for a metaphor for men in a marriage relationship (5:25), he underscores how Christ did not rule but served until he died.

Paul, under no illusions that his exhortations will be easy, uses a military analogy to reinforce his convictions. His readers' faithfulness will be attacked not only by social pressures, but also by spiritual forces hoping to undermine the church. Each believer must wear armor that soldiers used to protect them from enemy assault—such as a "helmet of salvation" (6:17), the "breastplate of righteousness" (6:14), and the "belt of truth" (6:14).

THE PROBLEM OF AUTHORSHIP

Ephesians and Colossians provide us with an opportunity to discuss the authorship questions circulating around some of Paul's letters. Since the nineteenth century, scholars have investigated whether Paul wrote all of the letters attributed to him. Few doubts have been raised for Galatians, Romans, and the two Corinthian letters. But for the other letters, critics have pointed to shifts in vocabulary, style, grammar, and general tone. They also suggest historical inconsistencies or anomalies in the letters or changes in ideas, theology, and general worldview. Ephesians and Colossians are often in the center of this debate. Since these two letters depart significantly from Paul's "usual" style, they are frequently viewed as written later, perhaps by one of Paul's students or by someone imitating the apostle.

Scholars argue that we see so many atypical words that the apostle could not have written the letter. For instance, in Ephesians Paul refers to the devil as *diabolos*, but elsewhere generally prefers *satanas*. Why the change? Only in Ephesians does Paul use the phrase "in the heavenly

THE AMANUENSIS OR SECRETARY IN ANCIENT LETTER WRITINGS
Cicero laments the absence of his trusted secretary Tiro, who edited his works. "My poor little studies (or if you like, ours) have simply pined away from longing for you.... When [Pompey] expresses a desire to hear something of mine, I tell him that, without you, I am altogether dumb" (Cicero, *Letters to Friends* 16.10.2 [43]). In rare cases, secretaries composed for their employers. Cicero asked Atticus to write several letters to mutual friends in Cicero's name: "I should like you to write in my name to Basilius and to anyone else you like, even to Servilius, and say whatever you think fit" (Cicero, *Letters to Atticus* 11:5 [216]).

realms" (1.3; 2.6; 3:10; 6:12). In fact, Ephesians has eighty *hapax legomena* (words or expressions that only occur here in his letters). However, note that the uncontested letters have *hapax legomena* as well. Galatians has thirty, and Romans and each Corinthian letter contain about a hundred each. A change in topic or audience may easily require a change in word choice.

Moreover, the style of Ephesians closely resembles those places in Paul's other letters where he is either praying or offering adoration to God (Rom. 8:38–39; 11:33–36). And since so much of Ephesians has a liturgical tone, this may explain the change in the letter's style. Paul tailors his terms to best meet his local audience's situation. Thus, when he speaks of "church" in Ephesians, he has two meanings in mind: a universal or heavenly gathering of believers in fellowship with Christ, and a concrete expression of this new relationship as seen in Jew/Gentile unity (Eph. 3:10).

Questions centering on vocabulary statistics and style must also come to terms with the use of secretaries in antiquity. If secretaries knew how to take dictation and were highly skilled, they used Greek or Latin shorthand (tachygraphy) and wrote down the message later. Some secretaries functioned as editors, with more or less input in the final product. The *amanuensis*, if trusted, could amend a letter so that it would fit the expectations of professional correspondence.

We know that early Christians used scribes. Peter wrote his first letter "with the help of Silas" (1 Peter 5:12). Most scholars agree that Paul used an amanuensis, though he never says *how* he used his secretaries. Tertius, the secretary of Romans, greets the Romans, which means that he was known to them (Rom. 16:22). Romans is a highly polished letter, suggesting that Tertius knew tachygraphy and could write as quickly as Paul spoke. Paul's other

A shield boss fits over the hand grip at the center of the shield. This example, made of silvered tin and bronze, was used by Junius Dubilatus from Legio VIII, in the second century AD.

letters do not show this level of secretarial sophistication. Paul signed his letters, using the standard formula of the time (1 Cor. 16:21; Gal. 6:11; Col. 4:18; 2 Thess. 3:17, Phlm. 19). We have no originals of Paul's letters, so we cannot see what would have been evident to the first readers—two different handwriting scripts. Some scholars even suggest that Luke may have written Ephesians, for he was with Paul in Rome (Col. 4:14), and of the many *hapax legomena* in Ephesians, twenty-five also appear in Luke-Acts.

Other questions have surfaced about Ephesians. If Paul spent over two years in this city, why does he seem unfamiliar with his audience (Eph. 1:15; 3:2–3; 4:21)? Why does he have so few greetings (6:21–24) compared with Romans (Rom. 16)? Note also that a few leading Greek manuscripts do not refer to "Ephesus" in 1:1. Perhaps Ephesians was an *encyclical letter* addressed to a number of churches in Asia Minor, and the name of Ephesus was later attached to it. This would explain its lack of historical detail. An interesting parallel can be found in Colossians 4:16, where Paul tells the Colossians to exchange letters with the Laodiceans. Letters were sometimes exchanged and could address a variety of audiences.

QUESTIONS FOR DISCUSSION ⊙⊙⊙⊙⊙⊙⊙⊙⊙⊙⊙⊙⊙⊙⊙⊙⊙⊙⊙⊙⊙⊙⊙⊙⊙⊙

1. Reconstruct the historical circumstances in Paul's life that lead us to refer to these letters as "prison epistles." What are these four letters?

2. What religious and philosophical pressures in Colossae contributed to Paul's Christology in Colossians?

3. What literary issues contribute to skepticism about Paul's authorship of these letters? How might they be answered?

4. Why were the Colossians interested in supplementing their Christian faith with religious rituals and festivals? What is Paul's answer?

5. What is revolutionary about the church? Does it always live up to its calling?

BIBLIOGRAPHY
Introductory

Arnold, C. E. *Power and Magic: The Concept of Power in Ephesians*. Grand Rapids: Baker, 1989.

_____. *The Colossian Syncretism*. Grand Rapids: Baker, 1996.

Garland, D. E. *Colossians and Philemon*. NIVAC. Grand Rapids: Zondervan, 1998.

Moule, C. F. D. *Studies in Ephesians*. Grand Rapids: Kregel, 1977.

Snodgrass, K. *Ephesians*. NIVAC. Grand Rapids: Zondervan, 1996.

Advanced

Barth, M. *Ephesians*. AB. 2 vols. New York: Doubleday, 1974

Barth, M., and H. Blanke. *Colossians*. AB. New York: Doubleday, 1994.

Best, E. *Essays on Ephesians*. ICC. Edinburgh: T. & T. Clark, 1997.

O'Brien, P. T. *The Letter to the Ephesians*. PNTC. Grand Rapids: Eerdmans, 1999.

_____. *Colossians*. WBC. Dallas: Word, 1982.

NOTES

1. See G. Rickman, *The Corn Supply of Ancient Rome* (Oxford: Clarendon, 1980).

2. See Apuleius, *Metamorphoses* 11:23.

3. Hippolytus, *Against Heresies* 9:11.

4. E. R. Richards, *The Secretary in the Letters of Paul* (Tübingen: Mohr Siebeck, 1991), 140–41, 207–8.

CHAPTER 20

PHILIPPIANS AND PHILEMON

The forum at Philippi in the province of Macedonia

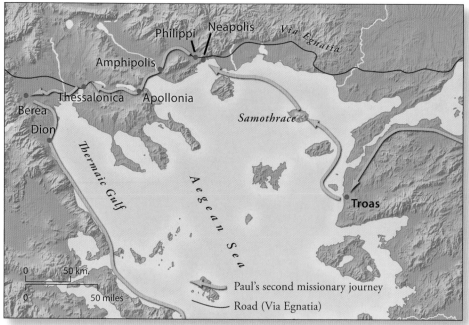

After landing at the harbor in Neapolis, Paul took the Via Egnatia to Philippi

On his second missionary journey, Paul founded the church in Philippi. His mission in the city landed both him and Silas in jail after having been beaten and publicly dishonored (Acts 16:22–32; 1 Thess. 2:2). When Paul writes to the Philippian church, he is again a prisoner, this time in Rome. The persecution he endured in Philippi is now also the experience of the Philippian believers.

Despite the pain he and the first readers suffer, the Philippian letter is filled with tremendous joy (mentioned twelve times in the letter). Paul pens the best-known words from

Left: This marble bollard was used to tie up ships at dock in the Neapolis harbor *Right*: Paul, Silas, Timothy and Luke traveled the Via Egnatia which passed through the center of Philippi.

the letter, "Rejoice in the Lord always" (4:4), while bound with chains and wondering whether he will live or die. He calls the Philippian church not to be afraid of their adversaries but to understand that "it has been granted to you on behalf of Christ not only to believe on him, but also to suffer for him" (1:29).

Paul is also troubled about the Judaizers (see below). In addition, the church is experiencing internal strife involving two female leaders. Nevertheless, Paul calls the congregation to humble service, presenting them Christ's example, and assures them that in the final day Christ will be recognized as Lord by every being in God's universe.

A tetradrachm minted at Amphipolis, the capital of the "first district" of Macedonia. The inscription reads *Makedonōn prōtēs* ("First of the Macedonians").

THE CITY OF PHILIPPI

Paul arrived at Philippi after crossing the Aegean Sea during his second missionary journey. He and his companions (Silas, Timothy, and Luke) had set sail from Troas to Philippi's port city, Neapolis (16:11).

From Neapolis, Paul and his companions traveled to Philippi, located some ten miles (sixteen kilometers) inland. Midway through the journey they would have stopped for water at an ancient inn (*mansio*) before finally passing through the Neapolis Gate to enter Philippi.

The victory of Mark Antony and Octavian over Brutus and Cassius at the Battle of Philippi is commemorated in this coin.

When the Romans defeated the Macedonian empire in the mid-second century BC, Philippi (named after the father of Alexander the Great) came under Roman control. The Romans divided the former Macedonian kingdom into four districts. Philippi was located in the first district, although the principal city there was Amphipolis (some late Latin manuscripts of Acts 16:12 say Philippi was "a city of the first district of Macedonia, a colony" instead of being "the leading city of that district").

Philippi became a Roman colony and was named *Colonia Iulia Philippensis*, in honor of Julius Caesar; shortly thereafter it became *Colonia Augusta Iulia Philippensis*, honoring Augustus. This city prospered since it presided over an extensive territory (*territorium*) and was granted legal status as an Italian city. This was legally *Italian soil* in Macedonia. Thus, no land or poll taxes were levied against the

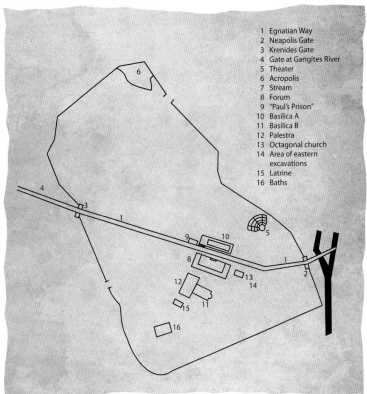

1 Egnatian Way
2 Neapolis Gate
3 Krenides Gate
4 Gate at Gangites River
5 Theater
6 Acropolis
7 Stream
8 Forum
9 "Paul's Prison"
10 Basilica A
11 Basilica B
12 Palestra
13 Octagonal church
14 Area of eastern
    excavations
15 Latrine
16 Baths

The city of Philippi

Since Philippi was a Roman colony, the majority of the inscriptions from the city are written in Latin. This one honors a Roman named Cornelius

colonists, who enjoyed full Roman citizenship. The law and judicial system were Roman. The main language in the streets was Latin, not Greek. However, four of the people we know from the Philippian story have Greek names (Lydia, Epaphroditus, Euodia, Syntyche; see Acts 16:14. Phil. 2:25; 4:2); only one was Latin (Clement in 4:3). This may say something about the social classes that were most open to the gospel, since in this city the Latin-speaking Romans held the wealth and the power.

THE SETTING OF PHILIPPIANS

Luke tells the story of the founding of the Philippian church in Acts 16. Paul arrived in the city around AD 49 or 50 after visiting the churches in Syria and Asia Minor where he delivered the decree of the Jerusalem Council (Acts 15:36, 41; 16:1, 4, 6). Paul headed east down the Cilician Road to the Roman province of Asia (Ephesus was likely his goal), but was "kept by the Holy Spirit from preaching the word in the province of Asia" (16:6). Silas accompanied Paul and, since he was a prophet, the prohibition was likely communicated through him (15:32). Likewise, "the Spirit of Jesus" did not allow Paul to head north to the province of Bithynia and Pontus (16:7). He, Silas, and Timothy (15:40; 16:1–3) traveled to the western port of Troas.

This city was a Roman colony and known as one of the great seaports of antiquity, having a population between 30,000 and 100,000. In a vision (Acts 16:9), Paul saw a Macedonian man (perhaps dressed in their well-known broad brimmed hat), urging him to travel to Macedonia to help them. Plutarch noted at the end of the first century AD that "in popular belief . . . it is only in sleep that men receive inspiration from on high"

When Paul entered Philippi he joined a group of Jews who worshiped at the river adjacent to the city (Acts 16:13). One possible site: the Krenides River.

Left: The harbor of Neapolis, the port city of Philippi. *Right*: The "Python spirit" which possessed the slave girl in Philippi was associated with the ancient oracular site Delphi in Greece.

(*Moralia* 589D). Paul and his companions responded to the vision as a divine summons (cf. Num. 12:6) and embarked by sea sailing west to Macedonia.

The trip from Troas to Neapolis was favored by appropriate winds, making this a mere two-day journey. Traveling the other direction took three days longer (cf. 20:6). Paul and his company depart from Neapolis and head to Philippi on the Via Egnatia, the great Roman military and commercial artery that traversed the whole province of Macedonia. Philippi did not have a large enough Jewish population to form a synagogue (ten men were required in order to establish a synagogue; cf. *m. Sanh.* 1:6; *Pirque Aboth* 3:6). Instead, a group of women gather by a river outside the city gate in "a place of prayer," a word that can denote a building but here refers simply to a place where prayers are offered.

Paul's first convert is, surprisingly, neither a Macedonian nor a man. Lydia (Acts 16:14) is from Thyatira (see Rev. 2:18–29), a city of the region of Lydia (hence her name) in Asia Minor. Thyatira was the center of a purple-dye industry, and Lydia has come to Philippi to ply her trade. She embraces the gospel, and both she and the members of her household (including slaves) believe and are baptized (16:14–15). She is wealthy enough to own a home and becomes the patroness of the gospel messengers while they are in the city. Her house is the meeting place of this first church in Macedonia (16:15, 40).

The second woman mentioned in Acts 16 is on the opposite end of the social spectrum. She is a slave girl possessed by a spirit and engaged in divination for pay, with all the profits going to her owners (Acts 16:16; in *De Divinatione* 1.5.9 Cicero defines "divination" as "the foreseeing and foretelling of events considered as happening by chance").

A high-order oracular spirit possesses the slave-girl. Her owners would have paid a great price for this woman with such supernatural talent. When Paul cast the spirit out of her, their profits are drastically cut. Both the spirit and their hopes of gain have "gone out" (lit.) (16:18-19)! According to Lucian, a Greek author who wrote *Alexander the False Prophet*, Alexander engaged in divination and was able to charge one drachma and two obols per question, which totaled something like 70,000 to 80,000 drachmas a year (a Greek drachma being equal to a Roman denarius, the wage for a day's labor). This was great profit, indeed.

The girl's owners extract revenge. They seize Paul and Silas and drag them "into the marketplace to face the authorities" (16:19). The accusation against them does not mention the financial loss but plays on prejudice and Roman pride. The first accusation is, "These men are Jews" (16:20). Anti-Jewish sentiments were rife in the Roman world. Men like Philostratus voiced the common prejudice that "the Jews have long been in revolt not only against the Romans but against humanity" (*Apollonius* 5.33).

Second, Paul and Silas "are throwing our city into an uproar" (16:20). The Romans loved order above everything else and were determined to maintain it.

Finally, the two are accused of "advocating customs unlawful for us as Romans to accept or practice" (16:21). In ancient society all people were expected to follow their ancestral traditions. The Roman Livy remarked, "How often ... has the task been assigned to the magistrates of forbidding the introduction of foreign cults ... and of annulling every system of sacrifice except that performed in the Roman way" (*Hist.* 39.8–19).

The scene that follows is frightening and a great affront to Paul and Silas's honor. They are attacked by the crowd, stripped, and beaten with rods under direction of the civil authorities. They are thrown into jail and confined to the innermost cell, feet secured in stocks (16:22–24; cf. 1 Thess. 2:2; Phil. 1:30). Not many months afterward, Paul recounts the incident to the Thessalonians: "We had previously suffered and been treated outrageously in Philippi, as you know" (1 Thess. 2:2), and later he reminds the Philippians of the suffering he experienced in the city (Phil. 1:30). The magistrates' actions, however, violate Roman law, for Paul and Silas are also "Roman citizens" (Acts 16:37). Beating a Roman citizen without due process was a great crime. "To bind a Roman citizen is a crime, to flog him is an abomination, to slay him is almost an act of murder" (Cicero, *Against Verres* 2.5.66.170). Heavy penalties were extracted on anyone who treated a Roman citizen in such an illegal manner (16:37–40).

Despite such hostility, humiliation, and suffering, Luke emphasizes God's intervention. As Paul and Silas sing hymns to God at midnight, an earthquake shakes the prison, opens the doors, and unfetters the chains (Acts 16:25–26). Most Romans would view this as a divine omen. Any guard who allowed a prisoner to escape was liable to the punishment of the prisoner (*Code of Justinian* 9.4.4); thus, the Philippian jailer seeks to take his own life (16:27). But he is assured by Paul that nobody has escaped. He therefore asks Paul and Silas, "Sirs, what must I do to be saved?" (16:29–30). The response has echoed through the church for centuries: "Believe in the Lord Jesus, and you will be saved—you and your household" (16:31; cf. 11:14; 16:15). His household would have included slaves as well as family members. In Roman culture the father of the family (*pater familias*) had a decisive role regarding the religious practices of the household. But Luke also adds that each member of the household hears the Word of God, believes, and is baptized (16:32–34). Before leaving town and heading to Thessalonica, Paul meets with the Philippian believers in Lydia's house (16:40).

Every tourist to Philippi is taken to this site and told that it is place where Paul was imprisoned. There is no evidence, however, that this structure was used as a prison in the first century

PAUL WRITES TO THE PHILIPPIANS

The Philippian church stayed in contact with Paul after his first visit by sending him offerings early on when he was in Thessalonica (Phil. 1:5; 4:15–16) and again while he was imprisoned in Rome (4:10–19). The church has recently dispatched Epaphroditus with this gift for Paul (2:25; 4:18). This church, along with other Macedonian congregations, also displayed extraordinary generosity in sending relief aid to the Jerusalem church (2 Cor. 8:1–5).

In his letter, Paul acknowledged the Philippians' generosity and offers commendation for Epaphroditus as he returns to Philippi (he is the one who likely carries this letter, though the explanation about his illness may indicate the need for some explanation about whether he accomplished his task for Paul). Paul also hopes soon to send Timothy to the church and

LETTERS OF COMMENDATION

Embedded in Philippians are two letters of commendation, one for Timothy (2:19–24) and another for Epaphroditus, the Philippians' messenger to Paul. Pseudo-Demetrius, who wrote on epistolary theory, described this type of letter:

> The commendatory type, which we write on behalf of one person to another, mixing in praise ... in the following manner:
>
> So-and-so, who is conveying this letter to you, has been tested by us and is loved on account of his trustworthiness. You will do well if you deem him worthy of hospitality both for my sake and his, and indeed for your own. For you will not be sorry if you entrust to him, in any matter you wish, either words or deeds of a confidential nature. Indeed, you, too, will praise him to others when you see how useful he can be in everything.[1]

offers another letter of commendation for him, who will gather news for Paul about the church (2:19–24).

While Paul acknowledges the gift he has received from the Philippians, he never specifically says "Thank you" (see 4:13–20). Note what Seneca writes: "Not to return gratitude for benefits is a disgrace, and the whole world counts it as such" (3.1.1). A person was socially obligated to return thanks. In acknowledging the Philippians' gift, however, Paul makes it clear that he is not seeking more benefits from them (4:17). He frames their generosity as a sacrifice to God and as participation in the cause of the gospel (4:18, 14–15). In the end, God is the One who will repay them for the benefit they have conferred on Paul (4:19). This is truly hearty thanks as the reciprocity comes from God himself.

OUTLINE OF PHILIPPIANS

I. Epistolary Greetings (1:1–2)

II. Thanksgiving and Prayers for the Philippians (1:3–11)

III. Body of the Letter (1:12–4:20)

    A. Paul's Imprisonment, Anticipated Release, Either through Life or Death (1:12–26)
    B. Exhortation to Unity (1:27–2:18)
        1. The Call for Unity (1:27–2:4)
        2. The Example of Christ (2:5–11)
        3. Corporate Conduct (2:12–18)
    C. Letters of Commendation for Timothy and Epaphroditus (2:19–30)
    D. Warning against Incursion of the Judaizers (3:1–21)
        1. Watch Out for the "Mutilators of the Flesh (3:1–4a)
        2. Paul's Past and Present Values and Credentials (3:4b–14)
        3. Following Paul's and Other's Example (3:15–21)
    E. Final Exhortations: Stand Firm, Be United, Follow Paul's Teaching and Example (4:1–9)
    F. Thanks for the Philippians' Generosity (4:10–20)

IV. Final Greetings and Blessing (4:21–23)

In addition, Philippians contains the marks of a letter of friendship. In the ancient world such letters stressed reciprocity in giving and receiving benefits and included notes about how physical absence did not imply absence in heart (1:27; 2:12). Psuedo-Demetrius presents a model of this kind of letter: "Even though I have been separated from you for a long time, I suffer this in body only. For I can never forget you or the impeccable way we were raised together from the childhood up."[2] Philippians abounds with expressions of affection (1:7–8; 4:1), emphasizes Paul's prayers for them and their prayers for him (1:4, 19), and stresses the church's partnership with him in suffering for the gospel (1:29–30; 2:17–18).

As Paul writes the Philippians, they are facing hostility in the city (1:27–30). The same antagonism Paul and Silas experienced in Philippi has spilled over into the church. Paul calls the church to hold firmly to their faith and to shine as lights in a dark world (2:14–16). Adherence to the gospel means participating in practices that appear anti-Roman (Acts 16:20–21). Perhaps this is why Paul emphasizes that "our citizenship is in heaven" (Phil. 3:20) and that "whatever happens to me, you must live in a manner worthy of the Good News about Christ, as citizens of heaven" (1:27 NLT). Paul reminds the church that the sufferings they endure for the gospel are the same as those he is presently facing in Rome (1:12–26, 30).

The Philippians' opponents are not confined to their persecutors. Paul warns them about the Judaizers (see Ch. 14 on Galatians), using rather strong language: "Watch out for those dogs, those evildoers, those mutilators of the flesh. For it is we who are the circumcision, we who serve God by his Spirit, who boast in Christ Jesus, and who put no confidence in the flesh" (3:2–3). These Judaizers are attempting to turn Gentile believers into Jewish proselytes in order to be saved, demanding especially the Gentiles' submission to circumcision and dietary laws (Acts 15:1). This letter simply warns the believers about them without suggesting that they have already put down roots in Philippi.

There is, however, another group of opponents mentioned in this letter, whom Paul characterizes as "enemies of the cross of Christ" (3:17–19). Are these the Philippians' persecutors (1:27–28) or are they the Judaizers (3:1–6)? Whatever their identification, Paul calls the Philippian church to follow his example and that of others (3:17) and conduct themselves as citizens of heaven, who live in expectation of the coming of the Savior, the Lord Jesus Christ (3:20–21).

The church is also experiencing some internal tensions. In 4:2–3 Paul calls on two leading women in the church, Euodia and Syntyche, "to be of the same mind in the Lord" (cf. 2:2). These women were Paul's co-workers (4:3). Earlier, Paul appeals for concord within the congregation (1:27; 2:1–4), so perhaps the dispute has spilled over into the church itself. Paul's exhortation does not imply that their relationship has degenerated into enmity; in fact, he commends these women highly: "They have contended at my side in the cause of the gospel, along with Clement and the rest of my co-workers, whose names are in the book of life" (4:3).

Paul writes this letter according to the ancient customs of letter writing, beginning with the name of the author, followed by the name of the recipient and an opening greeting (1:1–2). He begins the body proper with a thanksgiving for the church, woven with a prayer (1:3–11). The body of the letter comprises the bulk of the composition (1:12–4:20), after which Paul closes with final greetings (4:21–23). While ancient letters ended with good wishes for health, Paul prefers to end with a benediction (v. 23).

Authorship

Philippians very early received wide acceptance as an authentic letter of Paul. It was ascribed to Paul by Irenaeus, Clement of Alexandria, and Tertullian. Around AD 135, Polycarp wrote a letter to the church in which he mentions Paul's previous correspondence to them (*Philippians* 3:2). Most today consider this letter a genuine Pauline letter.

HUMILITY

Paul underscores Christ's self-humiliation and offers Christ's self-sacrifice as an example for the Philippian believers (2:1–8). But in the Roman world, the type of reversal of status that Christ willfully endured was considered degrading. The "humble" person was someone of inferior social status (James 1:9). Such a person had little social power in comparison with mighty rulers (Luke 1:52). They were unable to influence society by means of their wealth, social standing, or political position.

To "humble" others was to weaken them (Diodorus Siculus 19.67.3) and to "humble" oneself was to degrade oneself (Plutarch, *Moralia* 116E). Yet Christ came as someone who submitted himself to humiliation, to the point of taking the status of a slave and submitting to death. His honor came from the Father, who "exalted him to the highest place" (2:7–11).

Although Paul authored the book, he may have inserted a hymn into the letter. Philippians 2:6–11 has been identified by some as an early hymn to Christ. Most modern translations block out the section in poetic form (see also Col. 1:15–18; 1 Tim. 3:16). But the section diverges somewhat from ancient Greek hymns and should perhaps be viewed as prose that approaches poetic style. In any case, this section teaches about the self-humiliation and exaltation of Christ and is integral to the letter.

Date

One of the most vexing questions of Philippians has to do with its date. While we know that Paul was imprisoned when he wrote Philippians (1:7, 12–14, 17, 30), scholars cannot agree about where he was. While most consider he was in Rome (Acts 28:16, 30, between AD 60 and 62), some argue for an earlier date, either during Paul's captivity in Caesarea (Acts 23:33–26:32) or even in a presumed Ephesian imprisonment that took place during his three-year stay there (19:8, 10; 20:31; cf. 2 Cor. 1:3–11).

Both external evidence and Philippians itself support the Roman imprisonment. In the second century, the Latin prologue to this book (Anti-Marcionite Prologue) identified Rome as the place of composition, as do the postscripts added to a number of New Testament manuscripts. In Philippians, Paul refers to the *praetōrion* (1:13), a company of Caesar's elite personal guard, which numbered as many as a thousand men. This is another marker of the Roman origin of the letter.

This letter envisions various communications between Paul and the Philippians (see 2:25–30 for a number of messages that went back and forth). We should not suppose that special messengers were dispatched for each exchange of news. People heading in a certain direction were commonly encouraged to serve as messengers to carry news and letters. Cicero, for example, once quipped that, though he had no fresh news to share with Atticus, "I cannot refrain from entrusting letters to folk who are bound for Rome" (*Ad Atticum* 8.14.1 [164]).

Paul was imprisoned in Rome when he wrote Philippians. He refers to the elite praetorian guard (here pictured) in 1:13. These soldiers were charged with the protection of the emperor and the suppression of social elements which could cause unrest.

PHILEMON AND ITS SETTING

Philemon is Paul's shortest existing letter. It is about the length of typical personal correspondence in the Roman world. Its content is intensely personal, and we wonder why a letter like this was ever preserved by the early church. Yet one of the most recent commentaries on this book is 561 pages! Obviously, many in both the ancient and modern church have recognized the importance of this brief letter. Why? Philemon tells the story of the runaway slave Onesimus, who encountered Paul in Rome and was converted to Christ. Paul sends him back to his master, Philemon, making intercession on Onesimus's behalf. The story is replete with issues surrounding the intersection of grace and slavery.

In reading the letter, we discover a list of familiar names. Paul and Timothy appear in the opening greeting (v. 1; cf. Col. 1:1). The letter itself is filled with references to people we encounter in Colossians, such as Archippus (v. 2; Col. 4:17), Onesimus (v. 10; Col. 4:9),

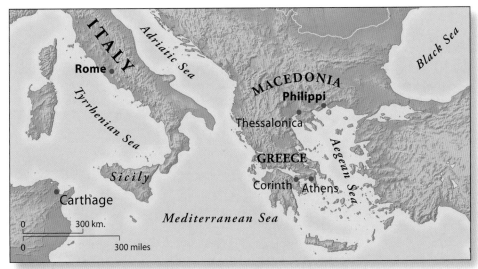

800 miles separated Rome from Philippi. An ordinary traveler could traverse this distance in four to five weeks.

Aristarchus (v. 24; Col. 4:10), Demas, Luke (v. 24; Col. 4:14), and Mark (v. 24; Col. 4:10). Epaphras, the founder of the Colossian church, is also mentioned in both letters (v. 23; Col. 1:7; 4:12). Presumably this letter is written to Philemon in Colossae, and at the same time as that larger letter to the whole church in the city.

Most important, however, is the social location of Philemon, Onesimus, and Paul. Onesimus is a slave (v. 16) who has become a believer, and Paul appeals to his master, Philemon, to receive him back as if he were the apostle himself (v. 17).

Slaves needed to be managed, and at times the control exercised over them turned cruel. Beatings were frequent and could be severe, including flogging and mutilation. If a slave was required to give testimony in court, torture preceded testimony so that, supposedly, the slave would speak the truth. Sexual abuse of slaves was common. If a slave killed, the penalty was burning at the stake or crucifixion. But it was not in the master's best interest to kill a slave, since slaves were a costly investment. Some masters were kind and could show genuine compassion to their slaves, yet others were capricious and cruel (1 Peter 2:18–20).

ROMAN SLAVES

At the beginning of the imperial period, there were approximately two million slaves in Italy alone, with one slave for every three free persons. People became slaves by being taken captive in war and by being kidnapped (1 Tim. 1:10). Convicted criminals and those unable to pay their debts could become slaves. Unwanted children were usually left exposed, where they either died or were found and raised as slaves. Children born to slave parents also became slaves.

Slaves were considered personal property and could be bought and sold. In fact, the more slaves a person had, the greater his or her social status. Slavery was not racial, however, as it was in the New World, nor were they necessarily uneducated. Some slaves were tutors and *paedagogues* (cf. Gal. 3:24). They cooked, cleaned, built buildings and roads, cut and styled hair, did laundry, made clothes, and even managed financial affairs.

Occasionally, slaves ran away, especially if they were treated severely or unjustly (see 1 Peter 2:18). An escaped slave could be crucified or given over to death in a gladiatorial show. To identify their slaves, masters sometimes branded them or required them to wear a metal ID tag (see sidebar). Rewards were offered for the capture of runaway slaves. Onesimus was clearly in a precarious position.

One of the wonders of early Christianity is its ability to absorb people of all genders, races, and socioeconomic classes. Note Galatians 3:28: "There is neither Jew nor Gentile, neither slave nor free, neither male nor female, for you are all one in Christ Jesus." Common faith in Christ leveled the usual stratified social distinctions that separated humanity in general and Roman society in particular.

THE LETTER TO PHILEMON

Paul is imprisoned when he writes this letter (vv. 1, 9–10, 13, 23), likely in Rome (see Colossians). During his captivity, he encounters Onesimus, who becomes a convert to Christ under Paul's ministry (v. 10). We have no idea how these two meet. Perhaps Onesimus is identified as a runaway and is imprisoned before being returned to his master. Another possibility is that Onesimus seeks Paul out since he is in trouble and surmises that Paul may have some influence with his Christian master. In any case, Onesimus responds to the gospel, and now Paul is able to call him a "dear brother," whom he even commends to the Colossian church (v. 16; cf. Col. 4:9).

OUTLINE OF PHILEMON

I. Epistolary Greeting (vv. 1–3)

II. Opening Thanksgiving (vv. 4–7)

III. The Body of the Letter (vv. 8–22)

    A. The Initial Appeal (vv. 8–11)
    B. Onesimus's Return (vv. 12–16)
    C. The Final Appeal (vv. 17–21)
    D. A Room Request (v. 22)

IV. Final Greetings and Blessing (vv. 23–25)

Things could be difficult for Onesimus upon returning to Colossae. But Paul appeals to his master, Philemon, to receive him not as a slave but as a brother (v. 16) and to treat him with leniency. He sends Onesimus back with clear signs of his deep affection for this new believer (v. 12), noting to Philemon that he would like to keep Onesimus as an assistant (vv. 12–14). Paul has a keen sense of God's sovereignty here. Although he makes no excuse for Onesimus's wrongdoing, Paul points out God's hand in the unfolding events. Onesimus was separated from Philemon for a short time in order that Philemon might have him back forever as a brother (vv. 15–16). This slave, whose name means "useful," has become truly that (v. 11).

Paul implies that Onesimus may have done some wrong to Philemon (vv. 17–19). Paul himself vows to pay any debt he owes, but also reminds Philemon of the spiritual debt he owes Paul (v. 20). In a rather astounding move, Paul takes then the pen from his secretary and writes the final highly personal appeal in his own hand (v. 19). But he is convinced of Philemon's generous character (v. 21). Paul announces a forthcoming visit since he expects his release from captivity (v. 22; cf. Phil. 1:19).

AUTHORSHIP AND DATE
While considerable debate has been generated over the years concerning the Pauline authorship of Colossians (see comments on that letter), few doubts have been raised concerning Philemon. Although Timothy is mentioned along with Paul in 1:1, the first person verbs are in the singular. Moreover, Paul writes in his own hand at one point (v. 19). Timothy does not seem to have had a significant role in the composition of this letter. Perhaps the amanuensis is Timothy himself.

Since the letter was penned at the same time as Colossians, the date can be fixed in the early 60s, during Paul's first Roman imprisonment (see the discussion of Colossians).

QUESTIONS FOR DISCUSSION ⊚⊚⊚⊚⊚⊚⊚⊚⊚⊚⊚⊚⊚⊚⊚⊚⊚⊚⊚⊚⊚⊚⊚⊚⊚⊚

1. In Philippians how does Paul understand the relationship between his imprisonment and his mission?

2. Look at Philippians 2:12–13. Is Paul's call to "work out your salvation with fear and trembling" a corporate or an individual task?

3. Why does Paul commend Epaphroditus and Timothy so highly to the believers in Philippi? What character traits mark them as exemplary servants of the gospel?

4. Do Paul's statements about loss and serving Christ in Philippians 3:1–14 mean we should give up all our plans and ambitions in order to be servants of the gospel?

5. What methods of persuasion does Paul use to encourage Philemon to receive Onesimus back as a brother? How does he use, and refrain from using, his authority as an apostle?

6. Slavery is still a reality in different parts of the world (see www.iAbolish.com; www.antislavery.org; and other internet sites on modern slavery). What should our Christian response be to this institution? Support your conclusions biblically and theologically.

BIBLIOGRAPHY

Philippians: Introductory

Martin, R. P. *Philippians*. NCB. Grand Rapids: Eerdmans, 1976.
Osiek, C. *Philippians, Philemon*. ANTC. Nashville: Abingdon, 2000.
Thielman, F. *Philippians*. NIVAC. Grand Rapids: Zondervan, 1995.

Philippians: Advanced

Bockmuehl, M. *The Epistle to the Philippians*. BNTC. Peabody, MA: Hendrickson, 1998.
Fee, G. D. *Paul's Letter to the Philippians*. NICNT. Grand Rapids: Eerdmans, 1995.
O'Brien, P. T. *The Epistle to the Philippians*. NIGTC. Grand Rapids: Eerdmans, 1991.
Silva, M. *Philippians*. BECNT. Rev. ed. Grand Rapids: Baker, 2005.

Philemon

Barth, M., and H. Blanke. *The Letter to Philemon*. Grand Rapids: Eerdmans, 2000.
Fitzmyer, J. A. *The Letter to Philemon*. AB. New York: Doubleday, 2000.
See also most commentaries on Colossians (which often include Philemon).

NOTES

1. A. Malherbe, *Ancient Epistolary Theorists* (Macon, GA: Scholars, 1988), 33.
2. Ibid.
3. J. Shelton, *As the Romans Did* (Oxford: Oxford Univ. Press, 1997), 177.

CHAPTER 21

THE PASTORAL LETTERS

Paul wrote to Titus when he led a church in Crete. Fair Havens harbor in South Crete would also host Paul on his imprisonment trip to Rome. (Acts 27:8–12)

Nero, shown above, was the adopted son of Claudius. Nero's mother, Agrippina the Younger, married Claudius, her uncle and convinced him to make Nero his heir to the throne over his own son, Britannicus.

Luke's story of Paul's missionary journeys ends with the apostle imprisoned in Rome (Acts 28). From here Paul wrote four letters: Ephesians, Colossians, Philippians, and Philemon. We can account for all of Paul's letters within Acts, except for 1 and 2 Timothy and Titus. These "Pastoral Letters," written to individual church leaders, suggest a context later than Paul's Roman imprisonment.

Paul did likely gain his freedom (see "Herald of the Gospel" in Ch. 13, above, for Paul's chronology after his release). Eusebius notes that "after defending himself the Apostle was again sent on the ministry of preaching.... Coming a second time to the same city [Paul] suffered martyrdom under Nero. During this imprisonment he wrote the second Epistle to Timothy" (*Eccl. Hist.* 2.22.2).

For the last hundred years Paul's authorship has undergone serious criticism. These letters are distinct in their literary style, historical setting, and theological perspective. Many conclude Paul could not have written them. They argue these letters are pseudepigraphic, that is, written by someone other than Paul, who used Paul's name to validate the content. We discuss this issue below.

Among conservative Christians these letters have also become a storm center of debate. Questions of gender equity and church leadership surface in these letters because they seem to limit the teaching authority of women in the church. This too deserves careful study.

THE CONTEXT OF THE PASTORALS
Timothy

Timothy's father was Greek and his mother a Jewish Christian (Acts 16:1). Timothy was considered Jewish because his mother was Jewish (see *m. Qidd.* 3.12). Paul praises Timothy's mother, Eunice, and his grandmother, Lois, as having "sincere faith" (2 Tim. 1:5). Timothy himself had a good reputation in Lystra and Iconium (Acts 16:2), and no doubt Paul discerned here a steadfast servant of God. One crucial problem, however, almost derailed Timothy's accompanying Paul: He was uncircumcised. Paul usually began his preaching in synagogues, and some Jews and/or Jewish Christians would have branded Timothy an "apostate." To defer such criticism and silence those who might say that Christ encouraged Jews to sin, Paul circumcised Timothy.

NOTES FROM ANTIQUITY

NERO: INFAMOUS PERSECUTOR OF CHRISTIANS
Born in AD 37, Nero Claudius Caesar ruled as Rome's fifth emperor from AD 54–68. His first five years of rule were comparatively peaceful since his able teacher Seneca ran the government. But Nero chafed under the supervision of wiser minds. He murdered his mother and his wife. Thereupon Seneca retired (Nero forced him to commit suicide in AD 65), and Nero, now free, ruined the Roman economy and thinned out the ranks of the senate by accusing many of treason.

Nero's unique evil was evident in condemning Christians as scapegoats for a fire that burned much of Rome in AD 64 (see sidebar on "Nero's Persecution of Christians" in Ch. 13).

In Ephesus, the Prytaneion functioned similarly to our town halls, where important meetings and banquets were held.

Timothy's name joins Paul's in the greetings of five of his letters (1–2 Thessalonians, Philippians, Colossians, and Philemon). Since at least two of these were written during Paul's Roman imprisonment, presumably Timothy went with him to Rome and helped with his needs. When Paul writes to Timothy, he is the leader of the church in Ephesus.

Titus

Titus is mentioned twelve times in Paul's letters and, like Timothy, was one of Paul's closest companions (Titus 1:4; cf. 1 Tim. 1:2). On one of Paul's earliest trips to Jerusalem, Titus accompanied Paul. When Jewish Christians demanded that Titus (a Gentile) be circumcised, Paul refused—which makes an interesting contrast with Paul's decision in Acts 16 to circumcise Timothy. Paul insisted that Gentiles need not undergo circumcision. To do so would suggest that to follow Jesus the Messiah, one must also become a Jew.

Titus was working on Crete when Paul asked that he join him in Nicopolis (Titus 1:5; 3:12). Eusebius writes that Titus later returned to Crete, where he served as bishop (*Eccl. Hist.* 3.4.5–6). Tradition recounts that Titus died at age ninety-four.

Crete is a large, mountainous island with fertile grazing land in its eastern region. It lies south of the Aegean Sea in the Mediterranean. Its most famous ancient king was the legendary King Minos, and the civilization (2600–1100 BC) is named "Minoan" by modern archaeologists. Rome took over the island in 67 BC.

Crete was well known for its moral faults. Paul paraphrases the famous seventh-century BC Greek writer Epimenides, "Cretans are always liars, evil brutes, lazy gluttons" (Titus 1:12). Paul's condemnation highlights common sentiment in the ancient world; note the remarks of Polybius (d. 122 BC), an ancient historian: "So much in fact do sordid love of gain and lust for wealth prevail among them, that the Cretans are the only people in the world in whose eyes no gain is disgraceful" (*Histories* 6:46). Jews lived on the island from at least the second century BC. The Hasmonean ruler Simon Maccabeus interceded on behalf

The ancient Minoan civilization prospered on the island of Crete, the mythological birthplace of Zeus, whose son was King Minos.

of a Jewish community in the city of Gortyna. This city has been excavated from its Roman period, revealing large public buildings and a church dedicated to St. Titus. Acts 2:11 tells us that some Jews from Crete were present on Pentecost.

THE MESSAGE OF THE PASTORALS

Prominently in the background of these letters are issues challenging the churches of Ephesus and Crete. Certain "teachers of the law" (1 Tim. 1:6–7) are seducing believers by their "myths" and mere speculations to compromise the true gospel (1 Tim. 1:4; 6:3–5; 2 Tim. 2:14–16, 23; 3:13; Titus 1:10, 14; 3:9). They are deceived by Satan (1 Tim. 4:1; 2 Tim. 2:26; 3:13) and are greedy (1 Tim. 6:5–10; Titus 1:11). These teachers reject marriage and certain foods, which "God created to be received with thanksgiving by those who believe" (1 Tim. 4:3; cf. 2:15; Titus 1:15). They preach that believers now live in a "new age" where the resurrection has already occurred and are not bound by limitations of the earthly body (2 Tim. 2:18). Only initiates have this salvation "knowledge" (Gk. *gnōsis*).

DIASPORA SYNAGOGUES

Outside Palestine, thriving Jewish communities worshiped God regularly in meeting places called "places of prayer." Archaeologists have excavated five ancient Diaspora synagogues: in Priene (Asia Minor), Stobi (Macedonia), Delos (in the Aegean), Ostia (near Rome), and Dura-Europos (Roman Syria). Each was built by renovating an existing house. Philo, a first-century AD Jew from Alexandria, writes:

Each seventh day in every city there stand wide open thousands of *didaskaleia* [institutes of learning] in good sense, temperance, courage, justice and all the virtues. They sit in them quietly and in order, with ears alert and with full attention, so much do they thirst for the drink which the teacher's words supply. (*Special Laws* 2:62)

Scholars have difficulty defining Paul's opponents because of his lack of specificity. He does not outline their false teachings. Instead, he insists on holiness based on right thinking. Paul's tactic is similar to that used to train agents battling counterfeiters. Instead of showing new recruits countless stacks of fake money, the trainers focus on getting the recruit to know real currency intimately.

1 Timothy

The Ephesian church is struggling with false teachings, so Paul instructs Timothy on how best to handle the situation. The letter falls into two parts. In chapters 1–3, Paul warns against the false speculations that pass for knowledge and redirects attention to the center of the gospel, that in Jesus Christ there is forgiveness of sins (1:15). The gospel also involves right actions, so Paul focuses on church fellowship and leadership. In chapters 4–6, Paul further characterizes the heresy and contrasts it with behaviors appropriate for the various social categories in the church, such as widows (a fast-growing group in the church) and slaves. He warns of the evils of money, "for the love of money is a root of all kinds of evil" (6:10). Wealthy believers must not depend on their wealth but on "God, who richly provides us with everything for our enjoyment" (6:17).

OUTLINE OF 1 TIMOTHY

I. Introduction (1:1–2)

II. Avoid False Doctrine (1:3–20)

III. Instructions for Prayer (2:1–15)

IV. Qualifications for Leaders in the Church (3:1–16)

V. Avoid False Teachings (4:1–16)

VI. Instructions for Groups within the Church (5:1–6:19)

    A. Instructions to Young Men and Widows (5:1–16)
    B. Instructions for Elders and Others (5:17–25)
    C. Instructions to Slaves (6:1–2)
    D. Seeking Contentment (6:3–19)

VII. Closing Remarks (6:20–21)

Paul reminds Timothy of Jesus' dual nature (completely human and completely divine, 3:16). He uses this truth to attack the heresy's condemnation of marriage and things of the body/creation. God has created everything good (4:4), and from this theological truth Paul encourages Timothy to stay the course God created for him. Timothy must not give into the heretics, but rather stand fast in the Lord (4:14). All believers are to honor each other in culturally appropriate ways, such as young people respecting their elders (5:1–2), students learning from their teachers (5:17), and slaves working diligently for their masters (6:1–2).

Because some of the earliest Christians were slaves, Paul must explain how the gospel relates to them. He does not mandate elimination of slavery. Rather, he works within the social framework of his day to teach slaves how to best demonstrate Christian love (6:1–2; see also commentary on Philemon and the sidebar "Roman Slaves" in Ch. 20).

Paul's social world also differs from ours in the area of gender expectations. Perhaps the most controversial passage in 1 Timothy is 2:8–15, where Paul writes that women should not teach or have authority over men. In this complex issue, the interpreter must be discerning, asking how Paul's teaching should be applied in our modern setting.

Some scholars argue Paul's context involves a schismatic movement in Ephesus, led by a few women who rejected cultural modesty (2:9) and instead promoted asceticism, including abstinence in marriage and avoidance of pregnancy (2:15). Paul reacts by reemphasizing the importance of modesty.[1]

Other scholars believe Paul attacks the basis of the women's heresy in his remarks about Adam and Eve, when he reinforces the truth that Eve and Adam did indeed sin when they ate of the forbidden fruit (Gen. 3:6–7). They contend that underlying the women's behavior is a proto-gnostic perspective that views creation as evil and elevates Eve as being the source of knowledge (1 Tim. 2:13–14). Paul stresses Genesis in his argument to remind them of Eve's sin. His encouragement to women to have children cuts to the root of the proto-gnostic heresy that denied any place to creation.

Paul requests that the Ephesian women who are opposing Timothy learn in submission (2:11). He then argues that they should not teach in the Ephesian church (2:12a) and not usurp leadership authority (2:12b), but be silent. Paul uses a rare, unusual verb for authority here (Gk. *authenteō*), which connotes aggression, even violence.

What does Paul mean when he tells women to "be quiet"? In a related passage, Paul asks the Thessalonians to live "a quiet life" (1 Thess. 4:11; cf. 2 Thess. 3:12), intending that they act respectably within the larger community. Being "quiet" was a mark of nobility, of gracious decorum. It also implied keeping oneself out of public life, avoiding any meddlesome or disruptive behavior. Perhaps Paul is asking these women to refrain from disorderly conduct and to respect social norms that limit women's public activities.

We should note Paul's references to a number of women who held leadership roles in his churches. In Romans 16 he commends nine women (see sidebar on "Nine Women in Romans 16" in Ch. 18). He encourages two female coworkers, Euodia and Syntyche (Phil. 4:2), to agree with each other. Lydia established a house church in her home (Acts 16:15, 40). Paul's good friend Priscilla taught Apollos (Acts 18:26). Paul's churches, then, had men and women leading, teaching, and making decisions in the church.

Titus

Paul's letters to Titus and 1 Timothy have numerous thematic connections. Titus is a leader in Crete and is likewise confronting teachings that are eroding the church's faith. False teachers use their religious roles for profit (1:10–14) and promote Jewish myths (1:14).

OUTLINE OF TITUS

I. Paul's Greeting (1:1–5)

II. Godly and Unsound Leaders (1:6–16)

III. Live Consistent, Self-Controlled Lives (2:1–15)

    A. Charge to Older Men and Women (2:1–5)
    B. Charge to Younger Men (2:6–8)
    C. Charge to Slaves (2:9–10)
    D. Charge to the Congregation (2:11–15).

IV. Live in the Spirit (3:1–8)

V. Warning Divisive People (3:9–11)

VI. Closing Remarks (3:12–15)

Paul tells Titus to confront false teachings initially by making sure that his own personal life will be free from criticism (2:7–8). He outlines how elders/bishops should conduct themselves if they intend to serve as leaders of the church and fight against false teaching (cf. 1 Tim. 3). Paul spares no sympathy for those who are dividing the church. He instructs Titus to "avoid foolish controversies and genealogies and arguments and quarrels about the law, because these are unprofitable" (Titus 3:9). Titus must warn divisive persons twice; "after that, have nothing to do with them" (3:10).

2 Timothy

In 2 Timothy, we find a much different letter. Paul is again in prison (1:8; 2:9; 4:6, 16) and speaks with remarkable candor about suffering and even martyrdom. His perseverance is buoyed by his conviction that even if he is martyred, he will be with the Lord for eternity (2:11). Paul is not ashamed of his life or his decisions, nor should Timothy (1:8). He writes, "I have fought the good fight, I have finished the race, I have kept the faith" (4:7). Timothy too must sustain the fight that will bring him to the close of his race.

Paul connects his life for Christ with the reward that awaits him for faithfully finishing the race laid out for him by God. Paul will receive a "crown of righteousness" given to him "on that day—and not only to me, but also to all who have longed for his appearing" (4:8). True life does not end with death; rather, death ushers the believer into full life. Twice Paul speaks of Jesus' "appearing," his entrance into time that made possible human salvation (1:10; 4:1). The Holy Spirit, who lives in us, will guard this priceless treasure for us (1:14).

Throughout the letter Paul intends to strengthen Timothy's faith so that he will "stay the course" despite his many opponents. He cites, for instance, the story of Jannes and Jambres from Exodus 7 (2 Tim. 3:8), two deceitful men who tried to subvert Moses. Despite Timothy's convictions, the quality of life he exhibits, and the truth he proclaims, Paul admits that people will gravitate to false teaching because they seek out teachers who will make them comfortable and affirm the values they desire (4:3). This reality of human nature can lead to despair. Paul's confidence does not waver since he understands that ultimately his strength comes from the Lord. In all of these struggles, God is at work, saving Paul (and Timothy) for his heavenly kingdom (4:18). For this reason, God deserves the fullest praise.

OUTLINE OF 2 TIMOTHY

I. Introduction (1:1 – 2)

II. Hold Fast to the Gospel (1:3 – 18)

III. Encouragement to be Strong (2:1 – 13)

IV. Rebuke of the Opponents (2:14 – 26)

V. Example of Paul before Ungodliness (3:1 – 4:8)

VI. Instructions for Timothy (4:9 – 18)

VII. Closing Remarks (4:19 – 22)

AUTHOR AND DATE

Few letters attributed to Paul have witnessed the level of debate surrounding authorship as the Pastorals. With these three letters many New Testament scholars feel that their case against Pauline authorship is assured: both external evidence (manuscripts, later Christian writers) and internal evidence (grammatical, literary, theological differences) suggest Paul did not write these letters. Are they right?

Preserved from first century AD Egypt is a personal letter from Sarapion to Diodoros. 2 Timothy reflects the openness and warmth of personal letters.

External Evidence

One of the earliest (about 200 AD) and most important papyrus manuscripts of Paul's letters (P^{46} [papyrus 46]) does not include the Pastorals. Yet evidence from this document remains inconclusive because the collection is incomplete; the manuscript breaks off in the middle of 2 Thessalonians with seven leaves missing. It is hard to determine if all of 2 Thessalonians and Philemon, plus the Pastoral Letters could fit onto seven papyrus pages. The scribe's handwriting gets smaller toward the end of the manuscript, as though he is attempting to fit in all the material. Perhaps the scribe intends to add more pages. It is unwise to make a definitive judgment from an incomplete manuscript.

Scholars also point to the collection of Paul's letters made by Marcion in the mid-second century, which does not include the Pastorals. Unfortunately we only know about Marcion's list through the later theologian-opponent Tertullian (ca. AD 160–225). Tertullian claims that Marcion *rejected* the letters. His phrasing implies that Marcion was aware of the Pastorals, but chose not to include them.

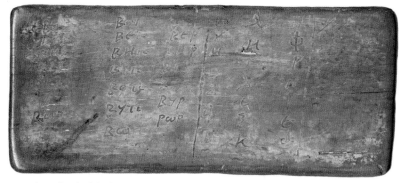

A wooden school tablet from Roman Egypt records an exercise in writing. Students practiced their script and spelling, and some might go on to become professional scribes.

A legitimate case can be made that the apostolic fathers knew and used these letters.[3] Polycarp in the early second century cites 1 Timothy 6:7, 10, "for he that has love is far from all sin. But the love of money is the beginning of all troubles. Knowing therefore that we brought nothing into the world, neither can we carry anything out, let us arm ourselves with the armor of righteousness and let us teach ourselves first to walk in the commandment of the Lord" (*To the Philippians* 3:3–4:1). Some scholars argue that Polycarp, Clement, Ignatius, and Barnabas show varying degrees of acquaintance with the Pastoral Epistles.[4]

Internal Evidence

Authorship can also be studied by looking for *internal* clues that may suggest its author or its context. Even a casual reading of the Greek text of these letters reveals genuine differences in tone, style and vocabulary from the rest of Paul's writings (especially Romans, Galatians, 1–2 Corinthians). Terms such as "piety," "sound teaching," and "good conscience" are unique to the Pastorals, while common Pauline words like "cross," "covenant," "my brothers," and "freedom" are absent. Why? Was Paul much older? This seems doubtful. Has he matured? If so, do we then think of Romans as *immature*?

Scholars commonly resolve these questions by arguing that Paul did not write the letters. Instead, theories suggest a disciple of Paul penned them years later, writing in the "spirit" of Paul to "update" him for a new generation of Christians. Others suggest that a disciple wrote these shortly after Paul's death, perhaps using some of Paul's own unpublished materials.

But a fully plausible view is that Paul used a professional scribe (or amanuensis) to write these letters. Due to the numerous similarities between the Pastorals and Luke-Acts, scholars have suggested that Luke was Paul's amanuensis (see sidebar). This is entirely possible; 2 Timothy 4:11 tells us that Luke was with Paul in his final imprisonment.

Pseudepigraphy / Pseudonymity

According to some scholars an ancient student often wrote letters or essays and ascribed them to his teacher (a practice called "pseudepigraphy"). While there is evidence that students in philosophical schools produced writings they signed in honor of a teacher's name, the early church does not seem to have done this. In the second century, Serapion called the *Gospel of Peter* pseudepigraphic because "the writings that falsely bear their names [such as Peter] we reject ... knowing that such were not handed down to us" (Eusebius, *Eccl. Hist.* 6.12.3; see also Tertullian, *On Baptism* 17). The crucial issue for the church was authority. How could they know for sure that a writing was true unless they could verify an apostle as its author? With so many pretenders and heretics proclaiming their versions of the gospel, the church needed to be able to trace each teaching back to an authoritative, apostolic source.

Another problem with maintaining the Pastorals as pseudepigraphic is the numerous personal details scattered throughout the letters. These are not abstract philosophical treatises; note 2 Timothy 4:13: "When you come, bring the cloak that I left with Carpus at Troas, and my scrolls, especially the parchments." To write this in Paul's name implies a level of dishonesty unparalleled in antiquity.[5]

Other scholars base pseudepigraphic authorship on the fact that the historical setting presupposed in the letter is so different. In 1 Corinthians 12–14 church structure is charismatic, based on the gifts of the Spirit. But in 1 Timothy and Titus Paul underscores the ecclesiastical offices of bishop, elder, and deacon. Does this sound like Paul? In fact it does. Paul refers to "deacons" in his earlier writings (e.g., Rom. 16:2–3), and Luke refers to "elders" in Acts 14:23; 20:17. Moreover, Paul's solution to church order is shaped by each situation. The Corinthians struggling with misuse of the Spirit need a solution that emphasized the Spirit. In the Pastorals, the churches need pragmatic rules to control access to leadership, so his solution is administrative structures.

Note too that these letters have much in common with Paul's theology and the practical Christian life outlined in his earlier letters (e.g., 1 Tim. 1:12–17; 6:1–2).

Date

The date of these letters is related to authorship. If Paul did not write them, the date can be pressed into the second century. If Paul did write them, the date must be somewhere in the mid- to late-60s. We suggest a likely date for 1 Timothy and Titus at AD 65/66 and 2 Timothy at 67/68, prior to his death under Nero (who died June 9, 68).

1. Why is the context and setting of the Pastorals different from Paul's prison letters? What evidence do we have?

2. Profile the nature of the controversies surrounding Timothy at Ephesus and Titus at Crete. What is Paul's solution?

3. Why would Paul call for the silence of women at Ephesus (1 Tim. 2:8–15)?

4. Explain the arguments for and against Pauline authorship of these letters.

BIBLIOGRAPHY
Introductory

Dunn, J. D. G. "Pseudepigraphy." In *Dictionary of the Later New Testament and Its Developments*. Ed. Ralph P. Martin and Peter H. Davids. Downers Grove, IL: InterVarsity Press, 1997.

Liefeld, W. L. *1 and 2 Timothy and Titus*. NIVAC. Grand Rapids: Zondervan, 1999.

Reicke, B. *Re-examining Paul's Letters: The History of the Pauline Correspondence*. Ed. David P. Moessner and Ingalisa Reicke. Harrisburg, PA: Trinity International, 2001.

Towner, P. H. *1 – 2 Timothy, Titus*. IVPNTC. Downers Grove, IL: InterVarsity Press, 1994.

Advanced

Johnson, T. L. *The First and Second Letters to Timothy*. AB. New York: Doubleday, 2001.

Knight, G. W., III. *The Pastoral Epistles: A Commentary on the Greek Text*. NIGTC. Grand Rapids: Eerdmans, 1992.

Marshall, I. H. *A Critical and Exegetical Commentary on the Pastoral Epistles*. ICC. Edinburgh: T. & T. Clark, 1999.

Meade, D. G. *Pseudonymity and Canon*. WUNT 39. Tübingen: Mohr, 1986.

Mounce, W. D. *1 and 2 Timothy, Titus*. WBC. Waco, TX: Word, 2000.

Towner, P. H. *The Letters to Timothy and Titus*. NICNT. Grand Rapids: Eerdmans, 2006.

NOTES

1. See B. W. Winter, *Roman Wives, Roman Widows* (Grand Rapids: Eerdmans, 2003).

2. Inscription from J.-B. Frey, *Corpus of Jewish Inscriptions 1* (New York, 1975), 741. Inscription quoted in R. Kraemer, ed., *Maenads, Martyrs, Matrons and Monastics: A Sourcebook on Women's Religions in the Greco-Roman World* (Philadelphia: Fortress, 1988), 218.

3. I. H. Marshall writes, "There is nothing unusual about the low degree of proven usage of the Pastoral Epistles in the context of the general difficulty of establishing knowledge and use of the accepted Pauline letters" (*A Critical and Exegetical Commentary on the Pastoral Epistles* [ICC; Edinburgh: T. & T. Clark: 1999], 5).

4. *The New Testament in the Apostolic Fathers*, written by A Committee of the Oxford Society of Historical Theology (Oxford: Clarendon Press, 1905). Newly released by Elibron Classics, 2000.

5. I. H. Marshall, *Commentary on the Pastoral Epistles*, 83 – 84.

CHAPTER 22

THE LETTER
OF JAMES

This fifth-century mosaic from Beth Shean synagogue uses all of the well-known symbols of Jewish religious life in the first century: the temple candelabra, incense shovel, and rams's horn.

The philosopher/theologian Søren Kierkegaard summed up the Christian life as "to will one thing."[1] James would likely agree with that. He summarizes the Christian life by urging his readers to devote their lives to God with a singleness of purpose that reflects their faith. Faith must be active; it cannot be simply an assent to doctrines (2:14–20). Those who hear the truth but do not act on it are like people who look in a mirror, but as soon as they turn away, they forget what they look like (1:22–24).

SETTING OF JAMES

James writes to the "twelve tribes in the Dispersion" (1:1 NRSV). Is James speaking to believers outside of Judea? Most scholars argue the term reflects this more literal meaning. That is, James is writing to those followers of Jesus who live perhaps in Egypt, Asia Minor, or even Rome. Acts 15:23–29 (a letter sent by James to Christian communities in Antioch, Syria, and Cilicia) indicates that James is well known outside Palestine (cf. Gal. 2:12).

Is James writing to Jews or Gentiles? Some scholars are convinced he is addressing Jewish Christians. Note the use of "*synagōgē*" (2:2) to designate their meeting, the reference to monotheism (2:19), and the central place of the law (2:8; 21–25; 4:11–12). But others argue that the metaphorical meaning of "twelve tribes" is dominant here, as it is in Paul, who designates "Israel" as including Gentiles (Gal. 6:16; see also 1 Peter 1:1; 2:9).

In other words, the language of Dispersion, twelve tribes, and Israel combine to reference the historic exile and the promised eschatological restoration (cf. Jer. 31:7–8). Because early Christians used this language when speaking of Gentiles, James here may be creating with the term "Dispersion" "a symbolic world: they [the readers] *become*, for the purposes of this composition, the hoped-for restored Israel among the nations."[2]

Clues within the text itself help create a picture of James's audience. They are living a Diaspora existence, which explains their poverty and oppression. They are tempted to show

In Pliny's *Natural History* (36.66 [193]), he notes that glass mirrors were invented in the first century AD in Sidon, located in what is now modern Lebanon. The earliest extant examples of glass mirrors date from the second century.

THE CONNECTION BETWEEN JAMES AND PAUL

NOTES FROM ANTIQUITY

In the late nineteenth century, F. C. Baur proposed a theory that pitted Paul's Gentile Christianity against Peter's Jewish Christianity, suggesting that the two were hostile enemies. He stuck James in Peter's camp. This reconstruction of first-century Christianity has led many to read James as a reaction to Paul.

But nothing in James itself suggests this. While the two men clearly knew each other, there is no reason to suggest that they write to challenge each other's teaching. James does not hold a "judaizing" position advocating circumcision of Gentiles, and Paul speaks of James with utmost respect and brotherly love (1 Cor. 15:7; Gal. 1:19, 2:9).

favoritism to the wealthy (2:1–7) in hopes of material rewards. The rich take advantage of them (5:4–6) and haul them off to court (2:6). Does anyone in the community have wealth? In 1:9–10 James compares a lowly brother to a rich man, who is probably a Christian, and he is speaking with prophetic warning—the rich must not rely on their wealth. Wealth is as transient as the flowers of the field (cf. Isa. 40:7–8).

We can infer several other characteristics of James's audience. His appeal for ethical behavior is not rooted in philosophical discourse, but stands over against it. Perhaps his readers are drawn to such pagan perspectives, and James is warning them that "friendship with the world means enmity against God" (4:4). James's audience has followed Jesus for some time, for he does not teach them doctrine. In fact, they assume right belief is all that God requires (see 2:14). Instead, James pushes them to live moral lives based on God's revelation. He makes it clear that right action is a necessary part of right belief: "I will show you my faith by what I do" (2:18).

THEMES IN JAMES

James proposes to be a mirror that exposes the wrinkles and blemishes Christians often try to conceal. He urges moral excellence, impartiality, and justice and forces his readers to look carefully at their actions.

James's exhortations have elements from both Jewish and Greco-Roman philosophical ethicists of the day. Scholars have noted a closeness to writings from both of these; some argue that James need not be a Christian work at all! However, this letter clearly displays the marks of a Christian work.

In this fresco from Pompeii, both the wife and her husband, Terentius Neo, are depicted as learned. The woman has a stylus (ancient pen) to her lips and holds a wax tablet. Her husband holds a scroll. Clearly this couple wanted to be seen as scholarly and well read. James's letter might have attracted such couples, given its similarities with aspects of Greco-Roman philosophies.

Greco-Roman philosophical writings. James shares common themes with contemporary moralists, such as virtue leading to joy and virtue being shown through testing. Seneca (d. AD 65) writes: "And yet I do not mean to say that the brave man is insensible to these [external things], but that he overcomes them, and being in all else unmoved and calm rises to meet whatever assails him . . . [for] without an adversary, prowess shrivels" (*On Providence* 2.2, 4 and James 1:2). The image of the mirror as an aid to moral assessment (1:23) occurs in Epictetus (*Discourse* 2.14.21).

The conviction that the tongue can be deadly is discussed in James 3:6 and Plutarch (first century A.D), who writes, "And yet there is no member of human bodies that Nature has so strongly enclosed within a double fortification as the tongue, entrenched within with a barricado of sharp teeth. . . . According to Euripides, 'Our miseries do not spring / From houses wanting locks and bolts, / But from unbridled tongues, / Ill used by prating fools and dolts" (*Concerning Talkativeness* 3 [503C]).

James's structure, like Greco-Roman moral philosophies, is organized around a central theme or *topos*. For example, James 3:13–4:10 may seem to be an assortment of ideas, but closer examination reveals that James centers his thoughts around the *topoi* of envy and friendship.

Yet in at least two distinct ways, James differs from the moral philosophies of his day. (1) James focuses on morals, not manners, which concerned the Greco-Roman philosophers. They stressed keeping one's place in the world, adhering to established social structures, obeying rules, and displaying proper honor and gratitude to one's superiors. James concentrates on doing good deeds irrespective of the honor or shame they will bring in the world's eyes (1:23–27). (2) The church in James is community-focused, not individualistic (2:14–16). Greco-Roman philosophers emphasize that those who are virtuous deserve honor, which elevates them above others. But for James, the church community concentrates on giving honor to God through Jesus.

Jewish moral writings. Other scholars focus on the close ties of James with Jewish moral writings. Philo (first century AD) uses the image of mirror in connection with his moral exhortations (*Migration of Abraham* 17 [97–98]; see 1:23–24). Philo raises the question "what good is it . . . ?" (cf. 2:14), as in "what is the good of having right intentions, and yet resorting to unfitting deeds and words. . . ?" (*Posterity and Exile of Cain* 24 [87]). James's injunction to "practice what you preach" is found in the first-century rabbinic *Pirke Aboth* 1:15: "Shammai said:—Make thy Torah a fixed *duty*. Say little and do much; and receive every man with a cheerful expression of face."

Drawing from both Greco-Roman and Jewish literary conventions, James's writing style is dynamic. He uses diatribe, a literary style of short questions followed by direct

---

THE LAW IN JAMES AND LEVITICUS 19

Citing Leviticus 19:18, James admonishes his readers, "If you really keep the royal law found in Scripture, 'Love your neighbor as yourself,' you are doing right" (2:8; cf. Gal. 5:14). Echoes of Leviticus 19 resonate throughout James, as he speaks against false swearing (James 5:12; Lev. 19:12), withholding a worker's earnings (5:4–5; Lev. 19:13), partiality (2:1–7; Lev. 19:15), and slander (4:11–12; Lev. 19:16). But James does not simply restate the Old Testament law; he understands it through Jesus' teachings. The law has been planted in the believer's heart (1:21), which reflects the new covenant theme of Jeremiah 31:31–34.

THE GOSPEL OF MATTHEW AND JAMES

Though James was likely written before Matthew's gospel, they share a similar understanding of Jesus' teachings. Many similarities are found in the Sermon on the Mount. Both emphasize the joy that comes with trials (Matt. 5:12; James 1:2). Matthew encourages, "Ask and it will be given to you" (Matt. 7:7), and James writes, "Ask from God ... and it will be given you" (James 1:5 NRSV). Both stress perfection: "Be perfect, therefore, as your heavenly Father is perfect" (Matt. 5:48), and "Let endurance have its full [*teleion*] effect so that you may be mature [*teleioi*] and complete" (James 1:4 NRSV).

Both praise meekness and endurance (Matt. 5:5, 9; 24:13; James 1:12; 3:17–18) and speak out against anger (Matt. 5:22; James 1:20), oath taking (Matt. 5:33–7; James 5:12), and divided loyalty (Matt. 6:24; James 4:4).

responses or a rhetorical question (3:13; 4:14; 5:13–14). The diatribe method uses comparisons extensively, cites famous heroes as exemplars (1:23; 3:6), and includes imaginary interlocutors (2:15–20; 4:13–16; 5:1–6). James writes in excellent Greek, quoting from the LXX. The letter is filled with alliterations and other mnemonic devices (see the judging theme in 2:12–13). These literary devices promote his argument, and his use of alliteration reminds us that ancient literature was meant to be read aloud.

Based on an alleged lack of Christian themes, some claim James is simply a Jewish moral text modified slightly by a Christian writer (1:1; 2:1). There is no specific reference to Jesus' life or death, his resurrection, the Holy Spirit, baptism, the Eucharist, or the church as Christ's body. Yet while it is true that James does not mention key elements of the Christian tradition and faith, this letter is not merely a touched-up Jewish text. He distinguishes his Christian perspective in stating explicitly Jesus' name in 1:1 and 2:1. Moreover, he identifies himself as a "slave" (Gk. *doulos*), a common self-appellation of Christian leaders (see Rom. 1:1; 2 Peter 1:1; Jude 1; Rev. 1:1). James draws on certain Christian phrases such as the "the Lord's coming" scattered throughout the New Testament (see 1 Cor. 15:23, 1 Thess. 2:19).

Moreover, although James does not quote Jesus' sayings directly, he provides teachings that stem directly from Jesus' words. For example, in the Beatitudes (Matt. 5:3–12; cf. also Luke 6:20–26), Jesus says blessed are the poor, the merciful, the pure in heart, and the peacemakers. James echoes these thoughts, noting that God has chosen the poor (2:5), that mercy triumphs over judgment (2:13), that the double-minded are to purify their hearts (4:8), and that those who make peace will reap a harvest of righteousness (3:18). We can be confident, then, in labeling James as a Christian work.

THE STRUCTURE OF JAMES

The structure of James has puzzled scholars. Some see him using prepackaged sections, cobbling them together with no rhyme or reason. Others find stylistic differences between the various units, and conversely, different vocabulary when speaking about the same issue. Yet woven throughout the letter is the strong sentiment that love of this world is hatred toward God (4:4). James is harshly critical of the world's wisdom, its evaluation of the poor, and its contentment to know the good but not do the good. In that sense, James reflects a dualism between the world and God's kingdom.

A close look at the opening chapter reveals the key ideas central to James. In 1:2–4, we read of testing, endurance, and perfection (completeness). These three ideas are fleshed out in the rest of the letter. Intimately connected to perfection is God's wisdom (1:5) reflected in the proper view of the poor (1:9–11). Wisdom involves right behavior based on understanding God's Word: "Who is wise and understanding among you? Let them show it by their good life, by deeds done in the humility that comes from wisdom" (3:13).

James connects testing and trials to a believer's faith, noting that testing produces endurance (1:12). Endurance is linked to perfection (*teleios*). James explains this concept further using Abraham's offering of his son, Isaac, as a demonstration that "faith was made complete by what he did" (2:22). He closes his letter with a call to patient endurance as the readers await the coming of the Lord (5:9), citing Job's endurance as an example for his readers (5:11).

James expands his idea of testing to poverty (1:9–11). Poor believers are wealthy beyond measure, for they "will receive the crown of life" (1:12). Conversely, the rich are doomed to fade. James also decries the favoritism shown to the rich (2:1–7) and strongly admonishes them (5:1–6).

OUTLINE OF JAMES

I. Greetings and Admonitions about Testing, Truth, and the Tongue (1:1–27)

II. Christian Service (2:1–26)

III. Wisdom and Truth (3:1–18)

IV. Charges against Sinful Behaviors (4:1–5:6)

V. Patience in Suffering (5:7–12)

VI. Power of a Prayer of Faith (5:13–20)

In the earliest preserved depiction of Jesus' family, a second-century Roman catacomb shows Mary holding the infant Jesus (ca. 100 AD), and the man to the left is identified by many as a prophet. The group is under a fruit tree. Jesus' siblings (including James) are rarely found in ancient Christian art.

James develops his concern for equality among the several social levels represented in the community. He decries the community's partiality, claiming that it breaks God's law to "love your neighbor as yourself" (2:8). He expands the discussion about behavior to include his important distinction between faith as an intellectual assent and faith lived out actively. Abraham (Gen. 22) and Rahab (Josh. 2) serve as examples. James includes as proper, active faith the ability to control what one says (ch. 3). Speaking wisely is related to "deeds done in the humility that comes from wisdom" (3:13).

The opposite of wisdom is pride and evil desires (4:1–2). True purity and perfection come from submission to God (4:7). Christians ought not to judge each other, for God alone is judge (4:12). James singles out those who boast about their future as another example of wrong speech (4:13–16). James enjoins that "if you know the good you ought to do and don't do it, you sin" (4:17).

James has no time for those who view their wealth as their safety net. He attacks their smug confidence by declaring that their life of pleasure is in fact a time of fattening for the slaughter (5:5). But for the followers of Jesus whose faith is evidenced in their works, James asks only that they be patient. He assures them that the Lord will return soon and will bless those who endure (5:7). As they wait for his return, they should continue to pray for healing and forgiveness (5:13–16).

In Sepphoris, in Galilee, wealthy Romans built elaborate villas. The mosaic above is found in the dining room (triclinium) of one such house. The influence of Greek speaking Romans in Sepphoris encourages the theory that Jews in Galilee could be well versed in Greek.

James can be read as a list of do's and don't's. It can be analyzed for its logic, its structure, its form. It can be compared to Paul, to Jewish texts, or to Greco-Roman writings. But to do so ultimately misses his main message. James demands that the reader ask, "What does faith look like?"

AUTHORSHIP, DATE, AND GENRE OF JAMES

The letter begins, "James, a servant [slave] of God and of the Lord Jesus Christ, to the twelve tribes scattered among the nations: Greetings" (1:1). Tradition has identified James as the brother of the Lord known to Paul (1 Cor. 9:5; 15:7; Gal. 1:19; 2:9) and in Acts 1:14; 12:17; 15:13–21; 21:18. Some dismiss this identification. They point to the letter's excellent Greek and conclude it could not have come from the pen of a Galilean laborer. The James in Acts 15 allegedly has a different perspective from this letter, for this letter shows no interest in cultic practices or initiation rites.

But recent studies of first-century Palestine weaken those arguments. Greek was widely used in Galilee. Recent excavations in Sepphoris (about an hour's walk from Nazareth) reveal how influential Greek was. Moreover, James might have used an amanuensis highly skilled in Greek.

Nor does Acts 15 reveal a different person from the one who wrote this letter. In Acts, James is defending the rights of Gentiles to enter the church *as Gentiles*. In this letter, the topic of Gentiles is not addressed. But both the letter and Acts 15 reveal an author well versed in the Old Testament. Interestingly, the quotation in Acts 15:16 begins with the promise that the Lord will return, a sentiment found throughout James, which consistently points to the "the Lord's coming" and the future judgment (5:7–9; cf. also 1:12, 18; 2:13; 4:12; 5:3).

Several other factors point to James, the Lord's brother, as the author of this letter. (1) Numerous signs mark it as an early composition. James has similarities to the hypothetical early Q source used by Matthew and Luke (see Ch. 5). Both Q and James emphasize wisdom and prophecy within a framework that foresees God's immanent return and judgment. (2) The letter does not elaborate about James's identity. One would expect such particulars if the author was a lesser known James. (3) Finally, the lack of details about church leadership and doctrinal issues points to an early stage in the church.

QUESTIONS FOR DISCUSSION ⊙⊙⊙⊙⊙⊙⊙⊙⊙⊙⊙⊙⊙⊙⊙⊙⊙⊙⊙⊙⊙⊙⊙⊙⊙⊙⊙

1. Describe the problems related to determining the author and audience of James.

2. How does James understand the law? How does he differ from Paul in Galatians and Romans? How do they both understand faith?

3. What should a Christian look like, according to James?

4. What does James have to say to the rich? To teachers?

BIBLIOGRAPHY
Introductory

Bauckham, R . *James*. New York: Routledge, 1999.

Johnson, L. T. *Brother of Jesus, Friend of God: Studies in the Letter of James*. Grand Rapids: Eerdmans, 2004.

Moo, D. J. *The Letter of James*. PNTC. Grand Rapids: Eerdmans, 2000.

Nystrom, D. P. *James*. NIVAC. Grand Rapids: Zondervan, 1997.

Penner, T. C. *The Epistle of James and Eschatology*. Sheffield: Sheffield Academic Press, 1996.

Advanced

Davids, P. H. *The Epistle of James*. NIGTC. Grand Rapids: Eerdmans, 1982.

Johnson, L. T.. *The Letter of James*. AB. New York: Doubleday, 1995.

Martin, R. *James*. WBC. Waco, TX: Word, 1988.

NOTES

1. S. Kierkegaard, *Purity of Heart Is to Will One Thing*, trans. by D. V. Steere (New York: Harper & Brothers, 1948), 31.

2. L. T. Johnson, *The Letter of James* (AB; New York: Doubleday, 1995), 171–72.

3. D. Moo, *The Letter of James* (PNTC; Grand Rapids: Eerdmans, 2000), 141.

CHAPTER 23

THE LETTER TO
THE HEBREWS

A seven-branched temple lampstand (or menorah) carved in plaster from first-century Jerusalem. These fragments were found in the Jewish Quarter Excavations amidst the debris of the ruins from Jerusalem's destruction in AD 70.

The Jewish temple candelabra or seven branch candlestick was a well known symbol of Judaism in the ancient world. It is displayed prominently on Titus' Arch, a monument commemorating the general's defeat of Jerusalem and destruction of the temple.

Hebrews presents Jesus as the unique high priest before God (5:5–6; 7:11–17). His "priestly lineage" is traced through the mysterious Melchizedek, king of Salem (see Gen. 14:17–24). Greater than the angels (1:4), Moses (3:3), and the Levitical priesthood (7:27–28), Jesus offers "for all time one sacrifice for sins" (10:12). Hebrews explains how Israel's tabernacle was an earthly copy of a "greater and more perfect tabernacle" (9:11). In offering himself as a perfect sacrifice, Jesus mediates a new and better covenant (10:14) and opens "a new and living way" to God (10:20). The author directs the reader to approach God "with a sincere heart in full assurance of faith" (10:22), to "run with perseverance the race" (12:1), and to struggle against drifting away from the gospel (2:1). The letter encourages a life of faith, one that emulates the past heroes of Israel (11:1–39).

WHO IS MELCHIZEDEK?

Genesis 14:17–21 describes the enigmatic Melchizedek. Abram is returning victorious against the kings who abducted Lot, his nephew. He meets "Melchizedek king of Salem [who] brought out bread and wine.... He blessed Abram ... then Abram gave him a tenth of everything." Psalm 110:4 refers to Melchizedek as a priest forever. Hebrews identifies the "Lord" of Psalm 110:1 with Jesus. It becomes a natural step to connect Jesus with the priesthood of Melchizedek.

Hebrews 7 develops an analogy based on assumptions about Christ's divinity. Though Melchizedek himself is human, his lack of genealogy is seen as foreshadowing Jesus' divine priesthood. Abram's tithe to Melchizedek shows the latter's superiority.

SETTING

Within Hebrews we find clues describing the community addressed here. The author speaks of their conversion to the message proclaimed by those who heard Jesus (2:3). Accompanying this message were signs and wonders, gifts of the Holy Spirit, and miracles from God (2:4). With this came a new social context. Their baptism created new boundary lines (10:22). A new group was formed with other Christians (10:24–25).

This new social relationship had led to serious hardships and persecutions. In some cases, property was confiscated (10:34); this implies that some were wealthy enough to have considerable belongings. Hebrews warns against seeking wealth (13:5), which may be directed at those who had it and lost it. Believers were also publicly abused and shamed. Yet many stayed together as a community, having compassion for those in prison and standing by those who lost everything (10:33–34).

Most scholars have understood the Hebrews' community as Jewish. Both its ancient title and extensive use of the Old Testament reinforce that claim. Many ancient commentators placed the audience in Jerusalem, but modern scholars have suggested Rome under Claudius as a better guess. Suetonius notes that in AD 49, Claudius expelled the Jews from Rome (see sidebar on "Edict of Claudius" in Ch. 18); note also the phrase "those from Italy" in 13:24, which may refer to those exiled from Rome under Claudius.

Recently, some scholars are rethinking the theory of a Jewish audience. They recognize that Gentile converts were knowledgeable of God's revelation in the Old Testament. Note how Paul deals with Old Testament events in his writings to Gentile Christians (e.g., 1 Cor. 10:1–11; Gal. 4:21–31). Second-century Gentile figures Tatian and Justin Martyr were converted to Christianity based on their reading of the Greek Old Testament (Tatian, *Address to the Greeks* 29; Justin, *Dialogue with Trypho* 8). The extensive discussion of Israel's past secures the current believers' hope in God's faithfulness (12:1–2).

In this theory, our author is not concerned that these Christians will turn to Judaism. For example, 13:9–10 does not hint that readers are being drawn back to the synagogue. Problems such as property confiscation (10:34) are allegedly best understood as an issue most likely faced by a Gentile leaving paganism. So our author encourages them: "We are not of those who shrink back and are destroyed, but of those who believe and are saved" (10:39).

Such scholars are less specific in defining a location for the letter's audience. They argue that by the time our author writes the letter, the community has endured public shame and suffering, and some are now rethinking their commitment to Christ. Some are in prison (13:3) and others are told to expect future attacks (13:13). The pressure is wearing them down. Our author encourages them to persevere through these hard times (2:1; 12:1).

Who is persecuting the community? Perhaps Jews are (note Acts 17:1–9, as well the enigmatic statements in Rev. 2:9; 3:9). Other scholars suggest that Gentile family, friends, coworkers, and neighbors are outraged at those who have rejected their former religion. If so, Hebrews declares that these Gentile believers are like Moses, who left Egypt to stand with God's people, Israel. Like Moses, they share the ill-treatment with God's people (Heb. 11:24–25).

Ostia, the port city of Rome, was a bustling commercial and military sea port in Paul's time. This third century AD relief of a candelabra and shofar from the synagogue in Ostia was added when the first century synagogue was renovated.

Hebrews 12:1–2 recalls a stadium filled with competing athletes and cheering crowds. Most athletic events were restricted to males in the ancient world, but Pausanius (mid-second century AD) writes of games for unmarried women, such as in the Heraea: "They run in the following way: their hair hangs down, a tunic reaches to a little above the knee, and they bare the right shoulder as far as the breast. These too have the Olympic stadium reserved for their games, but the course of the stadium is shortened for them by about one-sixth of its length. To the winning maidens they give crowns of olive and a portion of the cow sacrificed to Hera" (*Description of Greece* 5.16.2–8).

MESSAGE

Christians stand at the edge of the old world, looking forward to their new home, "the city of the living God, the heavenly Jerusalem" (12:22). Their hope is based on the new covenant (9:15). The coming of God's Son signals the last days (1:2). The present times bring suffering and sorrow, but perseverance will result in incalculable rewards to those who finish the race (12:2). Hebrews is filled with both encouragement and admonition to remain steadfast and not lose hope. The author clearly warns of what will happen to those who reject God's Son: "It is a dreadful thing to fall into the hands of the living God" (10:31).

The community is facing external pressures to follow the wisdom and culture of the day, to desire wealth and prestige. The steady assault on their status is wearing away at their steadfastness. The promises of God are growing dim in their minds. When their possessions were confiscated (10:34), they had few resources to regain or replace what

Athletic activities were usually reserved for men, but a few women participated in all-female events, as seen in this fourth century AD mosaic in Sicily. Both men and women would have related to Hebrews' references to athletics.

was taken. Quite possibly some lost the tools of their trade and thus could no longer earn a living. Also, money greases the social wheels, and without any belongings a person is dependent on others. Most pagans had little sympathy for a Christian's dilemma, believing that they brought such hardship on themselves by their own foolishness. They were getting their just rewards from the gods.

In addition, the members of this community are failing to encourage each other and strengthen their faith (10:25). They are stuck at the basic level of Christian learning (5:12). The author wants them to refocus on the eternal reward that awaits them, to recommit to Christ and their Christian community (10:24–25). They are to "move beyond the elementary teachings about Christ and be taken foward to maturity" (6:1).

Our author must persuade his audience that following Christ is worth it. To do so, he first shows how Jesus and his covenant are so much greater than Moses and the old covenant with its sacrifices and tabernacle priests. Next, he pulls out all the stops in using Greek rhetorical devices to convince his audience of his argument's value.

The greatness of Jesus. Hebrews begins with a lengthy explanation on the exaltation of the divine Jesus, who is esteemed above angels and Moses. Jesus is the "heir of all things," the one through whom God created the world (1:2). He is divine, "the radiance of God's glory and the exact representation of his being" (1:3). To reinforce this claim the author uses a common interpretive technique of *qal wahomer* (see sidebar on "The Old Testament in Hebrews").

Jesus' humanity is brought to bear on the community's grave situation. He models in his own sufferings what the Christians face, and "he is able to help those who are being tempted" (2:18). Only a human can truly suffer (5:7–8) and be sympathetic to other humans (2:18; 4:15). Jesus is fully human and thus able to restore the community. But the author warns against a "sinful, unbelieving heart that turns away from the living God" (3:12).

In developing a picture of God's rest and Israel's failure to enter it (4:6–7), the author draws from Numbers 14 and Psalm 95. Numbers 14 recounts how the Israelite spies returned from exploring the Promised Land with frightening pictures of fierce people inhabiting the region. Their apostasy spread to the entire community, so that God said: "As surely as I live . . . not one of those who saw my glory and the signs I performed in Egypt and in the wilderness but who disobeyed me and tested me ten times . . . will ever see the land I promised on

---

SOJOURNING IN ANOTHER LAND

In the ancient world, most travelers pined for their homeland. A person's identity was connected tightly to their native land, and aliens often were treated cruelly in a foreign city. Lucian (ca. AD 120–180) laments that "those who get on well [in a foreign land], however successful they may be in all else, think that they lack one thing at least, a thing of the greatest importance, in that they do not live in their own country . . . for thus to sojourn is a reproach" (*My Native Land* 8). To those who lost their citizenship, "life seems with good reason not worth living, and many choose death rather than life after losing their citizenship, for whoever so desires is free to strike them and there exists no private means of punishing him who treats them with contumely" (Dio Chrysostom, *Discourse* 66.15).

Hebrews emphasizes a Christian's citizenship in heaven. Just as aliens on earth suffer reproach, so too believers should not wonder at the vile treatment they endure. They are, like the patriarchs, "longing for a better country—a heavenly one. Therefore God is not ashamed to be called their God, for he has prepared a city for them" (11:16).

oath to their ancestors" (Num. 14:21–23). Hebrews warns against this sort of disobedience, which excludes the Christian community from God's rest (3:19; 4:11).

Hebrews also draws on the priesthood and tabernacle. The author lays out a detailed discussion of Israel's sacrificial system, including animal sacrifices and the tabernacle. Jesus is an excellent high priest; because of his "reverent submission" (5:7) and obedience (5:8), he was "made perfect" (5:9). Through his sufferings, he has become "the source of eternal salvation for all who obey him and was designated by God to be a high priest in the order of Melchizedek" (5:10).

Jesus is superior to the Levitical priests in that they were not perfect, but Jesus the "Son . . . has been made perfect forever" (7:28). The priests needed to offer sacrifices for their own sins, but Jesus was sinless; they had to offer continual sacrifices, while Jesus offered himself once for all (7:27, 9:12). With that sacrifice Jesus "has made perfect forever those who are being made holy" (10:14). Not only is his priesthood superior, but also the covenant he represents (see Jer. 31:31–34). With its fulfillment in Jesus, the old covenant is "obsolete and . . . will soon disappear" (8:13).

Persuasion through rhetoric. The author is not content simply to emphasize how Jesus supersedes the Mosaic covenant. He must persuade his audience that the cost of discipleship is not too high. In the ancient world, the art of persuasion involved rhetoric, and our author uses a variety of rhetorical devises such as alliteration, catchwords, *inclusios*, and repetitions. An ancient audience expected to be persuaded by the speaker's character and content of the speech as well as by the emotions raised through the speech.

The reader is treated to the author's rhetorical skill in 1:1–4 (part of the *exordium* or introduction). We find here alliteration (words sharing initial sounds) and *homoeoptaton* (words sharing ending sounds). The opening verse reveals a perfect parallelism of consistent clauses: "in the past" is balanced by "in these last days"; "to our ancestors" balanced by "to us," and "through the prophets" balanced by "by his Son." The author uses *inclusios* or foreshadowing of themes. Jesus is introduced as a high priest in 2:17 and 3:1, which is developed in 4:14–16 and 7:1–8:5. In chapter 11, our author employs *anaphora* or the repetition of a word—in this case, the term "faith."

Drawing on the rich tradition of rhetoric, the author focuses on logic, emotion, and integrity to convince the people to change course (see Aristotle, *Rhetoric* 1.2.3). He implicitly acknowledges a felt disconnection between God's sovereign glory and their current state of suffering. In his argument they see Jesus, the power of God's plan working itself out. Jesus suffered and now is glorified. Past generations of faithful followers waited patiently amidst suffering (11:39). So too, this community will experience the glory of God's heavenly city if they endure disappointment and affliction like Jesus (10:22–24; 13:14).

Not content with merely appealing to their minds, our author connects with their hearts. Cicero observes that people "decide far more problems by hate or love, or lust or rage, or sorrow or joy, or hope or fear" (*De Oratore* 2.42 [178]). Hebrews stresses both hope and fear. It offers a picture of God reaching out to his people with a sincere promise (6:17; see also 1:2).

Hebrews also sends strong warnings against drifting away from God and his promises (2:1–4). It advises against neglecting God's good favor (3:12; see also 6:4–8; 10:31). For those who know the truth but keep on sinning, "no sacrifice for sins is left, but only a fearful expectation of judgment" (10:26–27). "God is a consuming fire" (12:29; cf. Deut. 4:24), so believers must live in peace and holiness (12:14–17).

Hebrews excites the imagination with its vivid pictures. The reader can almost hear the cheering crowd of witnesses (12:1) or smell the sacred incense (9:4). We can see the rich red blood of the sacrifices made for human sins (9:18–22) and the awesome majesty of the heavenly Jerusalem with "thousands upon thousands of angels in joyful assembly" (12:22–23).

Aristotle (384-322 BC) was a Macedonian who studied in Athens with Plato, published numerous famous works, including *The Art of Rhetoric*. The author of Hebrews was adept at using rhetoric.

ATONEMENT AND JESUS' VOLUNTARY DEATH

In Leviticus 17:11 atonement comes through blood: "It is the blood that makes atonement for one's life." The Psalms promote a sacrifice of praise or obedience: "My sacrifice, O God, is a broken spirit . . . and contrite heart" (Ps. 51:17). Isaiah 52:13–53:12 speaks of God's servant as suffering vicariously for the sins of the people.

In the Hellenistic period, a martyr's innocence and obedience counted for forgiveness of sins. Eleazar the priest prays that his death will be sufficient for God's people: "Make my blood their purification, and take my life in exchange for theirs" (4 Macc. 6:28-29). His death is not, technically speaking, a sacrifice, but it counts *as* a sacrifice. Jesus' death is understood in these terms in Hebrews: "Jesus also suffered outside the city gate to make the people holy through his own blood. . . . Through Jesus, therefore, let us continually offer to God a sacrifice of praise" (13:12, 15).

OUTLINE OF HEBREWS

I. Introduction of God's Son (1:1–3)

II. Jesus Greater than Angels (1:4–2:9)

III. Jesus, Our Apostle and High Priest (2:10–6:20)

    A. Jesus Made Perfect through Suffering (2:10–18)
    B. Entering God's Rest (3:1–4:12)
    C. Jesus the High Priest (4:13–5:10)
    D. Warning and Encouragement to Mature (5:11–6:20)

IV. Jesus' Priesthood and New Covenant (7:1–10:18)

    A. Jesus Is High Priest in the Order of Melchizedek (7:1–28)
    B. Jesus Mediates a New Covenant (8:1–13)
    C. Jesus Brings a Better Sacrifice (9:1–10:18)

V. Call to Perseverance (10:19–12:29)

    A. Hold Fast to the Faith (10:19–39)
    B. Past Witnesses to the Faith (11:1–12:3)
    C. Endure Hardship (12:4–29)

VI. Call to Ethical Living (13:1–13:21)

VII. Postscript (13:22–25)

Engaging the mind, the heart, and the speaker's character, these three are essential in persuading an audience. God is the primary speaker; he "has spoken to us by his Son, whom he appointed heir of all things" (1:2), and he can be trusted, for "he who promised is faithful" (10:23).

Patron/client convention. Along with the rhetorical argument, our author draws heavily from the patron/client social convention and the code of reciprocity. Seneca notes that "the practice . . . constitutes the chief bond of human society" (*On Benefits* 1.4.2). In this social system, a patron gave gifts to the client—perhaps a job, or money or even an introduction to another patron. Seneca goes further than most, however, when he declares that the patron should expect nothing in return: "In benefits the book-keeping is simple—so much is paid out; if anything comes back, it is gain, if nothing comes back, there is no loss. I made the gift for the sake of giving" (*On Benefits* 1.2.3). The benefactor should give freely because that is the noble thing to do. The client should seek to repay the gift, but in most cases that is impossible. Thus, the client remains forever in the patron's debt and always seeks to build up his or her honor (*On Benefits* 2.10.4).

Hebrews applies this system of reciprocity to God's relationship with his people. Believers should recognize themselves as clients of God. As such, they have a sacred duty to honor God continually and to proclaim his greatness. But they are clearly slipping in this duty, neglecting the great promises and also sliding away from God's people. Such behavior would be unforgivable if they acted this way to a human benefactor. How much more should they be concerned that they are snubbing the God of the universe.

Summary. Hebrews encourages God's people to be faithful: "Fix your thoughts on Jesus, whom we acknowledge as our apostle and high priest. He was faithful to the one who appointed him" (3:1 – 2). In chapter 11, the "Hall of Faith," the author defines faith as "being sure of what we hope for and certain of what we do not see" (11:1). Believers show their faith by standing firm and by moving ahead. This is neatly summarized in 4:14 – 16 with the phrases: "Let us hold firmly to the faith we profess" and "let us then approach God's throne of grace with confidence."

Believers are encouraged to hold tightly to the gospel preached to them (3:6) and to persevere (10:36; 12:2). Fearful of their slipping (2:1; 3:12) and pursuing worldly wealth (13:5), the author of Hebrews stresses that to keep from moving backward, one must proceed forward. Faith is dynamic, not static. Therefore Christians should *strive* to enter the rest (4:11) or *pursue* maturity (5:12 – 6:1). Our author ties these two strands together in chapter 11, pointing to martyrs standing firm for the faith (11:35 – 37) and Abraham and Sarah moving forward in faith (11:8 – 11).

As believers move forward, Hebrews holds out a vivid picture of the goal — life with God and the exalted Christ. Jesus' exaltation at God's right hand confirms his power to save (2:10). For those who persevere, the wonderful promises of God await them. They will enjoy the Sabbath rest of God (4:9) and join the angels in the heavenly city, gathered before God and Jesus (12:22 – 24). For those who slip back, the judgment of God stands over them (12:17, 25).

AUTHOR AND DATE

Most church fathers accepted Paul as the author, but behind this authorship debate is the issue of canonicity. For a text to be included in the canon, not only did it need to represent correct (orthodox) teachings about the faith,

A replica of a statue of Eumachia from Pompeii highlights the patron/client system in the ancient world. "The fullers [dedicate this statue] to Eumachia, daughter of Lucius, public priestess." She acted as their patron, and the guild of those who wash and dye clothes (fullers) responded by honoring her. Hebrews draws on the patron/client relationship to explain a believer's relationship to God.

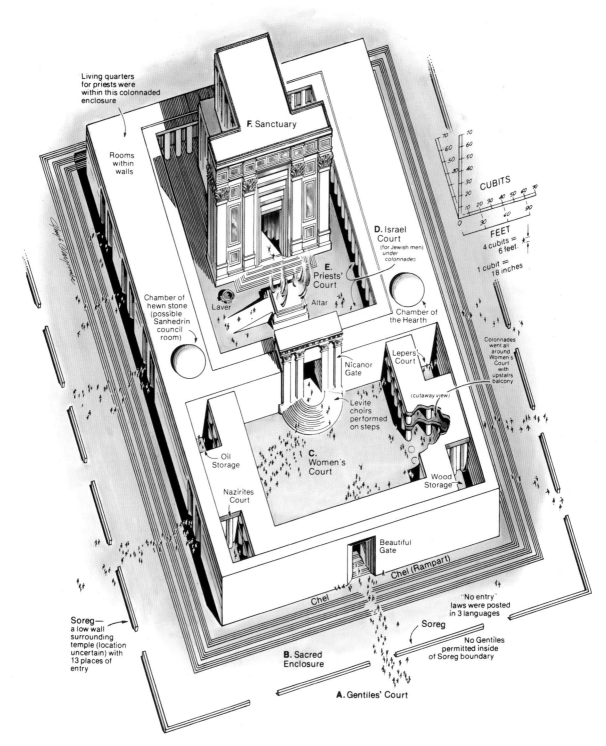

Living quarters for priests were within this colonnaded enclosure

Rooms within walls

F. Sanctuary

D. Israel Court (for Jewish men) under colonnades

Chamber of hewn stone (possible Sanhedrin council room)

Laver

E. Priests' Court

Altar

Chamber of the Hearth

CUBITS

FEET

4 cubits = 6 feet.

1 cubit = 18 inches

Colonnades went all around Women's Court with upstairs balcony

Lepers' Court

Nicanor Gate

Levite choirs performed on steps

(cutaway view)

Oil Storage

C. Women's Court

Wood Storage

Nazirites Court

Beautiful Gate

Chel (Rampart)

Chel

"No entry" laws were posted in 3 languages

Soreg— a low wall surrounding temple (location uncertain) with 13 places of entry

Soreg

No Gentiles permitted inside of Soreg boundary

B. Sacred Enclosure

A. Gentiles' Court

Hebrews reflects the practices of Jewish sacrificial worship from its beginnings in the tabernacle to Herod's temple. Jesus is portrayed as the great High Priest who brings himself as the sacrifice to God's altar, and thereby opens the veil which marked off the Holy of Holies.

but it also had to be written by or sponsored by an apostle. Hebrews is anonymous, and with that anonymity came a threat to its canonicity. Yet most church fathers were convinced that Paul was in some way related to the work. This letter was placed with Paul's letters in older manuscripts of the Bible. For example, the Egyptian manuscript P^{46} (ca. AD 200) includes Hebrews immediately after Romans.

Several particulars, however, point away from Pauline authorship. Its Greek is widely different from Paul's other letters, including the disputed Pastoral Letters. Hebrews uses elegant Greek with an expansive vocabulary. Moreover, Hebrews 2:1–3 states that its author did not hear Jesus' gospel directly, but rather it "was confirmed to us by those who heard him." In other words, the author heard the gospel from the first disciples. But Paul insists he knew Jesus directly, though he refers here to the resurrected Christ (see 1 Cor. 9:1; 15:8; Gal. 1:12).

If not Paul, then who? Ancient suggestions have been Barnabas and Clement of Rome. In the Middle Ages, Luke was suggested because of his command of Greek, and about three hundred unique words or expressions are shared between Luke/Acts and Hebrews. Silas, a coworker of Paul and Peter (Acts 15:40; 1 Peter 5:12), has also been a candidate. Martin Luther suggested Apollos, the eloquent speaker from Alexandria (Acts 18:24; 1 Cor. 1:12; 3:5–6). Finally, Priscilla has been suggested. For now, we might best conclude with Origen, who said, "Who wrote the epistle? God knows the truth" (Eusebius, *Eccl. Hist.* 6.25.14).

The dating of Hebrews is complicated by our inability to establish its author. Nevertheless, there are clues in the text. Suggesting an early date, some scholars point to the author's use of present tense when speaking of the sacrificial system (5:1; 8:3; 9:8; 10:8) and conclude that the Jerusalem temple is still functioning. This would date the letter earlier than AD 70. This interpretation, however, is inconclusive. Some ancient writers, working after the fall of Jerusalem, still used the present tense when speaking of the sacrificial system. Moreover, Hebrews refers to the tabernacle, not Herod's temple in Jerusalem.

A more solid reason for an earlier date is the author's claim that the community has not shed blood for Christ's sake. This puts the writing before Nero's persecution in the late 60s.

QUESTIONS FOR DISCUSSION ⊚⊚⊚⊚⊚⊚⊚⊚⊚⊚⊚⊚⊚⊚⊚⊚⊚⊚⊚⊚⊚⊚⊚⊚⊚⊚⊚

1. How does Hebrews use the Old Testament in its argument? How does this differ from Paul's use of the law in Galatians and Romans?

2. Describe how Hebrews pictures Jesus and highlight its uniqueness compared to the rest of the New Testament.

3. What are the problems of authorship for this letter? Problems of audience?

4. How does Hebrews enhance our understanding of God? Of Christian discipleship?

BIBLIOGRAPHY
Introductory

DeSilva, D. A. *Perseverance in Gratitude: A Socio-Rhetorical Commentary on the Epistle "to the Hebrews."* Grand Rapids: Eerdmans, 2000.

Guthrie, G. *Hebrews*. NIVAC. Grand Rapids: Zondervan, 1998.

Hagner, D. A. *Encountering the Book of Hebrews*. Grand Rapids: Baker Academic, 2002.

Johnson, T. L. *Hebrews*. NTL. Louisville: Westminster John Knox, 2006.

Advanced

Attridge, H. *Hebrews*. Hermeneia. Philadelphia: Fortress, 1989.

Ellingworth, P. *The Epistle to the Hebrews*. NIGTC. Grand Rapids: Eerdmans, 1993.

Koester, C. *Hebrews*. AB. New York: Doubleday, 2001.

Lane, W. L. *Hebrews*. WBC. 2 vols. Dallas: Word, 1991.

CHAPTER 24

1 AND 2 PETER AND JUDE

The temple of Augustus in Pisidian Antioch, located in the Roman province of Galatia.

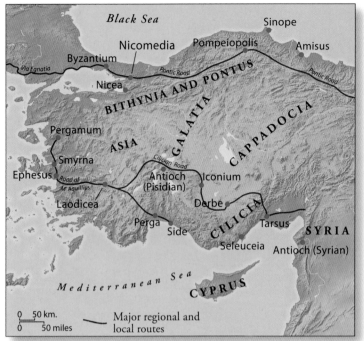

First Peter was sent to churches located in the Roman provinces of northern region of Asia Minor.

The early church faced two main crises: persecution and false teaching. These three small letters bring us into the swirl of these dangers. First Peter addresses believers in Asia Minor who are enduring hostilities and exhorts them to maintain the good way of life and to do good even to those who revile them for their faith. Both Jude and 2 Peter battle against heresies that diverge from the apostolic tradition and are leading believers into immorality.

These are not the only battles surrounding these books. In contemporary scholarship, the authorship of each has been debated. Did Peter write both 1 and 2 Peter; if so, why are their styles so different? Was Jude written by an early second-century author or is it truly a composition of Jude, brother of James and half-brother of Jesus? Doubts about these books today parallel those in the ancient church, which, for example, questioned the authenticity of 2 Peter. Moreover, both Jude and 2 Peter present an apocalyptic vision of coming judgment. That vivid portrayal of final doom stands in sharp contrast to contemporary notions of Christianity as "sweetness and light." How do we listen to their message today?

1 PETER: THE SETTING

Peter addresses his first letter "to God's elect, exiles scattered throughout the provinces of Pontus, Galatia, Cappadocia, Asia and Bithynia" (all Roman provinces in Asia Minor). He composes this letter while in "Babylon" (5:13), a common code name for Rome (e.g., Rev. 14:8; 16:19; 17:5, 9, 18).

While the many rural allusions may suggest these are not urban Christians (1:22–24; 2:25; 5:2–4, 8), at the beginning of the second century Pliny the Younger, governor of Bithynia, commented on the gospel spreading from urban centers to surrounding areas:

"It is not only the towns, but villages and rural districts too which are infected through contact with this wretched cult" (*Letters* 10.96). Peter addresses both men and women (3:1–7), and these churches have believers from divergent socioeconomic strata. Some are slaves (2:18) while others are free and even have sufficient economic power to be benefactors (2:13–17). Some women can afford costly apparel and jewelry (3:3). They have only recently become Christians (1:3, 12, 23; 2:2; 4:3, 15).

In this relief, two slaves hold a bull which has been prepared for the sacrifice about to take place.

Several passages suggest these are Jewish believers (e.g., "Diaspora" in 1:1; also citation of numerous Old Testament texts, such as 2:9–10). But 4:3 implies they are Gentiles, for they formerly participated in pagan banquets and engaged in idolatry, and their contemporaries are surprised that they no longer participate in such activities (4:4). They have broken from a traditional ancestral way of life along with its religious observances and civic cults (1:18). In a society that lauded duty and adherence to tradition, their conversion was a serious social breech indeed. They no longer attend banquets held under the auspices of the deities (4:3–4). Wives do not participate in the cult of their husbands (3:1–2), bringing them into a fearful position because of the threat of abuse (3:6). The power of fathers over their children (the *patria potestas*) extends into the area of religion.

Slaves too would encounter grave problems if they participated in religious activities not sanctioned by their masters. Columella (first century AD) gave this advice about slaves who served as overseers: "He shall offer no sacrifice except by direction of the master" (*On Agriculture*, 1.8.5). Cato says, "He must perform no religious rites," with only a few exceptions (*On Agriculture* 5.3).

Community reaction against Christian converts mainly takes the form of social ostracism and verbal abuse. Christians are reviled and reproached (3:9; 4:14, 4), and accused of doing evil (2:12; 3:16a). "Evildoers" are either criminals (4:15) or those engaged in practices like magic. People who do not fulfill their duties toward the gods can also be called "evildoers." These charges echo the slander heard in Rome where, according to Tacitus, the Christians were "loathed for their vices" (*Annals* 15.44). Such verbal attacks were a source of grave social humiliation or dishonor. Peter insists that such public ridicule is just the ignorance of foolish people (2:15).

The Christians' contemporaries are not adverse to call them to account for their new religious allegiance (3:15–16) since ancient religion was a public affair. The gods, after all, served as patrons and protectors of the communities. Noncompliance by Christians is a social threat.

But Peter does not seem to reflect any state-sponsored persecution, though physical attacks are not out of the picture (4:1), especially where authoritative relationships govern religious practice. Slaves are subject to beatings (2:19–20) and women face similar abuse (implied in 3:6).

The crux of the matter is the reaction of the Christians to their situation. Some have begun to be ashamed of their faith (4:16; cf. Rom. 1:16; 2 Tim. 1:8).

Some believers are tempted to retaliate (3:9; cf. 2:23). In the Roman world, revenge was a social obligation in order to maintain your honor in society; offering the other cheek was not an option. One Roman mother said, "You will say that it is wonderful to avenge yourself upon your enemies. I consider vengeance as important as anyone."[1] Fear and terror are setting in among these new Christians (3:6, 14), and they are tempted to conform to a more socially acceptable lifestyle (1:14; 4:2–3) and so commit apostasy. Peter identifies the force behind their persecutions as the devil, who "prowls around like a roaring lion looking for someone to devour" (5:8). The lion was used in funeral reliefs as a symbol of death (see 2 Tim. 4:17; cf. Ps. 22:13).

1 PETER: THE MESSAGE

Peter responds to this situation by making the Christians fully aware of the overarching grace of God toward them and calling them to stand firm in this grace instead of returning to their former way of life (5:12). "Grace" summarizes the message of the book. It embraces God's activity on their behalf as well as the call to a holy way of life. Grace is rooted in God's election (1:1–2), predicted through the prophets, and brought into history through the sufferings, death, and glorification of Christ (1:10–12). God's grace will be consummated at the final unveiling of Christ (1:13). It is proclaimed in the gospel (1:12), and through God believers are able to stand strong and firm in the face of hostility (5:10).

First Peter is an impassioned plea to maintain a holy way of life (1:14–16) in the midst of the moral and social problems of the believers. Peter calls them to live the "good lives among the pagans" (2:11–12), to meet evil with good and not retaliate (3:9), and to resist the devil by standing firm in the faith (5:8–9). But his message also shows how to change their status in the community. They must do "good deeds" in order to silence the opposition (2:12, 15) and live in such a way that their detractors will be ashamed of their ill-treatment (3:16). Good conduct will serve as a witness to the gospel and win over the opposition — whether a woman's unbelieving husband (3:1–2) or anyone opposed to the Christians (2:12). The "day [God] visits us" (2:12) is the time when God visits humanity, either to save or judge (Gen. 50:24–25; Ex. 3:16; Isa. 10:3; Luke 19:44). The hope that their persecutors will "glorify God" implies their conversion.

This call to good works is closely tied with civic benefaction in the ancient world (2:13–15). Peter reminds his readers that the governor will "commend those who do right." Benefactors in the ancient world were honored by public inscriptions that praised their good deeds for the community.

HONORING CIVIC BENEFACTORS

The city of Athens resolved to praise the benefactor Menelaus "because he is a good man and does whatever good he can for the people of Athens." Another inscription honors a benefactor who did "whatever good he is able to perform for the citizens." An inscription from the island of Cos illustrates the social obligation to honor benefactors: "so that we ourselves may be seen by those who propose to bestow benefactions on us to give appropriate rewards."[2]

Peter therefore calls the believers to participate in the life of their communities, seeking to "do good" for all, not just for those of the household of faith (cf. Acts 10:38; Gal. 6:10). Such social engagement might oblige the persecutors to change their opinion of Christians.

OUTLINE OF 1 PETER

I. Epistolary Salutation (1:1–2)

II. The Christian Existence (1:3–2:10)

    A. The New Life (1:3–12)
    B. The Call to Sanctification (1:13–2:3)
    C. The New Existence as the Elect and Holy People of God (2:4–10)

III. The Christian Obligations (2:11–5:11)

    A. In the Structures of Society: General Exhortations (2:11–3:12)
    B. In the Structures of Society: Under Persecution (3:13–4:6)
    C. In the Christian Community (4:7–11)
    D. In the Structures of Society: Under Persecution (4:12–19)
    E. In the Christian Community (5:1–7)
    F. In the Structures of Society: Under Persecution (5:8–11)

IV. Final Exhortation and Salutation (5:12–14)

COMPOSING 1 PETER

According to 5:12, Peter composed this letter "with the help of Silas, whom I regard as a faithful brother." The Greek text actually uses "Silvanus," the Latin form of the Greek name "Silas." This person is probably the same Hellenistic Jewish believer who traveled with Paul (Acts 15:40; 1 Thess. 1:1; 2 Thess. 1:1). As an amanuensis, Silvanus would have had some liberty in the composition, which likely includes adjustments to the grammatical style, a common scribal practice.

Peter, however, indicates he is responsible for the letter's content. He uses a variety of sources, such as the Old Testament (e.g., 1:16 [Lev. 19:2]; 2:6 [Isa 28:16]) and the teaching of Jesus, especially the Sermon on the Mount (cf. 4:14 with Matt. 5:10–11). The striking similarities between Peter and Paul's teaching on a Christian's obligation to the state (cf. 2:13–17 and Rom. 13:1–4) and the domestic code (cf. 2:18–3:7 with Eph. 5:21–6:9;

The wax tablets known as a diptych were used to make first drafts of compositions which were then transferred to papyrus. Silvanus, as Peter's scribe or amanuensis (5:12), would have written down the apostle's message on such tables before making the papyrus copy to be sent.

Col. 3:18–4:1) suggests that both authors draw on early Christian instruction for new believers. Affinities between 1 Peter and James on watchfulness and resisting the devil in light of the end (cf. 5:6–9 with James 4:6–10) likewise indicate common source material.

1 PETER: AUTHOR AND DATE

In 1:1 the author identifies himself as "Peter, an apostle of Jesus Christ" while 5:1 indicates that he is an "elder" and "a witness of Christ's sufferings." The early church was unanimous in recognizing this book as an authentic letter of Peter. The earliest testimony comes from 2 Peter 3:1, which states: "This is now my second letter to you." Eusebius groups the books that the church used into three categories: genuine, disputed, and false. He lists 1 Peter with the first group (*Eccl. Hist.* 3.3.1). Various second-century church fathers know of this letter, such as Papias (*Eccl. Hist.* 3.3.2), Irenaeus (who cites it), Tertullian (*Against Heresies* 5.7.2), and Clement of Alexandria (*Paedagogus* 1.6.43).

But many modern scholars question the book's authenticity, partly because of its fine Greek style. Could a Galilean fisherman have composed such a letter? We can attribute its grammatical style to Silvanus (5:12).

Another argument is that the persecutions reflected in the book are state-motivated, which does not occur until the time of Domitian (AD 95) or Pliny the Younger (AD 112) in Bithynia. But these believers are not facing state-organized persecution. In 3:15 the word answer or "defense" (*apologia*) need not imply legal proceedings (Acts 22:1; 1 Cor. 9:3); moreover, this defense is to be given "to everyone," not just civil authorities. To "suffer as a Christian" (1 Peter 4:16) does not necessarily reflect the situation under the governor Pliny, who discussed with Emperor Trajan "whether it is the mere name of Christian which is punishable, even if innocent of crime, or rather the crimes associated with the name" (*Letters* 10.96). From very early Christians understood their sufferings as being "for the Name" (Acts 5:41). The situation reflected in this letter is that of first-century Christians, regardless of where they lived.

As to date, the book was written sometime before Peter's death, which occurred during Nero's persecution of Christians, whom he blamed for the fire in Rome (AD 64). Some have even understood the "fiery ordeal" of 4:12 as a reference to that persecution since Nero used Christians as human torches to illuminate his garden at night (Tacitus, *Annals* 15.44). However, although Peter writes *from* Rome during Nero's reign (5:13), its recipients are scattered throughout Asia Minor, and the Neronian persecution did not extend outside the imperial city. Early church testimony confirms Peter was martyred in Rome (sometime between AD 64 when the fire broke out and AD 68 when Nero died). A likely date for the letter is in the early 60s.

2 PETER: SETTING

In 2 Peter 3:1 the author states: "This is now my second letter to you." His first letter took up the pressing problem of persecution; here the crisis is internal as heresy has crept in and threatens these congregations. This letter warns those who "are firmly established in the truth" (1:12) not to be persuaded to abandon the faith. Peter's appeal here is urgent since he knows his death is imminent (1:12–15).

The situation is also urgent since false teachers are exerting their influence on the church (1:5, 10, 15) just as false prophets had in Israel (2:1). Peter reveals their error: "They will secretly introduce destructive heresies, even denying the sovereign Lord who bought them." The heretics deny the coming of the Lord and future judgment, and this theological diversion is coupled with libertine morality (2:14, 18–19; 3:3–9). To bolster their case, they repudiate apostolic teaching, which they classify as *mythos* ("myth") (1:16), and question the divine inspiration of the prophets (1:20–21). Peter warns of the dire outcome of this heresy: "swift destruction" (2:1, 3; 3:7, 16).

The skepticism about the Lord's coming (3:3–10) is based on the apparent delay of his advent (3:4, 9; cf. 2:3). Their sexual immorality (2:2, 10, 14, 18), drunkenness, and gluttony (2:13) result from a distortion of Paul's teachings (3:15–16), turning "freedom" into moral license (2:19a). In reality, such people are enslaved to corruption (2:19b).

The heretics are motivated by greed (2:3, 14) as they exploit members of the church. Peter highlights their arrogance as they "despise authority" (2:10–12) and mock the teaching about the second coming (3:3–4). Their "denial" of "the sovereign Lord" is not only verbal since in their conduct they do not acknowledge him as the Master of their life (2:15; cf. 1 Tim. 5:8; Titus 1:16). This is shocking since the Master is the very one "who bought them" (2 Peter 2:1).

At one time the heretics were participants in the faith but "left the straight road and have gone astray, following the road of Balaam son of Bosor" (or Beor, 2:15 NRSV). These people have forgotten that they were cleansed from past sins (1:9). They entice others to their way, and as a result, unstable souls succumb to their error (2:14, 18–22). They are apostates who had "escaped the corruption of the world by knowing our Lord and Savior Jesus Christ" and yet were "again entangled in it and are overcome." Peter appeals to his readers not to be carried away with this error (3:18), as some already have. Two proverbs of the day described their condition: " 'A dog returns to its vomit,' and, 'A sow that is washed returns to her wallowing in the mud' " (2:20–22).

What is this error? Those who view 2 Peter as pseudepigraphic say that the letter is an attempt to curb Gnosticism, which believed in salvation via esoteric knowledge (1:2, 3, 5–6, 8; 2:20; 3:18). This movement did not arise until the second century AD (although certain elements were present in the first century). But there are no traces in the letter of the later Gnostic dualism, which viewed the material world as evil and the spiritual as good. Moreover, their immorality is linked with skepticism about final judgment and a distortion of Pauline teaching about Christian liberty, not with Gnostic dualism. Although Peter does

DENYING THE MASTER WHO BOUGHT THEM

The language in 2:1 evokes images drawn from ancient slavery, especially the act of freeing a slave known as manumission (see 1 Cor. 7:22–23). One manumission inscription reads: "Apollo the Pythian bought from Sosibius of Amphissa, for freedom, a female slave, whose name is Nicaea, by race a Roman, with a price of three minae of silver and a half-mina."[3] This slave became free by being sold, in effect, to the deity (Apollo). Though freed from the slavery to sin (Rom. 6:17–18), the Christian now belongs to another Master, Christ.

mention "knowledge" in the letter, he has in view personal knowledge of God and Christ (1:2 – 3, 8; 2:20; 3:18).

Another possible explanation of the heretics' teaching is the influence of Epicureanism (see Ch. 4). Epicureans rejected the notion of a future divine judgment and based their belief on the apparent delay in divine vengeance on evil. Peter appears to respond to their perspective in 3:8 – 10: "The Lord is not slow in keeping his promise, as some understand slowness. Instead he is patient with you, not wanting anyone to perish, but everyone to come to repentance."

The Epicureans also denied divine providence and believed that everything happened by chance. A corollary to their rejection of providence was their skepticism regarding predictive prophecy. How could even the gods predict that which happened by chance?

But Peter rejects these notions (3:3 – 4) and affirms that God was active in the world in the past, having brought it into being, and so he will act in the future (3:5 – 7). In fact, God has judged the world (2:4 – 10a), and he has not been absent from its history. Even if the heretics have not been influenced by Epicureans, a climate of skepticism in the first century brought into question the possibility of predictive prophecy, a trend that Cicero traces back to the Greek author Carneades (Cicero, *On Divination* 2.3.9-12).

2 PETER: MESSAGE

In light of the danger of apostasy, Peter urges his readers to be diligent in their moral progress (1:5 – 8) and so confirm their "calling and election" (1:10). His call to growth becomes his summary message: "But grow in the grace and knowledge of our Lord and Savior Jesus Christ" (3:18). He links this growth with the moral life of the believer (1:8). Second Peter is an impassioned plea to reject the heretics' notions about judgment and moral responsibility and to affirm that delay in divine judgment is due to nothing less than God's mercy as he calls people to repentance (3:8 – 10). But judgment will come, which should shape the present conduct of the believer (3:11 – 13). This was also Paul's message (3:14 – 16).

OUTLINE OF 2 PETER

I. Epistolary Greeting (1:1 – 2)

II. Letter Body: A Warning against False Teachers (1:3 – 3:17)

    A. Body Opening: God's Call to Glory and Virtue (1:3 – 11)

    B. Body Middle: The Apostolic Testimony and the False Teachers (1:12 – 2:22)

        1. A Call to Remember (1:12 – 21)

        2. The Coming and the Judgment of the False Teachers (2:1 – 22)

    C. Body Closing: A Call to Holiness (3:1 – 17)

        1. A Call to Remember Prophetic and Apostolic Teaching (3:1 – 2)

        2. Understand This: The Scoffers of the Last Day (3:3 – 7)

        3. Do Not Ignore This: One Day Is As a Thousand Years (3:8 – 10)

        4. Since All These Things Will Pass Away: Living in Light of the End (3:11 – 13)

        5. While Waiting For These Things: Diligence to Be Found Blameless (3:14 – 17)

III. Letter Closing: A Doxology (3:18)

THE EPICUREANS ON THE DELAY OF DIVINE JUDGMENT

In a fictitious dialogue, Plutarch discusses Epicurus's argument that delay in divine judgment is strong evidence against divine providence. Plutarch's son-in-law Patrocleas comments, "The delay and procrastination of the Deity in punishing the wicked appears to me the most telling argument by far." Olympichus adds that "his slowness destroys belief in providence" (*On the Delays of the Divine Vengeance* 548C-D, 549B)

COMPOSING 2 PETER

Peter is aware of a corpus of Paul's writings whose message the heretics have distorted (3:15–16). Our author admits that Paul's letters contain teachings that are difficult to understand, although he appears confident that the heretics' interpretation of those teachings is wide of the mark. Apart from this reference (2:19), 2 Peter is not otherwise dependent on Paul's writings.

But Peter does make extensive use of Jude, which he apparently has at hand. A good portion of Jude is reproduced in 2 Peter 2, and both letters present their material in roughly the same order. For example, Jude reminds his readers of God's past judgment of the angels, who are "bound with everlasting chains for judgment" (Jude 6), which Peter adapts: "God did not spare angels when they sinned, but sent them to hell, putting them in chains of darkness to be held for judgment" (2:4). Note the following comparison in the chart at the right.

It is unlikely that Jude used Peter. Were that the case, we would expect teaching from 2 Peter 1 and 3 to appear in Jude's letter. It is also unlikely that both authors used a common source. A careful comparison of these verses shows that Peter modifies material from Jude, shaping it in his refutation of the heretics. Neither should we assume that since Jude is Peter's source, the heretics denounced in both letters are the same people. The issues raised, while similar, are distinct.

Some have identified 2 Peter as a "testament" or a "farewell speech" (notes 1:12–15). Various examples of such literature from antiquity have been preserved (e.g., *Testaments of the Twelve Patriarchs*, *Testament of Abraham*), and testamentary material appears in other ancient writings (e.g., *1 Enoch*, *Jubilees*). This genre usually involves gathering family and friends around one's deathbed, reflecting on the dying person's character, calling them to avoid certain sins, and exhorting them to live a righteous life; it also contains blessings and cursings, and visions of the future.[4] Richard Bauckham observes that since testaments are always pseudepigraphical, 2 Peter cannot be an authentic work of Peter.[5] But although 2 Peter includes a testamentary section (1:12–15), it does not share other common features of this genre and we should not classify this entire letter as a testament.

2 PETER AND JUDE – A COMPARISON	
Jude	**2 Peter**
v. 4	2:1–3
v. 6	2:4
v. 7	2:6
v. 8	2:10
v. 9	2:11
v. 10	2:12
v. 11	2:15
v. 12a	2:13
vv. 12b–13	2:17
v. 16	2:18
vv. 17–18	3:2–3

2 PETER: AUTHOR AND DATE

The authorship of 2 Peter has been debated since ancient times. The *Apocalypse of Peter* knew of the book as did many of the church fathers. In the second century Justin Martyr referred to it, Clement of Alexandria wrote a commentary on it, and Irenaeus echoed it. A translation appeared in Egypt in the third century, and people such as Origen accepted it as genuine. But even Origen noted that some doubted its authenticity. In the fourth century Jerome commented that considerable doubt existed about its authenticity, citing stylistic differences with 1 Peter (Jerome accounts for the differences through different secretaries). Eusebius said most churches accepted it as authentic, although he entertained doubts. The book was, however, finally accepted into the canon.

In contemporary biblical scholarship, the debate over authorship revolves around different grammatical style in 1 and 2 Peter; sometimes the same concepts are expressed by different terminology (cf. 1 Peter 1:13 and 2 Peter 2:16 on Christ's coming). But since antiquity, stylistic differences have been attributed to Peter's amanuensis, Silvanus (1 Peter 5:12). Lexical differences may be accounted for by considering a distinct situation for each letter, evoking unique vocabulary. Second Peter 3:16 seems to point to a second-century date of composition since Paul's writings have been collected and classified as "Scripture." But Paul's letters were circulated and collected early (Col. 4:16), and the elevation of Paul's letters to "Scripture" is not out of line with Paul's own understanding of the inspired nature of his writings (1 Cor. 2:16; 7:40; 14:37; 2 Cor. 13:3). Some argue that concern over the delay in Christ's coming (3:4) reflects a second-century situation, but teaching about the delay has been woven into the earliest strata of Christian literature (see Matt. 25:1–13; Luke 12:35–48; James 5:7–8).

No compelling arguments have been forwarded against the authenticity of 2 Peter, and doubts that have arisen have reasonable explanations. We should consider this an authentic work of Peter since the accused has not been found guilty. The date of the letter is just before Peter's death (some time between AD 64 and 68).

JUDE: SETTING AND MESSAGE

Jude does not write the letter he originally intended. Apparently he was eager to compose a letter to a church or churches in Palestine to reflect on the "salvation we share" (v. 3). But Jude finds himself constrained to change his tone because some teachers have come from the outside whose conduct is ungodly. They pervert the teaching on grace (v. 4), transforming it into an excuse for licentious conduct that denies the only Master and Lord, Jesus Christ. Their theological novelty does not agree with the faith handed down as a sacred tradition (v. 3b).

Jude's letter pleads for the believers "to contend for the faith that the Lord has once for all entrusted to us, his people" (v. 3). It calls them to be built up and stand firm in the faith (vv. 20–21). But the troublers of the church are persuasive, and some members have been swayed. Jude calls the church to show mercy on those who are wavering (v. 22) but also to rescue those who have succumbed to the temptation (v. 23). Yet Jude is concerned that the rescuers themselves do not become ensnared by the heresy.

These heretics are promoting a theology that grace frees a person from moral constraint, but they deny the Lord by their immorality (v. 4). They reject any form of authority over their conduct (v. 8a) and are especially bombastic in their rejection of "glorious ones" (v. 8b, NRSV), a reference to angels whom Jewish theology understood as mediators of divine law (Acts 7:53; Gal. 3:19). They claim their teaching is inspired since it came to them in dreams (v. 8), a universally recognized form of divine communication. New, inspired revelation is set over against apostolic tradition (vv. 4, 17)

Some have broadly characterized the error as "antinomianism." Jude portrays the heretics as not only being in error (vv. 11b, 13) but also as corrupt people. He draws special attention to their unbridled sexuality (vv. 4–8, 12, 16, 18), avarice (v. 11), and pride-filled verbal excess (vv. 8–9, 10, 16, 18). What moves them are animal instincts (v. 10), not the Spirit (v. 19), the source of Christian virtue.

These heretics are also intent on persuading others to join with them. They stealthfully make their way in among the members of the church (v. 4) and act like friends (though they are nothing more than flatterers, v. 12). They have come to be recognized as leaders and, like Cain, Balaam, and Korah, are actively influencing others for ill (v. 11). They are effective in persuading members of the church to follow their ways, though not all who are tempted fully embrace their error (vv. 22–23).

Jude informs his readers/hearers that destruction awaits such people, as was predicted long ago (v. 4). Their presence, in effect, is a sign of the last times (v. 18). Yet Jude is confident that God is able to keep the disciples from falling into their trap (v. 24). They must avail themselves of faith and love (vv. 20–21) and mercifully come to the aid of any who are becoming ensnared (vv. 22–23). Jude is confident that this situation rests in God (vv. 24–25).

OUTLINE OF JUDE

I. Epistolary Greeting (1–2)

II. Letter Body: An Exhortation to Fight for the Traditional Faith (3–23)

    A. Disclosure of Jude's Purpose for Writing: An Exhortation to the Beloved (3–4)

    B. A Call to Remember: Predictions about the Heretics and Fulfillment (5–19)

        1. Text and Comment: Exodus, Angels, Sodom and Gomorrah, and Those Who Defile the Flesh, Reject Authority and Slander Glorious Ones (5–8)

        2. Text and Comment: Michael Did Not Blaspheme the Devil but These Blaspheme What They Do Not Understand (9–10)

        3. Text and Comment: Cain, Balaam, Korah, and Those Who Are Stains in the Community Meals (11–13)

        4. Text and Comment: The Prophecy of Enoch and Those Who Are Grumblers, Complainers, Flatterers (14–16)

        5. Text and Comment: The Apostolic Prophecy and Those Who Are Worldly, Lacking the Spirit (17–19)

    C. Exhortations to the Beloved (20–23)

III. Closing Doxology (24–25)

JUDE: COMPOSING THE STORY

A striking feature of Jude's letter is his use of pseudepigraphical literature. In verse 6 he refers to an angelic fall, which is an interpretive tradition based on Genesis 6:1–4 and elaborated extensively in *1 Enoch* 6–12 and other Jewish texts. In verse 9 Jude refers to the dispute over the body of Moses between the archangel Michael and the devil—a story is drawn from the *Assumption of Moses*. The most striking use of extrabiblical literature is in verses 14–15, where Jude quotes *1 Enoch* 1:9. New Testament authors sometimes make use of extrabiblical texts as they elaborate their arguments. Paul, for example, quotes Epimenides (Acts 17:28; Titus 1:12), Aratus (Acts 17:28), and Menander (1 Cor. 15:33). We should not conclude that such texts are inspired but only that they express something deemed true.

JUDE: AUTHOR AND DATE

The author identifies himself as Jude, "a brother of James" (v. 1), most likely the same person who is named, along with James, as one of Jesus' siblings (Matt. 13:55; Mark 6:3). Jude's reference to James is likely the well-known James, "the Lord's brother," one of the "pillars" of the Jerusalem church (Gal. 2:9). Since honor in the Mediterranean world is shared among family members, the honor ascribed to James as the leader of the Jerusalem church would enhance the status of Jude. In other words, in identifying himself as the "brother of James," Jude claims authority that parallels Paul's affirmations of his apostleship (Gal. 1:1).

Some confusion existed in the early church regarding Jude. But in his *Comments on the Epistle of Jude* (1–4), Clement of Alexandria not only states that Jude is the Lord's brother but comments on the author's reluctance to identify himself as such:

> Jude, who wrote the Catholic Epistle, the brother of the sons of Joseph, and very religious, whilst knowing the near relationship of the Lord, yet did not say that he himself was His brother. But what said he? "Jude, a servant of Jesus Christ,"—of Him as Lord; but "the brother of James." For this is true; he was His brother, (the son) of Joseph.

Jude was read early in the church and was accepted in the second-century Muratorian Canon and that of Athanasius in the mid-fourth century. Clement of Alexandria esteemed Jude highly enough to write a commentary on it. The letter was likely written around the middle of the first century.

QUESTIONS FOR DISCUSSION ⊚⊚⊚⊚⊚⊚⊚⊚⊚⊚⊚⊚⊚⊚⊚⊚⊚⊚⊚⊚⊚⊚⊚⊚⊚⊚⊚⊚⊚

1. First Peter presents a robust theology of suffering. Discuss this theology in relation to Peter's theology about God, Christ, and the end times. Is the theology of suffering a topic of reflection in the contemporary church?

2. Should Christians be engaged in social action in society? Integrate the teaching of 1 Peter into your response.

3. Is "heresy" a category that we can maintain in a pluralistic culture? Discuss the tension between theological novelty and apostolic tradition in light of 2 Peter and Jude.

4. What role does eschatology play in the field of Christian ethics? What insight can be gained from Jude and 2 Peter?

5. Examine Jude's use of pseudepigraphical literature. Does Jude consider such writings to be authoritative?

BIBLIOGRAPHY
Introductory
Davids, P. H. *The First Epistle of Peter*. NICNT. Grand Rapids: Eerdmans, 1990.

_____. *The Letters of 2 Peter and Jude*. PNTC. Grand Rapids: Eerdmans, 2006.

Green, M. *The Second Epistle of Peter and the Epistle of Jude*. TNTC. Grand Rapids: Eerdmans, 1987.

Grudem, W. *The First Epistle of Peter*. TNTC. Grand Rapids: Eerdmans, 1988.

Marshall, I. H. *1 Peter*. IVPNTC. Downers Grove, IL: InterVarsity Press, 1991.

Moo, D. J. *2 Peter and Jude*. NIVAC. Grand Rapids: Zondervan, 1996.

Schreiner, T. R. *1, 2 Peter, Jude*. NAC. Nashville: Broadman & Holman, 2003.

Advanced
Bauckham, R. J. *Jude, 2 Peter*. WBC. Waco, TX: Word, 1983.

Elliott, J. H. *1 Peter*. AB. New York: Doubleday, 2000.

Green, G. L. *Jude and 2 Peter*. BECNT. Grand Rapids: Baker, 2008

Jobes, K. *1 Peter*. BECNT. Grand Rapids: Baker, 2005.

Michaels, J. Ramsey. *1 Peter*. WBC. Waco, TX: Word, 1988.

Neyrey, J. H. *2 Peter, Jude*. AB. New York: Doubleday, 1993.

NOTES
1. Cited in D. F. Epstein, *Personal Enmity in Roman Politics 218–34 BC* (London: Croom Helm, 1987), 20.

2. B. Winter, *Seek the Welfare of the City* (Grand Rapids: Eerdmans, 1994), 28, 34–35.

3. A. Deissmann, *Light From the Ancient East*, 323.

4. J. Charlesworth, *The Old Testament Psuedepigrapha*, 1:773.

5. R. Bauckham, *Jude, 2 Peter* (WBC; Waco, TX: Word, 1983), 134.

CHAPTER 25

THE LETTERS OF JOHN

Early Christians such as John were competing with colossal religious temples throughout the empire. To speak of a God who appeared in a Jewish man named Jesus hardly compared with the glorious temple of Bacchus in Baalbeck (Lebanon).

Three short letters in the New Testament have been attributed to John. Unmistakable thematic connections with the Fourth Gospel suggest that the letters originated with the author of that gospel. The letters are an enigma, however. While 2 John and 3 John have the usual features of ancient letters, 1 John bears no such marks: it is more like a tract aimed at a problem.

To understand the letters, we must attempt to reconstruct the social and theological history of John's community by using clues in these letters. Threatening heresies are sweeping within John's churches. John's letters address these issues forcefully in order to protect the unity of the church and identify those undermining his authority. Rather than arming the com-

Tradition says that John was buried in Ephesus. In the 6th century, Justinian built a church in Ephesus to commemorate it.

munity for combat against *external* pressures, these letters indicate that the conflicts are now *internal*. John's letters address these issues forcefully in a manner that both protects the unity of the church and identifies those who are undermining his authority.

THE CONTEXT OF JOHN'S LETTERS

Eusebius was the leading church historian in the 4th century. His account of early church history survives today and has become an important source for understanding the apostolic age.

According to Ireneaus (130–200), bishop of Lyons, John was a leading figure in Asia Minor (Eusebius, *Eccl. Hist.* 3.23). Clergy traveled to Ephesus just to learn from him and hear his stories about Jesus. Irenaeus says he got this information from Polycarp, bishop of Smyrna, who himself received instruction from John (*Against Heresies* 2.22.5). Eusebius also notes that John, who reclined near the Lord at the Last Supper (John 13:25), was buried in Ephesus (*Eccl. Hist.* 3:31)

John's community of believers lives on the frontiers of Judaism. His church is heterogeneous: Jewish Christians with little knowledge of Greek live alongside Greeks, who know little of the Old Testament. Their common bond is a firm allegiance to Jesus, their Messiah, and John is their leader. Yet since John himself and his "Christian message" are rooted in Judaism, this community naturally lives in close proximity to the synagogues of Ephesus.

These were the formative years when prized stories about Jesus were being preserved, including a collection of John's personal accounts. John's gospel

JOHN'S TOMB IN EPHESUS

Eusebius cites a remarkable quote from Papias, bishop of Hierapolis in Asia Minor (c. AD 60–130), that he was mentored by John. But Eusebius also refers to a second John in Ephesus—"John the elder." Thus Ephesus had two tombs attached to the name "John" (*Eccl. Hist.* 3.39.6).

Today visitors to Ephesus can see the ruins of a large Byzantine church built by Emperor Justinian (483–565). This marks the traditional burial place of John.

offered generous amounts of teaching from Jesus, who predicted the sort of persecution the church was having. Among Jesus' teachings were those that promised an intimacy with him through the Holy Spirit; John includes phrases like "rebirth," "drinking living water," and "eating the bread of life." This was a gospel that encouraged those believers prone to mystical experiences of the faith.

Indeed John's gospel is an *empowering gospel* that shaped this Christian community. Jesus and the Father lived inside these spiritually reborn believers (John 14:23). The Holy Spirit promised to provide them with incredible powers: to recall Jesus' words (14:26), to work miracles greater than those of Jesus (14:12), to have prayer answered (14:13–14), and to confront a hostile world (16:8). They even had the power to forgive sin (20:23). Above all, the Spirit gave them the power of *prophecy*, to continue speaking with Jesus' voice, revealing *new things* not recorded in Scripture (16:13).

In other words, John's community was a *pneumatic* community — a community that made the Spirit (Gk. *pneuma*) a vital feature of its life. Believers were ready to experience the Spirit in its fullness. In short, John's theology established the context for a pneumatic/charismatic Christianity.

But something serious has happened to this church's life. The once-unified congregation is beginning to tear apart, and this crisis seems fueled by a misuse of the gospel's teachings about the Spirit. There are threats within the fellowship itself. John says that it is "the last hour" for the community (2:18).

Lengthy scholarly debate has tried to identify these dissenters. They are likely a group of John's former followers who know his gospel well, claim to be inspired by the Spirit, and challenge John's understanding of Jesus Christ's person and work. They are succeeding, because the community is splitting, harsh words are being exchanged, and the vocabulary once reserved for those in "the world" is now aimed at fellow Christians.

First John supplies our primary evidence for this division, where we read of the painful departure of this group (2:19–26) and warnings about "deceivers" and "liars" who twist the truth of Christ (2:22; cf. 2 John 7). We read of theological debates (1 John 5:5–8) being fought among teachers claiming to be filled with the Holy Spirit (2:20–21; 4:1–6). The letter's repeated emphasis on love hints at the severity of the situation.

John's letters are a response to those misinterpreting the Fourth Gospel. For some scholars these letters served as a commentary on the gospel. Others describe them as an "epilogue," designed to circulate with his gospel to root out erroneous interpretations.

Hippolytus, a third-century theologian, describes how Johannine language was used by his Gnostic opponents. The earliest commentaries on John were written by Gnostics (e.g., Heracleon; see sidebar). This is probably why the orthodox church only grudgingly

Claims for prophetic inspiration were common in antiquity and contributed to the confidence of John's opponents. Called "oracles," none were more famous than those at Delphi, Greece, which gave their utterances in the inner halls of the temple of Apollo.

embraced this gospel. There is a surprising lack of interest in John's writings among the second-century writers. As many scholars believe, it was the letters of John — 1 John in particular — that redeemed the Fourth Gospel for the New Testament.

LITERARY FORM

The letters of 2 and 3 John have all the usual features of first-century letters: the author and recipient identified at the beginning, a blessing or prayer ("Grace, mercy, and peace"), and a "greeting" at the end. The letters also contain personal references and allusions that suggest they are intended for a specific situation. Some suggest that 3 John is the best New Testament example of first-century epistolary format.

But the same cannot be said for 1 John, which is least like a first-century letter. It lacks any address or name. No conclusion ends the document — 5:21 sounds abrupt, as if the writer's thoughts are cut off. There are no personal comments. This is unusual when we consider the crisis in the church.

This absence of form has led many to suggest that 1 John is not a personal letter but a general treatise or a sermon for wide distribution (John uses the plural "you" twenty-two times). Perhaps it is a pamphlet engaged in some sort of polemic.

Discovering a recognizable structure of thought in 1 John has proven impossible. Scholars find either spirals of cyclical thought or unconnected units. Some see two main divisions each with a declaration: "God is light" (1:5) and "God is love" (4:8). The gospel of John, which also enjoys a bipartite form, may be the *structural model* for 1 John. Similarities between the two writings are numerous.

OUTLINE OF 1 JOHN

I. Prologue (1:1–4)

II. God Is Light (and We Should Walk Accordingly) (1:5–3:10)

    A. Thesis: The Light and the Darkness (1:5–7)
    B. Resist Sinfulness (1:8–2:2)
    C. Obey God's Commands (2:3–11)
    D. Defy the World and Its Allure (2:12–17)
    E. Renounce Those Who Distort the Truth (2:18–27)
    F. Live like God's Children (2:28–3:10)

III. God Is Love (and We Should Walk Accordingly) (3:11–5:12)

    A. Love One Another in Practical Ways (3:11–24)
    B. Beware of False Prophets (4:1–6)
    C. Love One Another as Christ Loves Us (4:7–21)
    D. Obey God and Thereby Conquer the World (5:1–5)
    E. Never Compromise Your Testimony (5:6–12)

IV. Conclusion (5:13–21)

It seems clear that 2 John and 3 John do not have a careful theological structure. As personal letters, they simply begin with a greeting and then develop one theme after another. Both letters are concerned about living the truth, which means loving those who abide in the family of God and chastising those who dismantle that family. In each case John warns against community destroyers.

AUTHORSHIP AND DATE

While Christian tradition has attributed these letters to John the apostle, the letters are anonymous (except that 2 and 3 John call their author "the elder"). This title may simply refer to a man of high esteem in the church, though elsewhere the apostles call themselves "elders" (1 Peter 5:1). This situation is complicated by Eusebius's reference to two Johns (see sidebar on "John's Tomb in Ephesus," above)

While 2 and 3 John appear to come from the same pen, does 1 John originate with this same author described as "the elder"? There are striking similarities of style and content among all three writings that suggest common authorship.[1] A more compelling question is whether the same pen wrote the gospel of John. As early as the third century church fathers were making this claim based on similarities of content and style, especially between 1 John and the gospel. These parallels are similar to those found between Luke and Acts or Colossians and Ephesians. Thus, most scholars today affirm common authorship for 1 John and the gospel. Therefore if John the apostle wrote the gospel, he most likely wrote all three letters.[2]

If this is indeed true, those who place the gospel in the late first century locate the letters anywhere from AD 90–110. However, arguments for such a late date are being seriously criticized, and increasingly the gospel has been given an earlier time frame (closer to AD 70 or 80). Allowing time for the development of the heresy described in the letters, a date between 70 and 90 is likely.

THEOLOGICAL THEMES IN JOHN'S LETTERS

The theological emphases of the letters are intimately tied to the controversy that has placed the community under siege. The reason why John repeatedly talks about love, sin, and the truth is rooted in the views of certain heretics.

The Views of the Heretics

It is impossible to name this movement with any specificity. We can only outline their beliefs using clues within these letters. But this is difficult. Writers rarely describe their opponents' views completely, and we have no first-hand documents from John's adversaries. Moreover, some things John opposes in his letters may not derive from his opponents. For instance, in 1 John 4:18 he says there is no fear in love because perfect love casts out fear; John may be chastising his followers here, not the heretics.

John returns repeatedly to two intimately connected themes: Christology and ethical behavior. The opponents have embraced an aberrant view of Christ that has led them to make wrong judgments about Christian living.

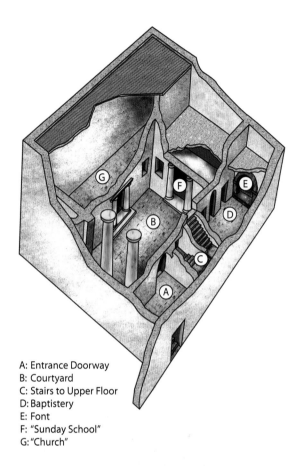

A: Entrance Doorway
B: Courtyard
C: Stairs to Upper Floor
D: Baptistery
E: Font
F: "Sunday School"
G: "Church"

John's "communities" were likely small gatherings of Christians in house churches. This artist's rendering shows the earliest Christian church building known, from Dura-Europas, Syria. Early third century.

Christology. John's opponents hold the following beliefs: They deny the Son (1 John 2:23), deny that Jesus Christ has come in the flesh (1 John 4:2; 2 John 7), and deny that Jesus is the Christ (1 John 2:22). Affirmations in the letters that buttress John's own Christology are: Jesus is the Christ (1 John 5:1), Jesus Christ has come in the flesh (4:2), Jesus is the Son (2:23; 3:23; 5:11) or the Son of God (1:3, 7; 3:8, 23; 4: 9, 10, 15), and Jesus Christ came "by water and blood" (5:6).

From these statements we can deduce that John's opponents are Christians who have begun to deviate from the traditional understanding of Jesus Christ. They affirm the idea of Christ, but doubt if he became flesh and if the man Jesus is indeed the incarnation of God.

Today many scholars conclude that John's opponents embrace a Christology that elevates Christ's divinity at the expense of his humanity. The Hellenistic world affirmed a cosmos populated by numerous deities, and elevating Christ into their company was easy. But this same world rejected the idea that such divinities entered our material world, since it is imperfect and subject to decay.

In this dualistic outlook, Christ is separated from our world and belongs with the deities of heaven. One variety of this view said that Christ may have "seemed" (Gk. *dokeō*; hence, Docetism) to appear in the flesh but did not. Although the earthly life of Jesus Christ is now irrelevant, these opponents still claim to have immediate access to God. They believe they have moved beyond the elementary teachings of Christianity and, inspired by the Spirit, can know God directly. The very gospel that gave birth to their faith is being jettisoned (cf. 2 John 9).

We have cautiously rebuilt the Christological context from which John's opponents are working. The incarnate Jesus Christ no longer occupies the central place in Christian faith. While the opponents may have a nominal

---

JESUS IS NOT THE CHRIST

In a polemical verse John writes: "Who is the liar? It is whoever denies that Jesus is the Messiah" (1 John 2:22). At first glance it would seem that John's opponents deny the messiahship of Jesus. But this is not what they are saying. They deny "that *Jesus* is the Messiah." That is, they believe in a redemptive revealer named Christ, but he was not made truly human in the man Jesus.

In 4:2 John reinforces his claim: "Every spirit that acknowledges that Jesus Christ has come in the flesh is from God." Note also 2 John 7: "Many deceivers, who do not acknowledge Jesus Christ as coming in the flesh, have gone out into the world. Any such person is the deceiver and the antichrist."

interest in the Jesus of history, they look for inspired spiritual experiences that lift them above the views of John.

Ethics. John's letters give a sustained critique of the moral disposition of the heretics, whose theology apparently makes ethical behavior of no consequence for the Christian life. John mentions that his opponents boast that they:

- are "without sin" (1:8, 10)
- "have fellowship" with God but walk in the darkness (1:6)
- "know" God but are disobedient (2:4)
- are "in the light" but hate their fellow Christians (2:9)
- "love God" but hate their brothers and sisters (4:20)

John also repeats affirmations that shed light on the nature of the opponents' ethical position:

- to abide in God is to obey him (2:6)
- to sin willfully shows you have not known God (3:3–6; 5:18)
- whoever acts sinfully belongs to the devil (3:7–10)
- we should love one another (3:11–12, 17–18)
- refusing to love your brother or sister means you have not inherited eternal life (3:14–15)
- God is love—and to know him is to love (4:8–10)

Christology is the main battleground in the community, but the tangible expression of these disagreements comes in the form of open conflict and hostility. In other words, faulty Christology spills over into unethical conduct.

What does John mean when he says that these people are "not obedient"? There is no evidence that they live immoral lives. But since they deny the significance of Christ's incarnation, they likely deny the significance of his earthly teachings and take no heed to Jesus' words in the gospel. Likewise, if they deny their own sinfulness, they feel no need for Christ's atoning death on the cross. Theirs is a "deeper" religion, fueled by nontraditional insights gleaned from the Spirit (2:20–23; 4:1). They refuse to submit to the leadership that promotes these teachings and are intolerant of those who disagree with them.

The themes of John's opponents find numerous echoes in a collection of Gnostic Christian writings discovered in Nag Hammadi, Egypt, in 1945

A typical bath in Ephesus. Polycarp wrote that John met the heretic Cerinthus at such a bath (see sidebar, p. 417).

The opponents are not simply indifferent to those who disagree with them; they are intolerant. This explains the repeated times that John refers to "hating" fellow Christians. Conflict has resulted from the opponents' superior spirituality. These people have become elitist in their view of themselves, and those who seek to exhort them, if they cannot catalogue similar experiences for themselves, have no credibility.

John's Secondary Concerns

Various secondary themes are evident throughout the letters. These appear by accident because they are a part of the refutation the author is making against his opponents.

The Holy Spirit. If John's gospel is central to this community's spiritual formation, the Spirit obviously plays a pivotal role in discipleship. In 4:13 John reassures his followers that possessing the Spirit is characteristic of those who "live in God." Such abiding is not simply a matter of orthodox confession (4:15) or loving conduct (4:16). Abiding in God is experien-

---

THE GOSPEL OF THOMAS, SAYING 29

The discovery of the *Gospel of Thomas* in Egypt (1945) has given us a poignant view into what happened to early Christians who jettisoned an orthodox framework for thinking theologically. Here we have 114 "secret sayings" claiming to be from Jesus. However in them are Gnostic categories that denigrate the material world. Saying 29 illustrates this well:

NOTES FROM ANTIQUITY

> Jesus said, "If the flesh came into being because of spirit, it is a wonder. But if spirit came into being because of the body, it is a wonder of wonders. Indeed I am amazed at how this great wealth has made its home in this poverty."

First John contradicts this sort of thinking. He embraces the material world: "That which was from the beginning ... which we have *seen with our eyes*, which we have looked at and our *hands have touched* — this we proclaim concerning the Word of life" (1:1).

---

tial—a personal experience with the Holy Spirit. Therefore, the false teachers must buttress their authority with some pneumatic experience. This explains why in 4:1–3 John calls the church to "test the spirits." Believers must be able to spot "false prophets" (4:1).

This is a pneumatic context. Note that John does not use his apostolic authority as Paul often does. Instead, he urges the church to test the spirits to see if they are affirming traditional beliefs about Jesus—thereby undercutting the authority of these prophets. His tactic, therefore, is characteristic of those struggling against rival leadership claims in a "charismatic" setting. One cannot deny the Spirit. Thus, one must teach discernment and urge Christians to weigh claims made in the Spirit.

But John goes further. If these secessionists are claiming a superior spirituality, he reminds the church that each member has been equally anointed with the Spirit (2:20, 27). In other words, spiritual discernment is the task of *every* person. No one may claim exclusive spiritual insight.

Discernment and tradition. These letters remind us that the church is the custodian of the truth. The believing community must discern false belief and practice and distinguish between truth and error. While this theme is explicit only in 4:1ff, it is presumed throughout 1 John (cf. also 2 John 8).

But how can we discern truth from falsehood? If a prophet urges something new under the authority of the Spirit, how can it be weighed? John believes that the church is accountable to the historic revelation given in Jesus Christ and passed down through the apostles. Individual inspiration must be weighed against truth revealed in Scripture and tradition.

Throughout 1 John the author affirms that what was "from the beginning" should be the anchor (1:1; 2:13–14; 3:11). John continually urges his readers to recall what they first learned and measure everything else by it. "Let what you heard *from the beginning* abide in you. If what you heard *from the beginning* abides in you, then you will abide in the Son and in the Father" (2:24 NRSV).

By "the beginning" John refers to the historic coming of Jesus Christ and the preservation of that revelation. What is revealed in the incarnation must be the litmus test for all new theological insights. Thus in 1:1–3 John points to what he saw with eyes and touched with hands—the incarnate Christ. *Historic Christology must be the touchstone for all Christian belief.* His exhortation in 2:12–14 twice reminds the fathers—those who are older—to rekindle their acquaintance with the ancient teachings.

This theological anchor in historic Christology is reminiscent of the gospel of John. In his farewell discourse, Jesus talks about the Spirit and the limits of what he will do. As Jesus' words cannot deviate from the Father's words (John 5:19), so too the Spirit will reiterate what Jesus himself has said (14:26; cf. 16:13). Father, Son, and Spirit provide a revelation that is self-consistent.

Since John did not possess the New Testament as we do today, he had to elevate "tradition" or historic teaching passed down with apostolic authority. No doubt his own record of Christ—the gospel of John—serves as a reservoir of such traditional teachings. Were John with us today, he would undoubtedly point to Scripture as an apostolic archive of teachings against which to weigh modern teachings. Yet other, more ancient Christian

John uses the language of the family (1 John 2:12-14, 28; 5:2) to describe Christian believers' relationships with each other. This was unconventional in antiquity and underscored the unique community early Christianity aspired toward.

The short letters of John remind us that the early Christians did not live in isolation but enjoyed a communications network of couriers that used the Roman road system. Pictured: A Roman road located in modern Algeria identical to Roman roads built throughout the eastern empire.

communities (such as the Catholic and Orthodox churches) would object to such a narrow explanation of "tradition." To them tradition means more — the archive of normative religious truth passed down through the church from generation to generation. John affirms that Christian wisdom and truth — anchored in right Christology — are cumulative and binding.

Love, unity, and fellowship. The gospel and letters of John place a high premium on the quality of Christian community. Jesus' command in John 13:34 and 15:12, 17 make clear that love should be the hallmark of his followers. In John 17 Jesus prays for harmony and unity among his followers so "that they may be one," based on the model of the oneness of the Father and the Son (17:20–23).

No doubt the division in John's church has placed unity and love on the ecclesiastical agenda. He even makes love a command: Christians who love God *must* love their brothers and sisters in the church (1 John 4:21). This teaching John anchors "from the beginning" as well (3:11; 2 John 5). In 1 John 3:23 he almost sums up the Christian life with two exhortations: believing in Jesus Christ and loving one another.

But John accompanies this exhortation with a theological basis. Initially, he says, God first loved us (4:19). Love cannot be fueled by human energy. It originates from God when we apprehend the depth of his love for us (4:7a) and when we are born anew by *his* Spirit (4:7b). Intimate knowledge of God is the same as enjoying the intimate reciprocity of God's love: He loves us, we love him, and this love spills over to those near us. Conversely, not to love is evidence that someone does not truly know God (4:8).

Christ Jesus is the material expression of God's tangible love. Once again, historic Christology addresses the issues of ethics. Because Christ laid down his life for us, we ought to do the same for one another (3:16; see especially 4:10).

John describes living in God's love, knowing him, and obeying his commands as "living in the light." When people live in the light together, they *corporately* experience God's love and unity, and fellowship results (1:5–7). But the reverse is also true. When people exhibit hostility and division, when they "hate" (to use John's term), they prove they live "in the darkness" (2:9–11). Such so-called Christians are "liars" and hypocrites (4:20).

THE CONTEXT OF 2 JOHN

The ongoing history of John's church is visible in 2 John and 3 John. Various theories have been offered for the chronological rearrangement of these three letters. Some suggest 2 John is John's original letter and 1 John is his expansion—a fulfillment of his wish to write much more (2 John 12). But how does 2 John make sense if the recipients have not read 1 John. Second John is an exhortation—a reminder—of things said in 1 John. The shorter letters should be interpreted in light of 1 John.

These letters show us a community that takes its faith seriously. Some have wondered if it fosters a sectarian outlook in which inner love and cohesion are as absolute as the boundary the community has erected between itself and the world. Christians are taught to reject the world (1 John 2:15–17; 4:4–5) and to practice a love within the community that has no natural counterpart (4:19–21; 2 John 5; 3 John 5–6). They must view themselves as elect of God (1 John 5:19–20; 2 John 7–9).

Does such a community finally collapse under its own internal pressures? The intensity of its vision arms its critics with an intolerance that finally tears the church apart. When we read 1 John 2:18–19, this group has departed, though John still views them from the doorway of the church as "former members." But by the time we read 2 John 7, the rupture seems complete. Now they are "in the world" and allied with the antichrist, and John forbids further contact (2 John 10–11).

These letters bear eloquent testimony to the vulnerability of the church when it lives on the frontiers of the world and is subject to its influences. They warn us of anyone "who runs ahead and does not continue in the teaching of Christ" (2 John 9)—particularly when such teachers are from within the ranks.

THE CONTEXT OF 3 JOHN

In 3 John, the church is in the grips of the theological struggle described in 1 John and confronted in 2 John. John himself once wrote to the church, but an influential man named Diotrephes rejected his letter (3 John 9). John then sent emissaries to the church, but Diotrephes refused to acknowledge them (v. 10). He even rejected John publicly (v. 9) and

ROMAN REST STOP DISCOVERED

The Roman road system, famous for its excellent construction and safety, recognized the need for rest stops. One road stretching across Europe gave up its secrets in December 2004 when an archaeological team discovered a Roman rest stop in Neuss, Germany. It offered a chariot service station, a gourmet restaurant, and a hotel with central heating.

Christians relied on the hospitality of other believers when they traveled. Thus John commends Gaius in 3 John 5 for welcoming his emissaries. To welcome someone meant hospitality, acceptance, friendship, and loyalty.

NOTES FROM ANTIQUITY

spread rumors about him. Diotrephes even forcefully stopped anyone who showed sympathy to the visitors or tried to speak with them.

The missionaries found a courageous host, however, in a man named Gaius. We cannot tell if Gaius belonged to Diotrephes's house church or lived nearby. Gaius knew Diotrephes but did not feel threatened by his power. He offered hospitality to traveling Christians and helped finance their journey (3 John 5–6). He sent them "on their way" (v. 6)—which means giving them money—and they returned to John with their report about the church's rebellion and Gaius's faithfulness (v. 3).

John wants to visit this church personally but cannot at the present (v. 14). He knows he must shore up the true believers there and encourage their faithfulness—those like Gaius who still walk in the truth, whom he calls "friends" (v. 14; cf. v. 1). So John plans a strategy: commend Gaius for his hospitality and encourage him to continue. Thus, when John comes for a visit, he has allies who will stand for Christ and against Diotrephes.

Verse 12 introduces the courier of the letter—Demetrius. The hospitality and financial support shown to other Christian travelers will undoubtedly be extended to Demetrius, a personal friend of John. Moreover, John says, even "the truth" speaks well of him.

This strong affirmation of Demetrius anticipates what Diotrephes might say about him. Since Diotrephes rejects John, he will reject Demetrius. John's testimony should strengthen Gaius's confidence in Demetrius, but the problem will only be solved when John confronts Diotrephes personally.

QUESTIONS FOR DISCUSSION ◉◉◉◉◉◉◉◉◉◉◉◉◉◉◉◉◉◉◉◉◉◉◉◉◉◉◉◉

1. What is the relationship between 1 John and the gospel of John?

2. Why was the early church reluctant to embrace the gospel of John fully?

3. How does John confront opponents who claim that their teaching stems from Jesus himself speaking through the Spirit?

4. How can a faulty understanding of the incarnation lead to a willingness to live immorally?

5. How do we balance a commitment to love with a commitment to separate ourselves from those who contradict the truth?

BIBLIOGRAPHY

Introductory

Bruce, F. F. *The Epistles of John*. Grand Rapids: Eerdmans, 1970.

Burge, G. M. *Letters of John*. NIVAC. Grand Rapids: Zondervan, 1996.

Kruse, C. G. *The Letters of John*. PNTC. Grand Rapids: Eerdmans, 2000.

Thompson, M. M. *1–3 John*. IVPNTC. Downers Grove, IL: InterVarsity Press, 1992.

Advanced

Brown, R. E. *The Epistles of John*. AB. New York: Doubleday, 1982.

Marshall, I. H. *The Epistles of John*. NICNT. Grand Rapids: Eerdmans, 1978.

Smalley, S. *1, 2, 3 John*. WBC. Waco, TX: Word, 1984.

NOTES

1. R. E. Brown, *The Epistles of John* (AB; New York: Doubleday, 1982), 14–35, 755–59 (charts).

2. For the credibility of this tradition, see G. M. Burge, *Interpreting the Gospel of John* (Grand Rapids: Baker, 1992), 37–54.

CHAPTER 26

THE REVELATION OF JOHN

A street in ancient Pergamum called "The Sacred Way" leading to the city's Asclepion. This well-known city had a Christian community whom John addresses in Rev. 2:2-17.

Island of Patmos in the Aegean Sea, John's home in exile.

Revelation is perhaps the least understood—and most misrepresented—book in the New Testament. Even its Greek name, The Apocalypse, is odd. It means "unveiling" or "revealing," but the clarity of that revelation is often in dispute. Beautiful scenes of the throne room of God (chs. 4–5) contrast with the evil of the many-horned beast (ch. 13) and the desperate calamity of the faithful witnesses (ch. 11). What do these pictures mean?

THE CONTEXT OF REVELATION

A man named John (1:4) received a vision on the island of Patmos, located in the Aegean Sea southeast of Miletus. The small island was barren and used by Rome to exile criminals and political prisoners.

Presumably John was banished to Patmos because of his faith (1:9). The shame of this treatment was no less extreme than his probable loss of private property. Public sentiment against Emperor Domitian's cruelty (AD 81–96) led his successor, Nerva (AD 96–98), to release all political prisoners, including Christians. John was then liberated and returned to his home in Ephesus (Eusebius, *Eccl. Hist.* 3.17–20).

IMPERIAL CULT

John's exile was probably connected to his resistance to Domitian's interest in promoting the imperial cult (emperor worship) This practice began when the Roman Senate deified Julius Caesar at his death. It initially flourished in the East, where worship of a living leader was already appropriate. In the West, some emperors declared themselves as gods while still living.

Emperor worship helped unify the empire and proved one's loyalty to Rome. All who sacrificed to the emperor received a certificate verifying their fidelity. This cult was a problem for Christians, who pledged allegiance to one Lord and Savior, Jesus Christ.

APOCALYPTIC SECT AT QUMRAN

The Essenes of Qumran thought of themselves as "sons of light" and everyone else as "sons of darkness." Their apocalyptic vision describes a mighty battle against the forces of evil.

> For the M[aster. The Rule of] War on the unleashing of the attack of the sons of light against the company of the sons of darkness, the army of Belial: against the band of Edom, Moab.... The sons of Levi, Judah, Benjamin, the exiles in the desert, shall battle against them.... The confusion of the sons of Japheth shall be [great] and Assyria shall fall unsuccoured. The dominion of the Kittim shall come to an end and iniquity shall be vanquished, leaving no remnant; [for the sons] of darkness there shall be no escape. [The sons of righteous]ness shall shine over all the ends of the earth. (*War Scroll* [1QM] 1:1–2, 6)

THE GENRE OF REVELATION

What is the genre of Revelation? Is it an apocalypse, a prophecy, or a combination of the two? *Apocalypse* is defined as revelatory literature with a narrative framework. The revelation is mediated by an angel, and its content concerns eschatological salvation. In an apocalypse, the supernatural world is described with vivid symbols as the author shows how events in heaven impact our world. The world is in crisis because of sin, but God will break into history to make all things right in the new age. The author's words inspire hope and exhort readers to remain faithful in the midst of suffering. The imminent end of the present age is anticipated. Many scholars see these characteristics in John's Revelation.

Not all scholars, however, are convinced that Revelation is best understood as an apocalypse. They suggest it is a *prophecy*, wherein God will work out his (future) will within history. Those who argue Revelation is of the prophetic genre point to John's claims in 1:3 and 22:6–7, which identify the book as prophecy. Others suggest that prophecy is a broad enough category to encompass apocalyptic views; apocalyptic is a "heightening and more intense clustering of literary and thematic traits found in prophecy."[1]

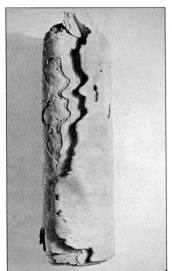 

Left: The War Scroll from Qumran is an apocalyptic account of the last battle between the "Sons of Light," the faithful Jews, and the "Sons of Darkness," all those who do not belong to the Essene community, including fellow Jews *Right*: Tradition says that John received his vision on the island of Patmos. In the 12th century, a monastery was built on the island to recall John's life and work.

Map of the Seven Churches to which John sent letters (Rev. 2-3).

The impulse behind Jewish apocalyptic works seems twofold. First, the author wants to reflect on God's redemptive work in history, continuing the prophets' messages. Second, he understands God's acts as having significance outside of history in a cosmic struggle against Satan and evil. Through the use of violent images and esoteric symbols, God's immanent judgment was anticipated by the righteous, who longed for vindication.

MESSAGE OF REVELATION

While on Patmos, John receives a revelation from God. His opening chapter is replete with vivid descriptions of God's majesty, Jesus Christ's glory, and the Holy Spirit's power. God is the one "who is, and who was, and who is to come" (1:4, 8; cf. Ex. 3:14, where God identifies himself as "I am"). Jesus Christ is "the First and the Last. I am the Living One; I was dead, and now look, I am alive for ever and ever!" (1:17–18). He is the "firstborn from the dead, and the ruler of the kings of the earth" (1:5; cf. Ps. 89:27, 37, a messianic psalm about David's kingdom that John sees fulfilled in Christ).

The Spirit is symbolically referred to as "the seven spirits before his throne" (1:4; cf. "seven lamps . . . blazing" in 4:5). John connects the power of the Holy Spirit with the witness of the church, for he refers to the churches as seven golden lampstands (1:12). The lamps burning on these lampstands portray the fire of the Holy Spirit empowering the church.

Jesus stands among seven lampstands (1:12), representing his presence among his churches. The letters to seven communities in Asia Minor (chs. 2–3) are connected to the opening vision of God, as well as to events and symbols relayed in the following chapters. For the growing number of Gentile Christians, the dangerous mix of Roman imperialism and Hellenistic Judaism led to difficult, even life-threatening social realities. Emperor worship continued to rise, and all Gentiles, including Christians, were expected to show loyalty to him through sacrifices.

EPHESUS TODAY

Today, Ephesus is one of the best preserved ancient cities. First-century remains include the large theater, the agora (marketplace), and the temple of Artemis. In the second century, more building took place, including a magnificent library, the fountain of Trajan, the temple of Hadrian, the Odeon (a small theater), public baths, and a gymnasium.

Ephesus

Ephesus, a city of 250,000, continued as an important center of Christian leadership after Paul's ministry there. As emperor worship increased in the late first century, Ephesus built a temple to Roman imperial religion and dedicated it to the Sebastoi (the family of Vespasian, Titus, and Domitian). Christians faced the pressure to honor past "divine" emperors.

The grand temple to Artemis dominated the city of Ephesus. Only one of its 127 columns remains standing

Ephesus was also home to the temple of Artemis, one of the seven wonders of the world. The goddess and her temple are often pictured with a palm tree on imperial coinage. John may be contrasting the tree of Artemis with the tree of life (2:7; 22:2–3).

Smyrna

John addresses Smyrna (modern Izmir), directly north of Ephesus on an important east-west trade route through the Hermes Valley. Smyrna rivaled Ephesus in influence along the eastern Aegean. It claimed to be the first city to perform emperor worship, dedicating a temple to Tiberias in AD 26. This stood alongside beautiful temples to Zeus and Cybele.

The name "Smyrna" may have come from its famous tree-lined streets. Many of these trees produced a resin from which myrrh was made for perfume or embalming (Matt. 2:11;

Left: The buildings of Smyrna were well known for their beauty, seen in the excavated marketplace or agora *Right*: The lower level archway of the agora in Smyrna

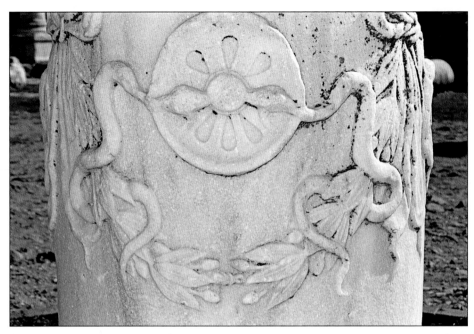
The cult of Asclepius was known for its snake symbol, as seen on this decoration from Pergamum's Asclepius sanctuary

John 19:39). The image of a crown was used in Smyrna to honor the dead. John perhaps uses "crown of life" (2:10) as a deliberate contrast.

Pergamon/Pergamum

Next John writes to Pergamum (modern Bergama), located sixty-five miles north of Smyrna and fifteen miles inland on a plateau. Pergamum was known for its production of parchment. The English word *parchment* and the Spanish *pergamino* stem from this city's name.

As an administrative center for the Roman Empire, many temples filled its public spaces. In 29 BC, Augustus bestowed the special honor of allowing a temple to be built there, dedicated to him. In front of Athena's temple stood a forty-foot altar to Zeus. When John refers to "where Satan has his throne" in 2:13, he may be thinking of this altar. The healing cult of Asclepius (and its snake symbol) was also prominent in Pergamum. This image of the snake may have led John to think of Genesis 3 and Satan since he refers to the city as the place "where Satan has his throne." John warns Christians in Pergamum to avoid pagan practices, particularly sexual immorality and idolatry. Those who persevere will be blessed with a "white stone with a new name written on it" (2:17).

Thyatira

Forty-five miles southeast of Pergamum stood Thyatira (modern Akhisar). This city enjoyed an excellent crossroads location along the trade route that connected Sardis and Pergamum. It was situated in a broad valley with no natural defenses. Not until the *pax Romana* did it enjoy prosperity and growth.

A curious feature of Thyatira is the preponderance of trade guilds,[2] which had a strong religious basis in the local patron god, Apollo Tyrimnaeus. Coins from the city depict this god together with the Roman emperor, combining local and imperial religion. Joining a guild secured one's livelihood, but it also included pagan religious rituals and meals. The pressure on Christians was enormous, for they were faced with financial ruin if they rejected the guilds. Perhaps "Jezebel" (2:20) suggested that an idol is nothing (see also 1 Cor. 8:1 – 4), so that Christian tradesmen and women could freely participate in the guild. John thinks otherwise (Rev. 2:22 – 23) and promises that the faithful will rule the nations with a rod of iron (2:27).

Sardis

The next city to the southeast is Sardis (modern Sart). This fortified city was the ancient capital of the region. Gold was found in the river, and the Romans mined it until it was gone. Residents of Sardis claimed that the precious metal originated with great King Croesus (560 – 546 BC), whose touch could turn anything into gold. In AD 17, Sardis suffered a major earthquake (cf. 6:12 – 17, 11:13; 16:18). Later chapters in Revelation may bring to mind this catastrophe (6:12 – 17, 11:13; 16:18).

Philadelphia

Nearby is Philadelphia (modern Alasehir), thirty miles from Sardis. Of the seven cities, Philadelphia has the fewest epigraphic and numismatic (coins) remains. In AD 17 it was devastated by the same earthquake that overwhelmed Sardis. John's promise of a heavenly city, the new Jerusalem, will bring much comfort to those Christians living among the ruins of this city (3:12).

Left: This plant was used to make the famous purple dye prized throughout the Roman world. Lydia of Thyatira, noted in Acts 16, was a dealer in purple cloth. *Upper Right*: The synagogue at Sardis is from the third century AD. It shares a wall with the city's bath complex. *Lower Right*: The water system in Laodicea included hollowed individual blocks that were sealed together with plaster and olive oil.

Laodicea

Laodicea lies forty-three miles southeast of Philadelphia, about a hundred miles due east of Ephesus. Like Colossae and Hierapolis, it was located in the Lycus River Valley. The city took its water from the hot springs in Hierapolis, but in the six miles of aqueduct, the water cooled to lukewarm. John exploits this image in 3:15 – 16.

In these seven letters we meet the John's immediate audience — Gentiles under assault from the larger pagan culture. His vision in chapter 1 encourages these Christians to keep their hope alive amidst the terrible persecution. Christ is indeed in their midst, watching over his churches. The remaining chapters engender hope that God will be victorious over all evil.

JOHN'S VISIONS IN CHAPTERS 4 – 22

After writing these letters, John is taken to heaven and witnesses the great throne room of God and of Christ (ch. 4 – 5). He describes "four living creatures" (4:6) and twenty-four elders who ceaselessly praise the One who sits on the throne. John watches as Christ the Lamb opens a sealed scroll (5:7; 6:1). At once, John sees events happen, though scholars debate whether John intends his readers to understand his narrative as happening sequentially.

As each seal is broken catastrophe occurs. With the breaking of the seventh seal, there is a half-hour of silence (8:1), after which seven trumpets sound in succession. These trumpets also bring disaster on the earth. Before the seventh trumpet sounds, John describes two witnesses (11:3), who are attacked by a beast from a bottomless pit (11:7). With the blowing of the last trumpet, "God's temple in heaven was opened, and within his temple was seen the ark of his covenant" (11:19).

Next John sees a woman "clothed with the sun," who is attacked by a great red dragon. War breaks out in heaven between Michael and his angels against the dragon (12:7). The dragon is joined by a seven-headed, ten-horned beast rising from the sea, who makes war on the saints (13:1). John breaks away from this terrifying picture of life on earth to the saints in heaven singing before Christ the Lamb (14:1 – 3). Three angels then declare to the earth three messages. The first speaks the "eternal gospel . . . to every nation, tribe, language and people" (14:6), the second declares "fallen is Babylon" (14:8), and the third warns against accepting the mark of the beast (14:9 – 11).

> ### NUMBERS IN THE ANCIENT WORLD
> In antiquity, numbers meant far more than their numerical value. They were symbols. Pythagoras considered 3, 5, and 7 as masculine; 2, 4 and 6 as feminine. Ten was the perfect number since it is a "triangular number" (from a triangle of dots with four on each side). The Pythagoreans followed Aristotle seeing 7 as symbolizing the first cause and itself was uncaused — hence, the Unmoved Mover.

Now comes the final series of seven — seven angels with seven bowls filled with plagues (chs. 15 – 16). These terrible judgments create agony; "people gnawed their tongues . . . and cursed the God of heaven because of their pains and their sores, but they refused to repent" (16:10 – 11). With the seventh bowl comes a terrible earthquake that shakes the great city of "Babylon" (perhaps a euphemism for Rome). At its destruction, John hears what sounds like the roar of a great multitude in heaven shouting: "Hallelujah!" (19:1).

"The Word of God" rides out from heaven on a white horse, executing judgment (19:11) and leading the armies of heaven (19:14). The dragon (Satan) is defeated and thrown into the bottomless pit, while those who have "not worshiped the beast or his image . . . came to life and reigned with Christ a thousand years" (20:4). After these years, Satan is released from the pit, and war ensues. Judgment is carried out, and Satan is thrown into "the lake of burning sulfur, where the beast and the false prophet had been thrown. They will be tormented day and night for ever and ever" (20:10).

John then sees the "Holy City, the new Jerusalem, coming down out of heaven from God" (21:3, 10). In this city are found the tree of life (22:2) and the water of life (22:1). Light shines not from the sun or moon, for God himself is the light (22:5). John concludes with a warning and encouragement to take to heart "the words of the prophecy of this scroll, because the time is near" (22:10). A closing promise comes from Christ: "Yes, I am coming soon." John responds, "Amen. Come, Lord Jesus" (22:20).

OUTLINE OF REVELATION

I. Introduction (1:1 – 5a)

II. Opening Vision (1:5b – 20)

III. Letters to the Seven Churches (2:1 – 3:22)

IV. The Heavenly Court (4:1 – 5:14)
    A. The Throne of God (4:1 – 11)
    B. The Lamb of God Opens the Scroll (5:1 – 14)

V. Judgment of the Seven Seals (6:1 – 8:1)
    A. Six Seals Opened (6:1 – 17)
    B. The 144,000 Sealed from Judgment (7:1 – 17)
    C. Seventh Seal Opened (8:1)

VI. Judgment of the Seven Trumpets (8:2 – 11:19)
    A. Prayers of God's People (8:2 – 5)
    B. Six Trumpets Sounded (8:6 – 9:21)
    C. The Little Scroll (10:1 – 11)
    D. The Two Witnesses (11:1 – 14)
    E. Seventh Trumpet Sounded (11:15 – 19)

VII. The Dragon and Beast Make War (12:1 – 13:18)

VIII. Three Angels Reap a Deadly Harvest (14:1 – 20)

IX. Judgment of the Seven Bowls (15:1 – 16:21)

X. Fall of Babylon (17:1 – 19:21)

XI. Final Judgment (20:1 – 15)

XII. New Jerusalem (21:1 – 22:9)

XIII. Epilogue and Exhortations (22:10 – 21)

INTERPRETING THE NARRATIVE STRUCTURE IN REVELATION 4 – 22

How should we read these chapters? In general, three basic positions have suggested reading strategies: premillennialism, postmillennialism, and amillennialism. Each reading strategy takes positions on four lead concepts: the Rapture, Millennium, Tribulation, and Second Coming of Christ.

Though *Rapture* is not found in the Bible, it refers to the bodily resurrection of Christians who are physically alive when Christ returns. Paul possibly speaks about the Rapture in 1 Thessalonians 4:13–18. At that time, Christians who have died will be raised, and those believers alive will be caught up or raptured "together with them in the clouds to meet the Lord in the air."

Millennium is a Latin word meaning one thousand. In 20:1–4, John uses this term to describe a reign of Christ with his saints. Does John mean a literal thousand years or an indefinite period of time? During the *Tribulation* evil seems to take an upper hand and Christians are severely persecuted (cf. 2 Thess. 2:3 with its "man of lawlessness," which some interpreters view as integral to the Tribulation). The church eagerly awaits Christ's *Second Coming*, when the last trumpet will sound and death will be swallowed up in victory (1 Cor. 15:51–56; cf. Acts 1:11; 1 Thess. 4:16).

Premillennialism

The *premillennial* position enjoys popularity among evangelicals. In the early church, this position was called *chiliasm* (*chilias* in Gk. means "thousand"). This view reads Revelation in four basic movements: the church age, the tribulation period, the millennial kingdom, and the final judgment culminating in the new heavens and earth. Currently believers live in the church age, who will be raptured either before or after a literal seven-year Tribulation,[3] which ends in Armageddon (16:16).

Then a literal thousand-year reign of Christ from his throne in Jerusalem begins. The glorified, resurrected saints will govern mortals with Christ (20:4). Old Testament prophecies of Isaiah are fulfilled (e.g., Isa. 65:20–25). Peace between nations and the centrality of Jerusalem will prevail (Isa. 2:2, 4; Mic. 4:1, 3). Nevertheless, many alive at the end of the Millennium will rebel against Christ (Rev. 20:7–9). They are defeated by "fire ... from heaven" (20:9–10); after this, all the dead will be raised and judged. Then God will usher in the new heavens and new earth.

Amillennialism

Amillennialism (which literally means "no millennium") does not believe in a literal thousand-year reign. Instead, it focuses on Christ's current dominion over sin and evil. Augustine believed that Christ's reign began over his church at his exaltation. The church is enjoying God's rule now, and believers at death will enjoy Christ's reign with him in heaven as they await the consummation of the present church age. No rapture is anticipated; rather, amillennialists look forward to Christ's Second Coming, when he comes not "to bear sin, but to bring salvation to those who are waiting for him" (Heb. 9:28).

There is likewise no seven-year Tribulation. The church suffers now the effects of sin and Satan's evil. These trials will escalate until the Second Coming, at which time Christ will completely defeat death and Satan. The eternal kingdom of God under Christ's perfect reign follows the Final Judgment. The redeemed will enjoy God's new heaven and new earth eternally. Amillennialism teaches that Jesus Christ fulfills Old Testament prophecies made to Israel.

Postmillennialism

Amillennialists live in hope, but also expect the worst. Postmillennialism views the world's situation much more positively. They gravitate toward the promises that Christ's church will grow and prosper. God's saints are reigning with him currently (Eph. 2:6; cf. Col. 3:1–2).

From John 12:31–32, postmillennialists believe a massive conversion will occur as Jesus draws all people to himself and creates a redeemed world, bringing about a time of peace and justice within society. At this point, the earth will enjoy the millennial kingdom of God, a thousand years of idyllic social and political life. After these years, Satan will make one last attempt to overthrow good with evil but will be thwarted by Christ's Second Coming and the Final Judgment. Then God will establish the renewed earth. As with the amillennial position, postmillennialism does not expect the Rapture or a seven-year Tribulation.

DECODING SYMBOLS

Having traced the three basic narrative structures for reading Revelation, we need to ask how to decode the symbols and images used by John. We will consider four hermeneutic theories.

Preterist Position

The Preterist (from *praeteritus*, "gone by, past") understands John's symbolic language to speak prophetically about specific historical events, most all of which were accomplished in the first century shortly after John's lifetime. Preterists usually identify Rome as John's enemy and think that John's vision was fulfilled at the fall of Rome in AD 476. They suggest John was describing Emperor Domitian (late 90s) in 2:9–11, 14, 20.

From AD 532-537, the Byzantine Emperor Justinian built the greatest church of his empire, called Hagia Sophia or the Holy Wisdom of Christ. For almost 1,000 years it was known as the "great church" of Byzantium. This mosaic of Christ dates to the 9th century and depicts Christ as ruling the world. Today some postmillennialists look for the gospel message to conquer and rule the world.

Preterists focus on John's context in the first-century Roman Empire, with particular emphasis on the seven letters to the churches in Asia Minor and their specific situations. Their position usually follows an amillennial narrative structure. This reading strategy holds that the church is currently in the "millennial age" (figuratively understood) and suggests that John is describing the first century or so of this "millennial age." The final judgment and return of Christ are not central to John's vision, and so he only briefly mentions them in 20:7–15.

Futurist Position

The Futurist believes that most prophecies in Revelation will be fulfilled within a brief time directly before Christ's return. This understanding of John's symbols is read from a premillennial position, in three basic interpretations: the classical dispensationalist, the progressive dispensationalist, and the covenant premillennialist.

The *classical dispensationalist* view of Revelation began with John Nelson Darby (1800–1882), whose ideas were promoted through the *Scofield Reference Bible* (1909). A distinct line is drawn between Israel and the church, with future prophecies still to be accomplished on earth in national Israel's history. The church age is an interlude until the full revival of the Jewish people. Then God will fulfill his promises to Israel and restore their

This Roman coin shows the Emperor Domitian's deceased infant son seated on a globe, playing with stars. The words on the coin read "The Deified Caesar, Son of the Emperor Domitian." The stars symbolize the child's divine status. The globe suggests that Romans believed the earth was a sphere. Eratosthenes (276-194 BC) of Cyrene (modern Libya) discovered this fact.

land "from the Wadi of Egypt to the great river, the Euphrates" (Gen. 15:18). The church will be raptured before the Tribulation (Rev. 4–5), and God's people, Israel, will endure the Tribulation. Many dispensationalists link the developments of the Middle East and the creation of the state of Israel in 1948 with end-time prophecies in Revelation. They look for a temple to replace the Muslim Dome of the Rock in Jerusalem.

The *progressive dispensationalist* accepts that much of John's Revelation has partial fulfillment in the first century AD (as do the Preterists). But it also holds that specific events are yet to be fulfilled. Not all progressive dispensationalists see the signs in chapters 6–18 as happening sequentially, nor will all argue for a literal seven-year Tribulation. Jesus Christ will reign a thousand years (though some do see this number symbolically) in an earthly kingdom before the eternal state. The place of Israel is disputed.

These dispensationalists hold these views together with an "already-not yet" eschatology. Christ's life, death, and resurrection have inaugurated the new age, but that new age will not fully come until Christ's second coming. The Christian lives in tension between these two eras.

The *covenant premillennialist* shares much in common with the progressive dispensationalist, with one important exception. They do not hold to a special place in redemptive history for a restored Israel, nor is Israel sharply distinguished from the church as God's people. They see a strong continuity in God's redemption history,

The Dome of the Rock, built by the Muslim Caliph Abd-al-Malik from 688-691, commemorates Muhammad's ascension into heaven after his Night Journey to Jerusalem (Koran, Sura 17). Jews believe this may be the location of David's temple and where Abraham nearly sacrificed Isaac (Gen. 22). Some Dispensationalists believe the Dome of the Rock will be destroyed and the new temple rebuilt on that site.

John describes the final battle of history as "Armageddon" (Rev. 16:12-16). This term is a Greek translation of the Hebrew "Mountains of Megiddo." This is the ancient city of Megiddo whose surrounding mountains and plains provide the setting of the battle.

especially highlighting Christ's first coming. They accept that prophecy may have an immediate, historical fulfillment and a future, eschatological fulfillment.

Idealist Position

For the Idealist, Revelation is a symbolic description of the perpetual struggle between good and evil. The church continually faces persecution and wonders whether evil will win. But Revelation affirms the ultimate destruction of Satan and evil and the final victory of God and his people. Most idealists are amillennialists. A Modified Idealist position argues that several specific events are perhaps prophesied in Revelation: the Second Coming of Christ, the final Judgment, and the kingdom of God. According to the Idealist the best way to interpret the book is with a nonliteral interpretive approach.

Eclectic Position

Few scholars today read Revelation through only one hermeneutical lens. Part of the reason for an eclectic reading of this book is the increased interest in matching hermeneutical approach with genre type. For example, some read chapters 1 – 3 as preterists (referring to the first century), and chapters 4 – 22 as a futurist. Those holding this hermeneutic generally understand the narrative framework from either a premillennial or a postmillennial perspective. Some premillennialists are even preterist or idealist regarding symbols, but futurist regarding the timing of what is signified. An eclectic amillennialist might see chapters 1 – 18 through the preterist lens, but view chapters 19 – 22 as a futurist.

AUTHOR AND DATE

The author of Revelation identifies himself as John (1:1, 4, 9; 22:8), but who is he? A variety of men were named John in early Christianity: John the Baptist, John the apostle (author of the Fourth Gospel), Simon Peter's father (John 21:15–17), and John Mark (Acts 12:12). Most early Christian leaders believed that the author of Revelation was John the apostle.

Today many scholars argue that John the apostle did not write Revelation. (1) The author never identifies himself as an apostle. (2) Critics point out that the author never hints that he knew the historical Jesus. (3) Some maintain that the apostle John was martyred early, perhaps in the early 60s, while they date Revelation to the 90s. (4) The differences in vocabulary and style between Revelation and John's gospel suggest different authors.

Those who accept that John the apostle wrote Revelation respond that John was already well known and did not require more identification. Failure to mention that he knew the historical Jesus is an argument from silence. The date of John's martyrdom is difficult to confirm with certainty. The differences in vocabulary and style may be explained through the different genres of the works or different secretaries. Or perhaps the consistently different use of conjunctions in the body of Revelation highlights the author's deliberate stylistic choice.[4]

Moreover, John's gospel and Revelation reflect similar motifs in their Christology and eschatology. Both see Christ as the Word (John 1:1; 1:14; Rev. 19:13), the Lamb (John 1:29; Rev. 5:6; 6:7), and the Son of Man (John 3:13; 6:27; Rev. 1:13). The evidence garnered by critics is not persuasive enough to overturn tradition's declaration that John the apostle wrote Revelation.

As to its date, Irenaeus said that John the apostle wrote the Apocalypse during Emperor Domitian's reign (AD 81–96). This matches general church tradition that promotes Domitian as a cruel tyrant against the church. Others date it in the 60s under Emperor Nero (though his maltreatment of the church was confined to Rome). A date in the 90s is fully plausible.

QUESTIONS FOR DISCUSSION ◉◉◉◉◉◉◉◉◉◉◉◉◉◉◉◉◉◉◉◉◉◉◉◉◉◉◉◉◉◉◉

1. Explain the three theories on the narrative framework of Revelation and the four views on decoding the symbols.
2. What was an "apocalypse" in the Jewish culture of antiquity?
3. Explain the importance of knowing the historical setting of Revelation's seven letters.
4. How does the description of God offered here differ from those in the Gospels?
5. How does an appreciation of the Roman imperial cult impact the study of Revelation?

BIBLIOGRAPHY
Introductory
Bock, D., ed. *Three Views on the Millennium and Beyond*. Grand Rapids: Zondervan, 1999.

Hemer, C. J. *The Letters to the Seven Churches of Asia in Their Local Setting*. Grand Rapids: Eerdmans, 2001.

Keener, C. S. *The Book of Revelation*. NIVAC. Grand Rapids: Zondervan, 2000.

Ladd, G. E. *A Commentary on the Revelation of John*. Grand Rapids: Eerdmans, 1972.

Pate, C. M., K. L. Gentry, Jr., S. Hamstra, and R. L. Thomas. *Four Views on the Book of Revelation*. Grand Rapids: Zondervan, 1998.

Advanced
Aune, D. *Revelation*. 3 vols. WBC. Nashville: Nelson, 1998.

Beale, G. K. *The Book of Revelation*. NIGTC. Grand Rapids: Eerdmans, 1999.

Mounce, R. H. *The Book of Revelation*. NICNT. Grand Rapids: Eerdmans, 1977.

Osborne, G. *Revelation*. BECNT. Grand Rapids: Baker, 2002.

NOTES
1. G. Beale, *The Book of Revelation* (NIGTC; Grand Rapids: Eerdmans, 1999): 37.

2. C. Hemer, *The Letters to the Seven Churches of Asia in Their Local Setting* (Grand Rapids: Eerdmans, 2001), 108–17.

3. Note that some post-tribulationalists do not take the seven years literally.

4. V. S. Poythress, "Johannine Authorship and the Use of Intersentence Conjunctions in the Book of Revelation," *WTJ* 47 (1985): 329–36. See also Beale, *The Book of Revelation*, 35.

CHAPTER 27

PRESERVATION AND COMMUNICATION OF THE NEW TESTAMENT

Codex Sinaiticus showing the final page of John's gospel. 4th Century AD. Located at the British Library, London.

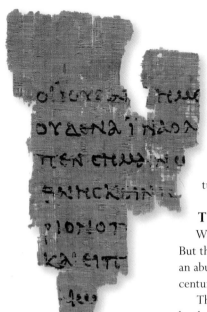

The New Testament that we read today is the end result of many centuries of effort. Manuscripts originally written on papyrus were copied and preserved from generation to generation. Leading authorities and church councils determined which writings should enter the church's final collection of twenty-seven books. And as the New Testament moved out of the Greek-speaking world, scholars had to translate its words into new languages.

Each of these three areas—text criticism, the canon, and translation theory—are important disciplines. A modern English translation has inherited a long history of debate and decision-making, and we now turn to these issues.

THE TEXT OF THE NEW TESTAMENT

We do not possess any of the original autographs of New Testament texts. But these originals were carefully copied and preserved, and today we possess an abundance of manuscripts—over 5,700 (from the second to the fourteenth centuries)—that give us some portion of the New Testament.[1]

The earliest copies of important New Testament writings were circulating by the late first century. The first formal printing of the Greek New Testament did not take place until 1516. For 1,400 years, therefore, the New Testament was subject to the hazards of hand-copying. In the earliest centuries, the Christians who produced these manuscripts were well-intentioned, pious believers who wanted to pass on to others copies of valuable Christian works. The evidence shows they were incredibly successful, but they did make inevitable minor mistakes, which textual criticism seeks to reverse.

Scholars believe that this is the earliest New Testament manuscript fragment in our possession (catalogued as P52). It is a very small papyrus piece (2.5 x 3.5 inches) dated from AD 125-150

Papyrus was grown in Egypt from the 3rd millennium BC. By the NT era it had become the chief source of writing material.

The Writing of Ancient Books

In antiquity a variety of materials was used for writing surfaces: wood, bone, broken pottery, papyrus, and parchment (treated animal skin). For the earliest New Testament period, papyrus is the most important for our study. Fifteen-foot stalks of papyrus were harvested from the Nile Delta, cleaned, flattened, and cut into twenty-inch strips. These were laid side by side, overlapping each strip so that its natural glue would bond the pieces together. Then a second layer running at right angles was laid down and glued. This final sheet was then trimmed, making a page about 20x9 inches. This page was polished into a smooth writing surface.

Next, workers glued numerous sheets side by side to make a commercial roll for consumers such as professional scribes, who cut off only the length he needed. The scribe used ink made of charcoal and water (along with a variety of acids). He marked a section with pin pricks to square and frame a writing area, and then began writing in columns about three inches wide.

The scroll made of either papyrus or parchment was the earliest and most important form of writing for official documents in the Hellenistic world ("volume" comes from the Latin *volumen*, "roll"). Late in the first century, however, another invention surfaces. For some time, secretaries had taken temporary notations on wood tablets with a waxed surface. These could be tied together at the margin, making a "book." Some scribes left the papyrus as sheets, folded them in the middle, and stitched sheets together at the center. This was called a "codex," which became a favorite form for the early Christians.

Scribal methods were well known in Judea as well. This ink well (along with four others) was discovered at Qumran near the Dead Sea. Since all were in one room, the area has been popularly called Qumran's "scriptorium."

Text Variants

Many copies of New Testament books circulated in the earliest centuries with varying levels of quality. Some copyists introduced errors by accident, and these were copied diligently by later scribes. In other cases, copyists intentionally made changes in order to improve the text. By comparing texts together, we can uncover errors and reconstruct what was in the

---

A SCRIBE'S COMPLAINT

Codex Vaticanus is one of the most important Biblical texts we own. It is a vellum (animal skin) codex from the fourth century and is located in the Vatican. It has 759 sheets (617 Old Testament, 142 New Testament). Each sheet has three columns with 42 lines to a column. It contains the entire Septuagint (except Maccabees and Manasseh). The New Testament lacks the Pastoral Epistles, Philemon, and Revelation. Because the ink was faded, at some point a later scribe decided to write over each letter. When something seemed unclear, he felt free to "correct" it.

There is an odd comment in the margin at Hebrews 11:3. A later scribe, frustrated that someone had changed something unnecessarily, scribbled the following in the margin:

> "Fool and knave!
> Can't you leave the old reading alone and not alter it?"[2]

NOTES FROM ANTIQUITY

original text. In this effort, New Testament scholarship has been extremely successful. Such "variant readings" are catalogued, organized, evaluated, and presented in any critical edition of the Greek New Testament.

Where do these variants come from? Inadvertent errors were common. Some came from simply seeing the text incorrectly. A scribe might misread an abbreviation. In 1 Timothy 3:16 some manuscripts tell us that "God was manifest in the flesh." Others read, "Who was manifest in the flesh" (RSV). In Greek, God was often abbreviated as $\overline{\Theta\Sigma}$; "who" is $O\Sigma$. These two words were easily confused.

Sometimes a line might end the same way a previous line ends and the copyist's eye skips a line. A variant reading of John 17:15 thus has Jesus praying the wrong prayer: "I do not pray that you should keep them from the evil one." Jesus actually prays, "My prayer is not that *you take them out of the world, but that* you protect them from the evil one."

The Greek letters ΠMA often abbreviate the word *pneuma* ("spirit"). But ΠOMA is the Greek word for drink. So at 1 Corinthians 12:13 some texts read: "All were made to drink of one drink" instead of "all [were] given one Spirit to drink." The error makes little sense.

Occasionally the scribe knows another New Testament text so well that his mind inserts words from elsewhere. Luke 11:1–2 offers a shorter version of the Lord's Prayer, which can be found in full form in Matthew 6:9–13. Here is the original abbreviated prayer, but placed in brackets are inserted scribal "harmonizations." The final addition in the last line is a remarkable expansion coming no doubt from the scribe's own piety.

[our] **Father** [who is in heaven]
Let your name be holy
Let your kingdom come
[let your Holy Spirit come upon us and cleanse us]

Sometimes the scribe cannot make sense of what he sees or he doesn't entirely like it, and he tries to improve it. These are *intentional* changes. John 5:4 does not exist in most modern New Testaments because a later scribe decided to explain why the lame man was trying

THE SOLDIER'S REMARK

Sometimes scholars suggest textual emendations to the New Testament when there is *no* evidence for them in any manuscript. For example, in Mark 15:35–36 Jesus calls out to God ("*Eloi! Eloi!*..."). Some of those standing nearby (likely including the Roman soldiers) misunderstand this Aramaic phrase and say, "Listen, he is calling *Elijah* ... let's see if Elijah comes to take him down." However, there is limited Jewish evidence for seeing Elijah as a rescuer, nor (if the Roman soldiers are involved) would they likely even know about Elijah.

Some scholars therefore suggest that the Greek text misrepresents what actually took place. The word for Elijah in Greek is *Helias*. But if we change one letter it becomes *Helios*, the "sun"—which represented a god in antiquity. When Jesus is on the cross, darkness covers Jerusalem (15:33). Therefore, these scholars insist, it would be natural for the soldiers and others around the cross to think that Jesus is calling on the sun to restore him. But earlier copyists of the gospel of Mark confused *Helios* for *Helias*, and soon the change was permanent.[3] This may be a creative suggestion, but it is purely speculative. There is no textual evidence to support it, and it is doubtful if it improves the text.

to get into the pool: "An angel of the Lord would stir the water. . . ." Scribes were also unclear about where this miracle occurred. Various manuscripts offer: Bethzatha, Bezatha, Belzetha, Bethsaida, Bethesda. Most text critics prefer Bethzatha.

Intentional changes like this in John 5 are benign. Sometimes scribes tried to clarify what seemed unclear or wrong. Mark 1:2 gives a composite quote from Isaiah and Malachi but credits it to Isaiah. Some scribes sought to improve this by changing Mark: "as it says in *the prophets*." Other scribes were motivated by doctrine. In Mark 13:32 Jesus says, "But about that day or hour no one knows, not even the angels of heaven, nor the Son, but only the Father." Scribes could not reconcile this statement of Jesus' ignorance with his divinity and their solution was simple. They removed the phrase "nor the Son."

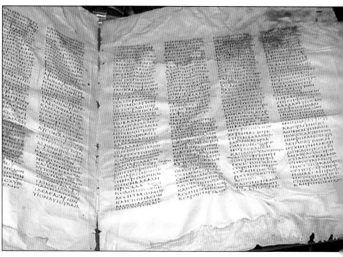

Codex Sinaiticus is an important uncial manuscript copied in the 4th century. It was discovered at St. Catherine's monastery on Mt. Sinai in the 19th century.

Text Types

The earliest manuscripts of the New Testament are papyrus fragments; we possess about 115 of these. These generally come from the period up to the fourth century and give us excellent insight into the earliest informal development of our texts. They are classified with a "P" and are numbered [P^{52}, P^{66}]. For instance, P^{66} dates to 200 and holds 104 6x5 inch pages containing numerous chapters from John's gospel. P^{72} is a third-century codex that gives us the earliest copies of Peter's two letters.

From the fourth to the ninth century we have 310 majuscule manuscripts written on parchment (made from animal skins). When Christianity became an official faith in the empire, the copying of manuscripts was done by professional scribes, who carefully produced beautifully embellished and formatted documents for study and worship. Some of these codices are classified with symbols (Sinaiticus is indicated by א [Hebrew letter *aleph*]) but each of these also receive a number preceded by a zero: 01 Codex Sinaiticus, 02 Codex Alexandrinus, 03 Codex Vaticanus, 032 Codex Washingtoniensis, and so on.

In the ninth century a smaller cursive handwriting style developed for more rapid copying. We have 2,877 of these, generally called "minuscules." These manuscripts are classified with simple Arabic numbers: Codex 1 is a twelfth-century codex now in Basel and was used by Erasmus to print the first Greek New Testament. Codex 565 is the Codex Purpureus Petropolitanus ("the purple codex of St. Petersburg") and comes from the tenth century.

Portions of the New Testament also appeared in the worship literature of the early church called "lectionaries." Here texts were arranged according to the sequence of desired readings for the church year. We now have 2,432 manuscripts of this order. These are classified by "*l*" (e.g., *l*45) or "Lect." (Lect.55).

Another source of information about the early New Testament is the "versions"—translations as early as the second century, such as Syriac, Latin, Coptic, and Armenian. An early version may reflect a text reading just like a Greek manuscript but do so indirectly. A second indirect source is the "patristic citation." The church fathers wrote

Perhaps the oldest continually occupied Christian monastery in the world, St. Catherine's was the home of the famous Codex Sinaiticus.

letters and sermons and cited the New Testament texts in their library. Thus if a bishop in Alexandria quoted a text in the early fourth century, that citation is one more witness to texts circulating in this period.

Text Families

Comparative analysis of text variants remained in its infancy until the seventeenth century (though Jerome refers to an edited Greek New Testament from Lucian of Antioch in the early fourth century). Desiderius Erasmus (1466–1536) was one of the earliest critical students of the Greek New Testament. His scholarship led to a publication of a variety of ancient texts (Jerome, Seneca, Plutarch), including the Greek New Testament in 1516. He based his

CODEX SINAITICUS DISCOVERED

The German scholar Constantin von Tishendorf pursued ancient manuscripts in the nineteenth century. In 1844 he visited St. Catherine's monastery on Mount Sinai and according to his report (disputed by the monks at St. Catherine's), in their library he saw parchment sheets piled and ready for the fire. He saved forty-three pages from the Greek Old Testament, urged the monks to stop, borrowed these texts, and returned to Leipzig where he published them in 1846.

In 1853 and 1859 Tishendorf returned to Mount Sinai with a copy of the published sheets he took in 1844. One monk said he had something better. From his closet he unwrapped a complete codex containing much of the Old Testament and the entire New Testament in pristine condition. Tishendorf studied it all night and after lengthy negotiations the monastery presented it to their protector, the Russian czar, as a gift. This text, Codex Sinaiticus, was published in 1862. Scholars now believe the codex originates from the fourth century. Subsequently St. Catherine's has offered up many more manuscripts, including twelve more sheets from Codex Sinaiticus.

text on Byzantine manuscripts resembling those coming from Lucian. By the late sixteenth century scholars felt this was the best text possible — called the Received Text or the *Textus Receptus*; it became the basis for the 1611 King James Version.

But soon scholars began to find other manuscripts outside the *Textus Receptus* tradition. For instance, in 1627 the patriarch of Constantinople presented King Charles I of England with Codex Alexandrinus, an exquisite fifth-century vellum codex containing 773 10x12 inch pages of text; most of the Old and New Testaments were there except for lost leaves from Matthew, John, and 2 Corinthians. Such discoveries convinced scholars that more had to be done. Theoretical principles had to be developed to bring order out of chaos.

The solution came in the eighteenth century when scholars agreed that a text variant could not be decided by the sheer number of manuscripts that supported it. They spoke of text "genealogies" or "families," where one early text reproduced by a scribe in turn became the source for multiple others. If twenty manuscripts were copied from a poor original, these twenty really only represented the one manuscript and did not bring twenty different readings. They belong to a family. Families were determined by tracking the errors and classifying the manuscripts that held them. Thus, manuscripts could be sorted and their relative value assessed.

By the early nineteenth century scholars began publishing Greek texts that rivaled the venerated *Textus Receptus*. Scholars were hunting for new manuscripts, and even the Vatican permitted the world to study its famous Codex Vaticanus. As the complexity of the problem increases, the science of textual criticism forced it to yield to principles of order and reason.

Today every New Testament student should be familiar with a critical edition of the Greek New Testament. Its heritage begins with the critical work of the great Cambridge scholars B. F. Westcott and F. J. A. Hort. They carefully explained their methodology and produced a Greek New Testament based on sound principles that are still used today. One rule controlled all they did: "The first step towards obtaining a sure foundation is the constant application of the principle that knowledge of documents should precede final judgment upon readings."[4] No other rule is more important. A text variant belongs to a document and that document belongs to a family whose heritage can be reconstructed and evaluated.

A critical edition of the Greek New Testament provides a recommended Greek text, but each page indicates where other manuscripts differ. This information is called a *critical apparatus*. In the widely used United Bible Society text, an editorial team has graded each variant reading ("A" for a certain reading to "D" for an uncertain reading). Even though many textual issues are still debated, the church has never had more reason for confidence in its New Testament Scriptures.

THE CANON OF THE NEW TESTAMENT

Not only did the early Christians preserve their Scriptures through a process of copying and distribution, but at some point the church's leadership had to give guidance concerning which writings were deemed beneficial. They had to develop criteria by which Christian leaders could adopt texts as "Scripture." This authoritative collection of New Testament books is called "the canon."

Definitions

The term *kanōn* ("canon") had two basic definitions in the ancient world. It could refer to a measuring ruler, something that guides or regulates belief or practice. But since a ruler has

3 τὸν ἄρτον ἡμῶν τὸν ἐπιούσιον δίδου ἡμῖν τὸ
καθ᾽ ἡμέραν·

4 καὶ ἄφες ἡμῖν τὰς ἁμαρτίας ἡμῶν,
καὶ γὰρ αὐτοὶ ἀφίομεν παντὶ ὀφείλοντι
ἡμῖν·
καὶ μὴ εἰσενέγκῃς ἡμᾶς εἰς πειρασμόν[4].[a]

5 Καὶ εἶπεν πρὸς αὐτούς, Τίς ἐξ ὑμῶν ἕξει φίλον
καὶ πορεύσεται πρὸς αὐτὸν μεσονυκτίου καὶ εἴπῃ αὐτῷ,
Φίλε, χρῆσόν μοι τρεῖς ἄρτους, **6** ἐπειδὴ φίλος μου
παρεγένετο ἐξ ὁδοῦ πρός με καὶ οὐκ ἔχω ὃ παραθήσω
αὐτῷ· **7** κἀκεῖνος ἔσωθεν ἀποκριθεὶς εἴπῃ, Μή μοι
κόπους πάρεχε· ἤδη ἡ θύρα κέκλεισται καὶ τὰ παιδία
μου μετ᾽ ἐμοῦ εἰς τὴν κοίτην εἰσίν· οὐ δύναμαι ἀναστὰς
δοῦναί σοι. **8** λέγω ὑμῖν, εἰ καὶ οὐ δώσει αὐτῷ ἀναστὰς
διὰ τὸ εἶναι φίλον αὐτοῦ, διά γε τὴν ἀναίδειαν αὐτοῦ
ἐγερθεὶς δώσει αὐτῷ ὅσων χρῄζει.[b] **9** κἀγὼ ὑμῖν λέγω,
αἰτεῖτε καὶ δοθήσεται ὑμῖν, ζητεῖτε καὶ εὑρήσετε,
κρούετε καὶ ἀνοιγήσεται ὑμῖν· **10** πᾶς γὰρ ὁ αἰτῶν
λαμβάνει καὶ ὁ ζητῶν εὑρίσκει καὶ τῷ κρούοντι ἀνοι-
γ[ήσ]εται[5].[c] **11** τίνα δὲ ἐξ ὑμῶν τὸν πατέρα αἰτήσει ὁ υἱὸς

cion[acc. to Tertullian]) Origen; Tertullian[vid] Augustine[vid] ‖ σου· γενηθήτω τὸ θέλημά σου it[a]
vg[mss] cop[sa. bo mss] geo ‖ σου· γενηθήτω τὸ θέλημά σου ὡς ἐν οὐρανῷ καὶ ἐπὶ τῆς γῆς
(see Mt 6.10) ℵ[1] (ℵ* οὕτω καί) (ℵ[2] A C D P.W Δ Θ 892 omit τῆς) Ψ f[13] 28 33
157 180 205 (565[supp] omit σου) 579 597 700 1006 1010 1071 1241 1243 1292 1424
1505 Byz [E F G H] Lect it[aur, b, c, d, e, f, ff2, i, (l), q, r1] vg[mss] syr[p. h] cop[bo] eth slav (Titus-Bostra)
Cyril

[4] **4** {A} πειρασμόν 𝔓[75] ℵ*.[2] B L 1 700 1342 vg syr[s] cop[sa, bopt] arm geo Marcion[acc. to Tertullian] Origen Cyril; Tertullian[vid] Augustine[vid] ‖ πειρασμόν ἀλλὰ ῥῦσαι ἡμᾶς ἀπὸ
τοῦ πονηροῦ (see Mt 6.13) A C D W Δ Θ Ψ f[13] 28 33 157 180 205 565 579 597 892
1006 1010 1071 1241 1243 1292 1424 1505 Byz [E F G H] Lect it[aur, b, c, d, f, ff2, i, l, q, r1]
vg[mss] syr[c. p. h] cop[bopt] eth slav Diatessaron[syr] (Titus-Bostra) ‖ *transposes* ἀλλὰ ῥῦσαι ...
πονηροῦ *after* γῆς (footnote 3) ℵ[1]

[5] **10** {C} ἀνοιγήσεται (see 11.9; Mt 7.8) 𝔓[45] ℵ C L Θ Ψ f[1] f[13] 28 33 157 180 579
597* 700 892 1241 1292 1342 1505 Byz[pt] Lect[pt. AD] arm geo Macarius/Symeon ‖

---

[a] **4** NO P: TR AD Lu ‖ SP: WH ‖ S: Seg NJB TOB   [b] **8** P: NIV Lu NRSV ‖ S: NJB TOB   [c] **10** P: NIV
VP REB

---

7 Μή ... πάρεχε Mt 26.10; Lk 18.5; Ga 6.17   **8** διά ... χρῄζει Lk 18.5

This page from the United Bible Society's Greek New Testament shows the Greek text and the textual apparatus for Luke 11. Note how footnotes point to textual data where variant readings are listed. Each entry in the apparatus is then given a letter grade.

units of measurement etched on it, that series of marks is also called a canon or a list. Today, we use both senses: "The 'canon' of scripture is understood to be the *list* of books which are acknowledged to be, in a unique sense, the *rule* of belief and practice."[5]

Most Jews in Jesus' day agreed on a common core of authoritative texts, including the Pentateuch, the Former Prophets (Joshua, Judges, Samuels, and Kings), the Latter Prophets (Isaiah, Jeremiah, Ezekiel, and the Minor Prophets), and writings such as the Psalms. But was there an official Jewish canon in the first century? Those who understand "canon" to mean a list from which nothing can be removed or nothing can be added believe the Jewish canon is later than Jesus' day. But those who see "canon" as recognition of a particular book's authority hold that Judaism in Jesus' day did operate with a canon.

Historical Evidence from Patristic Authors

Within the New Testament itself, we have hints of collections of writings and claims of authority about those writings. In 2 Peter 3:15–16, Peter declares that Paul's letters are collected and known among many churches. Paul himself encourages the Colossians to share his letter with the church in nearby Laodicea (Col. 4:16). Of course, Jesus' words were given the utmost authority, not only in the gospels but also in Paul (see 1 Cor. 7:10, 17; 1 Tim. 5:18).

Already in the second century we see a pattern of both revering New Testament Scripture and collecting it into an authoritative body of texts. Clement of Rome (ca. AD 95) asks his readers to "especially remember the words of the Lord Jesus which he spoke when he was teaching gentleness and long suffering" (*1 Clement* 13.1–4; see also 46.7–8). The *Epistle of Barnabas* announces, "As it is written, 'many are called, but few are chosen'" (4:14; see Matt. 22:14). Did this author have access to a copy of Matthew's gospel?

The author of *2 Clement* (mid-second century) writes: "Another scripture also says, 'I came not to call righteous, but sinners'" (2:4–6, citing Matt. 9:13 or Mark 2:17). Ignatius, bishop of Antioch (ca. AD 50–110), directly claims a superiority of Jesus' words over the Old Testament: "For I heard some men saying, 'If I find it not in the charters [Old Testament], I do not believe in the Gospel.'[6] ... But to me the charters are Jesus Christ, the inviolable charter is his cross, and death, and resurrection, and the faith which is through him" (*Phld.* 8.2). Each of these writers either knew of a gospel or at least of some collection of Jesus' sayings.

Justin Martyr (ca. AD 150) speaks of the Gospels as the "memoirs of the Apostles" useful to establish doctrine (*First Apology* 66.3; 67.3). These "memoirs" truthfully tell the story of Jesus (*Dialogue with Trypho* 103.8). For Irenaeus, the church has "the gospel in fourfold form, [but] held together by one Spirit," and he denounces those who "reject the form of the gospel and introduce either more or fewer faces of the gospels" (*Against Heresies* 3.11.8). He was referring to the four canonical Gospels (Matthew, Mark, Luke, and John), denouncing those

who would "reject the form of the gospel and introduce either more or fewer faces of the gospels" (ibid.). This "fourfold" gospel is presumably the accepted norm throughout the church.

In the second century Marcion not only edited Paul's letters but removed anything that validated the Old Testament and Jewish faith. He was declared a heretic, and his "canon list" survives only in the pages of his antagonist, Tertullian (*Against Marcion*).

Canon Boundaries

Throughout the second century, Christian writers also refer to texts not included ultimately in the canon, such as the *Shepherd of Hermas*, the *Didache*, *Wisdom of Solomon*, and the *Epistle of Barnabas*. For example, Irenaeus cites the Shepherd of Hermas in his *Against Heresies* 4.20.2. Gradually texts such as these were determined as outside canonical authority. An early canon list, the Muratorian Canon (ca. AD 200), is missing both its beginning and ending. What remains includes the following: the gospels of Luke and John, Acts, the letters of Paul

Ignatius was one of the first martyrs of the second century, killed during Emperor Trajan's rule (AD 98-117). He declared to the Roman Christians as he faced his martyrdom, "Let me be given to the wild beasts, for through them I can attain unto God. I am God's wheat, and I am ground by the teeth of wild beasts that I may be found pure bread [of Christ]" (Letter to the Romans 4.1, translation J.B. Lightfoot). This art piece was done by Francesca Francanzama (1612-1656).

(1 and 2 Corinthians, Ephesians, Philippians, Colossians, Galatians, 1 and 2 Thessalonians, Romans, Philemon, Titus, and 1 and 2 Timothy), Apocalypse of John, Jude, 1 and 2 John, Wisdom of Solomon, Apocalypse of Peter (though the list notes that some think this last work should not be read in church). By the fourth century, Athanasius spoke of the *Didache* and the *Shepherd* as important for teaching purposes, but not as part of the canon (*Festal Letter* 39).

In the early third century, Eusebius (ca. AD 263–339) referred to three categories of texts: "recognized, disputed, and spurious" (*Eccl. Hist.* 3.25.1–7). "Recognized books" included the four Gospels as well as Acts and the letters of Paul (14, including Hebrews, see 3.3.4), 1 John, and 1 Peter. He adds "if it seems right, the Apocalypse of John." James, Jude, 2 Peter, and 2–3 John were "disputed." He also claims that the *Acts of Paul*, *Shepherd of Hermas*, *Apocalypse of Peter*, *Epistle of Barnabas*, and the *Didache* are spurious (*Church History* 3.25.1–7).

Eusebius offers three criteria for identifying a "recognized" book. (1) The book must be true. Did its contents match the *regla fides* ("rule of faith"), a summary of essential tenets of Christianity as determined by the apostles who knew Jesus? This rule established that the historical figure Jesus of Nazareth was crucified for the sins of humanity, was raised by God's power, and is now seated at God's right hand. He is both fully God and fully human. In the second and third centuries, the *regla fides* was challenged by heresies, so many church fathers pointed to the traditions handed down from the apostles (see 1 Cor. 15:3–11; Ignatius, *Trall.* 7; Irenaeus, *Against Heresies* 3.2).

(2) A book must be genuine, that is, written by an apostle or their associate. For example, Mark wrote a gospel for Peter and Luke was connected with Paul. The early church would not have knowingly accepted a pseudepigraphic or anonymous writing (see Chs. 8, 9, and 21). Those writings claiming to be written by an apostle (e.g., *Gospel of Thomas*) but holding views that differed sharply with teachings of Matthew, John, and Paul, were rejected.

(3) The book must be widely used among all the churches. Augustine wrote: "Prefer those [writings] that are received by all Catholic Churches to those which some of them do not receive."

By ca. AD 325, the New Testament canon was essentially in place. In 367 Athanasius wrote the earliest complete New Testament list in his 39th *Festal Letter* 2, 7–10.

> I also resolved to set forth in order the writings that are in the list and handed down and believed to be divine.... Those of the New Testament ... are ... four gospels [Matthew, Mark, Luke, John]. Then after these are Acts of the Apostles and the seven letters of the Apostles called the 'Catholic' letters [James, 1 and 2 Peter, 1, 2, 3 John, Jude]. In addition, there are fourteen letters of Paul the apostle [Romans, 1, 2 Corinthians, Galatians, Ephesians, Philippians, Colossians, 1, 2 Thessalonians, Hebrews, 1, 2 Timothy, Titus, Philemon]. Last, from John again comes the Revelation. These are springs of salvation ... let no one add to them or take away aught of them.[7]

In 397 the Council of Carthage confirmed the twenty-seven books of the New Testament canon.

TRANSLATING THE NEW TESTAMENT
Translation in Antiquity

The Mediterranean world had a mix of languages with the two main tongues being Greek and Latin. The Romans were generally more willing to learn other languages than the Greeks and any educated Roman was expected to know these two. Archaeologists have discovered many bilingual inscriptions. In such a world, translation became a common practice. As noted in Chapter 3, the Greek-speaking Jews of the Diaspora used the Septuagint (LXX), a Greek translation of the Hebrew Scriptures.

The early Christians were the beneficiaries of ancient translations. The LXX became their Bible, even though other Greek translations took place later (e.g., those by Aquila, Theodotion, and Symmachus). In fact, the majority of the quotations of the Old Testament in the New Testament writings are based on the LXX. The multiple translators of the LXX did not hold a unified translation

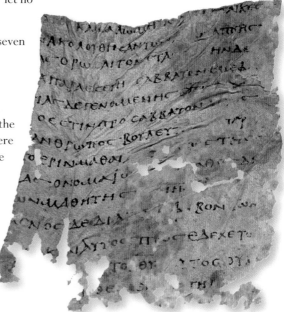

The Diatessaron compiled by Tatian was used extensively within the Syriac-speaking churches until the early fifth century. This is a photo of a Greek fragment of the Diatesseron found in 1933. It comes from the first half of the third century.

Greek and Latin were the principal languages of the Empire, as is contained in this bilingual inscription from Thessalonica

A portion of the Gospel of John in Coptic

theory and, as a result, some sections were translated literally (e.g., Judges and Ruth) while others were more of a paraphrase (e.g., Daniel and Job). We can sometimes recognize the influence of the LXX on the New Testament authors when we examine New Testament quotations of Old Testament texts (compare Mark 7:6–7, quoting Isa. 29:13 from the LXX, and Isa. 29:13 as translated from the Hebrew in a modern translation).

But even for those Jews living in Palestine translation was necessary since the language of the street was Aramaic rather than Hebrew. These translations from Hebrew to Aramaic were first done orally. The Mishnah's *Megillah* 4.1 instructs: "He that reads from the Law . . . may not read to the interpreter more than one verse, or, in [a reading from] the Prophets, three verses." In other words, the reader must not run too far ahead of the translator. Eventually these translations were written down and became known as the *targumim* (Ch. 3). It has been suggested that the interpretive traditions incorporated into the *targumim* even influenced the translators of the LXX.

Ancient authors discussed how translation should be done. Cicero, commenting on the translation of the Greek orators Demosthenes and Aeschines, said, "And I have not translated them as a literal interpreter, but as an orator giving the same ideas in the same form and mould, as it were, in words conformable to our manners; in doing which I did not consider it necessary to give word for word, but I have preserved the character and energy of the language throughout" (*De optimo genere oratorum* 14).

Cicero's concern to translate the ideas of the original and not give a word-for-word translation is echoed by Jerome (AD 347–420). He even noted that a literal translation may obscure the sense since the goal is to "look for the meaning" (*Letter* 57.6). Jerome quotes extensively from Cicero as his authority, affirming his statement, "If all that I have written is not to be found in the Greek, I have at any rate striven to make it correspond with it" (*Letter* 57.5).

Early Christian Versions

A Latin translation of the Christian Scriptures was needed since not everyone knew Greek. Jerome was specifically asked by Pope Damascus to revise the existing Latin translations of the Gospels (known as Old Latin), using the Greek text. He did the Old Testament as well, translating first from the LXX but then from the Hebrew text. Jerome's work became the Latin translation known as the Vulgate.

But not everyone spoke Latin or Greek, so other translations of the Scriptures, known as "versions," came into being. Christians in Egypt spoke Coptic, and so a Coptic version appeared (start of the third century). In Africa, an Ethiopic version of the Bible was done (cf. Acts 8:26–39).

The gospel took hold in Syria early on (cf. Syrian Antioch in Acts 11:19–30), so that some of the oldest versions are Syriac (Old Syriac in the second century, the Peshitta in the second and third centuries). Armenian, Georgian, and Arabic versions of the Bible survive from the early centuries as well. This robust enterprise of translation shows that the church understood that the message of Christ had to be brought to people in languages they could understand.

The Continuing Translation Tradition

At the heart of the church's response to the Great Commission is the work of the Bible translator. While Jesus did not specifically call for his disciples to engage in translation, the Great Commission (Matt. 28:16–20) makes the task necessary. Jesus emphasized the need for understanding the message of the kingdom of God (13:18–23). This mission of the church from its very beginning serves as the mother of translation.

The Bible was translated into Ethiopic

Today, agencies such as the United Bible Societies and SIL International/Wycliffe International facilitate this task globally. At times, translators learn the language into which they hope to translate Scripture and translate from the Hebrew and Greek. In other cases bilingual men and women translate the biblical text from a common language (e.g., Spanish) into a local tongue (e.g., Garufina, spoken in some parts of Guatemala), under the supervision of a translation consultant.

There are approximately 6,900 languages in the world, and around 2,300 have at least one book of the Bible translated. This represents 90 percent of the world's population. Despite the great advances in Bible translation techniques, much work remains to be done by those women and men who, as the seventh century bishop of Seville, Isidorus, said, stand *inter partes* ("between the two sides"; 10.123). At the same time, many language groups have multiple translations available to them, with new versions being produced at a rapid rate to address the concerns and needs of various readers. In fact, the large number of translations available to English readers makes selection between them difficult. While grateful for this abundance, students and church members may well wonder if supply has superseded the need.

The earliest translations of the Bible into English come from the Anglo-Saxon monk Caedmon (seventh century) and the great early church historian of England, the Venerable Bede (eighth century). John Wycliffe (fourteenth century) tried to make the Bible accessible to readers of his day as a hedge against abusive ecclesiastical authority. In the sixteenth

The gospel was also translated into Syriac. This is an example of a copy of the Old Syriac.

century William Tyndale, an Oxford graduate, was persecuted for his translation of Scripture based on the original Hebrew and Greek. These early translators displayed a passion for the gospel and the conviction that their labors and the personal cost were small in comparison to the great need.

The most well-known English translation, the King James Version (KJV), was completed in 1611. The Textus Receptus (see above on textual criticism) served as the textual base for this translation. But this is not the Greek text used by most contemporary Bible translators. Most translators today recognize that the Majority Text sometimes includes words, phrases, and sometimes even paragraphs that were not part of what the biblical author wrote. What appears to be an omission in contemporary translations is really a refusal to add what a biblical author did not write (see sidebar on "What Happened to the Verse"). They use either the critical edition of the New Testament published by the United Bible Societies or the Nestle-Aland text, both of which take into account the vast manuscript discoveries since the seventeenth century. They are examples of an eclectic text that represents the best application of the principles of textual criticism.

The Revised Standard Version (RSV, 1952), New English Bible (NEB, 1961, 1971), Living Bible (LB, 1966, 1971), Jerusalem Bible (JB, 1966), Good News Bible (GNB, 1966, 1976), New American Standard Bible (NASB, 1971), New International Version (NIV, 1973, 1978), New Jerusalem Bible (NJB, 1986), New Revised Standard Version (NRSV, 1990), New Living Translation (NLT, 1996), English Standard Version (ESV, 2001), Holman Christian Standard Bible (NCSB, 2004), and Today's New International Version (TNIV, 2005) are all based on the current editions of these Greek texts.

Translation Theory

How can we translate the New Testament in a way that is both faithful to the biblical author's meaning and understandable to the contemporary reader? This central question is simple and elusive. Bible translators must decide on a philosophy of translation to guide their work. This task is daunting since we can only approximate the meaning of the source language (in this case, Greek) in the receptor language (contemporary English). An Italian dictum voices a somewhat cynical view — "Tradductore, traditore" ("Translators, traitors") — since a translator can never get in all the meaning of the original.

When a person speaks or writes, the language or linguistic "code" supplies evidence of what she or he wishes to communicate. The process of understanding what someone says includes not only decoding the words and sentences but also making proper inferences. So, for example, if you say to a friend sitting next to you in class, "It's 8:30," what you may mean, "It's time to for class to begin," or, "The professor is late." You expect your classmate to understand what you mean by making the proper inferences. In both these cases contextual information comes into play (this particular class begins at 8:30 a.m. and the professor is not in the room).

We always communicate more than what our words say. So it is with the New Testament. When Paul said to the Philippians, for example, that one day every knee will bow and every tongue confess that "Jesus Christ is Lord" (Phil. 2:11), he expected the Philippians to understand his meaning of the term "Lord." "Lord" (*kyrios*) was how the LXX translated the name of God, Yahweh (see Isa. 45 for this very citation in Phil 2:11). Also, "Lord" was a common title given to multiple deities around the empire, such as the Egyptian "Lord Serapis" and sometimes even the emperor. For Paul and the Philippians, the claim that Jesus is "Lord" attaches to the concept of transcendent deity. In fact, he is the one who is above every other so-called god and lord (see 1 Cor. 8:4–6). The question the translator of any verse must wrestle with is whether to translate the words alone or whether to attempt, in a limited way, to supply some of the conceptual information for the contemporary reader that would have been accessible to the original readers.

The problem of translation is even more acute since the concept suggested by a term in one language is not usually equivalent to the translated word used in another language. Think about our ideas attached to the term "lord." The Merrian-Webster dictionary indicates that the term can refer to "one having power and authority over others" or "a man of rank or high position." But these concepts are not equal to the ancient concepts of deity and divine rule as suggested by *kyrios* in the Greek-speaking world of the first century. Translations can only approximate the meaning of the author's original utterance. The concept suggested by a term in one langue will overlap the concept of the equivalent word in another language, but the two concepts are rarely the same in all their dimensions.

ROMANS 8:4 – QUESTIONS OF TRANSLATION

What is the best way to translate Romans 8:4? Should translators render the Greek term *sarx* by the gloss "flesh," or should they explain the word in some brief way to the English reader? What did Paul mean by "walking"? Compare the following translations in light of the philosophy of translation they represent:

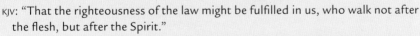

> KJV: "That the righteousness of the law might be fulfilled in us, who walk not after the flesh, but after the Spirit."
>
> TNIV: "in order that the righteous requirement of the law might be fully met in us, who do not live according to the sinful nature but according to the Spirit."
>
> NLT: "He did this so that the requirement of the law would be fully accomplished for us who no longer follow our sinful nature but instead follow the Spirit."
>
> J. B. Phillips: "so that we are able to meet the Law's requirements, so long as we are living no longer by the dictates of our sinful nature, but in obedience to the promptings of the Spirit."

Translators deal with these issues in various ways. Some argue that the best approach is to seek "formal equivalence," that is, to translate as much as possible word for word from the source language into the receptor language. Others attempt to produce a translation that has "functional" or "dynamic equivalence." As Eugene Nida, a scholar who has been highly influential in the field of translation, says, such translations try to reproduce "in a receptor language [i.e., English] . . . the closest natural equivalent of the source language [i.e., Hebrew or Greek] message, first in terms of meaning, and second in terms of style."[8] Such translators seek to render the original thought for thought. A version like the New American Standard falls clearly on the formal equivalence side while the New Living Translation has functional equivalence as its goal.

Much debate has taken place in recent years about whether translations should use "gender-inclusive language" (as do the NLT, NRSV, and TNIV). For example, Paul addresses the *adelphoi* in Philippi (Phil. 1:12); should we render this term "brothers" or "brothers and sisters"? What did Paul mean here? Did he intend to address both male and female believers, or only the men? While in the past "brothers" included both men and women, recent shifts in the English language indicate to many that "brothers" is more gender-marked today. Therefore many argue that in order to be faithful to Paul's meaning, *adelphoi* should be translated as "brothers and sisters."

Despite these challenges of translation, the church has been enriched through the centuries. Just as the LXX version of the Old Testament served the early church, so too in our day the global church is being served by the translations of the New Testament into the languages of the world. The message of Jesus is heard through these translations; by God's grace this message is indeed the "the power of God that brings salvation to everyone who believes: first to the Jew, then to the Gentile" (Rom. 1:16).

QUESTIONS FOR DISCUSSION ⊚⊚⊚⊚⊚⊚⊚⊚⊚⊚⊚⊚⊚⊚⊚⊚⊚⊚⊚⊚⊚⊚⊚⊚⊚⊚

1. What were the unique challenges to the preservation and copying of the New Testament text from AD 100 to 300?

2. If scholars discovered a new ancient manuscript that challenged the authenticity of some vital portion of the New Testament, how would we decide whether or not to change our Bibles? Who decides?

3. Explain the term "canon" and how it was used in the ancient world.

4. How did Eusebius (a fourth-century church historian) describe books being considered for inclusion in the New Testament?

5. Discuss the issue of gender-inclusive language translations, comparing the NIV with the TNIV. Which kind of translation should be used in the church today, and why? Be sure to reflect on the philosophy of translation that guides these decisions as well as whether changes in the English language warrant the use of gender-inclusive language.

BIBLIOGRAPHY

The Text of the New Testament

Aland, K., and B. Aland. *The Text of the New Testament*. Grand Rapids/Leiden: Eerdmans/Brill, 1987.

Black, D. A., ed. *Rethinking New Testament Textual Criticism*. Grand Rapids: Baker, 2002.

Comfort, P. *A Student's Guide to Textual Criticism*. Nashville: Broadman & Holman, 2006.

Greenlee, J. H. *An Introduction to Textual Criticism*. 2nd ed. Peabody, MA: Hendrickson, 1995.

Metzger, B., and B. Ehrman. *The Text of the New Testament: Its Transmission, Corruption, and Restoration*. 4th ed. Oxford: Oxford Univ. Press, 2005.

Wegner, P. D. *A Student's Guide to Textual Criticism*. Downers Grove, IL: InterVarsity Press, 2006.

Canon

Barton, J. *Holy Writings Sacred Text: The Canon in Early Christianity*. Louisville: Westminster John Knox, 1997.

Bruce, F. F. *The Canon of Scripture*. Downers Grove, IL: InterVarsity Press, 1988.

McDonald, L. M. *The Formation of the Christian Biblical Canon*. Peabody, MA: Hendrickson, 1995.

Patzia, A. G. *The Making of the New Testament*. Downers Grove, IL: InterVarsity Press, 1995.

Metzger, B. M. *The Canon of the New Testament: Its Origin, Development, and Significance*. Oxford: Clarendon, 1987.

Translation

Carson, D. A. *The Inclusive Language Debate*. Grand Rapids: Baker, 1998.

Comfort, P. W. *Essential Guide to Bible Versions*. Carol Stream, IL: Tyndale, 2000.

Wegner, P. D. *The Journey from Texts to Translations*. Grand Rapids: Baker, 1999.

NOTES

1. B. Metzger and B. Ehrman, *The Text of the New Testament: Its Transmission, Corruption, and Restoration*, 4th ed. (Oxford: Oxford Univ. Press, 2005), 50

2. B. Metzger, *Manuscripts of the Greek Bible: An Introduction to Greek Paleography* (New York: Oxford, 1981), 74. (see p. 75 for a photo of Codex Vaticanus at Heb. 11:3).

3. See C. H. Turner, *A New Commentary on the Holy Scripture* (1928), as cited by S. Neill, *The Interpretation of the New Testament, 1861–1961* (Oxford: Oxford Univ. Press, 1964), 79.

4. B. F. Wescott and F. J. A. Hort, *The New Testament in the Original Greek* (London: MacMillan, 1881), 31, cited by S. Neill, *The Interpretation of the New Testament, 1861–1961* (Oxford: Oxford Univ. Press, 1964), 73.

5. F. F. Bruce, *The Canon of Scripture* (Downers Grove, IL: InterVarsity Press, 1988), 18.

6. Lee McDonald's translation of the statement. The rest of the passage is from the LCL. L. M. McDonald, *The Formation of the Christian Biblical Canon* (Peabody, MA: Hendrickson, 1995), 146.

7. Translation from McDonald, *The Formation of the Christian Biblical Canon*, 221.

8. E. A. Nida and C. R. Taber, *The Theory and Practice of Translation* (Leiden: Brill, 1969), 210.

SCRIPTURE INDEX

NONCANONICAL INDEX

PHOTO CREDITS

Note: Those who have contributed multiple photos are listed first. Those are followed by single contributors in order of page numbers.

Todd Bolen/www.BiblePlaces.com . . . . 35, 36, 47, 48 (Masada), 54, 60 (Jordon River), 61 (all), 63 (synagogue), 67, 79, 82, 83 (paving stones), 94 (temple), 95, 96 (Tarsus), 98 (temple), 99 (both temples), 102 (temple), 103, 107, 108, 125, 129, 131 (aerial), 132 (both), 133, 134, 135, 136 (Jordan River), 137, 139 (temple model), 141 (temple model), 142 (Via Dolorosa), 145, 147, 148 (Mt. Arbel), 149, 150, 161 (crosses), 165, 166, 170, 173, 174, 175, 177, 180, 187 (boat), 188 (Kursi), 189, 195, 201, 202 (Bethlehem), 204, 207, 208 (all), 217, 218, 222, 223, 225, 226, 227, 232, 235, 238 (Samaria), 242 (both), 243 (both), 244, 245, 253, 256, 258, 260, 262 (temple), 267, 279, 282 (agora), 285, 293, 295 (temple), 296 (both), 297 (both), 298, 304, 333, 337, 349, 350 (Via Egnatia), 352 (river), 353 (both), 355, 363, 391, 397, 412 (grave of John), 413, 418, 425, 427 (monastery), 429 (temple of Artemis and Smyrna archway), 437, 446

Z. Radovan/www.BibleLandPictures.com . . . . 18, 19, 20, 21, 23, 24 (both), 25 (ishtar gate), 26, 32 (gold coin), 39, 40 (Herodium and temple platform), 41, 43, 44 (pottery), 48 (cloth), 49 (both), 50, 53, 55 (mosaic), 57 (both), 58, 59 (both), 63 (village), 64, 65, 70 (synagogue), 71, 74 (both), 75, 92, 109, 112, 126 (both), 127, 130, 131 (jars), 136 (millstones), 139 (fig), 140 (all), 141 (lamb slaughter and Sisters of Zion convent), 142 (thorns), 143 (ankle bone), 148 (ossuary), 151, 152, 155, 156, 157, 159, 161 (grapes), 162, 167, 171, 179, 181, 182, 184 (both), 185 (all), 187 (fish), 188 (coin), 190, 213, 215 (both), 216, 221, 224 (both), 239 (theater), 317 (both), 321, 323, 375, 381, 385, 443

© The Trustees of the British Museum . . . . 29, 30 (coin), 32 (silver coins), 90, 91, 98 (coin), 101, 246 (both), 263, 264, 283, 322 (coin), 347, 402

Copyright 1995-2009 Phoenix Data Systems . . . . 25 (cylinder seal), 30 (fortified tower), 37 (theater), 42, 44 (inscription), 97, 169, 205, 229, 251, 311, 364, 365, 386

Harlan J. Berk, Ltd. . . . . 93 (all), 96 (coin), 280 (both), 281 (all), 339 (coin), 342, 351 (coins), 436 (coin)

Images courtesy of www.HolyLandPhotos.org. . . . . 88, 135, 240, 249, 268, 270, 290, 295 (monument), 366, 431 (all), 436 (Dome of the Rock)

Gene L. Green . . . . 28, 81, 83, 89, 99 (ear tablets), 282 (gods), 305, 350 (bollard), 352 (inscription), 452 (bilingual inscription)

Courtesy of Wikimedia Commons . . . . 94 (coin), 115 (Griesbach), 325, 326, 332, 380, 412 (Eusebius)

Marie-Lan Nguyen/Wikimedia Commons . . . . 100, 102 (Epicurus), 197, 340 (Attis), 399

© Hugh Claycombe 138, 144, 394